Third Edition

A Customized Version of *Thriving in College and Beyond* by Joseph Cuseo, Designed Specifically for Dalton State College

Kendall Hunt
publishing company

Photo and Art Credits

pgs. 3, 42, 263
© Corbis

pgs. 5, 41
© Adobe

pgs. 10, 14, 21, 64, 83, 85, 101, 03, 162, 169, 179, 225, 228, 233, 262, 265, 271, 310
© 2007 JupiterImages Corporation

pg. 23
Copyright © by Ed Arno. Reprinted by permission.

pg. 27
© Diego Cervo

pgs. 38, 165, 266
Copyright © by Harley Schwadron. Reprinted with permission.

pgs. 43, 45, 95
© Comstock

pgs. 47, 90, 135, 229, 245, 313
© Stockbyte

pgs. 48, 197, 262
Copyright © by Scott Arthur Masear. Reprinted with permission.

pgs. 49, 78, 81, 97, 128, 155, 167, 214, 228, 278, 304, 324
© Shutterstock

pg. 65
Copyright © by George Abbott. Reprinted with permission.

pg. 119
© Digital Stock

pg. 211
Copyright © 2002 by Joel Pett. All rights reserved. Reprinted with permission.

pgs. 246
Copyright © by Benita Epstein. Reprinted with permission.

pg. 327
Copyright © by John Shanks. Reprinted with permission.

Kendall Hunt
publishing company

www.kendallhunt.com
Send all inquiries to:
4050 Westmark Drive
Dubuque, IA 52004-1840

Cover image courtesy of Dalton State College. Cover image courtesy of Linda Massey, Dalton State College Public Relations Specialist.

Copyright © 2007, 2008, 2009 by Kendall Hunt Publishing Company

ISBN: 978-0-7575-6533-5

All rights reserved. No part of this publication may be reproduced, stored in a retrieval system, or transmitted, in any form or by any means, electronic, mechanical, photocopying, recording, or otherwise, without the prior written permission of the copyright owner.

Printed in the United States of America
10 9 8 7 6 5 4 3 2 1

Contents

Acknowledgments ix
Letter to Students xi
Introduction xiii
Technology at Dalton State College xix
Campus Resources xxxi

1 Touching All the Bases
An Overview and Preview of the Most Powerful Principles of College Success 1

The Most Powerful Research-Based Principles of College Success 2
The Home Base of College Success:
   Active Involvement 2
      Time Spent in Class 3
      Time Spent on Coursework Outside the Classroom 3
      Active Listening and Note-Taking 4
      Active Class Participation 5
      Active Reading 7
Touching the First Base of College Success:
   Utilizing Campus Resources 8
      Learning Center 9
      Writing Center 9
      Disability Services or Office for Students with Special Needs 10
      College Library 10
      Academic Advisement 10
      Career Development Center 11
      Counseling Center 12
      Health Center 12
      Experiential Learning Resources 12
      Learning More about Your Campus Resources through Your Own Research 15
Touching the Second Base of College Success:
   Social Interaction and Collaboration 15
      Student-Faculty Interaction 16
      Student-Advisor Interaction 17
      Interaction with a Mentor 18
      Interaction with Peers (Student-Student Interaction) 19
      Collaboration with Peers 21
Touching the Third Base of College Success:
   Self-Reflection 24
      Self-Assessment 25
      Self-Monitoring 26
      Reflecting on Feedback 27
      Reflecting on Your Future 28
A Checklist Summary of Key College-Success Principles and Strategies 29
Learning More through Independent Research 30
      Web-Based Resources for Further Information on College Success 30
Exercise: Constructing a Master List of Campus Resources 31
Case Study: Alone and Disconnected: Feel Like Going Home 36

2 The Value of Liberal Arts and General Education
How the College Experience Develops You as a Whole Person and Improves Your Total Quality of Life 37

The Meaning and Purpose of a Liberal Arts Education 38
The Liberal Arts Curriculum 41
      Major Divisions of Knowledge and Subject Areas in the Liberal Arts Curriculum 42
What Is the Value of a Liberal Arts Education? 44
      Gaining a Multi-Dimensional Perspective and Multiple Thinking Tools 45
      Acquiring a Powerful Set of Fundamental Skills 46
Achieving Career Success 49
      Skills 49
Developing the Whole Person 51
      Skills and Abilities Associated with Each Element of Holistic Development 52
The Co-Curriculum 55
Broadening Your Perspective of the Whole World 57
      Elements of the Chronological Perspective 59
      Elements of the Social-Spatial Perspective 60
      The Synoptic Perspective: Integrating Diverse Perspectives to Form a Unified Whole 62
Summary and Conclusion 63
Learning More through Independent Research 67
      Web-Based Resources for Further Information on the Liberal Arts 67
Exercise: Planning Your Liberal Arts Education 69
Case Study: Dazed and Confused: General Education versus Career Specialization 72

3 Strategic Learning
Applying Research on Human Learning and the Human Brain to Acquire Knowledge Effectively and Comprehend It Deeply 73

Brain-Based Learning Principles 74
    The Brain Is Biologically Wired to Seek Meaning 74
    New Knowledge Is Built on Knowledge Already Possessed 76
    Shallow, Surface-Oriented versus Deep, Meaning-Oriented Approaches to Learning 76

Stages in the Learning and Memory Process 78
    Stage 1. Perception: Receiving Information from the Senses and Sending It to the Brain 78
    Stage 2. Storage: Keeping Information in the Brain 80
    Stage 3. Retrieval: Finding Information That's Been Stored in the Brain and Bringing It Back to Consciousness 81

Lecture Listening and Note-Taking Strategies 83
    The Importance of Taking Notes 83
    Taking Notes 85

Strategies for Improving Textbook-Reading Comprehension and Retention 90
    Before Beginning to Read 90
    While Reading 91
    After Reading 94

Study Strategies 95
    Minimize Distractions 95
    Find Meaning in Terms 96
    Compare and Contrast 96
    Integrate Information 97
    Divide and Conquer 97
    Use a "Part-to-Whole" Method of Studying 98
    Begin with a Review 99
    Change Things Up 99
    Use All of Your Senses 100
    Emotional Learning and Memory 103
    Form Study Groups 103

Self-Reflection and Self-Monitoring 104
    Comprehension Self-Monitoring Strategies 105
    Knowledge Awareness Strategies 106

Summary and Conclusion 107
    Active Involvement 107
    Self-Reflection 108
    Social Interaction/Collaboration 108
    Utilizing Campus Resources 108

Learning More through Independent Research 109
    Web-Based Resources for Further Information on Strategic Learning 109

Exercise: Self-Assessment of Learning Strategies and Habits 111

Case Study: Too Fast, Too Frustrating: A Note-Taking Nightmare 112

4 Educational Planning and Decision Making
Making Wise Choices about Your College Courses and Major 113

To Be or Not to Be Decided about a College Major: What the Research Shows 114

When Should You Reach a Firm Decision about a College Major? 115

The Importance of Long-Range Educational Planning 116

Myths about the Relationship between Majors and Careers 117
    Myth 1: When You Choose Your Major, You're Choosing Your Career 117
    Myth 2: If You Want to Continue Your Education After College, You Must Continue in the Same Field as Your College Major 119
    Myth 3: To Work in a Business or Corporation, You Need to Major in Business or a Technical Field 121
    Myth 4: If You Major in a Liberal Arts Field, the Only Career Available to You Is Teaching 121
    Myth 5: Having Specialized Skills Is More Important for Career Success than Having General Skills 121

Making Decisions about a College Major 122
    Step 1: Gaining Self-Awareness 122
    Step 2: Awareness of Your Options (the academic subjects available to you as choices for a college major) 131
    Step 3: Awareness of the Options that Best Match Your Personal Abilities, Interests, and Values 131
    Strategies for Discovering a Compatible Major 131

Summary and Conclusion 136

Learning More through Independent Research 139
    Web-Based Resources for Further Information on Educational Planning 139

Exercises:
    Assignment 1. Planning for a College Major 141
    Assignment 2. Developing a Comprehensive, Long-Range Graduation Plan 142

Case Study: Whose Choice Is It Anyway? 144

5 Academic Advising

The Advisor's Responsibilities 146
    Advisors Are Responsible to the Individuals They Advise 146

The Student's Responsibilities 146

Exercise: DSC Catalog 149

The Advising Process and the College Plan 151

Academic Advising Session Expectations 151

6 Improving Memory and Test Performance
Strategies for Remembering What You Have Learned and Demonstrating What You Know 153

Memory and Learning 154
Memorization Strategies 154
    Mnemonic Devices 154
    Meaningful Association 155
    Organization: Classifying or Categorizing What You're Trying to Remember 157
    Visualization 157
    Rhythm and Rhyme 159
    Acrostics 160
    Link System 161
    Loci System 162
Test-Taking Strategies 163
    Before the Test 164
    On the Day of the Test 169
    During the Test 171
    After the Test: Troubleshooting Test-Taking Errors and Sources of Lost Points on Exams 178
Summary and Conclusion 182
Learning More through Independent Research 183
    Web-Based Resources for Further Information on Improving Memory and Test Performance 183
Exercises:
    Self-Assessment of Learning Strategies 185
    Midterm Self-Evaluation 185
Case Study: Bad Feedback: Shocking Midterm Grades 186

7 Higher-Level Thinking
Moving Beyond Basic Knowledge and Comprehension to Higher Levels of Critical and Creative Thinking 187

What Is Thinking? 188
What Is Higher-Level Thinking? 189
Defining and Classifying the Major Forms of Higher-Level Thinking 190
    Analysis (Analytical Thinking) 191
    Synthesis 191
    Multidimensional Thinking 192
    Dialectical (Dialogic) Thinking 196
    Balanced Thinking 197
    Inferential Reasoning 199
    Critical Thinking 200
    Creative Thinking 205
Strategies for Developing and Applying Higher-Level Thinking Skills to Improve Academic Performance 207
    Self-Questioning Strategies 207
    Listening Strategies 211
    Reading Strategies 212
    Creating Cognitive Dissonance 212
    Creative Thinking Strategies 213
Summary and Conclusion 215
    Benefits of Higher-Level Thinking 215
Learning More through Independent Research 217
    Web-Based Resources for Further Information on Higher-Level Thinking 217
Exercises:
    Plan to Demonstrate Higher-Level Thinking in Your Courses 219
    Self-Assessment of Higher-Level Thinking 220
Case Study: Trick or Treat: Confusing or Challenging Test? 222

8 Diversity
Appreciating the Value of Human Differences for Enhancing Learning and Personal Development 223

The Spectrum of Diversity 224
    What Is Culture? 225
    What Is an Ethnic Group? 225
    What Is a Racial Group? 226
Diversity and the College Experience 228
Advantages of Experiencing Diversity 230
    Diversity Increases the Power of a Liberal Arts Education 230
    Diversity Promotes Self-Awareness 231
    Diversity Strengthens Development of Learning and Thinking Skills 231
    Diversity Enhances Career Preparation and Success 233
    Diversity Stimulates Social Development 233
Blocks to Experiencing Diversity 234
    Stereotyping 234
    Prejudice 234
    Discrimination 235
Causes of Prejudice and Discrimination 236
    The Influence of Familiarity and Stranger Anxiety 237
    The Tendency to Categorize People 238
    Group Perception 239
    Majority Group Members' Attitudes 239
    Group Membership and Self-Esteem 239
Strategies for Making the Most of Diversity 241
    Self-Reflection: Gaining Self-Awareness and Developing Diversity Tolerance 241
    Personal Action: Learning about Diversity by Acquiring Knowledge of Different Cultures 243
    Interpersonal Interaction: Learning through Interaction and Collaboration with Members of Diverse Groups 244

Summary and Conclusion 251
Learning More through Independent Research 251
    Web-Based Resources for Further Information on Diversity 251
Exercise: Diversity Self-Awareness 253
Case Study: Hate Crime: Racially Motivated Murder 254

9 Finding a Path to Your Future Profession
Career Exploration, Preparation, and Development 257

Why Career Planning Should Begin in the First Year of College 258
Career Exploration and Development Strategies 259
    Step 1. Self-Awareness 259
    Step 2. Awareness of Your Options 262
    Step 3. Awareness of What Career Options Best Fit You 270
    Step 4. Awareness of How to Prepare for and Gain Entry into the Career of Your Choice 273
Summary and Conclusion 285
Learning More through Independent Research 286
    Web-Based Resources for Further Information on Careers 286
Exercise: Conducting an Information Interview 287
Case Study: Career Choice: Conflict and Confusion 289

10 Majoring in Life and Career Management

Major = Career? 292
    True or False Quiz 292
Understanding the Difference between Majors and Careers 293
Why Create a Career Plan? 293
    1. Work and Worth 293
    2. Marketability 293
    3. Persistence and Degree Attainment 294
    4. Less Time to Graduate 294
How to Create a Career Plan 295
    Step 1: Understand Yourself 295
    Step 2: Research Career Options 297
    Step 3: Make a Decision and Map out Your Goals 298
    Where to Go for Assistance 298

11 Life-Management Skills
Managing Time and Money 301

The Importance of Time and Money Management 302
Managing Time 302
    Strategies for Improving Time Management 303
Elements of a Comprehensive Time-Management Plan 306
    Converting Your Time-Management Plan into an Action Plan 308
    Dealing with Procrastination 309
Managing Money 314
    Strategies for Managing Money Effectively 315
    Strategic Selection and Use of Financial Tools for Tracking Cash Flow 317
    Developing Personal Money-Saving Strategies and Habits 322
    Long-Range Financial Planning: Financing Your College Education 326
Summary and Conclusion 330
Learning More through Independent Research 331
    Web-Based Resources for Further Information on Managing Time and Money 331
Exercise: Financial Self-Awareness: Monitoring Money and Tracking Cash Flow 331
Case Study: Procrastination: The Vicious Cycle 335

12 Financial Planning

Part I. The Cost of Attending College 338
Part II. Dalton State College Financial Aid 339
    Types of Financial Aid 339
    Who Can Receive Financial Aid? 339
    How to Apply for Financial Aid 339
    Calculating Financial Need 343
    Financial Aid Disbursements 343
    Enrollment Status for Financial Aid 344
    Georgia HOPE Program 345
    Exercise: Calculating a HOPE GPA 347
    How Dropping and Withdrawing from Classes Affects Financial Aid 349
    Satisfactory Academic Progress (SAP) for Financial Aid 349
    Other Financing Options 352
Part III. Managing Your Money 353
Basic Rules of Money Management 353
Budgeting 353
Exercise: Creating a Budget 355
Money Saving Tips 359

The Credit Card Trap 359
    Selecting a Credit Card 359
    The Lure of the Minimum Payment 360
    Other Credit Card Tips 360

Student Loans 360
    Subsidized Stafford Loan 361
    Unsubsized Stafford Loan 361
    Annual Loan Limits 361
    How Do I Repay My Federal Stafford Loan? 361
    Private Loans 362

Identity Theft 362
Exercise: What Is Your Identity Theft Probability (ITP) Score? 363
    Minimize the Risk of Identity Theft 365
Maintaining Good Credit 365

References 369

Glossary 394

Index 407

Acknowledgments

There are a number of individuals at Dalton State College who assisted in the creation of this book. We are grateful for their support.

Dianne Cox —Director, Financial Aid

First Year Experience Committee

First Year Experience Instructors

Kristi Casey-Hart—MS, LAPC,—Counseling and Career Services

Holli Goodwin—Academic Advisor

Kim McCroskey—Instructional Technologist Academic Services

Amy Schmidt—Director, Academic Advsing

Jody Trost—Coordinator, First Year Experience and Peer Instruction

Linda Wheeler—Director, Academic Resources

Letter to Students

The first year of college is a composite of many experiences, uncertainties, decisions, and transformations which will influence you to ask yourself important questions regarding your life and academic career. At Dalton State College, we created The First Year Seminar to assist you in finding the answers to your questions, provide you with the academic skills you need to succeed, and connect you to faculty, peers, and the resources needed to transition smoothly to the college environment and to become a lifelong learner.

To succeed, you must have the tools and guidance to persist; without these instruments, you may ask questions which may not be answered. The First Year Experience staff and faculty hope to successfully provide you with the tools for success and with the guidance you need to carry out your academic and career goals.

Best Wishes,
Jody Trost
Coordinator First Year Experience and Peer Instruction

Introduction

Welcome to College

Congratulations and welcome! We applaud your decision to continue your education. You've made it to college, also known as "higher education" (because it's "higher" than high school), and you are about to begin a new and exciting journey in your life. While your previous attendance in school was required, continuing your education in college is your choice, and you have made a choice that will surely better your life.

Your movement into higher education represents an important life transition. Similar to an immigrant moving to a new country, you will be moving into a new culture with different expectations, regulations, customs, and "language" (Chaskes, 1996). Your transition to college means you will be moving into "higher education," where you will be moving up to higher levels of challenge, support, and development.

It is probably safe to say that, after college, you will never again be a member of any other organization or institution with as many resources and services available to you that have been intentionally designed to promote your learning, development, and success. Your college experience has the potential to be the most enriching and enjoyable stage of your life. If you capitalize on the numerous resources and opportunities that are available to you, and if you utilize effective learning strategies while in college, you are likely to create an experience that will bring you multiple, life-long benefits. (See Box 1.)

Your transition to college means you will be moving into "higher education," where you will be moving up to higher levels of challenge, support, and development.

BOX 1 — Snapshot Summary

Why College Is Worth It: The Economic and Personal Benefits of College

About 27 percent of Americans have earned a college (bachelor's) degree. Research comparing college graduates with individuals from similar social and economic backgrounds who have not continued their education beyond high school indicates that college is well worth the investment. It has been found that college graduates experience multiple advantages, such as the following.

1. **Career Benefits**
   - Security and Stability—lower rates of unemployment
   - Versatility and Mobility—more flexibility to move out of one position and into other positions
   - Advancement—better opportunity to move up to higher professional positions
   - Interest—more likely to find their work stimulating and challenging
   - Autonomy—greater independence and opportunity to be their own boss
   - Satisfaction—enjoy their work more and feel that it allows them to use their special talents
   - Prestige—higher career status (job desirability)

> **· CLASSIC QUOTE ·**
> *"If you think education is expensive, try ignorance."*
> —Derek Bok, former President, Harvard University

(continued)

> **CLASSIC QUOTE**
>
> *A bachelor's degree continues to be a primary vehicle of which one gains an advantaged socioeconomic position in American society.*
>
> —Ernest Pascarella & Patrick Terenzini, *How College Affects Students*

2. Economic Advantages
   - Higher income—the gap in income between high school and college graduates is *increasing*. Individuals with a bachelor's degree now earn an average salary of about $50,000 per year—40 percent higher than high school graduates, whose average salary is less than $30,000 per year. The lifetime income of families headed by persons with a bachelor's degree is about $1,600,000 more than families headed by persons with a high school diploma.
   - Make wiser consumer choices and decisions
   - Make more effective long-term investments

3. Advanced Intellectual Skills
   - Greater knowledge
   - More effective problem-solving skills
   - Better ability to deal with complex and ambiguous (uncertain) ideas
   - Greater openness to new ideas
   - More advanced levels of moral reasoning
   - A clearer sense of self-identity—more awareness and knowledge of personal talents, interests, values, and needs
   - More likely to continue learning throughout life

4. Better Physical Health
   - Better dietary habits
   - Exercise more regularly
   - Live longer and healthier lives

5. Social Advantages
   - Higher levels of social self-confidence
   - Understand and communicate more effectively with others
   - Greater popularity
   - More effective leadership skills
   - Greater marital satisfaction

6. Emotional Advantages
   - Lower levels of anxiety
   - Higher levels of self-esteem
   - Higher sense of self-efficacy—sense of control over their life
   - Higher levels of psychological well-being
   - Higher levels of personal happiness

7. More Effective Citizens
   - Greater interest in social and political issues
   - Greater knowledge of current affairs
   - Higher voting participation rates
   - Participate more frequently in civic affairs and community service

8. Better Quality of Life for their Children
   - Spend more time and energy on their children
   - Provide better health care for their children

(continued)

- More likely to involve their children in educational activities that stimulate their mental development
- Their children are more likely to graduate from college
- Their children are more likely to attain higher-status and higher-paying careers

References:
Astin, A. W. (1993). *What Matters in College?*
Bowen, H. R. (1977, 1997). *Investment in Learning: The Individual & Social Value of American Higher Education.*
Ottinger, C. (1990). *College graduates in the labor market: Today and the future.*
Feldman, K. A., & Newcomb, T. M. (1994). *The impact of college on students.*
Pascarella, E. T., & Terenzini, P. T. (1991). *How college affects students: Findings and Insights from Twenty Years of Research.*
Pascarella, E. T., & Terenzini, P. T. (2005). *How college affects students: A third decade of research* (volume 2). San Francisco: Jossey-Bass.
Postsecondary Education Opportunity (2000). *Private Benefit/Cost Ratios of a College Investment for Men and Women, 1967–1999.*
Tierney, W. G. (ed.) (1998). *The responsive university: Restructuring for high performance.* Baltimore: Johns Hopkins Press.
U.S. Census Bureau (2003). *Bureau of Labor Statistics.* Washington, D.C.: Author.

STUDENT PERSPECTIVE

"My 3-month old boy is very important to me, and it is important that I graduate from college so my son, as well as I, live a better life."

—First-year student in response to the question, "What is most important to you?"

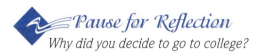

Why did you decide to go to college?

Why did you choose the particular college you're now attending?

••• Importance of the First Year of College

The *first* year of college is definitely the most critical stage of the college experience. It is the year during which students report the most change, the most learning, and the most development (MacGregor, 1991; Light, 2001). It is also the year during which students experience the most stress, the most academic difficulties, and the highest dropout rate (American College Testing, 2003; Cuseo, 1991). When graduating seniors look back on their college experience, many of them say that the first year was the time of greatest change and the time during which they made the most significant improvements in their approach to learning. Here is how one senior put it during a personal interview:

Interviewer: What have you learned about your approach to learning [in college]?

Student: I had to learn how to study. I went through high school with a 4.0 average. I didn't have to study. It was a breeze. I got to the university and there was no structure. No one checked my homework. No one took attendance to make sure I was in class. No one told me I had to do something. There were no quizzes on the readings. I did not work well with this lack of structure. It took my first year and a half to learn to deal with it. But I had to teach myself to manage my time. I had to teach myself how to study. I had to teach myself how to learn in a different environment (Chickering & Schlossberg, 1998, p. 47).

In many ways, the first-year experience in college is similar to ocean surfing or downhill skiing; it can be filled with many exciting thrills and also some potentially dangerous spills. The goal of skiing and surfing is to maximize the thrills, minimize the spills, and finish the run while still on your feet. The same is true for the first year of college; studies show that if you can complete your first-year experience in good standing, your chances for successfully completing the total college experience improves dramatically (American College Testing, 2003).

In a nutshell, college success depends on your taking advantage of what your college can do for you and what you can do for yourself. The research cited and the advice provided in this book point to one major conclusion: Success in college depends on **you**—i.e., you make it happen by what you **do**. The more motivated you are to get the most out of your college experience, the more successful you will be. In the graph below, you can see that there is a direct relationship between students' motivation and their college grades.

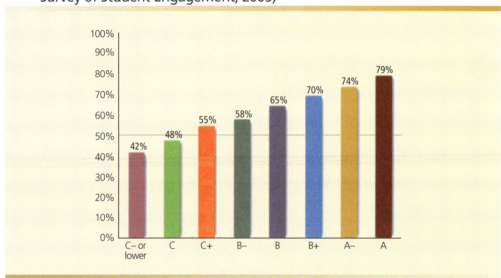

Percentage of Highly Motivated Students Attending a Particular College and the Average Grades Achieved by Students at that College (National Survey of Student Engagement, 2005)

After reviewing 40 years of research on how college affects students, two distinguished researchers concluded that:

> *The impact of college is largely determined by individual effort and involvement in the academic, interpersonal, and extracurricular [co-curricular] offerings on a campus. Students are not passive recipients of institutional efforts to "educate" or "change" them, but rather bear major responsibility for any gains they derive from their postsecondary [college] experience (Pascarella & Terenzini, 2005, p. 602).*

Compared to high school, your college experience will involve a much broader range of courses, far more resources to capitalize on, much more freedom of choice and many more decision-making opportunities. Your particular college experience will be different than that of any other college student because you will have the freedom to actively shape or create it in a way that is uniquely your own. So, don't let college happen *to* you; instead, make it happen *for* you—by taking charge of your experience and taking full advantage of all the resources that are at your command.

·—· **CLASSIC QUOTE** ·—·

Some people make things happen, while others watch things happen or wonder what has happened.

—Author unknown

Pause for Reflection

In order to be successful in college, what do you think you'll have to do differently than you did in high school?

••• Importance of a First-Year Seminar (also known as a College Success or Student Success Course)

If you're reading this book, you are already beginning to take charge of your college experience because you're probably enrolled in a course that is designed to promote your college success. Research strongly indicates that new students who participate in courses such as the one you're in are more likely to stay in college, complete their degree, and achieve higher grades. These positive effects have been found for:

- all types of students (under-prepared and well-prepared, minority and majority, residential and commuter, male and female),
- students at all types of colleges (2-year and 4-year, public and private),
- students attending college of different sizes (small, mid-sized, and large), and
- students attending college in different locations (urban, suburban, and rural).

(References: Barefoot, 1993; Barefoot et al., 1998; Boudreau & Kromrey, 1994; Fidler & Godwin, 1994; Glass & Garrett, 1995; Grunder & Hellmich, 1996; Hunter & Linder, 2005; Shanley & Witten, 1990; Sidle & McReynolds, 1999; Starke, Harth, & Sirianni, 2001; Thomson, 1998; Tobolowski, 2005).

It is fair to say that there has been more carefully conducted research on first-year seminars or college-success courses, and more evidence supporting their effectiveness for increasing students' college success, than there is for any other course that has ever been offered in the history of higher education. You are fortunate to be enrolled in such a course. Give it your best effort and take full advantage of what it has to offer. If you do, you will be taking a major step toward thriving in college and beyond.

As you begin your college journey . . .

> **Remember:** On the higher education highway, don't be a passive passenger; instead, take charge of your college experience and be an active driver of your own vehicle. Ultimately, your effort and energy will provide the high-mileage fuel that carries you all the way to graduation, and your goal-setting and strategic planning will provide the steering wheel that guides you in the direction of future success.

Have a good trip!

STUDENT PERSPECTIVES

"Every first-semester freshman needs a class like this—whether they think so or not."
—First-year student comment made when evaluating a first-year seminar (college success course)

"I am now one of the peer counselors on campus, and without this class my first semester, I don't think I could have done as well, and by participating in this class again (as a teaching assistant), it reinforced this belief."
—First-year student comment made when evaluating a first-year seminar (college success course)

Technology at Dalton State College

This chapter provides information related to technology and its support at Dalton State College. You will find detailed instructional handouts to help you through processes such as accessing your DSConnect account, sending emails, checking your grades, and contacting the Office of Computing and Information Services (OCIS).

The Office of Computing and Information Services

The Office of Computing and Information Services (OCIS) is responsible for the management and support of computing, networking, and information technology services at Dalton State College. Our goal is to empower you to utilize technology in your daily life. You can find our contact information and hours of operation below:

Contact Information

Phone: 706-272-2611
Location: Memorial 103
Email: helpdesk@daltonstate.edu
Web: http://www.daltonstate.edu/ocis

OCIS Hours of Operation

Regular Business Hours: 8:00 a.m.–5:00 p.m. (Monday–Friday)
After-Hours Support: 5:00 p.m.–8:00 p.m. (Monday–Thursday)

Wireless Internet Access

Wireless Internet access is available to the entire DSC campus. You will use your username and password for DSConnect to access the wireless Internet network.

Secure Data Management

The security of data at Dalton State College is very important. You should not store any sensitive information such as social security numbers, financial account information, or birth dates on any device that is not password protected. Do not disclose your username and password to anyone else. If you feel that your account information has been compromised, please contact the OCIS office immediately.

DSConnect

DSConnect is your information highway portal at Dalton State. Campus communications via email and announcements take place through the portal. You will have access your free campus email account. You will also have access to our student information system, Banner, which will allow you to check your grades, register for classes, and much more.

To access DSConnect, visit http://mydsc.daltonstate.edu. You can obtain your username and password by clicking on the link below the area where the information is to be typed in.

GeorgiaVIEW

Dalton State College utilizes GeorgiaVIEW to deliver online and hybrid (1/2 time online) classes. GeorgiaVIEW is also used to enhance a large number of classes on campus.

You can access GeorgiaVIEW through the link in your DSConnect portal, by visiting http://www.daltonstate.edu and clicking the Vista link, or by visiting https://daltonstate.view.usg.edu. Your username and password for GeorgiaVIEW is the same as that for DSConnect.

Campus Computer Labs

The Learning Commons

This computer lab is an open access lab for students and will be located in the Derrell C. Roberts Library. We also have a 40-station computer lab in the main library area.

Classroom Computer Labs

General and special purpose computer labs are located in the various buildings on campus. You can find out the location and software installations for the labs by visiting http://www.daltonstate.edu/ocis/labs.

Technology Training Tutorials and How-To Guides

While this chapter will provide you with some detailed handouts for accessing DSConnect, Banner, and GeorgiaVIEW, up-to-date training materials and handouts can be found by visiting http://www.daltonstate.edu/ocis/training.

Accessing DSConnect

1. Go to http://www.daltonstate.edu (or go to http://mydsc.daltonstate.edu) and bypass step 2.
2. Click on the link to Webmail, Banner.
3. Type in your username and password. If you do not know your password, click on the link the username and password area to find out your username and password.
4. You are now inside of DSConnect.

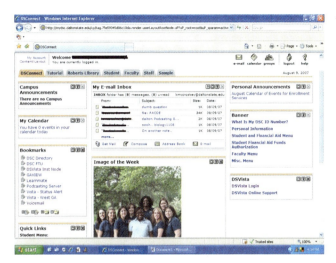

Using Email in DSConnect

Sending Mail

1. Click on Compose.
2. Type in the person's email address and message in the appropriate locations. (DSConnect has a file attachment limit of 5 mb.)
3. Click on Send.

DSConnect Address Book

If you are not sure of the person's email address on campus, you can use the DSC Directory in DSConnect to look it up.

1. Click on Address beside the To: field.
2. Change the Address Source to DSConnect Directory.

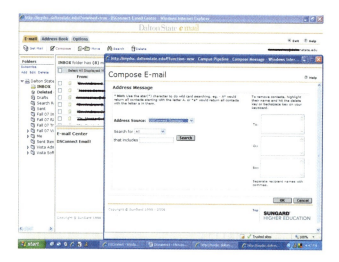

3. Type in the name of the person you are searching for and click Search. The results will be displayed. This may take a few minutes because all DSC students, faculty, and staff are being searched during this process.
4. When the results are provided, click on the To: beside the appropriate name and then click OK in the lower right corner.

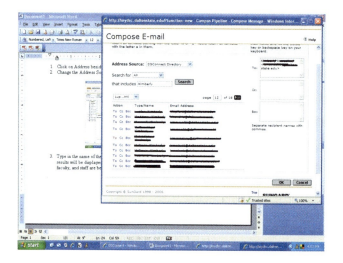

5. Finish your email message and click send.

Organizing Emails

Organization is the key to success. If you wish to organize your email messages, follow the steps below:

1. From the DSConnect entry page, click on Email.
2. On the left side of your window, you should see a list of folders. Click on the Add button to add a new folder. You will be asked to click on the folder where you wish to place your new folder. For example, all top level folders are under Dalton State College Mail (click on that to select it).

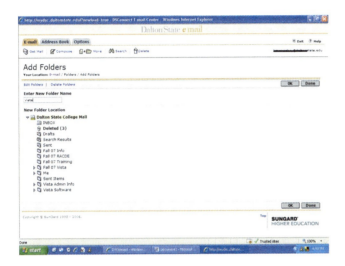

3. Click OK when you have typed in the new folder name.
4. Click Done when you have added all of your folders.

Tips to Consider When Using Email Programs

1. **Be professional when writing your email.** Be sure your email includes all the important information your reader will need to know the entire situation.
2. **Proper grammar, punctuation, and spelling** are crucial when communicating in the written format. Do not send an email with Internet slang such as TTL, LOL, or the number 2 instead of using the word to.
3. **Proofread before you send.** Be sure to proofread your email message before you send it. Make sure you have included all of the information needed and the tone is what you want it to be. Make sure that all of your grammar and spelling are correct.
4. **Add the email address last.** It is usually a good idea to add the email address as the last step to ensure you do not send an email prematurely.
5. **Utilize a strong subject line.** A strong, specific subject line will get your email message picked for reading quicker.
6. **Email is traceable.** It is important to remember that anything send in written format is traceable. Use common sense and do not write anything in an email you would not want to answer for later. Email in your workplace belongs to your employer and is not your private tool. It is recommended to not use your company account for any personal business.

7. **Watch your emotions.** Because email is a written form of communication, it is very easy to miss the emotion behind what is being said. It is very easy to misunderstand a message if it is written while you are feeling strong emotions. If your email has the potential to be misinterpreted, then you have the option not to send it. You can also pick up the phone and talk to the person to avoid this situation. AVOID ALL CAPS WHEN TYPING. IT IS CONSIDERED SHOUTING.
8. **Open attachments with caution.** Be sure to use extreme caution when opening attachments. This is how viruses are spread from company to company. Never open an attachment with an .exe file attached. They're usually bad.

Adding Bookmarks in DSConnect

1. Log into your DSConnect account.
2. Click the button for "add a bookmark" (The first button on the left under bookmarks).

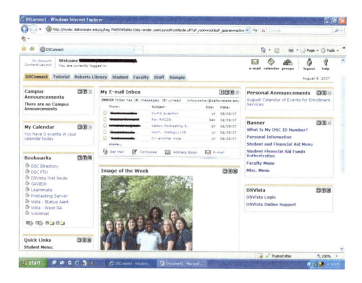

3. Type in the information requested which includes a title to be displayed and the Internet address.
4. Click Add. You should now see the title you typed in your list of addresses. You can delete bookmarks and organize bookmarks using the links as indicated in the bookmark channel.

••• DSConnect My Courses

What Is My Courses?

My Courses is a tool in DSConnect that allows instructors to post files, make announcements, and link to articles for the students to access. This tool can also be used for communication purposes such as class emails, chats, and discussion postings.

How Do I Access My Courses?

In order to access My Courses, you will need to log into your DSConnect account. Once you have logged into your account, click on the Student tab located at the top of the window.

After selecting the Student tab, you now have the option to access My Courses, Academic Services, Campus Life, and a listing of upcoming Student Activities events.

Click on the link for My Courses. You will now see a list of the courses you are enrolled in for the semester.

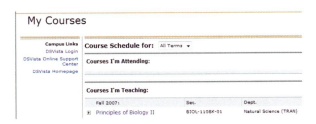

Technology at Dalton State College ♦ XXV

What Tools Can I Use in My Courses?

Below is a screen capture showing the options for My Courses.

Course Tools

These links will allow you to access information your instructor posts. If you are trying to access files posted by the instructor, click on the link for Files. If you are trying to access web links posted for your use, click on the link titled "Links" on the left side of the screen.

••• Banner—Financial Aid Menu

Banner is the student information system used at Dalton State College to store student data. You have access to your Banner information through your DSConnect account.

To access Banner, you will need to log into your DSConnect account and click on the link for Student and Financial Aid Menu on the right side of the screen under the Banner channel.

By clicking on the link for Financial Aid, you will be able to access all of the information related to your financial aid status at Dalton State College.

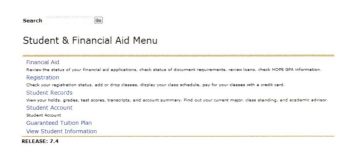

From the Financial Aid menu, you can perform many tasks such as identifying your current financial aid status, determining your Hope Eligibility, and apply for loans. Descriptions for each of the areas are located underneath the headings as shown above.

Banner—Registration Menu

Banner is the student information system used at Dalton State College to store student data. You have access to your Banner information through your DSConnect account.

To access Banner, you will need to log into your DSConnect account and click on the link for Student and Financial Aid Menu on the right side of the screen under the Banner channel.

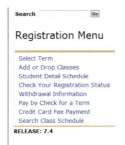

The Registration link will be one of your frequently used links. This powerful area will give you access to tools such as registering for classes, getting a copy of your schedule, and paying for classes. You can access any of these items simply by clicking on the link.

Technology at Dalton State College ◆ xxvii

Banner—Student Records Menu

Banner is the student information system used at Dalton State College to store student data. You have access to your Banner information through your DSConnect account.

To access Banner, you will need to log into your DSConnect account and click on the link for Student and Financial Aid Menu on the right side of the screen under the Banner channel.

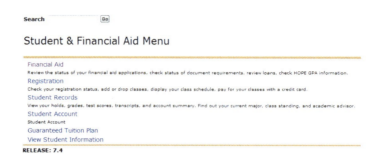

The Student Records link will take you to all of your student records. You will click on the Student Records link in order to access your mid-term and final grades. You will click on the link for Academic Transcript to see a copy of your transcript. Your transcript will provide you with information such as your transfer information, advisor information, and semester schedule. You can also get a detailed receipt from your Academic Transcript.

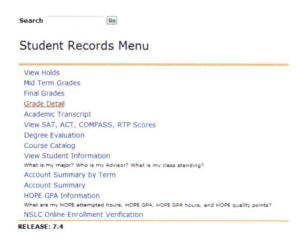

••• GeorgiaVIEW Access Information

How to Access GeorgiaVIEW

In order to access your class using GeorgiaVIEW, please complete the following steps:

1. Open your Internet browser (Netscape or Internet Explorer or Mozilla).
2. Type in the following URL (Internet Location): https://daltonstate.view.usg.edu.
3. Click on the Log In button.
4. Type in your username and password. Your username and password are the same as the username and password for DSConnect.
5. You will see a list of the courses you have assigned to your GeorgiaVIEW ID. You will click on the name of the course you wish to enter.

Using the steps above takes you directly to the GeorgiaVIEW server. You can also get to the same location by clicking on the link for GeorgiaVIEW inside of DSConnect. In the event DSConnect is unavailable, you will need to access GeorgiaVIEW using the steps above.

How to Get Help with GeorgiaVIEW

GeorgiaVIEW Online Support Center (24/7/365)

http://help.view.usg.edu.

DSC Technical Support

The Office of Computing provides technical support to faculty and students using GeorgiaVIEW. Please contact Kim McCroskey (kmccroskey@daltonstate.edu) for assistance. Helpful information and troubleshooting tips can be found at http://www.daltonstate.edu/ocis/training.

Java

You will need to have the latest version of Sun Microsystems Java Runtime Environment (JRE) software installed on your computer in order for certain areas of GeorgiaVIEW to function properly. To install this software, go to http://www.java.com to download the software.

Pop-up Blockers and Firewalls

Be sure to disable Pop-Up Blocking and Firewalls for the GeorgiaVIEW site. While using GeorgiaVIEW, if you are unable to view discussion postings, quiz windows, and download links, then you need to disable pop-up blocking for your GeorgiaVIEW site. Depending on the pop-up blocking software you are using, you may be able to set your GeorgiaVIEW site as an allowed site, or you may need to disable the pop-up blocker while using GeorgiaVIEW. Pop-up blockers work in the background while you browse the Internet. When they detect a pop-up window that may be an unwanted advertisement, they automatically close the window. This can prevent GeorgiaVIEW from performing properly.

Trusted Sites

To prevent an XP security feature from blocking attachments in the future, you must add https://daltonstate.view.usg.edu and https://c.view.usg.edu to your list of trusted sites. Directions for adding trusted sites can be found at http://www.daltonstate.edu/ocis/training.

Campus Resources

There are many resources and activities for students on campus. The following are brief descriptions of each. For an extensive description of all resources refer to your DSC Catalog or Website at http://www.daltonstate.edu/catalog.htm.

Academic Resources

Phone: 706-272-4429
Location: Lower level of the Pope Student Center
Website: **http://www.daltonstate.edu/ace**

The Academic Resources offers resources and support services to help students determine and pursue academic, career, social, and personal goals.

Academic Support Services

- Academic strategy workshops
- Assistance with study skills, test anxiety, and reading textbooks
- Books, videos, and audiotapes for academic success
- College transfer and testing information
- Course syllabi
- Peer Instruction and Tutoring in academic courses

Computer Lab

- Career and academic software
- Catalogs and applications for other colleges/universities online

Cooperative Education and Career Services

- Assistance for qualified students in locating cooperative education positions closely related to their fields of study
- Career advising for help in choosing a major or a career
- Career information and planning resources
- Fall and Spring Career Fairs
- Job placement bulletin board and online listings
- Resume, interview, and job search seminars
- Online seminars

Counseling and Career Services

The staff of Academic Resources can assist students with personal and career concerns and in acquiring assistance from appropriate agencies in the community.

The Testing Center

Phone: 706-272-2606
Location: Room 303 of the Lorberbaum Liberal Arts Building

- Responsible for the coordination of all standardized testing on campus
- Administers tests with accommodations for students with disabilities

Disability Support Services

Students with disabilities are invited to contact the Academic and Career Enhancement (ACE) Center of Dalton State College to request reasonable accommodations for academic programs and other activities at Dalton State College. Professional documentation must be provided to receive services. Students who are unable to come to Academic Resources to request services should call the ACE Center at 706-272-4429 for assistance. Some services available include:

- ADA seating
- Adaptive technology lab with specialized software
- Testing with accommodations
- Volunteer note-taking assistance

FYE First Year Experience

Phone: 706-272-4429
Location: Lower level of the Pope Student Center
FYE provides the Freshman Year Seminar and assists with freshman transition to college.

- Provides First Year Experience Learning Communities
- Provides FYE Common Reading Program
- Provides Peer Instruction

Academic Advising Center

Phone: 706-272-4458
Location: Room 107 of the Lorberbaum Liberal Arts Building
In the Academic Advising Center you can receive assistance with:

- Initial registration
- Education on Student Resources
- Assistance with registration of classes
- Education on Academic Programs offered at DSC

Financial Aid

Phone: 706-272-4545
Location: Lower level of the Pope Student Center
The primary purpose of the Office of Student Financial Aid and Veteran Services is to provide financial assistance to qualified and eligible students attending Dalton State College.

Food Service

Phone: 706-272-4441
Location: Upper level of the Pope Student Center

The "Skylight Cafe" is open Monday through Thursday, 7:00 a.m. to 5:00 p.m., and Friday and summer term from 7:00 a.m. to 1:00 p.m. Food Service offers breakfast, lunch (cafeteria style or sandwiches), and snacks.

Bookstore

Phone: 706-272-4548
Location: Upper level of the Pope Student Center

The Bookstore is open Monday through Thursday 7:30 a.m. to 6:00 p.m. and Friday 7:30 a.m. to 12:30 p.m. Services include textbook sales, textbook buy-back, best-sellers, reference materials, and sundries.

Library

Phone: 706-272-4547
Location: South end of campus
The Derrell C. Roberts Library is online at http://www.daltonstate.edu/library.

If you need assistance with an assignment or just have a question, stop by the Reference Desk or send a question via Ask-A-Librarian which is linked off the Library's main page. The Library is open over 73 hours a week during main semester hours and is open 24/7 through the Library's web page. Summer, holiday, and intercession hours can be found at http://gil.daltonstate.edu/calreq.php.

Main semester hours are: Monday through Thursday, 7:30 a.m. to 10:00 p.m.; Friday, 7:30 a.m. to 5:00 p.m.; and Sunday 1:00 p.m. to 7:00 p.m.

Some services provided by the Library are:

- Laptop check out
- Workstations
- Study rooms
- Printers
- Digital scanners
- Library media room
- Circulation materials, online materials, online catalog
- Inter-Library loan

••• Gym

Location: South side of campus

The Bandy Gymnasium provides health and physical education facilities for scheduled activities. The facility includes a heated, indoor swimming pool, basketball courts, a weight room, locker rooms, and classrooms. Intramural programs are conducted each term and are open to currently enrolled students, faculty, and staff. Facilities are also available for open recreation when no scheduled class or activity is in progress.

••• Student Activities

Phone: 706-272-4428
Location: Upper level of the Pope Student Center

Many clubs exist on the campus and, as interest develops among students, additional clubs will be recognized. The following groups are currently functioning on campus:

Bacchus Network	Baptist Collegiate Ministries
Black Student Alliance	Business Networking Club
Business Office Professionals Organization	Chemist Society
College Bowl	Circle K
College Republicans	Community Service Organization
Criminal Justice Society	D.I.R.T.
Environmental Club	
Funny Healers	Future Educators
History Club	International Students Association
LPN Club	Medical Laboratory Technicians
Music Club	
Phi Alpha	Phi Theta Kappa
Philosophy Club	Pre-Health Professional Club
President's Council	Psychology Club
Radiology Technology Club	Social Work Club
Spanish Club	Speech and Debate Society
Student Ambassadors	Surgical Technology Club
Tributaries	Young Democrats

Student Services also provides student IDs, campus recreation, intramural sports, and new student orientation.

Writing Lab

Location: Room 315 of the Lorberbaum Liberal Arts Building

The Writing Lab provides services to all students seeking assistance with writing assignments. Qualified faculty will assist you. Hours vary from semester to semester. See online at http://www.daltonstate.edu/faculty/mnielson.

Math Lab

Location: Room 140 of the Sequoya Building

The Math Lab tutors students in all levels of math and in all math courses offered at DSC. Qualified faculty and peer tutors are available Monday through Thursday, 8:00 a.m. to 8:00 p.m., and 8:00 a.m. to 12:00 p.m. on Fridays.

Public Safety

Location: Upper level of the Pope Student Center

Public Safety has the responsibility on campus for the safety and security of DSC students, staff, and faculty. There are seven full-time state-certified Police Officers. You can go to Public Safety for the following services:

- To report crime on campus
- Parking tickets
- To obtain parking decal

Touching All the Bases

An Overview and Preview of the Most Powerful Principles of College Success

Learning Goals

The major goal of this chapter is to supply you with a set of powerful learning strategies that you can immediately use to get off to a fast start in college and that you can continually use to achieve success throughout your remaining years of college.

Outline

The Most Powerful Research-Based Principles of College Success
The Home Base of College Success: Active Involvement
    Time Spent in Class
    Time Spent on Coursework Outside the Classroom
    Active Listening and Note-Taking
    Active Class Participation
    Active Reading
Touching the First Base of College Success: Utilizing Campus Resources
    Learning Center
    Writing Center
    Disability Services or Office for Students with Special Needs
    College Library
    Academic Advisement
    Career Development Center
    Counseling Center
    Health Center
    Experiential Learning Resources
    Learning More about Your Campus Resources through Your Own Research
Touching the Second Base of College Success: Social Interaction and Collaboration
    Student-Faculty Interaction
    Student-Advisor Interaction
    Interaction with a Mentor
    Interaction with Peers
    Collaboration with Peers
Touching the Third Base of College Success: Self-Reflection
    Self-Assessment
    Self-Monitoring
    Reflecting on Feedback
    Reflecting on Your Future
A Checklist Summary of Key College-Success Principles and Strategies
Learning More through Independent Research
Exercises: Constructing a Master List of Campus Resources

Activate Your Thinking

1. How do you think college will be *different* than high school?
2. What do you think it will take to be *successful* in college? (In other words: What personal characteristics, qualities, or strategies do you feel are most important for college success?)
3. What do you imagine your first year here will be like?

The Most Powerful Research-Based Principles of College Success

Research on human learning and student development indicates that there are four powerful principles of college success:

1. active involvement,
2. utilizing resources,
3. social interaction/collaboration, and
4. self-reflection (Astin, 1993; Kuh, 2000; Light, 2001; Pascarella & Terenzini, 1991, 2005; Tinto, 1993).

These represent the four basic principles of college success, and they are introduced and examined carefully in this chapter for two important reasons:

1. so you can *immediately* put these strategies into practice to get off to a fast start in college and establish good habits, and
2. because these principles provide the essential *foundation* for all the success strategies that are recommended throughout this book. These four key principles of college success can be represented visually in the form of a diamond with four bases (Figure 1).

Figure **The Diamond of College Success**

The Home Base of College Success: Active Involvement

Research indicates that active involvement is the most fundamental and most powerful principle of human learning and college success (Astin, 1993; Kuh, 2000). You could consider it to be the home base of college success, because it provides the basic foundation for all other college-success strategies. The bottom line is this: To maximize your success in college, you need to be an *active agent* in the learning process, not a passive sponge or spectator.

The basic principle of active involvement includes the following pair of key components or processes:

- the amount of personal *time* you devote to learning in college, and
- the degree of personal effort or energy (mental and physical) that you put into the learning process.

> **CLASSIC QUOTE**
>
> *Tell me and I'll listen. Show me and I'll understand. Involve me and I'll learn.*
>
> —Teton Lakota Indian saying

One way to ensure that you are actively involved in the learning process, and are expending high levels of energy or effort, is to act on what you are learning. In other words, you should perform some physical action on what you are attempting to learn. If you engage in any of the following physical actions with respect to what you are learning, you can be assured that you are investing a high level of involvement and energy in the learning process.

Writing—expressing what you are trying to learn in print

    ACTION: Write notes when reading, rather than passively underlining sentences.

Speaking—orally communicate what you are attempting to learn

    ACTION: Explain a course concept to a study-group partner, rather than just looking it over silently.

Organizing—grouping or classifying the concepts you are learning into logical categories that show how they are related.

    ACTION: Create an outline, diagram, or concept map (similar to Figure 1) that visually organizes concepts.

Writing notes while reading is one way to become actively involved in the learning process.

The following section explains how you can apply both components of active involvement—spending time and expending energy—to some of the major learning tasks that you will encounter in college.

Time Spent in Class

Since the total amount of time you spend on learning is associated with how much you learn and how successful you are in college, this association naturally leads to a very straightforward recommendation: Attend all class sessions in all your courses. It may be tempting to skip or cut classes because college professors are less likely to monitor your attendance or call roll like your teachers in high school. Do not let this new freedom fool you into thinking that missing classes will not affect your grades. College research indicates that there is a direct relationship between class attendance and course grades—as one goes up or down, so does the other (Anderson & Gates, 2002; Grandpre, 2000). For instance, one study revealed that every 10 percent increase in the number of student absences in college classes resulted in a .2 drop in students' overall grade-point average (Kowalewski, Holstein, & Schneider, 1989). Figure 2 represents the results of another study conducted at the City Colleges of Chicago, which shows the relationship between students' class attendance during the first five weeks of the term and final course grades.

Time Spent on Coursework Outside the Classroom

In college, you will spend fewer hours per week sitting in class than you did in high school. However, in college, there are higher expectations for the amount of time that you should commit to academic work outside of class time. Studies clearly show that the greater amount of time college students spend on academic work outside of class results in greater learning and higher grades. For example, one study of over 25,000 college students found that the percentage of students receiving grades that were mostly "As" was almost three times higher for students who spent 40 or more hours per week on academic work than it was for students who spent 20 or

STUDENT PERSPECTIVE

"You don't have to be smart to work hard."

—24-year-old, first-year student who has returned to college

STUDENT PERSPECTIVE

"My biggest recommendation: GO TO CLASS. I learned this the hard way my first semester. You'll be surprised what you pick up just by being there. I wish someone would have informed me of this before I started school."

—Advice to new students from a college sophomore (Walsh, 2005)

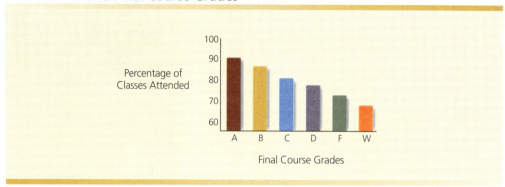

Figure 2 Relationship Between Class Attendance Rate and Final Course Grades

less. On the other hand, among students who spent 20 or fewer hours on academic work, the percentage of them receiving grades that were mostly "Cs" or below was almost twice as high as it was for students who spent 40 or more hours per week on academic activities (Pace, 1990a, 1990b).

Only 20 percent of first-year students expect to spend more than 25 hours per week studying, and although almost all (96%) first-year students agree that they can improve their academic ability through hard work and practice, almost one-third (30%) admitted that they did just enough work to get by (National Survey of Student Engagement, 2005).

Keep in mind that better grades in college equals better chances for career success after college. Research on college graduates indicates that the higher their grades were in college, the higher:

◆ the status (prestige) of their first job,
◆ their job mobility (ability to change jobs or move into different positions), and
◆ their total earnings (salary).

This relationship between college grades and career success exists for students at all types of colleges and universities, regardless of the reputation or prestige of the institution they are attending (Pascarella & Terenzini, 1991, 2005). In other words, how well you do academically in college matters more to your career success than where you go to college, or what particular college issues your diploma.

*Pause for Reflection*

In high school, how many hours per week did you spend on schoolwork outside of class?

Active Listening and Note-Taking

You will find that professors frequently use the lecture method, whereby the instructor speaks continuously and the students' job is to listen and take notes. This method of instruction places great demands on students' ability to listen carefully and take notes that are accurate and complete.

• CLASSIC QUOTE •

"*Success comes to those who hustle.*"

—Abe Lincoln, 16th American president and author of the "Emancipation Proclamation," which set the stage for the abolition of slavery in the United States

---

STUDENT PERSPECTIVE

"I thought I would get a better education if the school had a really good reputation. Now, I think one's education depends on how much effort you put into it."

—First-year college student (Bates, 1994)

Remember: Research shows that, in all subject areas, the majority of test questions on college exams come from the professor's lectures and that students who take better class notes get better course grades (Brown, 1988; Kierwa, 2000).

The best way to apply the strategy of active involvement during a class lecture is to engage in the physical action of writing notes. Writing down what your instructor is saying in class essentially forces you to pay closer attention to what is being said and reinforces your retention of that information. By taking notes, you not only hear the information (auditory memory), you also see it—on paper (visual memory) and feel it—in the muscles of your hand as you write it (motor memory).

STUDENT PERSPECTIVE

"I usually sit in the back [of class] because you can relax and possibly nap."

—*First-year student with Attention Deficit Disorder*

Remember: Your role in the college classroom is not to be a passive spectator or sponge; instead, take on the role of an aggressive detective or investigative reporter who is on a "search and record" mission. Actively search for information by picking your instructor's brain and recording your "pickings" in your notebook.

See Box 1 for top strategies on classroom listening and note-taking that you should put into practice immediately. "Take Action Now!" boxes contain top-priority academic strategies. Compared to high school, achieving academic success in college will require working harder—investing more time and energy—and working smarter—using more effective learning strategies. However, academic success not only depends on the quantity of time you devote to your studies, it also depends on the quality of the time you spend; and the quality of your learning time increases when you use high-quality learning strategies.

STUDENT PERSPECTIVE

"I sit in front because I have Attention Deficit Disorder, and it's a technique to keep me focused and involved in class."

—*First-year student*

Active Class Participation

You can become actively involved in the college classroom by coming to class prepared (e.g., having done the assigned reading), by asking relevant questions, and by contributing thoughtful comments during class discussions. Oral communication increases your level of active involvement because it requires you to exert both mental energy—thinking about what you are going to say—and physical energy—moving your lips to say it. Thus, thoughtful class participation increases the likelihood that you remain alert and attentive in class. It also sends a clear message to the instructor that you are a motivated student who takes the course seriously and really wants to learn. Since class participation accounts for a portion of your final grade in many courses, your attentiveness and involvement in class may have a direct, positive effect on your course grade.

If you do not feel confident or assertive enough to speak in class with many people present, consider contributing your questions and comments by e-mail to your instructor and/or classmates.

Participating in class increases the likelihood that you will remain alert and attentive, and lets the instructor know you are motivated to learn.

TAKE ACTION NOW! — Box 1

Top Strategies: Listening and Note-Taking

One of the tasks that you will be expected to perform at the very start of your first term in college is to take notes in class. Studies show that professors' lecture notes are the number-one source of test questions (and test answers) on college exams. So, get off to a fast start by using the following strategies to improve the quality of your note-taking.

1. **Get to every class.** Whether or not your instructor takes roll, s/he may still be aware of whether you are in class, and you are still responsible for all material covered in class. Think of your class schedule as a full-time job that requires you to show up only about 13 hours a week. (If you happen to miss class, leave space in your notebook as a reminder to get those notes from a classmate.)
2. **Get to every class on time.** The first few minutes of a class session often contain very valuable information, such as reminders, reviews, and previews.
3. **Get organized.** Come to class with the right equipment—get a separate notebook for each class, get your name on it, date each class session, and store all class handouts in it.
4. **Get in the right position:**
   - The ideal place to sit—front and center of the room—where you can hear and see most effectively;
   - the ideal posture—sitting upright and leaning forward—because your body influences your mind; if your body is in an alert and ready position, your mind is likely to follow.
   - the ideal position socially—sit near people who will not distract your focus of attention or detract from the quality of your note-taking.

Remember: These attention-focusing strategies are particularly important during the first year of college because you are more likely to have large-sized classes. When class size increases, each individual tends to feel more anonymous, which may reduce feelings of personal responsibility and the need to stay focused and remain actively involved. So, in large-class settings, it is especially important to use effective strategies that eliminate distractions and attention drift.

5. **Get in the right frame of mind.** Get psyched up, and come into the classroom with the attitude that you are going to pick your instructor's brain and pick up answers to test questions.
6. **Get it down** (in writing) by actively looking, listening, and recording important points. Pay special attention to whatever information the instructor puts in writing—on the board, on an overhead, on a slide, or in a handout.
7. **Do not let go of your pen**—if you're in doubt, write it out—it's better to have it and not need it than to need it and not have it. Keep in mind that most professors do not write out all the important information on the board for you; instead, they expect you to listen carefully to what they are saying and write it down for yourself.
8. **Finish strong**—the *last few minutes* of class often contain very valuable information—such as reminders, reviews, and previews.
9. **Stick around.** As soon as class ends, don't bolt out—hang out—and quickly review your notes (by yourself or with a classmate); if you find any gaps, check them out with your instructor before s/he leaves the classroom. Also, this quick end-of-class review will help your brain retain the information it just received.

Pause for Reflection

When you enter a classroom, where do you usually sit? Why do you think you sit there? Is it a conscious choice or more like an automatic habit? Do you think that your usual seat places you in the best possible position for listening and learning in the classroom?

Finish class with a rush of attention, not a rush out the door!

Active Reading

Just as writing promotes active listening in class, writing also promotes active reading outside of class. Taking notes on important information that you highlighted in your first read, ensures active involvement because it requires more mental and physical energy than merely reading the material or passively highlighting sentences with a highlighter. (See Box 2 for top strategies on improving textbook reading that you should put into practice immediately.)

> **STUDENT PERSPECTIVE**
>
> "I recommend that you read the first chapters right away because college professors get started promptly with assigning certain readings. Classes in college move very fast because unlike high school, you do not attend class five times a week, but two or three times a week."
>
> —First-year student's advice to new college students

TAKE ACTION NOW! — Box 2

Top Strategies: Improving Textbook-Reading Comprehension and Retention

You have already purchased textbooks for your courses, and you probably have already received reading assignments to complete. After lecture notes, information from reading assignments is the second most frequent source of test questions on college exams. In fact, your professors may deliver class lectures with the expectation that you have done the assigned reading; so, if you haven't done the reading, you may not be able to follow what your instructor is talking about in class. Also, college professors often expect you to relate or connect what they talk about in class to the reading they have assigned. Thus, it's important to start developing good reading habits right now. You can do so by using the following strategies to improve your reading comprehension and retention.

1. **Get the right equipment**
   - Pen or pencil to note important information that should be later reviewed and studied for exams.
   - Dictionary to find the meaning of unfamiliar words. This will not only help you understand what you are reading, it is also the most effective way to build your vocabulary, which will come in handy in all college courses and on all standardized tests, such as those required for entry to graduate schools and professional schools.
2. **Get in the right position**—sit upright and have light coming from behind you, over the opposite side of your writing hand. (This will reduce the distracting and fatiguing effects of glare and shadows.)
3. **Get a sneak preview** of the chapter by first reading its boldface headings and any chapter outline, summary, or end-of-chapter questions that may be provided. This will give you a mental map of the chapter's content before you begin reading, enabling you to see the big picture and helping you keep track of the chapter's most important concepts as you read through all the specific details.
4. **Use boldface headings and subheadings** as cues for important information. Turn these headings into questions, then read to find their answers. This will send you on an answer-finding mission , keeping you mentally active and helping you read with a purpose. This is also the ideal way to prepare for tests because you will be practicing exactly what you will be doing on tests—answering questions.
5. **Pay special attention to the first and last sentences** in sections of the text that lie beneath the chapter's major headings and subheadings. These sentences often contain an important introduction and conclusion to the material covered within that section of the text.
6. **Finish with a short review** of what you have highlighted or noted as important information (rather than trying to cover a few more pages). It is best to use the last few minutes of your reading time to lock in the most important information you have just read because most forgetting takes place immediately after you stop focusing and start doing something else (Underwood, 1983). So, read to find the most important information, but end your reading by re-reading your findings.

Touching the First Base of College Success: Utilizing Campus Resources

Successful performance in college, like successful performance in any human endeavor, is influenced by both the individual and the environment. Your environment (college campus) is chock full of specialized resources that are available to you (in print, in person, and online), all of which can strongly support your quest for educational and personal success. Studies show that students who utilize these resources report higher levels of satisfaction with, and get more out of, the college experience (Pascaralla & Terenzini, 1991, 2005).

For example, two researchers who conducted a comprehensive review of over 2,500 research studies reached the following conclusion. "The impact of college is not simply the result of what a college does for or to a student. Rather, the impact is a result of the extent to which an individual student exploits the people, programs, facilities, opportunities, and experiences that the college makes available" (Pascarella & Terenzini, *How College Affects Students,* pp. 610–611).

Described in this section are some of the most valuable campus services that can support and promote your success.

> **Remember:** Involvement with campus services is not only valuable, but it's also free because the cost of these services has already been covered by your college tuition. By investing time and energy in these resources, you are not only increasing your prospects for personal success, you are also maximizing the return on your financial investment in college.

Learning Center

Also known as the Center for Academic Support or Academic Success, this is the place on campus where you can obtain individual assistance to support and strengthen your academic performance. The one-to-one and group tutoring provided by the Center can help you master difficult course concepts and assignments, and the people working there have been professionally trained to help you learn "how to learn." While your professors may have expert knowledge of the subject matter they teach, learning resource specialists are experts on the process of learning. These specialists can show students how to adjust or modify their learning strategies to meet the demands of the different courses and teaching styles they encounter in college.

Studies show that students who become actively involved with academic support services outside the classroom, such as the Learning Center or Academic Support Center, are more likely to attain higher college grades and complete their college degree. This is particularly true if they began their involvement with these support services during the first year of college (Cuseo, 2003). Also, students who seek and receive assistance from academic-support services show significant improvement in academic self-efficacy—that is, they develop a greater sense of personal control over their academic performance and develop higher self-expectations for future academic success (Smith, Walter, & Hoey, 1992).

Despite the multiple advantages of getting involved with academic support services outside the classroom, these services are typically under-utilized by college students, especially by those students who could gain the most from using them (Knapp & Karabenick, 1988; Walter & Smith, 1990). This could be due to the fact that some students feel that seeking academic help is an admission that they are not smart, or that they cannot succeed on their own. Do not be one of these students.

Remember: The purpose of the Learning Center (Academic Support Center) is not just to provide remedial repair work for academically under-prepared learners, to save floundering or failing students, or to fix struggling students' with academic problems. It is a place where all learners can benefit, including well-prepared and highly motivated students who want to be the best they can be and who are striving to achieve the highest possible levels of academic excellence.

Personal Story

At my college, it has been found that the grade-point average of students who use the Learning Center is higher than the college average, and honor students are more likely to use the Center than non-honors students.

–Joe Cuseo, Professor of Psychology

Writing Center

Many college campuses offer specialized support that is expressly designed to help students improve their writing skills. Typically referred to as the Writing Center, this is the place where you can receive assistance at any stage of the writing process, whether it be collecting and organizing your ideas in outline form, composing your first draft, or proofreading your final draft. Since writing is an academic skill that you'll use in almost all your courses, improvements in your writing will improve your overall academic performance. Thus, we strongly encourage you to capitalize on this campus resource.

Disability Services or Office for Students with Special Needs

If you have a physical or learning disability that is interfering with your performance in college, or think you may have such a disability, this would be the resource on your campus to consult for assistance and support. Programs and services typically provided by this office include:

- assessment for learning disabilities,
- verification of eligibility for disability support services,
- specialized counseling, advising, and tutoring,
- authorization of academic accommodations for students with disabilities.

> **CLASSIC QUOTE**
>
> *The next best thing to knowing something is knowing where to find it.*
>
> —Dr. Samuel Johnson, famous English literary figure who authored the *Dictionary of the English Language* (1747)

College Library

Do not overlook the fact that librarians are educators who provide instruction outside the classroom. You can learn from them just as you do from faculty inside the classroom. Furthermore, the library is a place where you can acquire skills for locating, retrieving, and evaluating information that you may apply to any course you are taking or will ever take.

Academic Advisement

College students who have developed a clear sense of their educational and career goals are more likely to continue their college education and complete their college degree (Willingham, 1985; Wyckoff, 1999). However, most beginning college students need help with clarifying their educational goals, selecting an academic major, and exploring future careers. For instance, consider the following findings:

- three of every four beginning college students are uncertain or tentative about their career choice (Frost, 1991);
- less than 10 percent of new students feel they know a great deal about their intended college major (Erickson & Strommer, 1991);
- over half of all students who enter college with a declared major change their mind at least once before they graduate (Noel, 1985); and
- only one of three college seniors end up majoring in the same field that they preferred during their first year of college (Cuseo, 2005).

Working with your academic advisor can help you develop clear educational and career goals.

These findings point to the conclusion that the majority of college students do not make final decisions about their major before starting their college experience; instead, they make these decisions during the college experience. It is only natural for you, a first-year student, to feel uncertain about your intended major because you have not yet experienced the variety of subjects and academic programs that make up the college curriculum. In fact, you will encounter fields of study in college that you probably never knew existed in high school.

Remember: Being undecided or unsure about your major and career is nothing to be embarrassed about because the process of long-range academic planning and effective decision-making is challenging and complex. So, connect early and often with an academic advisor to help you work through this challenging process and to help you find a major that best taps your educational interests, talents, and values.

> **Pause for Reflection**
>
> *If you have decided on a major, how sure are you about your choice?*
>
> *If you haven't decided on a major, why have you chosen to delay your decision?*

Career Development Center

Research on college students indicates that they are more likely to stay in school and graduate when they have some sense of how their present academic experience relates to their future career goals (Levitz & Noel, 1989). Studies also show that the vast majority of new students are uncertain about what future careers they would like to pursue (Gordon & Steele, 2003). So, if you are uncertain about a career right now, welcome to the club. This uncertainty is entirely normal and understandable because you have not yet had the opportunity for hands-on work experience in the real world of careers. As Vincent Tinto, a nationally known scholar on student success, points out:

> *Among any population of young adults who are just beginning in earnest their search for adult identity, it would be surprising indeed if one found that most were very clear about their long-term goals. The college years are an important growing period in which new social and intellectual experiences are sought as a means of coming to grips with the issue of adult careers. Students enter college with the hope that they will be able to formulate for themselves a meaningful answer to that important question (1993, p. 40).*

The Career Center is the place to go for help in finding a meaningful answer to the important question of how to connect your current college experience with your future career goals. Although it may seem like beginning a career is light years away because you are just beginning college, the process of investigating, planning, and preparing for career success begins in the first year of college. You can start this important process by visiting the Career Center, which is a campus resource that has been explicitly created to help you:

- explore the rapidly changing world of careers,
- understand the often complex relationship between particular academic majors and related careers,
- identify what careers may be most compatible with your personal interests, abilities, or values,
- locate volunteer (service-learning) experiences and internships that will enable you to test your interest in different careers through direct, real-world experience, and
- develop your resume.

Your Career Center will typically provide such services as personal career counseling, workshops on career exploration and development, and "career fairs" where you are able to meet professionals working in different career fields. Although entering a career may appear to be a very long-term goal to you right now, successful career planning should begin in your first year. Thus, we strongly encourage you not to wait until your junior or senior year before taking advantage of this valuable campus resource.

Counseling Center

Students entering college today are reporting higher levels of stress than in years past (Astin, et al., 1997; Sax, et al., 2000). The first year in college can be particularly stressful because it represents a major life transition, which requires not only academic adjustments, but also involves significant changes in social relationships, emotional experiences, and personal identity. In fact, studies show that the vast majority of students who withdraw from college do not do so for strictly academic reasons. Most students who drop out do not flunk out; they leave because of other factors (Tinto, 1993).

These findings point to the importance of focusing not only on your academics, but also on non-academic aspects of your adjustment to college and your development as a whole person. In fact, studies of successful people indicate that social and emotional intelligence (EQ) are often more important for personal and professional success than intellectual ability (IQ) (Goleman, 1995).

Counseling services can provide you with a valuable source of support during your first year of college, not only for helping you cope with college stressors that may be interfering with your academic success, but also for helping you realize your full potential. Personal counseling can promote self-awareness and self-development in social and emotional areas of your life that are important for mental health, physical wellness, and personal growth.

Remember: College counseling is not just for students who are experiencing emotional problems. It is for all students who want to enrich their overall quality of life.

Pause for Reflection
Take a moment to visualize your campus environment. Can you "see" the locations of the following college services that are designed to support your academic success: Academic Advisement? College Library? Learning Center (Academic Support Center)? Career Center? Counseling Center?

Health Center

Making the transition from high school to college often involves taking more personal responsibility for your own health and wellness. In addition to making your own decisions about what to eat, when to sleep, and how to manage your own health, your stress level is likely to increase during times of change or transition in your life. Good health habits are one effective way to both cope with college stress and reach peak levels of performance. The Health Center on your campus is the key resource for information on how to manage your health and maintain wellness. It is also the place to go for help with physical illnesses, sexually transmitted infections or diseases, and eating disorders.

Experiential Learning Resources

The learning that takes place in college courses is primarily vicarious—that is, you learn from or through somebody else—by *listening* to the ideas professors present in class and by *reading* the print materials outside of class. While this academic learning is valuable, it should be complemented by experiential learning—that is, learning directly through first-hand experiences. This is supported by the work of two highly regarded scholars, who reviewed more than 2,500 studies on college students, and reached the following conclusion: "On the basis of the extensive body of evidence reviewed, one of the most inescapable conclusions we can make is that the impact of college is largely determined by the individual's quality of effort and level of involvement in both academic and nonacademic [experiential] activities" (Pascarella & Terenzini, 1991, 2005).

As a first-year college student, there are two major ways in which you can get involved in college life beyond academics and capitalize on experiential learning opportunities outside of the classroom:

1. through involvement in co-curricular experiences on campus, and
2. through volunteer experiences in the local community.

Here are some specific strategies for becoming actively involved in both of these important forms of experiential learning.

Co-Curricular Experiences on Campus

Colleges and universities no longer refer to involvement in campus life outside the classroom as "extra"-curricular activities, because these activities can be very powerful sources of experiential learning. Instead, they are referred to as "*co*"-curricular experiences, because the prefix "co" suggests that they are *equal* to curricular (course-related) experiences for promoting learning and development.

More specifically, research reveals that students who become actively involved in campus life are more likely to:

- enjoy their college experience,
- graduate from college, and
- develop leadership skills that are useful in the world of work after college (Astin, 1993).

For example, college graduates consistently report that their participation in co-curricular experiences involving leadership helped them to develop skills that were important for their work performance and career advancement. These reports have been confirmed by on-the-job evaluations of college alumni, which indicate that previous involvement in co-curricular activities on campus, particularly those involving student leadership, is the best predictor of successful managerial performance. In fact, these experiences are more strongly associated with the managerial success of college graduates than the prestige of the college they attended (Pascarella & Terenzini, 1991, 2005). Also, involvement in student leadership activities is associated with improved self-esteem (Astin, 1993).

Try to get involved in no more than two to three major campus organizations at any one time. Limiting the number of your out-of-class activities should enable you to keep up with your studies, and it is likely to be more impressive to future schools or employers because a long list of involvement with multiple activities may seem suspicious. As the director of a national bureau for college placement once said: "Just a [long] list of club memberships is meaningless; it's a fake front. Remember that quality, not quantity, is what counts" (Pope, 1990, p. 189). High-quality campus clubs and organizations to become involved with are those that relate to your academic major or career interests (for example, history or psychology club), and which place you in a position of providing leadership or help to others (for example: student government, college newspaper, college committees, peer counseling, or peer tutoring).

Remember: Co-curricular experiences are also resumé-building experiences, and campus professionals with whom you interact regularly while participating in co-curricular activities (for example, the Director of Student Activities or Dean of Students) are valuable resources for personal references and letters of recommendation to future schools or future employers.

Volunteerism and Service Learning

When you volunteer to serve others, you are also serving yourself. Your self-esteem is boosted by knowing that you are doing something good. Volunteering also enables you to:

- acquire learning skills through hands-on experience (hence the term, "service *learning*"),
- strengthen your resumé, and
- explore areas of work that may relate to your future career interests.

One of the benefits of volunteering at a local elementary school is that it will give you the experience to determine if you want to major in education.

Service-learning experiences can function as exploratory internships that enable you to test the waters and gain real-life knowledge about careers relating to your area of volunteer work, while simultaneously providing you with career-related work experience. Volunteer experiences also allow you to network with professionals outside of college who may serve as excellent resources, references, and sources for letters of recommendation. Furthermore, if these professionals are impressed with your initial volunteer work, they may also hire you on a part-time basis while you are still in college, or on a full-time basis after you graduate.

Do not worry that putting some time into experiential learning outside the classroom will subtract time from your studies and lower your grades. Keep in mind that, in college, you will be spending much less time in the classroom than you did in high school. For instance, a full load of college courses (15 units) only requires that you be in class about 13 hours per week. This leaves enough out-of-class time for other activities. Just don't overdo it. In fact, there is evidence that college students who are involved in co-curricular, volunteer, and part-time work experiences outside the classroom that total *no more than 15 hours per week* actually earn higher grades than students who do not get involved in any out-of-class activities (Pascarella, 2001; Pascarella & Terenzini, 2005). This is probably because students who have commitments outside the classroom learn to manage their out-of-class time better, because their structured out-of-class schedule essentially forces them to use their time well. On the other hand, students who do not have to show up for anything other than their 13 hours of classes per week may have so much unstructured out-of-class time that they do not get into a regular routine for organizing it. Apparently, instead of effectively using their out-of-class time, they end up wasting or abusing it. If you work, we strongly recommend limiting it to 15 hours per week, because students who work more than 15 hours are more likely to eventually switch from full-time to part-time enrollment and are less likely to continue in college and complete their degree (Pascarella & Terenzini, 2005).

Learning More about Your Campus Resources through Your Own Research

Utilizing your resources is an important, research-based strategy for college success. An essential first step toward putting this strategy into practice is to become fully aware of all the key support services that are available at your college. You can find this information in three major forms:

1. **In print**—information published in written form. For in-print information on campus resources, consult your College Catalog (also known as the College Bulletin), and your *Student Handbook*. If you do not have a copy of the college catalog, you should be able to obtain one from the Office of Admissions or Center for Academic Advising. If you do not have a copy of the student handbook, you should be able to obtain one from the Office of Student Life or Student Affairs.

2. **Online**—information posted electronically on the Internet. For online information on campus resources, check your college's Web site. Your college may have its entire Catalog and Student Handbook available online.

3. **In person**—information communicated directly to you by a knowledgeable person For in-person information on campus resources, speak with a professional in different offices or centers on your campus, such as:
   a. Academic Support Services (Learning Resource Center)—ask about the type of support it provides for improving course learning and increasing academic success (e.g., study and test-taking strategies);
   b. College Library—ask about the type of support it provides for finding information and completing research assignments (e.g., term papers and group projects); and
   c. Student Development Services (Student Affairs)—ask about the type of support it provides on issues relating to social and emotional adjustment, involvement in campus life outside the classroom, and leadership development.

Pause for Reflection

You have now reached the end of this unit on campus resources, so this is a good time to step back from your reading and reflect on what you have read thus far. Take a minute to look back at the major college resources that have been mentioned in this section, and identify two or three of them that you think you should use immediately. *Briefly explain* why *you have identified these resources as your top priorities at this time. (You might consider asking your course instructors what they think, and see what resources they would recommend for immediate use.)*

Touching the Second Base of College Success: Social Interaction and Collaboration

Learning is strengthened when it takes place in a social context that involves human interaction. As some scholars put it, human knowledge is socially constructed or built-up through interaction and dialogue with others. According to these scholars, our thinking is largely an internalization or internal incorporation of the conversations we have had with other people, and our personal knowledge is often a product of these interpersonal interactions (Bruffee, 1993). So, if we have frequent, high-quality dialogue with others, we increase the quality of our thinking and the quantity of our knowledge.

Modern advances in electronic technology (e-mail, instant messaging) now allow interpersonal interaction to occur at any time and any place—on or off campus. If you are a commuter student who does not live on campus, or if you are an adult student who is juggling family and work commitments along with your academic schedule, e-mail communication may be an especially effective and efficient mode of interaction for you.

Four particular forms of interpersonal interaction have been found to be strongly associated with improving students' performance in college and their motivation to complete college:

1. Student-faculty interaction,
2. Student interaction with academic advisors,
3. Student interaction with a mentor, and
4. Student-student (peer) interaction.

Student-Faculty Interaction

Many research studies demonstrate that students' college success is influenced heavily by the quality and quantity of their interaction with faculty members *outside the classroom*. More specifically, student-faculty contact outside of class is positively associated with the following student developments:

- improved academic performance,
- increased critical thinking skills,
- greater satisfaction with the college experience,
- increased likelihood of completing a college degree, and
- stronger desire to seek further education beyond college (Astin, 1993; Pascarella & Terenzini, 1991, 2005).

Because these positive results are so strong and widespread, we urge you to consciously seek interaction with college faculty outside of class time. Here are some of the most manageable ways to increase your out-of-class contact with college instructors during the first year of college.

1. Seek interaction with your course instructors *immediately after class*.

This may be an ideal time for you to interact with a faculty member because your interest, curiosity, or confusion may have been sparked by course material just covered in class. This is likely to be the time when you are most motivated to talk about a concept discussed in class, and it may also be the time when your instructor is most motivated to discuss it with you. Furthermore, interaction with your instructors immediately after class serves to increase their familiarity with you and their awareness of you as an individual, which in turn should increase your confidence and willingness to seek subsequent contact with them.

2. Seek interaction with your course instructors during their *office hours*.

One important piece of information on the syllabus you receive in college courses is your instructors' office hours. Make specific note of these office hours, and make an earnest attempt to capitalize on them. College professors spend most of their professional time outside the classroom preparing for class, grading papers, conducting research, and serving on college committees. However, some of their out-of-class time is reserved specifically for office hours, during which they are expected to be available for interaction with students.

National surveys reveal that 85 percent of first-year college students report having worked on academic matters with other students outside of class, but less than 20 percent have interacted with their instructors outside of class (Policy Center on the First Year of College, 2003). One way to be sure that you do not fall into this pattern is to schedule an office visit with your instructor during the early stages of the course. This is important for the purpose of discussing course assignments, term paper topics, and possible major or career choices. Try to make at least one visit to the office of all your instructors, preferably early in the term, because once midterm is reached, both instructors and students tend to become very busy, so quality time for student-faculty interaction is often harder to find.

Even if you meet with your instructors for only a few minutes, it will still serve as a valuable icebreaker that can help them to get to know you as a person, and help you to feel more comfortable about interacting with them again in the future.

STUDENT PERSPECTIVE

"I wish that I would have taken advantage of professors' open door policies when I had questions, because actually understanding what I was doing, instead of guessing, would have saved me a lot of stress and re-doing what I did wrong the first time."

–Advice to new students from a college sophomore (Walsh, 2005)

3. Seek interaction with your instructors through e-mail.

Electronic communication is another effective way to interact with your instructors, particularly if their office hours conflict with your class schedule, work responsibilities, or family commitments. Also, if you are shy or hesitant about "invading" your instructors' office space, e-mail can provide a less threatening way for you to interact with your instructors, and may give you the initial self-confidence to eventually seek contact with them on a face-to-face basis.

Student-Advisor Interaction

An academic advisor can be an effective referral agent who is well positioned to direct you to, and connect you with, campus support services that best serve your needs. An advisor can also help you understand college procedures and navigate the bureaucratic maze of college policies and politics.

> **Remember:** An academic advisor is not someone who you see just once per term—when you need to get a signature for class scheduling and course registration. An advisor is someone you should visit on a more regular basis than your course instructors. Your instructors will change from term to term, but your academic advisor may be the college professional with whom you have regular contact and a stable, ongoing relationship that can endure throughout your college experience.

Your academic advisor should be someone you feel comfortable talking to, who knows you by name, and who is familiar with your personal interests and abilities. Give your advisor the opportunity to get to know you personally, and seek that person's advice about courses, majors, and personal issues that may be interfering with your academic performance.

If your college does not assign you a personal advisor, but offers advising through an advisement center on a drop-by basis, this may result in your seeing a different advisor each time you visit the center. If you are not satisfied with this system of multiple advisors, find one advisor with whom you feel most comfortable and make him or her your personal advisor by scheduling your appointments in advance. This will enable you to consistently connect with the same advisor, with whom you can develop an ongoing relationship. On the other hand, if your college has assigned a personal advisor to you, and you find that you cannot develop a good relationship with this person, ask the Director of Advising or Academic Dean if you could

Make appointments to meet with an academic advisor at times other than during the "mad rush" of course registration and class scheduling.

be assigned someone else. If your college does not allow you to change from an advisor that you are unhappy with, then consider finding a *mentor* with whom you could develop a better relationship.

Do you have a personally assigned advisor?

If yes, do you know who this person is and where he or she can be found?

If no, do you know where you could go if you have questions about your class schedule or academic plans?

Interaction with a Mentor

A mentor may be described as an experienced guide who takes personal interest in you and the progress you are making toward your goals. (For example, in the movie "Star Wars," Yoda served as a mentor for Luke Skywalker.) Research in higher education is beginning to demonstrate that a mentor is someone who can make first-year students feel significant and who can encourage or enable them to stay on track until they complete their college degree (Campbell & Campbell, 1997). A mentor can assist you in trouble-shooting difficult or complicated issues that you may not be able to resolve on your own. A mentor is also someone with whom you can share good news, such as your success stories and personal accomplishments. Look for someone on campus with whom you can develop this type of trusting relationship. There are many people on campus who have the potential to be outstanding mentors, such as:

◆ Academic advisors
◆ Academic support professionals (e.g., professional tutors in the Learning Center)
◆ Your instructor for the first-year seminar or college-success course
◆ Faculty in your intended major
◆ Juniors, seniors, or graduate students in your intended field of study

- Working professionals in careers that interest you
- Career counselors
- Personal counselors
- Learning assistance professionals (for example, Learning Resource Center)
- Student Development professionals (for example, Director of Student Life or Residential Life)
- Residential Life advisors
- Work-study or volunteer-service supervisor
- Campus minister or chaplain
- Financial aid counselors or advisors

Pause for Reflection

Four general categories or types of people in your college community who can contribute to your success are:

1. *Peers (to be discussed in the next section),*
2. *Faculty (instructors),*
3. *Administrators (e.g., office and program directors), and*
4. *Staff (e.g., student support professionals and administrative assistants).*

Think about your first interactions with faculty, staff, and administrators. Do you recall anyone who impressed you as being very approachable, personable, or helpful? If you did, make a note of that person's name for future reference, in case you would like to seek out the person again. If you have not met such a person yet, be sure not to forget him or her when you do.

Interaction with Peers (Student-Student Interaction)

Studies of college students repeatedly point to the importance of the peer group as a powerful source of social and intellectual support (Pascarella, 2005). One study of over 25,000 college students revealed that when students interact with each other while learning, they achieve higher levels of academic performance and are more likely to complete their college degree (Astin, 1993). Another study, which involved in-depth interviews with more than 1,600 college students, found one particular study habit that was shared by almost all students who struggled academically: They always studied alone (Light, 2001).

Peer interaction is especially important during the first term of college because this is a stage in the college experience when feeling socially accepted and "belonging" are high-priority needs for new students—many of whom have left the long-time security of their family and hometown friends. As a new college student, it might be best to view your early academic performance in terms of the classic need hierarchy theory of human motivation that was formulated by American psychologist Abraham Maslow (1954) (Figure 3). According to this theory, humans cannot reach their full potential and achieve peak performance until their more basic emotional and social needs have been met (for example, their needs for personal safety, social acceptance, and self-esteem). Making early connections with your peers can help you meet these basic human needs by providing you with a base of social support that can ease your integration into the college com-

Figure 3 Abraham Maslow's Hierarchy of Needs Resembles a Pyramid

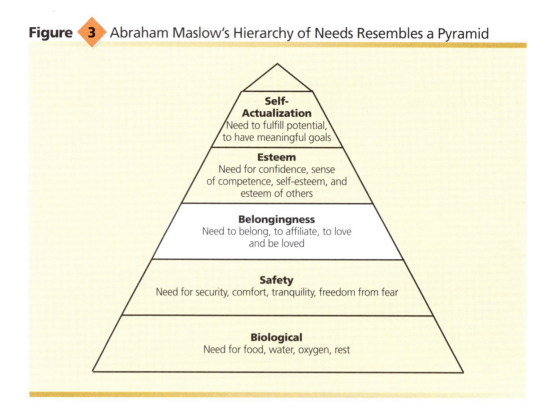

munity, and enable you to move up to higher levels of the need hierarchy (for example, striving for educational excellence and fulfilling your personal potential).

Studies repeatedly show that students who have become socially integrated or connected with other members of the college community are much more likely to complete their first-year of college and continue on to complete their college degree (Tinto, 1993). So, find ways to become involved with campus organizations or activities that connect you with other students. Also, try to get connected with experienced students who are at more advanced stages of college development. Sophomores, juniors, and seniors can often be a very valuable social resource for a new student, and they may be very willing to share their experiences with you because you have shown an interest in hearing what they have to say. In fact, you may be the very first person who has ever bothered to ask them what their experience has been like at your college. You can learn from their experiences by asking them about good courses they have taken, what instructors they would recommend, or what advisors they found to be most well informed and personable.

Remember: Your peers can be much more than competitors or sources of negative peer pressure; they can also be collaborators, a source of positive influence, and a resource for college success. Be on the lookout for first-year classmates who are motivated to learn and willing to learn with you, and keep an eye out for advanced students who are willing to assist you. Start building your own success-supporting social network by surrounding yourself with success-seeking and success-achieving students. They can be a stimulating source of positive "peer power" that can drive you to higher levels of academic performance and increase your motivational drive to complete college.

Collaboration with Peers

Simply defined, collaboration is the process of two or more people working interdependently toward the same goal, rather than working independently or competitively. Collaboration involves true teamwork, whereby individuals support each other's success and share equal responsibility for helping the team move toward its common goal. Research on students from kindergarten through college has shown that when students collaborate in teams, their academic performance and interpersonal skills improve significantly (Cuseo, 1996).

To maximize the power of collaboration, use the following guidelines to seek peers who will enhance the quality of your learning team.

Research shows that students who collaborate in teams improve their academic performance and their interpersonal skills.

1. Choose your teammates wisely; look for fellow students who are motivated and will contribute to your team's success, rather than those who are likely to be hitchhikers looking for a free ride. Observe your classmates with an eye toward identifying potentially good teammates.
2. Do not team-up only with peers who are similar to you, or have characteristics that are familiar to you. Instead, include teammates who are different than you in terms of age, gender, ethnic, racial, cultural or geographical backgrounds, learning styles, and personality characteristics. Such variety brings different life experiences, styles of thinking, and learning strategies to your team, which will serve not only to enrich its diversity but its quality as well. If you team-up only with friends or classmates whose interests and lifestyles are similar to your own, this familiarity and homogeneity can work against your team's performance because your common experiences can result in your learning group getting off track and on to topics that may have nothing to do with the learning task (for example, what you did last weekend or what you are planning to do next weekend).

Remember: Seek diversity—capitalize on the advantages of collaborating with peers from varied backgrounds and lifestyles. Simply stated, studies show that you learn more from people who are different than you than you do from people who are the same as you (Pascarella, 2001).

Another point to keep in mind about learning teams is that they are not simply study groups formed the night before an exam. Effective learning teams collaborate more regularly and work on a wider variety of academic tasks than late-night study sessions. Listed below is a series of important academic tasks and situations for which learning teams may be formed to improve your personal performance.

CLASSIC QUOTE

Surround yourself with only people who are going to lift you higher.

—Oprah Winfrey, actress and talk-show host

Note-Taking Teams

Immediately after class sessions end, take a couple of minutes to team-up with another student to compare and share notes. Listening and note-taking are demanding tasks, so what often happens is that one student will pick up an important point that others overlooked. Also, by teaming-up immediately after class, your team has the opportunity to consult with your instructor about any missing or confusing information before the instructor leaves the classroom.

> *Personal Story*
>
> During my first term in college, I was having difficulty taking complete notes in my biology course because the instructor spoke rapidly and with an unfamiliar accent. I noticed another student (Alex) sitting in the front row who was trying to take notes the best he could, but he was experiencing the same difficulty. Following one particularly fast and complex lecture, we both looked at each other and began to share our frustrations. We decided to "double-team" the instructor by pairing-up immediately after every class and comparing each other's notes to identify points that we missed or found confusing. First, we helped each other; then, if there were points that neither one of us could figure out, we went up together to consult with the instructor before he left the classroom. At the end of the course, Alex and I finished with the highest grades in class.
>
> —Joe Cuseo

Reading Teams

After completing your reading assignments, you can team-up with classmates to compare your highlighting and margin notes. You can consult with each other to identify major points in the reading and reach decisions about what information is most important to study for upcoming exams.

Writing Teams

Teammates can provide each other with feedback that can be used to revise and improve the quality of their writing. You could connect with a writing team of peers at any or all of the following stages in the writing process:

- topic selection and refinement—to help generate a list of potential topics and related subtopics,
- pre-writing—to clarify your purpose and audience,
- first draft—to improve your general style and tone, and
- final draft—to proofread and correct mechanical errors before submitting your work.

Library Research Teams

Many first-year students are unfamiliar with the process of conducting library research, and some may experience library anxiety. Forming library research teams is an effective way for you to develop a social support group that can make trips to the library more enjoyable and transform the process of library research from something you do alone into something you do as a team.

> **Remember:** It is ethical and acceptable for you to team-up with others to search for and share resources. This is not cheating or plagiarizing, as long as your final product is completed individually and what you turn into your instructor represents your own work.

Team-Instructor Conferences

Visiting course instructors during their office hours with other classmates is an effective way to get additional assistance in preparing for exams and completing assignments. This is a good team-learning strategy for the following reasons:

- You may feel more comfortable about visiting and soliciting help from instructors on their "turf" if you are accompanied by peers, rather than entering this unfamiliar territory on your own. As the old expression goes, "There's safety in numbers."
- When a team of students makes an office visit, the information shared by the instructor is heard by more than one person, so your teammates may pick up some useful information that you might miss, misinterpret, or forget.
- You save your instructors' time by enabling them to help multiple students simultaneously, rather than requiring them to engage in "repeat performances" for students who visit individually at different times.
- You send a message to instructors that you are serious about their course and are motivated to learn, because you have taken the time—in advance—to connect with your peers and prepare for the visit.

Test Results-Review and Assignment-Review Teams

After receiving results on your course examinations and assignments, you can collaborate with other classmates to review your results as a team. By comparing answers, you can better identify the sources of your mistakes. Also, observing the answers of teammates who received maximum credit on particular questions can provide you with a model for improving your future performance.

Teaming-up after tests and assignments given early in the term is especially effective, because it enables you to get a better idea of what the instructor expects from students throughout the remainder of the course. You can use it as early feedback to trouble-shoot problems, fine-tune your performance, and improve your grade—while there is still plenty of time left in the course to do so.

> **CLASSIC QUOTE**
>
> *Two heads are better than one, not because either is infallible, but because they are unlikely to go wrong in the same direction.*
>
> —C.S. Lewis, English novelist and essayist

Learning Communities

Your college may offer first-year students the opportunity to participate in a learning community program, in which the same group of students takes the same block of courses together during the same academic term. If this opportunity is available to you, try to take advantage of it because it's been found that students who participate in learning community programs are more likely to:

- become actively involved in classroom learning,
- form their own learning groups outside the classroom,
- report greater intellectual gains, and
- continue their college education (Tinto, 1997, 2000).

If learning community programs are not formally available to you on your campus, consider forming your own learning communities by identifying first-year students who are likely to be taking the same courses as you, and team-up with them to register for the same two to three courses. This will allow you to reap the benefits of a learning community, even though your college does not offer a formal learning-community program.

> **CLASSIC QUOTE**
>
> *TEAM = Together Everyone Achieves More*
>
> —Author Unknown

STUDENT PERSPECTIVE

"Stay the first month. The weekends of the first month are when I really connected with the people I'd met, learned to love the campus, and got involved the most. Besides, you'll figure out how to beat homesickness (it's all about staying busy)."

—Advice to new students from a college sophomore (Walsh, 2005)

Pause for Reflection

Think about the students who are in your classes this term. Are there any students who might be good members to join-up with and form learning teams? Do you have any classmates who are in more than one class with you, and who you would consider collaborating with, so that you might work together on the courses you have in common?

TAKE ACTION NOW! — Box 3

Top Strategies: Making Connections with Key Members of Your College Community

Studies consistently show that students who become socially integrated or connected with other people in the college community are more likely to remain in college and complete their degree. Below is a list of ten tips for making important interpersonal connections in college. We encourage you to start making these connections right now so that you can begin constructing a base of social support that can strengthen your performance during your first term and serve as a solid foundation for your future success in college.

1. Connect with a favorite peer or student development professional that you may have met during orientation.
2. Connect with peers who live in your student residence or who commute to school from the same community in which you live. If your schedules are similar, consider carpooling together.
3. Join a college club, student organization, campus committee, intramural team, or volunteer-service group whose activities match your personal or career interests.
4. Connect with a peer leader who has been trained to assist new students (e.g., peer tutor, peer mentor, or peer counselor), or with a peer who has more college experience than you (e.g., sophomore, junior, or senior).
5. Look for and connect with a motivated classmate in each of your classes and try working together as a team to take notes, complete reading assignments, and study for exams. (Look especially to team-up with a peer who may be in more than one class with you.)
6. Connect with your favorite faculty in fields that you may be interested in majoring in by visiting them during office hours, conversing briefly with them after class, or communicating with them via e-mail.
7. Connect with an academic support professional in your college's learning resource center to receive personalized academic assistance or tutoring for any course in which you want to improve your performance.
8. Connect with an academic advisor to discuss and develop your future educational plans.
9. Connect with a college librarian to get early assistance and a head start on any major research project that you have been assigned.
10. Connect with a personal counselor at your college or a campus minister to discuss any difficult college-adjustment or personal-life issues that you may be experiencing.

••• Touching the Third Base of College Success: Self-Reflection

Success requires not only action, but also reflection—that is, reflecting on what you have *done*, what you are *doing*, and what you *will do*. In our current, fast-paced, fast food, fast Internet society, we need to make a conscious effort to take time to step back and reflect on our experiences. Such reflection or thoughtful review is the flip side of active involvement.

Both processes are needed for learning to be complete. Active involvement is necessary for engaging your attention—which enables you to initially get information into your brain—and reflection is necessary for consolidation—keeping that information in your brain, by locking it into your long-term memory (Broadbent, 1970; Bligh, 2000). In fact, researchers have discovered that different brainwave patterns are associated with each of these two essential processes of human learning (Bradshaw, 1995) (Figure 4). This faster brain activity indicates that you are attending to the information and processing it in your brain. This slower brain activity indicates that you're taking the information that's reached your brain and are thinking deeply about it, which will consolidate or lock it into your memory. Thus, effective learning involves both active involvement and thoughtful reflection.

There are four specific forms of self-reflection that are particularly important for effective learning and college success:

1. Self-assessment,
2. Self-monitoring,
3. Reflecting on feedback, and
4. Reflecting on your future.

Figure 4

Faster Brain-Wave Pattern Associated with a Mental State of *Active Involvement*

Slower Brain-Wave Pattern Associated with a Mental State of *Reflective Thinking*

Self-Assessment

Simply defined, self-assessment is the process of evaluating your personal characteristics, traits, or habits, and their relative strengths or weaknesses. This process is essential for promoting self-awareness, which is a critical first step toward self-improvement, strategic planning, and decision-making. Listed below are key characteristics of the self that can strongly influence college success and, therefore, are important target areas for self-assessment.

- Personal Interests: What you like or enjoy doing.
- Personal Values: What is important to you; what you care about doing.
- Personal Abilities or Aptitudes: What you do well or have the potential to do well.
- Learning Habits: How you go about learning—the usual approaches, methods, or techniques you use when learning.
- Learning Styles: How you prefer to learn, that is, your preferred manner of:
  ◇ Receiving information (e.g., reading from books or listening to speakers),
  ◇ Perceiving information (e.g., through sight, sound, or touch), and
  ◇ Processing information—how you tend to deal mentally with information that you have received and perceived (e.g., thinking about it alone, or talking about it with others).
- Personality Traits: Your temperament, emotional characteristics, and social tendencies (e.g., whether you tend to be an introvert or extrovert).

- Academic Self-Concept: Your personal beliefs about what kind of student you think you are, and how you perceive yourself as a learner. In particular, two components of your academic self-concept play an important role in college success:
    1. Academic Self-Efficacy—whether you think your academic success depends largely on you (e.g., your self-motivation and determination) and that you can change for the better (e.g., by increasing your effort and improving your habits); or, whether you believe that academic success depends largely on factors beyond your control (e.g., your upbringing or present life circumstances) and that you cannot change or improve your performance (e.g., due to low ability or insufficient intelligence).
    2. Academic Self-Esteem—how you feel about yourself as a student (e.g., positive, negative, or neutral) and your level of self-confidence in academic situations (e.g., whether you expect success or fear failure).

Pause for Reflection

How would you rate your academic self-confidence at this point in your college experience? (Circle one)

VERY CONFIDENT   SOMEWHAT CONFIDENT   SOMEWHAT UNCONFIDENT   VERY UNCONFIDENT

Why did you make this choice?

Self-Monitoring

Research indicates that one key characteristic of successful college students is that they monitor their own performance. They maintain awareness of:

- How effectively they are learning—for example, they pay attention to whether they are really paying attention in class.
- Whether they are comprehending what they are attempting to learn—for example, if they are truly understanding the material they are studying or merely memorizing it (Weinstein, 1994; Weinstein & Meyer, 1991).
- What they are attempting to learn (for example, science or literature), and they self-regulate or adjust their learning strategies in a way that best meets the specific demands of the subject they are trying to learn (Pintrich, 1995). For instance, they read more slowly and stop to test their understanding more frequently when reading technical material in a science textbook than when reading a novel in a literature course. In contrast, unsuccessful students often do not maintain this high level of self-awareness during the learning process. This can result in their not being fully aware of what method they are using to learn, whether the method they are using is most effective for the type of material they are attempting to learn, or if they are actually understanding the material they are attempting to learn.

You can begin to establish good habits of self-monitoring right now by getting in the routine of periodically pausing to reflect on what you are doing in college. For instance, ask yourself these questions:

- Are you are really listening attentively to what your instructor is saying in class?
- Do you really comprehend what you are reading outside of class?
- Are you effectively utilizing campus resources that are designed to support your success?
- Are you interacting with campus professionals who can contribute to your current and future development?
- Are you interacting and collaborating with peers who can enhance your learning and social integration into the college community?
- Are you effectively implementing the key success strategies identified in this book?

It is important to periodically stop and reflect on whether you are actually comprehending what you are reading.

You can also engage in effective self-monitoring to reflect on what you should *not* be doing if you want to achieve academic excellence. In Box 4, the director of academic advising at a state university offers the list of behaviors to avoid if you want to excel in college.

How Not to Succeed in College: Self-Monitoring the Behaviors You Should Avoid

1. Either don't go to class at all or go very little. This way you won't be bothered with knowing anything about stuff that might be on exams.
2. After cutting class, be sure to ask the instructor, "Did I miss anything?"
3. Sit in the back of the classroom. This will immediately indicate a lack of interest in the class and a generally negative attitude toward school.
4. Forget to buy your textbooks.
5. Don't read your assignments before going to class. This way, you'll be nicely unprepared to answer questions, and you'll have no idea what the professor is lecturing about.
6. If you must take notes, let the reading and studying of them pile up until the night before an exam.
7. Ignore exam results. Throw them away. If you study them, you might do better next time.
8. Start term papers late. In fact, just throw them together.
9. Never visit with any of your professors during the term. That way you can avoid getting any valuable information that might help you.

Source: Bonnie Titley, *National On-Campus Report*, Aug. 12, 1994.

Reflecting on Feedback

Learning and decision-making are enhanced when you reflect on, and make use of information you receive from others on how to correct or improve your performance. In college, potential sources of valuable feedback include professors, academic advisors, academic support professionals, and student life professionals. While feedback from such experienced professionals is extremely valuable, do not overlook your peers as another potential source of useful academic and personal feedback.

Effective learning requires *self-monitoring*—periodically reflecting on whether you're truly understanding what you're learning, or simply "going through the motions."

Pause for Reflection

What positive feedback have you received from others about your personal characteristics or behavior?

Have you ever received feedback from others that you've used to improve yourself, your behavior, or your performance?

If yes, what type of feedback did you receive, and what changes did you make as a result of receiving this feedback?

Be alert and open to feedback that you receive from peers as well as professionals. Better yet, rather than just waiting and hoping that useful feedback floats your way, actively seek it out from people whose judgment you trust and value.

Reflecting on Your Future

Self-reflection not only involves reflecting on what you have done and what you are currently doing, it also involves self-projection—reflecting on what you will be doing in the more distant future. This process of futuristic thinking involves the twin tasks of goal-setting and long-range planning. To achieve success, you need to focus on the "big picture"—your long-term goals and dreams, which inspire motivation, and the "little details"—daily deadlines, due dates, and short-term commitments, that require perspiration. Try to view college as if you were using a dual-focus camera with two lenses: a narrow-angle lens to focus on the foreground that is immediately in front of you (e.g., completing your major assignment that is due next week) and a wide-angle lens to focus on the more distant background—one that enables you to keep in perspective how all your immediate academic chores and challenges are part of a larger picture (e.g., college graduation and a successful future). In other words, you need to periodically pick-up your head from the books in front of you and look farther ahead; then you need to shift back from this long-range vision to the here and now, lower your head again, put your nose to the grindstone, and refocus your sight on the day-to-day college tasks that immediately confront you.

By viewing college from both of these perspectives, you will not lose sight of how achieving your future goals connects with conquering your current challenges. Consider discussing your future plans on a regular basis with an academic advisor, career counselor, or mentor to help you stay focused and moving in the direction of your long-term goals, while simultaneously meeting your short-term objectives.

Remember: Keep both your future dreams and present realities in clear focus. Integrating these two perspectives will produce an image that can provide you with the inspiration to continue your college education and the determination to complete your day-to-day tasks.

Pause for Reflection

Before exiting this chapter, we ask you to do one last thing to "lock into" your brain some of the chapter's major ideas. Take a look at the following "Checklist Summary of College-Success Principles and Strategies," and take a minute to see how these ideas compare with those you recorded at the start of this chapter—in response to the questions we asked you about how college would be different from high school and what it would take to be successful in college. What ideas from your list and our checklist tend to match? Were there any ideas on your list that were not on ours, or vice versa?

••• A Checklist Summary of Key College-Success Principles and Strategies

1. **Active Involvement**

   Inside the Classroom:
   - ☑ Get to Class—treat it like a job—if you "cut," your pay (grade) will be cut.
   - ☑ Get Involved in Class—come prepared, listen actively, take notes, and participate.

   Outside the Classroom:
   - ☑ Read Actively—take notes while you read to increase attention and retention.
   - ☑ Spend a Significant Amount of Time on Academic Activities Outside of Class—make it a 40-hour work week (with occasional "overtime").

2. **Utilizing Campus Resources**

   Capitalize on Academic and Student Support Services:
   - ☑ Learning Center
   - ☑ Writing Center
   - ☑ Disability Services
   - ☑ College Library
   - ☑ Academic Advisement
   - ☑ Career Development
   - ☑ Personal Counseling
   - ☑ Health Center

Capitalize on Experiential Learning Opportunities:
- ☑ Participate in co-curricular experiences on campus.
- ☑ Participate in volunteer experiences and internships off campus.

3. **Social Interaction and Collaboration**

Interact with:
- ☑ Peers—by joining campus clubs and student organizations.
- ☑ Faculty—by connecting with them immediately after class, in their offices, or by e-mail.
- ☑ Academic Advisors—see them for more than just a signature to register; find an advisor you can relate to and with whom you can develop an ongoing relationship.
- ☑ Mentors—try to find experienced people on campus who can serve as trusted guides and role models.

Collaborate by:
- ☑ Forming Learning Teams—not only last-minute study groups, but teams that collaborate more regularly to work on such tasks as taking lecture notes, completing reading assignments, editing writing assignments, conducting library research, and reviewing results of exams and course assignments.
- ☑ Participating in Learning Communities—enroll in two or more classes with the same students during the same term.

4. **Self-Reflection**
- ☑ Self-Monitor Your Learning—maintain awareness of how you are learning, what you are learning, and if you are learning.
- ☑ Reflect on Feedback—seek information from others (professionals and peers) on the quality of your performance and what specifically you can do to improve it.
- ☑ Reflect on Your Future—take time from the daily grind to project yourself into the future, set long-term goals, and develop strategic plans for your major, your career, and your life.

••• Learning More through Independent Research

Web-Based Resources for Further Information on College Success

For additional information relating to the ideas discussed in this chapter, we recommend the following Web sites:

http://steele.instrasun.tcnj.edu/travers6/college_success_formula.html
http://www2.ncsu.edu/for_student/success/text/fundamentals.html
http://www.lifehack.org/article/lifehack/from-a-freshman-five-tips-for-success-in-college

Name _____ Date _____

 ## Constructing a Master List of Campus Resources

Use each of the following information sources to gain more in-depth knowledge about the specific support services available on your campus.

1. Information published in your College Catalog and Student Handbook.

2. Online information posted on your college's Web site.

3. In-person information gathered by speaking with a professional in different offices or centers on your campus.

ASSIGNMENT

Using the above information sources, construct a master list of all support services that are available to you at your college. Your final product should be a list that includes:

1. The names of different support services your college offers,

2. The specific types of support each service provides,

3. A short statement next to each specific support service listed, indicating whether you think you would benefit from this particular type of support, and

4. The name of a person whom you could contact for support from this service.

NOTE:

◆ You can pair-up with a classmate to work collaboratively on this assignment. Working together with a peer on a research task can often reduce your anxiety, increase your energy, and generate synergy—which results in a final product that is superior to what could have been produced by either of you working alone (independently).

◆ Save your master list of support services for future use after this course is completed. You might not have an immediate need or use for some of these services during your first term of college, but they can become very valuable and useful to you at later stages of your college experience.

Support Services

LEARNING CENTER

Types of Support

Will I benefit?	Contact Person:
Will I benefit?	Contact Person:
Will I benefit?	Contact Person:
Will I benefit?	Contact Person:
Will I benefit?	Contact Person:

WRITING CENTER

Types of Support

Will I benefit?	Contact Person:
Will I benefit?	Contact Person:
Will I benefit?	Contact Person:
Will I benefit?	Contact Person:
Will I benefit?	Contact Person:

DISABILITY SERVICES

Types of Services

Will I benefit?	Contact Person:
Will I benefit?	Contact Person:

Will I benefit? _____ Contact Person: _____

Will I benefit? _____ Contact Person: _____

Will I benefit? _____ Contact Person: _____

COLLEGE LIBRARY

Types of Services

Will I benefit? _____ Contact Person: _____

Will I benefit? _____ Contact Person: _____

Will I benefit? _____ Contact Person: _____

Will I benefit? _____ Contact Person: _____

Will I benefit? _____ Contact Person: _____

ACADEMIC ADVISEMENT

Types of Services

Will I benefit? _____ Contact Person: _____

Will I benefit? _____ Contact Person: _____

Will I benefit? _____ Contact Person: _____

Will I benefit? _____ Contact Person: _____

Will I benefit? _____ Contact Person: _____

CAREER DEVELOPMENT CENTER

Types of Services

Will I benefit? | Contact Person:

Will I benefit? | Contact Person:

Will I benefit? | Contact Person:

Will I benefit? | Contact Person:

Will I benefit? | Contact Person:

COUNSELING CENTER

Types of Services

Will I benefit? | Contact Person:

Will I benefit? | Contact Person:

Will I benefit? | Contact Person:

Will I benefit? | Contact Person:

Will I benefit? | Contact Person:

HEALTH CENTER

Types of Services

Will I benefit? | Contact Person:

Will I benefit? | Contact Person:

Will I benefit?   Contact Person:

Will I benefit?   Contact Person:

Will I benefit?   Contact Person:

EXPERIENTIAL LEARNING RESOURCES

Types of Services

Will I benefit?   Contact Person:

Will I benefit?   Contact Person:

Will I benefit?   Contact Person:

Will I benefit?   Contact Person:

Will I benefit?   Contact Person:

OTHER

Types of Services

Will I benefit?   Contact Person:

Will I benefit?   Contact Person:

Will I benefit?   Contact Person:

Will I benefit?   Contact Person:

Will I benefit?   Contact Person:

CASE STUDY

Alone and Disconnected: Feel Like Going Home

Josephine is a first-year student in her second week of college. She doesn't feel like she fits in with other students that she's met at the college thus far. She also feels separated from her family and former friends, and fears that her ties with them will be weakened or broken if she doesn't spend more time at home. In fact, Josephine is feeling so homesick right now that she is having thoughts about withdrawing from college altogether.

Reflection and Discussion Questions

1. What could you say to Josephine that might persuade her to stay in college?

2. Could your college have done more during her first two weeks on campus to make Josephine (and other students) feel more welcomed and less homesick?

3. What could Josephine do now to help herself feel less homesick and more at home at college?

The Value of Liberal Arts and General Education

How the College Experience Develops You as a Whole Person and Improves Your Total Quality of Life

Learning Goals

The primary goal of this chapter is to develop a deeper understanding of the meaning, purpose, and value of a *liberal arts* education. This is the part of your education that provides the essential foundation or backbone of the college experience because:

◆ it is the part that *all* students experience in common, no matter what their major may be, and
◆ it represents what *all* college students should *know* and be able to *do* by the time they graduate.

Outline

The Meaning and Purpose of a Liberal Arts Education
The Liberal Arts Curriculum
    Major Divisions of Knowledge and Subject Areas in the Liberal Arts Curriculum
What is the Value of a Liberal Arts Education?
    Gaining a Multi-Dimensional Perspective and Multiple Thinking Tools
    Acquiring a Powerful Set of Fundamental Skills
Achieving Career Success
    Skills
Developing the Whole Person
    Skills and Abilities Associated with Each Element of Holistic Development

The Co-Curriculum
Broadening Your Perspective of the Whole World
    Elements of the Chronological Perspective
    Elements of the Social-Spatial Perspective
    The Synoptic Perspective: Integrating Diverse Perspectives to Form a Unified Whole
Summary and Conclusion
Learning More through Independent Research
Exercises: Planning Your Liberal Arts Education
Case Study: Dazed and Confused: General Education versus Career Specialization

Activate Your Thinking

Which one of the following statements represents the most accurate meaning of the term *"liberal arts"* education?
a. Learning to be less conservative politically.
b. Learning to spend money more freely.
c. Learning to value the art of peace more than the martial arts.
d. Learning how to become a performing artist.
e. Learning skills for freedom.

The Meaning and Purpose of a Liberal Arts Education

If you are not certain about what the term "liberal arts" means, welcome to the club. Most first-year students do not have the foggiest idea about what a liberal arts education actually stands for (Hersh, 1997), and if they were to guess, they might say that it has something to do with liberal politics, as illustrated by the following story.

> **Personal Story**
>
> I was once advising a first-year student (Laura) who intended to major in business, and I was helping her plan what courses she needed to complete her degree. I pointed out to her that one course she still needed to take was philosophy. Here is how our conversation went after I made that point.
>
> *Laura (in a somewhat irritated tone):* "Why do I have to take philosophy? I'm a business major."
>
> *Dr. Joe:* "Because philosophy is one important component of a liberal arts education."
>
> *Laura (in a very agitated tone):* "I am not liberal and I don't want to be a liberal. I'm conservative and so are my parents. We all voted for Reagan in the last election!"
>
> —Joe Cuseo

Many students (and their parents) do not know what the term *"liberal arts"* truly means.

> **CLASSIC QUOTE**
>
> *It is such good fortune for people in power that people do not think.*
>
> —Adolf Hitler, German dictator

In the multiple-choice question that we asked at the start of this chapter, Laura probably would have picked choice "a" as her answer. She would have been wrong because choice "e" actually is correct. Literally translated, the term "liberal arts" derives from the Latin words "liberales"—meaning to *liberate* or *free*, and "artes"—meaning *skills*. Thus, "skills for freedom" is the most accurate meaning of the term "liberal arts."

The roots of the term "liberal arts" date back to the origin of modern civilization—to the ancient Greeks and Romans—who argued that political power in a democratic society rests with the people because, in a democracy, the people elect their own leaders. Thus, in a democracy, people are freed from uncritical dependence on, or blind obedience to, a dictator or autocrat. However, to ensure that a democratic society is successful and political freedom is preserved, citizens in a democracy must be *well educated* so they can ask intelligent questions of their potential political leaders and make wise choices about whom they elect as their leaders and lawmakers (Bishop, 1986; Cheney, 1989).

The founding fathers of America also shared the ancient Greco-Roman emphasis on the importance of education as typified by Thomas Jefferson, third president of the United States and founder of the University of Virginia, who wrote in 1801:

> *I know of no safe depository of the ultimate powers of a society but the people themselves; and if we think them not enlightened enough to exercise control with a wholesome discretion [ability to make responsible decisions], the remedy is not to take power from them, but to inform their discretion by education"* (Ford, 1903, p. 278).

Although its original purpose was to preserve freedom in a democracy, a liberal arts education has taken on the added meaning of liberating or freeing people to be *self-directed* individuals whose choices, decisions, and behavior are determined or driven by their own thoughts and values, rather than by others around them (Gamson, 1984). Self-directed human beings have the mental power to resist excessive control by outside influences, such as:

- Politicians—who may try to manipulate or dominate.
- Parents—who may attempt to make decisions for their children after they reach an age of independence.
- Peers—who can exert excessive influence or pressure for conformity.
- Mass media—which may try to manipulate people into thinking how they should vote, act, look, and spend their money.

A liberal arts education encourages you to be "your own person" and to always ask: "Why?" It is the component of your college education that is designed to equip you with the mental tools needed to think independently, along with the inquiring mind needed to question authority and resist thought control by all authority figures, including your instructors! This is one reason why students in college, compared to high school, spend less time per week sitting in class under the direction of instructors and have more free time to work independently outside the classroom. This greater freedom also brings with it greater expectations about the amount of time college students are to commit to their studies outside the classroom, plus greater personal responsibility for planning and managing their own time. For some tips on exercising this freedom responsibly, see Box 1.

CLASSIC QUOTE

Knowledge will forever govern ignorance; and a people who mean to be their own governors must arm themselves with the power which knowledge gives.

—James Madison, 4th president of the United States, and co-signer of the American Constitution and Bill of Rights

STUDENT PERSPECTIVE

"I want knowledge so I don't get taken advantage of in life."

—First-year student

TAKE ACTION NOW! — Box 1

Top Strategies for Exercising Personal Freedom Responsibly: Completing Tasks, Planning Time, and Preventing Procrastination

In high school, your educational time was frequently structured for you. In college, you will have more freedom and responsibility to structure your own time. For example, in college, you will typically spend only about 15 hours per week in class, and often you will not go directly from one class to the next; instead, you will often have gaps of "free time" between classes. To effectively manage your out-of-class time, consider implementing the following strategies.

1. **Plan Your *Term***
   - Review the *course syllabus (course outline)* for each course you are enrolled in this term, and highlight all major exams, tests, quizzes, assignments, papers, and the dates they are due.

STUDENT PERSPECTIVE

"High school can be an assembly line-like time-table. Everything you do is pre-planned; you are given a schedule you must follow. You wish you would have some free time."

—High school senior

(continued)

> **STUDENT PERSPECTIVE**
>
> "The amount of free time you have in college is much more than in high school. Always have a weekly study schedule to go by. Otherwise, time slips away and you will not be able to account for it."
>
> —First-year student's advice to incoming students (Rhoads, 2005)

Note: College professors are more likely to expect you to rely on your course syllabus to keep track of what you have to do and when you have to do it.

- Obtain a *large calendar* for the academic term (available at your campus bookstore or learning center) and record all your exams, assignments, etc. for all your courses in the calendar boxes that represent their due dates. To fit this information within the calendar boxes, use creative abbreviations to represent different tasks—e.g., "E" for Exam, "TP" for Term Paper (not toilet paper). When you are done, you will have a centralized chart or map of deadline dates, and a potential "master plan" for the entire term.

2. **Plan Your *Week***

   - Make a map of your *weekly schedule* that includes times during the week when you are in class, when you typically eat and sleep, and if you are employed, when you work.
   - If you are a full-time college student, find *at least 25 total hours per week* when you can do *academic work outside the classroom*. (These 25 hours can be pieced together any way you like, including time between daytime classes and work commitments, evening time, and weekend time.) When adding these 25 hours to the time you spend in class each week, you will end-up with a 40-hour workweek, similar to any full-time job.
   - Make good use of your *"free time" between classes* by working on assignments and studying in advance for upcoming exams. **Remember:** For the purpose of mastering course material and improving your course grade, out-of-class work includes such tasks as:
     - completing reading assignments,
     - reviewing class notes,
     - integrating information in your class notes with related information that you have highlighted in your assigned reading, and
     - breaking-up work for large, long-term assignments into smaller short-term tasks.

> **STUDENT PERSPECTIVE**
>
> "I was constantly missing important meetings during my first few weeks because I did not keep track of the dates and times. I thought I'd be told again when the time was closer, just as had been done in high school. Something I should have done to address that would have been to keep a well-organized planner for reference."
>
> —Advice to new students from a college sophomore (Walsh, 2005)

3. **Plan Your *Day***

   - Make a *daily "to do" list*. **Remember:** If you *write it out*, you are less likely to block it out and forget about it. Studies of effective people show that they are "list makers," and they make lists not only for grocery items and wedding invitations, but also for things they want to accomplish each day (Covey, 1990).
   - Attack daily tasks in *priority order*. **Remember:** "First things, first." So, *plan your work* by placing the most important and most urgent tasks at the top of your list, and *work your plan* by attacking tasks in the order that you have listed them.

4. **Carry *Portable* Work and Planning Materials with You at All Times**

   - Portable work is work that you can take with you and do in any place at any time, enabling you to take advantage of dead time during the day. For example, carry material with you that you can read while sitting and waiting for appointments or transportation during the day, which will resurrect this wasted time and transform it into productive time.
   - Carry a *small calendar or appointment book* with you at all times. This will enable you to record appointments that you may need to make on the run during the day, and it will also allow you to jot down creative ideas or memories of things you need to do—which can sometimes pop into your mind at the most unexpected times.
   - Wear a *watch* or carry a cell phone that can accurately and instantly tell you what *time* it is and what *date* it is. Obviously, you can't even begin to manage time if you don't know what time it is, and you can't plan a schedule if you don't know what date it is!

> **STUDENT PERSPECTIVE**
>
> "I believe the most important aspect of college life is time management. DO NOT procrastinate because, although this is the easy thing to do at first, it will catch up with you and make your life miserable."
>
> —Advice from first-year student to new college students

••• The Liberal Arts Curriculum

The first liberal arts *curriculum* was intended to provide the type of education that would best preserve political democracy and personal freedom. It was driven by the belief that individuals who experienced these courses would be equipped with a *broad* base of knowledge—ensuring that they would be well informed in a variety of different subjects, and that they would develop a wide range of mental skills—enabling them to think *deeply* and *critically*. Based on this educational philosophy of the ancient Greeks and Romans, the first liberal arts curriculum was developed during the Middle Ages and consisted of two major divisions of knowledge:

1. The Verbal Arts, which included logic, language, and rhetoric (the art of persuasion), and
2. The Numerical Arts, which included mathematics, geometry, and astronomy (Ratcliff, 1997).

The liberal arts curriculum has survived the test of time, and today's colleges and universities continue to offer a liberal arts curriculum for the purpose of providing students with a broad base of knowledge in different subject areas. However, the liberal arts curriculum today is sometimes referred to as:

A liberal arts education encourages students to ask questions.

- The *general education* curriculum—"general" representing "broad" rather than narrow education;
- The *core* curriculum—"core" standing for what is central or essential for all students to know, regardless of their particular major; or
- *Breadth requirements*—required courses that are "wide-ranging," spanning across different subject areas.

Also, the major divisions of knowledge that comprise the liberal arts curriculum today have changed and include more divisions than those that made up the original curriculum devised by the Greeks and Romans. The contemporary liberal arts curriculum usually consists of the general divisions of knowledge and specific subject areas listed below. The *divisions* of the liberal arts curriculum, and the *courses* that make up each division, may vary somewhat from one college to another. Also, colleges vary in terms of whether they require students to take specific courses within each division of knowledge, or whether students are allowed to choose from a menu of courses within each of the divisions. However, what the liberal arts curriculum represents at every college and university are the areas of knowledge and the types of intellectual skills that all students should experience and master, no matter what their particular major happens to be.

Pause for Reflection

What type of knowledge or skills do you think are needed to be successful in all majors and careers?

> **CLASSIC QUOTE**
>
> *Never mistake knowledge for wisdom. One helps you make a living; the other helps you make a life.*
>
> —Sandra Carey, lobbyist, California State Assembly

Pottery is a visual art, one of the subject areas of Fine Arts, which focuses on the art of human expression.

> **CLASSIC QUOTE**
>
> *Dancing is silent poetry.*
>
> —Simonides, ancient Greek poet

Major Divisions of Knowledge and Subject Areas in the Liberal Arts Curriculum

Humanities

Courses in this division of the liberal arts curriculum tend to focus on the human experience and human culture, asking important questions that arise in a human's life, such as: Why are we here? What is the meaning or purpose of our existence? How should we live? What is the good life? Is there life after death?

Primary Subject Areas:

- English Composition: improving written communication.
- Speech: public speaking (rhetoric).
- Literature: reading written works of artistic merit.
- Languages: learning foreign languages.
- Philosophy: understanding why logical thinking is essential for humans to live wisely, ethically, and achieve meaning or purpose in life.
- Theology: understanding how humans view their relationship with, and express their faith in, a transcendent or supreme being.

Fine Arts

Courses in this division of the liberal arts curriculum focus largely on the art of *human expression*, asking such questions as: How do humans express and appreciate what is beautiful? How do humans express themselves aesthetically (through the senses) with imagination, creativity, style, and elegance?

Primary Subject Areas:

- Visual Arts: creative expression through painting, sculpture, and graphic design.
- Musical Arts: rhythmical and creative arrangement of sounds.
- Performing Arts: creative expression through drama and dance.

Mathematics

Courses in this division of the liberal arts curriculum are designed to promote skills in numerical calculation, quantitative reasoning, and problem solving.

Primary Subject Areas:

- Algebra: mathematical reasoning involving symbolic representation of numbers with letters that can vary in size or quantity.
- Statistics: mathematical methods for summarizing, estimating probabilities, and drawing conclusions from numerical data.
- Calculus: higher mathematical methods for calculating the rate at which the quantity of one entity changes in relation to another, and for calculating the areas enclosed by curves.

Natural Sciences

Courses in this division of the liberal arts curriculum are devoted to observation of the *physical world* and explanation of *natural phenomena*, asking such questions as: What causes physical events in the natural world? How can we predict and control physical events and improve the quality of interaction between humans and the natural environment?

Primary Subject Areas:

- Biology: understanding the structure and vital processes of all living things.
- Chemistry: understanding the composition of natural and man-made substances, and how they may be changed or developed.
- Physics: understanding the structural properties of the physical world and how they produce energy.
- Geology: understanding the composition of the earth, and the natural processes that take place to shape its development.
- Astronomy: understanding the make-up and motion of celestial bodies that comprise the universe.

The natural sciences division of the liberal arts curriculum focuses on the observation of the physical world, and the explanation of natural phenomena.

Social and Behavioral Sciences

Courses in this division of the liberal arts curriculum focus on the observation of *human behavior*, individually and in groups, asking such questions as: What causes humans to behave the way they do? How can we predict, control, or improve human behavior and interpersonal interaction?

Primary Subject Areas:

- Psychology: understanding the human mind, its conscious and subconscious processes, and the underlying causes of human behavior.
- Sociology: understanding the structure, interaction, and collective behavior of organized social groups and societal institutions or systems (e.g., families, schools, and governmental services).
- Anthropology: understanding the cultural and physical origin, distribution, and classification of human beings.
- History: understanding past events, their causes, and their influence on current events.
- Political Science: understanding how societal authority is organized and how this authority is exerted to govern people, make collective decisions, and maintain social order.
- Economics: understanding how the monetary needs of humans are met by allocating limited resources, and how material wealth is produced and distributed.
- Geography: understanding how the place where humans live influences their cultural interactions and their interactions with the physical environment.

Physical Education and Wellness

Courses in this division of the liberal arts curriculum focus on the *human body* and how to best maintain health or develop physically, asking such questions as: How does the body function most effectively? What can we do to prevent illness, promote wellness, and improve the physical quality of our lives?

Primary Subject Areas:

- Physical Education: understanding the role of human exercise for promoting health and peak performance.

- Nutrition: understanding how nourishment is consumed by the body and is used to promote health and generate energy.
- Sexuality: understanding the biological, psychological, and social aspects of sexual relations.
- Drug Education: understanding how substances that alter the body and mind affect physical health, mental health, and human performance.

By the time you graduate from college with a bachelor's degree, roughly one-third of your total college credits will consist of required *liberal arts* courses, one-third will be required courses in your *major*, and one-third will be *electives*—courses in any subject that you choose or "elect" to take.

Pause for Reflection

Look back at the subject areas within each of the six divisions of the liberal arts (general education) curriculum, and list those subjects in which you have never had a course. Then look back at your list and highlight any courses that strike you as particularly interesting or intriguing.

What Is the Value of a Liberal Arts Education?

Most of the liberal arts courses required for general education are taken during your first and second year of college. Do not be disappointed if you see some general education courses that you have already taken in high school. College courses in these subject areas will not simply repeat what was covered in high school because, in college, you will examine these subjects at a higher level and in greater depth.

Also, if you have already decided on a specific major, do not assume that general education courses have nothing to do with your specialized field of study. Recall our story about Laura, the first-year student with a business major who questioned why she had to take a course in philosophy. Laura needed to take philosophy because she would encounter topics in her business major that relate either directly or indirectly to philosophy. For instance, in her business courses, she would likely encounter philosophical issues relating to (a) the logical assumptions and underlying values of capitalism, (b) business ethics—for example, hiring and firing practices, and (c) business justice—for example, how profits should be fairly or justly distributed to workers and shareholders. Philosophy would equip her with the fundamental logical and ethical thinking skills needed to understand these issues deeply and respond to them humanely. Similarly, other areas of the liberal arts would provide Laura, or any student in her major, with a foundation of knowledge and the fundamental thinking skills needed to succeed in the field of business. Some other courses in the liberal arts curriculum relevant to a business degree are:

- **History and Political Science**—understanding governmental policies toward business and regulations of industry;
- **Psychology and Sociology**—understanding what motivates individuals and groups, such as the work habits of employees and the purchasing habits of consumers;
- **Speech, English Composition, and Literature**—speaking confidently and persuasively at meetings, writing clear and concise memos, reading and interpreting business reports accurately and critically;
- **Mathematics**—analyzing statistical data from marketing surveys;

- **Natural Science**—determining effective and efficient ways to utilize energy and conserve natural resources;
- **Fine Arts**—devising creative and innovative advertisements;
- **Physical and Health Education**—selecting effective employee health-insurance plans and corporate-sponsored health services.

In addition to business, liberal arts subjects are relevant to successful performance in a wide variety of majors and careers, as is explained in the following section.

Gaining a Multi-Dimensional Perspective and Multiple Thinking Tools

Aside from helping with a business major, liberal arts courses provide a relevant foundation for success in any college major or professional career. The broad, balanced base of knowledge provided by a liberal arts education enables you to view issues or problems from *multiple* perspectives, angles, and vantage points.

Although you will specialize in one field (your college major), "real-life" issues and career challenges are not specialized into majors. For instance, such important issues as providing effective leadership, improving race relations, and promoting world peace, cannot be understood or solved by one single field of study. A narrow approach provides only a single-minded and often over-simplified explanation of, or solution to, complex issues. Similarly, the tasks that humans face in their personal lives and professional careers are also multi-dimensional, requiring perspectives and skills that go well beyond the boundaries of one particular field of study.

The different disciplines of a liberal arts education train your mind to think in different ways. An algebra class requires you to think symbolically.

The multiple subject areas that you are exposed to in the liberal arts provide you with these multiple perspectives and equip you with a wider repertoire of thinking tools to work on the tasks we face in our personal and professional lives. Keep in mind that liberal arts courses do not just expose you to different subject areas; they also train your mind to think in different ways. This is why different academic subjects are often referred to as *disciplines*, because by learning them, you are developing the "mental discipline" that faculty in these fields have spent years of their lives developing. For instance, when you study history, algebra, biology, and art, you are disciplining your mind to think in new and different ways—you are learning to think chronologically (history), symbolically (algebra), scientifically (biology), and creatively (art). You will find that subjects in different divisions of the liberal arts will ask you to think in very different ways. For example, some subjects will require you to think:

- in the form of words, numbers, or images,
- in terms of specific parts or whole patterns,
- individually or globally,
- concretely or abstractly,
- systematically (in sequential steps) or intuitively (in sudden leaps),
- objectively or subjectively, and
- factually or imaginatively (Donald, 2002; Katz & Henry, 1993).

Different disciplines will also train your mind to develop the habit of asking powerful questions. Some will be important fact-seeking and fact-finding questions, such as: Who, What,

When, and Where? Others will be deeper questions designed to get beyond the facts and beneath the surface, such as: Why? Why not? How come? What if? The diversity of thinking and questioning styles you experience by taking a broad array of courses in the liberal arts provide you with a wide range of intellectual resources to draw from, along with a large repertoire of thinking tools. This rich supply of mental resources equip you with the intellectual curiosity, versatility, and agility needed to "think on your feet."

> **CLASSIC QUOTE**
>
> *When the only tool you have is a hammer, you tend to see every problem as a nail.*
>
> —Abraham Maslow, humanistic psychologist, best known for his theory of self-actualization

Furthermore, the liberal arts enhance your creativity. The different thinking styles you develop supply you with a myriad of strategies that you can modify and adapt to solve problems you may encounter in a range of contexts or situations. These diverse strategies can also be combined or rearranged in ways that result in unique or innovative solutions to problems. Thus, ideas you acquire in separate subject areas of the liberal arts can often feed off each other and "cross-fertilize," giving birth to new approaches for solving old problems.

Another advantage of liberal arts is that it can accelerate your learning curve, enabling you to learn new material more rapidly. Learning occurs when your brain makes a connection between the new concept you are trying to learn and something you already know. The greater the number and variety of learned connections that your brain has already made, the more pathways it has to build on and connect new ideas to, and the faster you will learn new ideas.

Acquiring a Powerful Set of Fundamental Skills

Another key way in which the liberal arts provides a foundation for success in your major, your career, and your life is by equipping you with a *set of essential skills* that have two powerful qualities:

1. **Transferability**—skills that "travel" well, enabling you to apply them across a wide range of subjects, careers, and life situations, and
2. **Durability**—skills that are long-lasting and that can be continually used to learn new things throughout your entire lifetime.

To use an athletic analogy, what the liberal arts do for the mind is similar to what cross-training does for the body. In cross-training, you intentionally engage in a wide range of different exercises. As a result of this wide range of exercises, the body builds up a broad base of fundamental physical-performance skills, which include strength, endurance, flexibility, agility, and coordination. These physical skills are essential for successful athletic performance in all sports, whether it be basketball, baseball, tennis, or rowing.

Similar to cross-training, a liberal arts education builds-up the following set of basic academic and lifelong learning skills that can be applied to promote your success in any field of study or professional career.

Read each of the skills listed below and rate yourself according to the following scale:

4 = very strong
3 = strong
2 = needs some improvement
1 = needs much improvement

- **Communication Skills** for accurate *comprehension* and articulate *expression* of ideas.

    There are five particular types of communication skills that provide an important foundation for future success in any specialized field of study or work:
    1. **Reading Skills**: comprehending, interpreting, and evaluating writing in a variety of styles and subject areas.
    2. **Written Communication Skills**: writing in a clear, creative, and persuasive manner.
    3. **Oral Communication Skills**: speaking in a concise, confident, and eloquent fashion.
    4. **Listening Skills**: comprehending spoken language with accuracy and empathy.
    5. **Multi-Media Communication Skills**: comprehending and expressing ideas delivered through modes of communication other than language, which include visual representation (drawings, images) and technology-assisted communication (sound, film, and computer graphics).

- **Computation Skills** for accurate calculation and comprehension of quantitative information, and to analyze, summarize, interpret, or evaluate statistical data.
- **Research Skills** for locating, accessing, retrieving, organizing, and evaluating information from a variety of sources, including library and technology-based systems.
- **Critical Thinking Skills** that enable you to think at a deeper or higher level than merely memorizing facts.

    In particular, the following four types of thinking skills are essential for success in any field:
    1. **Analysis:** ability to break down or dissect information into its key parts and detect what is most important or relevant.
    2. **Creativity:** ability to imagine alternative ideas, original viewpoints, and new or innovative strategies for addressing old problems.
    3. **Evaluation:** ability to critically assess or judge the validity (truth), morality (ethics), or aesthetic (artistic) value of ideas, products, or practices.
    4. **Synthesis:** ability to build up or connect separate ideas and integrate them into a meaningful whole, resulting in a more complete understanding of the "big picture."

Reading skills are one of the five types of communication skills needed to provide an important foundation for future success.

 Memory Tips A useful mnemonic device (memory-improvement strategy) for recalling these four powerful thinking skills is to take the first letter of each skill and form one word "ACES."

"Education is what's left over after you've forgotten all the facts" is an old saying that carries a lot of truth. Studies do show that students' memory of specific facts learned in college often fades with the passing of time (Pascarella & Terenzini, 1991, 2005). What is left over are the lifelong learning skills that students develop in college, such as thinking deeply, writing clearly, and speaking persuasively. Just as the physical skills of bicycle riding or roller skating can be remembered throughout an entire lifetime, so can mental skills and thinking habits. Memorized facts often fade with time, but learning skills remain with you, and can be repeatedly retrieved and recycled continually throughout life. They are the "gift that keeps on giving."

Lifelong learning skills are more essential for success in today's work world than ever before, because with the help of computer technology, new information is now being generated and communicated at a faster rate than at any other time in human history (Dryden & Vos, 1999). Existing knowledge and traditional methods quickly becomes obsolete due to the rapid communication of new information (Naisbitt, 1982). Thus, it is necessary for workers to update their skills continually in order to remain employed and advance in their careers (Niles & Harris-Bowlsbey, 2002). This results in an increased need for people to continue to acquire new knowledge *for* themselves and *by* themselves throughout their lifetime (Daly, 1992).

Today's rapidly changing information society places a high value on, and creates a great demand for, individuals who have learned *how to learn*—one of the key skills you will acquire from a liberal arts education. Remember that the wide range of different thinking styles and the broad base of knowledge developed by the liberal arts will accelerate your "learning curve," enabling you to continue to learn new things more rapidly and more effectively.

Furthermore, since so much new information is being produced at such a rapid rate, the research skills you develop as part of a liberal arts education will allow you to effectively locate, select, and organize the information you need to learn. The ability to research, evaluate, and integrate information are lifelong learning skills that can provide the lifeboat you need to stay afloat and navigate the tidal wave of information generated by current technology. Since one primary goal of a liberal arts education is to "liberate" or free you to become an independent, self-reliant learner, your college librarians will not just simply supply you with this information; instead, they will educate you on *how* to find it on your own. Thus, you acquire a lifelong learning skill that can be used to locate any information you need whenever you need it, at any time or stage of your life.

CLASSIC QUOTE

If you give a man a fish, you feed him for a day. If you teach a man how to fish, you feed him for life.

—Author unknown

A liberal arts education develops *lifelong learning skills* that you can use to continue learning new things more effectively throughout life.

Pause for Reflection

Reflect on the four key skill areas developed by a liberal arts education (communication, computation, research, and critical thinking), and choose one that is most important or most relevant to you. Write a one-paragraph explanation about why you chose this skill.

••• Achieving Career Success

Studies show that college students, as well as their parents, are extremely concerned about majors and careers, but they often overlook or underestimate the relationship between liberal arts education and career performance (Hersh, 1994). They often believe that the "liberal arts" are something idealistic or impractical, which cannot be put to use in the "real world" and will not help you get a "real job" (Hersh, 1997). Actually, this is far from the truth. Just as the core skills developed by a liberal arts education prepare you for success in your major, they are also important for success in your eventual career.

Skills

The skills developed by a liberal arts education are strikingly similar to the types of skills that employers desire and seek in new employees. In many national surveys and in-depth interviews, employers and executives in both industry and government consistently report that they seek employees with skills that fall into the following three categories.

Writing skills are one of the communication skills employers look for when hiring.

1. **Communication Skills,** which include listening, speaking, writing, and reading (National Association of Colleges & Employers, 2003).

   "There is such a heavy emphasis on effective communication in the workplace that college students who master these skills can set themselves apart from the pack when searching for employment." Marilyn Mackes, Executive Director of the National Association of Colleges and Employers (Mackes, 2003, p. 1).

2. **Thinking Skills,** which include problem solving and critical thinking (Van Horn, 1995).

   "We look for people who can think critically and analytically. If you can do those things, we can teach you our business." Paul Dominski, Store Recruiter for the Robinson-May Department Stores Company (Indiana University, 2004, p. 1).

3. **Lifelong Learning Skills,** which include learning how to learn and how to continue learning (The Conference Board of Canada, 2000).

   "Employers are virtually unanimous that the most important knowledge and skills the new employee can bring to the job are problem solving, communication, and 'learning to learn' skills. The workers of the future need to know how to think and how to continue to learn." David Kearns, former Chief Executive Officer for the Xerox Corporation (Kearns, 1989, p. 8).

This trio of skills shows up in studies that ask employers for skills they are currently seeking in employees and skills they will be seeking from employees in the future. These same skills are also consistently cited by employers in different regions of the United States and in different countries around the world, including Canada (The Conference Board of Canada, 2000), England (QHE, 1993, 1994), Australia (Business/Higher Education Round Table, 1991, 1992), and Germany (Laur-Enrst, 1990).

If you compare the key work skills sought by employers with the key academic skills developed by a liberal arts education, you will find that there is a remarkable resemblance between the two. This similarity is not surprising when you think about the typical duties or responsibilities of working professionals. They need to have good communication skills because they listen, speak, and explain things to co-workers and customers. They read and critically interpret reports, and they write letters, memos, and reports. They need to have well-developed thinking skills to analyze problems, construct well-organized plans, come up with creative solutions to problems, and evaluate whether their plans and strategies are effective.

In his classic book, *The Idea of a University*, John Henry Newman (1852) eloquently explains how a liberal arts education prepares students for any career or any major:

> *It is the education which gives a man [woman] a clear conscious view of his own opinions and judgments, a truth in developing them, an eloquence in expressing them, and a force in urging them. It teaches him to see things as they are, to go right to the point, to detect what is sophisticated, and to discard what is irrelevant. It prepares him to fill any post with credit, and to master any subject with facility (1852, pp. 177–178).*

Remember: The liberal arts component of your college education is not only providing you with academic skills needed to succeed in your chosen major; it is simultaneously providing you with practical skills to succeed in your future career. Do not underestimate the importance of these fundamental skills: Work hard at developing them, and take pride in their development.

The academic skills developed by a liberal arts education are also *practical* skills that contribute to successful performance in *any career*.

Do not lose sight of the fact that these essential skills are durable and transferable, so they can be transported and applied to different types of careers throughout your entire working life. This is one way in which a liberal arts education "liberates"—freeing you from narrow job training or career overspecialization that only equip you with a small set of technical skills to perform a specific task.

Lastly, keep in mind that the transferability and durability of liberal arts skills serve not only to increase your chances of being hired immediately after college graduation (career entry); these skills also increase your freedom of career choice—the ability to move into different types of careers, and your career mobility—the ability to move out of a career or back into a career after taking time off from it.

Pause for Reflection

During your college experience, you might hear students state that they need to get their general education (liberal arts) courses out of the way so they can get into courses that relate to their major and career. Based on what you've read thus far in this chapter, what may be inaccurate or untrue about this statement?

••• Developing the Whole Person

While the development of intellectual skills are important for success in your major and career, there are other aspects of yourself that need attention and development in order to achieve success in both college and life. Your "self" is comprised of multiple elements or dimensions, and each one of them can affect your success and happiness. As you can see in Figure 1, there are a number of key elements of the self that join together to form the "whole person," and their development is an essential goal of a liberal arts education (Kuh, Shedd, & Whitt, 1987). These elements include the following eight aspects of self-development:

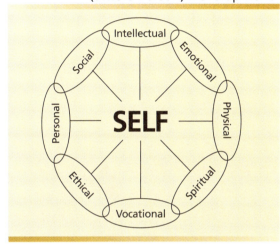

Figure 1 Key Elements of Holistic (Whole-Person) Development

1. intellectual
2. social
3. emotional
4. physical
5. spiritual
6. ethical
7. vocational
8. personal

We are not just intellectual beings or working beings; we are also social, emotional, physical, ethical, and spiritual beings. Furthermore, notice in the figure that all of these elements are joined or linked, and they are interrelated because they work interdependently (Love & Love, 1995). For instance, our intellectual performance can be influenced by our emotional state (e.g., whether we are bored or excited); our emotional state can be influenced by our social relationships (e.g., whether we feel lonely or loved); and our social relationships can be influenced by our physical condition (e.g., whether we have a positive or negative physical self-image). Thus, if we can strengthen one element of the self, other elements can often be strengthened simultaneously. In fact, research shows that when college students gain more knowledge, they also attain higher levels of self-esteem, greater social popularity, and greater popularity with the opposite sex (Pascarella & Terenzini, 1991, 2005).

Research also suggests that our quality of life depends on our attention to and integration of all the important elements of the self. It has been found that people who are healthy (physically and mentally) and successful are typically individuals who have effectively attended to and blended all key dimensions of the self, enabling them to lead well-balanced and well-rounded lives (Covey, 1990; Goleman, 1995; Heath, 1977).

Since wholeness seems so essential for wellness, success, and happiness, we ask you to carefully read the following descriptions and specific skills associated with each of the eight elements of holistic development. Keep in mind that even though these elements are discussed separately, in real life they are interrelated and influence each other.

• CLASSIC QUOTE •

"The research portrays the college student as changing in an integrated way, with change in any one area appearing to be part of a mutually reinforcing network or pattern of change in other areas."

—Pascarella & Terenzini, *How College Affects Students*

STUDENT PERSPECTIVE

"Being successful is being balanced in every aspect of your life."

—First-year college student

"I thought I was going to college to get a good job. Now they tell me I'm going to develop critical thinking, social intelligence, emotional intelligence, ethical perspective, personal wellness, and spiritual awareness! I don't think I'll even have enough time to sleep!!"

A liberal arts education is designed to develop your whole person.
(And still leave you enough time to sleep.)

Pause for Reflection

As you are reading the specific skills listed beneath each of the following eight elements of holistic development, place a checkmark in the space next to any skill that is especially important to you. You may check more than one skill within each area.

Skills and Abilities Associated with Each Element of Holistic Development

Intellectual Development: Acquiring knowledge, learning how to learn, and how to think deeply.

Key Skills and Specific Abilities:

- Becoming aware of your different intellectual abilities, interests, or learning styles.
- Attaining and maintaining attention and concentration.
- Using effective strategies for improving long-term learning and memory.
- Moving beyond memorization to think at a higher level.
- Using effective research skills to obtain information from a variety of sources and systems.
- Viewing issues from multiple angles or viewpoints (psychological, social, political, economic, etc.) in order to attain a balanced, comprehensive perspective.
- Critically evaluating ideas in terms of their truth and value.
- Thinking creatively or imaginatively.
- Responding rationally and constructively to differing viewpoints or opposing arguments.
- Resisting persuasion tactics that appeal to emotions, to responding to them logically or rationally.

Emotional Development: Strengthening skills for understanding, controlling, and expressing emotions.

Key Skills and Specific Abilities:

- Dealing with emotions in an honest, non-defensive manner.
- Maintaining a healthy balance between emotional control and emotional expression.
- Responding with empathy and sensitivity to emotions experienced by others.
- Dealing effectively with depression.
- Dealing effectively with anger.
- Using effective stress-management strategies to control anxiety or tension.
- Responding positively to life changes and challenges.
- Dealing effectively with fear of failure, criticism, or poor performance.
- Accepting feedback in a constructive, non-defensive manner.
- Being optimistic and enthusiastic.

Social Development: Enhancing the quality and depth of interpersonal relationships.

Key Skills and Specific Abilities:

- Using effective interpersonal communication skills.
- Relating effectively to others in one-to-one, small-group, and large-group situations.
- Overcoming shyness or loneliness and initiating new relationships.
- Forming meaningful friendships.
- Effectively handling interpersonal conflict in an assertive manner, rather than in a passive or aggressive manner.
- Providing advice and feedback to others in a constructive and considerate manner.
- Using effective collaboration and teamwork skills to work productively with others.
- Relating effectively to others from different cultural backgrounds and with different personal lifestyles.
- Using effective leadership skills.

Ethical Development: Acquiring a clear value system for guiding life choices and decisions, and developing consistency between moral convictions (beliefs) and moral commitments (actions).

Key Skills and Specific Abilities:

- Being self-aware of personal values and ethical assumptions.
- Making important personal choices and life decisions based on a meaningful value system (for example, decisions about majors, careers, and relationships).
- Having the courage to think and act with personal integrity or honesty, including honesty with respect to schoolwork, both inside and outside the classroom (academic integrity).
- Using electronic technology in an ethical and responsible manner.
- Fulfilling personal commitments and responsibilities to others.
- Knowing how to exercise individual freedom without infringing on the rights of others.
- Developing a concern and commitment for human rights and social justice.
- Becoming a responsible citizen.

Physical Development: Applying knowledge about how the human body functions to prevent disease, maintain wellness, and promote peak performance.

Key Skills and Specific Abilities:

- Being aware of your physical condition and state of health.
- Applying knowledge about exercise and fitness training to promote physical and mental health.
- Understanding the role of rest and sleep patterns for promoting health and increasing energy.
- Applying knowledge on nutrition and diet to enhance your health and physical performance.
- Maintaining healthy balance between work, relaxation, and recreation.
- Having a healthy and positive body image.
- Being aware of and avoiding eating disorders.
- Being aware of the effects of drugs on the body and how they affect physical and mental performance.
- Being knowledgeable about the biology and psychology of human sexuality and sexually transmitted diseases.
- Being knowledgeable about the physical and physiological differences between the sexes and their implications for male-female relationships and gender orientation.

Spiritual Development: Searching for the meaning or purpose of life and death, and exploring eternal relationships that transcend human life and the physical world.

Key Skills and Specific Abilities:

- Developing a personal philosophy or world view about the meaning and purpose of human existence.
- Appreciating what cannot be completely understood.
- Appreciating the mysteries associated with the origin of the universe.
- Exploring the connection between yourself and humanity.
- Exploring the connection between yourself and the physical world that surrounds you.
- Being open to examining questions relating to death and life after death.
- Being open to examining questions about the possible existence of a supreme being or higher power.
- Being aware of different approaches to spirituality and their underlying beliefs or assumptions.
- Understanding the difference and relationship between faith and reason.
- Being knowledgeable and tolerant of religious beliefs and practices.

Vocational Development: Exploring career options, making career choices wisely, and developing skills needed for lifelong career success.

Key Skills and Specific Abilities:

- Being knowledgeable about the relationship between college majors and careers.
- Using effective strategies for exploring and identifying potential careers.
- Selecting career options that are consistent with your personal values, interests, and aptitudes.
- Acquiring work experience in fields that relate to your career interests.

- Developing an effective resumé and portfolio.
- Adopting effective strategies for selecting individuals to serve as personal references and improving the quality of your letters of recommendation.
- Developing effective job-search strategies.
- Acquiring effective strategies for writing letters of inquiry and letters of application to potential employers.
- Developing effective networking skills for making personal contacts with potential employers.
- Learning strategies for effective job-interview preparation and performance.

Personal Development: Developing positive self-beliefs, personal attitudes, and personal habits.

Key Skills and Specific Abilities:

- Developing a sense of personal identity and a coherent self-concept. (Who am I?)
- Finding a sense of future direction and purpose. (Who am I becoming?)
- Developing self-respect and positive self-esteem.
- Acquiring self-confidence.
- Developing a strong belief that success is yours for the taking.
- Setting realistic goals and establishing personal priorities.
- Becoming self-motivated and self-disciplined.
- Developing the patience and perseverance to persist on tasks despite personal setbacks or frustration.
- Managing personal affairs effectively and efficiently.
- Becoming independent, self-reliant, and self-sufficient.

Pause for Reflection

Look back and count the number of checkmarks you placed in each of the eight general areas of self-development. Did you find that you placed roughly the same number of checks in all eight areas, or did you place a large number of checks in certain areas and very few checks in others?

Based on your answers to these questions, would you say that your interests in self-development are balanced across different elements of the self, or are they slanted toward strong interest in certain elements of self-development with little interest in others?

The Co-Curriculum

For the college experience to have maximum positive impact on all key areas of self-development, you need to take advantage of the "total" college environment. This includes not only courses in the curriculum, but also the learning experiences available to you outside the classroom (the co-curriculum) because research consistently shows that they are equally important to your overall development as the course curriculum (Kuh, 1995; Kuh et al., 1994). The co-curriculum includes all educationally-related discussions you have with your peers and professors outside the classroom, as well as the wide variety of support services and programs that are offered on college campuses. Listed below are some of the college services and programs that comprise the co-curriculum, preceded by the primary element of the self that they are designed to develop:

- **Intellectual development:** Academic Advising, Learning Center, Library, Tutoring Services, Information Technology Services, Campus Speakers, Publications, Concerts, Plays, and Galleries
- **Emotional development:** Counseling Services, Peer Counseling, and Peer Mentoring Programs
- **Social development:** Student Activities, Student Organizations, Campus Clubs, Residential-Life Programs, Commuter Programs
- **Physical development:** Student Health Services, Athletics, Intramural Sports
- **Spiritual development:** College Chaplain, Campus Ministry, Peer Ministry
- **Ethical development:** Judicial Review Board, Academic Integrity Committee, Student Government
- **Vocational development:** Career Development Services, Internships, Service Learning, Work-Study Programs, Major Fairs, Career Fairs
- **Personal development:** Counseling Services, Financial Aid Services, Campus Workshops, Peer Counseling, Peer Mentoring Programs

This list is just a sample of the total number of programs and services that may be available at your school. As you can see from this lengthy list, colleges and universities have been organized to promote your development in multiple ways, and a liberal arts education is the component of your college experience that has been intentionally designed to provide you with this multi-faceted, well-rounded form of development.

 Remember: To develop a "whole person," a liberal arts education relies on both the curriculum *and* co-curriculum, and requires student use of the *total* college environment.

Leadership skills cannot be developed solely by listening to lectures and reading books about leadership; they need to be accompanied by leadership *experiences*, such as those developed by "leading a [discussion] group in class, holding office in student government, or by being captain of a sports team" (Association of American Colleges & Universities, 2002, p. 30). Recall that using campus resources is one of the key bases for college success, so take full advantage of your whole college to develop yourself as a whole person.

Developing all aspects of yourself will not only help you become a more complete human being and improve the quality of your personal life, it will also help you prepare for a career and succeed in your professional life. You may recall that earlier in this chapter we identified three clusters of skills that employers consistently look for in college graduates: communication skills, thinking skills, and lifelong learning skills. While these three sets of intellectually oriented skills rank high in importance to employers, they do not account for the complete list of skills that employers seek in college graduates. There are other characteristics that employers value, which relate to different elements of the self, such as:

Interpersonal (Social) Skills, including leadership, ability to collaborate, negotiate, work in teams, and relate to others with diverse characteristics and backgrounds—such as people of different age, race, gender, and cultural backgrounds (National Association of Colleges & Employers, 2003).

Personal Attitudes and Behaviors, including motivation, initiative, effort, self-management, independence, personal responsibility, enthusiasm, flexibility, good work habits, and self-esteem (National Association of Colleges & Employers, 2000).

Personal Ethics, namely: honesty, integrity, and ethical standards of conduct (National Association of Colleges & Employers, 2003).

Pause for Reflection

Look at the above three skills and jot down something you could do in college to develop or demonstrate each of them.

1. Interpersonal (Social) Skills:

2. Personal Attitudes and Behaviors:

3. Personal Ethics:

Do you recognize that the qualities sought by employers correspond closely to different elements of holistic development promoted by a liberal arts education? Note also that some of the skills correspond closely to the liberal arts goal of developing the "liberating" skills needed for independence, such as personal initiative, self-management, and personal responsibility. You can start developing these skills right now by taking the initiative to assume personal responsibility for managing your independent work in college. See Box 2 on the following page, for some quick tips on how to do so.

••• Broadening Your Perspective of the Whole World

Thus far, the focus of this chapter has been on you, and how the liberal arts benefit you as an individual. However, another major goal of a liberal arts education is to help you step outside yourself and expand your perspective of the world around you. The components of this larger perspective are organized and illustrated in the following concept map (Figure 2).

In Figure 2, the center circle represents you as an individual. Fanning out to the right is a series of arches, labeled as the **social-spatial perspective**. This broadening perspective includes increasingly larger social groups and more distant places, ranging from the narrowest perspective (self) to the widest perspective (universe). A liberal arts education frees you from the narrow tunnel vision of an egocentric viewpoint and provides you with a panoramic perspective of the world, enabling you to move outside yourself and see yourself in relation to other people and other places.

STUDENT PERSPECTIVE

"College was not something I regarded as the next step after high school. It was not something I deemed important in order to be really rich later on in life. It was something I considered fundamental to learning about myself and the world around me."

—First-year student (Watts, 2005)

TAKE ACTION NOW! — Box 2

Top Strategies: Working Independently Outside the Classroom

Unlike high school, homework in college often does not involve turning things in to your instructor on a daily or weekly basis. Instead, the academic work you do outside the classroom may not be collected and graded, but is done for your own benefit to prepare yourself for upcoming exams and major assignments (e.g., term papers or research reports). Rather than formally assigning work to you as homework, your professors expect that you will do this work on your own and without supervision. Listed below are strategies for working independently and in advance of college examinations and assignments, which should serve to increase your performance on them.

INDEPENDENT WORK IN ADVANCE OF EXAMS

- **Complete reading assignments** in advance of lectures that will relate to the same topic as the reading. This will make lectures easier to understand and will prepare you to ask intelligent questions and make relevant comments in class.
- **Review your class notes** between class periods so you can construct a mental bridge from one class to the next and make each upcoming lecture easier to follow. When reviewing your notes before the next class, rewrite any class notes that may be sloppily written, and if you find notes relating to the same point that are all over the place, reorganize them by getting notes relating to the same point in the same place. Lastly, if you find any information gaps or confusing points in your notes, seek-out the course instructor or a trusted classmate to clear them up before the next class takes place.
- **Review information** that you have highlighted in your reading assignments in order to improve your memory of the information, and if there are certain points that are confusing to you, discuss them with your course instructor or fellow classmate.
- **Integrate key ideas** in your class notes with information that you have highlighted in your assigned reading that relate to the same major point or general category. For example, get related information from your lecture notes and your readings in the same place.
- **Use a part-to-whole study method,** whereby you study key material from your class notes and readings in small parts during short, separate study sessions that take place well in advance of the exam; then make your last study session prior to the exam a longer review session, during which you re-study all the small parts together (the "whole").

 The belief that studying in advance is a total waste of time because you will forget it all anyway is a myth. Information studied in advance of an exam remains in your brain and is still there when you later review it. Even if you cannot recall the previously studied information when you first start reviewing it, you will re-learn it much faster than you did the first time, thus proving that some memory of it was retained.

INDEPENDENT WORK IN ADVANCE OF TERM PAPERS OR RESEARCH REPORTS

Work on these large, long-term assignments by breaking them into the following smaller, short-term tasks:

- Search for and select a topic.
- Locate sources of information on the topic.
- Organize the information obtained from these sources into categories.
- Develop an outline of the report's major points and the order or sequence in which you plan to discuss them.
- Construct a first draft of the paper (and, if necessary, a second draft).
- Write a final draft of the paper.
- Proofread the final draft of your paper for minor mechanical mistakes, such as spelling and grammatical errors, before submitting it to your instructor.

In Figure 2, to the left of the individual, you see a different series of arches that are labeled the **chronological perspective**, which represents the perspective of time—past (historical), present (contemporary), and future (futuristic). A liberal arts education not only widens your perspective, it also lengthens it—by stretching your vision beyond the present, enabling you to see yourself in relation to those who have lived before us and those who will live after us.

Figure 2 The Broadening Perspectives of a Liberal Arts Education

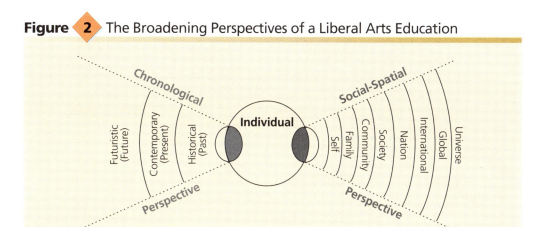

This chronological perspective gives you hindsight to see where the world has been, insight into where it is now, and foresight to see where it may be going.

The social-spatial perspective can be seen as providing you with a telescope for viewing aspects of the world that are far away, while a chronological perspective provides you with a mental "time machine" that you can use to flash back to the past and fast-forward to the future. We will now provide a brief description of the specific elements that make up each of these two major perspectives developed by a liberal arts education.

Elements of the Chronological Perspective

The **historical element** of the chronological perspective is an important one to understand because it represents the root causes of our current human condition and world situation. We are products of both social and natural history. Don't forget that our earth is estimated to be more than 4.5 billion years old, and our human ancestors date back more than 250,000 years (Knoll, 2003). Our current lives represent a very small frame in a very long reel of time, and every modern convenience we now enjoy reflects the cumulative knowledge and collective efforts of humans that span across thousands of years of history. By studying the past and understanding how it has influenced our present circumstances, we can learn to reproduce its achievements and avoid its mistakes.

The **contemporary element** of a chronological perspective focuses on understanding the current world situation and the current events that comprise today's news. For example, we are now living in a world of such rapid technological change that it is being referred to as the technology revolution (Glassman, 2000). So, it is important to understand how modern technology is affecting the world we currently live in, and how it will affect the world of tomorrow. One major goal of a liberal arts education is to increase your understanding of contemporary society (Miller, 1988) and its effectiveness for doing so is supported by research on college graduates, which consistently shows that they have greater knowledge of current affairs, popular culture, and contemporary news media than people who have not experienced a college education (Pascarella & Terenzini, 1991, 2005).

The **futuristic element** of the chronological perspective focuses on looking forward and envisioning what the world will be like years from now. It is concerned with such questions as: Will the world be in better shape and a better place for humans who will live after us, including our children and grandchildren? How can humans avoid short-term or shortsighted think-

·—· **CLASSIC QUOTE** ·—·

Those who cannot remember the past are damned to repeat it.

—George Santayana, Spanish-born American philosopher

ing and adopt a long-range vision that will enable them to anticipate, prepare for, and adapt to the future?

Thus, a complete chronological perspective enables us to see our lives, and the world we live in, as an ongoing process that began well before we arrived on the current scene and that will likely continue long after we have departed. "We all inherit the past. We all confront the challenges of the present. We all participate in the making of the future" (Boyer & Kaplan, 1977, p. 16).

> **CLASSIC QUOTE**
> *The future is literally in our hands to mold as we like. But we cannot wait until tomorrow. Tomorrow is now.*
> —Eleanor Roosevelt, United Nations diplomat, humanitarian, and wife of President Franklin D. Roosevelt

Pause for Reflection

How might you use the information you've just read to interpret or explain the meaning of the following statement: "We can't know where we're going until we know where we've been?"

Elements of the Social-Spatial Perspective

As you can see in Figure 2, the first element of the social-spatial perspective is the **self**. Among the many goals of a liberal arts education, the one that has the longest history and most frequent emphasis is "Know thyself" (Cross, 1982). To do so, you need to step outside yourself and view yourself objectively. This enables you to remove personal blinders and increase your self-awareness, which is the first step toward self-development and personal success. As an old saying goes, "It is difficult to see the picture when you are inside the frame."

> **CLASSIC QUOTE**
> *The unexamined life is not worth living.*
> —Socrates, Greek philosopher

Moving beyond the self, an individual is part of a larger social unit—the **family**. The people with whom you were raised have almost certainly influenced the person you are today and how you got to be that way. You also influence your family. For example, your decision to go to college may make your parents and grandparents proud, and may influence the decision of other members of your family to attend college. Furthermore, if you have children, graduating from college is likely to positively influence their future welfare. As mentioned in the introduction to this book, the children of college graduates experience improved intellectual development, physical health, and economic security (Bowen, 1977, 1997; Pascarella & Terenzini, 1991, 2005).

Moving beyond your family, you are also a member of a larger social unit—your **community**. This social circle includes your friends and neighbors at home, at school, and at work. These local communities are where you can begin to take action to improve the world around you. If you want to make the world a better place, this is the place to start—get involved in your home or college community.

> **CLASSIC QUOTE**
> *Be the change you want to see in the world.*
> —Mahatma Gandhi, Indian national leader

Moving beyond your local community, you are also a member of a larger **society** that includes people from different regions of the country, cultural backgrounds, and social classes. There is more diversity in our society today than at any other time in history. Being willing and able to understand, relate to, and learn from people with diverse backgrounds has become a critical skill for success in today's world (Smith, 1997; National Association of Colleges & Employers, 2003).

Not only are you a member of a society, you are a citizen of a **nation**. As such, you are expected to participate in its political system—as a voter—and in its judicial system—as a juror. It is noteworthy that American citizens between the ages of 18 and 24 consistently have the lowest voter turnout rate of any age group that is eligible to vote (Cummings, 2002). If you are a student in this age group, we strongly encourage you to involve yourself in the voting process because it is the foundation of a democratic nation and is the original purpose of a liberal arts education—to educate citizens broadly so they could vote wisely.

Moving beyond our nation of citizenship, we are members of an **international world** that includes citizens of other countries. Today, there is more interaction among citizens of different countries and more "international interdependence" among nations than at any other time in world history. Boundaries between countries are breaking down as a result of more international trading, more multinational corporations, more international travel, and more international communication—due to rapid advances in electronic technology (Dryden, & Vos, 1999; Smith, 1994). Employers of college graduates are beginning to place higher value on prospective employees who have international knowledge and foreign language skills (Fixman, 1990; Office of Research, 1994). Today's world truly is a small world, and your success in it will be enhanced if you gain an international perspective. You can do this by interacting with international students who may be attending your college, by taking foreign language and cross-cultural courses, or by participating in a study-abroad program. By learning from and about different nations, you become much more than a citizen of your own country, you become cosmopolitan—a citizen of the world.

Although you are expected to vote as a citizen of a nation, American citizens between the ages of 18 and 24 have the lowest voter turnout.

Even broader than the international perspective is the **global perspective**. This perspective goes beyond relations between people of different nations to include relationships among all life forms that inhabit planet earth, and the relationship between these life forms and their environment. Don't forget that humans share the earth and its natural resources (minerals, air, water) with millions of other animal species and several hundred thousand forms of vegetative life (Knoll, 2003). As members of this global village, we need to balance our human needs and our industrial-technological progress with the preservation of other life forms and the earth's natural resources. Striking this balance may be the only way to ensure long-term survival of our species and our planet.

Beyond the global perspective is the broadest of all perspectives—the **universe**. We should not lose sight of the fact that the earth is just one planet among other planets sharing the solar system and that our planet is just one celestial body sharing a galaxy with millions of other types of celestial bodies, which include stars, moons, meteorites, and asteroids. Also, we need to remember that our planet is not the center of the universe, and all these other heavenly bodies do not revolve around us! As one physics professor put it: "In astronomy, you must get used to viewing the earth as just one planet in the larger context of the universe" (Donald, 2002, p. 49).

Astronauts who have traveled beyond the earth's force of gravity and explored the universe from the perspective of outer space have often described this perspective as being a spiritual experience. Even mental exploration of the universe by contemplating its massive and mysterious nature, how it may have begun, where it may be going, and whether it will ever end, are issues that some educators have referred to as spiritual questions (Zohar & Marshall, 2000). Whether you view the universe through the physical telescope of astronomy or the spiritual scope of introspection (or both), it qualifies as the broadest of all social-spatial perspectives developed by a liberal arts education.

---· **CLASSIC QUOTE** ·---

A liberal [arts] education frees a person from the prison-house of class, race, time, place, background, family, and nation.

—Robert Hutchins, former president, University of Chicago

---· **CLASSIC QUOTE** ·---

Without exception, the observed changes [during college] involve greater breadth, expansion, and appreciation for the new and different. These changes are eminently consistent with values of a liberal [arts] education, and the evidence for their presence is compelling.

—Ernest Pascarella and Pat Terenzini, *How College Affects Students*

> ### ~*Pause for Reflection*
>
> *Think about the courses you are taking this term, and look back at the different broadening perspectives developed by a liberal arts education. List those courses that you think are designed to develop one or more of these broadening perspectives, and next to the courses you have listed, note the particular perspective that is being developed. If you are unsure or cannot remember whether a course is designed to develop any of these perspectives, take a look at the course goals or objectives that are cited in the syllabus.*

The Synoptic Perspective: Integrating Diverse Perspectives to Form a Unified Whole

By broadening your perspective on time, place, and people, a liberal arts education liberates you from the here and now, enabling you to view things "long ago and far away." In addition to this liberating purpose of a liberal arts education, it also has an *integrating* purpose. You are enabled to see how, as an individual, you are a single strand that is embedded within a progressively wider web of social-spatial interconnections with your family, community, society, nation, world, and universe—all of which are united along a chronological spectrum of time—past, present, and future. Seeing how these different perspectives of time, place, and person are interrelated to form a unified whole is sometimes referred to as a synoptic perspective (Cronon, 1998; Heath, 1977).

The term synoptic refers to a comprehensive, integrated perspective. The word derives from a combination of two different roots: "syn"—meaning 'together' (as in the word 'synthesize'), and "optic"—meaning 'to see.' Thus, a *synoptic* perspective literally means to "see things together" or to "see the whole."

| **Memory Tips** | Breaking down technical terms into smaller parts that contain the roots of their meaning is an effective strategy for making sense of what you are learning and locking it into your long-term memory. |

So, in addition to the wholeness that comes from integrating different elements of the self to develop the whole person, there is another type of wholeness that a liberal arts education attempts to develop—how you, as an individual, are integrated or connected with other people, places, and times to form the whole world.

•—•- **CLASSIC QUOTE** -•—•

A truly great intellect is one which takes a connected view of old and new, past and present, far and near, and which has an insight into the influence of all these on one another, without which there is no whole, and no center.

–John Henry Newman, English Cardinal and educator, *The Idea of a University*, 1852

When we view ourselves as connected with others from different places and different times, we become aware of the common humanity we all share, and this increased sense of integration with mankind serves to decrease our feelings of isolation or alienation (Bellah, et al., 1985). In his book, *The Perfect Education*, Kenneth Eble skillfully describes this benefit of a liberal arts education:

> *It can provide that overarching life of a people, a community, a world that was going on before the individual came onto the scene and that will continue on after [s]he departs. By such means we come to see the world not alone. Our joys are more intense for being shared. Our sorrows are less destructive for our knowing universal sorrow. Our fears of death fade before the commonness of the occurrence (Eble, 1966, pp. 214–215).*

Thus, by stepping outside ourselves to view the similarities we share with other people and other times, we then return to view ourselves from a new perspective and in a new light. Stepping outside ourselves and seeing how we differ from other people and other times provides us with reference points for comparison and contrast that sharpens our self-awareness and insight. We see what is distinctive about ourselves, and how we may be uniquely advantaged or disadvantaged. For instance, by seeing what limited opportunities there are for people to attend college in many countries today, and what limited opportunities there were for certain groups of people in our own country some time ago, we become instantly aware that the opportunity all Americans have today to attend college and advance themselves—regardless of their race, gender, age, or prior academic record—is truly a distinctive advantage that should neither be overlooked nor taken for granted.

By looking outside yourself and taking the perspective of other people and other times, you can acquire a sort of reflective mirror that also allows you to see yourself and your present situation more clearly by comparison. This dual vision provided by a liberal arts education supplies you with a double-purpose tool that you can use to simultaneously better yourself and the world in which you live. For example, by broadening your perspectives and widening your range of knowledge, you gain greater social self-confidence. You are able to relate to a wider range of people with different interests, and you can contribute to conversations on a wider variety of topics. You become a more interested and interesting person who is less likely to be left out of a conversation or to have the topic of conversation go over your head. Furthermore, broadening your perspectives and discovering new knowledge is simply a very stimulating mental experience, which can prevent you from becoming bored (and boring).

> **CLASSIC QUOTE**
>
> *Only boring people get bored.*
>
> —Graffiti written in men's room at the main library, University of Iowa (circa 1977), author unknown

Pause for Reflection

What information or ideas in this chapter might be used to support the following statement: "Knowledge is power."

••• Summary and Conclusion

Before leaving this chapter, there are three key ideas we hope you will take with you.

1. Being a generalist is as important for career success as being a specialist.

Studies show that college students, as well as their parents, are extremely concerned about what majors and careers to specialize in. However, they often overlook or underestimate the value of general education provided by the liberal arts (Hersh, 1994, 1997). As a result, liberal arts courses are sometimes seen as unnecessary requirements that students need to get out of the way before they can get into what is really important—their specialized major. This negative view probably stems from lack of knowledge about what the liberal arts stand for and what they are designed to do, as well as misinterpreting general education to mean something that is non-specific and without any particular value or practical purpose. However, as we have demonstrated repeatedly in this chapter, a liberal arts education develops very practical, durable, and transferable skills that provide the foundation for success in all majors and all careers.

Your general education classes provide you with skills that are stable and portable.

In fact, research indicates that as an individual's career progresses, specific skills learned in a major tend to decline in importance and are replaced by more general skills (Pascarella & Terenzini, 2005). Specific, technical skills may be important for moving you into a career, but general, professional skills are more important for moving you up the career ladder. They are the skills that prevent you from being stuck at a dead-end position and help you avoid the tendency to rise to a position that you cannot perform successfully because the position requires broader professional skills and responsibilities than those needed for success at a lower level. The importance of general professional skills will become even more important for people entering the workforce during the twenty-first century because the demand for upper-level positions that involve management and leadership will exceed the supply of people in the workforce who are prepared to fill these positions (Herman, 2000).

While many people see the career advantages of specializing in a particular field, they often fail to see its potential disadvantage—overspecialization. There is an old saying that goes something like this: "A specialist is someone who knows more and more about less and less until he knows a whole lot about very little (and isn't interested in learning anything outside his specialty because then he wouldn't be a specialist)." There is some truth to this old adage because when you are very narrowly trained, you are restricted by knowledge limited to one specific type of job or specialized position.

Furthermore, if changes in society create less demand for the specialized career you trained for, then your risk of unemployment is higher. You may end up preparing for a very specific career that will no longer be in demand (or may no longer exist) after graduation.

Personal Story

My father is a good example of someone whose education was too narrow and whose career was too specialized. He spent approximately two years of his life learning to be a horologist—a specialist in watch and clock repair. He found regular employment until the 1980s, when advances in technology at that time made it possible for companies to produce and sell high-performance watches at a much cheaper price than ever before. As a result, instead of having their watches repaired when they began to malfunction, people simply threw them away and bought new ones. This reduced society's need for watch repairmen, such as my father, who soon lost his position with the watch company he was working for and was eventually forced into early retirement.

—Joe Cuseo

Our society is undergoing rapid technological change and dramatic growth in knowledge. Existing jobs can become obsolete and unnecessary, while at the same time, entirely new positions get created that never existed before (Brown, 2003). Naturally, nobody is specifically trained or prepared to fill these new positions because no one knew they would come into existence. The growing number of such unanticipated positions is now creating a greater demand for generalists who have a broad base of knowledge, flexible lifelong-learning skills, plus the mental versatility needed to take on changing job responsibilities and different professional roles (Niles & Harris-Bowlsbey, 2002; Herman, 2000).

The best way to prepare for such a changing future is by equipping yourself with durable, transferable learning skills—those timeless skills that always have been and always will be useful, and that can be employed anywhere in any way. While certain technological skills may be "hot" right now, the specific technological skills needed for current technological tasks, such as word-processing programs and Web-page designs, will likely change considerably in the future. However, the general education (liberal arts) skills of clear writing and visual creativity are likely to withstand the test of time and continue to remain in demand.

Remember: Do not look at general education as something to get out of the way so that you can get into your major and career. Instead, look at it as something to get into and be ready to take away from general education those general, transferable skills that will remain *stable*—which you can continue to use during changing times, and which are *portable*—that you can take with you and use successfully to adapt to different work situations and career roles.

> **CLASSIC QUOTE**
>
> *The fixed person for the fixed duties, who in older societies was a blessing, in the future will be a public danger.*
>
> —Alfred North Whitehead, English mathematician and philosopher

"I hear this school likes to emphasize the value of a Classical Education."

Recent, rapid changes in information technology are increasing society's demand for the type of *timeless* and *flexible* mental skills developed by a liberal arts education.

2. Building your skills, broadening your perspectives, and keeping track of your development is as important as earning credits, completing courses, and checking off degree requirements.

While completing assignments, getting good grades, and getting a degree are all important accomplishments, it is equally important to step back, reflect, and keep track of what you are actually learning. More important than memorizing facts, figures, and formulas are the new skills you are acquiring or refining, the new perspectives or vantage points from which you are viewing things, and the different dimensions or elements of the "self" that you are developing. Save the lists of specific skills, perspectives, and areas of self-development that have been identified in this chapter, and use them as checklists to keep track of how many of them you are acquiring.

It is important to make a conscious attempt to increase your awareness and memory of your developing skills and perspectives because their improvement can often be subtle and subconscious. Development of these important skills and perspectives sometimes gets embedded within or buried below all the factual material you are consciously trying to learn. Skills and perspectives are mental habits, and like other habits that are repeatedly practiced, their growth can be so gradual, we often do not notice how much has actually occurred.

> **Remember:** Consciously keeping track of your areas of development serves as a strength-recognition exercise that can boost your self-esteem and your motivation to continue learning. Furthermore, it is an excellent way to sell yourself to potential employers, who are often more interested in what specific skills you have acquired and can bring with you to the job, rather than what courses you took or what major you had.

3. Attending college is not just about earning a better living; it is also about learning to live a better life.

CLASSIC QUOTE

The finest art, the most difficult art, is the art of living.

—John Albert Macy, American author, poet, and editor of Helen Keller's autobiography

---

Research shows that the primary reasons why students go to college are to "prepare for a career" and "get a better job" (Sax, et al., 2004). We acknowledge that these are important reasons and that your career is an important element of your life. However, as previously noted, a person's vocation or occupation represents just one element of the self. It also represents just one of many different roles or responsibilities that you are likely to have in life, such as being a son or daughter, a friend, a spouse, a parent, a co-worker, and a citizen.

> **Remember:** Living a successful and rewarding life depends on your ability to fulfill multiple roles effectively. The broad-based knowledge, wide-ranging perspectives, and transferable skills developed by a liberal arts education will help prepare you for these multiple life roles.

Personal Story

One life role that a liberal arts education helped prepare me for was the role of parent. Courses that I took in psychology and sociology proved to be very useful in helping me understand how children develop and how a parent can best support them at different stages of their development. Surprisingly, however, there was one course I took in college that I never expected would ever help me as a parent. That course was *statistics*, which I took to fulfill a general education requirement in mathematics. It was not a particularly enjoyable course; in fact, some of my classmates sarcastically referred to it as "sadistics" because they felt it was a somewhat painful or torturous experience. However, what I learned in that course really become valuable to me many years later as a parent when my 14-year-old son (Tony) developed a life-threatening disease, known as leukemia—a cancer that attacks blood cells. Tony's form of leukemia was a particularly serious one because it had only a 35% average cure rate; in other words, 65% of those who develop the disease do not recover and eventually die from it. This statistic was based on patients that received the traditional treatment of chemotherapy, which was the type of treatment that my son began receiving when his cancer was first detected.

Another option for treating Tony's cancer was a bone-marrow transplant, which involves using radiation to destroy all of his own bone marrow (that was making the abnormal blood cells) and replace it with bone-marrow donated to him by another person. My wife and I got opinions from doctors at two major cancer centers—one from a center that specialized in chemotherapy, and one from a center that specialized in bone-marrow transplants. The chemotherapy doctors felt strongly that drug treatment would have the best chance of curing Tony, and the bone-marrow transplant doctors felt strongly that his chances of survival would be much better if he had a transplant. So, my wife and I had to decide between two opposing recommendations, each made by a respected group of doctors.

To help us reach a decision, I asked both teams of doctors for research studies that had been done on the effectiveness of chemotherapy and bone-marrow transplants for treating my son's particular type of cancer. I read all of these studies and carefully analyzed their statistical findings. I remembered from my statistics course that when an "average" is calculated for a general group of people (for example, average cure rate for people with leukemia), it tends to "lump together" individuals from different subgroups of people (for example, males and females; children and teenagers). Sometimes, when separate statistics are calculated for different subgroups, the results may be different than the average statistic for the whole group. So, when I read the research reports, I looked to find any subgroup statistics that may have been calculated. I found that there were two subgroups of patients with my son's particular type of cancer that had a higher rate of cure with chemotherapy than the general (whole-group) average of 35%. One subgroup included people with a low number of abnormal cells when the cancer was first detected and chemotherapy first began, and the other subgroup consisted of people whose cancer cells dropped rapidly after their first week of chemotherapy. My son belonged to both of these subgroups, which meant that his chance for cure with chemotherapy was higher than the overall 35% average. Furthermore, I found that the statistics showing higher success rate for bone-marrow transplants were based only on patients whose bodies accepted the donor's bone marrow, and did not include those who died because their body "rejected" the donor's bone marrow. So, the success rates for bone-marrow patients were not actually as high as they appeared to be, because the overall average did not include the subgroup of patients who died because of transplant rejection. Based on these statistics, my wife and I decided not to have the transplant and to continue with chemotherapy.

Our son has now been cancer-free for almost five years, so we think we made the right decision. However, I never imagined that a statistics course, which I took many years ago to fulfill a general education requirement, would help me fulfill my role as a parent and help me make a life-or-death medical decision about my own son.

—*Joe Cuseo*

Remember:
A liberal arts education not only prepares you for a career, it prepares you for *life*.

••• Learning More through Independent Research

Web-Based Resources for Further Information on the Liberal Arts

For additional information relating to the ideas discussed in this chapter, we recommend the following Web sites:

http://www.aacu-edu.org/issues/liberaleducation/index.cfm
http://www.educationindex.com/liberal/

Name _____   Date _____

Planning Your Liberal Arts Education

The liberal arts are such an important component of your college experience that it should be intentionally planned. By so doing, you can become actively involved in shaping or creating your liberal arts education in a way that will have maximum impact on your personal development and career success.

STEPS:

1. **Become aware of the general education requirements at your college.** You can find this information by consulting your college catalog. Since college catalogs can sometimes be difficult to navigate, you might consider teaming-up with a classmate to make this task a little easier. You and your teammate will be pursuing a common goal of finding information that applies to both of you because general education requirements apply to all students. Another personal resource on campus that you can consult for help with interpreting the college catalog and accurately identifying general education requirements is an academic advisor.

2. Use the index in your college catalog to **find the general education or liberal arts requirements**, and go to the pages on which these requirements appear. You are likely to find that general education requirements are organized into general divisions of knowledge that make up the liberal arts curriculum, such as Humanities, Fine Arts, Natural Sciences, etc. Within each of these liberal arts divisions, you will see specific courses listed that fulfill the general education requirement for that particular division. In some cases, you will have no choice about what courses you must take to fulfill the general education requirement, but in most cases, you will have the freedom to choose from a group of courses. You can exercise this freedom of choice to plan and build a liberal arts experience that will have the most positive impact on your development. (Remember that courses you are taking this term may be fulfilling certain general-education requirements, so be sure to include them in your plan.)

3. **Highlight the specific courses** in the catalog that you plan to take to fulfill your general education requirements in each area of the liberal arts, and use the form at the end of this chapter to list these courses. Before making your final selections, be sure to read the descriptions of these courses that are provided in your college catalog. It is recommended that you use the following criteria or guidelines when selecting general education courses:

   ◆ Select courses that will expose you to **new areas of knowledge**, particularly those that capture your curiosity and interest. (Your answer to the "pause for reflection" in this chapter may help you identify these courses.) Exploring new fields of knowledge that attract your interest will stimulate your motivation to learn and may lead to discovery of fields in which you eventually want to major or minor.

   ◆ Select courses that will enable you to attain all of the **broadening perspectives** developed by a liberal arts education, which are described in this chapter. Use the perspectives provided on the form at the end of this chapter as a checklist to ensure that your overall perspective is comprehensive and that there are no blind spots in your liberal arts education. Remember that general education courses you are taking this term may already be developing some of these broadening perspectives. So, any general education courses that you listed in your "pause for reflection" could be included on the checklist.

   ◆ Select courses that will enable you to **develop elements of the whole person**. A list of these elements is provided on the planning form at the end of this chapter. Use this as a checklist to ensure that you are not overlooking any important area of self-development. Remember that development of your whole self also includes co-curricular learning experiences (for example, leadership and volunteer experiences) that take place outside the classroom. So, be sure to consider including these experiences as part of your plan to develop yourself as a whole person. Your *Student Handbook* probably represents the best resource for information about co-curricular experiences offered by your college. The best person to contact for this information on your campus would be the Director of Student Development, Student Life, or Student Activities at your college.

◆ Try to take courses that encourage you to **make connections** between different disciplines or fields of knowledge, and between academic learning in the classroom and service to the community. Courses that encourage these types of connections are described briefly below.

Interdisciplinary courses are courses that are designed to help you connect or integrate two or more different academic disciplines. For example, psychobiology is an interdisciplinary course that examines connections between the mind (psychology) and the body (biology). Research indicates that students who participate in interdisciplinary courses report greater gains in learning and greater satisfaction with the learning experience (Astin, 1993; Terenzini & Pascarella, 2004).

Service-learning courses are courses designed to help you integrate or connect classroom learning with volunteer service in the community. For example, a sociology course may include assignments that involve volunteer service in the local community, which students then reflect on and relate to course material through writing or class discussions. Research indicates that students who participate in such service-learning courses have been found to experience strong gains in multiple areas of self-development, including critical thinking skills and leadership skills (Astin, et al., 2000; Strage, 2000).

Enrolling in service-learning and interdisciplinary courses will help you develop the synoptic perspective described in this chapter, and will enable you to see how different pieces and parts of your learning experience connect together to form a more meaningful whole.

Liberal Arts Education-Planning Form

Division of the Liberal Arts Curriculum: _____
General education courses you are planning to take to fulfill requirements in this division:
(Record the course number and course title)

_____ _____ _____

_____ _____ _____

Division of the Liberal Arts Curriculum: _____
General education courses you are planning to take to fulfill requirements in this division:

_____ _____ _____

_____ _____ _____

Division of the Liberal Arts Curriculum: _____
General education courses you are planning to take to fulfill requirements in this division:

_____ _____ _____

_____ _____ _____

Division of the Liberal Arts Curriculum: _____
General education courses you are planning to take to fulfill requirements in this division:

_____ _____ _____

_____ _____ _____

Division of the Liberal Arts Curriculum: _____
General education courses you are planning to take to fulfill requirements in this division:

_____ _____ _____

_____ _____ _____

Division of the Liberal Arts Curriculum: _____
General education courses you are planning to take to fulfill requirements in this division:

_____ _____ _____

_____ _____ _____

Planning Checklist for Developing the Broadening Perspectives of a Liberal Arts Education

BROADENING CHRONOLOGICAL PERSPECTIVES
Course developing this perspective:

_____ Historical (Past) _____

_____ Contemporary (Current) _____

_____ Futuristic (Future) _____

BROADENING SOCIAL-SPATIAL PERSPECTIVES
Course developing this perspective:

_____ Self _____

_____ Family _____

_____ Community _____

_____ Society _____

_____ Nation _____

_____ International _____

_____ Global _____

_____ Universe _____

Planning Checklist for Developing Key Elements of the Whole Person

ELEMENTS OF THE WHOLE PERSON Course or co-curricular experience developing this element:

_____ Intellectual (Cognitive) _____

_____ Emotional _____

_____ Social _____

_____ Ethical _____

_____ Physical _____

_____ Spiritual _____

_____ Vocational _____

_____ Personal _____

▼ CASE STUDY

Dazed and Confused: General Education versus Career Specialization

Joe Tech was really looking forward to college because he thought he would have freedom to select the courses he wanted and the opportunity to get into the major of his choice (computer science). However, he is shocked and disappointed with his first-term schedule of classes because it consists mostly of required general education courses that do not seem to relate in any way to his major, and some of these courses are about subjects that he already took in high school (English, history, and biology). He's beginning to think he would be better off transferring out of college and going to a technical school where he could get right into computer science, and immediately begin to acquire the knowledge and skills he'll need to prepare him for his intended career.

Reflection and Discussion Questions

1. If this student decides to leave college for a technical school, what would be the possible short-term and long-term consequences of his decision?

2. Can you relate to this student, or know of other students who feel the same way as he does?

3. Do you see any way this student might strike a balance between pursuing his career interest and his college degree, so that he could work toward achieving both goals at the same time?

Strategic Learning

Applying Research on Human Learning and the Human Brain to Acquire Knowledge Effectively and Comprehend It Deeply

Learning Goals

The goal of this chapter is to supply you with a well-designed set of learning strategies that are supported by solid research on how humans learn and how the human brain works.

Outline

Brain-Based Learning Principles
    The Brain Is Biologically Wired to Seek Meaning
    New Knowledge Is Built on Knowledge Already Possessed
    Shallow, Surface-Oriented versus Deep, Meaning-Oriented Approaches to Learning

Stages in the Learning and Memory Process
    Stage 1: Perception
    Stage 2: Storage
    Stage 3: Retrieval

Lecture Listening and Note-Taking Strategies
    The Importance of Taking Notes
    Taking Notes

Strategies for Improving Textbook-Reading Comprehension and Retention
    Before Beginning to Read
    While Reading
    After Reading

Study Strategies
    Minimize Distractions
    Find Meaning in Terms
    Compare and Contrast
    Integrate Information
    Divide and Conquer
    Use a "Part-to-Whole" Method of Studying
    Begin with a Review
    Change Things Up
    Use All of Your Senses
    Emotional Learning and Memory
    Form Study Groups

Self-Reflection and Self-Monitoring
    Comprehension Self-Monitoring Strategies
    Knowledge Awareness Strategies

Summary and Conclusion
    Active Involvement
    Self-Reflection
    Social Interaction/Collaboration
    Utilizing Campus Resources

Learning More through Independent Research
Exercise: Self-Assessment of Learning Strategies and Habits
Case Study: Too Fast, Too Frustrating: A Note-Taking Nightmare

Activate Your Thinking

Do you think there is a difference between learning and memorizing?

If yes, what do you think the difference is?

You are likely to experience greater academic challenges in college than you did in high school. Studies show that the percentage of students earning "As" and "Bs" drops from about 50 percent in high school to about 33 percent in college (Astin, 1993; Sax et al., 2004). Learning strategies that enabled you to earn "As" and "Bs" in the past may not earn you those grades now. Thus, to maintain or exceed your level of academic performance in high school, you will need to elevate your performance to a higher level in college. Attaining this higher level of academic performance will probably not involve just working "harder"; it will involve working "smarter" and learning to use effective strategies that are supported by research on how humans learn and how the human brain works.

Brain-Based Learning Principles

Learning becomes more effective and efficient when it is "brain-based" or "brain-compatible" (Hart, 1983) and capitalizes on the brain's natural learning tendencies (Caine & Caine, 1994). Despite the fact that there are differences among us in terms of our intellectual talents and learning styles, we are all members of the human species and we all possess a human brain. Just as all humans have bodily organs that perform specific functions, such as our heart and liver, we also have a brain that functions as the "learning organ" of the body (Zull, 1998). By understanding how the human brain learns, we can capitalize on this knowledge to identify general principles or common themes of learning that work effectively for all humans. You can then convert these general principles into specific strategies that may be used to learn effectively in all subject areas to promote your success across the curriculum (Weinstein, 1982).

The Brain Is Biologically Wired to Seek Meaning

Perhaps the most distinctive and most powerful feature of the human brain is that it is biologically wired to seek meaning (Caine & Caine, 1994). The human brain naturally looks for meaning by trying to connect what it is trying to learn and understand to what it already knows. For instance, when the brain perceives the external world, it looks for meaningful patterns and connections rather than isolated bits and pieces of information (Nummela & Rosengren, 1986). In Figure 1, notice how your brain naturally ties together and fills in the missing information to perceive a meaningful whole pattern.

Figure 1 Triangle Illusion

You perceive a white triangle in the middle of this figure. However, if you use three fingers to cover up the three corners of the white triangle that fall outside the other (background) triangle, the white triangle suddenly disappears. What your brain does is take these corners as starting points and fills in the rest of the information on its own to create a complete or whole pattern that has meaning to you. (Notice also how you perceive the background triangle as a complete triangle, even though parts of its left and right sides are missing.)

The brain's natural tendency to seek whole patterns with meaning applies to words as well as images. The following passage once appeared (anonymously) on the Internet. See if you can read it and grasp its meaning.

> "Aoccdrnig to rscheearch at Cmabridge Uinverstisy, it deosn't mattaer in what order the ltteers in a word are, the only iprmoetnt thing is that the frist and lsat ltteer be at the rghit pclae. The rset can be a total mses and you can still raed it wouthit a porbelm. This is bcusae the human mind deos not raed ervey lteter by istlef, but the word as a wlohe. Amzanig huh?"

Notice how your brain found the meaning of the misspelled words by naturally transforming them into correctly spelled words that it already knew or understood. We tend to see whole patterns because the knowledge we have in our brain is stored in the form of a connected network of brain cells (Coward, 1990). Thus, whenever we learn something, we do so by connecting what we're trying to understand to what we previously know and what we have already stored in our brain.

When we learn by making meaningful connections, this is referred to as *deep learning* (Entwistle & Ramsden, 1983). To "deeply" learn the challenging concepts you'll encounter in college will require active mental involvement and personal reflection on the information you receive. You will need to move beyond shallow memorization to deeper levels of comprehension. When you learn deeply, you don't just take in information; you take the additional step of actively reflecting on it. This also involves a shift away from the old view that learning occurs by passively absorbing information like a sponge, whereby you receive it from the teacher or text and study it in exactly the same, pre-packaged form you received it. Instead, you want to adopt a different approach to learning that involves active transformation of information you receive into a form that is meaningful to you (Entwistle & Marton, 1984; Feldman & Paulsen, 1994).

Pause for Reflection

When you try to acquire knowledge or learn new information, do you tend to memorize it in the form in which it's presented to you, or do you usually try to transform it into your own words?

Personal Story

When my son was about 3 years old, we were riding in the car together and listening to a song by the Beatles titled, "Sergeant Pepper's Lonely Heart Club Band." You may be familiar with this tune, but in case you're not, there is a part in it where the following lyrics are sung over and over: "Sergeant Pepper's Lonely, Sergeant Pepper's Lonely, Sergeant Pepper's Lonely . . . ."

When this part of the song was being played, I noticed that my 3-year-old son was singing along. I thought that it was pretty amazing for a boy his age to be able to understand and repeat those lyrics. However, when that part of the song came on again, I noticed that he wasn't singing "Sergeant Pepper's Lonely, Sergeant Pepper's Lonely . . ." etc. Instead, he was singing: "Sausage Pepperoni, Sausage Pepperoni . . ." (which were his two favorite pizza toppings).

So, I guess my son's brain was doing what it tends to do naturally. It took unfamiliar information (song lyrics) that didn't make any sense to him and transformed it into a form that was very meaningful to him!

—Joe Cuseo

New Knowledge Is Built on Knowledge Already Possessed

Acquiring knowledge isn't a matter of pouring information into the brain, as if it were an empty jar; it's a matter of building new knowledge onto knowledge you already possess (Piaget, 1978; Vygotsky, 1978), or attaching it to information that is already stored in the brain.

When people understand a concept, a physical or biological connection is made between brain cells, whereby the new information gets connected into a network of connections that have already been made in the brain (Alnon, 1992). Thus, deep learning is learning that actually changes the brain. The following figure (Figure 2) shows a microscopic section of the human brain that specializes in the learning of language. Notice that the number of brain cells (black spots) in a newborn baby and a 6-year-old child are about the same. However, the 6-year-old's brain almost looks like a forest because there are many more connections between brain cells; these connections represent all the language (e.g., vocabulary words) the child has learned in six years of life.

Figure 2

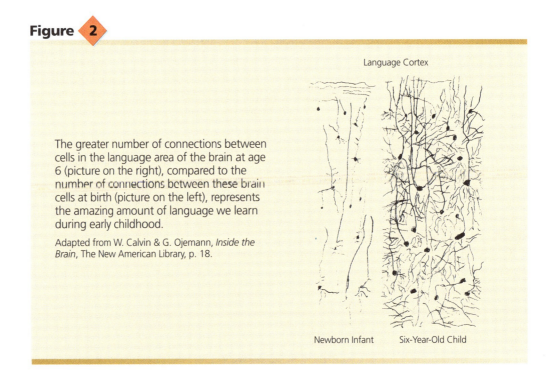

The greater number of connections between cells in the language area of the brain at age 6 (picture on the right), compared to the number of connections between these brain cells at birth (picture on the left), represents the amazing amount of language we learn during early childhood.

Adapted from W. Calvin & G. Ojemann, *Inside the Brain*, The New American Library, p. 18.

Shallow, Surface-Oriented versus Deep, Meaning-Oriented Approaches to Learning

It has been found that students have different methods of processing or handling information they are trying to learn (Schmeck, 1981; Entwistle & Marton, 1984). Some students take a shallow, surface-oriented approach to learning in which they spend most of their study time repeating and memorizing information in the exact form that it's presented to them. Other students use a deep, meaning-oriented style of learning in which they deal with new information by elaborating on it—changing it from the form they received it into a form of their own—by restating it in their own words and relating it to their own experiences. They spend most of their study time thinking about and trying to understand what they're learning, rather than repeating and memorizing it.

Figure 3 Memorizing Factual Information

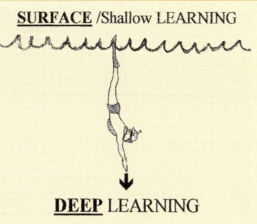

SURFACE /Shallow LEARNING

DEEP LEARNING
(Going beneath the surface to a deeper level of learning involves comprehension rather than memorization)

Studies show that academically successful students dive below the surface of shallow memorization to a deeper level of learning that involves seeking meaning and understanding.

Studies of these two methods of learning reveal that the shallow, surface-oriented approach tends to result in poorer memory for studied material (Watkins, 1983) and lower college grades than the deep, meaning-oriented approach (Ramsden, 2003). For example, in a study of engineering students, those students who used a surface approach to learning earned lower grades, even though they had high class-attendance rates and spent a great amount of time studying outside of class. Despite the fact that these students attended class regularly and put in sufficient study time, their method of study was not as effective as those students who took a deeper, meaning-oriented approach to learning (Kember, Jamieson, Pomfret, & Wong, 1995).

Although there may be times in college when you simply have to remember information that is presented to you, the primary goal of your studying should be to seek deep learning and comprehension, rather than settling for shallow memorization and repetition. Seeking meaning not only results in learning that is deeper, but also results in memory that is more *durable*—it's more likely to "stick" or remain in your brain for a longer period of time (Craik & Lockhart, 1972; Craik & Tulving, 1975).

 Remember: Deep, long-lasting learning requires an active search for meaning via personal reflection, rather than passive memorizing via mindless repetition.

Finding meaning in what you're learning means you truly understand it, which enables you to connect it with the knowledge you already possess and apply it to new situations you'll encounter in the future (Ramsden, 2003).

Since our brains naturally seek meaning, when you learn by searching for meaning, it also makes the process of learning more stimulating and more motivating than learning by memorizing and repeating, which can quickly become very monotonous, mindless, and boring. In fact, interviews with students show that those who use a deep approach to learning are more likely to report a higher level of personal satisfaction and interest in what they're learning than students who use a surface approach (Biggs, 1987; Marton, et al., 1997; Marton & Saljo, 1984).

> ### Pause for Reflection
> Look back at your response to the question asked at the very start of this chapter about whether there is a difference between learning and memorization. Based on the information you've read thus far in this chapter, would you modify or change your answer in any way?

••• Stages in the Learning and Memory Process

Although deep learning is the ultimate goal or final stage you want to achieve, to get there requires successful completion of a series of stages in the process of learning and memory. Learning deeply, and remembering what you've learned, is a process that involves three key stages:

1. getting information into your brain (*perception*),
2. keeping it there (*storage*), and
3. finding it when you need it (*retrieval*).

You can consider these stages of human learning and memory to be similar to the way information is processed by a computer: (a) information first gets typed onto the screen, (b) the information is kept or stored by saving it in a memory file, and (c) the information is found by calling up or retrieving that file when it's needed.

We'll now take a more detailed look at each of these three key stages in the learning-memory process and relate them to learning in college.

Stage 1. Perception: Receiving Information from the Senses and Sending It to the Brain

If you are not paying attention to a sign, you could drive right by it and not perceive it.

This is the first step in the learning process because we must first attend to and receive information in order to get it into our brain—where it is then registered or perceived. All information from the outside world gets to the brain through our senses (e.g., sight and sound), but it will only reach and get registered in our brain if we pay attention to it.

Contrary to popular belief, not all information that reaches our senses is received and registered in our brain (Rose, 1993). Although information may reach our eyes and ears, if we are not paying close enough attention to it, it will not register in our brain and we will not perceive it. Have you ever had the experience of driving right past an exit that you were supposed to take? Your eyes were fully open and the exit sign was in your field of vision when you passed it, but because you weren't paying close enough attention to it, it didn't register in your brain and you never perceived it.

Only information that we pay attention to gets registered by our conscious brain because the lower, subconscious part of our brain works as an attention filter by selectively letting in or keeping sensory information from reaching the upper parts of the brain—where it is consciously perceived (Figure 4).

Figure The Brain's Human Attention System

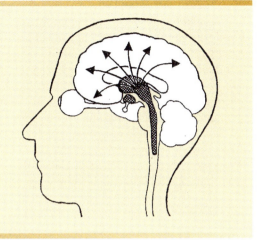

Information reaching our senses must pass through lower, subconscious parts of the brain that act as an attention filter or gatekeeper, determining whether sensory information will be sent to upper parts of the brain where it is consciously received (perceived).

 Pause for Reflection
People often forget the name of someone immediately after being introduced. What do you think causes this memory failure?

In fact, one of the major causes of forgetting is our failure to pay enough attention to what we want to remember; as a result, this information never registers in our brain in the first place. For example, forgetting where we put our keys or where we parked our car are classic examples of inattention or "absentmindedness." We forget these sorts of things because our brain never received the information in the first place. Our mind was not consciously present

As these examples illustrate, attention is a critical prerequisite for learning and memory to take place.

•—• **CLASSIC QUOTE** •—•
The true art of memory is the art of attention.
—Dr. Samuel Johnson, English author

Remember:
If there is no attention, there can be no retention.

In college, there are two key sensory channels or routes through which you will receive information:

1. Hearing—listening to lectures, and
2. Seeing—reading information from textbooks.

For learning to occur through either of these routes, the critical first step is to attend to and make note of the information you receive. Simply stated, you cannot learn and retain information that you've never attended to and acquired in the first place.

Chapter 3: Strategic Learning

CLASSIC QUOTE

We remember what we understand; we understand what we pay attention to; we pay attention to what we want.

—Edmund Bolles, *Remembering & Forgetting: An Inquiry into the Nature of Memory*

> **Personal Story**
>
> My son Michael is notorious for wanting to do everything that we ask his younger sister to do, and very little of what we ask him to do. A classic example is when we send him to any room to retrieve any object. My wife and I now measure how long it will take him to bring the wanted item back to us. (However, if we're in a hurry, we usually get it ourselves.) This is how it usually goes. "Michael, please go into the master bathroom and get the nail clippers." Michael, who will be seven at the time of this publication, walks slowly toward the bathroom. In a few minutes, he'll walk back into the room where we are, carrying some object he has started to construct (perhaps he'll grow up to be an engineer). When we ask him for the clippers, he'll say: "Oh, I forgot." In reality, he was not paying attention to our request, and it never registered in his brain. However, if we asked Maya (our daughter) to retrieve the item, Michael bowls her over to retrieve it. He listens well when Maya's name is called. The plan in our household now is to ask Maya for everything and let her actually get it when Michael is not around.
>
> —Aaron Thompson, Professor of Sociology

Stage 2. Storage: Keeping Information in the Brain

If information passes through our attention filter and is consciously perceived by our brain, it enters into one of the following memory systems:

◆ short-term memory—where it lasts for only a few seconds; or

◆ working memory—where you can consciously hold it in your mind and "work on it" for an extended period of time.

Have you ever walked into a room to do or get something, but once you got there, you had no idea why you were there? This experience illustrates the difference between short-term and working memory. What happened is that you had an idea in your short-term memory about something you were going to do or get in that room, but you then began thinking about something else after you had this thought, and by the time you got to the room, the thought had faded from your working memory. If you had kept that thought in your working memory, you would have been able to hold onto it and would have remembered why you went into the room after you got there.

To get information to stay in the brain for more than a short period of time, it has to be transferred from working memory, which is a temporary memory system, and moved into a different memory system known as *long-term memory*. Similar to a computer, we can get information onto the screen (short-term memory) and work on it (working memory), but if we want our computer to save the information we've worked on, we have to store it in the computer's long-term memory system.

The part of the brain that enables you to transfer memories from short-term to longer-term memory is known as the hippocampus (Squire, 1992) (Figure 5).

If the hippocampus is permanently damaged, an individual cannot store long-term memories. Or, if the hippocampus is temporarily slowed down by alcohol or marijuana, it can interfere with memory storage (for example, memory "blackouts" experienced by someone for events that occurred during a night of excessive drinking).

The process of storing information in long-term memory is referred to as *coding*, and the information that's stored is referred to as a *memory trace*—a physical or biological trace of the memory in the brain. (Note: The term memory "trace" is consistent with the word "learning"—which derives from the root word meaning "footprint" or "track.") Relating this to college learning, when you're studying, you are trying to register a memory trace by transferring

Figure 5 The Human Brain's Attention System

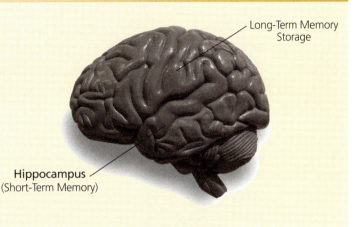

The hippocampus is the part of the brain that enables us to transfer information from short-term memory to association areas in the upper part of the brain where it is stored in long-term memory.

Long-Term Memory Storage

Hippocampus (Short-Term Memory)

© 2007, DAVID HUNTLEY, USED UNDER LICENSE FROM SHUTTERSTOCK, INC.

information from working memory to encode it in long-term storage so that you can recall it at test time. How well the information you have studied will stick in your brain depends on how effectively or deeply you learned it—the deeper the learning, the stronger its memory trace.

Memory Tips

The following strategies will help you better retain and more deeply learn new information while you are studying:

- connect or relate the information to something you already know;
- organize it into some classification system;
- take it in through multiple sensory modalities—e.g., see it, hear it, draw it, and feel it; and
- practice it at different times. (These strategies are discussed more fully later in the chapter.)

Pause for Reflection

It's common to hear students say, "I knew it when I studied it, but I forgot it on the test."

What do you think causes this common occurrence?

How might students study differently to prevent this from happening?

Stage 3. Retrieval: Finding Information That's Been Stored in the Brain and Bringing It Back to Consciousness

Getting information into the brain and getting it to stay there are the first two critical stages in the learning-memory process. The final stage is finding the stored memory and bringing it back to mind. To use the computer analogy, when your computer retrieves a file, it searches through the stored files, finds the particular file you need, and then brings it back to the screen in front of you. Relating this to college learning, the retrieval stage of memory corresponds to test taking. You first attend to and receive information from lectures and readings; you later study that information; and, finally, you attempt to retrieve that information at test time.

Evidence supporting the importance of the retrieval stage of memory comes from what researchers call the "tip of the tongue" phenomenon (Brown & McNeill, 1966). You've probably said to yourself: "Oh, I've got it (the memory) on the tip of my tongue." For example, you're taking an exam, you studied the material well, and you know the information that's being asked for in the test question, but you just can't quite get it to come back to you. However, after the test is over, it suddenly comes back to you when it's too late to use it! This demonstrates the memory trace was in your brain the entire time; you just weren't able to access and retrieve it.

Thus, retrieval represents the third and final stage of the memory process. All of the key stages in the processes of learning memory that we have discussed so far are summarized visually in Figure 6.

Figure 6 Key Stages in the Learning and Memory Process

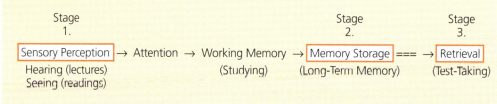

Pause for Reflection

For each of the three stages that make up the learning and memory process, how would you rate yourself in terms of your ability or past performance?

1. Attention to information presented in class and in reading assignments (strong, average, or weak?)

2. Studying—preparing for exams and getting information to "store" in your brain (strong, average, or weak?)

3. Test-taking—retrieving information that you've studied at test time and getting it down on paper (strong, average, or weak?)

This information about the key stages in the learning-memory process can be applied to generate a series of practical strategies that you can use to improve your performance on each of the following academic tasks:

- listening to lectures and note-taking,
- textbook reading, and
- studying.

Lecture Listening and Note-Taking Strategies

Information from class lectures represents one of the major sources of information that your brain must first take in for successful learning to eventually take place. Described are strategies for effective lecture listening and note-taking.

The Importance of Taking Notes

Studies show that information found in professors' lectures is the number-one source of test questions (and answers) on college exams (Brown, 1988; Kuhn, 1988). When lecture information appears on a test and has not been recorded in students' notes, it has only a 5 percent chance of being recalled (Kiewra, et al., 2000). This means that you should view each lecture like it is a test-review session during which your instructor is giving out test answers.

The importance of effective listening and note-taking for college success is highlighted by a study conducted with an entire freshman class of over 400 students who were given a listening test at the start of their first term in college. At the end of their first year, 49% of those students who scored low on the listening test were on academic probation at the end of their freshman year, compared to only 4.4% of students who scored high on the listening test. On the other hand, 68.5% of students who scored high on the listening test were eligible for the Honors program at the end of their first year, compared to only 4.17% of those students who had low listening-test scores (Conaway, 1982).

Contrary to popular belief that writing interferes with listening, students themselves report that taking notes actually increases their attention and concentration in class (Hartley & Marshall, 1974; Hartley, 1998). Studies also show that when students write down information that is presented to them rather than just listening to it, they are more likely to remember the most important aspects of that information when they are later given a memory test. Students who write notes during lectures have been found to achieve higher course grades than students who just listen to lectures (Kiewra, 1985), and students with a more complete set of notes tend to demonstrate higher levels of academic achievement (Kiewra & Fletcher, 1984). For instance, one study discovered that successful students (GPAs of 2.53 or higher) record more information in their notes and retain a larger percentage of the most important information than students with GPAs less than 2.53 (Einstein, Morris, & Smith, 1985). These findings are not surprising when you consider that *hearing* lecture information, *writing* it, and *seeing* it while writing, provide three different memory traces in the brain that can combine to improve your memory for that information. Furthermore, students with a good set of notes have a written record of that information, which can be re-read, reflected on, and studied later.

Students who take notes during lectures have been found to achieve higher class grades than those who just listen.

Remember: Come to class with the attitude that your instructors are throwing out answers to test questions as they speak; your purpose for being there is to pick-out and pick-up these answers. Take on the role of an active, investigative reporter who has an inquiring mind and an intense interest in acquiring important information.

·—· **CLASSIC QUOTE** ·—·

All genuine learning is active, not passive. It is a process in which the student is the main agent, not the teacher.

—Mortimer Adler, American professor of philosophy and educational theorist

Focus Your Attention

STUDENT PERSPECTIVE

"I never had a class before when the teacher just stands up and talks to you. He says something and you're writing it down, but then he says something else."

—First-year student quoted in Erickson & Strommer (1991) p. 8.

Attention is the critical first step to successful learning and memory. However, our attention span is limited, so it's impossible to attend to and make note of every piece of information that an instructor delivers in class. Thus, you need to use *selective attention* to attend to and select the most relevant or important information to record in your notes. Listed below are some key strategies for doing so.

- Pay special attention to any **information your instructors put in writing**—on the board, on an overhead, on a slide, or in a handout. If your instructor has taken the time and energy to write it out, that's usually a good clue that it is important information and you're likely to see it again—on an exam.

- Pay close attention to **information presented during the first few minutes and last few minutes of class**. Instructors are more likely to provide valuable reminders, reviews, and previews at the very start and very end of class.

- **Use your instructor's verbal and nonverbal cues** to detect important information. What the instructor writes out is not the only information that is important. It has been found that students record almost 90 percent of information that is written on the board, but they only record about 50 percent of important ideas that instructors state but don't write on the board (Locke, 1977). So, don't fall into the reflex-like routine of just writing something in your notes when you see your instructor writing something on the board. You also have to listen actively to record important ideas in your notes that you hear your instructor saying. In Box 1 are some specific strategies for detecting important information being delivered orally by your instructors during lectures.

TAKE ACTION NOW! Box 1

How to Detect When Instructors Are Delivering Important Information During Class Lectures

1. **Verbal cues:**
   - Phrases that signal important information, such as: "The key point here is . . ." "What's most significant about this is . . ."
   - Repeating information or rephrasing it in a different way (such as saying: "In other words, . . .").
   - Following stated information with a question to check students' understanding (e.g., "Is that clear?" "Do you follow that?" "Does that make sense?" "Are you with me?").

2. **Vocal (tone of voice) cues:**
   - Information that is delivered louder or at a higher pitch than usual, which may indicate excitement or emphasis.
   - Information delivered at a slower rate or with more pauses than usual, which may be your instructor's way of giving you more time to write down these especially important ideas.

3. **Nonverbal cues:**
   - Information delivered by the instructor with more than usual:
     a. facial expressiveness—e.g., raised or furrowed eyebrows;
     b. body movement—e.g., more gesturing and animation;
     c. eye contact—e.g., looking at the faces of students to see if they are following or understanding what is being said.
   - Information delivered with the instructor's body oriented directly toward the class—i.e., delivering information with both shoulders directly (squarely) facing the class.
   - Moving closer to the students—e.g., instructor moving away from the podium or blackboard to move closer to the class.

Taking Notes

Adopt a seating location that will maximize your focus of attention and minimize possible sources of distraction. Studies show that students who sit in the front and center of the classroom tend to attain higher exam scores (Rennels & Chaudhair, 1988). One study discovered a direct relationship between test scores and seating distance from the front of class: Students in the front scored 80 percent; those seated in the middle scored 71.6 percent; and those seated in the back rows of class scored 68.1 percent on course exams (Giles, 1982). Such results are found even when students are assigned seats by their instructor, so they are not simply due to the fact that more motivated students tend to sit in the front and center of the room. Instead, the higher academic performance of students sitting front and center is likely to have something to do with a learning advantage provided by these seating positions. Front-and-center seating probably improves academic performance by allowing students better vision of the blackboard, better hearing of what is being said by the instructor, and greater eye contact with the instructor—which may increase their sense of personal responsibility to listen and take notes on what their instructor is saying.

Studies show that students who sit in the front and center of a classroom tend to earn higher test scores.

When you enter the classroom, step up to the front of class and sit down. In large-sized classes, it is particularly important that you sit in front and "get up close and personal" with your instructors. This will not only improve your attention and note-taking; it should also improve your instructor's ability to remember who you are and how well you performed in class, which will work to your benefit if you ever need a letter of recommendation from that instructor.

Be aware of how your social seating position affects your behavior in the classroom. Intentionally sit near classmates who will not distract you or interfere with the quality of your note-taking. Attention comes in degrees or amounts; you can give all of it or part of it to whatever task you're performing. When you are in class trying to grasp complex information, this task demands your undivided attention.

> **Remember:** When you enter a classroom, you have a choice about where you are going to sit. Choose wisely by selecting a location that will maximize your focus of attention and the quality of your note-taking.

STUDENT PERSPECTIVES

"I tend to sit at the very front of my classrooms. It helps me focus and take notes better. It also eliminates distractions."
—First-year student

"I like to sit up front so I am not distracted by others and I don't have to look around people's heads to see the chalk board."
—First-year student

The evolution of student attention from the back to the front of class.

Adopt a seating posture that screams attention. Sitting upright and leaning forward is more likely to maximize your attention because these signals from your body will reach and influence your mind. If your body is in an alert and ready position, your mind tends to pick up these bodily cues and follow your body's lead by becoming more alert and ready to learn. Just as baseball players assume their "ready position" in the field before a pitch is delivered so that they are in a better postural position to catch batted balls, learners who assume a ready position in the classroom put themselves in a better position to mentally "catch" spoken ideas. Studies show that when humans are ready and expecting to capture an idea, greater amounts of the brain chemical C-kinase is released at the connection points between different brain cells, which increases the likelihood that a branched learning connection is formed between them (Howard, 2000).

Also, be aware that we may sometimes give others and ourselves the impression that we're actively listening because it is the polite thing to do; however, we may just be listening passively, partially, or not at all. For instance, when we're being introduced to someone for the first time, we may appear to be politely listening and paying attention to the person's name; however, we may not be listening carefully at all because we're thinking about what to say next or worrying about the type of impression we're making. When we run into that same person again five minutes later, we're embarrassed to learn that we've forgotten the person's name—which indicates that we weren't really listening and paying attention when we first heard it.

So, one aspect of effective listening in the classroom is to pay attention to whether you're really paying attention. Often the best way to do so is to check your own body language. Listed in Box 2 are some key nonverbal signals that often provide a good indication of whether or not you're listening actively and attending closely to what your instructor is saying in class.

Making a conscious effort to focus your attention in the classroom is particularly important during the first year of college because class sizes for introductory courses are often larger than other college courses or courses you had in high school. When class size gets larger, individuals tend to feel more anonymous, which may reduce their feelings of personal responsibility and their sense of active involvement. In large-class settings, it becomes especially important to fight off both distractions and the tendency to slip into "attention drift."

Lastly, there is another major advantage of maintaining your focus of attention in class: You send a clear message to your instructor that you're a motivated, conscientious, and courteous

---

TAKE ACTION NOW!   Box 2

Nonverbal Signals Indicating That You're Paying Close Attention During Lectures

1. Your body is oriented directly toward the instructor, so that your shoulders line up squarely with the instructor's shoulders (as opposed to one shoulder facing the instructor and your other shoulder facing away—which is known as giving someone "the cold shoulder").
2. Your body is upright or tilting slightly forward (rather than leaning back—which may mean you are "kicking back" and "zoning out").
3. You make occasional eye contact with the instructor—rather than making no eye contact at all (e.g., looking out the window) or continually staring/gazing at the instructor like you're in a mesmerized trance. Studies show that when a person makes periodic eye contact and then looks away for a moment to the left or right (referred to as "lateral eye movements" or "LEMS"), this indicates that the person is really listening to and thinking about what is being said (Glenberg, Schroeder, & Robertson, 1998).
4. Your head nods periodically and slowly—not continuously and rapidly—which usually means that you want the speaker to hurry up and finish so you don't have to listen anymore.

student. This can influence your instructor's perception and evaluation of your academic performance, either consciously or subconsciously. If you're on the border between two grades at the end of the term, you may get the benefit of the doubt. In contrast, inattentive or discourteous behavior in the classroom is likely to have the opposite effect on your instructors' perception and evaluation of you, which may lower your grade.

One survey revealed that college professors found the following student behaviors in the classroom to be especially irritating, so be sure to avoid them (Box 3).

BOX 3 Snapshot Summary — Pet Peeves of College Professors

Surveys show that professors really hate it when students:

1. Carry on personal conversations with others during a lecture.
2. Miss class and ask, "Did I miss anything important?"
3. Place their head on the desk or fall asleep during class.
4. Are excessively tardy.
5. Fail to bring required materials to class.
6. Are excessively absent.
7. Miss a lecture and then expect the professor to provide them with a personal encore.

Source: Larry Ludewig, college professor, cited in Vogt (1994).

Using cell phones and eating in class are both considered to be rude or uncivil behaviors (especially if both are done in the same class period!).

Question Frequently Asked by Students After Missing a Class

Responses from Tom Wayman, Professor of Creative Writing, University of Calgary

Nothing. When we realized you weren't here we sat with our hands folded on our desks in silence, for the full two hours.

Everything. I gave an exam worth 40 percent of the grade for this term and assigned some reading due today on which I'm about to hand out a quiz worth 50 percent.

Nothing. None of the content of this course has value or meaning. Take as many days off as you like: Any activities we undertake as a class I assure you will not matter either to you or me and are without purpose.

Everything. A few minutes after we began last time, a shaft of light descended and an angel or other heavenly being appeared and revealed to us what each woman or man must do to attain divine wisdom in this life and the hereafter. This is the last time the class will meet before we disperse to bring this good news to all people on earth . . .

And you weren't there.

"The student question that drove Professor Jenkins over the edge!"

Take organized notes. Keep taking notes in the same paragraph if the instructor is continuing on the same point or idea; for each new concept the instructor introduces, skip a few lines and shift to a new paragraph. Be alert to phrases that your instructor may state to indicate a shift to a new or different idea (e.g., "Let's turn to . . ."), and use these phrases as cues for taking notes in paragraph form. This will strengthen the organization of your notes, which, in turn, will improve your comprehension and retention of them. Also, leaving extra space between paragraphs will give you some room to add information that you may have missed and to add your own thoughts or to paraphrase lecture notes into your own words.

Take your own notes in class. Do not rely on someone else to take notes for you. Taking your own notes in your own words will ensure that they have meaning to you. You can rely on classmates for the purpose of comparing notes for completeness and accuracy, or to get notes if you are forced to miss class. However, do not routinely rely on others to take notes for you. Studies show that students who record and review their own notes earn higher scores on memory tests for that information than students who review the notes of others (Fisher & Harris, 1973). These findings point to the importance of taking and studying your own notes because they have personal meaning to you.

If you do not immediately understand what your instructor is saying, don't stop taking notes. Keep taking notes, even if you are temporarily confused, because this will at least leave you with a record of the information that you can reflect on later, when you will have more time to think about it and grasp it. If you still don't understand it after taking more time to reflect on it, then you can check with your textbook, your instructor, or a classmate.

Remember: Your primary goal during lectures is to get important information into your brain long enough to note it mentally and then physically—by recording it in your notes. Fully comprehending and deeply understanding that information may have to come later, when you have time to reflect on the ideas you've written.

Before individual class sessions, check your syllabus to see where you are in the course and determine how the upcoming class fits into the total course picture. This strategy will strengthen your learning by allowing you to see how the parts relate to the whole.

If possible, get to class ahead of time, so you can look over your notes from the previous class session and your notes from any reading assignment relating to the day's lecture topic. Research indicates that when students review information relating to a lecture topic before hearing the lecture, it improves their ability to take more accurate and complete notes during the lecture (Ladas, 1980). This research supports the strategy of reading textbook information relating to the lecture topic *before* hearing the lecture, because this will help you better understand the lecture and take better notes. A brief review of previously learned information serves to activate your previous knowledge, getting it into your working memory so you'll be in a better position to build a mental bridge from one class to the next. This will help you relate new information to what you've already experienced, which is essential for deep learning.

Pause for Reflection

What do you tend to do immediately after a class session ends?

Why?

As soon as class ends, quickly check your notes for missing information or incomplete thoughts. You can do this by yourself, or better yet, with a motivated classmate. If you both have gaps, check them out with your instructor before s/he leaves the classroom. Even though it may be weeks before you will be tested on this material, the quicker you address missed points and misunderstood ideas, the better, because you'll be able to avoid the last-minute, mad rush of students seeking help from the instructor just before test time. You want to reserve the critical time period just before exams to review a whole set of complete and accurate notes—rather than rushing around, trying to find missing information and trying to understand concepts that were presented weeks ago.

As soon as possible after the end of a class session, reflect on your notes and make them meaningful to you. In college, your professors will often be lecturing on information that you may have little prior knowledge about, so it is unrealistic to expect that you will understand everything that's being said the first time you hear it. Instead, you'll need to take time to reflect on and review your notes to make sense of them. During this review and reflection process, we recommend that you take notes on your notes by:

- translating technical information into your own words to make them more meaningful to you, and
- reorganizing your notes to get ideas relating to the same points in the same place or category.

Studies show that when students are instructed to organize lecture information into meaningful categories, they show greater recall on a delayed memory test for that information than students who were simply told to review their notes (Howe, 1970). We recommend that you do this review and reorganization of your notes as soon as possible after class because the information may still be fresh in your mind and will become more easily locked into memory storage before forgetting takes place.

> **Remember:** Look at note-taking as a two-stage process; stage one is aggressively taking notes in class (active involvement), and stage two occurs at a later point in time—when you think about those notes more deeply (personal reflection).

Pause for Reflection

Honestly rate yourself in terms of how frequently you use the following note-taking strategies, using the following scale: 4 = always, 3 = sometimes, 2 = rarely, 1 = never.

1. I take notes aggressively in class.	4 3 2 1
2. I sit near the front of the room in my classes.	4 3 2 1
3. I sit upright and lean forward while in class.	4 3 2 1
4. I take notes on what my instructors say, not just what they write on the board.	4 3 2 1
5. I pay special attention to information presented at the very start and very end of class.	4 3 2 1
6. I take notes in paragraph form.	4 3 2 1
7. I review my notes immediately after class to check if they are complete and accurate.	4 3 2 1

••• Strategies for Improving Textbook-Reading Comprehension and Retention

Following lecture notes, information from reading assignments is the second most frequent source of test questions on college exams (Brown, 1988). You will encounter test questions based on information found in your assigned readings that your professors may not have explicitly talked about in class. College professors often expect you to relate or connect what they are lecturing about in class with the reading they have assigned. Furthermore, professors often deliver class lectures with the assumption that you have done the assigned reading, so if you haven't done it, you may have great difficulty following what your instructor is saying in class. Unfortunately, studies show that only about 25 percent of students in class complete the course reading that their professor has assigned them to read before coming to class on any particular day (Hobson, 2004).

The bottom line is this: Do the assigned reading and do it according to the schedule that your instructors have assigned. This will help you comprehend lectures and improve the quality of your participation in class. Better yet, when you complete your reading assignments, use reading strategies that capitalize on the most effective principles of human learning and memory, such as those listed below.

Although keeping up with class reading is important, you should also utilize effective learning strategies to get the most from the material you read.

Before Beginning to Read

Before beginning to read, first see how the assigned reading fits into the overall organizational structure of the book and the course. You can do this efficiently by just taking a look at the book's table of contents to see where the chapter you're about to read is placed in the sequence of chapters in the book, particularly the chapters that immediately precede and follow it. This will give you a sense of how the particular part you're focusing on relates to the whole. Research shows that if learners have advance knowledge of how information is organized, and if they "see the whole" (how all the information is connected) before examining its parts, their ability to understand and remember that information is improved (Ausubel, 1978; Kintsch, 1994).

Before you begin to read a chapter, preview it by reading its boldface headings and any chapter outline, objectives, summary, or end-of-chapter questions that may be provided. Sometimes when you dive into details too quickly, you lose sight of how the details relate to the big picture. As we've previously discussed, the brain's natural tendency is to perceive and comprehend whole patterns rather than isolated bits of information. Start by seeing how the different parts of the text are integrated into the whole. In so doing, you're essentially seeing the total picture of a completed jigsaw puzzle. By seeing how its separate pieces will fit together, you can more effectively comprehend the content of the chapter.

So, get in the habit of previewing what is in a chapter to get an overall sense of its organization before jumping right into the content.

After previewing the chapter, take a moment to think about what ideas or knowledge you may already have that relates to the chapter's topic. By taking a minute to think about what you may already know about the topic you're about to read, you can activate the areas of your brain where that knowledge is stored, thereby preparing it to make meaningful connections with the information you are about to read.

While Reading

Read selectively by noting or highlighting the most important information for later review. Here are three key strategies that will help you decide what to note or highlight in your reading as important information.

1. Use boldface or dark-print headings and subheadings as cues for identifying important information.

    These headings serve to organize the chapter's content, and you can use them as "traffic signs" to direct you to the chapter's most important concepts. These headings are the key clues to finding the important information in the chapter.

    Better yet, turn the headings into questions, and then read the information beneath them to find their answers. This will send you on an answer-finding mission that can keep you mentally active and allow you to read with a purpose—to find answers to the questions you've created out of the headings.

     To help you remember to use this strategy, we recommend that you place a question mark after each heading while you're previewing or surveying the chapter.

    Creating and answering questions while you are reading is also motivating because you feel rewarded when you find answers to the questions you've created (Walter, Knudsbig, & Smith, 2003). Furthermore, answering questions while you are reading is an ideal way to prepare for tests because you're practicing exactly what you'll be doing on tests, which will be to answer questions. Also, you can conveniently use the heading questions as "flash cards" to review for exams by trying to remember the key information you've highlighted under each heading.

2. Pay special attention to the first and last sentences in each paragraph.

   These sentences often contain an important introduction and conclusion to the ideas covered in that passage of the text. In fact, when reading sequential or cumulative material that requires you to understand what was previously covered in order to understand what's covered next, it is a good idea to quickly reread the first and last sentences of each paragraph you've just finished reading before moving on to read the next paragraph.

3. Re-read the chapter after you've heard your instructor lecture on the chapter's topic.

   You can use your lecture notes as a guide to help you focus on what particular information in the chapter your instructor feels is most important. If you adopt this strategy, you will be able to read before lectures to help you better understand the lecture and take better class notes, and you can use your reading after lectures to help you better identify and understand the most important information contained in your textbook.

 Remember: Your goal when reading is not merely to "cover" the assigned pages, but to "uncover" the most important information and ideas contained in those pages.

Adjust your reading speed to the type of subject matter that you're reading. Academic reading is more technical and mentally challenging than popular reading, such as reading magazines or newspapers, so do not attempt to read college texts all at the same speed. Furthermore, certain academic subjects place greater demands on your working memory than others, so you cannot expect to read all types of academic material at the same rate. For instance, material in the natural and social sciences is likely to have more technical terminology and will need to be read at a slower rate than a novel or short story. For more technical subjects, you may not understand the material when you first read it, so you may need to reread what you have just read to get a better understanding of it.

Remain aware of your reading rate. If you find yourself reading different subjects at the same speed, you may need to better regulate and accommodate your reading speed to the type of material you are reading.

Find the meaning of unfamiliar words that you encounter while reading. Knowing the meaning of specific terms is important in any college course, but it is absolutely critical in courses whose subject matter builds on knowledge of previously covered information, such as math and science. If you do not learn the meaning of key terms as you read them, you cannot build upon this knowledge to understand information that is covered later.

Have a dictionary available, and if the textbook has a glossary, make regular use of it. In fact, you may want to make a photocopy of the textbook's glossary (typically located at the end of the text) because this will save you the hassle of having to repeatedly hold your place in the chapter with one hand while using the other to find the meaning of unfamiliar terms at the back of the textbook. The more effort it takes to look up words you don't know, the less likely you are to do it, so make your access to a glossary and dictionary as convenient as possible.

Take written notes on what you're reading. Just as you take notes in response to your instructor's spoken words in class, take notes in response to the author's written words in your text. For example, write short answers to the boldface heading questions in a reading notebook or in the text itself, using its side, top, and bottom margins. Writing requires more active thinking than highlighting because you are generating words on your own, which are words that have personal meaning to you (rather than passively highlighting words written by someone else). Try not to get into the habit of using your textbook as a coloring book, where you get so into the

CLASSIC QUOTE

The art of reading is the art of adopting the pace the author has set. Some books are fast and some are slow, but no book can be understood if it is taken at the wrong speed.

—Mark Van Doren, Pulitzer Prize winning poet, and former professor of English, Columbia University

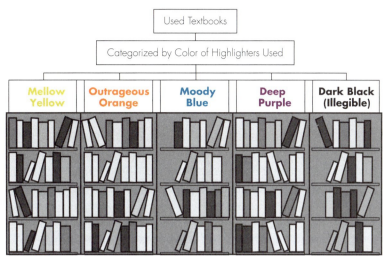

Highlighting textbooks in spectacular colors is a very popular reading strategy among college students, but it's a less effective strategy for producing deep learning than taking written notes on what you read.

artwork of highlighting in metallic, kaleidoscopic colors that the artistic process becomes more important than the process of thinking actively and deeply about what you are reading.

Remember that you can write in your textbook because you own it. Even if you intend to sell it at the end of the term, you can still write in it by using a pencil and you can even highlight it in pencil—by simply bracketing or underlining key sentences. If you eventually decide to sell your book back, then you can erase the pencil markings and probably end up with a book that will have higher resale value than one covered with hallucinogenic-like highlighting. In fact, pencils are more versatile reading tools than highlighters because they can be used more easily to do a variety of things, such as recording written notes, drawing figures or symbols, and making changes to your notes by erasing and rewriting.

> **·—· CLASSIC QUOTE ·—·**
>
> *I would advise you to read with a pen in your hand, and enter in a little book of short hints of what you find that is curious, or that might be useful; for this will be the best method of imprinting such particulars in your memory, where they will be ready.*
>
> —Benjamin Franklin, eighteenth-century inventor, politician, and co-signer of the *Declaration of Independence*

Pause for Reflection

When reading a textbook, which of the following items do you usually have on hand?

Highlighter: Yes   No

Pen or pencil: Yes   No

Notebook: Yes   No

Class notes: Yes   No

Dictionary: Yes   No

Make use of the visual aids that are provided in your textbooks. Don't fall into the trap of thinking that visual aids can or should be skipped because they merely supplement the written words of the text. Visual aids, such as charts, graphs, diagrams, and concept maps are powerful learning and memory tools for a couple of reasons:

1. They enable you to visualize information as a picture or image, and
2. They can organize many separate pieces of information into one meaningful whole.

Furthermore, viewing them gives you a periodic break from continually reading written words, allowing you to experience a different form of mental stimulation, which should increase your attention to what you're reading, as well as your motivation to read.

After Reading

Finish your reading session with a short review of the information that you've noted or highlighted. Forgetting information that your brain has just processed tends to occur most rapidly immediately after you stop focusing on it (Underwood, 1983). Taking a few minutes at the end of your reading time to review the most important information that you've noted or highlighted serves to lock in your memory of it before you turn your attention to something else and forget what you have just read.

Collaborate with peers to improve the effectiveness of your reading. The same benefits of participating in small-group discussions and study groups can be experienced when you form reading groups. After you complete your reading assignments, you can team-up with classmates to compare your highlighting and margin notes. You can consult with each other to identify major points in the reading, and help each other identify what information is most important to study for upcoming exams.

If you find that a certain concept explained in your text is difficult to understand, take a look at how another textbook explains that concept. Not all textbooks are created equally; some do a better job of explaining certain concepts than others. Another text may be able to explain a hard-to-understand concept much better than the textbook you purchased for the course. So, keep this option open by checking to see if your library has other texts in the same subject as your course, or check your campus bookstore for other textbooks in the same subject area as the course you're taking.

Pause for Reflection

Honestly rate yourself in terms of how frequently you use the following reading strategies according to the following scale:

4 = always, 3 = sometimes, 2 = rarely, 1 = never.

1. *I read the chapter outlines and summaries before I start reading a chapter.*   4   3   2   1
2. *I preview a chapter's boldface headings and subheadings before I begin to read the chapter.*   4   3   2   1
3. *I adjust my reading speed to the type of subject I am reading.*   4   3   2   1
4. *I look up the meaning of unfamiliar words and unknown terms that I come across before I read any further.*   4   3   2   1
5. *I take written notes on information I read.*   4   3   2   1
6. *I use the visual aids included in my textbooks.*   4   3   2   1
7. *I finish my reading sessions with a review of the important information that I noted or highlighted.*   4   3   2   1

••• Study Strategies

Effective note-taking and reading ensures that you receive and gain access to the information that will show up on exams. The next step is to get that information stored in your brain so that you can later retrieve it at test time. Described below is a series of strategies for effectively storing information in your brain while studying.

Minimize Distractions

Maximize your attention while studying by blocking out all distracting sources of outside stimulation. As mentioned earlier, attention comes in a fixed quantity or amount; you can give all of it or part of it to whatever task you're working on. When you're involved with the task of studying complex material, this requires your complete and undivided attention. You don't want to divide your attention among multiple tasks by trying to study and process other information at the same time, such as listening to music, watching television, or exchanging instant messages with a friend.

When studying complex material, you need to give your complete and undivided attention to this task. Listening to music is a distraction that will shift your focus away from the information you are trying to learn.

Research on such multi-tasking consistently shows that trying to do more than one task at the same time interferes with the performance of the primary task you're working on—especially if that primary task involves complex thinking (Crawford & Strapp, 1994). In fact, when people multi-task, studies show that they don't pay equal and maximum attention to different tasks at the same time; instead, what they do is alternate or shift their attention back and forth from one task to another (Howard, 2000). The result is that they lose attention to one of the tasks for a while before returning to it. Probably the most common example of the dangers of trying to focus on more than one task at the same time is driving a car while talking on a cell phone. Studies have repeatedly shown that a person's driving attention and performance are reduced when they try to drive and use a cell phone simultaneously (Redelmeier & Tibshirani, 1997).

Studies show that doing challenging academic work while multi-tasking divides up attention and drives down comprehension and retention.

·—· CLASSIC QUOTE ·—·

Receive, embrace, transform.

Sights and sounds unrelated to what we're trying to learn tend to compete for and interfere with our attention during the learning process. When people say that they learn just as well or better while they listen to music or watch TV, this doesn't turn out to be true when they are actually tested (Crawford & Strapp, 1994). Even all the hype about how listening to classical music while studying can accelerate learning is not supported by research (Wagner & Tilney, 1983). The bottom line is that when you are learning challenging concepts or performing mental tasks that you cannot do automatically, competing external stimulation interferes with the quiet, internal reflection time needed to form deep, long-lasting connections between brain cells (Jensen, 1998).

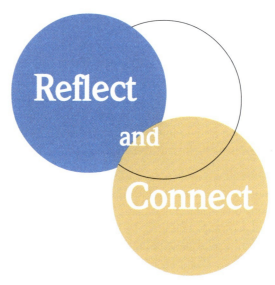

Find Meaning in Terms

Each academic field has its own specialized vocabulary that can almost sound like a foreign language to someone who has no experience in the subject area. Before you start to brutally beat these terms into your brain through sheer repetition, try to find some meaning in them, or in some part of them. You can make a meaningless term more meaningful to you by looking up its word root in the dictionary or by identifying its prefix or suffix that may give away the term's meaning. For instance, if you were studying the autonomic nervous system in biology, which is the part of the nervous system that operates without our conscious or voluntary control (e.g., our heart beating and lungs breathing), its meaning is given away by its prefix "auto"—which means self-controlling, as in the word "automatic."

If the term's root, prefix, or suffix does not give away its meaning, then see if you can make it more meaningful to you in some other way. For instance, suppose you looked up the root of the term "artery," and nothing about the origins of this term reveals its meaning or purpose. You could then create your own meaning for this term by taking its first letter ("a"), and have it stand for "away"—to help you remember that arteries carry blood *away* from the heart. Thus, you've taken a meaningless biological term and made it more personally meaningful (and memorable).

Compare and Contrast

When you're studying something new, get in the habit of asking yourself the following questions:

  Is this similar or comparable to something I've already learned?
  How does this differ from, or contrast with, what I already know?

Research indicates that this simple strategy is one of the most powerful ways to promote learning of academic information (Marzano, Pickering, & Pollock, 2001). The power of the compare-and-contrast strategy probably stems from the fact that asking yourself, "How is this similar to and different than something that I already know?" makes learning more personally meaningful by encouraging you to relate what you're trying to learn to what you already know.

Integrate Information

Pull together information from your class notes and your assigned reading that relate to the same major concept or category; for example, get them in the same place by recording them on the same index card under the same category heading. The category heading can function like the hub of a wheel, around which individual pieces of information are attached like spokes. This will improve your learning and memory by strengthening its organization, plus it will enable you to study all course material relating to the same topic at the same time.

In contrast, when information relating to different concepts is separated in physical space, it helps you to separate them mentally, and prevents all that information from running together in your mind and confusing you.

Divide and Conquer

Spreading out your studying into shorter sessions improves your memory by reducing loss of attention due to fatigue.

Effective learning depends not only on your study method, it also depends on when you learn—your timing. Although cramming just prior to exams is better than not studying at all, it is far less effective than studying that is spread out across time. Rather than cramming all your studying into one long session, use the *distributed practice* method, which spreads out study time into several shorter sessions. Research consistently shows that short, periodic practice sessions are more effective than a single marathon session. For instance, in one study of students who were learning Spanish, half of them studied many Spanish words in a single day, while another group studied the same number of words for the same amount of time, but their study time was broken up into a number of shorter sessions held at different times. Eight years later, the students were tested for their memory of these Spanish words. Those students who learned the words in the one-day cram session recalled an average of 6 percent of the words, while students who studied the words in several shorter sessions remembered 25 percent of the words—more than four times the amount remembered by the cramming group (Bahrick & Phelps, 1987).

Spreading out your studying into shorter sessions serves to improve your memory because it:

- reduces loss of attention due to fatigue or boredom, and
- reduces mental interference by giving the brain some "cool down" time to process and lock-in information that it has received without being interrupted by the need to take in additional information (Murname & Shiffrin, 1991).

If this downtime is interfered with by the need to process additional information, the brain gets overloaded and its memory for new information becomes impaired. This is exactly what cramming does—it interferes with the brain's need for downtime by overloading it with lots of information in a limited period of time. In contrast, distributed study does just the opposite—it spreads out learning into shorter sessions with downtime in-between sessions, which allows the brain to store information that has been previously studied. To illustrate this point, consider how difficult it would be to recall the names of ten new people you meet in one evening, compared with recalling the names of ten people you meet on ten separate evenings.

Another major advantage of distributed study is that it is less stressful and more motivating than cramming. You should feel more motivated to study because you know that you're not going to have to do it for a long stretch of time and lose any sleep over it. Furthermore, you should feel more relaxed because if you discover something that you don't understand, you know that you still have time to get help with it before you'll be tested and graded on it.

Distributing study time throughout the term is particularly crucial in college courses because tests are often given less frequently than in high school. In some college courses, you may take only two to three tests per term, and those tests will cover large amounts of material. So, resist the temptation to procrastinate and cram all information into your brain on the day (or night) before the exam; and don't buy into the belief that "I work better under pressure" (which often really means, "I *only* work under pressure because I procrastinate and have no other choice").

Use a "Part-to-Whole" Method of Studying

Divide your studying into small parts or units, and then learn these parts in several short, separate study sessions in advance of exams.

"Do not cram. If you start to prepare for a test about 3–5 days before, then you will only need to do a quick review the night before."

—Advice to freshmen from an experienced student, Walsh (2005)

The part-to-whole method of studying is consistent with and flows naturally from the distributed practice method of studying that we just discussed. With the part-to-whole method, your last study session prior to the exam is one in which you re-study what you previously studied in short sessions altogether at one time. Thus, your last study session is a review session, not a session during which you're trying to learn information for the first time.

Do not underestimate the power of studying small pieces of course material in short, separate study sessions in advance of exams. The part-to-whole study method is often resisted because of the following common (and dangerous) belief: Studying done in advance of an exam is a total "waste of time" because you'll "forget it all by the time you take the test." This is a flat-out fallacy because memory for information that you study in advance of an exam is still in your brain when you later review the day or night before the exam. Even if you cannot recall the previously studied information when you first start reviewing it, you will re-learn it much faster than you did the first time you studied it, thus proving that some memory of it was still retained in your brain (Kintsch, 1994).

The time you save when you review and re-learn something a second time is referred to by memory researchers as "relearning savings time" (Gordon, 1989) in other words, it is the amount of time saved when re-learning and remembering something a second time compared to the time it took to learn and remember it the first time. For example, suppose a student took French in high school and knew the French words for chair, table, floor, and ceiling, but two years later, this person can no longer recall the French translations of these words. So, it appears as if these French words learned in high school were completely forgotten. However, if you were to calculate the time this person would need to re-learn these French words and compare it to the amount of time it took to first learn them two years ago, much less time would be needed to re-learn these words the second time. The amount of time saved when re-learning the words the second time indicates that those French words learned in high school have not been totally forgotten; instead, traces of their memory are still in the student's brain, which enables them to be relearned much faster the next time around.

So, the old expression, "If you don't use it, you'll lose it," is not quite accurate when it comes to material that has been studied during the course of a term. Traces of these previous memories are not totally lost or erased from your brain; they are just weakened or lightened (Alnon, 1992). Often, all it takes is a mental "tune up" to get them up and working again. Thus, distributing studying into smaller parts in advance of a test is not a waste of time because it allows for re-learning savings time—plus reduced memory interference, reduced stress, and improved sleep that occur with distributed study compared to last-minute, late-night cramming.

Consuming large doses of caffeine or other stimulants to stay awake for all-night cram sessions is likely to maximize anxiety and minimize memory.

Begin with a Review

For sequential or cumulative subjects that build on understanding of previously covered information to learn new information (e.g., math), begin each study session with a quick review of what you learned in your previous study session.

Research shows that students of all ability levels learn course material more effectively when it's studied in small units, and when progression to the next unit takes place only after the previous unit has been mastered or understood (Pascarella & Terenzini, 1991, 2005). This strategy ensures that students build on their previous knowledge to understand what's coming next, and it enables *over-learning* to take place—that is, reviewing information that has already been learned further reinforces and strengthens its memory. This is particularly important in cumulative subjects that require memory for problem-solving procedures or steps, such as math and science. Continued practice of these procedures serves to make them become more automatic so you're able to retrieve them quicker (e.g., on a timed test) and use them without devoting all your mental energy to them (Newell & Rosenbloom, 1981). This frees up your working memory to focus on higher-level thinking and creative problem-solving (Schneider & Chein, 2003).

Change Things Up

Periodically change the type of academic tasks you're performing while studying. Change in work routine and in the type of mental task performed serves to increase your level of alertness and concentration by reducing "habituation"—attention loss that tends to occur after repeated exposure to the same learning task (McGuiness & Pribram, 1980). So, look to vary the type of task or work you're doing while studying. For instance, shift periodically across tasks that involve reading, writing, studying (e.g., rehearsing or reciting) and practicing skills (e.g., solving problems).

Study different subjects in different places. Different study locations provide different environmental contexts for learning, which tends to reduce the amount of interference that would normally build up if all the information was studied in the same place (Anderson & Bower, 1974). Memory research shows when lists of information are learned in different environments, memory interference is reduced. In one study, students who learned a group of 40 words in two separate study sessions held in the same room recalled an average of 15.9 words on a later memory test. In contrast, students who studied the words for the same amount of time, but whose study sessions took place in two distinctively different rooms, recalled an average of 24.4 words (Smith, Glenberg, & Bjork, 1978).

Thus, it may not only be a good idea to spread out your studying at different times, it may also be a good idea to spread out your studying in different places. In fact, ancient Greek and Roman speakers used this method of changing places to remember long speeches by walking through different rooms, mentally associating different parts of their speech with different rooms (Higbee, 1998).

The brain's attention system has a particular area that is specialized for attention to location (Ackerman, 1992), so changes in the place or space where learning occurs can stimulate greater attention (Schacter, 1992), in part because the change and novelty of the new environment provides greater sensory stimulation to the brain (La Berge, 1995). Even the act of standing up and moving to a new location can have positive effects on mental performance and brain functioning (Jensen, 1998) because it increases circulation of oxygen-carrying blood to the brain and stimulates areas of the brain that play a key role in learning (Middleton & Strick, 1994).

This research suggests that changes in the nature of the learning task and the learning environment provide changes of pace that infuse some variety into the learning process, which can improve your attention to and concentration on what you're studying. Although it may be useful to have a set schedule of study times during the week to get you into a regular, habit-forming work routine, this doesn't mean that learning occurs best by habitually performing the same learning tasks while sitting in the same seat at the same place. Instead, you should make periodic changes in the learning tasks you're performing and the environments in which you perform them to maximize attention and minimize interference (Druckman & Bjork, 1991).

 Remember: Studying will be more effective if:
- there is separation of your study material into smaller parts and separation of your study time into shorter sessions; and
- there is variation in the type of study tasks you perform and in the study places where you perform them.

Use All of Your Senses

When studying course material, try to use as many different sensory channels as possible because research clearly indicates that information stored through more than one sensory modality is better remembered (Bjork, 1994; Schacter, 1992). When a memory is stored in the brain, different sensory aspects of it are stored in different areas. For example, the visual, auditory, and motor sensations associated with what you're learning are all stored in different parts of the brain. Thus, when you use all of these sensory channels while learning, multiple "memory traces" of what you're studying are recorded in your brain, which leads to stronger memory (Education Commission of the States, 1996). Listed below are some of the major channels through which learning occurs and memories are stored, accompanied by specific strategies for using each of these channels while studying.

1. **Visual Learning**

   The human brain consists of two halves or hemispheres: the left hemisphere and the right hemisphere (Figure 7). Each of these hemispheres specializes in a different type of learning. In most people, the left hemisphere specializes in verbal learning, dealing primarily with words. In contrast, the right hemisphere specializes in visual-spatial learning, dealing primarily with images. Thus, if you use both words and images to learn the information you're studying, two memory traces are recorded in different halves of your brain: One memory trace is recorded in the left hemisphere—where words are encoded—and one in the right hemisphere—where images are encoded. This process of laying down a double memory trace (verbal and visual) is referred to as *dual coding* (Paivio, 1990). When this happens, memory for what you're learning is substantially strengthened, primarily because two memory traces are better than one.

   To capitalize on the advantage of dual coding, make use of any visual aids that are available to you. Use the visual aids provided in your textbook and by your instructor, and create your own by drawing pictures, symbols, or concept maps—such as flow charts or branching tree diagrams. Drawing is not just an artistic exercise; it can be used as a learning tool as well—you can draw to learn. By taking words and ideas and representing them in visual form, the resulting drawing enables you to dual code the information you're studying, doubling the number of memory traces recorded in your brain.

Figure 7

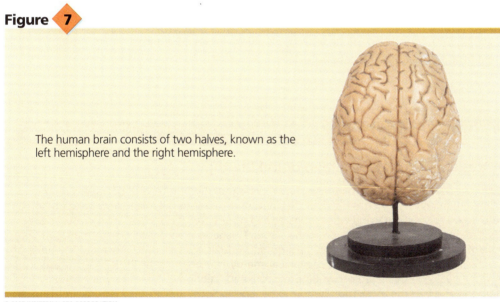

The human brain consists of two halves, known as the left hemisphere and the right hemisphere.

© 2007 JUPITERIMAGES CORPORATION

Pause for Reflection

People remember faces better than they do names. Why do you think this is?

2. **Motor Learning (also known as Muscle Memory)**

   In addition to hearing and seeing, movement is another sensory channel that provides the brain with kinesthetic stimulation—the sensations we get from our body's muscles as a result of physical movement. Memory traces for movement are commonly stored in the cerebellum—an area in the lower back of the brain. Brain research indicates that this part of the brain plays a major role in all types of learning (Middleton & Strick, 1994). Thus, associating movement with what you're learning can improve your ability to retain it because you record an additional "muscle memory trace" of it to another area of your brain.

   > *Personal Story* I was talking about memory in class one day and mentioned that if I forget how to spell a word, when I start to write it out, I often remember its correct spelling. One of my students then raised her hand and said the same thing happens to her when she forgets a phone number—it comes back to her when she starts dialing it. Both cases of memories coming back when movement began (writing and dialing) are classic cases of how a muscle memory trace can trigger recall of verbal or factual information that is associated with movement.
   >
   > —Joe Cuseo

STUDENT PERSPECTIVE

"I have to *hear* it, *see* it, *write* it, and *talk* about it."

—First-year student, responding to the question: "How do you learn best?"

   You can use movement to help you learn and retain academic information by using your body to act out what you're studying or to symbolize it with your hands (Kagan & Kagan, 1998). For example, if you're trying to remember five points about something (e.g., five key consequences of the Civil War), when you're studying these points, count them out on your fingers as you try to recall each of them. Also, remember that talking itself involves muscle movement of your lips and tongue. Thus, by speaking aloud when you're studying, either to a friend or to yourself, your memory of what you're studying should be improved by adding kinesthetic stimulation to your brain (along with the auditory or sound stimulation your brain receives from hearing what you're saying).

TAKE ACTION NOW! Box 4

Adjusting Your Academic Work to Your Biological Rhythms

- When planning your daily work schedule, be aware of your natural "biological rhythms"—your *peak periods* and *down times*. Studies show that humans vary in terms of when they naturally prefer to fall asleep and wake up; some are "early birds" who prefer to go to sleep early and wake up early, and others are "night owls" who prefer to stay up late at night and get up late in the morning (Natale & Ciogna, 1996). (Teenagers more often fall into the category of "night owls.") As a result of these differences in sleeping patterns, individuals will vary with respect to the times of day when they experience their highest and lowest levels of physical energy. Naturally, "early birds" are more likely to be "morning" people whose peak energy period occurs before noon; and "night owls" are likely to be more productive in the late afternoon and evening. Also, most people experience a "post-lunch" dip in energy in the early afternoon (Monk, 2005).

- Be aware of your most productive hours of the day and schedule your highest priority work and most challenging tasks at times when you tend to work at peak effectiveness. For example, schedule your out-of-class work so that you're tackling academic tasks that require intense thinking (e.g., technical writing or complex problem-solving) at times of the day when you tend to be most productive, and schedule lighter work (e.g., light reading or routine tasks) at times when your energy level tends to be lower. Also, keep your natural peak and down times in mind when you schedule your courses. Attempt to arrange your class schedule in such a way that you experience your most challenging courses at times of the day when your body and mind are most ready to accept that challenge.

Emotional Learning and Memory

Just as information reaches the brain through the senses and is stored in the brain as a memory trace, the same is true of emotions. There are numerous connections between brain cells in the emotional and memory centers of the human brain (Zull, 1998). For instance, when we're experiencing emotional excitement and energy about what we are learning, adrenaline is released and is carried through the blood stream to our brain. Once adrenaline reaches the brain, it increases blood flow and glucose production, which can stimulate learning and strengthen memory (LeDoux, 1998; Rosenfield, 1988). In fact, if an experience is very emotionally intense, the amount of adrenaline that is released can immediately and permanently store the memory in the brain for the remainder of a person's life. For instance, most people can remember exactly what they were doing at the time they experienced such emotionally intense events as the September 11th terrorist attack on the United States, or their first kiss, or when their favorite team won a world championship.

What does this emotion-memory link have to do with helping you remember academic information that you're studying? Research on human emotions suggests that emotional intensity, excitement, and enthusiasm do make a real difference for learning and memory. If you get "psyched up" about what you're learning, you have a much better chance of learning and remembering it. Even telling yourself that you want to learn and that you intend to remember what you're learning can increase your memory of it (Minninger, 1984; Howard, 2000).

> **CLASSIC QUOTE**
> *Education is not the filling of a pail, but the lighting of a fire.*
> —William Butler Yeats, Irish poet and playwright

Form Study Groups

Group learning is a natural, "brain compatible" form of learning. The human brain is biologically wired for interpersonal communication because social interaction and collaboration are critical to survival of the human species (Jensen, 1998). In fact, brain-imaging studies reveal that more activity occurs in thinking parts of the brain when people learn through social interaction than when they are learning alone or in isolation (Carter, 1998).

Research has shown that college students learn as much, or more, from peers than they do from instructors and textbooks (Astin, 1993; Pascarella, 2005). When seniors at Harvard University were interviewed, nearly every one of them who had been part of a study group considered this experience to be crucial to their academic progress and success (Light, 1990, 1992).

> **STUDENT PERSPECTIVE**
> "I learn best through teaching. When I learn something and teach it to someone else, I find that it really sticks with me a lot better."
> —College sophomore's response to the question: "How do you learn best?"

To fully capitalize and maximize the power of study groups, each member should study individually *before* studying in a group. Research on study groups indicates that they are effective only if each member has done required course work in advance of the group meeting—for example, if each group member has done the required readings and other course assignments (Light, 2001). All members should come prepared with specific information or answers to share with teammates as well as specific questions or points of confusion about which they hope to receive help from the team. This ensures that all group members are individually accountable or personally responsible for their own learning and for contributing to the learning of their teammates.

Forming a study group is an excellent learning strategy.

STUDENT PERSPECTIVE

"I would suggest students get to know [each] other and get together in groups to study or at least review class material. I find it is easier to ask your friends or classmates with whom you are comfortable with 'dumb' questions."

—Advice to first-year students from college sophomore (Walsh, 2005)

Personal Story

When I was in my senior year of college, I had to take a theory course by independent study because the course would not be offered again until after I planned to graduate. There was another senior who found himself in the same situation. Thus, the theory instructor allowed both of us to take this course together and agreed to meet with us every two weeks. My fellow student and I studied independently for the first two weeks. I prepared for the bi-weekly meeting by reading thoroughly, yet I had little understanding of what I had read. After our first meeting, I left with a strong desire to drop the course; however, I stayed with it. Over the next two weeks, I spent many sleepless nights trying to prepare for our next meeting and had feelings of angst about not being the brightest theory student in my class of two. During the next meeting with the instructor, I found out that the other student was also having difficulty. Not only did I notice this, but the instructor also noticed. After that meeting, the instructor gave us study questions and asked us to read separately and then get together to discuss the questions. During the next two weeks, my classmate and I met several times for some stimulating discussions on theory. By being able to communicate with each other about the issues we were studying, we both ended up gaining greater understanding. Our instructor was delighted to see that he was able to suggest a learning strategy that worked for both of us.

—Aaron Thompson

CLASSIC QUOTE

We are born for cooperation, as are the feet, the hands, the eyelids, and the upper and lower jaws.

—Marcus Aurelius, Roman Emperor, 161-180, A.D.

Pause for Reflection

Honestly rate yourself in terms of how frequently you use the following study strategies, according to the following scale:

4 = always, 3 = sometimes, 2 = rarely, 1 = never.

1. I block out all distracting sources of outside stimulation when I study. 4 3 2 1
2. I look for meaning in technical terms by looking at their prefix or suffix, or by looking up their word root in the dictionary. 4 3 2 1
3. I compare and contrast what I'm currently studying to what I've already learned. 4 3 2 1
4. I organize the information I'm studying into categories or classes. 4 3 2 1
5. I integrate or pull together information from my class notes and readings that relate to the same concept or general category. 4 3 2 1
6. I distribute or "spread out" my study time into several short sessions in advance of the exam and use my last study session before the test to review the information I previously studied. 4 3 2 1
7. I participate in study groups with my classmates. 4 3 2 1

••• Self-Reflection and Self-Monitoring

Rather than mindlessly going through the motions of learning, *deep* learning requires self-reflection. Effective learners reflect and check on themselves to see if they're really understanding what they're attempting to learn, monitoring their comprehension as they go along by asking themselves questions such as, "Am I following this?" "Do I really understand it?"

How do you know if you really know it? Probably the best answer to this question is: you know if you really know it and truly comprehend it when you find meaning in it—that is, when you can relate to it personally or can understand it in terms that make sense to you

(Ramsden, 2003). When you comprehend a concept, you've learned it at a deeper level than mere memorization; and when you comprehend it, you're more likely to remember it because learning that is deep is also more durable—it stays in long-term memory for a greater length of time (Kintsch, 1970).

Discussed below are some specific strategies for checking to see if you truly understand what you're learning. These can be used as indicators or checkpoints for determining whether you've moved beyond memorization to deeper understanding of what you're studying.

Comprehension Self-Monitoring Strategies

- Can you paraphrase what you're learning? Can you restate or translate it into your own words? When you can paraphrase what you're learning, you're able to describe it by completing the sentence that begins with the phrase, "In other words, ..." This is a good indication that you've moved beyond memorization to comprehension because you have transformed what you're learning into words that are meaningful to you. Even better than saying it in your own words is writing it in your own words, because this will reinforce your memory of it and give you a record of it for later review.

- Can you explain what you're learning to someone else who is unfamiliar with it? If you can explain to a friend what you've learned, this is a good sign that you've moved beyond memorization to comprehension because you are able to translate it into less technical language that someone hearing it for the first time can understand. Studies show that students gain deeper levels of understanding for what they're learning when they are asked to explain it to someone else (Chi, et al., 1994). Often, we don't realize how well we know or don't know something until we have to explain it to someone else who's never heard of it before (just ask any teacher). If you cannot find anyone to explain it to, then explain it aloud as if you were talking to an "imaginary friend."

- Can you think of an example of what you've learned? If you can provide an example or instance that is your own—not one that has already been given by your teacher or text—this is a good sign that you truly comprehend it because you're taking a general and abstract concept or principle and applying it to a specific and concrete experience. In fact, research indicates that when humans recall technical terms they have learned, they don't retrieve the definition first; instead, they retrieve an example or concrete instance of the term and use that example or instance to reconstruct the term's meaning (Norman, 1982; Tulving, 1985). This illustrates how important concrete examples are to understanding and retaining abstract concepts. (Have you ever noticed that when students are having trouble understanding something abstract or theoretical, they often ask their instructor: "Can you give me an example?")

- Can you represent or describe what you've learned in terms of an analogy or metaphor, which compares it to something else that has similar meaning or works in a similar way? Analogies and metaphors are basically ways of learning something new by understanding it in terms of something else that is similar and that we already understand. For instance, in this chapter we used the computer as a metaphor for the human brain to better understand learning and memory as a three-stage process. If you can use an analogy or metaphor to represent what you're learning, this is a good sign that you understand it at a deep level because you've built a mental bridge to connect what you're trying to understand to something that you already understand.

- Can you apply what you're learning to solve a particular problem that you've never encountered before? Perhaps the strongest sign of deep learning and comprehension is the ability to transfer something you've learned in one situation and apply it in a different context. Learning specialists sometimes refer to this mental process as "de-contextualization"—taking what has been learned in one context or situation and applying it to another (Bransford, Brown, & Cocking, 1999).

For instance, you know that you've really understood a mathematical concept when you can use that concept to solve math problems that are different than those which were used by your instructor or textbook to help you learn it in the first place. This is why it's unlikely that your math instructors will include on exams the exact same problems they solved in class or were solved in your textbook. They're not trying to trick you at test time; they're just trying to test your comprehension to determine if you've deeply learned the concept or principle, rather than simply memorized it. Similarly, if you took a course in human relations and learned the principles of conflict management, and you were later able to use those principles to settle a dispute between yourself and your roommate, this suggests you have deeply learned and understood those principles.

In fact, one of the key differences between deep learning and surface memorization is that when you've learned something deeply, you're able to continually put that learning to use in future situations that you have never encountered before (Anderson & Krathwohl, 2001). When you have simply memorized something, its future use is restricted to the same, exact situation in which you originally learned it.

> **CLASSIC QUOTE**
> "The habit of active utilization of well-understood principles is the final possession of wisdom."
> —Paul Ramsden, Chancellor of Teaching and Learning, University of Sydney (Australia)

Knowledge Awareness Strategies

Remain aware of the type of knowledge that you're trying to acquire and adjust your study strategy accordingly. Knowledge comes in different forms and involves different learning and memory systems. The key types of knowledge you will acquire in college usually fall into one of the following major categories.

Declarative (Semantic) Knowledge: knowing what is accurate or true and that you can "declare" or state it in words (e.g., factual information). Acquiring this type of knowledge requires studying that involves effective use of recitation or memory-improvement strategies, such as meaningful association, acrostics, or rhythm and rhyme.

Procedural (Skill) Knowledge: knowing how to do something, which usually involves procedures or skills that have multiple steps (e.g., solving math problems, conducting science experiments). Acquiring this type of knowledge requires repeated practice or rehearsal, such as practicing delivery of a speech or lines in a play. However, this repeated practice should be reflective practice, not mindless repetition. Although repetition is needed to develop certain skills, they are often developed more deeply and more rapidly if you reflect on and remain aware of the learning and thinking *process* that you are using while practicing.

> **CLASSIC QUOTE**
> "We learn to do neither by thinking nor by doing; we learn to do by thinking about what we are doing."
> —George Stoddard, former professor of psychology and education, University of Iowa

Studies show that students who consciously attend to their own thought processes when solving math and science problems become more effective problem solvers than those who just go through the motions (Resnick, 1986). For instance, expert problem-solvers ask themselves such questions as, "How did I go about solving this problem correctly?" "What were the key steps I took to arrive at the correct solution?" These are important questions to ask yourself while practicing any problem-solving skill, because you want to understand and recall the thought process behind the skill so you can use that successful thought process again in the future (e.g., on upcoming exams).

Episodic Knowledge: knowing where something is located—its place in space. The term episodic derives from "epi" meaning "on" or "at" and "odic" meaning "path." So, literally, it refers to knowing the specific place or space where something is located in relation to other things along the same path. For example, if you are taking a course in anatomy and you are trying to learn the location of each one of the internal organs of the body or each major part of the human brain, you are trying to acquire episodic knowledge. Acquiring this type of knowledge requires study strategies that make effective use of visual learning techniques, such as diagrams, concept maps, and visual imagery.

Pause for Reflection

Do you change or adjust your studying strategy, depending on the type of test you're going to take, or do you tend to study the same way for all tests?

> **CLASSIC QUOTE**
>
> *Each problem that I solved became a rule which served afterwards to solve other problems.*
>
> —René Descartes, seventeenth-century French philosopher and mathematician

Summary and Conclusion

We covered a lot of territory in this chapter, moving through all stages of the learning and memory process—from the very first stage of perceiving and receiving information through lectures and readings, to studying and storing information in the brain, and finally, to the stage of retrieving and recalling information.

The major principles and strategies associated with academic success at all stages in the learning and memory process are consistent with, and strongly reinforce, the four major bases of college success that we discussed in the first chapter of this text, namely: active involvement, self-reflection, social interaction/collaboration, and utilizing campus resources. These four bases can be used to summarize the most important learning and memory strategies that were discussed in this chapter.

Active Involvement

This principle of college success suggests that college students need to be active agents in the learning process (rather than passive sponges or spectators), and that academic success depends on the amount or degree of personal time, effort, and energy invested in learning. The importance of this principle emerged at the very start of this chapter when it was noted that deep learning involves active building of knowledge, whereby you shape and mold information to be learned into a form that has personal meaning for you. This importance of active involvement was also evident throughout all three key stages of the learning and memory process that were discussed in the chapter. First, active attention is needed for information to be perceived and received by your conscious brain. Second, information is saved in the brain through the investment of mental, physical, and emotional energy. Third, information is actively retrieved from the brain and brought back to consciousness when taking exams.

> **Remember:** We learn most effectively when we actively involve all our senses, and when we learn with passion and enthusiasm. In other words, learning becomes deeper and lasts longer when you put your "whole self" into it—your mind, your body, and your heart.

Self-Reflection

Deep learning not only requires action, it also requires reflection. Both mental processes are needed for learning to be complete. Active involvement is necessary for engaging our attention—which enables us to initially get information into our brain—and quiet reflection is necessary for consolidation—keeping that information in our brain, by locking it into our long-term memory. Rather than immediately jumping in and pounding in what we're trying to learn through mindless repetition, we need to take a pause for a worthy cause—to reflect and connect it with something that's already in our brain.

Reflection also involves awareness of ourselves as learners. We need to periodically pause and reflect on what is going on in our mind during different learning tasks. For instance, you should occasionally step back and think about whether you are actively listening to what your instructor is saying in class, and whether you are deeply understanding what you're studying outside of class. Also, you should occasionally step back and reflect on whether you are using learning strategies that are effective for the type of material you're studying and the type of test you'll be taking.

Said in another way, you want to be a self-regulated learner (Pintrich, 1995) who is self-aware and is in control of your own effort and attention, and who can regulate or adjust:

- *how* you learn to what you are learning—adjusting your study strategies to the type of subject you're studying and the type of test you're taking,
- *when* you are learning—adjusting your study time and timing, and
- *where* you are learning—adjusting your study situation or environment.

Social Interaction/Collaboration

One of the four key bases of college success is interpersonal interaction and collaboration. Learning is strengthened when it takes place in a social context that involves human interaction.

Your two primary sources for social interaction relating to your classes are your faculty instructors and your classmates. Student interaction with faculty is positively associated with improved academic performance and increased likelihood of completing a college degree (Astin, 1993; Tinto, 1993), so take advantage of opportunities to discuss course material with your instructors immediately after class and during their office hours. The educational benefit of interacting and collaborating with your peers is well supported by research (Johnson, Johnson, & Smith, 1991). As we noted earlier in this chapter, you can collaborate with your classmates at any stage of the learning and memory process. You can form:

- **note-taking teams** immediately after class by taking a few minutes to team up with a classmate to compare your notes for accuracy and completeness;
- **reading teams,** teaming up with classmates to compare your highlighting and margin notes;
- **study teams** to prepare for upcoming exams, and
- **test-results review teams** by collaborating with other classmates to review your results together, compare answers, and identify the sources of your mistakes.

Utilizing Campus Resources

The professionals who work in the Learning Resource or Academic Success Center on your campus have been professionally trained to help you learn "how to learn." These professionals are experts on the process of learning and can help you adjust or regulate your learning strategies to meet the demands of different courses and teaching styles. This Center provides learning support in multiple formats, including instructional videos, self-assessment instruments for assessing your personal learning habits, strategies or styles, and peer tutors—who can be especially effective teachers because they are developmentally closer to you in terms of their stage of intellectual development and level of communication (Vygotsky, 1978; Whitman, 1988).

Take full advantage of the multiple forms of support that your Learning Resource or Academic Success Center can offer you. Utilizing its services should strengthen your learning and elevate your grades.

Before you exit this chapter, we would like to remind you that the learning and memory strategies discussed here are more than just "study" skills or "academic" success skills; they are *life success* skills or *lifelong learning* skills that you can and will use throughout the remainder of your personal and professional life. For example, the skills of focusing attention and active listening are not only useful in the classroom, but in social relationships outside of class and throughout life; and note taking itself is a skill that you will continue to use throughout your career (e.g., during professional meetings and committee work).

Furthermore, these lifelong learning skills are probably more important today than at any other time in history because we are now living in an era characterized by rapid technological change and dramatic growth of knowledge. This information and communication explosion is creating a greater need for people to learn continuously throughout life and a higher demand for working professionals who are skilled learners—who have learned how to learn (Niles & Harris-Bowlsbey, 2002; Herman, 2000).

> ·—· **CLASSIC QUOTE** ·—·
>
> *In a world that is constantly changing, the most important skill to acquire now is learning how to learn.*
>
> —John Naisbitt, futurologist and author of *Megatrends: Ten New Directions Transforming Our Lives*

 Remember: Putting into practice the learning strategies discussed in this chapter will not only help you prepare for college tests, it will also help you prepare for lifelong learning.

••• Learning More through Independent Research

Web-Based Resources for Further Information on Strategic Learning

For additional information relating to the ideas discussed in this chapter, we recommend the following Web sites:

www.Dartmouth.edu/~acskills/success/index.html

www.utexas.edu/student/utlc/lrnres/handouts.html

www.muskingum.edu/~cal/database/general/

www2.gsu.edu/~wwwrld/Resources/helpfultips.htm

Name _____ Date _____

Self-Assessment of Learning Strategies and Habits

Look back at the ratings you gave yourself for effective note-taking strategies, reading strategies and studying strategies. Add up your total score for each of these three sets of learning strategies (maximum score for each set would be 28):

                Note Taking   _____

                Reading   _____

                Studying   _____

Total Learning Strategy Score = _____

SELF-ASSESSMENT QUESTIONS

1. In what learning strategy area did you score lowest?

2. Do you think that the strategy area in which you scored lowest has anything to do with your lowest course grade at this point in the term?

3. Of the seven specific strategies listed within the area that you scored lowest, which ones could you immediately put into practice to improve your lowest course grade?

4. What is the likelihood that you will put the above strategies into practice this term?

CASE STUDY

Too Fast, Too Frustrating: A Note-Taking Nightmare

Joanna Scribe is a first-year student who is majoring in journalism, and she's currently enrolled in an introductory course that is required for her major (Introduction to Mass Media). Her instructor for this course lectures at a very rapid rate and uses vocabulary words that go right over her head. Since she cannot get all the instructor's words down on paper and can't understand half the words she does manage to write down, she has become frustrated and has now stopped taking notes altogether. She wants to do well in this course because it's the first course in her major, but she's afraid she will fail it because her class notes are so pitiful.

Reflection and Discussion Questions

1. Can you relate to this case personally, or know any students who are in the same boat as Joanna?

2. What would you recommend that Joanna do at this point?

3. Why did you make the above recommendation?

Educational Planning and Decision Making

Making Wise Choices about Your College Courses and Major

Learning Goals

The primary goals of this chapter are to help you achieve a balance between academic exploration and commitment to a specific academic field, and develop a plan for making educational decisions that is best for attaining your personal and professional goals.

Outline

To Be or Not to Be Decided about a College Major: What Research Shows
When Should You Reach a Firm Decision about a College Major?
The Importance of Long-Range Educational Planning
Myths about the Relationship between Majors and Careers
    Myth 1: When You Choose Your Major, You're Choosing Your Career
    Myth 2: If You Want to Continue Your Education After College, You Must Continue in the Same Field As Your College Major
    Myth 3: To Work in a Business or Corporation, You Need to Major in Business or a Technical Field
    Myth 4: If You Major in a Liberal Arts Field, the Only Career Available to You is Teaching
    Myth 5: Having Specialized Skills is More Important for Career Success than Having General Skills
Making Decisions about a College Major
    Step 1: Gaining Self-Awareness
    Step 2: Awareness of Your Options
    Step 3: Awareness of the Options that Best Match Your Personal Abilities, Interests, and Values
    Strategies for Discovering a Compatible Major
Summary and Conclusion
Learning More through Independent Research
Exercises:
    Planning for a College Major
    Developing a Comprehensive, Long-Range Graduation Plan
Case Study: Whose Choice Is It Anyway?

Activate Your Thinking

Regarding your college major, are you decided or undecided? If you selected "undecided," please list any subjects that you would consider to be possibilities for a major:

If you selected "decided," note your choice here _____, and indicate how *sure* you are about that choice by circling one of the following options.

a. absolutely sure
b. fairly sure
c. not too sure
d. likely to change

113

••• To Be or Not to Be Decided about a College Major: What the Research Shows

Whether you have or have not decided on a major, here are some research findings related to student decisions about college majors that may be worth keeping in mind:

- Less than 10 percent of new college students feel they know a great deal about the field that they are intending to major in.
- As students proceed through the first year of college, they grow more uncertain about the major they chose when they began college.
- Over two-thirds of new students change their mind about their major during the first year of college.
- Only one in three college seniors eventually major in the same field that they chose during their first year of college (Cuseo, 2005).

These findings point to the conclusion that the vast majority of students entering college are truly undecided about a college major. They do not make a final decision about their major before starting college; instead, they reach a final decision during their college experience. Even if you think you're absolutely sure about a major, you will still need to explore specialized fields within your major to identify one that is most compatible with your personal interests, abilities, and values.

Thus, whether or not you have decided on a college major, you still need an action plan that will allow you to continue exploring and testing your options while you make steady progress toward a final decision. In other words, you need an action plan that allows you to strike a balance between exploration and commitment.

As a beginning college student, it is only natural to feel at least somewhat uncertain about your intended major because you have not yet experienced the variety of subjects or fields of study that make up the college curriculum. Being uncertain about a major is nothing to be embarrassed about. The term "undecided" or "undeclared" doesn't mean that you have somehow failed or are lost.

As a new student, you may be undecided for a variety of good reasons. For instance, you may be undecided simply because you have interests in a variety of subjects. This is actually a healthy form of indecision because it shows that you have a broad range of interests and a high level of motivation to learn about different subjects. You may also be undecided simply because you are a careful, reflective thinker whose decision-making style is to gather more information before making any long-term commitments. In one study of students who were undecided about a major when they started college, 43 percent had several ideas in mind but were not yet ready to commit to one of them (Gordon & Steele, 2003). These students were not "totally clueless"; instead, they had some ideas but still wanted to explore them and keep their options open, which is a very effective way to go about making decisions.

While it is true that decisions sometimes can be put off too long, resulting in procrastination, it is also true that they can be made too quickly, resulting in premature decisions that are reached without taking enough time to carefully think through all options. Judging from the large number of students who end up changing their minds about a college major, it is probably safe to say that more students make the mistake of reaching a decision about a major too quickly, rather than procrastinating about it indefinitely. This may be due to the fact that students hear the same question over and over again, even before they step a foot on a college campus: "What are you going to major in when you go to college?" You probably also saw this question on your college applications, and you are likely to hear it again during your first term

---

STUDENT PERSPECTIVE

"I see so many people switch [their] major like 4 or 5 times; they end up having to take loads of summer school just to catch up because they invest time and money in classes for a major that they end up not majoring in anyway."

—Advice to new students from a college sophomore (Walsh, 2005)

• — • CLASSIC QUOTE • — •

"All who wander are not lost."

—J. R. R. Tolkein, *Lord of the Rings*

in college. This is a prime time in your college experience for meeting new people, and when you meet them, almost immediately after they ask the typical opening question: "What's your name?", get ready for the typical follow-up question: "What's your major?" Also, if members of your family are helping you pay for the rising cost of a college education, they may frequently ask this same question—hoping you will have a definite answer to it—because paying for college becomes a little easier for them if they know you have a definite idea about what you're going to do while you're there (your major) and what you'll do with it after you leave (your career).

Despite any pressure you may be receiving from others to make an early decision, we encourage you not to officially commit to a particular major until you gain more self-knowledge and more knowledge of your options. Even if you think you're sure about your choice of major, before you make a commitment to it, take a course or two in the major to test it out.

"The best words of wisdom that I could give new freshmen is not to feel like you need to know what you want to major in right away. They should really use their first two years to explore all of the different classes available. They may find a hidden interest in something they never would have considered. I know this from personal experience."

—Advice to new students from a college sophomore (Walsh, 2005)

 Pause for Reflection

If you have chosen a major or are considering a particular major, what has led you to choose or consider this option?

Remember: Make sure that your *first* choice is your *best* choice—the one that is most compatible or consistent with your personal abilities and interests.

Studies show that students learn more when the material covered in their courses tends to match their personal interests and abilities (Cook, 1991; Dunn et al., 1995). Furthermore, research indicates that students are more likely to continue in college and graduate when they choose majors that reflect their personal interests (Leuwerke, et al., 2004).

In fact, it may be unrealistic for you, a first-term student, to make a final decision about a college major before you've had at least some experience with the courses that comprise the liberal arts curriculum. One key purpose of a liberal arts education is to help new students develop the critical thinking skills needed to make wise choices and well-informed decisions, such as choice of your college major. The liberal arts curriculum is also designed to introduce you to a variety of academic subjects, and as you progress through this curriculum, you may discover subjects that really captivate you and capture your interest. Some of these subjects may represent fields of study that you never experienced before, and all of them represent possible choices for a college major.

 CLASSIC QUOTE

Education is learning what you didn't even know you didn't know.

—Daniel J. Boorstin, renowned Jewish-American historian and prize-winning author

In addition to finding new fields of possible interest, as you gain experience with the college curriculum, you are likely to gain more self-knowledge about your academic strengths and weaknesses. This is important knowledge to take into consideration when choosing a major, because you want to select a field that builds on your academic abilities and talents.

••• When Should You Reach a Firm Decision about a College Major?

National surveys indicate that colleges and universities vary in terms of when they expect students to make a decision about their college major. Some institutions require or strongly en-

"I've decided to change my major."

courage first-year students to declare a major, some discourage or forbid it, and others leave it entirely up to the student (Policy Center on The First Year of College Year, 2003). If you have been pressured or forced to make an early decision, try to remain flexible and open to the possibility of changing your original choice. Changing decisions about a major is not necessarily a bad thing; it may represent your discovery of other academic fields that are more interesting to you or that are more compatible with your personal skills and abilities. Exercise your right to change your mind and don't lock yourself in a situation where you feel trapped or believe there is no turning back.

Naturally, there is a downside to changing majors—if you make the change late in your college experience. This can result in added time to graduation (and added tuition costs) because you may need to complete additional courses required for your newly chosen major.

Remember: As a general rule of thumb, you should reach a fairly firm decision about your major during your second (sophomore) year in college. However, in order to reach a good decision within this time frame, the process of exploring and planning should begin now—during your first term in college.

••• The Importance of Long-Range Educational Planning

Compared to high school, college will allow you more choices about what courses to enroll in and the choice of what field to specialize in. Your advisor's job, as the job title implies, is to "advise." Advisors are not academic dictators who tell you what to do; ultimately, you are in charge of making your own academic choices and decisions. Through advanced planning, you can actively take charge of your academic future, *making* it happen *for* you, rather than passively *letting* it happen *to* you. By looking ahead and developing a tentative plan for your courses beyond the first term of college, you're able to view your college experience as a full-length movie and get a sneak preview of the total picture. In contrast, scheduling your classes one term at a time just prior to each registration period (when everyone else is making a mad rush to get their advisor's signature for the following term's classes) forces you to view your academic experience as a series of separate snapshots that do not come together to form a big picture.

Furthermore, long-range educational planning enables you to take a proactive approach to your future. Being proactive means you are taking early, preventative action that anticipates your future before it sneaks up on you and forces you to react to it without enough time to plan and develop your best strategy. As the old saying goes, "If you fail to plan, you plan to fail."

Lastly, by doing some advanced educational planning, you reduce your anxiety about the future because you gain some control over it. To begin this process of advanced planning and gaining control of your educational future, you are strongly encouraged to complete the exercises at the end of this chapter. Remember that any long-range plan you develop is not set in stone—it can change—depending on changes in your academic interests and future plans. The purpose of long-range planning is not to lock you into a particular plan; instead, its purpose is to free you from shortsightedness, which if uncorrected, can lead to procrastination or denial.

Don't take the denial and avoidance approach to planning your educational future.

> **CLASSIC QUOTE**
>
> *Education is our passport to the future; for tomorrow belongs to the people who prepare for it today.*
>
> —Malcom X, African-American civil rights leader

⌇Pause for Reflection

Choosing a major is a life-changing decision because it will determine what you do for the rest of your life.

Would you agree or disagree with the above statement? Why?

••• Myths about the Relationship between Majors and Careers

Good decisions are informed decisions that are based on accurate information, rather than misconceptions or myths. Since there is a relationship between majors and careers, to be able to plan effectively for a college major, you first need to have an accurate understanding of this relationship. Described below are some common myths about the relationship between majors and careers that can lead to uninformed or unrealistic choices of a college major.

Myth 1: When You Choose Your Major, You're Choosing Your Career

While some majors lead directly to a particular career, most do not. Those majors that do lead directly to specific careers are often called pre-professional majors, which include such fields as accounting, engineering, and nursing. However, the vast majority of college majors do not channel you directly down one particular career path. Instead, they leave you with a variety of career options. The career path of most college graduates is not like walking a straight line directly from your major to your career. For instance, all physics majors do not become physicists, all philosophy majors do not become philosophers, all history majors do not become historians, and all English majors do not become Englishmen (or Englishwomen). The trip from your college experience to your eventual career(s) is more like climbing a tree. As illustrated in Figure 1, you begin with the tree's trunk (the foundation of liberal arts), which grows into separate limbs (choices for college majors), which in turn, lead to different branches (different career paths or options).

Figure 1 The Relationship between General Education (Liberal Arts), College Majors, and Careers

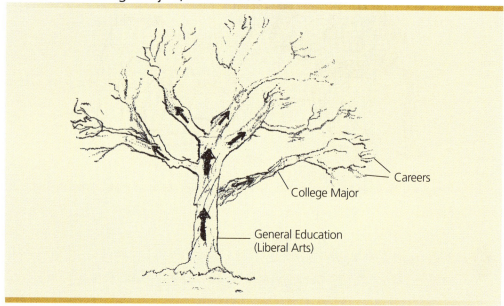

Note that the career branches grow from the same major limb, so typically a particular major will lead to a "family" of related careers. For example, an English major will often lead to careers that involve use of the written language (e.g., editing, journalism, publishing), while a major in art will often lead to careers that involve use of visual media (e.g., illustration, graphic design, art therapy). The Web site, MyMajors.com, provides useful information on what groups or families of jobs tend to be related to different majors.

Furthermore, different majors can lead to the same career. For instance, many different majors can lead a student to law school and to an eventual career as a lawyer, because there really is no law or pre-law major. Similarly, there really is no pre-med major. Students interested in going to medical school after college typically major in some field in the natural sciences (e.g., biology or chemistry); however, it is possible for students to go to medical school with majors in other fields, particularly if they take and do well in certain science courses that are emphasized in medical school (e.g., general biology, general chemistry, organic and inorganic chemistry).

Your major does not equal your career (major ≠ career), nor does it automatically turn into your career (major → career), but this is why some students may procrastinate about choosing a major; they think they are making a lifelong decision. They are afraid that if they make the "wrong" one, then they will be stuck doing something they hate for the rest of their lives. The key point we are making here is that the relationship between most majors and careers is not a direct, one-to-one relationship.

STUDENT PERSPECTIVE

"Things like picking majors and careers really scare me a lot! I don't know exactly what I want to do with my life."

—First-year student

 Remember: Do not assume that choosing your college major means that you're choosing what you will do for a living for the remainder of your working life.

Research on college graduates indicates that they change careers numerous times, and the further they continue along their career path, the more likely they are to work in a field that is unrelated to their college major (Millard, 2004). While this may seem hard to believe, remember that the liberal arts curriculum is a significant part of your college education and exposes you to different subjects, promotes your development of key skills (e.g., writing, speaking, organizing), and serves to qualify you for a number of different careers—regardless of what your particular major happens to be.

> **Remember:** Deciding on a major and deciding on a career are typically different decisions that are made at different times.

The order in which decisions about majors and careers are covered in this book reflects the order that they are made in life. First, you make a decision about your major, and later, you make a decision about your career. Although it is important to think about the relationship between your choice of major and your choice of career(s), these are different choices that are made at different times. Both choices do relate to your future goals, but they involve different timeframes: Choosing your major is a short-range goal, whereas choosing your career is a long-range goal.

Myth 2: If You Want to Continue Your Education After College, You Must Continue in the Same Field as Your College Major

After college graduation, you have two main options or alternative paths available to you:

1. You can enter a career immediately, or
2. You can continue your education in graduate school or professional school. (See Figure 2 for a visual map of the signposts or stages in the college experience and the basic paths available to you after college graduation.)

Although this man holds an MBA, he did not major in business as an undergraduate.

Once you complete your bachelor's degree, you can continue your education in the same field as your college major, or in a field that is different than your college major. This is particularly true for students majoring in fields that do not lead directly to a particular career after graduation (Pascarella & Terenzini, 2005). For example, if you major in English, you can still go to graduate school in a subject other than English, or go to law school, or get a master's degree in business administration. In fact, it is common to find that the majority of graduate students in master's of business administration (MBA) programs were not business majors in college (Dupuy & Vance, 1996).

Reflecting back on the timeline above:

1. *Do you see yourself completing your bachelor's degree in* four years?

2. *What do you think will help you the most to stay* on track *and finish your degree in four years?*

3. *Do you see any possible* interfering *factors or potential* obstacles *that might* prolong *the time you need to complete your degree?*

Figure 2 Timeline to the Future: A Snapshot of the College Experience and Beyond

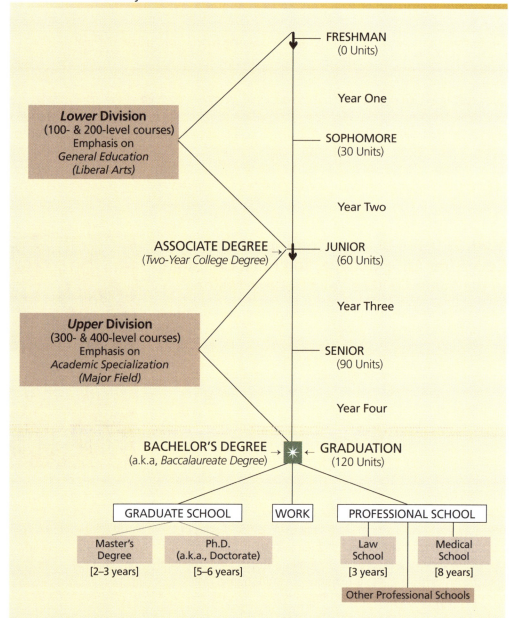

Notes:
1. The total number of *general education* units and the total number of units needed to *graduate* with a bachelor's degree may vary somewhat from school to school. Also, the total number of units required for a *major* will vary somewhat from major to major and from school to school.
2. It often takes college students longer than four years to graduate due to a variety of reasons, such as working part-time and taking fewer courses per term, needing to repeat courses that were failed or dropped, or making a late change to a different major and needing to fulfill additional requirements for the new major.
3. *Graduate* and *professional* schools are options for continuing to higher levels of education after completion of an undergraduate (college) education.
4. Compared to graduate school, *professional* school involves advanced education in more "applied" professions (e.g., pharmacy or public administration).

Myth 3: To Work in a Business or Corporation, You Need to Major in Business or a Technical Field

The former director of a national college-placement bureau puts it this way: "Employers are far more interested in the prospect's ability to think and to think clearly, to write and speak well, and how he works with others than in his major or the name of the school he went to. Several college investigating teams found that these were the qualities on which all kinds of employers, government and private, base their decisions" (Pope, 1990, p. 213). So, do not restrict your range of choices for a major by believing in the myth that you must major in business to work for a business after graduation. Research shows that in the long run, the career mobility and career advancement of non-business majors in the business world are equal to those attained by business majors (Pascarella & Terenzini, 1991, 2005).

Myth 4: If You Major in a Liberal Arts Field, the Only Career Available to You Is Teaching

Liberal arts majors enter and advance in careers other than teaching. There are many college graduates with majors in liberal arts fields who have proceeded to, and succeeded in, careers other than teaching. Among these graduates are such notable people as:

- Jill Barad (English major), CEO, Mattel Toys
- Steve Case (political science major), CEO, America Online
- Brian Lamb (speech major), CEO, C-Span
- Willie Brown (liberal studies major), Mayor, San Francisco

(Source: Indiana University, 2004).

In fact, studies show that students in liberal arts majors are just as likely to advance to the highest levels of corporate leadership as majors in pre-professional fields, such as business and engineering (Pascarella & Terenzini, 2005). If you are considering a major in a liberal arts field, you should not be dismayed or discouraged by those who may question your choice by asking: "What are you going to do with a degree in *that* major?"

(A good career-information Web site for liberal arts majors can be found at: www.eace.org/networks/liberalarts.html)

Myth 5: Having Specialized Skills Is More Important for Career Success than Having General Skills

You may find that liberal arts courses are sometimes viewed by students as unnecessary requirements, which they have to get out of the way before they can get into what is really important—their major or academic specialization. A liberal arts education develops very practical, durable, and transferable skills that provide a strong foundation for success in any major or any career.

Also, don't forget that the general skills and qualities developed by the liberal arts serve to increase career mobility (your ability to move into different career paths) and career advancement (your ability to move up the career ladder). While specific, technical skills may be important for getting into a career, the general, professional skills are more important for moving up the career ladder. The courses you take as part of your liberal arts education will prepare you for your advanced career positions, not just your first one (Boyer, 1987; Miller, 2003). Furthermore, general professional skills will grow even more important for college graduates who enter the workforce in the twenty-first century because the demand for upper-level positions that

STUDENT PERSPECTIVE

"They asked me during my interview why I was right for the job and I told them because I can read well, write well and I can think. They really liked that because those were the skills they were looking for."

—English major hired by a public relations firm (Source: Los Angeles Times, April 4, 2004)

involve management and leadership will exceed the supply of workers available to fill these positions (Herman, 2000).

Pause for Reflection
How do you think your general education courses will strengthen your performance in your chosen major?

Making Decisions about a College Major

Reaching an effective decision about a college major involves three steps:

1. Gaining awareness of yourself—your personal abilities, interests, and values;
2. Becoming aware of your options—the academic fields that are available to you as choices for a college major; and
3. Developing awareness of what options best match your personal abilities, interests, and values.

Strategies relating to each of these steps in the decision-making process for selecting a college major are discussed below.

Step 1: Gaining Self-Awareness

This is a critical first step in making decisions about a college major, or any other important decision. You must know yourself before you can know what choice is best for you. While this may seem obvious, self-awareness and self-discovery are often overlooked aspects of the decision-making process. Being true to yourself is the first and foremost step when choosing a major or making any other important choice.

"Know thyself" is the most frequently cited purpose of a liberal arts education. The wide range of courses that you will experience in the liberal arts curriculum will help you become more deeply aware of different dimensions of yourself. However, you can begin to deepen your self-awareness right now by engaging in some introspection. No one is in a better position to know who you are, and what you want, than *you*. One of the most effective ways to access information about yourself is through effective self-questioning—asking yourself key questions that trigger deep thinking about who you are and what matters most to you. Effective self-questioning launches you on a quest that leads to valuable personal insights and self-discoveries. When your goal is self-awareness for the purpose of choosing a college major that best fits you, good questions are those that increase self-awareness of your:

- interests—what you like doing,
- abilities—what you're good at doing, and
- values—what you feel good about doing.

Select one question from each of the following three categories that you can relate best to, or which brings to mind the most ideas about yourself. Record your ideas in the space provided

CLASSIC QUOTE

In order to succeed, you must know what you are doing, like what you are doing, and believe in what you are doing.

—Will Rogers, American actor and humorist

at the end of each category. When thinking about your answers to these questions, consider all areas of your life—home, school, jobs, volunteer experiences, athletics, hobbies, etc.

Personal Interests

1. What do you really enjoy doing and tend to do as often as you possibly can?
2. What do you look forward to or get excited about?
3. What tends to grab your attention and hold it for long periods of time?
4. What sorts of things are you naturally curious about or do you tend to seek more information about?
5. What are your favorite hobbies or pastimes?
6. When you're with your friends, what do you like to talk about or do together?
7. What has been your most stimulating or enjoyable learning experience?
8. If you've had previous work or volunteer experience, what jobs or tasks did you most enjoy doing?
9. What do you like to read about?
10. When you open a newspaper, what do you tend to read first?
11. When time seems to "fly by," what are you usually doing?
12. If you daydream about your future, does it tend to be about anything in particular?

Pause for Reflection
Choose one of the above questions relating to your personal interests, and record your response to it in the space below.

Personal Abilities

1. What comes easily or naturally to you?
2. What would you say is your greatest gift or talent?
3. What do you really excel at when you apply yourself and put forth your best effort?
4. What are your most advanced or well-developed skills?
5. What would you say has been the greatest accomplishment or achievement in your life thus far?
6. What about yourself are you most proud of, or take most pride in doing?
7. Do you notice people coming to you for advice or assistance with anything? (If yes, what do they usually come to you for advice or help with?)
8. What would your best friend(s) say is your most positive quality?
9. What have you had the most success doing?
10. What has been your most successful learning experience?
11. In what types of courses do you tend to earn the highest grades?
12. If you have received any special awards or other forms of recognition, what have they been for?

◆ Pause for Reflection

Choose one of the above questions relating to your personal abilities, and record your response to it in the space below.

_____

_____

> **CLASSIC QUOTE**
>
> *Never desert your line of talent. Be what nature intended you for and you will succeed.*
>
> —Sydney Smith, 18th-century English writer, and defender of the oppressed

Personal Values

1. What do you really care about?
2. What would be one thing that you really stand for or believe in?
3. What would you say are your highest priorities in life?
4. What makes you feel good about yourself when you're doing it?
5. If there was one thing in the world you could change, or could make a difference in, what would it be?
6. When you have extra spending money, what do you usually spend it on?
7. When you have free time, what do you usually find yourself doing?
8. What does living a "good life" mean to you?
9. How would you define success?
10. Do you have any heroes or anyone you admire, look up to, or feel has set an example worth following? (If you do, why do you admire this person?)
11. Would you rather be thought of as:
    a. smart,
    b. wealthy,
    c. creative, or
    d. caring?

    (Rank from 1 to 4, with 1 being the highest)
12. What would you say is your strongest conviction or commitment?

> **CLASSIC QUOTE**
>
> *Do what you value; value what you do.*
>
> Sidney Simon, author, *Values Clarification* and *In Search of Values*

◆ Pause for Reflection

Choose one of the above questions relating to your personal values, and record your response to it in the space below.

_____

_____

> **CLASSIC QUOTE**
>
> *If you do not live the life you believe, you will believe the life you live.*
>
> —Anonymous

Multiple Intelligences: A Tool for Identifying Your Personal Abilities and Talents

Intelligence was once considered to be a single, general intellectual trait that could be detected and measured by an IQ (Intelligence Quotient) test. Now the singular word "intelligence" has been replaced by the plural word "intelligence*s*" because humans can display intelligence or mental ability in many forms other than just their intellectual performance on an IQ test.

Listed in Box 1 are different forms of intelligence that have been identified by Howard Gardner (1983; 1993), based on his studies of gifted and talented individuals, experts in different lines of work, and a variety of other sources. As you read through these different types of intelligence, think about which types seem to best reflect your personal talents or abilities. (You can possess more than one type.) Keep your type(s) of intelligence in mind when you are deciding on a college major. Ideally, you want to select a major that most closely taps into and builds on your strongest skills or talents. Choosing a major that is compatible with your strongest abilities may enable you to master the concepts and skills required by your major more easily, rapidly, and deeply, as well as strengthen your academic self-esteem.

Multiple Forms of Intelligence

1. *Linguistic* Intelligence: ability to communicate through words or language. For example: verbal skills in the areas of speaking, writing, listening, or reading.
2. *Logical-Mathematical* Intelligence: ability to reason logically and succeed in tasks that involve mathematical problem-solving. For example, skill for making logical arguments and following logical reasoning or the ability to think effectively with numbers and make quantitative calculations.
3. *Spatial* Intelligence: ability to visualize relationships among objects arranged in different spatial positions and the ability to perceive or create visual images. For example, forming mental images of three-dimensional objects; detecting detail in objects or drawings; artistic talent for drawing, painting, sculpting, or graphic design; or skills related to sense of direction and navigation.
4. *Musical* Intelligence: ability to appreciate or create rhythmical and melodic sounds. For example, playing, writing, or arranging music.
5. *Interpersonal (Social)* Intelligence: ability to relate to others, to accurately identify others' needs, feelings, or emotional states of mind; or ability to effectively express emotions and feelings to others. For example: skills involving interpersonal communication and emotional expression; ability to accurately "read" the feelings of others, or to meet the emotional needs of others.
6. *Intrapersonal (Self)* Intelligence: ability to self-reflect, become aware of, and understand one's own thoughts, feelings, and behavior. For example: capacity for personal reflection, emotional self-awareness, and self-insight into personal strengths and weaknesses.
7. *Bodily-Kinesthetic (Psychomotor)* Intelligence: ability to use one's own body skillfully and to acquire knowledge through bodily sensations or movements. For example: skilled at tasks involving physical coordination; ability to work well with hands; mechanical skills; talent for building models and assembling things; or skills relating to technology.
8. *Naturalist* Intelligence: ability to carefully observe and appreciate features of the natural environment. For example: keen awareness of nature or natural surroundings; ability to understand causes or results of events occurring in the natural world.

Source: Howard Gardner (1993). *Frames of Mind: The theory of multiple intelligences* (2nd ed.)

Learning Styles: A Tool for Identifying Your Personal Interests and Learning Preferences

In contrast to multiple intelligences, learning styles refers to differences in learning preferences, or different ways in which individuals prefer to perceive information (receive or take it in) and process information (deal with it after taking it in). For instance, different individuals may prefer to take-in information by reading about it, listening to it, seeing an image or diagram of it, or physically touching and manipulating it. Individuals may also vary in terms of whether they like to receive information in a form that is very structured and orderly, or in an unstructured form that allows them the freedom to explore, play with, and restructure it in their own way. After information has been received, individuals may also differ in terms of how they prefer to process or deal with it. For instance, some might like to think about it on their own, while others may prefer to talk about it with someone else, make an outline of it, or draw a picture of it.

> *Personal Story*
>
> In my family, whenever there's something that needs to be assembled or set-up (e.g., a ping-pong table or new electronic equipment), I've noticed that my wife, my son, and myself have different learning styles in terms of how we go about doing it. I like to read the manual's instructions carefully and completely before I even attempt to touch anything. My son prefers to look at the pictures or diagrams in the manual and uses them as models to find parts; then he begins to assemble those parts. My wife seems to prefer not to look at the manual at all! Instead, she prefers to figure things out as she goes along by grabbing different parts from the box and trying to assemble parts that look like they should fit together—like piecing together pieces of a jigsaw puzzle.
>
> —Joe Cuseo

There are specially designed tests that you can take to assess your particular learning style and how it compares with others. If you're interested in taking a learning styles test, the Learning Center or Career Center are the two most likely sites on campus where you can take one. Perhaps the most frequently used learning styles test is the *Myers-Briggs Type Indicator (MBTI)* (Myers, 1976; Myers & McCaulley, 1985), which is based on the personality theory of psychologist Carl Jung. It consists of four dimensions, each of which has a pair of opposite traits or preferences, along which people vary on a scale or continuum (lower to higher). The four dimensions and opposite traits are illustrated in Figure 3.

Pause for Reflection

As you read the following scales, place a mark along the line where you think you fall with respect to these traits. For example, place a mark in the middle of the line if you think you are midway between these opposite traits, or place a mark at the far left or far right if you think you lean very strongly toward the trait listed on either end.

Figure 3 Traits and Learning Styles Measured by the Myers-Briggs Type Indicator (MBTI)

Extraversion	*Introversion*
Prefer to focus on "outer" world of persons, actions, or objects	Prefer to focus on "inner" world of thoughts and ideas
Sensing	*Intuition*
Prefer interacting with the world directly through concrete, sensory experiences	Prefer dealing with symbolic meanings and imagining possibilities
Thinking	*Feeling*
Prefer to rely on logic and rational thinking when making decisions	Prefer to rely on human needs and feelings when making decisions
Judging	*Perceiving*
Prefer to plan for and control events	Prefer flexibility and spontaneity

Figure 4 Students With Each MBTI Learning Style Have a Preferred Style of Writing

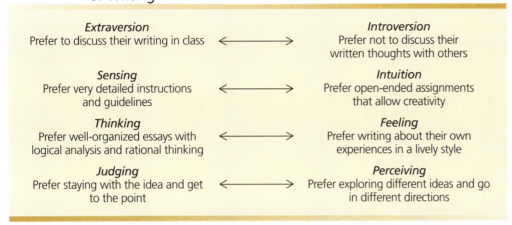

In one study, it was found that college students who score differently on the MBTI have different learning styles when it comes to the style of writing and type of writing assignments they prefer (Jensen & Ti Tiberio, as cited in Bean, 2001). See Figure 4 for the details on the findings.

These research findings clearly indicate that students have different learning styles, which in turn influence the type of writing assignments they feel most comfortable doing. This may be important to keep in mind when choosing your major because different academic fields emphasize different styles of writing. Some fields place heavy emphasis on writing that is structured and tightly focused (e.g., science and business), while other fields encourage writing with personal style, flair, or creativity (e.g., English and art). How your writing style meshes with the style emphasized by different academic fields may be one key factor to consider when making decisions about your college major.

Another popular learning styles test that may be available on your campus is the *Learning Styles Inventory (LSI)* (Dunn, Dunn, & Price, 1990), which was originally developed by David Kolb, a professor of philosophy (Kolb, 1976; 1985). It is based on how individuals differ with respect to the following two key elements of the learning process:

How Information Is *Perceived* (Taken in)

Concrete Experience
Learning through direct involvement or personal experience

Reflective Observation
Learning by watching or observing

How Information Is *Processed* (Dealt with after it has been taken in)

Abstract Conceptualization
Learning by thinking about things and drawing logical conclusions

Active Experimentation
Learning by taking chances and trying things

When these two dimensions are crisscrossed to form intersecting lines, four sectors (areas) are created, each of which represents a different learning style, as illustrated in Pause for Reflection. As you look at the four styles in Figure 5, circle the style that you think reflects your most preferred way of learning.

Figure Learning Styles Measured by the *Learning Styles Inventory (LSI)*

Concrete Experience

Accommodators
Prefer to learn through trial-and-error, hands-on experience; act on gut feelings; get things done; and rely on or accommodate the ideas of others.

Divergers
Prefer to observe, rather than act; generate many creative or imaginative ideas; view things from different perspectives; and pursue broad cultural interests.

Active Experimentation — *Reflective Observation*

Convergers
Prefer to use logical thinking to focus on solutions to practical problems and to deal with technical tasks rather than interpersonal issues.

Assimilators
Prefer to collect and evaluate lots of information, then systematically organize it into theories or conceptual models; prefer to deal with abstract ideas rather than people.

Abstract Conceptualization

People working in the medical field are most often found to be convergent thinkers.

Research indicates that students majoring in different fields tend to display differences in these four learning styles (Svinicki & Dixon, 1987). For instance, "assimilators" are more frequently found majoring in mathematics and natural sciences (e.g., chemistry and physics), probably because these subjects stress reflection and abstract thinking. In contrast, academic fields where "accommodators" tend to be more commonly found are business, accounting, and law, perhaps because these fields involve taking practical action and making concrete decisions. "Divergers" are more often attracted to majors in the fine arts (e.g., music, art, drama), humanities (e.g., history, literature) or social sciences (psychology, political science), possibly because these fields emphasize different viewpoints and multiple perspectives. In contrast, "convergers" are more likely found in fields like engineering, medicine, and nursing, probably because these fields focus on finding specific solutions to practical and technical problems (Kolb, 1976). This same clustering of fields took place when faculty were asked to classify different academic fields in terms of what learning styles they emphasized (Biglan, 1973; Carnegie Commission on Higher Education, cited in Svinicki & Dixon, 1987).

The Engineering and Humanities majors settle their differences in the Fine Arts quad!

Personal Story

The first time I noticed that students in different academic fields may have different learning styles occurred when I was teaching a psychology course that was required for students majoring in nursing and social work. I noticed that some students in class seemed to lose interest (and patience) when we got involved in lengthy class discussions about controversial issues or theories, while others seemed to love it. On the other hand, whenever I lectured or delivered information for an extended period of time, some students seemed to lose interest (and attention), while others seemed to get "into it" and took great notes. After one class period that involved quite a bit of class discussion, I began thinking about who the students were that seemed most involved in the discussion and who seemed to drift off or lose interest. I suddenly realized that the students who did most of the talking and seemed most enthused during the class discussion were the students majoring in social work. On the other hand, most of the students who appeared disinterested or a bit frustrated were the nursing majors.

When I began to think about why this happened, it dawned on me that the nursing students were accustomed to gathering factual information and learning very practical skills in their major courses, and that was the learning style they were expecting to use in my psychology course. The nursing majors felt more comfortable with structured class sessions in which they received lots of factual, practical information from the professor. On the other hand, the social work majors were more comfortable with unstructured class discussions because courses in their major often emphasized debating about social issues and hearing different viewpoints or perspectives.

I left class that day with the following question on my mind: Did nursing majors and social work majors select their major because the style of learning it emphasized tended to "match" their preferred learning style?

–Joe Cuseo

CLASSIC QUOTE

Minds differ still more than faces.

—Voltaire, 18th-century French philosopher, historian, and poet

The point we're making here is that students do have different learning styles, and academic fields do emphasize different styles of learning. Thus, if you are thinking about majoring in a particular field, it is important to consider how your learning style matches up with the style of learning emphasized by that field. If the match seems to be close or compatible, then the "marriage" between you and that major could be one that leads to a satisfying or enjoyable learning experience.

We recommend taking a trip to the Learning Center or Career Center on your campus, where you can take a test designed to assess your learning style. Even if the test doesn't help you choose a particular major, it will at least help you become more aware of your particular learning style. This alone could contribute to your academic success because studies show that just becoming more self-aware of your learning style can improve your academic performance in college courses (Claxton & Murrell, 1988).

Pause for Reflection

In addition to taking formal tests to assess your learning style, you can gain some awareness of your learning styles or preferences through some simple introspection or self-examination. Please take a moment to complete the following sentences that are designed to stimulate some awareness of your learning style:

I learn best if. . . .

I learn most from. . . .

I enjoy learning when. . . .

The most important factor to consider when reaching decisions about a major is whether it is compatible with four key characteristics of your "self": your *learning style*, your personal *abilities*, your personal *interests*, and your personal *values* (Figure 6). These are the four pillars that provide the foundation for effective decisions about a college major.

Figure 6 Personal Characteristics that Provide an Effective Foundation for Choice of a College Major

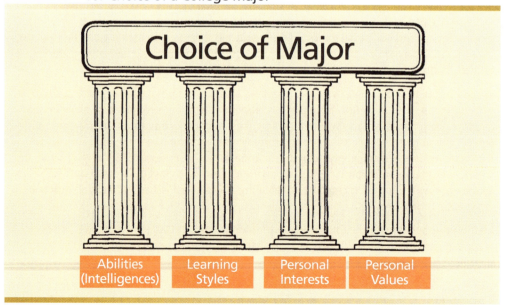

Chapter 4: Educational Planning and Decision Making

Step 2: Awareness of Your Options (the academic subjects available to you as choices for a college major)

The second critical step in any effective decision-making process is to gain awareness of the options available to you as possible majors. Here again, your trip through the liberal arts will help you take this step. These courses help you examine yourself and gain greater self-awareness. Your trip through the liberal arts curriculum may result in discovery of new personal interests and new possibilities for majors, some of which may be in fields that you didn't even know existed.

Also, your exposure to a wide range of subjects in the liberal arts curriculum will provide you with a general context for making an intelligent selection of your specific major. This will enable you to understand how your particular major fits into the bigger picture.

Lastly, experiencing these different fields of study may lead you to discover a second field of interest, which you could pursue as a *minor* to complement your major. (More details about college minors are contained later in this chapter.)

Before moving on to Step 3 in the decision-making process, be sure you have taken the first two steps: Knowing yourself (step 1) and knowing your options (step 2) should take place before making a firm decision and final commitment.

Step 3: Awareness of the Options that Best Match Your Personal Abilities, Interests, and Values

This is the final step in our three-step process for making decisions about a college major. When linked together, these three steps form the following chain of explorations and discoveries:

1. Exploring and discovering your personal abilities, interests, and values;
2. Exploring and discovering your range of options for a college major;
3. Exploring and discovering what college major best matches your personal abilities, interests, and values.

In the following section, we identify some key strategies for completing the last step in this process.

Strategies for Discovering a Compatible Major

If you are currently undecided about a major, this is perfectly fine because you are at the earliest stage of your college experience. Although you are postponing your decision about a major, this does not mean you are postponing the process of exploring and planning for your major. You shouldn't put all thoughts about your major on the back burner and drift until the time comes when a choice must be made. Now is the time to start the process of exploring and developing a game plan that will lead you to a good decision about your major.

Similarly, if you have already chosen a major, this doesn't mean that you'll never have to give any more thought to the decision you've made, and that you can just shift into cruise control and go along for a thought-free ride in the major you've chosen. Instead, you should continue the exploration process while you carefully test drive your first choice, making sure it's the choice that best fits your abilities, interests, and values. In other words, you should adopt a strategy that enables you to either verify or modify your first decision.

> **CLASSIC QUOTE**
>
> *When you have to make a choice and don't make it, that is in itself a choice.*
>
> —William James, American philosopher and psychologist

When exploring majors, consider using the following specific strategies.

- Think about what subjects you've been successful at in high school and during your first year of college.

    As the old saying goes, "Nothing succeeds like success itself." If you have done well, and continue to do well in a certain field of study, this may indicate that your mental skills and learning style correspond well with the academic skills required by that particular field. This could spell future success and satisfaction in that field if you decide to pursue it as your college major.

    You can enter information about your learning experiences with high school courses at a Web site (e.g., MyMajors.com), which will analyze this information and provide you with several majors that may be a good match for you, based on your academic experiences in high school.

- Use your elective courses to test your interests and abilities in subjects that you are considering as a major.

    As its name implies, elective courses are those that you elect or choose to take. In college, electives come in two forms: free electives and restricted electives.

    Free electives are courses that you may elect to enroll in, if you choose to, which count toward your college degree but are not required for either general education or your major.

    Restricted electives are courses that you must take, but you choose them from a restricted list of possible courses that have been specified by your college as fulfilling a requirement in general education or your major. For example, your school may have a general education requirement in the area of Social or Behavioral Sciences that requires you to take two courses in this area, but you are allowed to choose them from a menu of different subjects, such as anthropology, economics, political science, psychology, or sociology. If you are considering one of these subjects as a possible major, you can take an introductory course in this subject and test your interest in it, while simultaneously fulfilling a general education requirement needed for graduation. In addition to using your restricted electives in this way, you can use your free electives to select courses in fields that you are considering as possible majors. By using some of your free and restricted electives in this manner, you can test your interest and ability in these fields, and if you find one that is a good match, you may have found yourself a major.

    Naturally, you don't have to use all your electives in this fashion. Depending on your major, you may have as many as 40 units (credits) of elective courses in college. This leaves you with a great deal of freedom to shape your college experience in a way that best meets your personal needs and interests. For suggestions on how to make the best use of your free electives, see Box 2.

- Be sure you know the specific courses that are required for the major you're considering.

    In college, it is expected that students know the specific requirements for the major they have chosen, and these requirements can vary considerably from one major to another. Be sure to review your college catalog carefully to determine what specific courses are required for the major you are considering. If you have trouble tracking the requirements in your college catalog, don't become frustrated. These catalogs are often written in a very technical manner that can sometimes be difficult to follow or interpret. If you need help identifying or understanding the requirements for a major that you're considering, don't be embarrassed about seeking assistance from a professional in your school's Academic Advisement Center.

TAKE ACTION NOW! — Box 2

Top-Ten Suggestions for Making the Most of Your College Electives

Your elective courses in college will give you some degree of academic freedom and personal control of your college coursework. You can exercise this freedom of choice by strategically selecting your electives in a way that will enable you to get the most out of your college experience and degree.

As you read these 10 suggestions, select two that represent your top-two strategies for using your electives. In the space below this box, write a short explanation about why you chose each of these strategies.

Use Your Electives to:

1. Complete a minor or build an area of concentration that will complement and strengthen your major, or that will allow you to pursue another field of interest in addition to your major.

2. Help you make a career choice.
   Just as you can use electives to help you choose a college major, you can use them to help you choose a career. For instance, you could enroll in
   - career planning or career development courses,
   - courses that involve internships or service learning experiences, or an independent study course that allows you to study a career that you are considering.

3. Strengthen your skills in areas that may appeal to future employers.
   For example, courses in leadership development, foreign language, or argumentation and debate are educational experiences that may be attractive to future employers and may improve your employment prospects.

4. Help you develop practical life skills that you can use now or in the near future.
   For instance, you might take courses in managing personal finances, marriage and family, or child development to help you manage your money and your future family.

5. Seek personal balance and develop yourself as a whole person.
   You can use your electives strategically to cover all the key dimensions of self-development. For instance, you could take courses that promote your *emotional* development (e.g., stress management), *social* development (e.g., interpersonal relationships), *mental* development (e.g., critical thinking), *physical* development (e.g., nutrition, self-defense), and *spiritual* development (e.g., world religions; death and dying).

Remember: Choose college courses that will not only contribute to your major and career, but also to your quality of life.

6. Make connections across different subjects and academic disciplines.
   Courses that are specifically designed to connect or integrate two or more academic disciplines are typically referred to as interdisciplinary courses. For example, psychobiology is an interdisciplinary course that combines or integrates the fields of psychology (focusing on the mind) and biology (focusing on the body), thus enabling you to see how the mind influences the body and vice versa. Making connections across different subjects and seeing how they can be combined to provide a more complete understanding of a subject or issue can be a stimulating experience. Furthermore, the presence of interdisciplinary courses on your college transcript may also be attractive to future employers.

7. Help you develop broader perspectives on life and the world in which we live.
   You can take courses that progressively widen your perspective. For example, you could strategically select courses that provide you with a *societal* perspective (e.g., sociology), a *national* perspective (e.g., political science), an *international* perspective (e.g., cultural geography), or a *global* perspective (e.g., ecology). These broadening perspectives serve to widen your scope of knowledge and deepen your understanding of the world.

8. Appreciate different cultural viewpoints and improve your ability to communicate with people from diverse cultural backgrounds.
   For instance, you can take courses relating to diversity across nations (e.g., international or cross-cultural awareness), or ethnic and racial diversity within America (e.g., multicultural awareness).

(continued)

9. Stretch beyond your familiar or customary learning style to experience different ways of learning and to develop new skills.

   Courses are likely to be available to you in college that were never previously available to you, and which focus on skills that you've never had a chance to test-out or develop.

10. Learn something you were always curious about, or something you simply wanted to know more about.

    For instance, if you've always been curious about how members of the other sex think and feel, you could take a course on the psychology of men or the psychology of women; or, if you've always been fascinated by movies and how they are made, you might elect to take a course in film-making or cinematography.

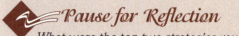

Pause for Reflection
What were the top-two strategies you selected from the above list? Why?

After you have accurately identified the requirements for the major you're considering, ask yourself the following two questions:

1. Do the course titles and descriptions appeal to my interests and values?
2. Do I have the abilities or skills needed to do well in these courses?

Also, be aware that college majors often require courses in fields outside of the major. For instance, psychology majors are often required to take at least one course in biology, and business majors are often required to take calculus. If you are interested in majoring in any particular subject area, be sure you are fully aware of such outside requirements and are comfortable with them. You don't want to be surprised by unexpected requirements after you have already committed to a major, particularly if these unanticipated requirements do not match-up well with your personal abilities, interests, or learning styles.

• **Look over an introductory textbook in the field that you're considering as a major.**

  Find an introductory book in a major that you are considering, review its table of contents, and ask yourself if the topics are compatible with your academic interests and talents. Read a few pages of the text to get some sense of the writing style used in the field and how comfortable you are with it. You should easily find introductory textbooks for all courses in your college bookstore, the college library, or by asking a faculty member in the field.

• **Talk with students majoring in the field that you're considering as a major and ask them about their experiences.**

  Try to speak with several students in the field so that you get a balanced perspective that goes beyond the opinion of just one individual. A good way to find students in the major you're considering is by visiting Major Clubs (e.g., psychology club, history club, etc.) on campus. Also, you could check the catalog for required courses in the major you're considering, and then check the schedule of classes to see when and where these classes meet. This would enable you to find and speak with students who are taking these classes (e.g., by conversing with them before or after the class period). The following questions may be good ones to ask students in a major that you're considering:

• CLASSIC QUOTE •

Before I came to college, I wish I had known that Psychology is really Biology; Biology is really Chemistry; Chemistry is really Physics; and Physics is really Math.

—Anonymous

- ◇ What first attracted you to this major?
- ◇ What do you think are the advantages and disadvantages of majoring in this field?
- ◇ Knowing what you know now, would you choose the same major again?

Also, ask these students about the quality of teaching and advising in the department. Studies show that different departments within the same college or university can vary greatly in terms of the quality of teaching, as well as their educational philosophy and attitude toward students (Pascarella & Terenzini, 1991).

◆ Sit in on some classes in the field you're considering as a major.

If the class you want to visit is a large class, you probably could just slip into the back row and listen. However, if the class is small, you should ask the instructor's permission. When visiting a class, focus on the content or ideas being covered in class, rather than the instructor's personality or teaching style. (Keep in mind that you're trying to decide if you will major in the subject, not in the teacher.)

◆ Discuss the major you are considering with an academic advisor.

It is probably best to speak with an academic advisor who advises students in a variety of majors, rather than someone who advises only students in one particular academic department or major field. You want to discuss the major with an advisor who is more likely to be neutral and will give you unbiased feedback about the pros and cons of majoring in that field.

Speaking with students majoring in the discipline you are considering is a good way to get a balanced perspective.

◆ Speak with some faculty members in the department that you're considering as a major. Consider asking them the following questions:
- ◇ What academic skills or qualities are needed for a student to be successful in your field?
- ◇ What are the greatest challenges faced by students majoring in your field?
- ◇ What do students seem to like most and least about majoring in your field?
- ◇ What can students do with a major in your field after college graduation?
- ◇ What types of graduate programs or professional schools would a student in your major be well prepared to enter?

◆ Visit your Career Center to see if information is available on what college graduates majoring in the field you're considering have gone on to do with that major after graduation. This will give you some idea about the type of careers the major can lead to, or what type of graduate and professional school programs that students may enter after completing a major in the field you're considering.

◆ Surf the Web site of a professional organization associated with the field that you're considering as a major. For example, if you are thinking about becoming an anthropology major, check out the Web site of the American Anthropological Association. If you're considering history as a major, take a look at the Web site of the American Historical Association. The Web site of a professional organization often contains useful information for students who are considering that field as a major. For example, the Web site of the American Philosophical Association contains information about non-academic careers for philosophy majors, and the American Sociological Association's Web site identifies a variety of careers that sociology majors are qualified to pursue after college graduation.

To locate the professional Web site of the field that you might want to explore as a college major, ask a faculty member in that field or complete a search on the Web by simply entering the name of the field, followed by the word "association."

◆ Be sure you know what academic standards must be met for you to be accepted for entry into the major that you're considering. Because of their popularity, certain college majors are oversubscribed, that is to say, there are more students interested in majoring in these fields than there are openings for them. For instance, pre-professional majors that lead directly to a particular career path can frequently become oversubscribed (e.g., accounting, education, engineering, pre-med, nursing, or physical therapy). On some campuses, these majors are called restricted majors, meaning that departments control their enrollment by limiting the number of students they let into the major. For example, departments may restrict entry to their major by admitting only students who have achieved an overall grade-point average of at least a 3.0 or higher in certain introductory courses required by the majors or by ranking all students who apply by their GPA and counting down until they have filled their maximum number of available spaces (Strommer, 1993).

Students who would like to major in one of these restricted fields, but have not yet been accepted or admitted to it, are sometimes called "shadow majors." In effect, shadow majors are students who have been admitted to their college or university, but have not yet been admitted to their intended major. These students may eventually be admitted to their preferred major, or they may be shut out if they fail to meet the specific standards of the department.

So, be sure you know whether the major you are considering is oversubscribed and has special standards that must be met before you can be admitted. As you complete courses and receive grades, check to see if you are meeting these standards. If you are, then continue your pursuit of that major. If you find yourself failing to meet these standards, increase the amount of time and effort you devote to your studies, and seek assistance from your campus Learning Center. If you are working at your maximum level of effort and are regularly using the learning assistance services available on your campus, but are still not meeting the academic standards of your intended major, then consider consulting with an academic advisor to help you identify an alternative field that may be closely related to the restricted major that you were hoping to enter.

Pause for Reflection

What major(s) at your school are oversubscribed, i.e., have more students wanting to major in the field than there are openings in the field?

◆ Consider the possibility of a college minor in a field that may complement your major.

A college minor usually requires about one-half the number of credits (units) that are required for a college major. Most schools allow you the option of completing a minor along with your major. Check your college catalog to determine which minors are available at your school and what courses are required to complete any minor that appeals to you.

If you have strong interests in two different fields, a minor will allow you to major in one of these fields while minoring in the other. Thus, you can pursue two fields that interest you without having to sacrifice one for the other. Furthermore, a minor can be completed along with most college majors without delaying your time to graduation. (In contrast, a "double major" will typically lengthen your time to graduation because you must complete the separate requirements of two different majors.) Other ways in which you can pursue another field of study along with your major without delaying your time to graduation are through completion of a *cognate* area—which requires fewer courses to complete than a minor (e.g., 4 to 5 courses)—or a *concentration* area—which may require only two to three courses.

Taking a cluster of courses in another field outside your major can be an effective way to strengthen your resume and increase your employment prospects because you demonstrate versatility and gain experience in areas that may be missing or underemphasized by your major. For example, students majoring in the fine arts (music, theatre) or humanities (English, history) may take courses in the fields of mathematics (e.g., statistics), technology (e.g., computer science) and business (e.g., economics), which are not emphasized by their major. In fact, some colleges and universities offer business classes that are open only to liberal arts majors. Employment and career opportunities for non-business majors are enhanced if they have some course work in business (e.g., economics, business administration) (The Board of Trustees, 2005).

Similarly, students majoring in such fields as business or computer science could take a cluster of courses in fine arts or humanities to develop skills and perspectives that are not strongly emphasized in their own major. For instance, they could take foreign language or cross-cultural courses to enhance their career prospects in today's global economy.

••• Summary and Conclusion

This chapter has focused on the *curriculum*, which refers to the total set of courses that your college offers. By the time you graduate, the total set of courses that appear on your college transcript will represent your curriculum. You will have much more choice and control of your curriculum in college than you did in high school. You will choose what field to specialize in (your major), and you will decide what particular electives to take within your major and within the academic areas required for general education.

One of the primary advantages of taking the wide range of courses that make up the liberal arts curriculum is that they enable you to become more aware of different aspects of yourself, while at the same time, you become more aware of the variety of academic disciplines and subject areas that are available to you as possible majors. Your trip through the liberal arts curriculum will likely result in your discovery of new personal interests and new choices for majors, some of which may be in fields that you didn't even know existed.

Also, your exposure to a wide range of subjects provides you with the general context that is needed to make an intelligent selection of your specific major and to understand how your particular major fits into the bigger picture. In other words, you need to take a trip through the forest before you can select the right tree. So, look at your trip through the liberal arts curriculum as an exploratory journey in which you are searching to make three key discoveries:

1. Discovering the full range of choices for majors that are available to you,
2. Discovering where your special interests, values, needs, and abilities lie, and
3. Discovering what specialized major best matches your special interests, values, talents, and abilities.

Remember: Finding yourself and your options should take place before you find a major and future career. You don't build your life around a major and a career; you build a major and career around your life.

Even if you have already decided on a major, you will still need to explore specialized fields within your major to find one that is most compatible with your personal interests, abilities, and values. For instance, if you have decided to major in communications, you will still need to select what particular field or communication media to specialize in, such as visual media, print media, or sound media. Similarly, if you are interested in pursuing a career in law, you will eventually need to decide what branch of law you wish to practice.

Choosing courses that best enable you to achieve your long-term educational and personal goals should take precedence over creating a class schedule that leaves your Fridays free for three-day weekends.

So, if you have decided on a major field of study, the liberal arts component of your college experience will help you explore specializations within that field by exposing you to a wide variety of subject areas and by testing your skills and interests in these areas. Furthermore, your exposure to different fields of study in the liberal arts curriculum may result in your discovery of a second field that interests you, which you may decide to pursue as a *minor* to accompany your major.

Lastly, keep in mind that approximately one of every three or four courses you'll take in college will be a free elective—your choice of any of the many courses that are listed in your college catalog. This freedom of choice will allow you the opportunity to shape and create an academic experience that is uniquely your own. Seize this opportunity, and exercise your freedom responsibly and reflectively. Do not make choices thoughtlessly, randomly, or solely on the basis of scheduling convenience (e.g., choosing courses to create a schedule with no early morning or late afternoon classes). Instead, make strategic choices of courses that will contribute most to your educational, personal, and professional development. Intentionally select courses with one or more of the following purposes in mind:

- to choose a major or confirm whether your first choice is a good one;
- to acquire a minor or build a concentration that will complement your major;
- to broaden your perspectives on the world around you;
- to become a more balanced or complete human being;
- to handle the practical life tasks that face you now and in the future; and
- to strengthen your career development and employment prospects after graduation.

With "higher" education comes a "higher" degree of freedom of choice and a greater opportunity to determine your own academic course of action. *Enjoy* it and *employ* it—use your freedom strategically to make the most of your college experience and college degree.

••• Learning More through Independent Research

Web-Based Resources for Further Information on Educational Planning

For additional information relating to the ideas discussed in this chapter, we recommend the following Web sites:

College majors: www.Mymajors.com

Careers for liberal arts majors: www.eace.org/networks/liberalarts.html

Name _____ Date _____

Assignment 1. Planning for a College Major

If you have not already done so, make a tentative plan for the liberal arts (general education) component of your college experience. We now ask you to consider developing a plan for your college major.

STEPS:

1. Go to your college catalog and use its index to locate pages containing information relating to the major you have chosen or are considering. Even if you are "totally undecided," select a field that you might consider as a possibility. To help you identify possible majors, you can use your catalog, or go online and complete the short interview at the following Web site: http://www.Mymajors.com.

   The point of this assignment is not to force you to commit to a major right now, but to familiarize you with the process of developing a plan, so that you can apply it when you do make a firm decision about the major you intend to pursue.

2. Once you've selected a major for this assignment, use your college catalog to identify what courses are required for the major you selected. Use the form below to list the course number and course title of all courses that are required by the major you've selected.

   You will find certain courses required by the major that you must take; these are often called *"core" requirements* for the major. For instance, at most colleges, all business majors must take the course microeconomics. In other cases, you will find that there are courses required for a certain area within your major, but you are allowed to choose them from a list of possible courses (e.g., "choose any three courses from among the following six courses"). Such courses are often called *"restricted electives"* in the major. When you find restricted electives in the major you've selected, read the course descriptions and choose those courses from the list that appeal most to you. Just list the course titles and numbers of these courses on the planning form. You don't need to write down all the possible choices that are listed in the catalog.

   College catalogs can sometimes be tricky to navigate or interpret, so if you run into any difficulty, don't panic. Seek help from an academic advisor, or check with the department secretary in the field you selected as a major to see if the department has created any summary sheets of requirements for a major in that field. Your college may also have a "degree audit" program that allows you to track your degree requirements electronically. If your college has such a program, take advantage of it.

Major Selected _____

Major Core Course Requirements:
Specific courses in your major that you must take

Course #	Course Title	Course #	Course Title

Restricted Electives in the Major:
Courses required for your major that you choose to take from a specified list.

Course #	Course Title	Course #	Course Title

PERSONAL REFLECTIONS ON THIS ASSIGNMENT

After competing this assignment, take a moment to think back on it and answer the following questions.

1. Looking over the courses required for the major you've selected, would you still be interested in majoring in this field?

2. Were there courses required by this major that you were surprised to see, or that you did not expect would be required?

3. Are there any unanswered questions that remain in your mind about this major?

Assignment 2. Developing a Comprehensive, Long-Range Graduation Plan

A comprehensive, long-range graduation plan includes all three key types of courses you need to complete a college degree:

1. Liberal arts requirements,
2. College major requirements, and
3. Free electives.

By combining your plan for required liberal arts courses and your plan for a college major (Assignment 1 of this chapter), you could then add in your free electives to create a comprehensive graduation plan.

Use the form on the following page to develop this complete graduation plan. Use the slots to pencil in the liberal arts courses you're planning to take to fulfill your general education requirements, your major requirements, and your free electives. (Use a pencil so that you can easily make any changes to this plan as you develop or implement it.)

SUGGESTIONS:

1. If you haven't decided on a major, a good strategy might be to concentrate on taking liberal arts courses to fulfill your general-education requirements during your first year of college. This will open more slots in your course schedule during your sophomore year. By that time, you may have a better idea of what you want to major in, and you can fill these open slots with courses required by your major. This may be a particularly effective strategy if you choose to major in a field that has many requirements, because it may be necessary for you to complete several of those requirements before the end of your sophomore year.

2. For ideas on choosing your free electives, see Box 2 in this chapter.

3. Keep in mind that the course number indicates the year in the college experience that the course is usually taken. Courses numbered in the 100s (or below) are typically taken in the first year of college, 200-numbered courses in the sophomore year, 300-numbered courses in the junior year, and 400-numbered courses in the senior year. Also, be sure to check if the course you are planning to take has any pre-requisites—which are courses that need to be completed before you can enroll in the course you're planning to take. (For example, if you're planning to take a course in literature, it is likely that you cannot enroll in it until you have completed at least one pre-requisite course in writing or English composition.)

4. To complete a college degree in four years, you should complete about 30 credits each academic year. Summer term is considered part of an academic year, and we encourage you to use that term to help keep you on a four-year timeline.

5. Check with your course instructor or an academic advisor to see if your college has developed a "projected plan of scheduled courses" for the next few years, which indicates when courses listed in the catalog are scheduled to be offered (e.g., fall, spring, summer). If such a long-range plan of scheduled courses is available, take advantage of it because it will enable you to develop a personal educational plan that includes not only what courses you will take, but also *when* you will take them. This can be a very important advantage because some courses you may need for graduation will not be offered every term. For example, if you're planning to take a course that you need to graduate during your final term in college, and that course is not offered during your final term, you may have to wait until it is offered again. While you wait for the term when that course is offered again, you end-up delaying your graduation and taking a longer time to complete your college degree. So, we strongly encourage you to inquire about and acquire any long-range plan of scheduled courses that may be available at your college or university, and use it to develop your personal, long-range graduation plan.

6. Don't forget to include out-of-class learning experiences as part of your educational plan, such as volunteer service, internships, and study abroad.

This long-range graduation plan is not something set in stone. Like clay, its shape can be molded and changed into a different form as you gain more experience with the college curriculum. Nevertheless, your development of this initial plan will remain useful because it provides you with a blueprint to work from. Once you have created slots specifically for your general education requirements, your major courses, and your electives, then you have all the key categories of courses covered and changes to your plan can often be made easily by simple substitution of different courses into the slots you've already created for the three categories of courses.

Remember: The purpose of this long-range planning assignment is not to "lock" you into a "rigid" plan, but to help you create a rough "map" that will enable you to visualize your future years in college. Vision can provide you with a sense of direction that leads to a plan of action, which, in turn, enables you to see a connection between where you are now and where you want to be. Furthermore, this process of visualizing can be energizing, because when you're able to see what's ahead of you, you can see the finish line and what it will take to get you there.

PERSONAL REFLECTIONS ON DEVELOPING A LONG-RANGE GRADUATION PLAN

After completing this assignment, take a moment to think back on it and answer the following questions.

1. Do you think this was a useful assignment? Why? (Or, why not?)

2. Do you see any way in which this assignment could be improved or strengthened?

CASE STUDY

Whose Choice Is It Anyway?

Ursula, a first-year student, was in tears when she showed up at the Career Center. She had just returned from a weekend visit home, where she informed her parents that she was planning to major in art or theatre. When Ursula's father heard about her plans, he exploded and insisted that she major in something "practical," like business or accounting, so she could earn a living after she graduates. Ursula replied that she had no interest in these majors, nor did she feel she had the skills needed to complete the level of math required by them, which included calculus. Her father shot back that he had no intention of "paying four years of college tuition for her to end up as an unemployed artist or actress!" He went on to say that if she wanted to major in art or theatre, she'd "have to figure out a way to pay for college herself."

Reflection and Discussion Questions

1. What options (if any) do you think Ursula has right now?

2. If Ursula were your friend, what would you recommend she do?

3. Do you see any way(s) in which Ursula might pursue a major that she's interested in, while at the same time, ease her father's worries that she will end up jobless after college graduation?

Academic Advising

Amy Schmidt, *Director, Academic Advising*
Holli Goodwin, *Academic Advisor*

Outline

The Advisor's Responsibilities
    Advisors Are Responsible to the Individuals They Advise
The Student's Responsibilities
DSC Catalog
The Advising Process and the College Plan
Academic Advising Session Expectations
Sources

Academic advising is a resource available to students to assist them in planning a successful academic journey. The academic advisor is well versed in college policies and program requirements. Successful academic advising requires that the advisor and the advisee work well together. During the first semesters of college, the advisor plays a greater role in explaining educational requirements, college policies and resources, registering the student for classes, and following up with the student after classes have begun. After the initial semesters, the advisee takes on more responsibility in developing an individual college plan and scheduling classes; students may meet less frequently with the advisor.

The Advisor's Responsibilities

Academic Advising is a profession with professional guidelines. The National Academic Advising Association (NACADA) has published a statement of core values of academic advising. The statement serves as a professional guideline for advisors and delineates the responsibilities of an academic advisor as described below:

Advisors Are Responsible to the Individuals They Advise

Academic advisors work to strengthen the importance, dignity, potential, and unique nature of each individual within the academic setting. Advisors' work is guided by their beliefs that students

- have diverse backgrounds that can include different ethnic, racial, domestic, and international communities; sexual orientations; ages; gender and gender identities; physical, emotional, and psychological abilities; political, religious, and educational beliefs;
- hold their own beliefs and opinions;
- [be] responsible for their own behaviors and the outcomes of those behaviors;
- can be successful based upon their individual goals and efforts;
- have a desire to learn;
- have learning needs that vary based upon individual skills, goals, responsibilities, and experiences; and
- use a variety of techniques and technologies to navigate their world.

In support of these beliefs, the cooperative efforts of all who advise include, but are not limited to, providing accurate and timely information, communicating in useful and efficient ways, maintaining regular office hours, and offering varied contact modes.

Advising, as part of the educational process, involves helping students develop a realistic self-perception and successfully transition to the postsecondary institution. Advisors encourage, respect, and assist students in establishing their goals and objectives.

Advisors seek to gain the trust of their students and strive to honor students' expectations of academic advising and its importance in their lives.[1]

The Student's Responsibilities

During the 2004/2005 academic year, the faculty at Dalton State College developed the Academic Advising Mission which appears in the ***Dalton State College Catalog 2006–2007***. It includes the following list of advisee responsibilities:

Advisees should

- become familiar with the course-of-study requirements, reviewing the catalog, course descriptions, course prerequisites, previous sequencing of course offerings, and schedule of classes prior to meeting with the advisor;
- come prepared to advising/registration sessions with a tentative schedule of classes and, if possible, an alternate schedule;
- seek out the advisor for academic assistance and guidance and communicate academic concerns;
- make use of campus resources if undecided about a major;
- accept responsibility for their academic goals;
- learn to use BANNER and take advantage of pre-registration;
- be aware of drop/add/withdrawal policies;
- initiate graduation procedures;
- see division secretaries to change advisors/majors prior to registration;
- make the most of their college experience by taking advantage of campus resources (labs, library, tutoring, recreational facilities);
- update personal information at the records office;
- meet appointments punctually as scheduled;
- have reasonable expectations;
- be courteous and flexible.[2]

The Dalton State College Catalog is a valuable resource when gathering information and self advising. The catalog explains how the college works, just as the owner's manual describes how the computer works. The **Dalton State College Catalog** contains a variety of information about the academic calendar, academic policies, programs of study, tuition and fees, etc. Students are responsible for knowing the information contained in the catalog or, at a minimum, knowing how to find information in the catalog.

Name _____ Date _____

DSC Catalog

Referring to your copy of the DSC Catalog, please answer the following questions and notate the correct page number from the catalog.

1. What do the three numbers to the right of each course description tell a student about the course being described?

   _____

   _____

   _____ p. _____

2. Describe two instances in which a student will be required to satisfy the program of study requirements from a catalog other than the catalog in effect during his/her initial enrollment.

   _____

   _____ p. _____

3. How can a student satisfy the computer literacy requirement?

   _____

   _____

   _____ p. _____

4. If a student receives a grade of "I" for a course, when must it be removed?

   _____

   _____

   _____ p. _____

5. What is academic probation?

   _____

   _____

   _____ p. _____

6. Name two "Area C" electives.

   _____

   _____

   _____ p. _____

7. What is the prerequisite for EDUC 4261?

   _____

   _____ p. _____

8. Who is the President of Dalton State College?

   _____

   _____

   _____ p. _____

9. What happens if a student has not exited a learning support area after attempting 12 semester hours in that area?

   _____

   _____ p. _____

10. List two reasons for which a student will be granted an exemption to the physical education requirement.

    _____

    _____

    _____ p. _____

The Advising Process and the College Plan

An understanding of the programs and policies described in the ***Dalton State College Catalog*** is only one factor in effective advising. Whether the student is studying Medical Transcriptionist, Radiologic Technology, English, or Business Administration, s/he should have a plan for the college years. Because students' lives vary drastically, the plan that works well for one individual may not work at all for another.

Before beginning to develop an academic plan a student should consider his/her lifestyle, responsibilities and goals. Answering the following questions should assist the student in preparing to develop an academic plan.

- How does college fit in with the rest of your life?
- Is college your primary focus?
- Are you working full or part-time?
- Do you have family responsibilities?
- What kind of schedule will you need in order to be a successful student: part-time or full-time, morning classes or evening, every term or only one term a year?
- How long will it take for you to complete your program of study?
- What will you do with your certificate or degree?
- Will you be looking for a job or continuing your education with a bachelor's or graduate degree?

After becoming familiar with the ***Dalton State College Catalog*** and answering many of the preceding questions, the student should schedule an appointment with an academic advisor to begin creating an academic plan.

Academic Advising Session Expectations

First Session/First Advisement and Registration

- Advisor explains catalog, program of study, college policies, academic calendar, etc.
- Advisee/student is registered for needed/desired courses
- Schedule is explained to student
- General college questions are answered
- Advisor assumes the majority of responsibility during session

Second Session/Follow-Up Appointment

- Advisor discusses student's progress toward academic goals and career goals, reviews college policies, program of study, etc.
- Potential course options are reviewed for future semesters
- Advisee is shown how to use the Interactive Course Schedule and catalog to plan future semester schedules. See "How To" section
- Advisees are encouraged to make an appointment to register for the following semester

Third Session/Second Advisement and Registration

- Discussion will occur to review advisee's program of study
- Advisee should be prepared with a potential list of courses for the semester, for which he/she is being registered
- The courses will be reviewed to ensure they are appropriate for student's program of study
- A review of policies will take place
- Advisee is expected to play an active role with the responsibility for his/her advising and registration

Fourth and Future Session(s)/Advisement and Registration

- Advisee should verify who his/her advisor is through using the "Who is my Advisor" link on DSConnect. See "How To" section
- The advisee should be responsible for determining his/her courses
- The advisee should be prepared with a course schedule and CRN r registration
- The above takes place as a transition from the Academic Advising Center to a faculty advisor. An advisee is expected to understand his/her program of study, course requirements, and have the ability to plan his/her schedule

Sources

1. NACADA. (2004). NACADA statement of core values of academic advising. Retrieved 9/21/2006 from the *NACADA Clearinghouse of Academic Advising Resources* Web site: http://www.nacada.ksu.edu/Clearinghouse/AdvisingIssues/Core-Values.htm.
2. Dalton State College Catalog 2006–2007. p. 106.

Improving Memory and Test Performance

Strategies for Remembering What You Have Learned and Demonstrating What You Know

Learning Goals

In this chapter, we will focus on the final stage of the memory process, which involves finding and retrieving information that has been stored in the brain. The primary goals of this chapter are to strengthen your ability to remember information that you've studied and to effectively demonstrate your knowledge of that information on college exams.

Outline

Memory and Learning
Memorization Strategies
    Mnemonic Devices
    Meaningful Association
    Organization: Classifying or Categorizing What You're Trying to Remember
    Visualization
    Rhythm and Rhyme
    Acrostics
    Link System
    Loci System
Test-Taking Strategies
    Before the Test
    On the Day of the Test
    During the Test
    After the Test: Troubleshooting Test-Taking Errors and Sources of Lost Points on Exams
Summary and Conclusion
Learning More through Independent Research
Exercises:
    Self-Assessment of Learning Strategies
    Midterm Self-Evaluation
Case Study: Bad Feedback: Shocking Midterm Grades

Activate Your Thinking

Are learning and remembering the same?

How are they similar?

How are they different?

••• Memory and Learning

If you are not sure about the answers to the "Activate Your Thinking" questions, welcome to the club. There is still debate among scholars about the similarities and differences between learning and memory. Certainly, these are not totally different mental processes. When we learn something, it's stored in our brain as a memory, so learning and memory are definitely related; we can only remember things that we've learned. However, if we've learned something and stored it in our brain, we cannot always recall it; thus, learning and remembering are not identical. Deep learning and long-term memory is a multi-step process that involves three distinct stages:

1. Getting information into your brain (perception),
2. Keeping it there (storage), and
3. Finding it later when you need it (retrieval).

Although college courses will often emphasize comprehension and higher-level thinking skills, there will be numerous occasions when you'll be asked just to recall information. Memory, like any other learning skill, can be improved by using effective strategies or techniques. Contrary to popular belief, most people with good memories do not possess any extraordinary ability, such as photographic memory. The vast majority of people with outstanding memory have successfully developed a set of effective memory strategies and practiced them diligently.

If you can learn to use memory-improvement methods effectively, you will not only reduce the risk of forgetting information that you've studied, but you'll also reduce the amount of study time spent on trying to memorize information through sheer repetition; this will open up more time for comprehension and "higher" forms of thinking. Furthermore, using memory-improvement methods, such as those we are about to discuss, are simply more stimulating and motivating than memorizing by repetition.

••• Memorization Strategies

Mnemonic Devices

Mnemonic devices, also known as mnemonics (pronounced "neh-mon-iks"), are specific memory-improvement methods designed to prevent forgetting. The mnemonic devices we are about to discuss should not be viewed as tricks or gimmicks but as legitimate strategies that are based on one or more of the following research-based, memory-improvement principles:

- meaning
- organization
- visualization
- rhythm and rhyme

What all mnemonic devices have in common is that they help us remember by providing us with a partial *cue* to bring the memory back to mind. When humans try to retrieve memories that have been stored, studies show they usually do not remember all parts or pieces of the information in one shot; instead, they "build back" their memory around one or two points that they do remember (Loftus, 1979). For instance, when college students are asked to recall stories, pictures, or geometrical designs that they have been shown days or weeks before, they tend to organize their recall around one or two major details—for example, they'll remember one character or episode in a story and will then try to fill in the missing details. This process

Figure 1 — A "Map" of the Functions Performed by the Outer Surface of the Human Brain

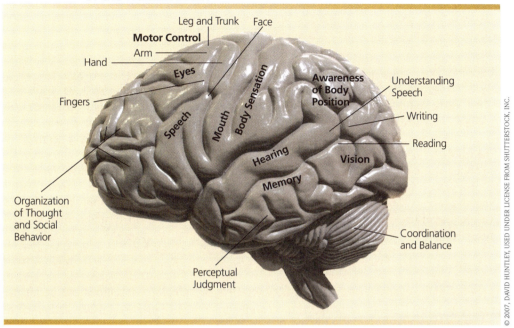

of building up and building back a memory piece-by-piece is called *reconstruction*. Retrieval works this way because different elements of a memory are stored in different parts of the brain (Pribram, 1991). For example, you may store the place where you saw the information in the part of our brain specialized for visual memory, the words you heard your instructor speak about it in an area of the brain specialized for auditory memory, and the printed words you read about it in an area of the brain involved with reading. See Figure 1, a map of the surface of the human brain, to get an idea of how different parts of the brain are specialized for different mental activities. When we retrieve a memory, we often retrieve different parts of the memory that are stored in different areas of the brain, and we use the process of reconstruction to try to rebuild the whole memory.

The effectiveness of mnemonics for reconstructing memory has been demonstrated in many research studies. For instance, one study showed that college students using mnemonics remembered 72 percent of words they studied, compared to an average of 28 percent for students who tried to memorize these words through mere repetition (Bower, 1973). Listed below are seven mnemonic devices that you could use to recall hard-to-remember information in any field of study (Buzan, 1991; Higbee, 1998; Lorayne & Lucas, 1974). These mnemonics can be adapted to remember information in different subject areas, whether it is a single piece of information, multiple ideas, or a sequence of steps in a procedure. Some of them may work more effectively on certain types of information than others, but the variety should give you a menu to choose from, allowing you to select different ones for different learning tasks or situations. (For additional mnemonics designed for remembering information in particular academic subjects, see: www.eudesign.com. To find mnemonics specifically for medical and health-related fields, see: www.medicalmnemonics.com.)

Meaningful Association

Relating what you're trying to remember to something that you already know can be a powerful memory aid because learning is all about making connections in the brain. So, the first and most effective way to improve memory would be to find *meaning* in what you're learning. Before starting to repeatedly pound what you're learning into your head like a hammer and nail, first look for a hook to hang it on by relating it to something already stored in your brain. It may take a little while to discover the right hook, but once you've found it, the information will store in your brain quickly and remain there for a long period of time.

> **Personal Story** Some time ago, I had to give up running because of damage to my right hip, so I decided to start riding a stationary bike instead. My wife found an inexpensive, used stationary bike at a garage sale. It was an old and somewhat rusty bike that made a noise when I rode it that sounded like "ee-zoh" over and over again as the wheel spun. One evening I was riding it and I noticed that, after about 10 minutes, I was hearing the words "zero," "rosy," and "Rio" off and on in my head. Now that I think about it, what my brain was doing was taking a meaningless sound ("ee-zoh"), which apparently it was becoming bored with hearing over and over again as the wheels spun, and transformed that sound into actual words that provided it with variety and meaning. Perhaps this was a classic case of how the human brain naturally seeks meaning and variety, and naturally resists mindless repetition.
>
> —Joe Cuseo

CLASSIC QUOTE

"The extent to which we remember a new experience has more to do with how it relates to existing memories than with how many times or how recently we have experienced it."

—Morton Hunt, *The Universe Within: A New Science Explores the Human Mind*

There are many everyday examples of how effective meaningful associations can be for improving memory. Here are some of the most well-known uses of meaningful association to improve recall of information.

- Remembering to turn the clock one hour ahead in the spring and one hour back in the fall by associating it with: "Spring forward, fall back."
- Remembering how to spell the word "principal" (as opposed to principle) by associating it with the idea that a principal should be a "pal."
- Remembering Italy's geographic location at the bottom of Europe because it's shaped like a boot.
- Remembering dates—for example, remembering that the Magna Carta (a key historical document that led to constitutional laws designed to protect personal freedoms and rights) was written in the year 1215—by associating it with a "free lunch" given at lunchtime (12:15 p.m.).

Here is a meaningful association we recommend for remembering one of the most frequently misspelled words in the English language: Remember to spell "separate" correctly (instead of the frequently misspelled "seperate,") by remembering that "par" means to divide, as in the words "*par*ts," "*par*tition," and "se*par*ate."

STUDENT PERSPECTIVE

"I like to associate what I have to remember with something that I already know/care about."

—First-year student's response to the question: "When you need to remember information, what strategy works best for you?"

Pause for Reflection

Can you think of information you're learning in a course this term that you could form a meaningful association to remember?

What is the information you're attempting to learn?

What is the meaningful association you could use to help you remember it?

Organization: Classifying or Categorizing What You're Trying to Remember

Bits or pieces of information are more easily learned and better remembered if they are organized into a classification system. Studies show that if students study a list of words that fall into different categories (e.g., 12 grocery items that fall into categories like fruit or meat), their recall is much better than when they study 12 unrelated words that cannot be grouped into categories (Mandler, 1967).

The memory advantage for categorized information is even greater if the words that belong to the same category are grouped or clustered together in blocked form (Bower et al., 1969). For instance, it's easier to remember "10-10-987" than it is to remember "1-0-1-0-9-8-7."

So, look for categories and sub-categories to organize information you're studying. For example, create a mental filing system by using index cards, with each card containing a separate category of information. Research suggests that we can hold up to about six items in our working memory, so try to create categories of no more than six items (Cowan, 2001). If you end up with a category that contains seven or more items then use a "divide and conquer" strategy by subdividing it into two smaller groups of six or fewer items.

The power of organization on learning and memory is so strong that some studies have shown that when college students are instructed simply to "organize" information, they tend to remember that information just as well as students who are specifically instructed to "study" or "memorize" the same information (Mandler, 1967; Kintsch, 1982). Although it may take you a little extra time to organize the information at first, you save study time in the long run because you're actually learning the information at the same time that you're organizing it. Furthermore, once the information has been organized, it is much less time-consuming to review at a later date because you've got all the parts together in a file system. In fact, if you organized the information on index cards, with each index card representing a separate category of information, you could put a rubber band around the cards and carry them with you to review at any time or any place. This not only makes studying more convenient, it also tends to reduce your level of test anxiety because you've got it altogether in a neat package, which is a lot more comforting than having it all over the place.

Personal Story

Whenever I meet a new class of students at the start of the term, the first thing I try to do is learn their names as quickly as possible. I have found that I can learn student names more rapidly if I do not study the names individually, but group them into certain categories. I first divide the names by gender, putting all the male and female students into separate groups. Then I subdivide the male and female names into two subgroups: American student names and international student names. Thus, I end up with four groups: (1) American male students, (2) American female students, (3) international male students, and (4) international female students. I have found that I can learn and remember student names faster when I group them into these categories than by trying to learn them one name at a time.

—Joe Cuseo

Visualization

This mnemonic involves:

- visualizing a mental *image* or *picture* of what you want to remember, or
- imagining what you want to remember in a familiar *place* or *location*.

Visual imagery strengthens memory because it allows you to "see" what you're learning. This improves memory by making abstract ideas more concrete and tangible. Also, visualizing an idea puts it in a concrete place or physical location that gives it a spatial dimension. Have you ever had the experience of first remembering the place on a page where a certain piece of information was located (e.g., upper-right-hand corner) which then triggered your memory of the information you were trying to recall? This example points to the important role that space and place can play in improving our memory.

Studies also show that visual images takes less rehearsal and are more easily recalled than words and sentences (Buzan, 1991; Roediger & McDermott, 2000). In fact, images can be recalled instantly because all of the parts can be "seen" at once (Nadel & Welmer, 1980). This power of visual memory may be due to the fact that it is the oldest form of human memory. Before humans were able to speak, write, and remember words, our early ancestors relied on site and visual memories of objects and places. The ability to visualize may have been critical for enabling early humans to survive, such as using their visual memory to recall places where food and shelter were located (Milner & Goodale, 1998). Thus, the human brain may be biologically wired for effective visual memory, so capitalize on it to reduce forgetting.

STUDENT PERSPECTIVE

"I use anything visual—usually drawings or pictures—anything visual!"

—First-year student's response to the question: "When you need to remember information, what strategy works best for you?"

You can use *visual imagery* as a mnemonic device by imagining visual scenes depicting the information you want to remember. This is illustrated by the common strategy for remembering that the mathematical symbol ">" means "greater than" by imagining it as a mouth taking a bite out of something smaller. Studies show that when students are asked to associate two words (e.g., "cow" and "ball"), they display better memory for the associated words if they visually imagine the two words interacting in some way (e.g., the cow chasing the ball). In learning foreign languages, it has been found that visual imagery improves learning word translations. For example, one student effectively learned and remembered the Spanish word caballo (pronounced "cab-eye-oh"), which means "horse," by associating it with a visual image of a horse with a huge eye (Atkinson, 1975). Visual images that are vivid, emotional, humorous, outrageous, or action-packed are often the most effective ones for improving memory (Bower, 1972; Carney & Levin, 2001).

Another way to capitalize on the memory-improving power of visualization and organization is to create *concept maps*, which organize all the pieces of information you're trying to remember into a visual map. Figure 2 represents a concept map that could be used to remember the parts and functions of the human nervous system.

STUDENT PERSPECTIVE

"When I have to remember something, it is better for me to do something with my hands so I could physically see it happening."

—First-year student's response to the question: "When you need to remember information, what strategy works best for you?"

Drawing concept maps help improve your memory by enabling you to become actively involved with the material you're trying to remember and by providing you with a visual picture of that information.

Pause for Reflection

Think of a course you're taking this term in which you're learning related pieces of information that could be joined together to form a concept map. Below, make a rough sketch of this map that includes the information you need to remember.

158 ♦ Chapter 6: Improving Memory and Test Performance

Figure 2 Concept Map for the Human Nervous System

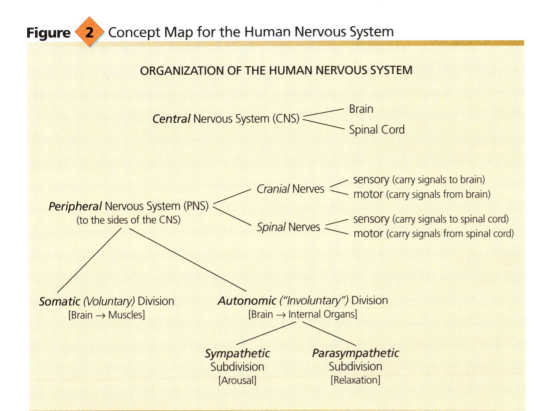

Rhythm and Rhyme

This mnemonic device involves creating a short poem, song, or jingle that ties together the pieces of information you're trying to remember. Studies show that if information is arranged in a rhythmical-rhyming pattern, it is better remembered (Higbee, 1998). You may have had the experience of hearing a song or melody that you hadn't heard in years, but as soon as you hear the melody, the song lyrics immediately come back to mind. There are many well-known examples of using rhythm and rhyme to improve memory, such as the following:

- Remembering the letters of the alphabet by singing the alphabet song—"A, B, C, D, E, F, G, . . . H, I, J, K, L, M, N, O, P," etc.
- Remembering the correct number of days in each month—"Thirty days hath September, April, June, and November," etc.
- Remembering spelling rules—for example, "i" before "e" except after "c" or when sounded like "a" as in "neighbor" and "weigh."
- Remembering directions—for example, when using a screwdriver: "left-loose, right-tight" or, the more rhythmic: "lefty-loosey, righty-tighty."
- Remembering dates—for example, "In fourteen hundred and ninety-two, Columbus sailed the ocean blue."

There are many other examples that could be added to this list, which suggests that rhythm and rhyme can be applied to almost any information you're trying to remember. So, be on the lookout for how you could use this powerful mnemonic to remember course information by converting that information into a short poem or jingle.

> **Personal Story**
>
> In 1993, there was a famous murder trial involving a sports celebrity in southern California. Much of the trial, including witness testimony and lawyer arguments, was covered live on national television. Today, the only thing I still remember about that trial was a poetic line used by the defense lawyer, which he used to make the case that the bloody glove found near the scene of the crime did not fit the hand of the defendant. His words were: "If the glove does not fit, you must acquit." I think that my long-term memory of this one sentence serves as clear testimony to the memory-promoting power of rhythm and rhyme.
>
> —Joe Cuseo

The following mnemonic devices are effective for remembering multiple pieces of information in their correct order or sequence.

Acrostics

The term acrostic stems from the same root as the words "order" or "line," and refers to a mnemonic device that involves lining up the first letter of each item you're trying to remember in an order that creates a word (acronym), phrase, or sentence. Some of the most famous acrostics are:

- "HOMES"—to remember the names of the Great Lakes: Huron, Ontario, Michigan, Erie, and Superior;
- "Roy G Biv"—to remember the colors of the visual spectrum: Red, Orange, Yellow, Green, Blue, Indigo, and Violet;
- "Every Good Boy Does Fine"—to remember the notes on the musical scale's treble clef: E-G-B-D-F;
- FOIL—to remember how to multiply algebraic expressions—First Outer, Inner Last.

You can create an acrostic for anything that you're studying that has multiple parts or pieces. For instance, there are five different indicators or signs that you could use to see if you really comprehend or understand something at a deeper level than memorization. We could take the first letter of each indicator of comprehension to form the sentence, "I RATE"—to remember: I = Illustration (give an example of it), R = Representation (represent it in a different form, such as an analogy or metaphor), A = Application (apply it to solve a problem), T = Translation (paraphrase it in your own words), and E = Explanation (explain it to a friend).

> **Personal Story**
>
> I once had trouble remembering the names of the planets in their correct order of distance from the sun, so I developed the following acrostic almost 25 years ago, and I've never forgotten it. "Men Very Easily Make Jugs Serving Useful Nighttime Pleasures–to remember: Mercury, Venus, Earth, Mars, Jupiter, Saturn, Uranus, Neptune, and Pluto. After I shared this mnemonic in class, one student raised her hand and shared the following acrostic that she used to remember the classification system of living species in her Biology course: "Kings Play Chess on Fat Girls' Stomachs"–to remember: Kingdom, Phylum, Class, Family, Genus, and Species.
>
> —Joe Cuseo

An acrostic can be an invaluable memory aid when you are trying to remember any information that can be arranged in a list or sequence. A good strategy would be to list the first letters of individual items you're attempting to remember and rearrange their order until you come up with a sequence that spells out an acrostic, just as you would rearrange the letters in a "word jumble" that you see in newspapers. Be creative; it may take a while, but once you've found one, it's likely to be an effective way to store information in long-term memory that can help you prepare for exams. In fact, when you take exams, as soon as you receive the test, immediately write down your acrostics so you don't forget them once you begin to turn all your attention to taking the test. Then, you can just refer to the acrostics when you need them during the exam. Once you've got an acrostic down on paper, it can serve as a powerful memory trigger for the information associated with it.

Pause for Reflection

Take a few moments and try to create an acrostic (word, phrase, or sentence) to serve as a mnemonic device for remembering the four key memory-improvement strategies that we've discussed thus far, namely: (1) meaningful association, (2) organization, (3) visualization, and (4) rhythm and rhyme.

(For one possibility, go to the bottom of the last page in this chapter.)

Link System

This mnemonic device uses meaningful associations to create a *story* containing the pieces of information that need to be remembered in a set order or sequence. It consists of two basic steps:

1. Make a list of the items you want to remember, arranging them in the order that you want to recall them.
2. Make an association between each successive pair of items on the list—that is, between the first and second items, then the second and third items, then the third and fourth items.

In other words, you associate two items at a time—linking each pair of items together until you form a complete association chain, which links all the items into one logically sequenced story.

For instance, suppose your biology course requires you to remember the following taxonomy of living organisms: (1) Kingdom, (2) Phylum, (3) Class, (4) Order, (5) Family, (6) Genus, and (7) Species. You might use the link system to weave all seven of these classifications into a meaningful story sequence, such as the following: "A mad ruler wanted to take over the world and create his own intelligent kingdom, so he decided to take his people and file 'em (phylum) into different classes of intelligence. He then delivered an order requiring that only members of the brightest groups be allowed to marry and have a family because they would be more likely to have genius (genus) children, which would improve the intelligence of the human species."

By linking all seven items into a short story such as this, seven unrelated bits of information are organized into one meaningful chunk. Thus, the link or chain system capitalizes on the power of the brain-based learning principles of organization and meaningfulness to improve memory.

You can also use the link system to help you remember parts of a speech you're planning to deliver, or the parts to a long essay answer you're preparing. You can do this by picking out a key phrase or catchword to represent the major point of each section of your speech or essay, and then devise a link between each of these catchwords, connecting them in the order in which you want to recall them. Thus, successive catchwords serve as memory cues to help you recall the specific piece of information associated with each of them, as well as their correct order or sequence.

Loci System

The word loci means place or location. This mnemonic device involves thinking of a natural sequence of places or locations along a path that you regularly travel and visually associating the items of information you're trying to remember at each of these sites. More specifically, this method consists of the following three steps:

1. Take a familiar location you pass through quite often and note the natural sequence of various sites (loci) you see along the way. For example, the location could be your home and the typical sequence of sites might be: the flower in your front yard, the concrete front steps, the oak front door, a narrow hallway, the numbered door leading to your room or apartment, etc.
2. Associate each of the items you want to remember with one of the sites along your route—in the order that you want to recall them. Associate the first item to be remembered with the first site on the route, the second item to be remembered with the second site, etc.
3. When you want to recall all the items in their proper sequence, just take an imaginary walk along your route, using each site as a cue to recall the item you associated with it.

The loci system mnemonic device uses a familiar location to trigger memory.

This memory strategy was discovered and used by famous Greek and Roman orators who delivered their speeches as they walked through their mansions, using each successive room as a visual cue to remember each successive part of their long speeches (Lofus, 1980). One current carry-over from this old tradition is the expression, "in the first place," which we tend to say when we're about to make a number of different points.

If you were to use the loci system to remember the Ten Commandments, you would visually associate one of the commandments with each successive site along your familiar route. To briefly illustrate: First, you could visualize a statue of a pagan god sitting in your front yard (for commandment #1: Thou shalt have no other gods before me). Second, you might imagine a salesman standing on your front steps cursing because your mother has just rejected his attempt to sell her a new encyclopedia (for commandment #2: Thou shalt not take the name of the Lord in vain), etc.

The loci system can be used to remember anything that comes in a series or sequence, such as:

- lists of information (e.g., Bill of Rights) or amendments to the Constitution,
- parts of a speech (letting each site stand for each section of your speech), or
- major sections of your answer to an essay question.

It is recommended that you visualize the images you want to remember as if you were seeing them with your own eyes, rather than watching yourself walking through the rooms as if you were a spectator. Also, as you go from place to place, try to feel the actual sensations you get

> **TAKE ACTION NOW!** **Box 1**
>
> ### Key Questions to Guide Creation of Your Own Mnemonic Devices
>
> 1. Can you relate or associate what you're trying to remember with something you already know, or can you create a short meaningful story out of it? (Meaningful Association)
> 2. Can you remember it by visualizing an image of it, or by visually associating the pieces of information you want to recall with familiar places or sites? (Visualization)
> 3. Can you represent each piece of information you're trying to recall as a letter and string the letters together to form a word, phrase, or short sentence? (Acrostic)
> 4. Can you rhyme what you're trying to remember with a word or expression you know well, or can you create a little poem, jingle, or melody out of it that contains the information? (Rhythm and Rhyme)

from moving, because this will add a kinesthetic memory trace to your visual memory trace. Studies show that when people not only visualize a movement, but also imagine making the movement, it enhances their performance (Garfield, 1984). This technique is referred to as visual-motor behavior rehearsal (VMBR), and athletes have used it successfully to improve their recall of motor (muscle) memories (Suinn, 1985).

Some of the mnemonic devices we've just described may appear to be very involved or elaborate. However, the best strategy for using them effectively is to keep the process simple. Use Box 1 as a guide to developing mnemonic devices that are likely to be more effective than trying to memorize the information through continual repetition.

Pause for Reflection

Have you ever created a mnemonic of your own for information that you were studying and trying to remember?

If yes, what was it?

If no, why do you think that you've never created one?

••• Test-Taking Strategies

The last stage in the learning-and-memory process involves remembering what you've learned and demonstrating that knowledge on tests or exams. The first stage of the process involves attention to and reception of key information from lectures and readings; the second stage involves studying that information and storing it in your brain; and the third stage involves remembering that information by either recognizing or recalling it on exams. Described below is a series of test-taking strategies for improving your ability to remember information at test time, which in turn, should improve your test performances and course grades.

Before the Test

Be well prepared for the exam.

Studies show that college students who are well prepared for exams not only achieve higher test scores; they also experience lower test anxiety (Zohar, 1998). For instance, not cramming before the exam will reduce the usual anxiety associated with the frantic rush to obtain and retain information in a very short period of time.

There is evidence that college students who display greater amounts of procrastination also experience higher levels of test anxiety (Rothblum, Solomon, & Murakami, 1986). High levels of pre-test tension associated with rushing and late-night cramming are likely to carry over to the test itself, resulting in higher levels of test-taking tension. Furthermore, loss of sleep caused by previous-night cramming is likely to decrease your amount of dream (REM) sleep, which in turn, will likely increase the level of anxiety you experience the following day—i.e., test day. Also, research on test anxiety indicates that the most effective strategy for reducing high levels of test anxiety is the use of effective learning strategies prior to the exam (Benjamin, McKeachie, Lin, & Holinger, 1981; Jones & Petruzzi, 1995; Zeidner, 1995).

Adjust your study strategies to the type of test you will be taking.

Your memory for information you have studied will depend not only on how you studied, but also on how your memory will be tested (Stein, 1978). It may be that you can remember what you've studied and demonstrate knowledge of it in one way (e.g., multiple-choice test), but not if you are tested in a different format (e.g., essay test). So, in addition to adjusting your study strategies to the type of knowledge you're acquiring, you also need to adjust your study strategies so that they match the type of test you'll be taking.

College test questions tend to fall into either one of two general categories, and there are study strategies that work most effectively for each type.

1. **Recognition Test Questions**

This category of test questions asks you to select or choose the correct answer from answers that are provided to you. Falling into this category are multiple-choice, true-false, and matching questions. These test questions do not require you to retrieve and produce the correct answer entirely on your own. Instead, you're asked to recognize the correct answer by identifying it or picking it out—similar to identifying the "correct" criminal from a line-up of potential suspects.

2. **Recall Test Questions**

In contrast to recognition test questions, recall test questions require you to go into your memory bank, retrieve the information you've stored in your brain, and reproduce it on your own at test time. As the root term for recall implies, you have to "call back" to mind what you are trying to remember. Falling into the category of recall test questions are essay and short-answer questions that ask you to write your own response.

Recall test questions ask you, "What is it?" In contrast, recognition test questions ask you, "Is it this one?" As you probably already know, we can usually remember information on recognition tests more easily than we can on recall tests (Gordon, 1989), because recognition just involves identifying the correct answer; it does not demand that we retrieve and provide the answer on our own. For instance, we can remember faces more easily than names because seeing someone's face is similar to being given a recognition test—the only thing we have to do is

Multiple-choice questions require recognition memory similar to that used to identify the correct criminal from a line-up of possible suspects.

say, "Yes, I recognize you (your face is familiar)." However, when we try to remember the name that goes with the face, it's similar to taking a recall test—now we have to come up with the name on our own, which is a more difficult memory task than simply recognizing a face that's presented to us. You have probably heard people say, "I've got a great memory for faces, but I'm terrible with names." However, you never hear them say, "I've got a great memory for names, but I'm terrible with faces!" It's also common to hear people say, "You're face is familiar, but I can't recall your name." But, you never hear them say, "Your name is familiar, but I can't recall your face!"

What does all this have to do with how you prepare for tests in college? Since recognition test questions ask you to recognize or identify the correct answer from among answers that are provided for you, a study strategy that involves looking over your notes and becoming familiar with key information may be an effective way to prepare for tests containing these questions. This study strategy works because reading over, becoming familiar with, and understanding the information written in your class notes and textbook matches the type of mental activity that you'll be asked to perform on the exam—reading over and identifying correct answers.

In contrast to recognition, recall test questions that require you to retrieve information and generate correct answers on your own (e.g., writing essays), require more elaborate study strategies. Recall test questions require *you* to generate or produce the correct answer, such as short-answer questions (e.g., "Explain what happens during photosynthesis") and longer essay questions (e.g., "Trace the causes and consequences of the industrial revolution").

Your recall memory may be tested in three basic ways:

1. **Paired-Associate Recall:** memory for one single piece of information that is "paired" or "associated" with another piece of information. For example, a test question that asks you to recall the Spanish word for "head," or the capital of Alaska.
2. **Free Recall:** memory for two or more pieces of information, which you are free to recall in any order or sequence that you like. For example, a test question that asks you to, "Name the countries of South America" or, "List and describe the major causes of World War I."

"When I looked at the first essay question, my whole life flashed before my eyes, then my whole mind went totally blank!"

Students can go "completely blank" on essay tests because they face a blank sheet that requires them to provide information on their own—as opposed to multiple-choice tests, which ask students to recognize or pick-out a correct answer from information that is provided for them.

3. **Serial Recall:** memory for two or more pieces of information in a specific series (order or sequence). For example, a test question that asks you to recall the names of all the vertebrae in the spinal column—in their correct order, from top to bottom.

What these three forms of recall memory have in common is that they require you to retrieve information on your own—a task that places greater demands on your memory than recognition. So, your study strategy for tests that require recall memory should be to practice retrieving the information on your own without looking at it, rather than just reading over information while it is in front of you. Research shows that practicing retrieval while studying information results in better recall memory for that information than just looking it over or re-reading it (Bjork, 1994). Simply reviewing information when studying for a recall test is similar to a football team reading the playbook or reviewing game films prior to a game, rather than actually practicing the plays. Or, imagine if actors were to prepare for their roles in a play by just looking over their lines—without practicing dress rehearsals during which they actually retrieve and say their lines without looking at the script. Obviously, these practice strategies do not match the actual performance situation, so the performance results will be much weaker. Similarly, studying for essay tests by looking over your class notes and highlighted reading will not prepare you to retrieve and recall information on your own, because it does not simulate what you'll actually be doing on the test itself.

Two of the most effective strategies for practicing memory retrieval while studying for recall tests are:

1. **Recitation**

Recitation involves saying to yourself the information you need to recall—*without looking at it*. Research studies indicate that memory for information is significantly strengthened when students study by trying to generate that information on their own, rather than reviewing or re-reading it (Graf, 1982). In particular, recitation strengthens recall memory in three key ways:

- Reciting essentially forces you to actively retrieve the information on your own, instead of just looking at that information while it's right in front of you. When preparing for recall tests that involve essay questions, it is more effective to write out what you are reciting so your practice will more closely match what you'll be expected to do on the test.
- Reciting gives you clear feedback on whether or not you can actually recall the information you're studying. If you cannot retrieve and recite the information to yourself without looking at it, then you know for sure you will not be able to recall it at test time, so you need to study it further. One way to ensure that you give yourself this feedback is to put the question on one side of an index card and the answer on the other side. If you find yourself turning over the index card to look at the answer before saying it, this is a good sign that you're not able to recall the information and it needs additional study.
- Reciting encourages you to use your own words, which gives you feedback on whether you are able to paraphrase it, which is one good indicator of whether you really understand what you're studying. Also, this is a good sign that you will be able to recall the information because if it is more deeply comprehended, it's more likely to be remembered.

Reciting while studying can be done silently, by speaking aloud, or by writing what you are saying. We recommend speaking aloud and writing out what you're reciting because these strategies involve physical action, which will keep you more actively involved or engaged with what you're studying. Speaking and writing also increases the number of sensory channels you use while learning, which, in turn, will increase the number of memory traces stored in your brain. For example, speaking aloud provides auditory stimulation and writing allows for motor and visual stimulation where you can feel and see what you have written.

2. **Creation of Retrieval Cues**

Suppose you're trying to remember a person's name that you know, but you just cannot seem to recall it. If a friend gives you a clue (e.g., the first letter of the person's name or a name that rhymes with it), this will suddenly trigger your memory of the person's entire name. What your friend did was provide you with a "retrieval cue." A retrieval cue can be considered to be a type of memory clue or reminder (like a string tied around your finger), which brings back to your mind what you've temporarily forgotten. The retrieval cue represents a piece of information that is connected to a whole chunk of information you're trying to recall; it helps you build back or reconstruct the total memory, because human memories are stored as parts in an interconnected network (Pribram, 1991) (Figure 3).

 Figure 3

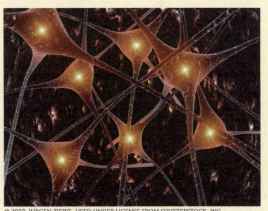

Human memories are stored in the brain as parts of an interconnected system or network. A retrieval cue represents one piece or part of a memory network that can activate and trigger your memory for other information stored in the same network.

© 2007, JURGEN ZIEWE, USED UNDER LICENSE FROM SHUTTERSTOCK, INC.

If you're able to recall one key piece or segment of an interconnected network, it has the potential to trigger total recall by spreading and activating other pieces of information contained within the same organizational network (Collins & Loftus, 1975).

Relating this to studying for recall tests, studies show that students who are unable to remember information they studied will recall it if they are given a retrieval cue. For instance, suppose students have studied a list of items that includes some animals, but are unable to recall these animals on a later memory test. If these students are given a retrieval cue, such as "animals" at the time of the recall test (e.g., if the term "animals" is listed on the answer sheet), what often happens is that the student will then be able to recall some or all of the animals that they had temporarily forgotten (Kintsch, 1968). These research findings suggest that category names can serve as powerful retrieval cues. By taking information that you'll need to recall on an essay test and organizing it into categories, you can then use their category names as retrieval cues at the time of the test.

Pause for Reflection

Think of a course you're taking this term that contains information that could be easily grouped into categories.

What is the course?

What are the categories that could be used to organize information contained in that course?

Also, if you are studying for a recall test, you can intentionally create retrieval cues in the form of catchwords or catchphrases as a net to "catch" related ideas that you want to recall. You can then use that catchword or phrase to trigger your memory of the related information at the time of the exam. For example, an acronym can serve as a catchword, with each letter serving as a retrieval cue for a set of related ideas. Suppose you are studying for a test in abnormal psychology that will include essay questions that ask you to write about different types of mental illness. You might create an acronym like "SCOT" that could serve as a retrieval cue to help you remember to discuss *symptoms* (S), *causes* (C), *outcomes* (O), and *therapies* (T) for each type of mental illness you'll be writing about on the test.

Try to match your study environment as closely as possible to the test environment.

Athletic teams hold their last practice sessions on the field where they will actually play so that their practice environment and performance (game) situation match as closely as possible. Theatrical performers also practice their dress rehearsals on the same set where they will actually perform. Similarly, you want to make your last study (practice) session as similar to the test environment as possible in order to maximize transfer of what you've learned in your study situation to the test situation. For example, if you know how many essay questions you'll need to answer and the total amount of time you'll have to answer them, it would be ideal to practice writing the same number of essays under the same time deadline that you will encounter in the actual test situation.

Studies show that when students take a test in the same environment that they studied in, they tend to remember more of that information at test time than do students who study in one place and take the test in a different place (Smith, Glenberg, & Bjork, 1978). While it is unlikely that you'll be able to do all your studying in the same room that you will take your test in, it may be possible to do your final review in your classroom or in an empty classroom with similar features. This could strengthen your memory for the information you studied because the features of the room in which you studied the information may become associated with the information you studied, and seeing these features again at test time may help trigger memory of the information you studied (Tulving, 1983).

Studying or doing a final review in the classroom where you will take a test could make recall easier during the exam.

Other studies demonstrate that if students are exposed to a distinctive or unique aroma while they are studying (e.g., the smell of chocolate) and are exposed to that same smell again during a later memory test, they display better memory for the information they studied than do students who didn't study and take the test with the same aroma present (Schab, 1990). Perhaps one practical application of this finding is to wear a distinctively smelling cologne or perfume while studying, and use it again on the day of the test. This might improve your memory for the information you studied by matching the scent of your study environment with the scent of your test environment. Although this strategy may seem silly, keep in mind that the area of the human brain where smell is perceived has connections with the brain's memory pathways (Jensen, 1998). This may account for why people commonly report that certain smells can trigger memories of past experiences (e.g., the smell of a summer breeze triggering memories of summer games played during childhood). Thus, don't underestimate the sense of smell's potential for promoting memory.

On the Day of the Test

- **Come to the test room fully equipped** with all the test-taking tools you'll need (e.g., #2 pencil, pen, blue book, Scantron, calculator, etc.). Also, bring back-up equipment in case you experience equipment failure (e.g., an extra pen in case your first one runs out of ink, or extra pencils in case your original one breaks); this will ensure that you don't lose test time and elevate your text anxiety while searching for replacements.
- **Avoid consuming caffeine prior to the test** because it's a drug that stimulates the nervous system and can elevate your level of nervousness during the test. (Caffeine also is a diuretic, meaning that it tends to increase the body's flow of urine, which may increase your urge to urinate during the test.)

Sit in the same seat that you normally occupy in class.

As previously mentioned, there is some research indicating that memory is improved when information is recalled in the same place or environment where it was originally perceived and studied (Sprenger, 1999). Taking the test in the same seat that you normally occupy during lectures, which is the place where you originally heard much of the information that appears on the test, may also improve your test performance.

TAKE ACTION NOW! — Box 2

Using Nutritional Strategies to Strengthen Your Academic Performance

Is there a "brain food" that can strengthen our mental performance? Can we "eat to learn?" Some animal studies suggest that memory may be improved by consumption of foods containing lecithin, which is a substance that helps the brain produce acetylcholine—a brain chemical that plays an important role in memory formation (Ulus & Wurtman, 1977). Fish contains a high amount of lecithin, which may have something to do with why some people refer to fish as "brain food."

> **CLASSIC QUOTE**
>
> "To keep the body in good health is a duty, otherwise we shall not be able to keep our mind strong and clear."
>
> —Hindu Prince Gautama Siddharta, a.k.a., Buddha; founder of Buddhism, 563-483 BC

Despite the results of some animal studies, there is not enough research yet available to conclude that there is any one miraculous food item humans can consume that will dramatically increase their ability to comprehend and retain knowledge. However, there is evidence that the following nutritional strategies may be used to improve mental performance on days when our knowledge is tested.

1. **Eat breakfast on the day of the exam.**

   Numerous studies show that students who eat a nutritious breakfast on the day they are tested typically attain higher test scores than students who do not (Martin & Benton, 1999; Smith, Clark, & Gallagher, 1999).

   Breakfast on the day of an exam should include grains, such as whole-wheat toast, whole-grain cereal, oatmeal, or bran, because those foods contain complex carbohydrates that will deliver a steady stream of energy to the body throughout the day; this should help sustain your test-taking endurance or stamina. Also, these complex carbohydrates should help your brain generate a steady stream of serotonin, which may reduce your level of nervousness or tension on test days.

> **CLASSIC QUOTE**
>
> "No man can be wise on an empty stomach."
>
> —George Elliot, 19th-century English novelist

2. **Make the meal you eat before an exam a light meal.**

   You don't want to take tests while feeling hungry, but the meal you consume nearest test time should not be a large one. Humans tend to get sleepy after consuming a large meal because it elevates our blood sugar to such a high level that large amounts of insulin are released into the bloodstream in order to reduce our high blood-sugar level. This draws blood sugar away from the brain, which results in a feeling of mental fatigue.

3. **If you feel you need an energy boost immediately before an exam, eat a piece of fruit rather than a candy bar.**

   Candy bars are processed sweets that can offer a short burst of energy provided by the sugar. Unfortunately, however, this short-term rise in blood sugar and quick jolt of energy is accompanied by an increase in nervous tension and is followed by a sudden, sharp decrease in energy and increase in sluggishness (Haas, 1994).

   The key is to find a food that can produce a state of elevated energy without elevating tension (Thayer, 1996) and maintains that state of energy at an even level. The best nutritional option we have for accomplishing this sustained level of energy is the natural sugar contained in a piece of fruit, not processed sugar that's artificially slipped into a candy bar.

4. **Avoid consuming caffeine before an exam.**

   Even though caffeine is a stimulant that increases alertness, it's also a legal drug that can increase your level of tension and make you jittery, which is not what you want to be feeling during a test, particularly if you tend to experience test anxiety. Also, caffeine is a diuretic, which means it will increase your urge to urinate. Naturally, this is an urge that you could do without during an exam when you're confined to a classroom for an extended period of time, sitting on your butt (and bladder).

Try to get to the test a few minutes early.

Getting to the test ahead of time will give you time to review any mnemonic devices or memory-improvement shortcuts that you may have created, as well as hard-to-remember terms, formulas, equations, etc. This strategy will help get them on your mind and into your short-term memory, so that you can retrieve them as soon as you receive the exam. Arriving early will also allow you to take a few minutes to get into a relaxed pre-test state by thinking positive thoughts, taking slow, deep breaths, or stretching and relaxing your muscles. Try to avoid discussing the test with other students just before the test begins because their last-minute questions, confusion, and anxiety may "rub off" on you. (Anxiety can be contagious.)

During the Test

As soon as you receive the test, write down any mnemonic devices or memory-improvement shortcuts that you may have created, as well as hard-to-remember terms, formulas, equations, etc.

This strategy ensures that you don't forget key information after you begin the test and get involved in the process of reading and answering questions, which can create memory interference for information you studied prior to the exam.

STUDENT PERSPECTIVE

"Avoid flipping through notes (cramming) immediately before a test. Instead, do some breathing exercises and think about something other than the test."

—Advice to first-year students from a college sophomore (Walsh, 2005)

Answer the easier test questions first.

As soon as you receive the test, before launching into the first question, take a moment to check out the layout of the test. Note the questions that are worth the most points and the questions that you know well. Studies show that when easier questions are answered at the start of a test, students tend to perform better on more difficult questions that come later (Savitz, 1985) and achieve higher overall test scores (Roos et al., 1996). A good test-taking strategy is to place a checkmark by any difficult questions that you encounter and come back to them later. This strategy is recommended for several reasons:

- It will prevent you from devoting so much time trying to answer difficult questions that you end up running out of time before getting to questions you know well and would earn you full credit.

- After you've answered and obtained full credit for all the questions you know well, you will feel more confident and relaxed because you already have a good number of points "under your belt." This should reduce your anxiety level when you return to the more difficult items. Research shows that our ability to solve difficult problems and think creatively is improved when our anxiety levels are not high (Teigen, 1994).

- It allows you to put the difficult questions out of your mind for a while before coming back to them. Sometimes, answers or solutions suddenly pop into your mind after you get away from them and come back to them later (Csikszentmihalyi, 1996).

- By skipping difficult questions and proceeding to the more manageable ones, you may find information in the easier questions that relate to the more difficult ones and may help you answer them. You could then take this information and go back to solve some of the difficult questions that you previously skipped.

If you experience "memory block" for information that you know you've studied and have stored in your brain, try using the following strategies:

- Mentally put yourself back in the environment or situation in which you studied the information. Recreate the steps in which you learned the information that you've temporarily forgotten by mentally picturing the place where you first heard or saw it and where you studied it, including its sights, sounds, smells, time of day, etc. This memory-improvement strategy is referred to as "guided retrieval," and research supports its effectiveness (Glenberg et al., 1983). In fact, people use it all the time to help them remember a lost item by retracing their steps and trying to recall where they saw it last. Also, detectives use guided retrieval to help witnesses recall details of a crime that they are having difficulty remembering (Czaja, et al., 1994).

- Think of any idea or piece of information that may be related to the information you cannot retrieve. This related piece of information may trigger your memory for the forgotten information because related pieces of information are usually stored as memory traces within the same network of brain cells. Studies show when students experience temporary forgetting, they're more likely to suddenly recall that information if they first recall partial information that relates to it in some way (Reed, 1996).
- Take your mind off the question and turn to another question. Just taking your mind off it for a while may allow your subconscious to work on it and trigger your memory. Also, you may find information appearing in later *test questions* that may serve as a retrieval cue for stimulating your recall of the information you've forgotten.

Pause for Reflection

During tests, when I experience memory block, I usually _____.

I am most likely to experience memory block in the following subject areas:

STUDENT PERSPECTIVE

"Taking tests are for the most part a constant battle for me, as I tend to get anxious during a test or exam. The anxiety issue causes me to then forget the information retained prior to the test."

—First-year student's response to the question "Do you consider yourself to be a good test-taker?"

To manage test anxiety, consider the following practices and strategies.

1. Focus your attention on the here and now—concentrate fully on the process of answering the test question that you're currently working on, and avoid thinking or worrying about what the future outcome may be—i.e., your eventual test grade.

2. Focus your vision on the test in front of you, not the students around you. Do not spend valuable test time looking at what others are doing and wondering whether they are doing better than you are. If you came to the test well prepared and are still finding the test to be difficult, it's very likely that other students are finding it difficult too. (And if you happen to notice that other students are finishing before you do, don't assume they "breezed through" the test or that they're smarter than you. Their faster finish may simply reflect the fact that they didn't know many of the answers and decided to give up and get out, rather than prolong the agony.)

3. Do not focus an excessive amount of attention to the amount of time remaining to complete the exam. Repeatedly checking the clock during the test can distract your thought process and increase your stress level, so only check the time periodically. Also, do your time checking after you've completed test questions, rather than during your answers and interrupting your train of thought. (You might also consider taking off your wristwatch or taking out your cell phone and laying it on your desk during the test, so you can check the time more easily during the exam.)

4. Control your thoughts—focus on thinking positively and showing what you know, rather than worrying about what answers you don't know and how many points you have lost. Our thoughts can influence our emotions (Ellis, 1995), and positive emotions, such as those associated with optimism and a sense of accomplishment, can improve mental performance by enhancing the brain's ability to process, store, and retrieve information (Rosenfield, 1988).

5. Keep the test in perspective. The exam does not represent a test of your general intelligence or your overall academic ability, and the score you receive is not a reflection on you as a person (e.g., your character or self-worth). In fact, a low test-grade may not

reflect lack of effort or ability on your part, but instead may reflect the complexity of the course material or the complexity of the test itself. College exams are going to be more difficult than high school tests, and it's less likely that college students will get 90 to 100 percent of the total points on any given exam. Remember that you can achieve good grades on college exams without having to achieve near-perfect test scores.

BOX 5.3 Snapshot Summary — Test Anxiety

- Understand what test anxiety is and what it's not. Do not confuse anxiety with stress. Stress is something that cannot be completely eliminated when you are involved in situations where your performance is being evaluated. Instead of trying to block out stress altogether, your goal should be to control it, contain it, and maintain it at a level that maximizes the quality of your performance. Actually, it is beneficial to experience a moderate amount of stress during tests and other performance situations because moderate stress tends to improve your levels of alertness, concentration, and memory (Sapolsky, 2004). Stress is a physical reaction that prepares your body for action by arousing and energizing it, and this arousal and energy can be used productively to strengthen your performance. In fact, if you were totally stress-free during an exam, this may indicate that you are too laid back and could care less about how well you're doing. Thus, your goal should not be to eliminate or ignore the stress you experience during exams; instead, your goal should be to remain aware of it and keep it at a moderate level, capitalizing on its capacity to help you get "psyched up" and "pumped up," but preventing it from reaching such a high level that you become "psyched out" or "stressed out."

- Identify the symptoms of test anxiety. If your stress level gets too high during exams, you may begin to experience test anxiety—a negative emotional state that can weaken your mental performance by producing mental interference (Tobias, 1985), such as interfering with your attention (Jacobs & Nadel, 1985), memory (O'Keefe & Nadel, 1985), and the ability to think at a higher level (Caine & Caine, 1991). If you experience the following symptoms during tests, your stress level may be at a level high enough to be accurately called test anxiety.
  1. You feel physical symptoms of anxiety during the test, such as: pounding heartbeat, rapid pulse, muscle tension, sweating, or an upset stomach.
  2. You having difficulty concentrating or focusing your attention while answering test questions.
  3. Negative thoughts and feelings run through your head (e.g., fear of failure or self-putdowns such as: "I always mess up on exams").
  4. You rush through the test just to get it over with (and alleviate the anxiety you may be experiencing).
  5. Even though you studied and know the material, you go blank during the exam and forget what you studied. However, you're able to remember the information after you turn in your test and leave the test situation.

- One final note on the topic of text anxiety: If you continue to experience test anxiety after implementing the strategies we have just suggested, seek assistance from a student support professional in your Learning (Academic Support) Center or Personal Counseling Office.

Pause for Reflection

How would you rate your general level of test anxiety during most exams?

High _____

Moderate _____

Low _____

Do you tend to experience different levels of anxiety depending on the type of test you're taking?

On what type(s) of tests do you tend to experience the most anxiety?

Consider the following test-taking strategies for multiple-choice questions.

◆ Read all of the choices that are listed and use a process-of-elimination strategy, whereby you eliminate choices that are clearly wrong and continue doing so until you narrow them down to one answer that seems to be the best choice.

Keep in mind that the correct answer is often the one that is *most probably* true; it does not have to be absolutely true—just "more true" than the other choices listed.

A *process-of-elimination* approach is an effective test-taking strategy to use when answering difficult multiple-choice questions.

◆ Use *test wise* strategies when you do not know the correct answer.

Your decision to choose a particular answer on a multiple-choice question should first be based on your knowledge of the material, rather than an attempt to outsmart the test by figuring out the correct answer based on how the question is worded. However, if you have used all your knowledge and the process-of-elimination strategy still leaves you with two or more answers that appear to be correct, then you should rely on being "test-wise," which is the ability to use the characteristics of the test question itself (such as its wording or format) to increase the probability of choosing the correct answer (Millman,

Bishop, & Ebel, 1965). Listed below are three key, test-wise strategies for making wise choices on a multiple-choice question whose answer you do not know or cannot remember.

1. Pick an answer that contains qualifying words, such as: "usually," "probably," "likely," "sometimes," "perhaps," or "may." Truth often does not come in absolute statements, so options that contain broad generalizations or definitive words are more likely to be false. For example, answers containing words such as: "always," "never," "only," "must," and "completely" are more likely to be false than true.

2. Pick the longest answer. True statements often require more words to make them true.

3. Pick a middle answer rather than the first or last answer. For example, on a question with four choices, select answer "b" or "c" rather than "a" or "d." Studies show that instructors have a greater tendency to place correct answers as middle choices, rather than as the first or last choice (Linn & Gronlund, 1995), perhaps because they think the correct answer will be too obvious or "stand out" if it's listed as the very first or very last choice.

♦ When reviewing your test and checking answers to multiple-choice (or true-false) questions, be especially careful to check for any questions that you may have skipped and intended to go back to later.

In some cases when students skip a question, they forget to skip the number of that question on the answer form, so it throws off the order of their remaining answers by one space or line. On a computer-scored test, this can result in answers being marked wrong because they are off by one space or line on the answer form.

When checking your answers on multiple-choice or true-false tests, do not be afraid to change an answer after you have re-read it and given it more thought.

Since 1928, there have been over 30 studies on the topic of changing answers on multiple-choice and true-false tests (Kuhn, 1988). These studies consistently show that most changed test answers go from an incorrect to a correct answer, and the majority of students who changed answers improved their test scores (Benjamin, Cavell, & Shallenberger, 1984; Shatz & Best, 1987). For example, in one study of more than 1,500 students' midterm exams in an introductory psychology course, it was found that when students changed their answers, 51 percent of the time they went from wrong to right and only 25 percent of the time they went from right to wrong (Kruger et al., 2005). This is probably because students may catch a mistake they made when they read the question the first time, or they discover some information later in the test that causes them to reconsider their first answer. However, you should not go overboard on your answer-changing. If you find yourself changing a large number of your original answers, this may indicate that you were not well prepared for the exam and are just doing a lot of guessing and second-guessing.

On exams, do you ever change your original answers?

If you do change answers, what is the usual reason why you make a change?

Consider the following test-taking strategies for essay questions.

- Make a brief outline or list of bullet points representing the main ideas to be included in your answers before you begin to write them. This strategy is effective for several reasons:
  - An outline will help you remember the major points you intend to make and the order in which you intend to make them. This should help prevent forgetting of any major points once you begin writing and focusing your attention on your sentences and word selection.
  - An outline will improve your answer's organization, which is one key aspect of your essays that your instructor will likely take into consideration when grading them. (You can make your answers' organization even clearer by underlining your major sections or numbering your major points.)
  - Having some advanced idea about what you're going to write about should reduce your test anxiety. The outline will take care of the answer's organization in advance, so you don't have to pay attention to both organizing and explaining your answer at the same time while writing it out.
  - By making an outline for your answers to each essay question before beginning to write any of them, if you happen to run out of test time, your instructor will be able to see your outline for any questions that you didn't have time to complete. Your outline should earn you points, even if you didn't have the opportunity to convert it into sentence form, because it demonstrates your knowledge of the major ideas relating to that unfinished question. (In contrast, if you begin the test by writing out your answers to essay questions one at a time, you run the risk of running out of time before getting to questions you knew well and having nothing on your test to show that you knew them.)

- Get directly to the point on each essay question.
  Avoid elaborate introductions to your answers that take-up your test time (as well as your instructor's grading time) and don't earn you any points. For example, don't start your answers by writing something like, "This is a very interesting question that we had a great discussion on in class . . . ." Your time on essay tests is often limited, so you cannot afford to spend valuable test time on flowery introductions. One strategy for getting right to the point of the question is to immediately include part of the question in the first sentence of your answer. For example, if the question asks, "Discuss how capital punishment may or may not reduce the nation's murder rate," your first sentence might be, "Capital punishment may not reduce the murder rate for the following reasons . . ."

- Answer all essay questions as precisely and completely as possible.
  Do not assume that your instructor already knows what you're talking about, or will be bored by details. Instead, take the approach that you are writing to someone who knows little or nothing about the subject—as if you are a teacher and the reader is a student.

 Remember: As a general rule, it is better to *over*-explain than to under-explain your answers to essay questions.

- Whenever possible, cite specific evidence—facts, stats, quotes, and figures—rather than general statements and personal opinions.
  Assume the role of a criminal lawyer who is making a case by presenting concrete evidence ("exhibit A," "exhibit B," etc.). Also, keep in mind that the time allotted for

Exhibit 1

Margin notes: Identical twins / adoption / Parents/family tree

6/6

1. There are several different studies that scientists conduct, but one study that they conduct to find out how genetics can influence human behavior is in <u>identical twins</u>. Since they are identical, they will most likely end up very similar in behavior because of their identical genetic makeup. Although environment has some impact, genetics are still a huge factor, and will more likely than not, behave similarly. Another type of study is with <u>Parents and their family trees</u>. Looking at a subjects family tree will alleviate why a certain person is bi-polar or depressed. It is most likely a cause of a gene in the family tree, even if it was last seen decades ago. Lastly, another study is w/ adopted children. <u>If adopted children act a certain way, that is unique to that child, and researchers find the parents/family tree, they will most likely see similar behavior in the parents/siblings as well.</u>

Margin notes: No freewill / No afterlife

6/6

2. The monistic view of the mind-brain relationship is so strongly opposed and criticised because there is belief or assumption that freewill is taken away from people. For example, if a person commits a heinous crime, it can be argued "monistically" that the chemicals in the brain were the reason, and that a person cannot think for themselves to act otherwise. This view limits responsibility.
Another reason that this view is opposed is because it has been said that there is no afterlife. If the mind and brain are one in the same, and there is NO difference, then once the brain is dead, and is no longer functioning, so is the mind, thus, it cannot continue to live beyond what we know today as life. And this goes against many religions, which is why this reason, in particular, is heavily opposed.

Written answers to two short essay questions given by a college sophomore, which demonstrate effective use of bulleted lists or short outlines to ensure recall of most important points.

essay tests may not allow you to write down all the evidence you know. Be selective and choose to write down your most powerful or persuasive pieces of evidence first.

- Leave extra space between your answers to each essay question. This strategy will enable you to easily add information to your original answer that you may happen to recall at a later point in the test.
- When reviewing and checking your answers on essay test questions, proofread what you have written and correct any spelling or grammatical errors that you find. Elimination of such errors is likely to improve your test score. Even if your instructor does not explicitly state that grammar and spelling will be counted in determining your grade, these mechanical mistakes may still subconsciously influence your professor's overall evaluation of your written work.
- Neatness counts. Research indicates that neatly written essays tend to be scored higher than sloppy ones, even if the answers are essentially the same (Klein & Hart, 1968). This is understandable when you consider that grading essay answers is a time-consuming task that forces your weary-eyed instructor to plod through multiple styles of handwrit-

ing—whose readability may range from crystal clear to cryptic code. So, make a point of writing as clearly as possible; and if you happen to finish the test with time to spare, "clean up" your writing by re-writing any sloppily written words or sentences.

◆ Before turning in your test, carefully review and double-check your answers.

This is the critical last step in the process of effective test taking. Sometimes the rush and anxiety of taking a test can cause test-takers to overlook details, misread instructions, unintentionally skip questions, or make absentminded mistakes. When taking essay tests, there may also be a natural tendency to grow tired of writing toward the end of the test and fall into the mindset that you just want to finish it up, turn it in, and get the whole thing over with. Try to avoid this tendency, as well as any ego-trip tendency to be among the fastest students in class to turn in their test. Instead, take some time after you're done to systematically review your answers and be sure that you didn't make any mindless mistakes. If you take into account the amount of time and effort you put into preparing for the exam, it certainly makes good sense to take just a few more minutes to be sure that you get the "maximum mileage" out of the time and effort you spent on test preparation.

Pause for Reflection

Honestly rate yourself in terms of how frequently you use the following test-taking strategies, according to the following scale:

4 = always, 3 = sometimes, 2 = rarely, 1 = never.

1. I take tests in the same seat that I usually sit in to take class notes.   4 3 2 1
2. I answer the easier test questions first.   4 3 2 1
3. I use a "process-of-elimination" approach on multiple-choice tests by eliminating choices until I find one that is correct or most accurate.   4 3 2 1
4. On essay test questions, I outline or map-out my ideas before I begin to write the answer.   4 3 2 1
5. I look for information included on the test that may help me answer difficult questions, or may help me remember information I've forgotten.   4 3 2 1
6. I leave extra space between my answers to essay questions in case I want to come back to them to add more information later.   4 3 2 1
7. I carefully review my work, double-checking for errors and skipped questions before turning in my tests.   4 3 2 1

•—• CLASSIC QUOTE •—•

"People can't learn without feedback. It's not teaching that causes learning. Attempts by the learner to perform cause learning, dependent upon the quality of the feedback and opportunities to use it."

—Grant Wiggins, Feedback: How Learning Occurs, 1997

After the Test: Troubleshooting Test-Taking Errors and Sources of Lost Points on Exams

Your test results represent a potential source of valuable feedback that you can use to improve your future test performances and your final course grade. Examine your tests carefully when you get them back, being sure to note any written comments that your instructor may have made. See where you went right—so you can do it again, and see where you went wrong—so you can avoid making the same mistake again.

Consider reviewing your test with other classmates. In particular, review your test with a classmate who did exceptionally well because it can provide you with a model that you can learn from and get a better idea about the type of work your instructor expects on exams. Also, con-

Seeking feedback from your peers is a good test-review strategy to identify correct answers after exams, but it's a violation of academic integrity to use it *during* exams.

sider making an appointment with your course instructor to seek feedback on how you might improve your performance on the next test.

When seeking feedback from others, seek quality feedback, which has the following features:

◆ Quality feedback is specific—it precisely identifies what you should do to improve your performance and how you should go about doing it. For example, after a test, seek feedback from your instructors that provides you with more than just information about what your grade is, or why you lost points; instead, seek specific information about what you could do to improve your performance next time.

◆ Quality feedback is prompt—it comes soon after completing a task, because this is the time when you are most motivated to receive it and most likely to retain it. For example, as soon as possible after completing tests or assignments, review your performance with classmates or your professor.

◆ Quality feedback comes early in the learning process—when you still have plenty of time to use it to improve your performance. For example, seek feedback from instructors early in the term, so you have more time to use that feedback to improve your course performance and course grade.

Whatever you do, try not to let a bad test grade get you mad or sad, particularly if it occurs during the first half of the term. Look at mistakes in terms of what they can do *for* you, rather than *to* you. A poor test performance can be turned into a valuable learning experience by using test results as feedback or as "error detectors" for locating the specific source of your mistakes.

Remember: Your past mistakes shouldn't be ignored or neglected; instead, they should be inspected, detected, and corrected so you don't replay them on future tests.

Receiving feedback from your instructor can be an excellent way to improve future performance.

·—· **CLASSIC QUOTE** ·—·

When you make a mistake, there are only three things you should do about it: admit it; learn from it; and don't repeat it.

—Paul "Bear" Bryant, legendary college football coach

Chapter 6: Improving Memory and Test Performance

On those test questions where you lost points, try to pinpoint what stage in the learning process the breakdown occurred by asking yourself the following key questions about the source of lost points on exams:

1. **Did you *have* the information you needed to answer the question correctly?**

    If you didn't have the information, what was the source of the missing information? Was it information presented in class that didn't get into your notes? If so, take a look at the strategies for improving listening and note-taking habits. If the missing information was from your assigned reading, check whether you're using effective reading strategies.

2. **Did you have the information, but did not study it because you didn't think it was important?**

    If this occurred, then you might want to review the study strategies for finding and focusing on the most important information in class lectures and reading assignments.

3. **Did you know the information, but not well enough?**

    This may mean one of three things:
    a. You didn't store the information adequately in your brain, so your memory trace for it wasn't strong enough for you to recall it at the time you took the test. This suggests that more study or practice time needs to be spent on recitation or rehearsal.
    b. There may have been too much interference built-up across all the information you studied, because you crammed too much of it in just before the test. The solution here would be to distribute your study time more evenly in advance of the next exam, and take advantage of the effective "part-to-whole" study method.
    c. You put in enough study time and you spread out your study time well enough, but you didn't study effectively or strategically. For example, you may have studied for essay questions by just reading over your class and reading notes, rather than writing them out and rehearsing them. The solution to this type of error would be to adjust or align your study strategy to better match the type of test you are taking.

4. **Did you study the material but didn't really understand it or comprehend it deeply?**

    If so, you may need to self-monitor your comprehension more carefully while studying to monitor whether you truly understand the material.

5. **Did you know the information but were not able to retrieve it during the exam?**

    If you had the information on the "tip of your tongue" during the exam, this indicates that the memory of it was stored in your brain, but the problem was that you couldn't get at it when you needed it. This error may be corrected by making more use of retrieval cues and mnemonic devices.

6. **Did you know the answer but just made a careless test-taking mistake?**

    If so, the solution may be simply to take more time to review your test after finishing it, double-checking it for absentminded mistakes before turning it in.

STUDENT PERSPECTIVE

"When I have to retain knowledge, I do not procrastinate; I can usually slowly remember everything. The knowledge is in [my] long-term memory, so I usually have no problems retaining it."

—First-year student's response to the question: "When you need to remember information, what strategy works best for you?"

BOX 4 Snapshot Summary

How to Compute Your Grade-Point Average (GPA)

Most colleges and universities use a grading scale that ranges from 0 to 4.0 to represent a student's grade-point average (GPA) or quality-point average (QPA). Some schools use letter grades only, while other institutions use letter grades with pluses and minuses.

Grading System Using Letters Only

Grade = Point Value
A = 4
B = 3
C = 2
D = 1
F = 0

GRADE POINTS Earned Per Course = Course Grade Multiplied by the Number of Course Credits

GRADE POINT AVERAGE (GPA) = Total Number of Grade Points for All Courses Divided by Total Number of Course Units

SAMPLE/EXAMPLE GPA

Course	Units	×	Grade	=	Grade Points
Roots of Rock 'n' Roll	3	×	C (2)	=	6
Daydreaming Analysis	3	×	A (4)	=	12
Surfing Strategies	1	×	A (4)	=	4
Wilderness Survival	4	×	B (3)	=	12
Sitcom Analysis	2	×	D (1)	=	2
Love and Romance	3	×	A (4)	=	12
	16				48

GPA = 48 / 16 = 3.0

Grading System Using Letters with Pluses and Minuses

Grade = Point Value
A = 4.0
A– = 3.7
B+ = 3.3
B = 3.0
B– = 2.7
C+ = 2.3
C = 2.0
C– = 1.7
D+ = 1.3
D = 1.0
D– = .7
F = 0

GRADE POINTS Earned Per Course = Course Grade *Multiplied* by the Number of Course Credits

GRADE POINT AVERAGE (GPA) = Total Number of Grade Points for All Courses *Divided* by Total Number of Course Units

(continued)

SAMPLE/EXAMPLE

Course	Units	×	Grade	=	Grade Points
Roots of Rock 'n' Roll	3	×	C (2.0)	=	6.0
Daydreaming Analysis	3	×	A (4.0)	=	12.0
Surfing Strategies	1	×	B (3.0)	=	3.0
Wilderness Survival	4	×	B+ (3.3)	=	13.2
Sitcom Analysis	2	×	C– (1.7)	=	3.4
Love and Romance	3	×	A– (3.7)	=	11.1
	16				48.7

$$GPA = \frac{48.7}{16} = 3.04$$

Semester or *Quarter* GPA = GPA for one academic term (semester or quarter)*
Cumulative GPA = GPA for *all* semesters or quarters combined

Academic *Sanctions* or *Penalties***
Academic Probation = GPA less than 2.0 in first term
Academic Dismissal = Cumulative GPA continuing to remain below 2.0 beyond first term

Awards for Academic Excellence**
Dean's List = Achieving an outstanding semester GPA (e.g., *3.5* or higher)
Summa Cum Laude = Graduating with Highest Honors (e.g., achieving a cumulative GPA of *3.8*)
Magna Cum Laude = Graduating with High Honors (e.g., achieving a cumulative GPA of *3.5*)
Cum Laude = Graduating with Honors (e.g., achieving a cumulative GPA of *3.3*)

* An academic term at most colleges and universities is either a *semester* (15 weeks) or *quarter* (10 weeks)

** The criteria or standards for academic sanctions/penalties and academic awards can vary from college to college. See your *College Catalog* (*Bulletin*) or *Student Handbook* for details.

Pause for Reflection

When this term began, what grade-point average (GPA) were you hoping to attain?

Based on your grades thus far this term, what GPA do you think you'll end-up with at the end of the term?

••• Summary and Conclusion

We started this chapter by noting that learning and memory are interrelated mental processes, both of which are critical for academic success. It may be said that learning relates more to the *input* (storage) of information into our brain, and memory relates more to the *output* (retrieval) of that stored information when we need it. However, strategies that are effective for improving information storage (learning) and information retrieval (remembering what we've learned) involve similar principles. Both learning and memory can be improved by implementing three key principles:

1. meaningful association—relating what you want to learn and remember to something you already know,
2. organization—grouping or classifying it into categories (also, chunking information into a rhythmic and rhyming pattern, such as a short poem or jingle, can strengthen your ability to remember it), and
3. visualization—creating a visual image of it in your mind.

Furthermore, the way in which your memory is tested may influence your ability to remember what you've learned. You are able to remember information more easily when you're asked to recognize or identify it, such as identifying the correct answer on a multiple-choice test. In contrast, it is more difficult to remember information when you have to recall it entirely on your own, such as recalling information on an essay test or short-answer test. When you are asked to recall information, you are being asked to retrieve it on your own—without any cues or clues provided for you. To handle this more demanding memory task, you need to create your own retrieval cues. In fact, all the effective memory-improvement strategies or mnemonic devices discussed in this chapter have one thing in common: they provide you with a retrieval cue that effectively triggers recall.

We conclude this chapter with a reminder of three key ingredients of successful test performance:

1. Be aware of how your knowledge will be tested and employ memory-improvement strategies that will best enable you to remember and demonstrate what you know.
2. Be "test wise"—maintain awareness of how the characteristics and formats of the test itself, such as the way test questions are worded, can provide clues to correct answers.
3. Manage test anxiety—maintain awareness of the amount of stress you're experiencing during exams and keep it at a moderate level to produce optimal performance.

••• Learning More through Independent Research

Web-Based Resources for Further Information on Improving Memory and Test Performance

For additional information relating to ideas discussed in this chapter, we recommend the following Web sites:

For improving memory:
www.utexas.edu/student/utlc/class/mkg-grd/memory.html
http://memory.uva.nl/memimprovement/eng/

For improving test-taking:
http://web.mit.edu/arc/learning/modules/test/testtypes.html
http://cws.unc.edu/content/view/71/0/1/2/

Name _____ Date _____

Exercise #1. Self-Assessment of Learning Strategies

Look back at the ratings you gave yourself for effective test-taking strategies. Add up your total score for this set of strategies (maximum score for the set would be 28):

Test-Taking Strategy Score: _____

SELF-ASSESSMENT QUESTIONS

1. In what strategy area did you score lowest?

2. Do you think that the strategy area in which you scored lowest is related to your lowest course grade at this point in the term?

3. Of the seven specific strategies listed within the area that you scored lowest, do you see any that you could immediately put into practice to improve your lowest course grade?

Exercise #2. Midterm Self-Evaluation

You are likely to experience a crunch at the midpoint of your first term in college—a wave of midterm exams and due dates for certain papers and projects. This may be a good time for you to step back and assess your academic progress thus far.

Use the form below to list the courses you're taking this term and the grades you are currently receiving in each of these courses. If you do not know what your grade is, take a few minutes to check your syllabus for your instructor's grading policy, and check your scores on completed tests and assignments. This should give you at least a rough idea of where you stand in your courses. If you're having difficulty determining your grade in any course, even after checking your course syllabus and returned tests or assignments, then ask your instructor how you could estimate your current grade.

Course No.	Course Title	Instructor	Grade
1.			
2.			
3.			
4.			
5.			

SELF-ASSESSMENT QUESTIONS

1. Were these the grades you were *hoping* to get? Are you pleased or disappointed?

2. Were these the grades you *expected* to get? (Or, were they better or worse than expected?)

3. If these grades turn out to be your final course grades for the term, what would your overall Grade Point Average (GPA) be? (See "How to Compute Your GPA.")

4. Do you see any patterns in your performance that suggest specific things you are doing well or things that you need to improve?

5. If you had to pinpoint one action step you could immediately take to improve your lowest course grades, what would it be?

CASE STUDY

Bad Feedback: Shocking Midterm Grades

Joe Frosh has really enjoyed his first weeks on campus. He has met lots of interesting people and feels that he really fits in socially. He also likes the fact that his college schedule does not require that he be in class for five to six hours per day, like it did in high school. This is the good news. The bad news is that, unlike high school where his grades were all "A's" and "B's", his first midterm grades in college are three "C's", one "D," and one "F." He was totally stunned and a bit depressed by his midterm grades because he thought he was doing well. Since he never received grades this low in high school, he's beginning to think that he is not college material and may flunk out.

Reflection and Discussion Questions

1. What factors may have caused or contributed to Joe's bad start?

2. What are Joe's options at this point?

3. What do you recommend Joe do now to get his grades up and avoid being placed on academic probation?

4. What might Joe do in the future to prevent this midterm setback from happening again?

Higher-Level Thinking

Moving Beyond Basic Knowledge and Comprehension to Higher Levels of Critical and Creative Thinking

Learning Goals

The primary goal of this chapter is to increase your awareness and understanding of the thinking process, and help you develop the type of higher-level thinking skills needed to excel in college.

Outline

What is Thinking?
What is Higher-Level Thinking?
Defining and Classifying the Major Forms
   of Higher-Level Thinking
      Analysis
      Synthesis
      Multidimensional Thinking
      Dialectical (Dialogic) Thinking
      Balanced Thinking
      Inferential Reasoning
      Critical Thinking
      Creative Thinking
Strategies for Developing and Applying
   Higher-Level Thinking Skills to Improve
   Academic Performance
      Self-Questioning Strategies
      Listening Strategies

      Reading Strategies
      Creating Cognitive Dissonance
      Creative Thinking Strategies
Summary and Conclusion
Benefits of Higher-Level Thinking
Learning More through Independent Research
Exercises:
   Plan to Demonstrate Higher-Level Thinking
      in Your Courses
   Self-Assessment of Higher-Level Thinking
Case Study: Trick or Treat: Confusing or
   Challenging Test?

Activate Your Thinking

Please start this chapter by completing the following sentence:

To me, *critical thinking* means . . .

_____

_____

(At a later point in this chapter, we will discuss critical thinking and flash back to your response to this incomplete sentence.)

What is Thinking?

"Thinking" refers to the mental process of consciously experiencing thoughts, ideas, and images. Psychologists often refer to thinking as "cognition" or as "cognitive" activity (from "cogito," meaning "to think" or "to know"), and distinguish it from emotions (e.g., anger or anxiety) or drives (e.g., hunger or sex). Brain research confirms that thought and consciousness occur in the upper part of the brain, nearer its outer surface, whereas emotions and drives originate from deep within the middle area of the brain (LeDoux, 1996) (Figure 1).

• CLASSIC QUOTE •

Cogito ergo sum
("I think therefore I am.")

—René Descartes, 17th-century French philosopher and mathematician

Figure 1 Where Thoughts, Emotions, and Drives are Experienced in the Brain

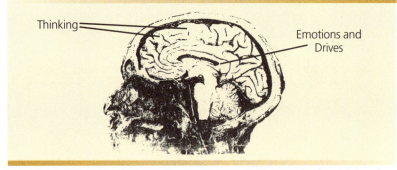

From *The Evolving Brain*, Prof. Ed. 1st edition by Dixon, T. 1978. Reprinted with permission of Brooks/Cole, a division of Thomson Learning: www.thomsonrights.com. Fax 800 730-2215.

The ability to think at higher levels is a key characteristic that distinguishes human beings from other living creatures. When the human brain is compared to the brains of other animals, it is clear that the area that is most responsible for higher thinking—the frontal lobe—is much larger in humans than other animals. This gives humans a distinctive biological advantage in intelligence and enables us to think at higher levels than any other living species (Figure 2).

Some scholars argue that it is the presence of thinking that defines a "living" or an "alive" human being. In contrast, prolonged absence of any electrical activity (flat line) in the upper parts of the human brain that are responsible for conscious awareness and thinking is referred to as "cerebral brain death" (Figure 3).

Figure 2

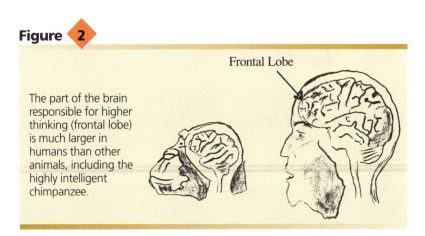

The part of the brain responsible for higher thinking (frontal lobe) is much larger in humans than other animals, including the highly intelligent chimpanzee.

Figure 3

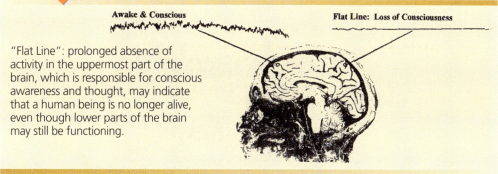

"Flat Line": prolonged absence of activity in the uppermost part of the brain, which is responsible for conscious awareness and thought, may indicate that a human being is no longer alive, even though lower parts of the brain may still be functioning.

From *The Evolving Brain*, Prof. Ed. 1st edition by Dixon, T. 1978. Reprinted with permission of Brooks/Cole, a division of Thomson Learning: www.thomsonrights.com. Fax 800 730-2215.

••• What is Higher-Level Thinking?

Thinking includes all those mental processes that are involved in learning, acquiring knowledge, and comprehending ideas. However, when we use the term "higher-level" thinking, we are referring to thinking that is "higher" than that used for basic learning, and which involves a more advanced level of thought. For instance, reviewing textbook information that you've highlighted and taken notes on does involve thinking, and it will help you learn and remember that information. However, *higher-level* thinking occurs when you reflect on that information and perform a more advanced mental act, such as evaluating its usefulness or integrating it with your class notes to create a larger, more comprehensive product. When you see contestants perform on TV quiz shows (e.g., "Jeopardy" or "Who Wants to Be a Millionaire?"), they are responding with factual knowledge to questions asking for information about who, what, when, and where. If these contestants were to be tested for higher-level thinking, they would be answering more challenging questions, such as: "Why?" "How?" or "What if?"

As its name implies, higher-level thinking involves setting the bar higher and "jacking up" your thinking to levels that go beyond merely remembering, reproducing, or regurgitating factual information. In college, simply remembering information may get you a grade of "C," comprehending the information at a deeper level may get you a "B," and going beyond comprehension to demonstrate higher-level thinking should get you an "A."

Remember: Your college professors want you to do more than just *retain* information; they want you to *attain* higher levels of thinking. So, don't stop thinking as soon as you understand something; instead, take it a step higher and analyze it, evaluate it, build on it, or connect it with other concepts you've learned.

Also, your future employers will expect you to apply higher-level thinking skills to meet challenges and solve problems that arise in the workplace (Business/Higher Education Round Table, 1991, 1992; Secretary's Commission on Achieving Necessary Skills, 1992; Education Commission of the States, 1995).

This is not to say that basic knowledge and comprehension are unimportant. Factual knowledge and basic comprehension in different subject areas provide the necessary foundation for the steps that enable you to climb up to reach higher levels of thinking (Figure 4).

For example, we cannot do higher-level thinking in math until we've acquired factual knowledge (e.g., memorizing our multiplication tables) and basic comprehension (understanding

STUDENT PERSPECTIVE

"To me, thinking at a higher level means deep thought. It is when you have to put your time and effort into whatever you are thinking or writing."
—First-year college student

STUDENT PERSPECTIVES

"To me, thinking at a higher level means to think and analyze something beyond the obvious and find the deeper meaning."
—First-year college student

"To me, thinking at a higher level means going beyond understanding something on a superficial and general level; it requires a deep and profound thought process."
—First-year college student

> **CLASSIC QUOTE**
>
> *What is the hardest task in the world? To think.*
>
> Ralph Waldo Emerson, 19th-century American essayist and lecturer

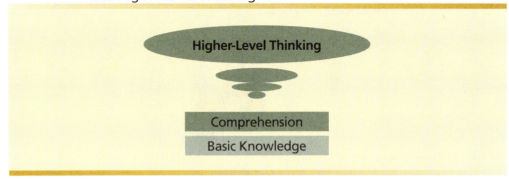

Figure 4 The Relationship between Knowledge, Comprehension, and Higher-Level Thinking

what the concept of multiplication really means). However, higher-level thinking doesn't stop there. It builds on this basic knowledge to reach higher levels of thought, which enables us to solve more complex mathematical problems.

Defining and Classifying the Major Forms of Higher-Level Thinking

> **CLASSIC QUOTE**
>
> *There are one-story intellects, two-story intellects, and three-story intellects with skylights. All fact collectors who have no aim beyond their facts are one-story men. Two-story men compare, reason, and generalize, using the labor of fact collectors as their own. Three-story men idealize, imagine, and predict—their best illumination comes from above the skylight.*
>
> —Oliver Wendell Holmes, 19th-century American poet and physician

Self-awareness or to "know thyself" is a major goal of a liberal arts education. One important aspect of yourself that you should know well is *how you think*. Consequently, our first major objective in this chapter is to dissect the process of higher-level thinking in order to help you gain a deeper understanding of what this thought process consists of, and to help you gain greater self-awareness about whether you're actually using it.

Thinking often takes the form of a private monologue in which we speak silently to ourselves, or sometimes speak out loud to ourselves. The language or vocabulary words we hear and learn to speak with also become part of our "thinking vocabulary," and can strongly influence what or how we think (Carroll, 1964). So, by understanding the "language" of higher-level thinking, such as the words we'll use to define and describe the different forms of higher thinking that we provide in this chapter, you will be taking an important first step toward training your mind to think at higher levels. This will help you demonstrate higher-level thinking in your college courses, which in turn, should help you earn higher grades.

College professors in different academic disciplines will define and emphasize higher-level thinking in different ways (Gardiner, 2005). We think that the various forms of higher-level thinking emphasized in college are most effectively described and classified in terms of seven types of mental skills, each of which will be explained in upcoming sections of this chapter. Our hope is that this classification system may be used as a guide to promote your awareness and use of higher-level thinking skills when you read, write, speak, listen, and study. Here is an overview of the seven major types of thinking skills that will be discussed in this chapter:

1. **Analysis (Analytical Thinking):** *breaking down* information and identifying its key parts or underlying elements.
2. **Synthesis:** *building up* ideas by integrating separate pieces of information to form a larger whole or more comprehensive product.
3. **Multidimensional Thinking:** taking *multiple perspectives* and considering *multiple theories*.

4. **Balanced Thinking:** carefully considering reasons *for and against* a particular position or viewpoint.
5. **Inferential Reasoning:** Using *deductive* and *inductive* reasoning to formulate arguments and reach conclusions.
6. **Critical Thinking:** making well-informed *evaluations* or *judgments* of arguments and conclusions.
7. **Creative Thinking:** producing *new* and *different* ideas, works, methods, or strategies.

We will first describe and illustrate each of these forms of higher-level thinking and then discuss specific strategies for using these skills to improve your academic performance in college.

Analysis (Analytical Thinking)

When you analyze something, you break it down or take apart the whole to identify its key parts or elements. For example, an analysis of a novel would involve identifying such elements as its main protagonist(s), key passages, or its underlying themes. Analysis of a textbook chapter would go beyond simply reading to "cover" the assigned content; it would involve attempting to "uncover" the author's main ideas. We are using analytical thinking in this chapter right now as we attempt to break down the whole process of higher-level thinking into its key elements or forms. Analysis may also involve identification of underlying reasons or causes, which is referred to as *causal analysis.* For instance, a causal analysis of the September 11th attack on the United States would involve identifying the factors that caused or motivated the attack, or the reasons why the attack took place.

STUDENT PERSPECTIVE

"In Physics, you have to be analytical and break it [the problem] down into its parts, and not look at the question all at once."

—*Physics student (quoted in Donald, 2002, p. 1)*

Pause for Reflection

A TV commercial for a particular brand of liquor (which shall remain nameless) shows a young man getting out of his car in front of a house where there's a party. The driver gets out of his car, takes out a knife, slashes his tires, and goes inside to join the party. Using the higher-level thinking skill of analysis, identify the underlying messages that you think this commercial is sending to viewers.

Synthesis

Synthesis is a form of higher-level thinking that is just the opposite of analysis. When you analyze something, you break it down; when you synthesize, you build it up by integrating separate pieces of information to form a larger whole or more complete product. For example, you would be using synthesis if you took related ideas discussed in separate sections or units of a course and connected them together to form a single, unified product—such as a speech, paper, or concept map. You would also be engaging in synthesis if you were to connect ideas presented in different courses; for instance, integrating ethical concepts you learned in a philosophy course with marketing concepts you learned in a business course to produce a set of ethical guidelines for business marketing and advertising practices.

As you may be able to tell from these examples, synthesis involves more than a summary of information on a topic. Instead, it involves finding and forming meaningful connections among separate pieces of information and weaving them together to form a bigger picture. When you are synthesizing you are thinking *conceptually* by converting isolated facts and separated bits of information and integrating them into a *concept*—a larger system or network of related ideas. For instance, when you connect separate facts you know about the sun, the earth, and how the earth rotates and tilts toward the sun at different times of the year, they can be synthesized to form the larger concept of "season" (Anderson & Krathwohl, 2001).

Although synthesis and analysis are opposite thought processes, they work well together. When you analyze, you disassemble wholes into their key parts. When you synthesize, you reassemble these parts to build a new whole. For instance, when writing this book, we analyzed published material in many different fields (e.g., psychology, education, philosophy) and identified parts of these fields that were most important for beginning college students to know. We then synthesized or reassembled these parts to create a new whole—the textbook that you're now reading.

Multidimensional Thinking

A multidimensional thinker is someone who draws conclusions and makes decisions by:

- taking multiple perspectives and
- considering multiple theories.

We will discuss both of these characteristics of multidimensional thinking in the following sections of this chapter.

Taking Multiple Perspectives

This feature of multidimensional thinking involves viewing ourselves, and the world around us, from different angles or vantage points. In particular, multidimensional thinkers consider issues from four key perspectives:

1. Person
2. Place
3. Time
4. Culture

Multidimensional thinkers consider how these four perspectives influence, and are influenced by, the issue they are discussing or debating. For example, they would ask the following types of questions:

1. How would this issue affect my personal health? (The perspective of Person)
2. What impact would this issue have on people living in different countries? (The perspective of Place)
3. How would future generations of people be affected by this issue? (The perspective of Time)
4. How would this issue be interpreted or experienced by groups of people who share different social customs and traditions? (The perspective of Culture)

For instance, global warming is a current issue that refers to the earth's atmosphere gradually thickening and trapping more heat due to a collection of greenhouse gases, which are produced primarily by the burning of fossil fuels. It is theorized that the increase of man-made pollution is causing temperatures to rise (and sometimes fall) around the world and is contributing to natural disasters, such as droughts, wildfires, and dust storms (National Resources Defense Council, 2005; Joint Science Academies Statement, 2005).

A comprehensive understanding and solution to this problem involves taking each of the four major perspectives we just cited, as depicted in Figure 5.

PERSPECTIVE	IMPLICATION
Person	Global warming involves us on an individual level because our personal efforts at energy conservation in our homes and our willingness to purchase energy-efficient products can play a major role in solving this problem.
Place	Global warming is an international issue that extends beyond the boundaries of one's own country to all countries in the world, and its solution will require worldwide collaboration.
Time	If the current trend toward higher global temperatures caused by global warming continues, it could seriously threaten the lives of future generations of people who inhabit our planet.
Culture	The problem of global warming has been caused by industries in technologically advanced cultures, yet the problem of rising global temperatures is likely to have its most negative impact on less technologically advanced cultures that lack the resources to respond to it (Joint Science Academies Statement, 2005). To prevent this from happening, technologically advanced cultures will need to use their advanced technology to devise alternative methods for generating energy that does not continue to release heat-trapping gases into the atmosphere.

Each one of these four key perspectives has different dimensions or elements embedded within it. The four major perspectives, along with the key dimensions that comprise each of them, are listed and described in the box below. (Note how these perspectives are consistent with those developed by a liberal arts education.)

Key Perspectives Associated with Multidimensional Thinking

Perspective 1: PERSON
Individual or Self

Key Dimensions:
- Cognitive—personal knowledge, thoughts, and self-concept.
- Emotional—personal feelings, emotional adjustment, and mental health.
- Social—personal relationships and interpersonal interactions.
- Physical—personal health and bodily wellness.
- Vocational (Occupational)—personal means of making a living and earning an income.
- Ethical—personal values and moral convictions.
- Spiritual—personal beliefs about the meaning or purpose of life and the hereafter.

(continued)

Perspective 2: PLACE
Broader perspectives representing wider circles of social and spatial distance beyond the individual

Key Dimensions:

- Family—perspective of parents, children, and relatives.
- Community—perspective of local communities and neighborhoods.
- Society—perspective of societal institutions (e.g., schools, churches, hospitals) and different groups within society (e.g., groups that differ in age, gender, race, or social class).
- Nation—perspective of one's country or place of citizenship.
- International—perspective of different nations or countries.
- Global—perspective on the planet Earth (e.g., all its life forms and natural resources).
- Universe—perspective on the relationship between earth and its place in a galaxy that includes all other planets and heavenly bodies.

Perspective 3: TIME
The chronological perspective

Key Dimensions:

- Historical—perspective of the past.
- Contemporary— perspective of the present.
- Futuristic—perspective on the future.

Perspective 4: CULTURE
The distinctive way or style of living of a group of people who share the same social system, heritage, and traditions

Key Dimensions:

- Language—how its members communicate through written or spoken words, and through nonverbal communication (body language).
- Political—how the group organizes societal authority and uses it to govern themselves, make collective decisions, and maintain social order.
- Economic—how the material wants and needs of the group are met through the allocation of limited resources, and how wealth is distributed among its members.
- Geographic—how the group's physical location influences the nature of their social interactions and affects the way they adapt to and use their environment.
- Aesthetic—how the group appreciates and expresses artistic beauty and creativity through the fine arts (e.g., visual art, music, theater, literature, and dance).
- Scientific—how the group views, understands, and investigates natural phenomena through systematic research (e.g., scientific tests and experiments).
- Ecological—how the group views the interrelationship between the biological world (human beings and other living creatures) and the natural world (surrounding physical environment).
- Anthropological—how the group's culture originated, evolved, and developed over time.
- Sociological—how the group's society is structured or organized into social subgroups and social institutions.
- Psychological—how its individual members tend to think, feel, and interact; and how their attitudes, opinions, or beliefs have been acquired.
- Philosophical—the group's ideas or views on wisdom, goodness, truth, and the meaning or purpose of life.
- Theological—its members' conception of or beliefs about a transcendent, supreme being, and how they express shared faith in a supreme being.

Most real-life issues, problems, and challenges do not exist in isolation, but as parts of interconnected systems. Using global warming again as an example, this is an issue that is intertwined with ecology—the interrelationship between humans and their natural environment; science—research and development of alternative sources of energy; economics—cost to industry to change their existing sources of energy; national politics—laws may need to be created to encourage or enforce changes in industry's use of energy sources; and international relations—collaboration among all countries that are currently contributing to the problem and could contribute to its future solution.

Reaching conclusions and making decisions that are both accurate and effective requires use of what some scholars call "systems thinking"—taking into account how our decisions affect and are affected by other parts of a larger, interrelated system (Senge, 1990). Systems thinking highlights the importance of viewing issues from multiple perspectives, such as those contained in the lists we have just provided. It is unlikely that you will need to consider all the perspectives on these lists for each issue you study or discuss. Issues you examine in college will probably have implications for some of these perspectives and not for others. It is best to use the four lists of perspectives as checklists; they can be easily scanned to check for perspectives that relate to the issue you're examining and to identify whether an important perspective has been overlooked in your thinking, or in the thinking of others.

> **STUDENT PERSPECTIVE**
>
> "To me, thinking at a higher level is when you approach a question or topic thoughtfully. When you fully explore every aspect of that topic from all angles."
>
> *First-year college student*

Pause for Reflection

Think of a problem in today's world other than global warming. Look back at the key perspectives of multidimensional thinking in Box 1, and briefly explain how one dimension within each of these perspectives may be involved in causing it or providing a potential solution to it.

Considering Multiple Theories

In addition to taking multiple perspectives, multidimensional thinking also involves considering multiple theories. A *theory* may be defined as a body of related concepts and general principles that help us organize, understand, and apply knowledge that has been acquired in a particular field of study. Information-processing theory can be used to organize a large amount of research in the field of learning and memory, so that it can be delivered in a form that is connected and coherent, rather than random and piecemeal. Information-processing theory helps us understand the concepts of learning and memory by explaining it in terms of a three-stage process (input, storage, and retrieval) similar to that used by a computer. We can also use this theory to generate a series of practical strategies that can be applied to improve academic performance.

One major misconception about a theory is that it's impractical. When people hear the word "theoretical," they often interpret it as being the opposite of practical, and they mistakenly conclude that a theory has no practical use, value, or benefit. However, theories do have practical benefits; they help us organize and make sense of research so that we can apply its results to improve the quality of our lives (for example, information-processing theory can improve the quality of our learning and memory).

> **CLASSIC QUOTE**
>
> *Nothing is more practical than a good theory.*
>
> —Kurt Lewin, social psychologist, and first well-known authority on group dynamics

Another common misconception about a theory is that it's nothing more than an opinion or guess. However, scholars in an academic field will not label something a theory until its ideas have been supported by at least some evidence. Don't confuse theory—which is supported by some evidence, with a *hypothesis*—which is an informed guess that *might* be true, but still needs to be tested to confirm whether it *is* true.

Although theories are supported by evidence and have practical value, no single theory can account for the whole truth or tell the whole story. This is why more than one theory exists in virtually every field of study. Different theories explain different portions of the total truth or knowledge that exists in any given field. For instance, information-processing theory alone cannot explain all aspects of human learning and memory. This theory is based on a computer model, and since computers do not experience emotions or feelings, it does not adequately account for the influence of motivation on human learning—for example, how humans often learn information more quickly and retain it longer if they're excited about it or interested in it. So, we also need to consider another theory (motivational theory) to account for how human interest and motivation affects learning and memory.

Although no single theory can account for the whole truth, the good news is that elements of different theories may be combined to explain a larger portion of the total truth. Also, elements of different theories may be combined to give us a more complete and versatile set of tools to use for practical purposes. We are able to generate a wide variety of strategies for improving learning and memory by combining elements of the following theories:

- information-processing theory—e.g., strategies for creating memory cues to retrieve stored information,
- brain-based learning theory—e.g., strategies for using the left and right halves of the brain to record dual (verbal and visual) memory traces, and
- constructivist learning theory (which takes the position that we learn by constructing or building new knowledge on what we already know)—e.g., strategies for using analogies and metaphors that relate what we're trying to learn to what we already know.

If you find yourself thinking or asking the question, "Why do we need all these theories anyway?" keep in mind that scholars in different fields are attempting to understand, explain, and improve the human experience and the world around us. These are not simple, one-dimensional subjects; they are complex, multi-dimensional subjects that involve many factors and perspectives. Thus, multiple theories are needed to understand these multiple factors and perspectives, and to help us develop a more comprehensive set of strategies for improving the human and world condition.

Dialectical (Dialogic) Thinking

Don't be surprised if you find that scholars in the same field disagree about what particular theory accounts for the largest portion of "truth" in their field. Don't be frustrated by such disagreement; it's just part of the normal process of intellectual dialogue that gradually brings us closer and closer to a more complete understanding of the issues and questions found in any field of study. This thought process is referred to as *dialectical* or *dialogic thinking* (Paul & Elder, 2002) (from the root word meaning "conversation"). When you think dialectically, you consider opposing viewpoints—a *thesis* and an *antithesis*; then you engage in an exchange of arguments for and against each viewpoint. During this dialogue, the thesis and antithesis are cross-examined and tested for their strengths and weaknesses. This process of cross-examination gradually leads to a *synthesis*—an integrated and intermediate viewpoint, which is closer to the truth than either the thesis or antithesis.

The mental confusion or contradiction caused by considering opposing viewpoints simultaneously helps reduce oversimplified, "dualistic" (black-or-white) thinking.

Dialectical thinking stimulates and sharpens our thinking skills by forcing the mind to consider the strengths of opposing viewpoints simultaneously, creating a mental experience called cognitive *dissonance*—a state of mental contradiction or disequilibrium (Kurfiss, 1988; Meyers, 1986). When you consider the strengths of opposing positions at the same time, it reduces *dualistic* thinking—an oversimplified form of thinking in which "truth" is seen as something that is always clear-cut and black-or-white, with one answer or position being right and all the others wrong (Perry, 1970, 1999). Thus, your first step in the process of seeking truth is not to immediately jump in and look to take an either-or (for-or-against) stance on a debatable issue. Instead, your first step should be to look at the pros and cons of each position, acknowledge the strengths and weaknesses of each, and identify what additional information may still be needed to reach a conclusion.

Studies consistently show that the majority of first-year college students think in a dualistic (black-white) manner, believing their professors' role is to give them the correct answers and their role is to learn (or memorize) these answers (Baxter-Magolda, 1992; Belenky, et al., 1986; King & Kitchener, 1994). However, in college (and in reality), truth often does not come in the form of absolute answers that are either true or false and conveniently packaged in boxes that are marked "right" or "wrong." This is not to say that there are only opinions and "everybody has a right to their own opinion," or that "everything is relative," or "anything goes." What we are saying is that although there may not be one absolutely correct answer, there are still some answers that are better than others because they are more accurate, and some viewpoints are better than others because they're more *informed*—that is to say, they are based on more accurate information or stronger evidence. Answers are usually not black or white but come in different shades of gray, ranging from lighter to darker, with some answers being closer to the truth than others because they are better supported by evidence.

So, when you encounter multiple theories in college, try not to look at them in dualistic (right-or-wrong) terms. Instead, take an *eclectic* approach, which means that you are open to different theories and are ready to borrow elements from each of them in order to create a more comprehensive understanding of complex issues, and are open to acquiring a more complete set of tools for solving practical problems.

Balanced Thinking

Balanced thinking involves seeking out and giving careful consideration to evidence for and against a particular position. The process of supporting a position with evidence is technically referred to as *adduction*; when you "adduce," you offer reasons *for* a particular position. The process of arguing against a position by presenting contradictory evidence is called *refutation*; when you "refute," you supply evidence against a particular position.

Balanced thinking involves both adduction and refutation. The goal of a balanced thinker is not to stack-up evidence for one position or the other, but to be an impartial investigator who looks at both supporting and contradictory evidence, and attempts to reach a conclusion that is neither biased nor one-sided. If that conclusion favors one position over another, the opposing position's stronger arguments are acknowledged and its weaker ones are refuted (Fairbairn & Winch, 1995).

Balanced thinking requires more than just adding up the number of arguments for and against a position; it also considers the degree of importance of each argument. For instance, suppose you find the following three arguments for a particular position: (1) it would be profitable (economic advantage), (2) it would beautify the environment (aesthetic advantage), and (3) it would help us understand how our environment works (scientific advantage). The only sound argument against this position is that it will increase the risk of cancer for people living in the nearby environment (health disadvantage). Although there are three times as many arguments for this position than against it, its one opposing argument outweighs the combined weight of all three of its supporting arguments, because the preservation or protection of human life is much more important than economic gain, artistic beauty, or scientific advancement. Because preserving human life is such an important or heavily weighed value, this case represents a rather clear-cut example of why arguments for and against a position need to be weighed, not merely added up or tallied like a debit-credit sheet. However, in other cases, the weights that should be assigned to different arguments may be more subtle and subject to disagreement; for example, whether or not to build needed housing for a growing community in a location that may cause the extinction of a rare species of butterfly. In such debatable cases, the weight given to opposing arguments will depend on the value system of the individual who is judging and weighing them.

Remember: A key characteristic of balanced thinking is being aware of the value you place on different arguments, and acknowledging how you weighed them when you reach a conclusion (e.g., in a written report or class presentation).

In some cases, after reviewing both supporting and contradictory evidence for a particular position, balanced thinking may lead you to conclude that you cannot reach a firm conclusion for or against it. For instance, as a balanced thinker, you may occasionally reach conclusions such as, "Right now, I see equally strong arguments for and against this position" or, "I need more information or evidence before I can make a final judgment or reach a firm conclusion." This is not being wishy-washy; it is a perfectly legitimate conclusion to draw, as long as it is an informed conclusion that is supported with sound reasons or evidence. In fact, it is better to hold an undecided, but informed viewpoint that's based on balanced thinking than to hold a definite, but uninformed opinion that's based on emotion—such as those often displayed by people on radio and TV talk shows.

• —• **CLASSIC QUOTE** •—•

Too often we enjoy the comfort of opinion without the discomfort of thought.

—John F. Kennedy, U.S. President, 1961-63

Personal Story

For years I really didn't know what I believed. I always seemed to stand in the no man's land between opposing arguments, yearning to be won over by one side or the other, but finding instead degrees of merit in both. But in time, I came to accept, even embrace, what I called "my confusion," and to recognize it as a friend and ally, no apologies needed. I preferred to listen rather than to speak; to inquire, not crusade.

—"In Praise of the 'Wobblies'" by Ted Gup (2005), *journalist who has written for* Time, National Geographic, *and* The New York Times

Remember: When you combine balanced thinking with multidimensional thinking, you become a comprehensive thinker who views ideas and issues from both sides and all angles.

Pause for Reflection

Consider the following positions:

1. *Course requirements should be eliminated; college students should be allowed to choose the classes they will take for their degree.*
2. *Course grades should be eliminated; college students should take classes on a pass-fail basis.*

Choose one of these positions and use balanced thinking to make two arguments: one for and one against this position.

Inferential Reasoning

Inferential reasoning is a thought process for making arguments and drawing conclusions; it starts with a premise (a statement or an observation) and uses it to *infer* or "step to" a conclusion. For example, the following sentence starters demonstrate the inferential reasoning process:

"Because this is true, it follows that . . . "
"Based on this evidence, I can conclude that . . ."

If you were to represent inferential reasoning in the form of a flow chart, it would look something like this:

     Premise   →   Inference   →   Conclusion
(because/since)   (thus/therefore)   (it can be concluded that . . .)

In college, you will frequently be required to reach conclusions and support those conclusions with evidence. For example, if you are asked to formulate an *argument*, you are being asked to use inferential reasoning to reach a conclusion and support your conclusion with logical reasons or evidence. In a sense, you're being asked to take on the role of a lawyer who is trying to build a strong case by supporting it with solid logic and concrete evidence (exhibit A, exhibit B, etc.).

Inferential reasoning takes place through either of two routes:

1. Deductive reasoning (deduction) or
2. Inductive reasoning (induction).

Since these are the primary ways that humans make arguments and reach conclusions, we will take a close look at both of these forms of inferential reasoning.

Deductive Reasoning (deduction)

When we reason *deductively*, we start with a general statement (the premise); we then infer (step to) a conclusion about a specific instance or particular case by arguing for what follows

> **CLASSIC QUOTE**
>
> *The trouble with English is that there are no answers. There are only evaluations and critical judgments backed up with evidence and strong argument. It requires the ability to make a case through reasoned, logical argument, and the ability to marshal evidence.*
>
> —English professor
> (quoted in Donald, 2002, p. 1)

logically from the general premise. A clear-cut example of deductive reasoning is the *syllogism*—a formal argument that involves a major premise, a minor premise, and a conclusion, such as the following:

> All college students like pizza. (Major premise)
> Greg is a college student. (Minor premise)
> Therefore, Greg likes pizza. (Conclusion)

Notice that this argument starts with a general statement (about college students and pizza), then proceeds to a conclusion about a more specific instance or example (Greg).

When you deduce a conclusion, your logic flows from top to bottom—in other words, it trickles down from a general premise and steps down to infer a conclusion about something more specific. Deduction derives from the same root as the word "deduct," which means to "take away" or "reduce"; thus, deductive reasoning takes from something larger (general premise) to reach a conclusion about something smaller (a specific instance or example).

Inductive Reasoning (induction)

When we reason *inductively*, we start with an observation of a specific instance or case (the premise); we then infer a conclusion that consists of a general statement by arguing that the conclusion follows logically from the specific instance. Here is an example of inductive reasoning that will allow us to compare and contrast it with deductive reasoning:

> I questioned fifty college students and found that each of them likes pizza.
>   (Observation of specific instances)
> Therefore, all college students like pizza. (Conclusion)

Notice that this argument starts with a specific observation (individual college students and pizza), and proceeds to a conclusion about something more general (all college students and pizza). Thus, inductive reasoning moves in a direction that's opposite to deductive reasoning. When you induce a conclusion, your logic flows from bottom to top—in other words, it bubbles up to a more general conclusion by taking an inferential step up from individual instances or specific examples. Induction derives from the same root word as "induct," meaning to "take into." Just as an individual can be inducted or taken into a larger group (e.g., an honor society or the hall of fame), inductive reasoning involves taking an individual instance to reach a larger (more general) conclusion.

Both deductive and inductive reasoning are important forms of higher-level thinking because they represent the primary mental processes humans use to reach conclusions about themselves and the world around them. These are also the two key thought processes that you will use to make arguments and reach conclusions about ideas presented in your college courses. For example, in an art history class, you may be asked to provide specific examples of artwork that represent the same general artistic style; this mental process requires deductive reasoning. Or, you may be shown specific works of art and asked to identify what general style or form of art that each of these instances represent; this mental process requires inductive reasoning.

Critical Thinking

Critical thinking is a higher-level thought process that involves making a judgment or evaluation. This evaluation can be either positive or negative; for example, a movie critic can give a good ("thumbs up") or bad ("thumbs down") review of a film.

Pause for Reflection

Flash back to the first page of this chapter and take a look at your response to the incomplete sentence. How does it match up with the definition of critical thinking we've just provided?

If you wrote that critical thinking means "being critical" or negatively criticizing something or somebody, don't feel bad. Many students think that critical thinking has this negative meaning or connotation.

Critical thinking can also be applied to many things besides judging films, art or music; it's also used to evaluate ideas, beliefs, choices, and decisions, whether they are our own or belong to others. Often, we use critical thinking to make judgments about something's:

- validity (Is it accurate or true?)
- morality (Is it fair or just?)
- beauty (Is it artistic or aesthetic?)
- practicality (Is it useful?)
- priority (Is it the best or most important?)

"Critical thinking is an evaluative thought process that requires deep thinking."

—First-year student's response to the question, "What does critical thinking mean to you?"

Critical thinking may be considered to be one of the highest forms of thinking because we use it to evaluate the quality of other forms of higher-level thinking. For instance, we use critical thinking to judge the quality of our analysis and synthesis, or to evaluate whether our thinking is multidimensional and balanced. In particular, critical thinking is most frequently used to evaluate the inferential reasoning process involved in making arguments and reaching conclusions (King & Kitchener, 1994; Paul & Elder, 2004). Since this is probably the most common function or purpose of critical thinking, we will provide a detailed description of how critical thinking is used to evaluate the two key forms of inferential reasoning: deductive and inductive reasoning.

Using Critical Thinking to Evaluate Deductive Reasoning

When critical thinking is used to evaluate arguments that involve deductive reasoning, two key elements of the argument require careful judgment:

1. Is the premise true? (In other words: Does the argument begin with and build on a statement that is accurate?)
2. Is the conclusion logically consistent with the premise? (In other words: Does the conclusion logically follow or flow from the premise?)

For example, let's apply critical thinking to evaluate the deductive reasoning used in the following argument.

> Mind-altering drugs are harmful to you. (Major premise)
> Alcohol is a mind-altering drug. (Minor premise)
> Therefore, alcohol is harmful to you. (Conclusion)

In this argument, there are two premises that may not be true:

1. The major premise states, "Mind-altering drugs are harmful to you." This is not necessarily true, because taking mind-altering drugs may not be harmful to someone who is

experiencing extreme physical pain (e.g., morphine given to a patient who has just recovered from a major operation), or for someone experiencing extreme emotional pain (e.g., giving an anti-depressant drug to someone who's extremely depressed and suicidal, due to a chemical imbalance in the brain).

2. The minor premise that alcohol is a mind-altering drug is not true in all cases. It is a mind-altering drug if taken in sufficiently large doses; however, if taken in small doses, alcohol may be classified as a beverage (e.g., drinking a glass of wine with dinner). So, a critical thinker would judge the quality of this argument to be weak because its conclusion is built on weak premises.

Now, let's apply critical thinking to evaluate a second key element of deductive reasoning: whether an argument's conclusion is logically consistent with its premises. Consider the following argument:

Alcohol is a dangerous drug because it increases the rate of violent and sexual crimes committed in our society. (Premise)
During the prohibition, drinking alcohol was illegal and people still continued to make alcohol illegally and abuse it. (Premise)
This proves that alcohol is a dangerous drug that should be banned. (Conclusion)

In this argument, both of the premises are true. Studies do show that drinking alcohol does increase the rate of violent and sexual crimes (e.g., date rape). The second premise is also true: During prohibition, people did continue to make alcohol and get drunk. However, the conclusion that alcohol should be banned does not follow logically from the second premise. If alcohol was banned during the prohibition and people still used and abused it, why would there be any reason to conclude that banning it now would provide a solution to the problem? (In fact, it could be argued that it would make the problem worse, because prohibition led to the birth and growth of organized crime groups whose booming illegal business was the selling of illegal or "bootleg" alcohol.) Thus, critical thinking would lead us to question this argument because its conclusion does not logically follow from one of its premises. (In the field of logic, this type of thinking error is referred to as a *non-sequitir*, which literally means: "It does not follow.")

Using Critical Thinking to Evaluate Inductive Reasoning

When critical thinking is used to evaluate arguments that involve inductive reasoning, two different aspects of the argument require careful judgment:

1. Is the size of the sample large enough to make a generalized statement?
2. Is the sample representative—does it accurately reflect the characteristics of the larger group that's referred to in its conclusion?

For example, let's apply critical thinking to evaluate the quality of inductive reasoning used in the following argument.

My father drank alcohol and became an alcoholic. (Specific instance)
My uncle drank alcohol and became an alcoholic. (Specific instance)
Therefore, people should not drink alcohol. (General conclusion)

In this argument, the conclusion is based on just two instances or cases. Critical thinking would lead us to judge this argument as weak, because the number of cases or size of the sample on which it is based is too small to reach a conclusion about people in general. In the field of logic, this reasoning error is sometimes referred to as a *hasty generalization*.

Another criticism of the above argument is that its conclusion refers to people in general; however, the particular instances that have been observed (the two brothers), which form the basis of its conclusion, may not accurately represent or reflect people in general. Said in another way, the argument may be using apples to draw a conclusion about oranges. The two brothers have something in common (their genes), so it is very possible that they may share the same genetic tendency toward alcoholism because they share similar genes. Other people who are unrelated to these brothers are likely to have an entirely different set of genes; thus, it is questionable whether the two brothers can be used as a representative sample to reach the general conclusion that, "People (in general) should not drink alcohol." In the field of logic, this type of "comparing apples to oranges" reasoning error is referred to as a *false* or *weak analogy*.

Logical Fallacies: Errors of Reasoning

As you read the following list of logical errors, make a brief note in the margin of any example of these errors that you have personally observed or experienced.

- **Dogmatism:** Stubbornly clinging to a personally held viewpoint that is not supported by evidence and remaining totally closed-minded (non-receptive) to other viewpoints.

    For example, believing that capitalism is the only economic system that can work in a successful democracy, and not acknowledging the existence of other countries with capitalistic economies, which are successful democracies.

- **Selective Perception:** The tendency to focus on and perceive instances that confirm one's position or conclusion, while overlooking those that contradict it.

    For example, two groups of people that have opposing moral viewpoints on an issue, yet each of them interprets the Bible in a way that supports their own viewpoint. Or, someone believing in astrology who only notices and talks about people whose personalities fit their astrological sign, but fails to notice those who don't.

- **Double Standard:** Having two sets of standards for judgment—a higher standard for judging others and a lower standard for judging oneself.

    This is the classic, "Do as I say, not as I do" hypocrisy. For example, people who critically evaluate and challenge the opinions of others, but not their own.

- **Denial:** Ignoring factual evidence that contradicts one's personal opinions or beliefs.

    For example, saying to someone who presents evidence that contradicts our own opinion: "Anybody can find evidence to support anything they want to believe."

- **Wishful Thinking:** Thinking that something is true, not because logic or evidence indicates that it's true, but because the person *wants* it to be true.

    For example, a teenage girl who does not want to become pregnant and believes that she will not become pregnant, even though she and her boyfriend always have sex without using any contraceptive.

- **Hasty Generalization:** Reaching a general conclusion based on a very limited number of observations or experiences.

    For example, concluding that people belonging to a group are "all that way" or "most of them are that way" on the basis of only one or two personal experiences.

> **CLASSIC QUOTE**
>
> *It's better not to know so much than to know so many things that ain't so.*
>
> —Josh Billings, pen name of Henry Shaw, nineteenth-century American humorist

> **CLASSIC QUOTE**
>
> *Belief can be produced in practically unlimited quantity and intensity, without observation or reasoning, and even in defiance of both by the simple desire to believe.*
>
> —George Bernard Shaw, Irish playwright and Nobel Prize winner for literature, 1925

(continued)

- **Jumping to a Conclusion:** Making a huge leap of logic to reach a conclusion that is based on only one reason or factor, and ignores other possible reasons or contributing factors.

    For example, after being rejected for a date or a job, the rejected person concludes that, "I must be a real loser." (While this may be a possible explanation for the rejection, there are many other reasons or factors that could have been responsible for it.)

- **Glittering Generality:** Making a positive general statement without supplying specific details or evidence to back it up.

    For example, writing a letter of recommendation for someone and claiming that the person is a "wonderful human being" with a "great personality," but not providing any specific reasons or evidence indicating why this person is so "wonderful" or has such a "great" personality.

- **Straw Man Argument:** Distorting an opponent's argument position and then attacking it.

    For example, a politician attacks an opposing candidate for supporting censorship and restricting civil liberties, when the opponent merely supported a ban on violent pornography.

- **Ad Hominem Argument:** Aiming an argument at the person who is being debated, rather than at the issue being debated. (Literally translated, the term "ad hominem" means "to the man.")

    For example, an older person telling a younger person, "You're too young and inexperienced to know what you're talking about." Or, a younger person telling an older person, "You're too old and behind the times to understand this issue."

- **Red Herring:** Bringing up an irrelevant issue that disguises or distracts attention from the real issue being discussed or debated. ("Red herring" derives from an old practice of dragging a herring—a strong-smelling fish—across a trail to distract the scent of pursuing dogs.)

    For example, someone responds to criticism of former president Nixon's involvement in the Watergate scandal by arguing that, "He was a good president who accomplished many good things while he was in office." (Nixon's effectiveness as a president is an irrelevant issue or a "red herring"; the real issue being discussed is Nixon's behavior in the Watergate scandal.)

- **Smoke Screen:** Intentionally disguising or covering up one's true reasons or motives with reasons that are designed to confuse or mislead others.

    For example, a politician opposes gun control legislation by arguing that it is a violation of our constitutional right to bear arms; however, his true reason for opposing it is that he's receiving financial support from gun manufacturing companies.

- **Slippery Slope:** Basically a fear tactic, whereby the person argues that not accepting his or her position will result in a "domino effect"; that is, it will result in a negative event, which will lead to another negative event, which in turn, will lead to yet another negative event, etc. (like a series of falling dominoes).

    For example, "If you experiment with marijuana it will automatically lead to harder drugs, you will lose your motivation, drop out of college, end up in rehab, and ruin your life."

- **Rhetorical Deception:** Using deceptive language to conclude that something is true, without actually providing any reasons or evidence that it is true.

    For example, confidently making such statements as: "*Clearly* this is . . ." or, "It is *obvious* that . . ." or, "Any *reasonable* person can see . . ." without ever explaining why it is so "clear," "obvious," or "reasonable."

- **Begging the Question** (*Circular Reasoning*): Arguing in circles whereby the conclusion is nothing more than a rewording or restatement of the premise.

    For example, concluding that, "Cursing is immoral because it's a sinful thing to do."

- **Appealing to Authority or Prestige:** If someone in authority or who has prestige says it's true or should be done, then it is true and we should do it.

    For example, "Buy product X because this famous and prestigious actor or athlete uses it." Or, "My supervisor told me to do it, so I must do it, whether it's right or wrong, otherwise I wouldn't be following orders."

(continued)

- **Appealing to Tradition or the Familiar**: Concluding that what currently *is* or what has traditionally been is what *should* be or *ought to* be.

  For example, "This is the way it's always been done, so this is the way we should do it."

- **Appealing to Popularity or the Majority** *(Jumping on the Bandwagon)*: Concluding that if a belief is very popular or is held by the majority, then it is true.

  For example, "So many people believe in psychics, it has to be true; they can't all be wrong."

- **Appealing to Emotion** (rather than reason): Reaching conclusions on the intensity of feelings experienced rather than the quality of reasons considered.

  For example, "If I feel strongly about something, it must be true." The expressions, "always trust your feelings" and "just listen to your heart" may not always lead to the most accurate conclusions and the best decisions, because emotions can overpower rational thinking. For instance, when people become involved in a romantic relationship (an emotionally intense experience), their quality of thinking can become seriously impaired, as reflected in expressions such as:

  ☐ "*madly* in love"—losing ability to think rationally;

  ☐ "love is *blind*"—failing to see obvious flaws in the partner

  ☐ "*insanely* jealous"—having irrational thoughts about the partner "cheating."

Sources: Bassham, et al., (2005); Ruggiero (2004); Wade & Tavris (1990).

Creative Thinking

To think creatively is to develop something new or different, whether it may be a product, an idea, a method, or a strategy. In contrast to critical thinking, which leads you to ask the question, "*Why?*" (For example, Why are we doing it this way?), creative thinking leads you to ask the question, "*Why not?*" (For example, "Why not try doing it this different way?"). When you think critically, you look "inside the box" and evaluate the quality of its particular content; when you think creatively, you look "outside the box" to imagine other possible packages containing different types of content. Your past schooling may have trained you to answer questions that other people ask. However, when you think at a higher level, you're the one asking the questions; and when you think creatively, you're asking new or original questions.

Creative ideas have changed the course of human history and are responsible for many modern conveniences, medical advances, and cultural arts we enjoy today. In a world that is rapidly changing due to advances in technology and faster production of new information, the ability to think creatively is a skill that may be more valuable today than at any other time in history (Pink, 2005). Surveys of employers indicate that they place high value on creativity (BCA, 2006) and personal qualities related to creativity, such as "thinking on your feet," "finding the right problems to solve," and "identifying new solutions" (Education Commission of the States, 1995).

Although creative and critical thinking represent different forms of higher-level thinking, they go hand-in-hand. We use creative thinking to ask new questions and generate new ideas, and we use critical thinking to evaluate the ideas we create (Paul & Elder, 2004). A creative idea must not only be different or original; it must also be effective (Sternberg, 2001; Runco, 2004). If critical thinking reveals that the quality of what we've created is poor, we then shift back to creative thinking to generate something that's new and improved. Or, we may start by using critical thinking to evaluate an old idea or approach and come to the judgment that it's not very good. This unfavorable evaluation naturally leads to and turns on the creative thinking process, which tries to come up with a new idea or different approach that is better than the old one.

> **CLASSIC QUOTE**
>
> *The principle mark of genius is not perfection but originality, the opening of new frontiers.*
>
> —Arthur Koestler, Hungarian novelist and philosopher

> **CLASSIC QUOTE**
>
> *Creativity is allowing oneself to make mistakes; art is knowing which ones to keep.*
>
> —Scott Adams, creator of the Dilbert comic strip and author of *The Dilbert Principle*

Creative and critical thinking often involve complementary mental processes, known as *divergent* and *convergent* thinking (Guilford, 1967). When you think creatively, you are using divergent thinking—that is, your thinking "diverges" (spreads out) in different directions, with the goal of generating many different possibilities. In contrast, when you think critically, you are using convergent thinking—that is, your thinking "converges" (narrows in) on each particular idea that you've created and evaluates it. In other words, creative thinking involves generating ideas that *could* be used; critical thinking involves determining which of these ideas *should* be used.

The problem-solving process of *brainstorming* is a classic example of how creative and critical thinking work together. See Box 3 for the key steps or stages involved in the process of brainstorming.

BOX 3 Snapshot Summary

The Process of Brainstorming

Steps:

1. Produce and list as many ideas as you possibly can, generating them rapidly without stopping to evaluate the quality of the ideas. Studies show that worrying about whether an idea is correct often blocks creativity (Basadur, Runco, & Vega, 2000). So, let your imagination run wild; don't worry about whether the idea you generate is impractical, unrealistic, or outrageous.

2. Use the ideas on your list as a springboard to think about and generate additional ideas. In other words, use your listed ideas to trigger new ideas and build on them to produce other ideas.

3. After you run out of ideas, review and evaluate the list of ideas you've generated and eliminate those that you think are least effective.

4. From the remaining list of ideas, choose the best idea or best combination of ideas.

Note that the first two steps in the brainstorming process involve divergent thinking, which goes off in different directions to generate multiple ideas. These first two steps represent the creative thinking stage of the brainstorming process. In contrast, the last two steps in the process involve *convergent* thinking that narrows-in, evaluates, and selects the best idea(s) generated. These final steps represent the *critical* thinking stage of the brainstorming process.

Personal Story

Several years ago, I was working with a friend to come up with ideas for a grant proposal that he was going to write. We started out by sitting at his kitchen table, sipping coffee, and then we both got up and began to pace back and forth, walking all around the room while throwing out different ideas and bouncing ideas off each other. Whenever a new idea was thrown out, one of us would jot it down (whoever was pacing closer to the kitchen table at the moment).

After we ran out of ideas, we shifted gears, slowed down, and sat down at the table to carefully review each of the ideas we just generated during our "binge-thinking" episode. After some debate, we finally settled on an idea that we judged to be the best one of all the ideas we produced, and he made it his grant proposal.

Although I was not fully aware of it at the time, the stimulating thought process we were using was called brainstorming, which first involved creative thinking—our fast-paced walking and idea-production stage, followed by critical thinking—our slower-paced sitting and idea-evaluation stage.

—Joe Cuseo

As the brainstorming process suggests, creativity does not just happen suddenly or effortlessly, like the so-called "stroke of genius"; instead, it takes conscious mental effort (Torrance, 1963; Paul & Elder, 2004). Although it may involve some sudden or intuitive leaps, it also involves carefully reflecting on those leaps and critically evaluating whether any of them actually landed on a good idea.

Furthermore, to think creatively doesn't mean that you have to be an artistic genius. Creative thinking is not restricted to the arts; it can occur in all subject areas, even in fields that seek precision and definite answers. For example, in math, creative thinking may involve using new approaches or strategies for arriving at a correct solution to a problem. In science, creative thinking takes place whenever a scientist uses imaginative thinking to create a hypothesis or logical hunch ("What might happen if . . .?"), then conducts an experiment and collects evidence to see if the hypothesis turns out to be true.

Anytime you combine two old ideas to generate a different idea or a new product, you are engaging in creative thinking. In fact, creative thinking can be viewed as just an extension or higher form of synthesis, whereby parts of separate ideas are combined or integrated, resulting in a final product that turns out to be significantly different from what existed before (Anderson & Krathwohl, 2001). Even in the arts, products that are created are not totally original or unique. Instead, creative art typically involves a combination or rearrangement of previously existing elements to generate a new "whole"—a different total product. For instance, Bob Dylan combined elements of acoustic folk music and amplified rock music to help create a new musical form or genre, which became known as folk rock (Shelton, 2003).

> **CLASSIC QUOTE**
>
> *Imagination should give wings to our thoughts, but imagination must be checked and documented by the factual results of the experiment.*
>
> —Louis Pasteur, French microbiologist, chemist, and founder of "pasteurization" (method for preventing milk and wine from going sour)

••• Strategies for Developing and Applying Higher-Level Thinking Skills to Improve Academic Performance

This section of the chapter is devoted exclusively to practical strategies for developing and applying higher-level thinking skills to improve your performance on academic tasks you face in college, such as: note-taking, reading, discussions, studying, and writing papers or reports. We offer these strategies for the dual purpose of elevating your thinking skills and raising your course grades.

Self-Questioning Strategies

Effective learners are effective self-monitors—they watch themselves while learning and monitor whether they are really understanding what they're attempting to learn (Weinstein & Underwood, 1985). Similarly, effective thinkers engage in a slightly different form of self-monitoring known as *meta-cognition*—they think about how they are thinking (Flavell, 1985).

One simple but powerful way to think about your thinking is through self-questioning. Since thinking often involves talking silently to yourself, if you remain consciously aware of the types of questions you ask yourself, you can become more aware of the types of thinking you are using and more able to control the quality of your thinking. In fact, one standard for judging the quality of any question you ask yourself is its ability to stimulate your thinking and elevate it to a higher level. It could be said that a good question is one that provides rocket fuel for the mind—it launches your thinking upward to higher levels in a quest to answer it.

> **CLASSIC QUOTE**
>
> *The blues are the roots. Everything else are the fruits.*
>
> —Willie Dixon, blues songwriter; commenting on how all forms of contemporary American music contain elements of blues music, which originated among African-American slaves

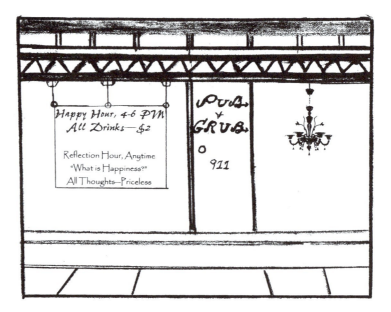

Asking yourself a good question can stimulate your higher-level thinking about almost any experience, whether it takes place inside or outside the classroom.

Pause for Reflection

In the above cartoon, what do you think are the advantages and disadvantages associated with the common practice of bars selling alcoholic drinks at reduced prices?

What do you think are the assumptions or implications of calling this practice "happy hour?"

Since questions have the power to activate and elevate our thinking, you can capitalize on their power by intentionally asking yourself good questions. The higher the level of thinking called for by the questions you regularly ask yourself, the higher the level of thinking you will display in class discussions, on exams, and in the papers you write. Listed in Box 4 is a set of questions that have been intentionally designed to promote the major forms of high-level thinking that have been discussed in this chapter. These questions are constructed in a way that will allow you to easily "fill in the blank" with any type of idea or issue that you may be discussing in almost any college course and academic discipline. Considerable research evidence indicates that students can use questions such as these as effective triggers for stimulating their use of higher-level thinking skills in a variety of academic subjects (King, 1990, 1995).

We recommend that you save a copy of these higher-level thinking questions so that you can use them regularly to monitor and strengthen your own thinking skills on academic tasks, such as studying or writing papers, and to stimulate the thinking of others during class discussions or study-group sessions.

> **TAKE ACTION NOW!** Box 4
>
> ## Questions for Stimulating Different Forms of Higher-Level Thinking
>
> **Analysis (Analytical Thinking):** to break down information into its essential elements or parts.
>
> *Trigger Questions*
>
> - What are the main ideas contained in _____?
> - What are the important aspects of _____?
> - What are the key issues raised by _____?
> - What are the major purposes of _____?
> - What assumptions or biases lie hidden within _____?
> - What were the reasons behind _____?
>
> **Synthesis:** to combine and integrate separate bits or pieces of information to form a larger product or pattern.
>
> *Trigger Questions*
>
> - How can this idea be joined or integrated with _____ to create a more complete or comprehensive understanding of _____?
> - How could these different _____ be grouped together into a more general class or category?
> - How could these separate _____ be reorganized or rearranged to produce a more comprehensive understanding of the "big picture?"
>
> **Taking Multiple Perspectives:** thinking that involves viewing ourselves, and the surrounding world, from different angles or vantage points.
>
> *Trigger Questions*
>
> - How would _____ affect different dimensions of myself (e.g., emotional, physical, etc.)?
> - What broader impact would _____ have on the social and physical world around me?
> - How might people living in different times (e.g., past and future) view _____?
> - How would people from different cultural backgrounds interpret or react to _____?
> - Have I taken into consideration all the major factors that could influence _____ or be influenced by _____?
>
> **Balanced Thinking:** carefully considering reasons for and against a particular position or viewpoint.
>
> *Trigger Questions*
>
> - What are the strengths/advantages and weaknesses/disadvantages of _____?
> - What evidence supports and contradicts _____?
> - What are the arguments for and the counterarguments against _____?
> - Have I considered both sides of _____?
>
> **Adduction:** arguing for a particular idea or position by supplying supporting evidence.
>
> *Trigger Questions*
>
> - What proof is there for _____?
> - What are logical arguments for _____?
> - What research evidence supports _____?
>
> **Refutation:** arguing against a particular idea or position by supplying contradictory evidence.
>
> *Trigger Questions*
>
> - What proof is there against _____?
> - What logical arguments indicate that _____ is false?
> - What research evidence contradicts _____?
>
> *(continued)*

Deductive Reasoning: inferring conclusions about specific instances or particular cases that follow logically from a general statement.

Trigger Questions
- What specific conclusion can be drawn from the general statement that _____?
- What particular actions or practices would be consistent with the general statement that _____?
- If the general statement _____ is true, it logically follows that _____.

Inductive Reasoning (Induction): inferring conclusions that involve a general statement, which follows logically from observation of specific instances or examples.

Trigger Questions
- What are the broader implications of _____?
- What are the common themes or patterns in _____?
- What general concept or principle can be drawn from _____?

Critical Thinking: making well-informed evaluations or judgments.

Trigger Questions for Evaluating Validity:
- Is _____ true or accurate?
- Is there sufficient evidence to support the conclusion that _____?
- Is the reasoning behind _____ strong or weak?

Trigger Questions for Evaluating Morality:
- Is _____ fair?
- Is _____ just?
- Is _____ ethical?
- Is this action consistent with the professed or stated values of _____?

Trigger Questions for Evaluating Beauty (Aesthetics):
- What is the artistic merit of _____?
- Does _____ have any aesthetic value?
- Does _____ contribute to the beauty of _____?

Trigger Questions about Practicality (Usefulness):
- Will this _____ work?
- Can this _____ be put to good use?
- How would _____ provide help or benefit for _____?

Trigger Questions about Priority (Order of Importance or Quality):
- Which one of these _____ would be most effective?
- Is this _____ the best option or choice available?
- How should these _____ be ranked from first to last (best to worst) in terms of their quality?

Creative Thinking: producing new or different ideas, products, methods, or strategies.

Trigger Questions
- What could be invented to _____?
- What might happen if _____?
- What might be a different way to _____?
- How would this change if _____?
- What would be an original idea for _____?

Pause for Reflection

Look back at the forms of thinking described in Box 4. Take one question listed under each of these forms of thinking and fill in the blank with a concept or issue you're learning about in a course you're taking this term.

Personal Story When I teach classes or give workshops, I often challenge students or participants to debate me on either politics or religion. I ask them to choose a political party affiliation, a religion or a branch of religion for their debate topic, and a social issue that they have a stance on that can be backed up politically or religiously. The ground rules are as follows: I will let them choose the topic for debate, they can only use facts to pose their argument and/or rebuttal, and they can only respond in an analytical, balanced manner without letting emotions drive their answers. This exercise demonstrates that the topics we feel strongly about are often the topics we don't look at critically. People often say they are Democrat, Republican, Independent, etc., and argue that they are sure this is where they stand, and who they are. However, very few people actually spend time critically thinking about whether that description really fits. Have they read the core document (i.e., party platform) that outlines the party stance? Have they determined whether those core documents hold up to higher-level thinking processes? What kind of examination has this belief been through (thought, debate, discussions, etc.)? Do *your* beliefs hold up to careful examination?

—Aaron Thompson

Listening Strategies

When listening to lectures and professional presentations, pay attention not only to the content of the message, but also to the thinking process that lies behind it.

You can use the list of higher-level thinking questions in Box 4 to help you detect the type of thinking your instructors are using and to keep your thinking at higher levels during lectures.

Asking yourself higher-level thinking questions during lectures should prevent you from asking questions like this one.

Reading Strategies

When completing reading assignments and listening to class lectures, try to get in the habit of *cross referencing* or connecting ideas you come across that relate to ideas you've previously encountered.

When you discover information that relates to something you've learned about elsewhere, make a note of it in the margin of your text or your class notebook. This practice will help you develop and demonstrate synthesis on course exams and writing assignments.

Creating Cognitive Dissonance

To increase your ability to engage in balanced thinking, intentionally hold opposing ideas in your mind at the same time to put yourself in a mental state of cognitive dissonance.

Studies show that this type of cognitive contradiction or friction serves to decrease dualistic thinking and increase balanced thinking (Kurfiss, 1988; Meyers, 1986). Listed below are some specific strategies for creating cognitive dissonance.

- Find arguments for a position, then reverse your thinking and switch sides to argue for the opposing viewpoint.

- When doing research on a controversial issue, proceed as if you are going to defend and refute both sides of the issue. For instance, seek out readings that take opposing viewpoints and compare or contrast them. This will enable you to develop and demonstrate balanced thinking in your assignments and discussions.

- During group discussions with classmates, seek out different viewpoints or positions. For example, ask questions such as: "Who doesn't agree with what's being said?" or, "Would someone else like to express an opposing viewpoint?"

    Studies show that the positive impact of interacting with peers on developing higher-level thinking skills is greatest when peers challenge each other's beliefs, which promotes personal reflection and re-evaluation (Pascarella & Terenzini, 2005). Seeking out different ideas doesn't mean that you are indecisive, looking to conform to someone else's viewpoint, or that you want to be a "yes man" who always agrees with others. Nor does it mean that you don't want to be a "no man" who always disagrees with others or ignores their viewpoints. Instead, you want to be an "open person" who seeks out and listens to different viewpoints in order to gain access to additional ideas that may make your viewpoint more balanced and complete.

    By seeking out and discussing opposing viewpoints during group discussions, your group benefits by what social psychologists call the "group depolarization" effect—the tendency for each group member's position to become less extreme (depolarized) as a result of being exposed to an alternative viewpoint (Taylor, Peplau, & Sears, 2006). This strategy is not only valuable for improving the balance and quality of your group discussions in college, but it will also improve the group discussions you're likely to become involved in beyond college (e.g., committee work and jury duty).

- During group discussion, periodically play the role of *devil's advocate*—the person who points out the shortcomings or weaknesses in the position that everyone else seems to be taking. This will promote your group's awareness of the limitations or disadvantages of its viewpoint, and will help them avoid what social psychologists call "group think"—the tendency for a tight-knit group of like-minded people whose thinking is so much alike that they become blind to its weaknesses (Janis, 1982). Even if you are persuaded by your group's position, always be on the lookout to find and acknowledge its possible limitations or weaknesses.

CLASSIC QUOTE

The test of a first rate intelligence is the ability to hold two opposed ideas in the mind at the same time, and still retain the ability to function.

—F. Scott Fitzgerald, early 20th-century novelist and short-story writer

CLASSIC QUOTE

I make progress by having people around who are smarter than I am—and listening to them. And I assume that everyone is smarter about something than I am.

—Henry Kaiser, successful industrialist, known as the "Father of American shipbuilding"

Remember: The goal of group work is not to encourage rigid conformity or blind loyalty among its members, nor is it to discourage disagreement or dissent. As a responsible group member, one of your key roles is to encourage other members to express their individual viewpoints, even if they differ from the majority. If you are the person who holds a view that differs from other members, your role is to help your group seek *consensus*—which means one of three things:

1. you change your mind and agree with other members of your group,
2. group members change their minds and agree with you, or
3. you and the other group members agree to disagree and move on.

Complete the following sentence with the first idea that comes to your mind:

To come up with creative ideas, you should _____

Creative Thinking Strategies

- Carry a small notepad or packet of post-its with you at all times because creative ideas can come to mind at the most unexpected times. The process of having a creative idea suddenly pop into your mind is referred to as *incubation*—because, just like an egg, an idea can suddenly hatch and emerge from your subconscious after you've sat on it for a while. However, just as creative ideas can suddenly slip into your mind, they can just as quickly slip out of your mind when you start thinking about something else. So, be sure to have the right equipment on hand to record and save your creative ideas before you lose them.

- When working on a problem that you cannot seem to solve, stop working on it for a while, and come back to it later. Creative solutions to a problem can sometimes appear after you stop thinking about it, take your mind off it, and return to it at a later point in time. Sometimes, when you're working intensely on a problem or challenging task, your attention may become mentally set or rigidly fixed on one aspect of it (Maier, 1970). Taking your conscious mind off it for a while may relax you and allow the problem to incubate in your subconscious, which may produce a sudden insight. Also, when you come back to the task later, your focus of attention is likely to shift to a different feature or aspect of it. This new focus point may enable you to view the problem from a different angle or vantage point, which can sometimes lead to a breakthrough idea that was blocked by your previous perspective (Anderson, 2000).

- When you're stuck on a problem, try rearranging its parts or pieces. The rearrangement can transform the problem into a different pattern and provides you with a new perspective. This new perspective may, in turn, allow you to suddenly see a solution that you previously missed, just like changing the order of letters in a word jumble may suddenly enable you to see the hidden, scrambled word. Similarly, you may increase your creative insights by changing the wording of any problem you're working on, or by recording ideas on index cards (or post-it notes) and laying them out in different orders and arrangements.

- If you are having trouble solving problems that involve a sequence of steps (e.g., math problems), try changing the sequence by reversing their order and working backwards, or starting in the middle. The new sequence may change your approach to the problem

> **CLASSIC QUOTE**
>
> *Eureka! (Literally translated, 'I have found it!')*
>
> —Attributed to Archimedes, ancient Greek mathematician and inventor, after he suddenly discovered a solution to the problem of how to measure the purity of gold

> **CLASSIC QUOTE**
>
> *Creativity consists largely of re-arranging what we know in order to find out what we do not know.*
>
> —George Keller, prolific American architect, and originator of the Union Station design for elevated train stations

There are several strategies for coping with a difficult problem, such as coming back to it later, rearranging its parts, or working at the problem backwards.

by forcing you to come at it from a different direction, which could provide you with an alternative path to its solution.

- ◆ Represent what you're thinking about in different sensory modalities. For instance, take verbal information and represent it in visual form, such as a diagram, flow chart, or idea map. This will increase the number of brain areas that become stimulated and engaged in the creative thinking process.

- ◆ Use multiple sources by drawing on ideas from different people and different fields of study. Trading ideas with different people and bouncing ideas off them is a good way to generate energy, synergy, and serendipity (accidental discoveries). Studies show that creative people have a wide range of knowledge and interests, and they tend to combine ideas from different sources (Riquelme, 2002). For instance, creative people in specialized fields often build on a large store of knowledge that goes beyond the boundaries of their particular area of specialization and seek connections across different subject areas (Baer, 1993; Kaufman & Baer, 2002). The broad base of knowledge and wide range of thinking skills you acquire from the liberal arts will enhance your creativity. The general knowledge acquired from different subject areas that comprise the liberal arts can be combined and connected to form bridges to new ideas.

- ◆ Be flexible. Think about ideas and objects in unusual or unconventional ways. The power of flexible and unconventional thinking was well illustrated in the nonfiction movie, "Apollo 13," when an astronaut saved his life by creatively using duct tape as an air filter. Johannes Gutenberg discovered the idea of a printing press when he was watching a machine being used to crush grapes at a wine harvest. He thought that the same type of machine could be used to press letters onto paper (Dorfman, Shames, & Kihlstrom, 1996).

- ◆ Be experimental. Play with different ideas. Try out new ideas to see if they will work, and whether they will work better than the status quo. Studies show that creative people tend to take risks by experimenting with different ideas and techniques (Sternberg, 2001). Don't take the attitude that "it won't work" or "if it ain't broke, don't fix it." Instead, adopt an experimental attitude that asks: "How do we know it won't work until we try it?" And if it's already working, how might it work even better—more effectively, efficiently, or aesthetically. In other words, strive for continuous quality improvement by continually thinking about ways to create new and improved versions of what already exists. Actively resist settling for the security of familiarity. Doing things the way they've always been done doesn't mean you're doing them the best way they could be done. It may mean that it's just the most habitual (and mindless) way to do them. When we cling rigidly or stubbornly to what is conventional or traditional, we may be clinging to the comfort and security of what is most familiar and predictable while resisting the challenge of creativity and change.

- ◆ Be mobile. Get up and move around. By just standing up, studies show that our brain gets approximately 10 percent more oxygen than it does when we're sitting down (King, 1996). Since oxygen provides fuel for the brain, our ability to think creatively may be enhanced when we think on our feet and move around, rather than thinking while sitting down for extended periods of time.

- Be persistent. Studies show that creativity takes time, dedication, and hard work (Ericsson & Charness, 1994). Creative thoughts do not often emerge in one sudden stroke of genius, but evolve after continuous reflection and persistent effort.

> **CLASSIC QUOTE**
>
> *Genius is 1% inspiration and 99% perspiration.*
>
> —Thomas Edison, scientist and creator of over 1,000 inventions, including the light bulb, phonograph, and the motion picture camera

Pause for Reflection

Post-It® Notes are very popular, perhaps because they stick on almost anything and can be stuck in any place; then they can be removed (without a mess) and re-stuck in a different place. Think creatively for a minute and come up with as many possible ways that students could use Post-Its to handle different tasks they face in college.

Summary and Conclusion

In this chapter, we analyzed the process of higher-level thinking and examined its individual forms separately in order to highlight their differences. However, in reality, these different forms of thinking typically work together in pairs, with one skill complementing the other. The various forms of higher-level thinking that have been discussed in this chapter may be concisely summarized in terms of the following complementary pairs of mental processes:

- **Analysis and Synthesis:** we use *analysis* to break down ideas into their parts or elements, and we use *synthesis* to build-up larger ideas (concepts) by connecting or integrating separate pieces of information.
- **Multidimensional and Balanced Thinking:** we look at issues from all angles (different perspectives and theories) to attain *multidimensional* thinking, and from both sides (pros and cons) to attain *balanced* thinking.
- **Dialectical and Dualistic Thinking:** we look at opposing arguments at the same time (dialectical thinking) to prevent us from thinking in overly simplistic, black-or-white terms (dualistic thinking).
- **Deductive and Inductive Reasoning:** we use *deductive* reasoning to move logically from general principles to reach conclusions about specific instances, and we use *inductive* reasoning to move logically from specific instances to reach conclusions that involve general statements or principles.
- **Divergent and Convergent Thinking:** we use *divergent* thinking to spread out our thinking in different directions to consider multiple ideas, and we use *convergent* thinking to narrow in and focus our thinking on a single idea.
- **Critical and Creative Thinking:** we use *critical* thinking to evaluate existing ideas, and we use *creative* thinking to generate new ideas.

Benefits of Higher-Level Thinking

Higher-level thinking is the most important teaching goal of college faculty.

Simply stated, college professors are more concerned about teaching you *how* to think than teaching you *what* to think (e.g., what facts to remember, or what position to take). In a national survey of 40,000 college professors teaching freshman-level through senior-level courses in a wide variety of fields, 97 percent of them reported that the most important goal of a college education is to develop students' ability to think critically (Milton, 1982). Similarly, college professors who teach introductory courses to freshmen and sophomores indicate that the primary educational purpose of their courses is to develop students' critical thinking skills (Stark et al., 1990).

Since thinking skills are valued by professors who are teaching students at all stages in the college experience and all subjects in the curriculum, if you work on developing these skills, it should be time well spent and should improve your academic performance significantly.

Higher-level thinking and research skills are increasingly important in today's information age, in which increasing amounts of information are being produced at increasingly faster rates.

As futurologist John Naisbitt (1982) predicted in *Megatrends*, "Running out of [information] is not a problem, but drowning in it is" (p. 24). The tidal wave of factual information currently being produced cannot be simply remembered or memorized, and even if it could, most of it would soon become outdated and replaced by the next wave. Thus, acquiring factual knowledge is less important than developing:

- information-literacy skills—which will allow you to efficiently search for and find information that is most relevant to your needs, and
- critical thinking skills—which will enable you to evaluate and select only the best information from the overwhelming amount that's at your fingertips (Cross, 1993).

The majority of new workers in the information age will no longer work with their hands but with their heads (Miller, 2003), and employers will value college graduates who have inquiring minds and possess higher-level thinking skills (Harvey, et al. 1997).

Higher-level thinking skills are vital for citizens in a democracy.

Authoritarian political systems, such as dictatorships and fascist regimes, suppress critical thought and demand submissive obedience to authority. In contrast, citizens living in a democracy are expected to control their political destiny by choosing (electing) their political leaders; thus, judging and choosing wisely is a crucial civic responsibility in a democratic nation. Citizens living and voting in a democracy must use higher-level reasoning skills, such as balanced and critical thinking, to make wise choices.

Research indicates that political campaigns in America are making more frequent use of manipulative media advertisements. These ads rely on short sound bites, one-sided arguments, and powerful visual images, which are intentionally designed to appeal to emotions and encourage simplistic thinking (Goleman, 1992). The need for Americana citizens to develop and deploy higher-level thinking skills may be more important today than at any other time in the nation's history, because these are the mental skills that empower voters to detect and resist the growing use of political propaganda.

Higher-level thinking is an important safeguard against prejudice, discrimination, and hostility.

Racial, ethnic, and national prejudices often stem from narrow, self-centered, or group-centered thinking (Paul & Elder, 2002). Prejudice often results from oversimplified, dualistic thinking that can lead individuals to categorize other people into either in-groups ("us") or out-groups ("them"). This type of dualistic thinking can lead, in turn, to ethnocentrism—the tendency to view one's own racial or ethnic group as the superior "in-group," while other groups are seen as inferior "out-groups." Development of higher-level thinking skills, such as taking multiple perspectives and using balanced thinking, counteracts the type of dualistic, ethnocentric thinking that can lead to prejudice, discrimination, and hatred.

••• Learning More through Independent Research

Web-Based Resources for Further Information on Higher-Level Thinking

For additional information on concepts covered in this chapter, see the following Web sites.

Critical Thinking: www.criticalthinking.org

Creative Thinking: www.amcreativityassoc.org

Name _____ Date _____

Exercise 1: Plan to Demonstrate Higher-Level Thinking in Your Courses

Take a look at the syllabus for each course you're enrolled in this term. Find a major assignment or exam that will strongly influence your grade in each course. List four of these assignments or exams in the space below. If you are taking fewer than four courses, you can choose more than one assignment or exam from the same course.

Course   Major Assignment/Test

1. _____

2. _____

3. _____

4. _____

Using the matrix below, place a check mark in the boxes representing forms of higher-level thinking that you feel you can demonstrate on each of these major assignments or tests. (See the higher-level definitions and the higher-level thinking questions earlier in this chapter, to help you determine what form(s) of higher-level thinking you could use on each assignment or test.)

MAJOR COURSE ASSIGNMENT/TEST

HIGHER-LEVEL THINKING SKILL	1.	2.	3.	4.
Analysis				
Synthesis				
Multiple Perspectives				
Multiple Theories				
Balanced Thinking				
Critical Thinking				
Creative Thinking				

Choose one box you checked in each column, and use the spaces provided below to explain how you would demonstrate that particular form of higher-level thinking on that particular assignment or test. For instance, if you checked a box indicating that you will use multiple perspectives in assignment #1, note the particular course concept or topic you will apply these multiple perspectives to, and what particular perspectives you will apply.

Exam/Assignment #1: _____

Form of Higher-Level Thinking: _____

How This Form of Thinking Will Be Demonstrated:

Exam/Assignment #2: _____

Form of Higher-Level Thinking: _____

How This Form of Thinking Will Be Demonstrated:

Exam/Assignment #3: _____

Form of Higher-Level Thinking: _____

How This Form of Thinking Will Be Demonstrated:

Exam/Assignment #4: _____

Form of Higher-Level Thinking: _____

How This Form of Thinking Will Be Demonstrated:

NOTES:

- Save the matrix on the previous page and use it as a visual reminder to ensure that you are using at least one form of higher-level thinking in your course assignments and exams.

- Use the matrix in study groups and group projects by having each member of your team take a different thinking role (e.g., analysis, synthesis, or balanced thinking). After each group member works individually, he or she could then share their thinking with the rest of the team. This would enable your team to pool the individual efforts of all its members to create a final product that demonstrates a variety of higher-level thinking skills.

Exercise 2: Self-Assessment of Higher-Level Thinking

Listed below are four general characteristics of higher-level thinkers along with a set of specific traits relating to each characteristic. When you read the specific traits listed beneath each of the general characteristics, place a checkmark in the space next to any specific trait that you think is true of you.

CHARACTERISTICS OF A HIGHER-LEVEL THINKER

1. **Tolerant and Accepting**

    ___ Keeps emotions under control when someone criticizes his or her viewpoint.

    ___ Does not tune-out ideas that conflict with one's own.

    ___ Feels comfortable with disagreement.

    ___ Is receptive to hearing different points of view.

2. **Inquisitive and Open-Minded**

   ___ Eager to continue learning new things from different people and different experiences.

   ___ Has an "inquiring mind" that's curious, inquisitive, and ready to explore new ideas.

   ___ Finds differences of opinion or opposing viewpoints interesting and stimulating.

   ___ Attempts to understand why people hold very different viewpoints and tries to find common ground between them.

3. **Reflective and Tentative**

   ___ Suspends judgment until all the evidence is in, rather than making snap judgments before knowing the whole story.

   ___ Acknowledges the complexity, ambiguity, or uncertainty of some issues and may say things like, "I need to give this more thought" or "I need more evidence before I can draw a conclusion."

   ___ Takes time to think things through before drawing conclusions, making choices, and reaching decisions.

   ___ Periodically reexamines personal viewpoints to see if they should be maintained or changed as a result of new experiences and evidence.

4. **Honest and Courageous**

   ___ Gives fair consideration to ideas that other people may instantly disapprove of, or find distasteful.

   ___ Willing to express personal viewpoints that may not conform with the majority.

   ___ Willing to change old opinions or beliefs when they are contradicted by new evidence.

   ___ Willing to acknowledge the limitations or weaknesses of one's own attitudes and beliefs.

Look back at the list and count the number of checkmarks you placed underneath each of the four general areas.

1. Tolerant and Accepting   _____
2. Inquisitive and Open-Minded   _____
3. Reflective and Tentative   _____
4. Honest and Courageous   _____

Under which characteristic did you have the most checkmarks?

Under which did you have the fewest checkmarks?

How would you interpret this difference?

Why do you think this difference occurred?

▼ CASE STUDY

Trick or Treat: Confusing or Challenging Test?

Students in a philosophy course just got their first exam back, and Professor Plato is going over the test with students in his class. Some students are really angry because they feel that Professor Plato deliberately made up a test that was designed to confuse them by creating "trick questions." In his defense, Professor Plato states that he did not construct a confusing test with trick questions, but a college-level test that was designed to "challenge students to think!"

Reflection and Discussion Questions

1. Why do you think the students may have felt that the professor was trying to "trick" or "confuse" them on the exam?

2. What do you think the professor meant when he said that his test questions were designed to "challenge students to think?"

3. What might these students do to reduce the likelihood that they'll feel tricked on future tests?

4. What might the professor do to reduce the likelihood that students will feel tricked on future tests?

Diversity

Appreciating the Value of Human Differences for Enhancing Learning and Personal Development

Learning Goals

The primary goal of this chapter is to show how experiencing diversity in college can promote your learning, personal development, and career success.

Outline

The Spectrum of Diversity
    What is Culture?
    What is an Ethnic Group?
    What is a Racial Group?
Diversity and the College Experience
Advantages of Experiencing Diversity
    Diversity Increases the Power of a Liberal Arts Education
    Diversity Promotes Self-Awareness
    Diversity Strengthens Development of Learning and Thinking Skills
    Diversity Enhances Career Preparation and Success
    Diversity Stimulates Social Development
Blocks to Experiencing Diversity
    Stereotyping
    Prejudice
    Discrimination

Causes of Prejudice and Discrimination
    The Influence of Familiarity and Stranger Anxiety
    The Tendency to Categorize People
    Group Perception
    Majority Group Members' Attitudes
    Group Membership and Self-Esteem
Strategies for Making the Most of Diversity
    Self-Reflection
    Personal Action
    Interpersonal Interaction
Summary and Conclusion
Learning More through Independent Research
Exercise: Diversity Self-Awareness
Case Study: Hate Crime: Racially Motivated Murder

Activate Your Thinking

Complete the following "sentence starter":

When I hear the word "diversity," the first thoughts that come to my mind are . . .

••• The Spectrum of Diversity

As you may have already detected by the title of this chapter, diversity simply means "variety" or "difference." Thus, human diversity refers to the variety or differences that exist among people that comprise humanity (the human species). When we use the word "diversity" in this chapter, we will be referring primarily to *different groups* of humans. The relationship between humanity and diversity is represented visually in Figure 1.

Figure 1 Humanity and Diversity*

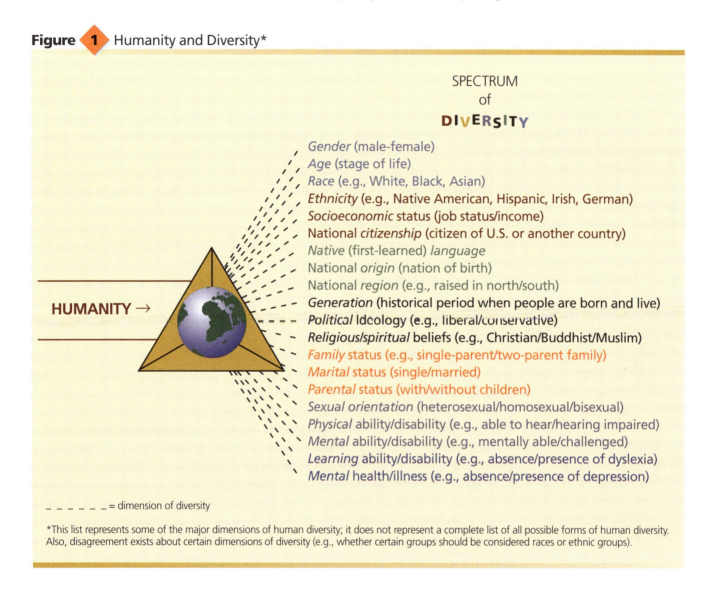

_ _ _ _ _ _ = dimension of diversity

*This list represents some of the major dimensions of human diversity; it does not represent a complete list of all possible forms of human diversity. Also, disagreement exists about certain dimensions of diversity (e.g., whether certain groups should be considered races or ethnic groups).

The relationship between humanity and human diversity is similar to the relationship between sunlight and the spectrum colors. Just as sunlight passing through a prism reflects all the different groups of colors that make up the visual spectrum, humanity occupying planet earth reflects all the different groups of people that make up the spectrum of human diversity. As you can see in Figure 1, groups of people can differ from one another in a wide variety of ways, including their physical features, values, beliefs, abilities, geographical locations, social backgrounds, and other personal dimensions.

Diversity has been viewed by some people to be a "political" issue. However, we view diversity as an *educational* issue—a learning experience that can have a powerful impact on an individual's college and career success. Since there have been different interpretations (and misinterpretations) about what diversity actually is, we would like to begin by clarifying some key terms that are essential to an accurate understanding of the meaning and value of diversity.

What Is Culture?

"Culture" can be broadly defined as a distinctive pattern of beliefs and values that develop among a group of people who share the same social heritage and traditions. Culture is the whole way in which a group of people has learned to live (Peoples & Bailey, 1998), which includes style of speaking (language), fashion, food, art, and music, as well as values and beliefs. Different cultures exist across different nations—often referred to as *cross-cultural* differences; and different cultures can exist within the same nation—commonly called *multicultural* differences. Thus, cultural diversity may take the forms of *international* diversity and *national* (*domestic*) diversity. Although the terms "culture" and "society" are used as if they have the same meaning, they refer to different things. *Society* refers to a group of people who are organized under the same social system. For example, all members of American society are organized under the same system of government, justice, and education. On the other hand, culture is what members of certain groups of people in a society actually share with each other in terms of traditions and lifestyle (Nicholas, 1991). So, within the same society, multiple cultures can exist; hence, we use the term "multicultural society."

Culture is a distinctive pattern of beliefs and values that develop among a group of people who share the same social heritage and traditions.

What Is an Ethnic Group?

An *ethnic group* (or *ethnicity*) refers to a group of people who share the same culture. Thus, culture refers to *what* an ethnic group shares in common, and ethnic group refers to the particular group of people *who* share a common culture. Major ethnic groups in the United States include Native Americans (American Indians), African Americans, Hispanic Americans (Latinos), Asian Americans, and European Americans. Ethnic subgroups also exist within each of these major ethnic groups. For example, Hispanic Americans include people who have cultural roots in Mexico, Puerto Rico, Central America, South America, etc.; Asian Americans include cultural descendents from Japan, China, Korea, Vietnam, etc.; and European Americans include descendents from Scandinavia, England, Ireland, Germany, Italy, etc. In the United States, European Americans are the *majority* ethnic group, meaning that the majority of the American population belongs to this ethnic group. Native Americans, African Americans, Hispanic Americans, and Asian Americans are considered to be ethnic *minority* groups.

Pause for Reflection

What ethnic group(s) do you belong to, or identify with? What common cultural values do you think are shared by your ethnic group(s)?

CLASSIC QUOTE

"We are all the same, and we are all unique."

–Georgia Dunston, African-American biologist and research specialist in human genetics

The different cultures associated with different ethnic groups may be viewed simply as variations in the way groups of people express the same theme: being human. You may have heard the question: "We're all human, aren't we?" The answer to this important question is, "yes and no." Yes, we are all the same, but not in the same way.

One way to understand this apparent paradox is to visualize humanity as a quilt in which all humans are joined together by the common thread of humanity—we are all human beings; yet, the different patches that makes up the quilt represent diversity—the distinctive or unique cultures that comprise our common humanity. This quilt metaphor acknowledges the identity and beauty of all cultures. It differs from the old American "melting pot" metaphor—which viewed differences as something that should be melted down or eliminated, and the "salad bowl" metaphor—which suggests that America is a hodgepodge or mishmash of different cultures thrown together without any common connection. In contrast, the quilt metaphor suggests that the cultures of different ethnic groups can and should be recognized. Yet these differences may be woven together to create a unified whole—as in the Latin expression: "E pluribus Unum" ("Out of many, one"). This expression has become a motto of the United States, and you will find it printed on all its coins.

Personal Story

When I was 12 years old and living in New York, I returned from school one Friday afternoon, and my mother asked me if anything interesting happened at school that day. I mentioned to her that the teacher went around the room, asking students what we had for dinner the night before. At that moment, my mother began to become a bit agitated and nervously asked me: "What did you tell the teacher?" I said: "I told her and the rest of the class that I had pasta last night because my family has a tradition of eating pasta on Thursdays and Sundays." My mother then exploded and yelled back at me: "Why couldn't you tell her that we had steak or roast beef!" For a moment, I was stunned and couldn't figure out what I had done wrong or why I should have lied about eating pasta. Then it suddenly dawned on me: My mother was extremely embarrassed about being an Italian American. She wanted me to hide our family's ethnic background and make it sound like we were very "American." After this became clear to me, a few moments later, it also became clear to me why her maiden name was changed from the very Italian-sounding "DeVigilio" to the more American-sounding "Vigilis."

I never forgot this incident because it was such an emotionally intense experience. For the first time in my life, I became aware that my mother was ashamed of being a member of the same group to which every other member of my family belonged, including me. After her outburst, I felt a combined rush of astonishment and embarrassment. However, these feelings didn't last long because, in the long run, my mother's reaction actually had the opposite effect on me. Instead of making me feel inferior or ashamed about being Italian-American, my mother's reaction that day caused me to become more aware of, and take more pride in, my Italian heritage.

Although I have never forgotten this incident, I have since forgiven my mother, because I later learned why she felt the way she did. She grew up in America's "melting pot" generation—a time when different American ethnic groups were expected to melt down and melt away their ethnicity. They were not to celebrate diversity; they were to eliminate it.

—Joe Cuseo

• — • **CLASSIC QUOTE** • — •

"*We have become not a melting pot but a beautiful mosaic.*"

—Jimmy Carter, thirty-ninth president of the United States and winner of the Nobel Peace Prize

What Is a Racial Group?

A *racial group (race)* refers to an ethnic group that also shares some distinctive physical traits, such as skin color or facial characteristics; however, there continues to be disagreement among scholars about what groups of people actually constitute a human "race," or whether totally distinctive races truly exist (Wheelright, 2005). Unlike an ethnic group, whose shared culture has been passed on through social experiences, a racial group's shared physical characteristics are those that they are born with and which have been passed on genetically. The United States Census Bureau (2000) identifies three races: White, Black, and Asian. Nevertheless, Anderson & Fienberg (2000) caution that racial categories are social-political constructs (concepts) and are not scientifically based.

> **Remember:** There are no specific genes that differentiate one race from another. In other words, there is no way you could do a blood test or any type of "internal" genetic test to determine a person's race. Humans have simply decided to categorize people into "races" on the basis of certain external differences in physical appearance, particularly the color of their outer layer of skin.

The differences in skin color that exist among humans is likely due to biological adaptations that evolved among groups of humans. These differences helped them survive in different environmental regions where they were living and breeding. For instance, darker skin tones were more likely to develop among humans who inhabited and reproduced in hotter regions nearer the equator (e.g., Africans), where darker skin may have enabled them to adapt and survive in that environment. Their darker skin provided their bodies with better protection from the potentially damaging effects of the sun (Bridgeman, 2003) and better ability to use the sun's source of vitamin D (Jablonski & Chaplin, 2002). In contrast, lighter skin tones were more likely to develop among humans inhabiting colder climates more distant from the equator (e.g., Scandinavians) to allow their bodies to absorb greater amounts of sunlight because it was less plentiful and direct.

While humans may display racial diversity, the biological reality is that all members of the human species are remarkably similar. There is much less genetic variability among us than members of other animal species; in fact, approximately 98 percent of our genes are exactly the same (Bridgeman, 2003; Molnar, 1991). This accounts for all the similarities that exist among humans, regardless of what differences in color appear at the surface of our skin. For example, all humans have similar external features that give us a "human" appearance and clearly distinguish us from other animal species; we have internal organs that are similar in structure and function; and we have similar facial expressions for expressing our emotions (Figure 2).

Other human characteristics that anthropologists have found to be shared across all groups of people in every corner of the world include storytelling, poetry, adornment of the body, dance, music, decoration of artifacts, families, socialization of children by elders, a sense of right and wrong, supernatural beliefs, explanations of diseases and death, and mourning of the dead (Pinker, 1994).

It is important to realize that human *variety* and human *similarity* exist side-by-side. For instance, humans all over the world communicate verbally via language; in fact, newborn babies in all cultures babble by using the same wide range of sounds. However, these babies will eventually speak only in the sounds of the language(s) they are exposed to in their particular culture and other sounds they used while babbling will eventually drop out (Oller, 1981). Thus, language is a characteristic that all humans share as part of their common humanity, but the variety of languages spoken by people around the world is a reflection and expression of their diverse cultural experiences.

It is also important to keep in mind that *individual* differences *within* the same group of people are *greater* than the average differences between different groups of people. For example, although we live in a world that is very conscious of differences between races, the fact is that physical differences (e.g., height and weight) and behavioral differences (e.g., personality char-

Figure 2

Humans all over the world display the same facial expressions when experiencing certain emotions. See if you can detect the emotions being expressed in the following faces. (To find the answers, turn your book upside down.)

Answers: The emotions shown. Top, left to right: anger, fear, and sadness. Bottom, left to right: disgust, happiness, and surprise.

PHOTOS © 2007 JUPITERIMAGES CORPORATION AND TOP MIDDLE PHOTO © FRED GOLDSTEIN, 2007, USED UNDER LICENSE FROM SHUTTERSTOCK, INC.

•—• **CLASSIC QUOTE** •—•

Every human is, at the same time, like all other humans, like some humans, and like no other human.

—Clyde Kluckholn, American Anthropologist

---

acteristics) among individuals within the same racial group are actually greater than the average differences between different racial groups (Caplan & Caplan, 1994).

As you proceed through this chapter, keep in mind the following distinctions among humanity, diversity, and individuality:

- **Humanity**—we are all members of the *same group* (the human species).
- **Diversity**—we are all members of *different groups* (e.g., our gender and ethnic groups).
- **Individuality**—each of us is a *unique person* who is different from any person in any group to which we may belong.

Diversity and the College Experience

The ethnic and racial diversity of students is increasing in American colleges and universities. In 1960, Whites comprised almost 95 percent of the total college population; in 2005, the percentage decreased to 69 percent. At the same time, the percentage of Asian, Hispanic, Black, and Native American students attending college increased (Chronicle of Higher Education, 2003). Approximately 35 percent of today's 18- to 24-year-olds are non-white, making it the most diverse generation in American history (The Echo Boomers, 2004).

American colleges are also becoming more diverse in terms of gender and age. In 2000, the percentage of females enrolled in college was almost 66 percent, compared to 25 percent in 1955 (Postsecondary Education Opportunity, 2001). The percentage of students enrolled in college today that are 24 years of age or older has grown to 44 percent (Chronicle of Higher Education, 2003).

You are also likely to find students on your campus from different nations. From 1990 to 2000, the number of international students attending American colleges and universities increased by over 140,000 (Institute of International Education, 2001).

Colleges and universities often intentionally recruit students with different cultural experiences and geographical backgrounds in order to create a campus environment that enriches the variety and quality of your learning experience. Thus, your campus may be the ideal environment for experiencing diversity. The college experience can provide you with the time, the place, the variety of people, and the quality of educational resources (courses, programs) needed to learn the most about and from diversity.

The ethnic and racial diversity of students in American colleges is increasing.

As a first-year student, this may be the first time in your life that you are a member of a community that includes so many people from such a variety of backgrounds. In fact, students report more experience with diversity during their first year of college than at any other time in the college experience (Kuh, 2002). So, this year may be the prime time for you to capitalize on the diversity around you and take full advantage of its many educational and personal benefits.

 Pause for Reflection

1. What diverse groups do you see represented on your campus?

2. Are there groups on your campus that you did not expect to see, or to see in such large numbers?

3. Are there groups on your campus that you expected to see, but do not see, or see in smaller numbers than you expected?

 STUDENT PERSPECTIVE

"I am very happy with the diversity here, but it also frightens me. I have never been in a situation where I have met people who are Jewish, Muslim, atheist, born-again, and many more."

—First-year student (Erickson, Peters, & Strommer, 2006)

Advantages of Experiencing Diversity

Diversity Increases the Power of a Liberal Arts Education

An effective liberal arts education should liberate or free you from the "tunnel vision" of an egocentric (self-centered) viewpoint and enable you to move outside yourself and see yourself in relation to the world around you. There is simply no way you can gain this global perspective without understanding human diversity. If we could reduce the world's population to a village of precisely 100 people, with all existing human ratios remaining the same, the demographics would look something like this:

> The village would have 60 Asians, 14 Africans, 12 Europeans, 8 Latin Americans, 5 from the United States and Canada, and 1 from the South Pacific.
>
> 51 would be male, 49 would be female
>
> 82 would be non-white; 18 white
>
> 67 would be non-Christian; 33 would be Christian
>
> 80 would live in substandard housing
>
> 67 would be unable to read
>
> 50 would be malnourished and 1 dying of starvation
>
> 33 would be without access to a safe water supply
>
> 39 would lack access to improved sanitation
>
> 24 would not have any electricity (and of the 76 that do have electricity, most would only use it for light at night)
>
> 7 would have access to the Internet
>
> 1 would have a college education
>
> 1 would have HIV
>
> 2 would be near birth; 1 near death
>
> 5 would control 32 percent of the entire world's wealth; all 5 would be citizens of the United States
>
> 33 would be receiving—and attempting to live on—only 3 percent of the income of "the village"
>
> (Source: *State of the Village Report* by Donella H. Meadows, originally published in 1990 as "Who lives in the Global Village?" and updated in Family Care Foundation, 2005.)

Another perspective that should be developed as part of your liberal arts education is a *national* perspective, which involves understanding and appreciating your own nation. To appreciate the United States as a nation is to appreciate human diversity. Today, the United States is more ethnically and racially diverse than at any other time in its national history, and it will continue to grow more diverse throughout the twenty-first century (Torres, 2003). In 1995, about 75 percent of America's population was White; by 2050, it will shrink to about 50 percent (U.S. Census Bureau, 2004).

Because of this increasing diversity, "multicultural competence"—the ability to understand cultural differences and to interact effectively with people from different cultural backgrounds—has become an important liberal arts skill that is critical for success in today's world (Pope et al., 2005).

Just as the different subjects you take in the liberal arts curriculum opens your mind to multiple perspectives, so does experience with people from different backgrounds. Exposure to the different perspectives of people with different cultural experiences serves to expand your con-

---

• ── CLASSIC QUOTE ── •

It [liberal arts education] shows you how to accommodate yourself to others, how to throw yourself into their state of mind, how to come to an understanding of them. You are at home in any society; you have common ground with every class.

—John Henry Newman, English Cardinal and educator

sciousness; it stretches your perspective and liberates you from viewing the world through the narrow perspective of a single culture—your own.

One cultural viewpoint cannot provide a complete understanding of any issue because it represents a one-sided viewpoint that is likely to be partial to its particular vantage point (Elder & Paul, 2002). Obtaining a wide range of cultural perspectives allows you to detect the partiality and weaknesses of partial viewpoints, but also allows you to combine their particular strengths to form a multi-sided perspective that is more comprehensive and balanced.

One of the major divisions of the liberal arts curriculum is the humanities. Courses in this division of knowledge focus on understanding humanity—the common elements of the human experience that are shared by all human beings.

> **CLASSIC QUOTE**
> *The mind is like a parachute; it works best when it is open.*
> —Anonymous

Remember: By learning about diversity (our differences), we simultaneously learn more about what we have in common—our shared humanity.

Experiencing diversity not only enhances your appreciation of the unique features of different cultures, it also provides you with a larger perspective on the universal aspects of the human experience that are common to all people, no matter what their particular cultural background happens to be.

Pause for Reflection
List three human experiences that you think are universal, i.e., that are experienced by all human beings in all cultures.

1.

2.

3.

Diversity Promotes Self-Awareness

Learning from people with diverse backgrounds and experiences also serves to sharpen your self-awareness and self-understanding by allowing you to compare and contrast your life experiences with people whose life experiences differ sharply from your own. This *comparative perspective* can give you an important reference point, putting you in a better position to see more clearly how your unique cultural experiences have influenced the development of your personal beliefs, values, and lifestyle. When students around the country were interviewed about their diversity experiences in college, many of them reported that these experiences enabled them to learn more about themselves. Some said that their interactions with students from different races and ethnic groups produced "unexpected" or "jarring" self-insights (Light, 2001).

Diversity Strengthens Development of Learning and Thinking Skills

Just as the quality of your physical health and performance are improved by consuming a varied and balanced diet of foods from different food groups, the quality of your mental performance is improved by helping yourself to a balanced diet of ideas obtained from different groups of people. Experiencing their rich variety of cultural perspectives nourishes your mind with good "food for thought." Research consistently shows that we learn more from people who are different from us than we do from people who are similar to us (Pascarella, 2001; Pascarella & Terenzini, 2005). This result is probably best explained by the fact that when we encounter what is unfamiliar or uncertain, we are forced to stretch beyond our mental comfort zone to actively compare and contrast it to what we already know in order to understand it (Acredolo & O'Connor, 1991; Nagda, Gurin, & Johnson, 2005).

> **CLASSIC QUOTE**
>
> *The more eyes, different eyes, we can use to observe one thing, the more complete will our concept of this thing, our objectivity, be.*
>
> —Friedrich Nietzsche, German philosopher

Keep in mind that learning is strengthened when it takes place in a social context that involves human interaction. As some scholars put it, human knowledge is "socially constructed"—it is built up through interaction and dialogue with others (Bruffee, 1993). According to these scholars, our thinking is largely an "internal" (mental) representation of conversations we have had with other people (Vygotsky, 1978). So, the nature and quality of our conversations with others affects the nature and quality of our own thinking. If we have multiple conversations with humans from very different backgrounds, then the nature of our thinking becomes more diverse and complex. In contrast, when we restrict the diversity of people who we interact with, we artificially restrict the range and complexity of our thought—by limiting the variety of lenses or angles we can use to view issues and solve problems.

Research on first-year college students shows that students who experience the highest level of exposure to different dimensions of diversity (e.g., interactions and friendships with peers of different races, or participating in multicultural courses and events on campus) report the greatest gains in:

- thinking complexity—the ability to think about all parts and all sides of an issue (Gurin, 1999),
- reflective thinking—the ability to think deeply (Kitchener et al., 2000), and
- critical thinking—the ability to think logically (Pascarella et al., 2001).

Lastly, experiencing diversity can enhance your ability to think *creatively*. Just as experiences with academic disciplines (subjects) can equip you with different thinking styles and strategies that may be combined to generate new ideas, so do experiences with different dimensions of diversity. Although a major advantage of culture is that it helps bind people together, it can also blind people from other perspectives. Since culture shapes the way we think, it can cause groups of people to view the world solely through their own cultural frame of reference (Colombo, Cullen, & Lisle, 1995). Diversity experiences supply us with different thinking styles that can help us think outside the boundaries of our own cultural framework. These experiences also help us to be aware of our perceptual "blind spots" and to avoid the dangers of group think—the tendency for tight, like-minded groups of people to think so much alike that they overlook the flaws in their own thinking—which can lead to poor choices and faulty decisions (Janis, 1982).

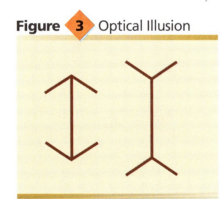

Figure 3 Optical Illusion

Optical illusions are a good illustration of how our cultural perspectives can blind us or cause us to misperceive things. For instance, compare the length of the two lines in Figure 3.

If you perceive the line on the right to be longer than the line on the left, welcome to the club. Virtually all Americans and people from Western cultures perceive the line on the right to be longer. Actually, both lines are equal in length. (If you don't believe it, take out a ruler and check it out.) However, people from non-Western cultures who live in environments with circular architecture rather than buildings with lines and corners, do not make this perceptual error (Segall, Campbell & Herskovits, 1966).

The key point underlying this optical illusion is that our cultural experiences shape and sometimes distort our perceptions or interpretations of reality. We think we are seeing things objectively or "as they really are," but we are often seeing things subjectively from our limited cultural vantage point. Being open to people from different backgrounds who perceive the world from different cultural vantage points opens up our range of perception and helps us overcome our cultural blind spots. As a result, we can see and think about the world around us with greater clarity and balance.

Diversity Enhances Career Preparation and Success

Learning from diversity also has a very practical benefit: It better prepares you for the world of work. Whatever career you may choose to enter, you will likely find yourself working with employers, employees, co-workers, customers, and clients from diverse cultural backgrounds. America's workforce is now more diverse than at any other time in its history, and work today takes place in a global economy that involves greater economic interdependence among nations (e.g., international businesses), more international trading (imports/exports), more multinational corporations, more world travel, and more effective worldwide communication—due to advances in the World Wide Web (Dryden, & Vos, 1999; Smith, 1994). Consequently, employers of college graduates have begun to place higher value on job candidates with international knowledge and foreign language skills (Fixman, 1990; Office of Research, 1994).

The people who live in these circular huts would not be fooled by the optical illusion in Figure 3.

> **CLASSIC QUOTE**
>
> *When all men think alike, no one thinks very much.*
>
> —Walter Lippmann, distinguished journalist, and originator of the term, "stereotype."

Successful career performance in today's diverse workforce requires sensitivity to human differences and the ability to relate to people from different cultural backgrounds who work in the United States and across different nations (National Association of Colleges & Employers, 2003; Smith, 1997). One national survey of business leaders and policymakers revealed that they want college graduates to have more than just "awareness" or "tolerance" of diversity; they want graduates to have actual *experience* with diversity (Education Commission of the State, 1995). Today's world truly has become a "small world," and your success in it will be enhanced if you gain a multicultural and cross-cultural perspective.

Diversity Stimulates Social Development

Experiencing diversity also promotes your social development. When you interact with people from a variety of groups, you widen your social circle by expanding the pool of people with whom you can associate and develop relationships. As the old American proverb goes, "Variety is the spice of life." Or, as the French might say: "Viva la difference!" (Long live difference!)

Just as the quality of your dining experiences are enriched by the range and variety of ethnic foods you can choose from to stimulate your taste palate, so too can the quality of your learning experiences be enriched by the range and variety of ethnic groups with which you can choose to interact. In fact, research indicates that students who have more diversity experiences in college report higher levels of satisfaction with their college experience (Astin, 1993).

> **CLASSIC QUOTE**
>
> *Empirical evidence shows that the actual effects on student development of emphasizing diversity and of student participation in diversity activities are overwhelmingly positive.*
>
> —Alexander Astin, *What Matters in College*

••• Blocks to Experiencing Diversity

Although there are multiple benefits associated with diversity, there are also some human tendencies that can interfere with or block us from experiencing diversity and reaping its benefits. Three of these potential stumbling blocks are *stereotyping*, *prejudice*, and *discrimination*.

Stereotyping

The word stereotype is a combination of two root words: "stereo" (to look at in a fixed way) and "type" (typical). It is the tendency to view individuals of the same type (group) in the same (fixed) way. In effect, stereotyping ignores or disregards a person's individuality; instead, all individuals who share a similar group characteristic (e.g., race or gender) are viewed as having similar personal characteristics—as in the expression: "You know what they are like; they're all the same." If virtually all members of a stereotyped group are judged or evaluated in the same way, this results in *prejudice*.

Pause for Reflection

1. Have you ever been stereotyped, based on your appearance or group membership? If so, how did it make you feel and how did you react?

2. Have you ever unintentionally perceived or treated someone in terms of a stereotype rather than as an individual? What assumptions did you make about that person? Was that person aware of, or affected by, your stereotyping?

Prejudice

STUDENT PERSPECTIVE

When you see me, do not look at me with disgrace.

Know that I am an African-American
  Birthed by a woman of style and grace.

Be proud
  To stand by my side.

Hold your head high
  Like me.

Be proud.
  To say you know me.
  Just as I stand by you, proud to be me.

—A poem by Brittany Beard, first-year student

The word "prejudice" literally means to "pre-judge." It represents a judgment, attitude, or belief about another person or group of people, which is formed before the facts are known. Stereotyping and prejudice often occur together because individuals who are placed in a stereotyped group are commonly pre-judged in a biased (slanted) way. When this bias is negative, it is referred to as *stigmatizing*—associating inferior or unfavorable traits with people who belong to the same group. Although, technically, prejudice may be either positive or negative, the term is most often used to refer to negative pre-judgment or stigmatizing, which is the way it will be used in this chapter.

Someone with a prejudice toward a group typically avoids contact with individuals from the stigmatized group. Thus, the prejudice continues because there is little or no chance for the prejudiced person to have positive experiences with a member of the group that could contradict or disprove the prejudice. Thus, a vicious cycle is established in which the prejudiced person avoids contact with the stigmatized group, and this lack of contact keeps the prejudice going by not allowing any opportunities for it to be contradicted.

A prejudice can also remain intact because facts that contradict it are often ignored through the psychological process of *selective perception*—the tendency for the prejudiced person to see what he or she *expects* to see (Hugenberg & Bodenhausen, 2003). This results in the prejudiced person choosing to pay attention to information that is consistent with the prejudice and "seeing" that information, while ignoring or overlooking information that contradicts the prejudice. Have you ever noticed that fans rooting for their favorite sports team tend to focus on and "see" the calls or decisions of referees that go against their own team, but do not seem to notice or react to calls that go against the other team? This is a classic, everyday example of selective perception. It could be said that selective perception changes the process of "seeing is believing" into "believing is seeing." Even if a contradictory piece of information happens to slip through the prejudiced person's attention filter, it is likely to be dismissed as an "exception to the rule," or as an exception that "proves" the general rule (Aronson, et al., 2005).

—· CLASSIC QUOTE ·—

We see what is behind our eyes.

–Chinese proverb

Selective perception can also be accompanied by *selective memory*—the tendency to remember only information that is consistent with the prejudice, while forgetting information that is inconsistent or contradictory (Judd et al., 1991). It is possible for the psychological processes of selective perception and selective memory to operate *unconsciously*, so the prejudiced person may not be fully aware that they are using them or that they are resulting in prejudice (Baron, Byrne, & Brauscombe, 2006).

Whether prejudice is conscious or unconscious, the bottom line is that it can cause a person to minimize or cut off interaction with a whole group of people. As a result, the prejudiced person fails to experience and profit from the particular dimension of diversity (e.g., ethnic, racial, or national) that members of the stigmatized group have to offer. Worse yet, the person's prejudice can lead to acts of *discrimination* against members of the stigmatized group.

Discrimination

Literally translated, the term discrimination means division or separation. While prejudice is an attitude or belief, discrimination is an *action* taken toward another individual, which results in that person receiving different treatment. So, it could be said that discrimination is prejudice put into action.

"Hate crimes" represent an extreme form of discrimination. These are crimes motivated solely by prejudice against members of a stigmatized group—for example, damaging their personal property or physically assaulting them (e.g., "gay bashing"). Hate crimes are acts of discrimination that are committed consciously and maliciously. However, just like prejudice, some forms of discrimination can be very subtle and may take place without people being fully aware that they are discriminating. For example, there is some evidence that white, male college professors tend to treat female students and students from ethnic or racial minority groups differently than they do males and non-minority students. In particular, females and minority students tend to:

- receive less eye contact from the instructors,
- be called on less frequently in class,
- be given less time to respond to questions asked by instructors in class, and
- have less contact with instructors outside the classroom (Hall & Sandler, 1982, 1984; Sedlacek, 1987; Wright, 1987).

In the vast majority of these cases, the discriminatory treatment that these students received was subtle and not done consciously or deliberately by the instructors (Green, 1989). Nevertheless, these unintended actions are still discriminatory, and they may send a message to these students that their ideas are not worth hearing, or that they are not as capable as other students (Sadker & Sadker, 1994).

Pause for Reflection

Have you noticed classroom teaching behaviors or strategies used by instructors that clearly treated all students equally and promoted appreciation of student diversity?

What did these instructors do?

Personal Story

Being African American and living in southeastern Kentucky, the heart of Appalachia, did not provide for the grandest of living styles. Even though my father worked twelve hours a day in the coal mines, he earned only enough pay to supply staples for the table. Our family also worked as tenant farmers to have enough vegetables for my mother to can for the winter and to provide a roof over our heads.

My mother was a direct descendent of slaves and moved with her parents from the deep south at the age of seventeen. My father lived in an all-black coal mining camp, into which my mother and her family moved in 1938. My dad would say to me, "Son, you will have opportunities that I never had. Many people, white and black alike, will tell you that you are no good and that education can never help you. Don't listen to them because soon they will not be able to keep you from getting an education like they did me. Just remember, when you do get that education, you'll never have to go in those coal mines and have them break your back. You can choose what you want to do, and then you can be a free man."

My father lived through a time when freedom was something he dreamed his children might enjoy someday, because before the civil rights movement succeeded in changing the laws, African Americans were considerably limited in educational opportunities, job opportunities, and much else in what was definitely a racist society. My father remained illiterate because he was not allowed to attend public schools in eastern Kentucky.

In the early 1960s my brother, my sister, and I were integrated into the white public schools. Physical violence and constant verbal harassment caused many other blacks to forgo their education and opt for jobs in the coal mines at an early age. But my father remained constant in his advice to me: "It doesn't matter if they call you n_____; but don't you ever let them beat you by walking out on your education."

Being poor, black, and Appalachian did not offer me great odds for success, but constant reminders from my parents that I was a good and valuable person helped me to see beyond my deterrents to the true importance of education. My parents, who could never provide me with monetary wealth, truly made me proud of them by giving me the gift of insight and an aspiration for achievement.

—Aaron Thompson

· — · CLASSIC QUOTE · — ·

"Let us all hope that the dark clouds of racial prejudice will soon pass away and the deep fog of misunderstanding will be lifted from our fear-drenched communities, and in some not too distant tomorrow the radiant stars of love and brotherhood will shine over our great nation."

—Martin Luther King, Jr., civil rights activist and clergyman

••• Causes of Prejudice and Discrimination

There is no single or definitive answer to the question of what causes people to be prejudiced and to discriminate against other groups of people. However, research indicates that the following factors can play an influential role.

The Influence of Familiarity and Stranger Anxiety

Research has repeatedly demonstrated that when humans encounter things that are unfamiliar or strange, they tend to experience feelings of discomfort or anxiety. In contrast, what is familiar tends to be more accepted and better liked (Zajonc, 2001).

When we encounter people who are not familiar to us, experiencing at least some feeling of discomfort is a natural human tendency that probably occurs automatically. In fact, these feelings may be "wired into" our bodies because it was once important to the survival and evolution of our species (Figure 4). When we encountered strangers in our primitive past, it was to our advantage to react with feelings of anxiety and a rush of adrenaline, known as the "fight or flight" response, because those strangers may have been potential predators who were about to threaten or attack us. This evolutionary response may also explain why "stranger anxiety" is a very normal part of human development during infancy. Between about 8 and 18 months of life, virtually all infants when seeing a stranger will react with anxiety (increased heart rate, breathing, crying) (Papalia & Olds, 1990).

Familiarity and stranger anxiety may contribute to prejudice by causing members of the same group to favor members of its own group and to be "on guard" to defend them from members of other groups who are less familiar or strange (Aronson, et al., 2005). Members of minority groups are less familiar to the majority group because they are fewer in number. Also, members of minority groups are less likely to have regular contact with members of the majority group because they are less likely to live in the same area (e.g., the same neighborhood), due to residential segregation of racial and ethnic groups, which is still common today (Massey,

Figure 4 "Fight-or-Flight" Reaction

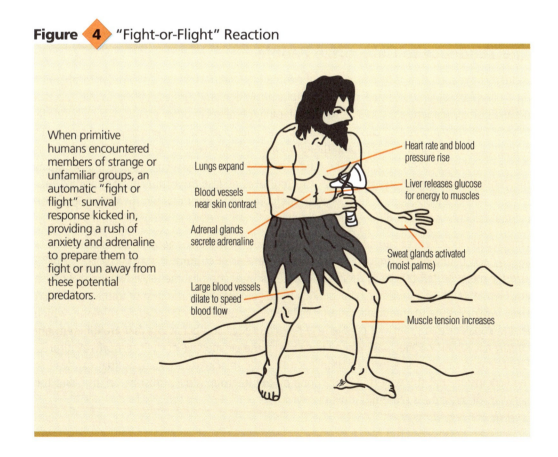

2003; Tienda & Cortes, cited in Nagda, Gurin, & Johnson, 2005). Thus, members of the majority group may view minority group members as "unfamiliar," and this lack of familiarity may automatically trigger negative feelings of uncertainty and anxiety. These negative feelings may then become associated with the minority group, which can lead to negative prejudices toward that group.

Pause for Reflection

Prejudice can be subtle and only begin to surface when the social or emotional distance between members of different groups grows closer. Rate your level of comfort (high, medium, low) with the following situations.

Someone from another racial group:

1. going to your school	high	medium	low
2. working in your place of employment	high	medium	low
3. living on your street as a neighbor	high	medium	low
4. living with you as a roommate	high	medium	low
5. socializing with you as a personal friend	high	medium	low
6. being your most intimate friend or romantic partner	high	medium	low
7. being your partner in marriage	high	medium	low

For any item you rated "low," why do you think it received that rating?

The Tendency to Categorize People

Humans have a tendency to put groups of people into mental categories in order to organize their complex social world and make it simpler to understand (Jones, 1990). While this is a normal human tendency, it can lead to stereotyping members of other groups, which blinds us to their individuality. It also can contribute to prejudice because we tend to create categories of *in*-groups ("us") and *out*-groups ("them"). One negative consequence of this tendency is that it can lead to *ethnocentrism*—the tendency to view one's own culture or ethnic group as the central or "normal" in-group and other cultures as less important or "abnormal" out-groups. This tendency can, in turn, lead to prejudice and discrimination toward people with cultural backgrounds that differ from our own.

Our cultural experiences can affect our judgments and conclusions about what is perceived as socially acceptable or "normal." For instance, in American culture, it may be socially acceptable for males to tell others of their achievements or accomplishments; however, in English and German cultures, such behavior is likely to be perceived as immodest or immature (Hall & Hall, 1986). Failure to appreciate cultural differences can lead to ethnocentric thinking, which fails to consider that groups of people may have attitudes and behaviors that are different but equally acceptable or "normal" when viewed from the perspective of their respective cultures. Ethnocentric thinking is a form of simplistic, dualistic (black-white) thinking that can lead to the conclusion that the way things are done by the in-group ("us") must be "right," and the behavior of out-groups ("them") must be "wrong."

Group Perception

Research studies show that humans are more likely to see members of groups that they do not belong to as more similar to each other in attitudes and behavior than members of their own group (Baron, Byrne, & Brauscombe, 2006). For instance, individuals perceive people older than themselves as being more alike in their attitudes and beliefs than members of their own age group (Linville, Fischer, & Salovey, 1989).

One explanation for this tendency to see members of other groups as being more alike than members of our own group is that we have more experience with members of our own group, so we have more opportunities to observe and interact with a wide variety of individuals within our group. In contrast, we have less experience with members of other groups, so the variety of individuals we have had contact with is narrower, perhaps leading us to conclude that the individual differences among them are narrower, i.e., they are more alike in attitudes and behavior than members of our own group. This effect can be so strong that we often fail to detect differences in the faces of individuals who are members of groups that we're unfamiliar with, i.e., "They all seem to look alike" (Levin, 2000). A dramatic example of this tendency is the case of Lenell Geter, an African-American engineer, who spent over a year of a life sentence in prison for a crime he didn't commit. Four of five non-black witnesses misidentified him for another black man who actually committed the crime and was later apprehended.

Majority Group Members' Attitudes

Research shows that if negative behavior occurs at the same rate among members of both majority and minority groups (e.g., the rate of criminal behavior in both groups is 10 percent), members of the majority group are more likely to develop negative attitudes (prejudice) toward the minority group than their own group (Baron, Byrne, & Brauscombe, 2006). For example, it has been found that whites in the United States tend to overestimate the crime rates of African-American men (Hamilton & Sherman, 1989).

One possible explanation why the negative behaviors of minority group members are more likely to produce negative views of their group is the tendency for majority group members to better remember instances of negative behavior associated with members of the minority group. Since minorities are more likely to be seen as different or distinctive, their behavior is more likely to stand out in the minds of majority group members, which makes it more likely that these negative behaviors will be remembered (McArthur & Friedman, 1980). Since these negative behaviors are more likely to be retained in the minds of the majority group, they are more likely to negatively influence their view of the minority group, thus increasing the possibility of prejudice.

Although prejudice on the part of the majority group toward minority groups has led to the most extreme form of discrimination and domination (Baron, Byrne, & Brauscombe, 2006), any group can become a target for prejudice. (See Box 1 for a snapshot summary of the many different groups of people that have been the target for prejudicial theories and beliefs.) Members of a minority group can also be prejudiced toward the majority group, as illustrated by the student perspective in the margin.

Group Membership and Self-Esteem

Self-esteem—how you feel about yourself—can be influenced by group membership. If people think that the group they belong to is superior, it enables them to feel better about themselves (Tafjel, 1982). In other words, "My group is superior, and since I belong to it, I am superior." This type of thinking is even more likely to occur when an individual's self-esteem has been threatened or damaged as a result of some personal frustration or failure. When this happens,

STUDENT PERSPECTIVE

"My friend said that he 'hates white people because they try to dominate people of color.' I, on the other hand, feel differently. One should not blame all white people for the mistakes and prejudiced acts that white people have made. Unfortunately, my friend has yet to learn this."

Student of color, quoted in Nagna, Gurin, & Sohnson, 2005, p. 102.

the person whose self-esteem has been threatened or damaged can boost it by stigmatizing or putting down members of another group (Rudman & Fairchild, 2004), or by blaming them and making them the "scapegoat" (Gemmil, 1989). For example, they might say, "If it weren't for 'them,' we wouldn't have this problem." Probably the most extreme example of "scapegoating" in human history took place in Nazi Germany, where Jews were blamed for the country's economic problems and became targets of the Holocaust. Studies have shown that when times are tough (e.g., when unemployment is high) and people are frustrated, prejudice and discrimination tend to increase (Aronson, et al., 2005).

Although the causes of prejudice are still not completely understood, we can help guard ourselves against it by remaining aware of the five tendencies discussed in this section, namely:

1. The tendency to favor familiarity and fear strangers;
2. The tendency to mentally categorize people into "in" and "out" groups;
3. The tendency to perceive members of other groups as more alike than members of our own group;
4. The tendency for the attitudes of majority group members to be more influenced by negative behaviors committed by members of minority groups than members of their own (majority) group; and
5. The tendency to build our self-esteem through group membership.

> **CLASSIC QUOTE**
>
> *We need every human gift and cannot afford to neglect any gift because of artificial barriers of sex or race or class or national origin.*
>
> —Margaret Mead, American anthropologist

BOX 1 Snapshot SUMMARY

Stereotypes and Prejudiced Belief Systems about Group Inferiority

As you read this list, make a note next to each item indicating: (a) whether you've heard of this form of stereotype or prejudice, and (b) whether you've observed or experienced it.

Ethnocentrism: considering one's own culture or ethnic group to be "central" or "normal," and viewing cultures that are different as "deficient" or "inferior."

For example, claiming that another culture is "weird" or "abnormal" for eating certain animals that we consider unethical to eat, even though we eat certain animals that they consider unethical to eat.

Racism: prejudice or discrimination based on skin color.

For example, Cecil Rhodes (Englishman and empire builder of British South Africa), once claimed: "We [the British] are the finest race in the world and the more of the world we inhabit the better it is for the human race."

Apartheid: a strict system of racial separation and discrimination against non-white people, which was once national policy in South Africa.

Classism: prejudice or discrimination based on social class, particularly toward people of low socioeconomic status.

For example, focusing only on the contributions made by politicians and wealthy industrialists to America, while ignoring the contributions of poor immigrants, farmers, slaves, and pioneer women.

Nationalism: excessive interest and belief in the strengths of one's own nation without acknowledgment of its mistakes or weaknesses, and without concern for the needs of other nations or the common interests of all nations.

For example, "blind patriotism" that blinds people to the shortcomings of their own nation, and views any questioning or criticism of their nation as being disloyal or "unpatriotic." (As in the slogan, "America: right or wrong!")

Regionalism: prejudice or discrimination based on the geographical region of a nation in which an individual has been born and raised.

For example, a northerner thinking that all southerners are racists.

> **CLASSIC QUOTE**
>
> *A fanatic is one who can't change his mind and won't change the subject.*
>
> —Winston Churchill, Prime Minister of the United Kingdom during World War II, and Nobel Prize winner in Literature

> **STUDENT PERSPECTIVE**
>
> "I would like to change the entire world, so that we wouldn't be segregated by continents and territories."
>
> —College sophomore

(continued)

Xenophobia: extreme fear or hatred of foreigners, outsiders, or strangers.

For example, someone believing that all immigrants should be kept out of the country because they will increase the crime rate.

Anti-Semitism: prejudice or discrimination toward Jews.

For example, the mass murdering of Jews in Nazi Germany.

Religious Bigotry: stubborn and total intolerance of any religious beliefs that are different from one's own.

For example, people who believe that members of their own religion are "favored" or "chosen" by God and will be saved, while those of other religious faiths are sinners and will (or should) be punished.

Terrorism: intentional acts of violence against civilians that are motivated by political or religious prejudice.

For example, the September 11th attacks on the United States.

Ageism: prejudice or discrimination based on age, particularly toward the elderly.

For example, believing that all "old" people are bad drivers with bad memories.

Ableism: prejudice or discrimination toward people who are disabled or handicapped.

For example, avoiding interaction with handicapped people because of anxiety about not knowing what to say or how to act around them.

Sexism: prejudice or discrimination based on sex or gender.

For example, believing that no one should vote for a woman president because she would be too "emotional."

Heterosexism: belief that heterosexuality is the only acceptable sexual orientation.

For example, using the phrase, "You're so gay" as an insult or put down; or believing that gays should not have the same legal rights and opportunities as heterosexuals.

Homophobia: extreme fear and/or hatred of homosexuals.

For example, people who create or contribute to anti-gay Web sites.

STUDENT PERSPECTIVE

"Most religions dictate that theirs is the only way, and without believing in it, you cannot enter the mighty kingdom of heaven. Who are we to judge? It makes more sense for God to be the only one mighty enough to make that decision. If other people could understand and see from this perspective, then many religious arguments could be avoided."

—First-year student

••• Strategies for Making the Most of Diversity

We can learn the most from diversity by taking each of the following three steps:

1. Self-reflection,
2. Personal action, and
3. Interpersonal interaction.

Each of these steps represents a progressively higher level of involvement with diversity, so the higher you go, the more you will learn.

Self-Reflection: Gaining Self-Awareness and Developing Diversity Tolerance

The first step to learning from diversity is to develop self-awareness about our attitudes toward diversity, particularly awareness of any stereotypes and prejudices we may have that are biasing our perceptions of, or behaviors toward, different groups of people. At the bare minimum, we want to behave in a way that demonstrates tolerance or acceptance of diversity.

By writing a constitution that failed to grant female citizens the right to vote, America's founding fathers forgot their mothers (along with all other women) and provided a very vivid example of sexism.

As previously mentioned, research indicates that prejudice and discrimination can occur unconsciously or unintentionally (Baron, Byrne, & Branscombe, 2006). Listed below are some specific strategies for increasing your conscious awareness of attitudes and feelings about diversity.

Keep a journal or diary of your personal reflections on diversity.

Studies show that students learn most effectively from diversity experiences when they take time to reflect on these experiences, particularly when they record these reflections in writing (Lopez, et al., 1998; Nagda, et al., 2003). If you decide to reflect on your diversity experiences, it might be useful to keep the following questions in mind:

- What type of feelings or emotions did you experience?
- When and where did you experience these feelings? (What was the situation or context?)
- Why do you think you felt that way?

Becoming aware of our subtle and sometimes subconscious prejudices is the first step toward eliminating them. Reducing prejudice not only benefits those who are the targets of prejudice, it also benefits those who reduce their own prejudice. Research indicates that people who are less prejudiced report more satisfaction with their lives (Feagin & McKinney, 2003)—perhaps because they are more open to social experiences and less distrustful or fearful of the people around them (Baron, Byrne, & Branscombe, 2006).

·—·CLASSIC QUOTES·—·

Stop judging by mere appearances, and make a right judgment.

—The Bible, John 7:24

You can't judge a book by the cover.

—Hit record, 1962, by Ellas Bates, a.k.a., Bo Diddley

(Note: a "bo diddley" is a one-stringed African guitar.)

 *Pause for Reflection*

Have you ever been prejudiced against a certain group of people?

If you have, what was the group, and why do you think you held that prejudice?

Consciously avoid preoccupation with physical appearances.

Go deeper and get beneath the superficial surface of appearances to view people in terms of *who* they really are and how they really act, not in terms of how they look. Remember the old proverb: "It's what's inside that counts." Judge others by the quality of their personal character, not by your familiarity with their physical characteristics.

> *Personal Story*
>
> When I was a new college student at a large university in the south, I encountered a student who talked loudly, had her ears pierced all around the lobes, and used words my mom never allowed me to use. At first, I was turned off by these differences, but I was also absolutely intrigued by her. It appeared that other students were too, because she seemed to be "together" and very cool. I'm ashamed to admit it, but it took me the whole year to realize that my way was not necessarily the right way (it was just more familiar), and her way was not really wrong or deficient (it was just different).
>
> —Viki Sox Fecas, Program Manager for Freshman
> and Pre-Freshman Programs and co-author of this text

Make a conscious attempt to perceive people as individuals—not as group members, and form your impressions of them on a case-by-case basis—not by using a "general rule."

This may seem like an obvious and easy thing to do, but remember, research shows that there is a natural tendency for humans to consider members of another group as being more alike (or all alike) than members of our own group (Taylor, 2006). Thus, we may have to deliberately fight off this grouping or "lumping together" tendency and consciously focus on each person's individuality.

Personal Action: Learning about Diversity by Acquiring Knowledge of Different Cultures

While self-awareness is an important first step toward learning from diversity, we also need to step outside ourselves and make an active attempt to learn about other social groups and cultures. Our perception of reality is a blending of fact (objectivity) and our interpretation (subjectivity)—which is shaped and molded by our particular cultural perspective (Paul, 1995). Viewing issues from different cultural perspectives allows you to perceive "reality" and see "truth" from different vantage points, which advantages your thinking by making it more comprehensive and less ethnocentric.

Thus, to think in a balanced and unbiased fashion, we need to acquire knowledge about the diverse groups that make up our social environment and how their experiences may be different from our own. In order to acquire this knowledge, we must first acknowledge that diversity exists. It means not being blind to, or in denial about human differences, and it is more than simply saying, "We're all human, so let's get over our differences and move on." This comment ignores the fact that different groups of people have had very different life experiences and continue to face different challenges. More importantly, it denies their group identity, which is an important element of their self-concept and self-esteem.

> **Remember:** Don't let cultural differences get in the way of potentially rewarding relationships. The more opportunities you create to learn from others who are different from yourself, the more opportunities you will create to learn about yourself.

• CLASSIC QUOTE •

"The common eye sees only the outside of things, and judges by that. But the seeing eye pierces through and reads the heart and the soul, finding there capacities which the outside didn't indicate or promise."

—Samuel Clemens, a.k.a., Mark Twain;
writer, lecturer, and humorist

Someone who merely tolerates diversity (level 1) might say things like, "Let's just get along," "live and let live," or "to each his own." Learning about diversity (level 2) involves taking a step beyond diversity tolerance to the higher level of diversity *appreciation*—becoming interested in the cultures and experiences of different groups of people and wanting to learn more about them. Listed below are some strategies for taking this second step.

To increase your understanding and empathy for the experiences of members of another group, imagine yourself as a member of a different group, and attempt to visualize what the experience might be like.

Better yet, see if you can place yourself in the position or situation of someone from that group. For instance, ride in a wheelchair to experience what it is like for someone who is physically disabled, or wear blinders to experience what it's like to be visually impaired.

Incorporate diversity into your work on course assignments.

If you have a choice about what topic to do research on in a particular course, consider choosing a topic relating to diversity; or, consider discussing the diversity implications of whatever topic you may be writing or speaking about (e.g., use multicultural or cross-cultural examples as evidence to illustrate your points).

Take courses that cover material relating to diversity.

You can actively plan to do this by reviewing your college catalog for course descriptions and identify courses that are designed to promote understanding or appreciation of multicultural diversity within the United States or cross-cultural diversity across different nations.

Strongly consider taking a foreign language course.

This will not only benefit you educationally, but it should also benefit you professionally because employers of college graduates are placing increasing value on employees who have foreign language skills (Fixman, 1990; Office of Research, 1994).

Participate in co-curricular activities on campus that relate to diversity.

You can actively plan to do this by reviewing your student handbook for co-curricular programs, student activities, or student clubs that promote diversity awareness and appreciation. Planning in advance to attend some of these programs may be easy to do, because they often coincide with annually scheduled "national" weeks or months, such as Black History Month, Women's History Month, Latin Heritage Month, and Asian American Month.

Studies indicate that taking diversity courses and participating in co-curricular programs helps to reduce unconscious prejudice (Blair, 2002) and strengthens mental development (Pascarella & Terenzini, 2005). Furthermore, what you learn in these courses and programs can provide you with the preparation and confidence to move on to the next step—direct interaction with people from diverse backgrounds.

Interpersonal Interaction: Learning through Interaction and Collaboration with Members of Diverse Groups

Through formal courses and programs, you can learn about diversity. However, you can also learn through diversity experience—direct, first-hand interaction with people from diverse groups and backgrounds. Studies show that learning is maximized when students step beyond just learning about diversity through reading and attending lectures to actually experiencing diversity by interacting with others from diverse groups (Nagda et al., 2003). Such interpersonal experiences move you from the level of multicultural or cross-cultural awareness to a higher level that involves intercultural interaction. This represents a significant increase in your level of involvement with diversity. It is almost like the difference between learning about a foreign country by taking a class or reading about it and actually traveling to the country, interacting with its natives, and immersing yourself in its culture.

This third step involves actively seeking out interaction with members of diverse groups of people who can contribute to your learning and who can learn from you. It requires being open to interaction, dialog, and cultivation of personal relationships with individuals from diverse groups. If you have taken the previous step and learned about different cultures, you may now be more confident about interacting with people from different cultural backgrounds. However, your comfort level with this level of involvement may depend on how much experience you have had with diversity prior to college.

Cultivating relationships with others from diverse groups increases your awareness and comfort level when interacting with those from different cultural backgrounds.

Pause for Reflection

How would you rank the amount or variety of diversity you have experienced in the following settings?

1. The neighborhood in which you grew up
2. The places where you have worked or been employed
3. The high school you attended
4. The college or university you now attend

Which setting had the most and least diversity? What do you think accounts for this difference?

If there is diversity on your campus that you have had little previous exposure to, seeking out and initiating interaction with members of unfamiliar groups may not come easily or naturally for you. On the other hand, if you have had little or no prior experience with diverse groups, you also have the most to gain from experiencing the diversity that is now available on your campus. Research on human learning consistently shows that new experiences that differ from an individual's prior experiences are those that tend to produce the greatest learning and the greatest gains in mental development (Piaget, 1985; Acredolo & O'Connor, 1991).

Even if you had experience living in diverse environments prior to college, you may not have experienced the particular types or dimensions of diversity that exist on your campus, or you may have not yet developed the most effective ways for interacting with and learning from members of diverse groups. Whatever your prior experience with diversity may be, look at the diversity on your campus as a new educational opportunity. Consider it to be a campus resource, and capitalize on this social resource to promote your educational and personal success.

Listed below is a series of strategies for increasing the quantity and quality of your interaction with members from diverse groups on campus.

Intentionally create opportunities for interaction and conversation with students from diverse groups.

Fight off the natural tendency to associate only with people who are similar to you. One way to do this is by placing yourself in situations where you are close enough for conversation to take place with individuals from diverse groups. Research indicates that meaningful interpersonal interactions and friendships are more likely to develop among people who are within close distance to one another (Latané, et al., 1993). So, make an intentional attempt to create this condition. For example, in class, sit near a student from another country; or, at lunch, sit near a student from a different ethnic or racial group.

> **CLASSIC QUOTE**
>
> *All that is necessary is to take an interest in other persons, to recognize that other people as a rule are much like one's self, and thankfully to admit that diversity is a glorious feature of life.*
>
> —Frank Swinnerton, British novelist and literary critic

Keep in mind that the definition of discrimination is giving unequal treatment to different groups of people. If we interact solely with members of our own group and separate ourselves from members of a group who are different than us, we are treating these two groups unequally. This qualifies as discrimination, even if we are not doing it maliciously or consciously.

"I have a love of words, too."

COPYRIGHT © BY BENITA EPSTEIN. REPRINTED WITH PERMISSION.

Make an earnest attempt to learn the names and interests of students from diverse groups.

This will enable you to establish early, personal rapport that can serve as a foundation for further interaction and deeper conversation. Pay particular attention to interests that you may have in common, because shared interests can provide a source of interesting conversation, and perhaps, lead to the development of a long-term friendship.

Consider spending some time at the multicultural center on your campus, or join a campus club or organization that is devoted to diversity awareness (e.g., international student club).

This will enable you to make contact with members of groups other than your own, and clearly sends a message to them that you are interested in doing so, because you have taken the initiative to visit them on "their turf."

Participate in a multicultural or cross-cultural retreat sponsored by your college.

A retreat setting can provide a comfortable environment for getting to know people at a personal level, without the everyday interference and distractions that take place on campus.

Become involved in volunteer or community service activities that may allow you to work in diverse communities or neighborhoods.

Research suggests that college students who participate in volunteer experiences report significant gains in learning and leadership development (Astin, et al., 2000).

Attempt to locate and participate in an internship in a company or organization that will allow you the opportunity to work with people from diverse backgrounds and cultures.

This will not only provide you with a good learning experience, it will also improve your preparation and qualifications for career entry after college. Surveys of employers indicate that they value college graduates who have actual "hands on" experience with diversity (Education Commission of the States, 1995).

If possible, participate in a study abroad program that allows you to live in another country and interact directly with its natives.

In preparation for this international experience, take a course in the language, culture, or history of the nation to which you will be traveling.

Take advantage of the Internet to "chat" with students from diverse groups on your campus, or with students in different countries.

Electronic communication can be a more convenient and more comfortable way to initially interact with members of diverse groups with whom you have had little prior experience. After you've communicated successfully online, you may then feel more comfortable about communicating in person.

Deliberately seek out the views and opinions of students from diverse backgrounds.

For example, ask students from different backgrounds if there was any point made or position taken in class that they would strongly question or challenge. Seeking out divergent (diverse) viewpoints has been found to be one of the best ways to develop critical thinking skills (Kurfiss, 1988).

Join or form discussion groups with students from diverse backgrounds.

You can experience diverse perspectives by joining groups of students who may be different from you in terms of such characteristics as gender, age, race, or ethnic group. When ideas are generated freely in groups comprised of people from diverse backgrounds, a powerful "cross-stimulation" effect occurs, whereby one group member's idea often triggers different ideas from other group members (Brown et al., 1998).

You might begin by forming discussion groups of students who are different with respect to one characteristic but similar with respect to another. For instance, join a group of students of your gender but who differ with respect to race, ethnicity, or age. This strategy can give your diverse group some common ground to build on, as well as increase their awareness that humans who are members of different groups can, at the same time, be members of the same group—and share similar experiences, needs, or concerns.

Remember: Including diversity in your discussion group not only increases its social variety, it also increases the quality of the group's thinking. Diverse discussion groups allow each member to access the different perspectives and thinking styles of people with different background experiences.

For instance, older students may have more life experience for younger students to draw upon and learn from, while younger students may bring a fresh, idealistic perspective to group discussions with older students. Also, males and females tend to contribute different thinking styles to group discussions. Studies show that males are more likely to be "separate knowers" who have a greater tendency to "detach" themselves from the concept or issue being discussed so they can analyze it, whereas females are more likely to be "connected knowers" who have a stronger tendency to relate personally to concepts and connect them to their own experiences. For example, when confronting a poem, males are more likely to ask themselves, "What techniques can I use to analyze it?" In contrast, females are more likely to ask themselves, "What is the poet trying to say to me?" (Belenky, et al., 1986, p. 101). It has also been found that females generally adopt a more collaborative style during group discussions and are more likely to collect ideas of others in a group-learning situation, whereas males are more likely to adopt a competitive approach and debate the ideas of others (Magolda, 1992).

Pause for Reflection
How would you define teamwork?

What do you think are the key factors that make study groups or group projects successful?

Form collaborative learning teams.

A learning team is much more than a discussion group; it moves beyond discussion to collaboration—whereby teammates rely on each other as part of a united effort to reach a shared goal.

Studies show that interpersonal contact between members of different ethnic and racial groups, which takes place while they work collaboratively to achieve a common goal, tends to reduce racial prejudice and promote interracial friendships (Allport, 1954; Amir, 1976). This may be due to the fact that when these individuals from diverse groups work collaboratively on the same team, they become members of the same group. Thus, they all become members of the "in group," with no one being an "outsider."

The greatest gains in reducing prejudice and improving relationships among members of different ethnic and racial groups take place when collaboration occurs under the six conditions described in Box 2. Research also indicates that these are the same conditions that are most likely to produce the largest gains in learning among team members (Slavin, 1995; Johnson, et al., 1998).

At the conclusion of collaborative teamwork and group discussions, take some time to pause and reflect on the social interaction that took place.

Ask yourself questions that cause you to think back on the ideas that emerged from diverse members of the group and think about what impact these ideas had on you. For instance, after group discussions you could ask yourself the following questions:

- What major differences did you detect among group members during your discussion?
- What major similarities in viewpoints or background experiences did all group members share?
- Did the discussion cause you to reconsider or change any ideas you previously held?

Take a leadership role with respect to promoting diversity.

There are a variety of ways in which you can demonstrate diversity leadership, such as those listed below.

- During group discussions, take on the role of a moderator, who ensures that the ideas of people from minority groups are included, heard, and respected.

    For example, encourage and reinforce the contributions of students who may be reluctant to speak up because of their minority status. Putting members with diverse cultures on the same team may serve to reduce prejudice, but only if each member's cultural identity and perspective is sought and acknowledged, not ignored or abolished (Baron, Byrne, & Brauscombe, 2006).

> **TAKE ACTION NOW!** Box 2
>
> ### Tips for Teamwork: Creating Successful Collaborative Learning Groups
>
> 1. **Teammates should have a common goal.**
>
>   To help your team identify and work toward a common goal, plan to produce a final product that can serve as visible evidence of the group's effort and accomplishment (e.g., a completed sheet of answers to questions, a list or chart of specific ideas, or an outline). This will help keep the team focused and moving in a common direction.
>
> 2. **Teammates should have equal opportunity and individual responsibility for contributing to the team's final product.**
>
>   For example, each member of the team should have equal opportunity to participate during group discussions and should be responsible for contributing something specific to the team's final product—such as a different perspective (e.g., national, global, or ethical) or a different form of thinking (e.g., application, synthesis, evaluation).
>
> 3. **Teammates should work interdependently—that is, they should depend on or rely upon each other to achieve their common goal.**
>
>   Similar to a sports team, each member of the learning team has a specific position and role to play. For instance, each member of the team could assume a different role, such as:
>   - manager—who assures that the team stays focused on their goal and doesn't get off track,
>   - moderator—who assures that all members have equal opportunity to contribute,
>   - summarizer—who identifies what the team has accomplished and what remains to be done, or recorder—who keeps a written record of the team's ideas.
>
> 4. **Before beginning their work, teammates should take some time to interact informally with each other to develop a sense of team identity and group solidarity.**
>
>   For example, take some "warm up" time for teammates to get to know each other's names and interests before tackling the learning task. Teammates need to feel comfortable with each other in order for them to feel comfortable about sharing personal thoughts and feelings, particularly if the team is comprised of individuals from diverse backgrounds.
>
> 5. **Teamwork should take place in a friendly, informal setting.**
>
>   The surrounding atmosphere can influence the nature and quality of interaction among members of the group. People are more likely to work openly and collaboratively with others when they are in a social environment that is warm and friendly. For example, a living room or a lounge area would provide a more informal and friendlier atmosphere than a classroom or library.
>
> 6. **Learning teams should occasionally change membership so that each member gets an opportunity to work with different individuals from other ethnic or racial groups.**
>
>   If someone with a prejudice toward a certain ethnic or racial group has the experience of working on multiple teams, which include different individuals from the same racial or ethnic group, the prejudiced person is less likely to conclude that any positive experience was due to having interacted with someone who was an "exception to the rule."
>
> When contact between people from diverse groups takes place under the above conditions, it can have the most powerful effects on diversity appreciation and team learning. Working in teams under these conditions is a win-win situation: Prejudice is decreased, and at the same time, learning is increased.
>
> References: Amir (1969); Allport (1979); Aronson, Wilson, & Akert (2005); Cook (1984); Sherif et al. (1961); and Wilder (1984).

- Serve as a community builder by identifying similarities or recurring themes you see across the ideas and experiences of students from varied backgrounds.

  For example, all humans live in communities, develop relationships, have emotional needs, and undergo life experiences that affect their self-esteem and personal identity. So, be on the lookout for patterns of unity that underlie diversity.

  Diversity without unity allows for no sense of community and can lead to feelings of group separation and divisiveness, because we fail to detect the deeper similarities that

> **CLASSIC QUOTE**
>
> *The nation's future depends upon leaders trained through wide exposure to that robust exchange of ideas which discovers truth out of a multitude of tongues.*
>
> —William J. Brennan, former Supreme Court Justice

lie beneath our more obvious differences. We need to dig more deeply to find the common ground from which our differences grow. By raising your fellow students' consciousness of the common or universal themes that bind different groups of people together, you can help ensure that highlighting diversity will not heighten divisiveness.

> **Remember:** Diversity represents variations on the common theme of humanity. Although people have different cultural backgrounds, they are still cultivated from the same soil—they are all grounded in the common experience of being human.

- Take a stand against prejudice or discrimination by constructively expressing your disagreement with those who make stereotypical statements or prejudicial remarks. You may avoid risk by saying nothing, but your silence may be perceived by others to mean that you agree with the person who made the remark. A number of studies have shown that when a person in a group observes others making prejudiced comments, that person's prejudice can increase, perhaps due to the pressure of group conformity (Stangor, Sechrist, & Jost, 2001). On the other hand, if a prejudiced person sees that his views are out of line with others, particularly others who are liked or respected, the person's prejudice can be reduced (Baron, Byrne, & Brauscombe, 2006). So, by taking a leadership role and not remaining silent when people make prejudiced remarks, you may not only help reduce that one person's prejudice, you may also reduce the prejudice of others who heard the remark.

- Take the initiative in forming friendships with members of diverse groups. These friendships not only enrich your social life, they can also help reduce prejudice among members of your own group. Research indicates that when people see a member of their own group develop a positive relationship with someone from a group that they are prejudiced against, their prejudice tends to decline (Paolini, et al., 2004).

> **Remember:** When you take a leadership role in modeling appreciation of diversity and combating prejudice in others, you are taking a stand for social injustice and for the ethical principle of *equity*—equal opportunity and impartial treatment of all people.

· — · CLASSIC QUOTE · — ·

Americanism is a question of principles, of idealism, of character: it is not a matter of birthplace or creed or line of descent.

—Theodore Roosevelt, American soldier, president, and Nobel Prize winner

Furthermore, you are demonstrating responsible citizenship by doing something good for your community and, ultimately, your country. Let us not forget that the United States is a nation that was originally built and developed by members of diverse immigrant groups, many of whom left their native countries to escape different forms of prejudice and discrimination, and to experience the freedom of equal opportunity in America (Levine, 1996).

As a democracy, the United States is a nation that is built on the foundation of individual rights and freedom of opportunity, which are guaranteed by its constitution. When the personal rights and freedom of fellow citizens are threatened by prejudice and discrimination, the political stability and survival of any democratic nation is threatened.

Diversity and democracy go hand-in-hand; by appreciating the former, you preserve the latter.

Pause for Reflection

Turn back to the diversity spectrum (Figure 1) and look over the list of groups that make up the spectrum. Do you notice any groups that are missing from the list that should be added, either because they have distinctive cultures or because they have been targets of prejudice and discrimination?

> **CLASSIC QUOTE**
>
> *A progressive society counts individual variations as precious since it finds in them the means of its own growth. A democratic society must, in consistency with its ideal, allow intellectual freedom and the play of diverse gifts and interests.*
>
> —John Dewey, U.S. educator, philosopher, and psychologist

Summary and Conclusion

The growing diversity in America and on American college campuses represents a social resource that we can intentionally capitalize on to promote our personal development. By seeking out and learning from diversity, rather than separating ourselves from it, we gain a more complete understanding of our nation and our world; we sharpen our self-awareness and self-insight; we learn to think with greater complexity and creativity; we acquire cultural knowledge and intercultural communication skills that are relevant to career success; and we enrich our social lives by increasing the variety of human beings with whom we interact, network, and develop relationships.

Last, but certainly not least, diversity is an opportunity to develop your personal character and leadership. By serving as a moderator, mediator, and community builder, you assume the role of a leader who helps to build bridges of unity across islands of diversity.

Remember: By being open to diversity and opposed to prejudice and discrimination, you also demonstrate character. You become a role model whose actions visibly demonstrate to others that diversity has both educational and ethical value and that it's not only the *smart* thing to do, but also the *right* thing to do.

Learning More through Independent Research

Web-Based Resources for Further Information on Diversity

Learn more about current issues relating to prejudice and discrimination by exploring the information provided at the following two Web sites.

Tolerance.org

This is the site of an educational and public service organization for people interested in fighting bigotry in America and creating communities that value diversity. It tracks hate groups, hate crimes, hate Web sites, and hate music, and it supplies research-based strategies for promoting social justice on campus and in the community. You can subscribe to a free newsletter that provides updates on the latest social, educational, and legal news relating to bigotry and diversity.

If you visit this site, try taking one of the *Hidden Bias Tests* that have been developed by psychologists at Harvard, the University of Virginia, and the University of Washington.

Amnesty.org

This is the Web site of Amnesty International (AI), which is a worldwide organization of people who are committed to preserving human rights. While Tolerance.org is a national organization, AI is an international movement that includes almost 2 million members from over 150 countries in every region of the world. Many of these people have very different political and religious beliefs, but they share the common concern and goal: to prevent violation of human rights. Its Web site includes strategies for protecting and promoting human rights, and information on how you can join this organization or its local volunteer groups.

If you visit this site, consider reading AI's *Universal Declaration of Human Rights*, which has been translated into more than 300 different languages for worldwide use.

Name _____ Date _____

Diversity Self-Awareness

Further your diversity self-awareness by completing the following four exercises.

1. **Diversity Spectrum**

   We are members of different groups at the same time, and our membership in these groups can influence our personal development and self-identity. In the figure below, the shaded center circle represents yourself, and the six non-shaded circles represent six different groups that you belong to, which you feel have influenced your personal development.

   Fill in these circles with the names of those groups to which you belong that have had the most influence on your personal development. You can use the diversity spectrum that appears on the first page of this chapter to help you identify different groups. Do not feel you have to come up with six groups to fill all six circles. What is most important is to identify those groups that you think have had significant influence on your personal development or identity.

   After you identify these groups, take a moment to reflect on the following questions:

   a. Which one of your group memberships has had the greatest influence on your personal identity and why?

   b. Have you ever felt limited or disadvantaged by being a member of any group(s)?

   c. Have you ever felt that you experienced advantages or privileges because of your membership in any group(s)?

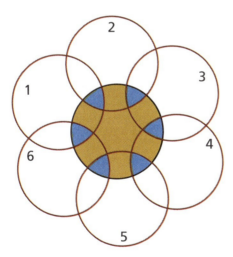

2. **When Have You Felt Different?**

   Describe an experience in your life when you felt that you were different from, or didn't fit in with, the majority of people around you.

   Why did you feel that way? How do you think members of the majority felt about you?

3. **Questions about Other Groups or Cultures**

   Write down, in question form, anything that you have wondered about people from a particular group or culture that is different than your own.

   Would you feel comfortable approaching and posing these questions to someone from this group or culture? Why or why not?

4. **Personal Experience**

   Have you ever been the personal target of prejudice or discrimination?

   What happened? Who was involved? How did you feel?

CASE STUDY

Hate Crime: Racially Motivated Murder

Jasper County, Texas, has a population of approximately 31,000 people, 80 percent of whom are White, 18 percent Black, and 2 percent are of other races. The county's poverty rate is considerably higher than the national average, and its average household income is significantly lower. In 1998, the mayor, president of the Chamber of Commerce, and two councilmen were Black. From the outside, Jasper appeared to be a town with racial harmony, and its Black and White leaders were quick to state there was racial harmony in Jasper.

However, on June 7, 1998, James Byrd, Jr., a 49-year-old African-American male, was walking home along a road one evening and was offered a ride by three White males. Rather than taking Mr. Byrd home, Lawrence Brewer (31), John King (23), and Shawn Berry (23), three individuals linked to white-supremacist groups, took Mr. Byrd to an isolated area and began beating him. They then dropped his pants to his ankles, painted his face black, chained Mr. Byrd to their truck and dragged him for approximately 3 miles. The truck was driven in a zigzag fashion in order to inflict maximum pain on the victim. Mr. Byrd was decapitated after his body collided with a culvert in a ditch alongside the road. His skin, arms, genitalia, and other body parts were strewn along the road, while his torso was found dumped in front of a Black cemetery. Medical examiners testified that Mr. Byrd was alive for much of the dragging incident.

While in prison awaiting trial, Lawrence Brewer wrote letters to King and other inmates. In one letter, Brewer wrote: "Well, I did it and am no longer a virgin. It was a rush and I'm still licking my lips for more." Once the trials were completed, Brewer and King were sentenced to death. Both Brewer and King, whose bodies were covered with racist tattoos, had been on parole prior to the incident, and they had previously been cellmates. King had spent an extensive amount of time in prison where he began to associate with White males in an environment where each race was pitted against the other.

As a result of the murder, Mr. Byrd's family created the James Byrd Foundation for Racial Healing in 1998. On January 20, 1999, a wrought iron fence that separated Black and White graves for more than 150 years in Jasper Cemetery was removed in a special unity service. Members of the racist Ku Klux Klan have since visited the gravesite of James Byrd, Jr. several times, leaving stickers and other markers that have angered the Jasper community and Mr. Byrd's family.

Sources: *San Antonio Express News*, September 17, 1999, *Louisiana Weekly*, February 3, 2003, *Houston Chronicle*, June 14, 1998, Two Towns of Jasper, PBS.

Reflection and Discussion Questions

1. What social factors (if any) do you think led to the incident?

2. Could the incident have been prevented? If yes, how? If no, why not?

3. What do you think will be the long-term effects of this incident on the town?

4. How likely do you think it is that an incident such as this could occur in your hometown or near your college campus?

5. How would you react if it did happen?

Finding a Path to Your Future Profession

Career Exploration, Preparation, and Development

Learning Goals

The primary goal of this chapter is to supply you with specific strategies that you can use now and throughout your remaining years of college to promote your career exploration, preparation, and development.

Outline

Why Career Planning Should Begin in the First Year of College
Career Exploration and Development Strategies
    Step 1: Self-Awareness
    Step 2: Awareness of Your Options
    Step 3: Awareness of What Career Options Best Fit You
    Step 4: Awareness of How to Prepare for and Gain Entry into the Career of Your Choice
Summary and Conclusion
Learning More through Independent Research
Exercise: Conducting an Information Interview
Case Study: Career Choice: Conflict and Confusion

Activate Your Thinking

Before you start digging into the meat of this chapter, take a moment to answer the following question: Have you decided on a career?

a. If yes, why did you pick this career? (Was your decision influenced by anybody or anything?)

b. If no, are there any careers you're considering as possibilities?

●●● Why Career Planning Should Begin in the First Year of College

We know what you might be thinking: "Have I decided on a career? Give me a break; I've barely begun college!" This is probably the way most college seniors felt when they were first-year students. However, if you ask these seniors how they feel now, they would probably say something like: "I can't believe I'm about to graduate. How did time fly by so fast?" For these seniors and other students who will be graduating in this century, they are likely to continue working until age 75 (Herman, 2000). Also, consider the fact that once you begin full-time work, you will spend the majority of your waking hours at work. The fact is, the only other single activity that you will spend more time doing in your lifetime is sleeping. When you consider that such a sizable amount of our lifetime is spent working, plus the fact that work can influence our sense of self-esteem and personal identity, it is never too early to start thinking about your career choices.

Remember: When you are doing *career* planning, you're also doing *life* planning; you are planning how to spend your future life doing what you want to do.

It is true that college graduation and career entry are years away, but the process of investigating, planning, and preparing for career success should begin during your first year of college. If you are undecided about a career, or have not even begun to think about what you'll be doing after college, don't be discouraged. In fact, you can join the club, because research indicates that the majority of college students are in the same boat. Three of every four beginning students are uncertain or have doubt about their career choice (Frost, 1991; Cuseo, 2005).

Even if you may have already decided on a career that you've been dreaming about since you were a preschooler, you will still need to make decisions about what specific type of specialization within that career you will pursue. For example, if you are interested in pursuing a career in law, you will eventually need to decide what branch of law you wish to practice (for example, criminal law, corporate law, or family law). You will also need to decide about what employment sector or type of industry you'd like to work in, such as: for profit, non-profit, education, or government. Each of these sectors will provide you with different options relating to the same career. For example, a student who is interested in an advertising career may work for an advertising agency (for profit) to encourage the purchase of a certain product, or may work in the non-profit sector to create a campaign for increasing public awareness of safety issues (e.g., persuade the public not to drink and drive). This student could also decide to create an effective advertisement designed to increase reading (education sector), or attempt to persuade people to enter public service positions (government). As these examples illustrate, there are still many options to consider and decisions to be made, even if you have decided on a particular career path.

Thus, no matter how certain or uncertain you are about your career path at this point in time, you will need to begin exploring different career options and start taking your first steps toward formulating a career development plan.

••• Career Exploration and Development Strategies

Reaching an effective decision about a career involves four steps:

Step 1. Awareness of yourself—such as your personal abilities, interests, and values.

Step 2. Awareness of your options—the variety of choices (career fields) available to you.

Step 3. Awareness of what particular options (careers) best fit you—that is, deciding on what are the best matches for your personal abilities, interests, and values.

Step 4. Awareness of how to prepare for and gain entry into the career of your choice.

Step 1. Self-Awareness

The more you know about yourself, the better your choices and decisions will be. Self-awareness is a particularly important step to take when making career decisions because the career you choose to pursue says a lot about who you are and what you want from life. Your personal identity and life goals should not be based on or built around your career choice; instead, it should be the other way around: **Your personal identity and life goals should be considered first and should provide the foundation on which you build your career choice.**

One way to gain greater self-awareness of your career interests, abilities, and values is by taking psychological tests or assessments. These assessments allow you to see how your interest in certain career fields compares with other students who have taken the same assessment, and how your interests compare with people working in different career fields who have experienced career satisfaction and success. These *comparative perspectives* can give you important reference points for assessing whether your level of interest in different careers is high, average, or low, relative to other students and working professionals. By seeing how your results compare with others, you may become aware of your distinctive or unique interests. Your Career Development Center is the place on campus where you can find these career-interest tests, as well as other instruments that may allow you to assess your career-related abilities and values.

In addition to career assessments, the learning styles instruments may sharpen self-awareness of your personal interests and preferences, and may provide useful information for making career choices. Also, self-assessment questions about your personal interests, abilities, and values to help you select a college major may also be used to help you select a career path.

Lastly, when making choices about a career, you may also have to consider one other important aspect of yourself: your personal needs. A personal "need" may be best understood as something stronger than an interest. When you satisfy a personal need, you are doing something that makes your life more satisfying or fulfilling. Psychologists have identified a number of important human needs that vary in strength or intensity from one individual to another. Listed in Box 1 are personal needs that we feel are the most relevant or important ones to consider when making decisions about careers.

Pierce Howard, author of *The Owner's Manual for the Brain*, puts it this way: "It is stressful to attempt to be someone different from who we are, to try to be solitary when our nature is to be gregarious. Being true to our nature is, in some ways, the ultimate goal. Attempting to be something different is an obstacle to that goal. Don't expect a recluse to be motivated to sell, a creative thinker to be motivated to be a good proofreader day in and day out, or a sow's ear to be happy in the role of a silk purse" (2000, pp. 386–387).

TAKE ACTION NOW! — Box 1

Personal Needs to Consider When Making Career Choices

As you read the needs listed in the box below, make a note after each one, indicating how strong the need is for you (high, moderate, or low).

When exploring career options, keep in mind how different careers may or may not satisfy your level of need for autonomy, affiliation, competence, and sensory stimulation, each of which is described below.

1. **Autonomy:** Need to work independently, without close supervision or control.

    Individuals high in this need may experience greater satisfaction working in careers that allow them to be their own boss, make their own decisions, and control their own work schedule. Individuals low in this need may be more satisfied working in careers that are more structured and involve a supervisor who provides direction, assistance, and frequent feedback.

2. **Affiliation:** Need for social interaction, a sense of belongingness, and the opportunity to collaborate with others.

    Individuals high in this need may be more satisfied working in careers that involve frequent interpersonal interaction and teamwork with colleagues or co-workers. Individuals low in this need may be more satisfied working alone, or in competition with others, rather than careers that emphasize interpersonal interaction or collaboration.

3. **Achievement:** Need to experience challenge and achieve a sense of personal accomplishment.

    Individuals high in this need may be more satisfied working in careers that push them to solve problems, generate creative ideas, and continually learn new information or master new skills. Individuals low in this need may be more satisfied with careers that do not continually test their abilities, and do not repeatedly challenge them to stretch their skills by taking on new tasks or different responsibilities.

4. **Sensory Stimulation:** Need to experience variety, change, and risk.

    Individuals high in this need may be more satisfied working in careers that involve frequent changes of pace and place (e.g., frequent travel), unpredictable events (e.g., work tasks that vary considerably from day to day), and moderate stress (e.g., working under pressure of competition or deadlines). Individuals with a low need for sensory stimulation may feel more comfortable working in careers that involve regular routines, predictable situations, and minimal levels of risk or stress.

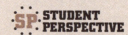 **STUDENT PERSPECTIVE**

"To me, an important characteristic of a career is being able to meet new, smart, interesting people."
—First-year student

STUDENT PERSPECTIVE

"I want to be able to enjoy my job and be challenged by it at the same time. I hope that my job will not be monotonous and that I will have the opportunity to learn new things often."
—First-year student

 **STUDENT PERSPECTIVE**

"For me, a good career is very unpredictable and interest-fulfilling. I would love to do something that allows me to be spontaneous."
—First-year student

Personal Story

While enrolled in my third year of college with half of my degree completed, I had an eye-opening experience. I wish this experience had happened in my first year, but better late than never (although earlier is best)! Although I had chosen a career during my first year of college, the decision-making process was not a good critical thinking, systematic one. I chose a major based on what sounded best, and would pay me the most money. Although these are not necessarily bad variables, the lack of a good process to determine these variables was bad. In my junior year of college I asked one of my professors why he decided to get his Ph.D. and become a professor. He simply answered, "I wanted autonomy." This was an epiphany for me! He explained that when he looked at his life he determined that he needed a career that offered independence, so he began looking at career options that would offer that. After that explanation, autonomy became my favorite word, and this story became a guiding force in my life. After going through a critical self-awareness process, I determined that autonomy was exactly what I desired, and a professor is what I became.

—Aaron Thompson, Professor of Sociology, and co-author of this text

Figure 1 Personal Characteristics Providing the Foundation for Effective Career Choice

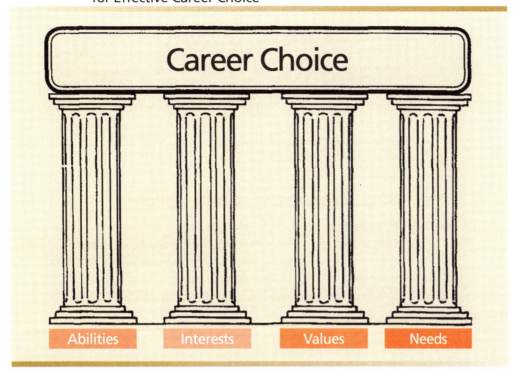

Taken altogether, there are four key aspects of yourself that should be considered when exploring careers: your personal *abilities*, *interests*, *values*, and *needs*. As illustrated in Figure 1, these are the four pillars that provide a solid foundation for effective career choices and decisions. You want to choose a career that you're good at, interested in, passionate about, and that fulfills your personal needs.

Lastly, since a career decision is a long-range decision that will involve your life beyond college, self-awareness should not only involve personal reflection about who you are now, it also involves *self-projection*—reflecting on how you see yourself in the more distant future. When you engage in the process of self-projection, you begin to see a connection between where you are now and where you want to be.

Pause for Reflection

Project yourself ten years into the future and visualize your ideal career and life.

Try to answer the following questions about your ideal future-life scenario:

1. What are you spending most of your time doing during your typical workday?
2. Where and with whom are you working?
3. How many hours are you working per week?
4. Where are you living?
5. Are you married? Do you have children?
6. How does your work influence your home life?

STUDENT PERSPECTIVE

"I think that a good career has to be meaningful for a person. It should be enjoyable for the most part [and] it has to give a person a sense of fulfillment."

—First-year student

CLASSIC QUOTE

"You've got to be careful if you don't know where you're going because you might not get there."

—Yogi Berra, former all-star baseball player

Your career choice should make you look forward to going to work each day.

Ideally, your choice of a career would be one that leads to a future career scenario in which your typical workday goes something like this: You wake up in the morning and hop out of bed enthusiastically—eagerly looking forward to what you'll be doing at work that day. When you're at work, time flies by, and before you know it, the day's over. When you return to bed that night and look back on your day, you feel good about what you did and how well you did it. For this ideal scenario to have any chance of really happening or even coming close to happening, you have to select a career path that is true to yourself—that closely matches your abilities (what you do well), your interests (what you like to do), your values (what you feel good about doing), and your needs (what brings you satisfaction and fulfillment in life).

Step 2. Awareness of Your Options

In order to make effective decisions about your career path, you need to have accurate knowledge about the nature of different careers and the realities of the work world. The Career Development Center is the first place to go for this information, as well as for help with career exploration and planning. In addition to helping you explore your personal career interests and abilities, the Career Development Center is also your key campus resource for learning about the nature of different careers and for strategies on how to locate career-related work experiences.

There are many more career choices in today's work world than there were for our early ancestors.

The federal government lists more than 30,000 different career fields, many of which you may have never heard of, but which may represent good career options for you. You can learn about careers through nine major routes or avenues:

1. Reading about careers,
2. Becoming involved in co-curricular programs on campus relating to career development,
3. Taking career development courses,
4. Interviewing people in different career fields,
5. Observing people at work in different careers,
6. Internships,
7. Co-op programs,
8. Volunteer service, and
9. Part-time work.

Strategies for using each of these routes to acquire accurate information about careers are discussed below.

1. Reading about Careers

Your Career Development Center and your College Library are key campus resources where you can find a wealth of reading material on careers, either in print or online. Here are some of the most useful sources of written information on careers:

- *Dictionary of Occupational Titles (DOT)*
  (http://www.occupationalinfo.org)

  This is the largest printed resource on careers; it contains concise definitions of over 17,000 jobs. It also includes such information as:
  - specific work tasks that people in the career typically perform on a regular basis;
  - type of knowledge, skills, and abilities that are required for different careers;
  - the interests, values, and needs of individuals who find working in their careers to be personally rewarding; and
  - background experiences of people working in different careers that qualified them for their positions.

- *Occupational Outlook Handbook (OOH)*
  (http://www.bls.gov/oco)

  This is one of the most widely available and frequently used resources on careers. It contains descriptions of approximately 250 positions, including information on the nature of work, work conditions, places of employment, training/education required for career entry and advancement, salaries, careers in related fields, and sources of additional information about particular careers (e.g., professional organizations and governmental agencies). A distinctive feature of this resource is that it contains information about the future employment outlook for different careers.

- *Encyclopedia of Careers and Vocational Guidance* (Chicago: Ferguson Press)

  As the name suggests, this is an encyclopedia of information on qualifications, salaries, and advancement opportunities for a wide variety of careers.

- *Occupational Information Network (O*NET) Online* (http://online.onetcenter.org)

  This is America's most comprehensive source of online information about careers. It contains an up-to-date set of descriptions for almost 1,000 different careers, plus lots of other information similar to that found in the *Dictionary of Occupational Titles (DOT)*.

There are many resources for finding information on careers, many of which can be accessed on the Internet.

In addition to these general sources of information, the Career Development Center or College Library should have books and other published materials relating to specific careers or occupations (e.g., careers for English majors). You can also learn a lot about careers by simply reading advertisements for position openings. You can find them in your local newspaper or at online sites, such as careerbuilder.com and monstertrak.com. When reading job descriptions, note the particular tasks, duties, or responsibilities that they involve, and ask yourself if these positions fit your profile of abilities, interests, needs, and values.

2. Becoming Involved in Co-Curricular Programs on Career Planning and Development

Periodically during the academic year, co-curricular programs devoted to career exploration and career preparation are likely to be offered on your campus. For example, your Career Development Center may sponsor career exploration or career planning workshops, which you can attend free of charge. Also, your Career Development Center may organize a "career fair" in which professionals working in different career fields are given booths on campus where you can visit with them and ask them questions about their careers. (See the end-of-chapter assignment for questions that you could ask.)

We strongly encourage your involvement in co-curricular programs that relate to career exploration and development. They have already been covered by the cost of your tuition, so get your money's worth and take advantage of them. Research suggests that such programs have positive effects on college students' career planning and decision-making (Brown & Krane, 2000; Hildenbrand & Gore, 2005).

3. Taking Career Development Courses

Many colleges offer career development courses for elective credit. These courses typically include self-assessment of your career interests, information about different careers, and strategies for career preparation. The things that students do in these courses are what they should do anyway (on their own), so why not do them as part of a career development course and receive academic credit for doing them? Studies show that students who participate in career development courses experience significant benefits in terms of their career choice and career development (Pascarella & Terenzini, 2005).

It might also be possible for you to take an *independent study* course that will allow you to investigate issues in the career area you are considering. An independent study is a project that you work out with a faculty member, which usually involves writing a paper or detailed report. It allows you to receive academic credit for an in-depth study of a topic of your choice, without having to enroll with other students in a traditional course that has regularly scheduled classroom meetings. You could use this independent-study option to choose a project that relates to a career you may be interested in pursuing. (To see if this option is available at your campus, check the college catalogue or consult with an academic advisor.) Also, if you have a free choice of a topic to write about in a writing course or to speak about in a speech course, consider researching your career interest and use this as a topic for your paper or presentation.

4. Information Interviews

One of the best and most overlooked ways to get accurate information about careers is to interview professionals who are actually working in careers that you are considering. Career development specialists refer to this strategy as "information interviewing." Although you might think that working professionals would have little interest in taking time out of their day to speak with a student, most of them do not mind being interviewed about their careers; in fact, they often enjoy it (Crosby, 2002).

Information interviews provide you inside information about what careers are really like, because you're getting that information directly "from the horse's mouth." Participating in information interviews can also help you gain experience and confidence with interview situations, which may help you prepare for future job interviews. Furthermore, if you make a good impression during the information interview, the person you interviewed may suggest that you contact him or her again after graduation in case there are any position openings. If there are, you might be the person being interviewed and possibly being hired.

Because information interviews can be a source of valuable information about careers (and provide possible contacts for future employment), we strongly recommend that you complete the information interview assignment that is included at the end of this chapter.

5. Observing People at Work in Different Careers

In addition to learning about careers from reading and interviews, you can experience careers more directly by placing yourself in workplace situations or environments that enable you to observe workers actually performing their jobs. Two college-sponsored programs that may allow you to observe working professionals are the following:

- Job Shadowing Programs: These programs allow you to follow around ("shadow") and observe a professional during a "typical" workday.
- Externship Programs: An externship is basically an extended form of job shadowing, which lasts for a longer period of time (e.g., 2–3 days).

Visit your Career Development Center to find out about what job shadowing or externship programs may be available at your college. If none are available in a career field that interests you, then consider finding one on your own, using strategies similar to those we recommend for information interviews in the end-of-chapter assignment. The only difference would be that, instead of asking the person for an interview, you would be asking if you could observe that person at work. In fact, you might ask the same people who were willing to give you an information interview if they would also be willing to let you observe them at work. Just remember that one or two days of observation will give you some first-hand information, but not a thorough understanding of that field.

Pause for Reflection

If you were to observe or interview a working professional in a career that interests you, what position would that person hold?

6. Internships

In contrast to job shadowing or externships, whereby you observe someone at work, an internship program involves you with the work itself; that is to say, you actually *participate* and *perform* work duties related to the career. The word "internship" implies that you are involved "internally" with the work process, and actually doing the work—as opposed to an "externship" where you are "external" to the work process, observing someone else doing the work.

Another distinguishing feature of internships is that you can receive academic credit, and, sometimes, financial compensation for the work you do. An internship usually totals 120 to 150 work hours, which may be completed at the same time you're enrolled in a full schedule of classes; or, internship hours could be completed during the summer.

An internship is an excellent way to get experience in a career before you graduate.

A key advantage of an internship is that it enables college students to avoid the classic "catch-22" situation they often run into when interviewing for their first career position after graduation. The interview scenario often goes something like this: Employer asks the college graduate, "What work experience have you had in this field?" The recent graduate replies, "I haven't had any work experience because I've been a full-time college student." This situation can be avoided if students have an internship *during* their college experience. We strongly encourage you to participate in an internship while in college; this will enable you to beat the "no experience" rap after graduation and will distinguish yourself from many other college graduates. In fact, research reveals that students who have internships while in college are more likely to experience positive gains in development of career-related skills and find employment immediately after college graduation (Pascarella & Terenzini, 2005).

Although internships are typically available to students during their junior or senior year, there may also be internships available to first- and second-year students on your campus. If your school offers internships only for juniors or seniors, or does not offer internships that relate to your particular career interests, you can pursue an internship on your own. There are published guides that describe a wide variety of career-related internships, along with information on how to apply for them (e.g., *Peterson's Internships* and the *Vault Guide to Top Internships*). You could also search for internships on the Web (e.g., www.internships.com and www.vaultreports.com). Another good resource for possible information on internships is the local Chamber of Commerce in the town or city where your college is located, or the local Chamber of Commerce in your hometown.

"Got Experience?"—The "killer question" that college graduates can't answer after college unless they've had some career-related work experience during college (e.g., internships or volunteer service).

7. Cooperative Education (Co-op) Programs

A co-op is similar to an internship, but involves work experience that lasts longer than one academic term and often requires students to stop their course work temporarily in order to participate in the program. There are, however, some co-op programs that allow students to continue to take classes while working part time at their co-op position; these are sometimes referred to as "parallel co-ops." Students are paid for participating in co-op programs, but do not receive academic credit—just a notation on their college transcript (Smith, 2005).

Typically, co-ops are only available to juniors or seniors, but you can begin now to explore co-op programs by looking through your college catalog and visiting your Career Development

Center to see if your school offers co-op programs in career areas that may interest you. If you find any, plan to get involved with one, because it can provide you with an authentic source of career information and work experience.

The value of co-ops and internships is strongly supported by research, which indicates that students who have these experiences during college:

- are more likely to report that their college education was relevant to their career,
- receive higher evaluations from employers who recruit students on campus,
- have less difficulty finding an initial position after graduation,
- are more satisfied with their first career position after college,
- obtain more prestigious positions after graduation, and
- report greater job satisfaction (Gardner, 1991; Knouse, Tanner, & Harris, 1999; Pascarella & Terenzini, 1991, 2005).

In one statewide survey, which asked employers to rank a variety of factors in terms of their importance for hiring new college graduates, internships and cooperative education programs received the highest ranking from employers (Education Commission of the States, 1995). Furthermore, employers often report that when full-time positions become available in their organization or company, they are more likely to turn first to their own interns and co-op students (NACE, 2003).

8. Volunteer Service

In addition to helping your community, volunteer service can help *you*. It can serve to promote your career exploration and preparation by allowing you to experience different work environments and to gain work experience in fields related to your areas of service. For example, volunteer service to different age groups (e.g., children, adolescents, or the elderly) and service in different environments (e.g., hospital, school, or laboratory) can provide you with first-hand work experience, while simultaneously giving you a chance to test out your interest in possibly pursuing future careers relating to these areas of service. Volunteer experiences also enable you to network with professionals outside of college who may serve as excellent references and resources for letters of recommendation. Furthermore, if these professionals are impressed with your volunteer work, they may become interested in hiring you on a part-time basis while you're still in college, or on a full-time basis after you graduate from college.

Personal Story

I am an academic advisor and was once advising two first-year students, Kim and Christopher. Kim was thinking about becoming a physical therapist, and Chris was thinking about becoming an elementary school teacher. I suggested to Kim that she visit the hospital nearby our college to see if she could do volunteer work in the physical therapy unit. The hospital did need volunteers, so she volunteered in the physical therapy unit, and she absolutely loved it. That volunteer experience confirmed for her that physical therapy is what she wanted to pursue as a career. She completed a degree in physical therapy and is now a professional physical therapist.

I suggested to Chris, the student who was thinking of becoming an elementary school teacher, that he visit some of the local schools to see if they could use a volunteer teacher's aide. One of the schools did need his services, and Chris volunteered as a teacher's aide for about 10 weeks. At the halfway point during his volunteer experience, he came into my office to tell me that the kids were just about driving him crazy and that he no longer had any interest in becoming a teacher! He ended up majoring in communications.

> Kim and Chris were the first two students whom I ever advised to get involved in volunteer work for the purpose of testing their career interests. Their volunteer experiences proved so valuable for helping both of them—in different ways—to make their career decision that I now encourage all students I advise to get volunteer experience in the field they're considering as a career.
>
> —Joe Cuseo

It might also be possible to do volunteer work on campus by serving as an informal teaching assistant or research assistant to a faculty member. Such experiences are particularly valuable for students intending to go to graduate school. If you have a good relationship with any faculty members on campus who are working in an academic field that interests you, consider asking them if they would like some assistance, either with their teaching or research responsibilities. It is possible that your volunteer work for a college professor may enable you to make a presentation with your professor at a professional conference, or may even result in your name being included as a co-author on an article published by the professor you assisted.

Pause for Reflection

Have you done volunteer work prior to college? If you have, did you learn anything from your volunteer experiences that might help you decide what types of work best match your interests or talents?

---

9. Part-Time Work

Jobs that you hold during the academic year or during the summer should not be overlooked as sources of career information and as resume-building experiences. Part-time work can provide you with opportunities to learn or develop skills that may be relevant to your future career (e.g., organizational skills, communication skills, and ability to work effectively with co-workers from diverse backgrounds or cultures).

Also, work in a part-time position may eventually turn into a full-time career. The following personal story illustrates how this can happen.

> *Personal Story*
>
> One student of mine, an English major, worked part time for an organization that provides special assistance to mentally handicapped children. After he completed his English degree, he was offered a full-time position in this organization, which he accepted. While working at his full-time position with handicapped children, he decided to go to graduate school on a part-time basis and eventually completed a Master's Degree in Special Education, which qualified him for a promotion to a more advanced position in the organization, which he also accepted.
>
> —Joe Cuseo

It might also be possible for you to obtain part-time work experience on campus through your school's *work-study program*. A work-study job allows you to work on campus in a variety of possible work settings, such as the Business Office, college library, Office of Public Relations, or Computer Services. On-campus work can provide you with valuable career-exploration and resume-building experiences, and the professionals for whom you work can serve as excellent references for letters of recommendation to future employers. To see if you are eligible for your school's work-study program, visit the Financial Aid Office on your campus.

Learning about careers through first-hand experience in actual work settings (e.g., shadowing, internships, volunteer services, and part-time work) is critical to successful career exploration and development. These first-hand experiences represent the ultimate "career-reality test." They allow you direct access to information about what careers are truly like—as opposed to how they are portrayed on television or in the movies, which often paint an inaccurate or unrealistic picture of careers, making them appear more exciting or glamorous than they actually are. We strongly recommend using the strategies suggested in this section to get direct, first-hand experiences in real work environments, so you can make realistic career choices, rather than unrealistic choices that are based on second-hand information that reaches you indirectly—after passing through the sanitized and fantasized filter of popular media.

In summary, first-hand experiences in actual work settings equip you with five powerful career advantages. Such experiences enable you to:

1. Learn about what work is really like in a particular field,
2. Test your interest and skills for certain types of work,
3. Strengthen your resume by adding experiential learning to your classroom learning,
4. Acquire references for letters of recommendation, and
5. Make personal contacts that allow you to network with employers who may refer or hire you for a position after graduation.

So, get actively involved in first-hand work experiences. Use your campus resources (e.g., Offices of Career Development Center and your Financial Aid Office), read items posted on campus kiosks and hallway bulletin boards, use your local resources (e.g., Chamber of Commerce), and use your personal contacts (family and friends) to locate and participate in work experiences that are related to your career interests. When you land an internship, work hard at it, learn as much as you can from it, and build relationships with as many people as possible because these are the people who can provide you with future contacts, references, and referrals.

If you start gaining work experience early in college through volunteerism and part-time work, and participate later in an internship or cooperative education program as junior or senior, you will be able to graduate from college with an impressive amount of work experience under your belt (and on your resume).

CLASSIC QUOTE

Give me a history major who has done internships and a business major who hasn't, and I'll hire the history major every time.

—William Ardery, senior vice president, investor communications company (quoted in The New York Times)

Pause for Reflection

1. Have you had first-hand work experiences?

2. Did you learn anything from these previous work experiences that may influence your future career plans?

3. If you could get first-hand work experience in any career right now, what career would it be?

Step 3. Awareness of What Career Options Best Fit You

When considering your career options, do not be misinformed and mislead by popular myths about careers. The following myths can lead students to make poor career choices or decisions.

Myth #1. Once you have decided on a career, you have decided on what you'll be doing for the rest of your life.

This is simply and totally false. The term "career" derives from the same root word as "racecourse," and like a racecourse, a career involves movement that typically takes different turns and twists. Like any race on any course, it's not how fast you start, but where you finish that matters most. This ability to move and change direction is what distinguishes a professional career from a dead-end job. According to the United States Bureau of Labor, Americans average four different careers in a lifetime; it also predicts that today's college graduates will change jobs 12 to 15 times, and these jobs will span across 3 to 5 different career fields (United States Bureau of Labor Statistics, 2005). You might find these statistics hard to believe because one of the reasons you are going to college is to prepare for a particular career. However, don't forget that the liberal arts component of your college education provides you with general, transferable skills that can be applied to many different jobs and careers.

Remember: It is highly unlikely that your first career choice after college is what you will be doing for the remainder of your working life. Instead, your first career choice is likely to be a temporary choice, not a permanent choice that determines how you will make a living until the day you die (or retire).

Myth #2. I need to pick a career that's in demand, which will get me a job with a good starting salary right after graduation.

Looking only at careers that are "hot" now and have high starting salaries can distract students from also looking at themselves, causing them to overlook the most important question of whether or not these careers are truly compatible with their personal abilities, interests, needs, and values.

Starting salaries and available job openings are factors that are external to us that can be easily "seen" and "counted," so they may get more attention and be given more weight in the decision-making process than things that are harder to see or put a number on, such as our inner qualities and whether they are really compatible with the choices we're considering. In the case of career decision-making, this tendency can result in college students choosing careers based exclusively on external factors (salaries and openings) without giving equal consideration to internal factors such as personal abilities, interests, and values. This, in turn, can lead some college graduates to choose and enter careers that eventually leave them bored, frustrated, or dissatisfied.

Also, keep in mind that careers which may be in high demand now may not be in such high demand by the time you graduate, nor may they remain in high demand for many years after you graduate. On the other hand, there will always be at least some demand for employees in almost all careers, because there will always be natural attrition (loss) of workers due to retirement or death.

The number of job offers you receive immediately after graduation and the number of dollars you earn as your first (starting) salary are very short-term and short-sighted standards for judging whether you've made a good career choice. Keep in mind the distinction between career *entry* and career *advancement*. Some college graduates may not bolt out of the starting gate

> **CLASSIC QUOTE**
> *Money is a good servant but a bad master.*
> —French proverb

> **CLASSIC QUOTE**
> *There is perhaps nothing worse than reaching the top of the ladder and discovering that you're on the wrong wall.*
> —Joseph Campbell, American professor and writer

and begin their career path with a well-paying first position, but they will steadily work their way up and get promoted to more advanced positions. Beware of advice from others who may tell you that you need to pick a career that's in demand. All this means is that you may be able to enter the field immediately and easily after graduation; it does not necessarily mean you will advance in that field just as quickly and easily. In other words, what is good in the short run (career entry) may not necessarily be good in the long run (career advancement).

Criteria to Consider When Evaluating Career Options

Effective decision-making requires identification of important factors that should be taken into consideration when evaluating your options, plus determining how much weight each of these factors should carry. As we have emphasized throughout this chapter, the factor that should carry the greatest weight or amount of influence in career decision-making is how compatible your choice is with your personal abilities, interests, needs, and values.

Suppose you have discovered more than one career option that is compatible with these four key dimensions of yourself. What other aspects of a career should be considered to help you reach a decision or make a selection? Many people would probably say money, but as the length of the following list suggests, there are other important aspects or characteristics of careers that should be factored into the decision-making process.

STUDENT PERSPECTIVES

"A big paycheck is a plus but it is not necessary. I would rather be inspired."
—First-year student

"I would rather make little money doing something I love than be rich doing something that makes me miserable."
—First-year student

1. Work Conditions

These would include such considerations as:

◆ the nature of the work environment (e.g., physical and social environment);
◆ geographical location of the work (e.g., urban, suburban, rural);
◆ work schedule (e.g., number of hours per week, flexibility of hours); and
◆ work-related travel (opportunities to travel, frequency of travel, locations traveled to).

2. Career Entry

Can you enter into the career without much difficulty, or does the supply of people pursuing the career far exceed the demand (e.g., professional acting), thus making entry into that career very competitive and difficult? If your first and ideal career choice is very difficult to enter, this doesn't mean you should automatically give up on it, but you should have a career to fall back on—in case you can't (or until you can) break into your ideal career.

3. Career Advancement (Promotion)

An ideal first job educates and prepares you to advance to an even better one. Does the career provide opportunities to be promoted to more advanced positions?

4. Career Mobility

Is it easy to move out of the career and into a different career path? This may be an important factor to consider because careers may rise or fall in demand, and because your career interests or values may change as you gain more work and life experience.

When evaluating career options, be sure to take into account things like the amount of travel required.

5. Financial Benefits

This includes salary—including both starting salary and expected salary increases with greater work experience or advancement to higher positions; it also includes fringe benefits—such as: health insurance, paid vacation time, paid sick-leave time, paid maternity- or paternity-leave time, paid tuition for seeking advanced education, and retirement benefits.

6. Impact of Career on Personal Life

How would the career affect your family life, your physical and mental health, or your self-concept and self-esteem? Remember that you should not build your life around a career; you should build your career around your life. Your work life and personal life have to be considered simultaneously when making career choices, because the nature of your work can affect the nature (and quality) of your personal life.

> **Remember:** A good career decision should involve consideration of how the career may affect all key dimensions of your "self" (social, emotional, physical, etc.) at all key stages of your life cycle—young adulthood, middle age, and late adulthood.

Think about a career you are considering, and answer the following questions:

1. Why are you considering it? (*What* led or caused you to become interested in this choice?)

2. Would you say that your interest in this career is motivated primarily by intrinsic factors—that is to say, factors "inside" of you, such as your personal abilities, interests, needs, and values? Or, would you say that your interest in the career is influenced more heavily by extrinsic factors—that is to say, factors "outside" of you, such as starting salary, pleasing parents, meeting family expectations, or meeting an expected role for your gender (male role or female role)?

3. If money was not an issue and you could earn a comfortable living in any career, would you choose the same career?

· — · CLASSIC QUOTE · — ·

Students [may be] pushed into careers by their families, while others have picked one just to relieve their anxiety about not having a career choice. Still others may have picked popular or lucrative careers, knowing nothing of what they're really like or what it takes to prepare for them.

—Lee Upcraft, Joni Finney, and Peter Garland, Student Development Specialists

---

Don't let gender stereotypes limit your choice of a major or career.

Since the cost of college can be very high, family members paying this hefty cost (or helping you pay it) may sometimes get nervous about making such a steep financial commitment if you choose a career path that they are not familiar with, do not agree with, or do not understand (Helkowski & Shehan, 2004). If you happen to choose such a path, they may strongly oppose it, or may pressure you to change your mind. It may be tempting to reduce their anxiety, or your guilt about causing their anxiety, and conform to their wishes. However, **the decision you make about what career path to follow should really be *your* choice, because it's really a decision about *your life*.** Although you should be grateful to those who have provided you with the financial support to attend college and should be open to their input, the final decision is yours to make.

Step 4. Awareness of How to Prepare for and Gain Entry into the Career of Your Choice

Whether you're keeping your career options wide open, or if you think you've already decided on a particular career, you can start preparing for success in any career field right now. In this section, we will discuss specific strategies that you can begin using immediately to prepare for successful career entry and development.

Self-Monitoring: Watching and Tracking Your Personal Skills and Positive Qualities

Many students think that a college credential or diploma itself is the passport to a good job and career success (Ellin, 1993; Sullivan, 1993). However, for most employers of college graduates, what matters most is not the credential but the specific skills and personal qualities an applicant possesses and can bring to the position (Educational Commission of the States, 1995). You can start building these personal skills and qualities by *self-monitoring*—watching or observing yourself, and keeping track of the skills you are using and developing during your college experience.

Although completing assignments, getting good grades, and getting a degree are all important end products, it is equally important to reflect on and keep track of the particular skills you've used, learned, or developed in the process of completing these products. More important than memorizing facts, figures, and formulas are the new skills you are acquiring or refining, the new perspectives or vantage points from which you are viewing things, and the different dimensions or elements of the "self" that you are developing. We suggest you create a list of specific liberal arts skills, perspectives, and areas of self-development associated with a liberal arts education. Save that list and use it periodically as a checklist to keep aware of, and to keep track of, the skills and perspectives you are developing in college. It is important to make a conscious and deliberate attempt to do so, because the development of skills and perspectives can occur subtly and subconsciously, often getting embedded within or buried below all the factual material you are consciously trying to learn. Skills and perspectives are mental habits, and like other habits that are repeatedly practiced, their development can be so gradual that you may not even notice how much growth is actually taking place (like watching grass grow).

Don't overlook the fact that *learning* skills are also *earning* skills. The skills you are acquiring in college may appear to be just *academic*-performance skills, but they are also *career*-performance skills. For instance, in the process of completing such academic tasks as taking tests and writing papers, you are often using a variety of career-relevant skills, such as: analyzing, organizing, communicating, and problem-solving.

> **· — · CLASSIC QUOTE · — ·**
> *Whoever wants to reach a distant goal must take many small steps.*
> —Helmut Schmidt, former Chancellor of West Germany

Career development specialists recommend that you track your skills and "sell" them to employers and enhance your career prospects (Lock, 2000). Be sure to make a conscious effort to track the specific skills and perspectives you are developing in college, so you will be able to showcase and sell them to future employers.

One specific strategy you can use to track your developing skills is to keep a *career-development journal* of your completed academic tasks and assignments, accompanied by the specific skills you used to complete them. Also, be sure to record skills in your journal that you are developing in non-academic situations, such as those skills used while performing part-time jobs, personal hobbies, co-curricular activities, or volunteer services. Keep in mind that a skill is any positive or productive action that you can apply in different situations, which usually include most work situations. Since skills are actions, it is best to record them as action verbs in any career-development journal you may be keeping.

> *Personal Story*
>
> One day after class I had a conversation with one of my students (Max) about his personal interests. He said he was considering a career in the music industry and was now working part time as a disc jockey at a night club. I asked him what it took to be a good disc jockey, and in less than five minutes of conversation, we discovered that there were many more skills involved in doing his job than either of us had realized. He was responsible for organizing 3–4 hours of music each night he worked; he had to "read" the reactions of his audience (customers) and adapt or adjust his selections to their musical tastes; he had to arrange his selections in a sequence that periodically varied the tempo (speed) of the music he played throughout the night; and he had to continually research and update his music collection to track the latest trends in hits and popular artists. Max also said that he had to overcome his fear of public speaking in order to deliver announcements that were a required part of his job.
>
> Although we were just having a short, friendly conversation after class about his part-time job, Max wound up reflecting on and identifying multiple skills that were involved in doing it. We both agreed that it would be a good idea to get these skills down in writing, so he could use them as selling points for future jobs in the music industry, or in any industry.
>
> —Joe Cuseo

In addition to reflecting on your developing skills, also reflect on and keep track of your positive traits or personal qualities. While it is best to record skills as verbs because they represent actions, it may be best to record positive traits or qualities as adjectives because they are descriptions.

The key to discovering career-relevant skills and qualities is to get in the habit of stepping back from your academic work and out-of-class experiences to reflect on the skills and qualities you're developing, and then get them down in writing before they slip your mind. You are likely to find that many of the performance skills and personal qualities that you develop in college will be the very same ones that your future employers will seek from you in the workforce. Box 2 contains lists of some important career-success skills and personal qualities that you are likely to develop during your college experience.

BOX 2 Snapshot Summary: Personal Skills Relevant to Successful Career Performance

The following behaviors represent a sample of useful *skills* that are relevant to success in a wide variety of careers (Bolles, 1998). As you read these skills, underline or highlight any of them that you have performed, either inside or outside of school.

advising	assembling	calculating	coaching	coordinating
creating	delegating	designing	evaluating	explaining
measuring	motivating	negotiating	operating	planning
researching	supervising	initiating	mediating	producing
proving	resolving	sorting	summarizing	synthesizing
translating				

The following represent a sample of *personal traits* or *qualities* that are relevant to success in multiple careers. As you read these traits, underline or highlight any of them that you feel you possess.

energetic	enthusiastic	ethical	outgoing	imaginative
industrious	loyal	precise	observant	open-minded
patient	persuasive	positive	productive	reasonable
reflective	sincere	tactful	thorough	flexible
broad-minded	cheerful	congenial	conscientious	considerate
courteous	curious	dependable	determined	prepared
punctual	persistent	productive		

Remember: Keeping track of your developing skills and your positive qualities is as important to your career success as completing courses, earning credits, and obtaining a diploma.

Self-Marketing: Packaging and Presenting Your Personal Strengths and Achievements

There are many more advantages and benefits associated with the college experience than "getting a better job" and "making more money." However, national surveys of new college students indicate that these are the primary reasons why they're attending college (Sax, et al., 2004). We acknowledge that this is an important goal for beginning students, so we devote this section to a discussion of strategies for packaging and presenting the skills you've developed in college to future employers. To do this most effectively, it might be useful to view *yourself* (a future college graduate), as an eventual "product" and *employers* as future "customers" who could potentially purchase you and your skills. As a first-year student, it could be said that you are in the early stages of the product-development process. You want to begin the process of developing yourself into a high-quality product, so that by the time you graduate, your "finished product" will be one that employers will be interested in purchasing.

All the career-development strategies we've discussed thus far may be viewed as strategies for developing yourself into a quality product that will be attractive to future employers (or future schools) after graduation. However, using these strategies effectively to develop yourself into a high-quality product may still not close the deal. You also have to effectively *market* yourself so that employers or schools will notice your product, be attracted to it, and be persuaded to purchase it. An effective marketing plan will allow you to give employers a clear idea of what you have to offer and will reduce the likelihood that you will accept the first job you are offered (if it does not match your capabilities).

The major routes or channels through which you can effectively "advertise" or market your personal skills, qualities, and achievements to future employers are your:

1. College transcript
2. Co-curricular experiences
3. Personal portfolio
4. Personal resume
5. Letters of application (cover letters)
6. Letters of recommendations (letters of reference)
7. Networking skills
8. Personal interviews.

These are the primary tools you will use to showcase yourself to employers and that employers will use to evaluate you. We'll now discuss how you can strategically plan, prepare, and sharpen each one of these tools in a way that maximizes its power and persuasiveness.

1. Your College Transcript

A college transcript is a listing of all the courses you enrolled in, along with the grades you received in those courses. There are two key pieces of information included on your college transcript that can influence decisions to hire you, or influence decisions to admit you to graduate or professional school: (1) the grades you earned in your courses, and (2) the types of courses you completed.

Simply stated, the better your grades are in college, the better are your employment prospects after college. Research on college graduates indicates that the higher their grades are, the higher:

- the prestige of their first job,
- their total earnings, and
- their job mobility.

This relationship between college grades and career success exists for students at all types of colleges and universities, regardless of the reputation or prestige of the institution they are attending (Pascarella & Terenzini, 1991; 2005). In other words, research indicates that *how well* students do academically in college has a greater influence on their career success than does the name of the school that appears on their diploma.

The particular types of courses that are listed on your college transcript can also influence employment and acceptance decisions. Listed below are the types of courses that should be good selling points if they appear on your college transcript.

- **Honors Courses**

If you achieve excellent grades during your first year of college, you may apply or be recommended for the honors program at your school, which qualifies you to take courses that are more academically challenging. If you qualify for the honors program, we recommend that you accept the challenge. Even though "A" grades may be more difficult to achieve in honors courses, the presence of these courses on your college transcript clearly shows that you were admitted to the honors program and that you were willing to accept this academic challenge.

◆ Leadership Courses

Many employers hire college graduates with the hope or expectation that they will advance and eventually assume important leadership positions in their company or organization. Although a leadership course is not likely to be required for general education, or for your major, it is an elective course worth taking. It can enrich the quality of your college experience and the quality of your college transcript.

◆ Interdisciplinary Courses

An interdisciplinary course is one that interrelates or integrates two or more disciplines (academic fields). Most career challenges cannot be fully addressed or understood by any one single field of study. For instance, careers that involve the challenge of effective management and leadership rely on principles drawn from multiple fields of study, including psychology (e.g., understanding human motivation), sociology (e.g., promoting harmonious group relationships), business (e.g., managing employees effectively), and philosophy (e.g., incorporating social ethics).

We recommend that you strongly consider taking at least one interdisciplinary course while in college. Even if interdisciplinary courses are not required for general education or your major, taking them will enable you to see connections across different subjects, which can be a very stimulating learning experience in its own right. Also, their appearance on your college transcript would clearly distinguish your transcript from those of most other college graduates. Furthermore, interdisciplinary courses may enhance your employment prospects because studies indicate that executives value new employees who have interdisciplinary experiences and who take an interdisciplinary approach to solving work-related problems. For instance, national surveys have shown that, "Business leaders point to the need for entry-level employees who have the practical ability to reach across artificial disciplinary boundaries to bring all relevant information to bear on concrete problems" (Daly, 1992).

◆ International or Cross-Cultural Courses

International or cross-cultural courses are those that cross national and cultural boundaries. The importance of such courses is highlighted by the fact that today's world is characterized by more international travel, more interaction among citizens from different countries, and more economic interdependence among nations than at any other time in world history (Office of Research, 1994). Boundaries between countries are also breaking down as a result of more international trading (importing-exporting goods), more multinational corporations, and more international communication—resulting from rapid advances in electronic technology (Dryden & Vos, 1999; Smith, 1994). As a result, employers have begun to place higher value on employees who have international knowledge and foreign language skills (Fixman, 1990; Office of Research, 1994). Taking courses that have an international focus, or which focus on cross-cultural comparisons, can help you develop the type of global perspective that strengthens the quality of your liberal arts education and the attractiveness of your college transcript to potential employers. In addition to gaining a global perspective from courses that emphasize international knowledge and foreign language skills, you might also consider participating in a study-abroad program in a country outside of the United States, which may be available to you during the regular academic year or during the summer.

Pause for Reflection

Are you aware of what study-abroad opportunities are available at your college or university?

Are you seriously considering a study-abroad experience? If not, why not?

◆ Diversity (Multicultural) Courses

America's workforce is more ethnically and racially diverse today than at any other time in history, and it will grow even more so in the years ahead (United States Bureau of Labor Statistics, 2005). Successful career performance in today's diverse workforce requires sensitivity to human differences and the ability to relate to people from different cultural backgrounds (National Association of Colleges & Employers, 2003; Smith, 1997). Your participation in college courses relating to diversity awareness and appreciation, and your involvement in courses emphasizing effective multicultural interaction and communication, represent valuable additions to your college transcript that will strengthen your career preparation.

◆ Senior Seminars or Senior Capstone Courses

These courses are designed to put a "cap" or final touch on your college experience, helping you tie it all together and make a smooth transition from college to life after college. They may include such topics as resume building, portfolio preparation, job-interview strategies, job-location strategies, development of a college-to-career plan, and strategies for applying to and preparing for graduate or professional school after college. Some capstone courses may also involve a senior thesis or research project in your major field, which can provide a powerful finishing touch to your major and may be particularly valuable for helping you gain acceptance to graduate or professional school.

2. Your Co-Curricular Experiences

Participation in student clubs, campus organizations, and other types of co-curricular activities can be a very valuable source of experiential learning that can complement classroom-based learning and contribute to your career preparation and development. When college graduates are asked to look back at their college experience and identify what aspects of it helped prepare them for their career, they frequently report that their co-curricular experiences helped them develop skills that enhanced their work performance and career advancement (Marchese, 1990; Kuh, 1993). These personal reports have been confirmed by employers' on-the-job evaluations of college graduates, which indicate that the best predictor of success in careers involving management or leadership was previous involvement in co-curricular experiences during college, particularly those involving student leadership (Howard, 1986; Pascarella & Terenzini, 1991, 2005). It has also been found that student involvement in leadership experiences during college is associated with increased self-esteem (Astin, 1993).

Participation in campus organizations can be a valuable source of experience that contributes to your career preparation and development.

Because there is such a solid body of research supporting the value of co-curricular experiences, we strongly recommend your involvement in campus clubs and organizations. We especially recommend involvement with co-curricular activities that:

◆ allow you to develop leadership and helping skills (e.g., leadership retreats, student government, college committees, peer counseling, or peer tutoring),

◆ enable you to interact with others from diverse ethnic and racial groups (e.g., multicultural club, international club), and

◆ provide you with out-of-class experiences that relate to your academic major or career interests (e.g., student clubs relating to your college major or intended career field).

Keep in mind that co-curricular experiences are also resume-building experiences that provide evidence of involvement in your educational community and commitment to your school. So, be sure to showcase these experiences to prospective employers. Furthermore, the campus professionals with whom you may interact while participating in co-curricular activities (e.g., the Director of Student Activities or Dean of Students) can serve as valuable references for letters of recommendation to future employers, or graduate and professional schools.

Lastly, some colleges allow you to officially document your co-curricular achievements on a special transcript, often referred to as a *student development transcript* or *co-curricular transcript*. If your college offers such a transcript, we recommend that you take full advantage of it. When the idea of such a transcript was first introduced, national surveys were conducted to assess its potential usefulness. These surveys revealed that college admissions officials and employers of college students both thought the transcript would be very useful in helping them select applicants (Bryan et al., 1981). If your college does not offer such a transcript, be sure to describe your co-curricular experiences on your resume and your letters of application. Do not just cite or list the names of these activities. Provide details about the duties you performed and the specific skills that were required of you and acquired by you.

3. Personal Portfolio

You may have heard the word "portfolio," and associated it with a collection of artwork that professional artists put together to showcase or advertise their artistic talents. However, a portfolio can be a collection of any materials or products that illustrates an individual's skills and talents, or demonstrates an individual's educational and personal development. For example, a portfolio could include such items as written papers, exam performances, research projects, senior thesis, audiotapes or videotapes of oral presentations, artwork, DVDs of theatrical performances, or CDs of musical performances.

You can start the process of portfolio development right now by saving your best work and performances. Store them in a traditional portfolio folder, or save them on a computer disc and create an electronic portfolio. Another option would be to create a Web site and upload them there. Eventually, you should be able to build up a well-stocked portfolio that documents your skills and demonstrates your development for possible presentation to future employers or future schools. (For useful information and assistance on how to develop an elec-

The ritual of burning completed coursework in high school is not recommended in college. (Instead, save your best work, and include it in a personal portfolio.)

tronic portfolio, starting early in your first year and continuing through your senior year, go to www.kzoo.edu/pfolio.)

Pause for Reflection

If you were to predict what your best "work products" in college will be—those most likely to appear in your personal portfolio—what do you think they'd be?

---

4. Personal Resume

Unlike a portfolio, which contains actual products or samples of your work, a resume may be described as a listed summary of your most important accomplishments, skills, and credentials. If you have just graduated from high school, you may not have accumulated enough experiences to construct a fully developed resume. However, you can start now to build a "skeletal resume," which contains major categories or headings (the skeleton), under which you'll eventually include your specific experiences and accomplishments. See Box 3 for a sample skeleton resume. As you acquire experiences, you can then flesh-out the resume's skeleton by gradually filling in its general categories with specific skills, accomplishments, and credentials.

This process can be an excellent strength-recognition exercise that elevates your self-esteem. It essentially forces you to focus on your accomplishments by providing a visual record of them. Furthermore, developing a framework for organizing your accomplishments will also provide an outline for your personal goal setting—by serving as a visible reminder of the things you plan to do or accomplish. As you fill in and build up your resume, you can literally see how much you have achieved, which, in turn, can boost your confidence and motivation to continue achieving. Every time you look at your growing resume, you are reminded of your past accomplishments, which, in turn, can energize and motivate you to reach your future goals.

5. Letters of Application (a.k.a., Cover Letters)

A letter of application refers to the letter you write when applying for an employment position or acceptance to a school. When writing this letter, we recommend that you demonstrate your knowledge of:

- *you*—e.g., your personal interests, abilities, and values (use specific, concrete examples);
- the *organization* or *institution* to which you are applying—show them that you know something specific about its purpose, philosophy, programs, and the position you are applying for; and
- the *"match"* or *"fit"* between you and the organization (e.g., between the skills you possess and the skills that the position requires).

Focusing on these three major points should make your letter complete, and will allow the letter to flow in a natural sequence that moves from a focus on *you*, to a focus on *them*, to a focus on the *relationship* between you and them. Here are some suggestions for developing each of these three points in your letter of application.

- **Organize information about yourself into a past-present-future sequence of personal development.**

For instance, point out:

> **TAKE ACTION NOW!** Box 3
>
> ### Constructing a Resume
>
> Use this "skeletal resume" as an outline or template for beginning construction of your own resume and for setting your future goals. (If you have already developed a resume, use this template to identify and add categories that may be missing from your current one.)
>
>
> Name (First, Middle, Last)
> e-mail address
>
>
> | Current Address: | Permanent Address: |
> |---|---|
> | P.O. Box or Street Address | P.O. Box or Street Address |
> | City, ST | City, ST |
> | Phone # | Phone # |
>
> EDUCATION: Name of College or University, City, State
> Degree Name (e.g., Bachelor of Science)
> College Major (e.g., Accounting)
> Graduation Date, GPA
>
> RELATED WORK EXPERIENCES: Position Title, City, State   Start and stop dates
> (begin list with most recent date)
>
> VOLUNTEER (COMMUNITY SERVICE) EXPERIENCES:
>
> NOTABLE COURSES
> (e.g., leadership, international, or interdisciplinary courses)
>
> CO-CURRICULAR EXPERIENCES
> (e.g., student government, peer leadership)
>
> PERSONAL SKILLS and POSITIVE QUALITIES:
> List as bullets, and list as many as you think relate (directly or indirectly) to the position.
>
> HONORS/AWARDS: In addition to those received in college, you may include those received in high school.
>
> PERSONAL INTERESTS: Include items that showcase any special hobbies or talents that are not directly related to school or work. (Employers may use this information to see how well you may fit in with the work culture or relate to current employees.)

- where you have been—your past history or background experiences that qualify you to apply (academic, co-curricular, and work experiences)
- where you are now (why, at the present point in time, you've elected to apply to them)
- where you intend to go (what you hope to do or accomplish for them once you get there).

This past-present-future strategy should result in a smooth chronological flow of information about you. Also, by focusing on where you've been and where you're going, you demonstrate the ability to self-reflect on your past and self-project to your future.

When describing yourself, try to identify specific examples or concrete illustrations of your positive qualities and areas in which you have grown or improved in recent years. While it is important to highlight all your major strengths, this doesn't necessarily mean you must cover up any area in which you feel you still need to improve or develop. No human being is perfect; in fact, one indication of someone with a healthy self-concept is that person's ability to recognize and acknowledge both personal strengths and personal weaknesses—areas in need of further development. Including a touch of honest self-assessment in your letter of application demonstrates both sincerity and integrity. (And it may reduce the risk that your letter will be perceived or interpreted as a "snow job" that piles on mounds and pounds of self-flattery, under which even the tiniest ounce of self-honesty or personal humility is totally buried and concealed.)

◆ **Do some advanced research about the particular organization to which you're applying.**

In your letter of application, mention some specific aspects or characteristics of the organization that you've read or learned about; for example, one of its programs that impressed you or attracted your interest to them. This sends the message that you have taken the time and initiative to learn something about their organization, which is a very positive message for them to receive about you.

Pause for Reflection

Have you met a faculty member or other professional on campus who is getting to know you well enough to write a personal letter of recommendation for you?

If yes, who is this person, and what position does he or she hold on campus?

◆ **Make it clear why you feel there is a good fit or match between you and the organization to which you've applied.**

Point out how your specific qualities, skills, interests, or values are in line with the organization's needs or goals. By doing some research on the particular institution or organization that you're applying to, and including this information in your letter of application, you will immediately distinguish your application from the swarms of standard form letters that companies receive from applicants who mail-out multiple copies of the exact same letter to multiple companies.

6. Letters of Recommendation (a.k.a., Letters of Reference)

Your letters of recommendation can be one of your most powerful selling points. However, to maximize the power of your recommendations, you need to give careful thought to:

◆ *who* you want to serve as your references,
◆ *how* to approach them, and
◆ *what* to provide them.

Specific strategies for improving the quality of your letters of recommendation are suggested in Box 4.

7. Networking Skills

Would it surprise you to learn that 80 percent of jobs are never advertised? This means that the jobs you see listed in a classified section of the newspaper and posted in a career development office or employment center represent only 20 percent of available openings at any given time. Almost one-half of all job hunters find employment through people they know or have met, such as friends, family members, and casual acquaintances. When it comes to locating

TAKE ACTION NOW! — Box 4

The Art and Science of Requesting Letters of Recommendation: Effective Strategies and Common Courtesies

- **Select recommendations from people who know you well.**

  Think about people with whom you've had an ongoing relationship, who know your name, and who know your strengths; for example, an instructor who you've had for more than one class, an academic advisor whom you see frequently, or an employer for whom you've worked for an extended period of time.

- **Seek a balanced blend of letters from people who have observed you perform in different settings or situations.**

  The following are key settings in which you may have performed well and key people who may have observed you perform well in these settings:
  a. *the classroom*—for example, a professor for an academic reference
  b. *on campus*—for example, a student life professional for a co-curricular reference
  c. *off campus*—for example, a professional for whom you've performed volunteer service, part-time work, or an internship.

- **Pick the right time and place to make your request.**

  Be sure to make your request well in advance of the letter's deadline date (e.g., at least two weeks). First, ask the person if s/he is willing to write the letter, then come back with forms and envelopes. Do not approach the person with these materials in hand because this may send the message that you have assumed or presumed the person will automatically say "yes." This is not the most socially sensitive message to send someone whom you're about to ask for a favor.

  Lastly, pick a place where the person can give full attention to your request. For instance, make a personal visit to the person's office, rather than making the request in a busy hallway or in front of a classroom full of students.

- **Waive your right to see the letter.**

  If the organization or institution to which you are applying has a reference-letter form that asks whether or not you want to *waive* (give-up) your right to see the letter, waive your right—as long as you feel reasonably certain that you will be receiving a good letter of recommendation.

  By waiving your right to see your letter of recommendation, you show confidence that the letter to be written about you will be positive, and you assure the person who receives and reads the letter that you didn't inspect or screen it to see if it was a good one before sending it off.

- **Provide your references with a fact sheet about yourself**, which includes your specific experiences and achievements—both inside and outside the classroom.

  This will help make your references' job a little easier by giving them points to focus on. More importantly, it will help you because your letter becomes more powerful when it contains concrete examples or specific illustrations of your positive qualities and accomplishments (rather than sweeping generalizations or glittering generalities that could be said about anybody).

  On your fact sheet, be sure to include any exceptionally high grades you may have received in particular courses, as well as volunteer services, leadership experiences, special awards or forms of recognition, and special interests or talents that relate to your academic major and career choice. Your fact sheet is the place and time for you to "toot your own horn," so don't be afraid of coming across as a braggart or egotist. You're not being conceited; you're just documenting your strengths.

- **Provide your references with a stamped, addressed envelope.**

  This is a simple courtesy that makes their job a little easier and demonstrates your social sensitivity.

- **Follow up with a thank-you note** to your references about the time your letter of recommendation should be sent.

  This is simply the right thing to do because it shows your appreciation, and it is the smart thing to do because if the letter hasn't been written yet, the thank-you note serves to gently remind your reference to write the letter.

- **Let your references know the outcome of your efforts** (e.g., your successful admission into graduate school or acceptance of a job offer). This is a courteous thing to do, and your references are likely to remember your courtesy, which could strengthen the quality of any future letters they may write for you.

positions, *who* you know can be as important as *what* you know or how good your resume looks. Consequently, it's important to continually expand the circle of people who know your career interests and abilities, because they can be a powerful source of information about employment opportunities.

You can start expanding your circle of contacts by visiting the Career Development Center on your campus to find out what employers come to campus to interview graduating seniors. See if it is possible to obtain the names of representatives from those companies who have come to your college. Some of this information may also be available on your Career Center's online job listings. Also, ask if it is possible to receive the names of college alumni who may be working in fields related to your career interests. Some career centers have an online database that allow you to network with alumni who are working in careers that relate to your interests. Once you have selected a major, you may begin networking with seniors who will be graduating in your major by joining a club or organization that involves students majoring in the same field as you (e.g., philosophy club, business club). Lastly, be sure to share copies of your resume with friends and family members, just in case they may come in contact with employers who are looking for somebody with your career interests and qualifications.

8. Personal Interviews

A personal interview is your opportunity to make a positive "in-person" impression. You can make a positive first impression during any interview by showing that you've done your homework and have come prepared. In particular, you should come to the interview prepared with knowledge about yourself and your audience.

You can demonstrate knowledge about yourself by bringing a mental list of your strongest selling points to the interview and being ready to speak about them when the opportunity arises. You can demonstrate knowledge of your audience by doing some homework on the organization you are applying to, the people who are likely to be interviewing you, and the questions they are likely to ask. Try to acquire as much information as possible about the organization and its key employees that may be available to you online and in print.

To prepare for interviews, visit your Career Development Center and inquire about questions that are commonly asked during personal interviews. You might also try to speak with seniors who have interviewed with recruiters and ask them if certain questions tended to be frequently asked. Once you begin to participate in actual interviews, try to recall and make note of the questions you were asked. Although you may be able to anticipate some of the general questions that are asked in almost any interview, it's likely there will be unique questions asked of you that relate specifically to your personal qualifications and experiences. If these questions are asked in one of your interviews, there is a good chance they may be asked again in a future interview. So, try to get in the habit of mentally reviewing your interview as soon as you complete it, and attempt to recall the major questions you were asked while they're still fresh in your mind. This will also make it much easier to explain why you are a good candidate in a thank-you letter you may send the person who interviewed you. Consider developing an index-card catalog of questions that you've been asked during interviews—with the question on one side and your prepared response on the reverse side. The better organized and prepared you are for personal interviews, the quality of your answers will increase and the level of your anxiety will decrease.

When you know yourself (what about yourself you're going to say), and when you know your audience (who they're likely to be and what they're likely to ask), you should then be ready to answer what probably is the most important interview question of all: "What can *you* do for *us*?"

••• Summary and Conclusion

When it comes to converting a college degree into successful career entry, studies show that students who make this conversion most successfully have two characteristics in common: a *positive attitude* and *personal initiative* (Pope, 1990). They do *not* take a passive approach that assumes a good position will just fall into their lap, nor do they feel that they are owed a good career simply because they have a college degree. Instead, they become actively involved in the job-hunting process and use multiple job-search strategies (Brown & Krane, 2000).

In national surveys, employers rank attitude of the job applicant as the number-one factor in making hiring decisions, rating it higher in importance than such other factors as reputation of the applicant's school, previous work experience, and recommendations of former employers (Education Commission of the States, 1995; Institute for Research on Higher Education, 1995). Graduation from college with a diploma is not a guarantee that you'll be hired immediately after graduation, nor is it an automatic passport to a high-paying job. Your college degree will open career doors, but it's your attitude, initiative, and effort that will enable you to step through those doors and into a successful career.

This scenario can be avoided when students take a *proactive* approach to *career planning* before their senior year, and take an *active* approach to *job-hunting* during their senior year.

One study tracked a large number of college students after graduation to determine how successful they were in finding jobs. The results of this study indicated that those students who were most successful in getting outstanding career positions after graduation had two characteristics in common:

1. They engaged in career preparation and career development activities while in college, and
2. They took personal initiative during the job-hunting process.

These successful graduates were later interviewed and asked what advice they would give new college students. The advice they gave is nicely summarized in the following statement issued by a nationally known college advisor:

> *A big reason for their success, which shines through their answers and the advice they give, is initiative. They tell students to get involved in campus activities, but for substance, not for show; to take some career-related courses; to get internships and to have summer work experiences; and finally, to use initiative in investigating career possibilities and in looking for an actual job. Eighty-six percent of them said their own personal initiative was crucial to their being hired for their first job (Pope, 1990, p. 57).*

The advice of these successful graduates reinforces the key points made in this chapter: Your career success *after* college depends on what you do *during* college. Touching all the bases that lead to *college* success will also lead to *career* success, namely:

1. **Get actively involved in the college experience**—get good grades in your classes and get work-related experiences outside of the classroom.

•—• CLASSIC QUOTE •—•

I'm a great believer in luck, and I find the harder I work the more I have of it.

—Thomas Jefferson, third president of the United States, author of the Declaration of Independence, and founder of the University of Virginia

·—· **CLASSIC QUOTE** ·—·

Know thyself, and to thine own self be true.

—Plato, ancient Greek philosopher

2. **Use your campus resources**—capitalize on all the career preparation and development opportunities that your Career Development Center has to offer.

3. **Interact and collaborate with others**—network with students in your major, college alumni, and career professionals.

4. **Take time for personal reflection**—deepen awareness of who you are, so you follow a career path that's true to you, and maintain awareness of your developing skills and personal qualities, so that you can successfully sell yourself to future employers.

 Remember: When you make the most of your college experience, you get the most out of your college degree, and you maximize the value of both for your future career.

••• Learning More through Independent Research

Web-Based Resources for Further Information on Careers

For additional information relating to the ideas discussed in this chapter, we recommend the following Web sites:

For career descriptions and future employment outlook:
www.bls.gov/oco

For internships:
www.internships.com and www.vaultreports.com

For information on electronic portfolios:
www.kzoo.edu/pfolio

Name _____ Date _____ _____

Conducting an Information Interview

One of the best and most overlooked ways to get accurate information about a career is to interview professionals who are actually working in that career, which is known as "information interviewing." An information interview has multiple advantages for your career exploration and development, which include:

- getting inside information about what a career is really like,
- networking with professionals in the field, and
- enabling you to gain experience and confidence with interview situations that may help you prepare for future job interviews.

STEPS

1. **Select a career that you may be interested in pursuing.**

   Even if you are currently keeping your career options wide open, pick a career that might be a possibility. You can use the resources cited in this chapter to help you identify a career that may be most appealing to you.

2. **Find someone who is working in the career you selected and set up an information interview with that person.**

   To help locate possible interview candidates, consider members of your family, friends of your family members, and family members of your friends. Any of these people may be working in the career you selected and may be good interview candidates, or they may know other people who could be good candidates. The Career Development Center and the Alumni Association on your campus may also be able to provide you with graduates of your college, or professionals working in the local community near your college, who are willing to talk about their careers with students. Lastly, you might consider using the Yellow Pages or the Internet to find names and addresses of possible candidates. Send them a short letter or e-mail, asking about the possibility of scheduling a short interview. Mention that you would be willing to conduct the interview in person or by phone, whichever would be more convenient for them.

   If you do not hear back within a reasonable period of time (e.g., within a couple of weeks), send a follow-up message; if you do not receive a response to the follow-up message, then consider contacting someone else.

3. **Conduct an information interview with the professional who has agreed to speak with you.**

   Use the suggested strategies and potential questions in the following box.

Suggested Strategies for Conducting Information Interviews

- **Thank the person for taking the time to speak with you.**
  This should be the first thing you do after meeting the person, before you officially begin the interview.

- **Take notes during the interview.**
  This not only benefits you—by helping you remember what was said; it also sends a positive message to the person you're interviewing—by showing the person that his or her ideas are important and worth writing down.

- **Prepare your interview questions in advance.** Here are some questions that you might consider asking:
  1. How did you decide on your career?
  2. What qualifications or prior experiences did you have that enabled you to enter your career?
  3. How does someone find out about openings in your field?
  4. What specific steps did you take to find your current position?
  5. What advice would you give to beginning college students about things they could start doing now to help them prepare to enter your career?
  6. During a typical day's work, what do you spend most of your time doing?
  7. What do you like most about your career?
  8. What are the most difficult or frustrating aspects of your career?
  9. What personal skills or qualities do you see as being critical for success in your career?
  10. How does someone advance in your career?
  11. Are there any moral issues or ethical challenges that tend to arise in your career?
  12. Are members of diverse racial and ethnic groups likely to be found in your career field?
      This is an especially important question to ask if you are a member of an ethnic or racial minority group.
  13. What impact does your career have on your home life or personal life outside of work?
  14. If you had to do it all over again, would you choose the same career?
  15. Would you recommend that I speak with anyone else to obtain additional information or a different perspective on this career field? (If the answer is "yes," you may follow-up by asking: "May I mention that you referred me?") This question is recommended because it's always a good idea to obtain more than one person's perspective before making an important choice or decision, especially one that can have a major influence on your life—such as a career choice.

If the interview goes well, consider asking if it might be possible to observe or "shadow" your interviewee during a day at work.

PERSONAL REFLECTION QUESTIONS

After completing your interview, take a moment to reflect on it and answer the following questions:

1. What information did you receive that impressed you about this career (if any)?

2. What information did you receive that distressed or depressed you about this career (if any)?

3. What was the most useful thing you learned from conducting this interview?

4. Knowing what you know now, would you still be interested in pursuing this career? (If "yes," why?) (If "no," why not?)

CASE STUDY

Career Choice: Conflict and Confusion

Josh is a first-year student whose family has made a great financial sacrifice to send him to college. He deeply appreciates the tremendous sacrifice his family has made for him and wants to pay them back as soon as possible. Consequently, he has been looking into careers that offer the highest starting salaries to college students immediately after graduation. Unfortunately, none of these careers seem to match Josh's natural abilities and personal interests, so he's confused and starting to get stressed out. He knows he'll have to make a decision soon because the careers with high starting salaries involve majors that have a large number of course requirements, and if he expects to graduate from college in four years, he'll have to start taking some of these courses during his first year.

Reflection and Discussion Questions

1. If you were Josh, what would you do?

2. Do you see any way that Josh might balance his desire to pay back his parents as soon as possible with his desire to pursue a career that's compatible with his interests and talents?

3. What other questions or factors do you think Josh should consider before making his decision?

Majoring in Life and Career Management

Kristi Casey-Hart, MS, LAPC, *Counseling and Career Services*

Outline

Major = Career?
    True or False Quiz
Understanding the Difference between Majors and Careers
Why Create a Career Plan?
    1. Work and Worth
    2. Marketability
    3. Persistence and Degree Attainment
    4. Less Time to Graduate
How to Create a Career Plan
    Step 1: Understand Yourself
    Step 2: Research Career Options
    Step 3: Make a Decision and Map Out Your Goals
    Where to Go for Assistance
Sources

••• Major = Career?

For some students, choosing a major is a simple decision. For others, choosing a major can be a difficult, even stressful, process. Many students find themselves overwhelmed at what seems to be endless possibilities and can't decide which major to select or which career they are best suited for. For students in the latter category, don't worry. No one says you should know what you are going to major in before you start college. In fact, you can use your first year of college to explore all the possibilities.

Before we begin learning how to develop a career plan, let's explore the myths and truths about majors and careers. Take the true/false quiz below. While you think about your answer, consider why you believe that answer to be true or false.

True or False Quiz

1. When you chose a major, you are choosing a career.
2. If you want to work in a business or a corporation, you need to major in business or in a technical field (like computer science).
3. The earlier you choose a major the better.
4. There is only one "right job" for you in terms of your ability.
5. Your GPA is the most important criteria employers look for when hiring.
6. My major will limit my choices for graduate or professional schools.

Answers

1. *FALSE*—Even someone in a highly structured major like nursing or electrical engineering might end up doing a variety of things. More than half of all college graduates pursue careers that are not directly related to their major.
2. *FALSE*—Most career fields don't require a specific major. For example, if you major in history or English, you might still choose to become a bank manager.
3. *FALSE*—Approximately 50% of college students will change majors at least once before they graduate. The most important part of choosing a major is found in understanding yourself—your interests, your skills, your personality—and that takes time.
4. *FALSE*—Conservative estimates show that most people change careers an average of 2–3 times during a lifetime. Your abilities, interests, and values change as you grow older, meaning that you may develop new career interests over time.
5. *FALSE*—Your GPA is actually 7th out of 10 criteria used by employers surveyed. Related experience, communication, leadership, teamwork, and computer skills are more important.
6. *FALSE*—Most college grads do not know what their long-term career objectives will be until 3 to 5 years of experience in the job market. Knowing this, most universities and educational institutions make allowances for graduate students with an unrelated undergraduate degree. **However**, there may be prerequisites and other admission criteria that a graduate student would be expected to obtain before beginning courses related to the graduate degree. For example, no one would be able to begin medical school without the required science and math prerequisites.

••• Understanding the Difference between Majors and Careers

Most college students frequently assume that a corresponding academic major exists for every career field and that in order to enter most career fields they must choose a matching major. In actuality, the relationship between a college major and a particular career field is not always so closely linked. Granted, some career fields do dictate that a specific major must be obtained in order to work in that field. For example, if you want to be a nurse, you have to major in nursing. However, most career fields don't require such a specific major. Furthermore, people with specific majors don't have to use them in ways that are commonly expected. For example, someone with a degree in psychology could be a bank manager.

It is important to note that your choice of major is only one of a number of factors that determine your future career path and job prospects. Other factors include the electives you choose, relevant experience (such as internships and cooperative education programs, or "co-ops"), and extracurricular activities like professional organizations and volunteer work. All of these experiences demonstrate to any potential employer that you have knowledge and interest in that career field and will play a large part in determining an employer's response to you.

••• Why Create a Career Plan?

1. Work and Worth

Have you ever noticed that one of the first questions people ask each other when meeting for the first time is "What do you do?" According to Donald Super (1976), Professor Emeritus of psychology and education at Teacher's College at Columbia University, these interactions reinforce the belief that in a fluid industrial society, occupation is one of the principal determinants of social status. Sigmund Freud once stated that "work is the individual's link to reality." Therefore, it is not such a leap to recognize that our career choice is often the measure used by others, and ourselves, to define who we are as individuals.

Work, and the meaning we give it, plays a central role in our lives, not only in the United States, but in other countries as well. Cross-national studies suggest that people in the U.S. and other countries view work as being more important than leisure, community, and even religion. Itzhak Harpaz (1999) found that in several multinational studies work was second in importance only to family activities.

Considering that so much emphasis is placed on work, it becomes evident why creating a career plan is beneficial. *We identify ourselves based on the work we do and it directly contributes to our overall feelings of satisfaction with life.*

2. Marketability

In this day and age, it's not enough just to have a degree. Employers are looking for students who are graduating with work-related experience. According to the research conducted by Michigan State University's Collegiate Employment Research Institute (2007), 50% of employers surveyed indicated they believed students should have at least one work-related experience (co-op or internship). However, the other 50% believed students should have at least *two*. Employers garner this information from resumes and it is used to determine which students can get off to a faster start if hired, and also used to differentiate students quickly when dealing with a large applicant pool. This means entering the workforce as a new graduate can be very competitive. Getting that *great* job right out of college and making a *large* salary becomes less of a reality when a student is competing against other graduates who are more qualified because they have more work-related experience. This is where having a career plan can help you become a commodity for potential employers. *A career plan will help you focus your efforts during college on obtaining knowledge and work experience related to your chosen career field.* The more knowledge and experience you acquire while in college, the more marketable you become to potential employers. Having work-related experience plus a degree can be the difference between settling for any job that will pay the bills and landing that great job that gives you tremendous satisfaction.

3. Persistence and Degree Attainment

It is a widely held belief that having a career plan can contribute to a student's persistence in college and completion of a degree program. The need for academic and career planning is supported by numerous research findings, which indicate that:

a) three out of four students are uncertain or tentative about their career choice at college entry (Titley & Titley, 1980; Frost, 1991).

b) only 8% of new students feel they know "a great deal about their intended major" (Lemoine, cited in Erickson & Summers, 1991), and,

c) more than half of all students who enter college with a declared major change their mind at least once before they graduate (Foote, 1980; Gordon, 1984).

These findings suggest that most students' *final* decisions about majors and careers do not occur before entering college, but typically develop *during* the college experience.

The importance of career decision-making and a student persisting in a degree program until graduation is empirically documented by Astin (1975), whose research indicates that *prolonged* indecision about an academic major and career goals is correlated with increased incidences of stopping out or dropping out of college. Lenning, Beal, and Sauer (1980) also report that students' motivation and commitment to an academic goal correlates positively with persistence to graduation. In addition, Levitz and Noel (1989) found that "lack of certainty about a major and/or career" to be the number one reason cited by high-ability students for their decision to drop out of college. Conversely, other research studies on student retention in higher education suggest that a student's commitment to educational and career goals is perhaps the strongest factor associated with student persistence to degree completion (Wyckoff, 1999). We can conclude then that if educational goals and career plans remain unformulated over extended periods of time, students are more likely to depart without completing their degree programs.

Napoleon Bonaparte once said, *"Few things are brought to a successful issue by impetuous desire, but most by calm and prudent forethought."* Choosing a major and having a career goal will give you a sense of direction. It will enable you to remain focused and persevere through potential academic "burn-out."

4. Less Time to Graduate

The U.S. Census Bureau first reported in 1994 that the length of time it takes college students to complete their graduation requirements have been extended (U.S. Bureau of Census, 1994). For example, the number of students who take 5 or more years to graduate from college has doubled since the early 1980s (Kramer, 1993). Student indecisiveness and late major-changing can result in delayed progress toward degree completion brought about by the need for students to complete additional courses to fulfill specific degree requirements for their newly chosen major. It is reasonable to expect that being proactive with career planning will promote earlier and more complete crystallization of a major and career plan, thereby reducing the average time to degree completion. If career planning becomes a goal for first year students, they may make more thoughtful and accurate choices about majors and careers. This will serve to reduce prolonged indecisiveness and premature decision-making, which can result in changing majors at later stages in the college experience. *Changing majors in later stages of a degree will increase the amount of time it takes to complete a degree.*

How to Create a Career Plan

Creating a career plan can be like building a bridge. A bridge is a structure built over an obstacle, like a body of water, to allow passage. With bridges, sometimes you can see the opposite shore and sometimes you can't. As it relates to career planning, you probably have dreams about the future but they may be vague and indistinct. You may not know how to get to the other side. Your obstacle may be obtaining a degree or some type of training. So, if a career plan is the bridge between your current reality and your dreams of the future, you will first need to know where you are going (your dream job), understand your obstacle (training/education), and recognize the materials (your skills, interests, and values) you can use to build that bridge. There are three basic steps to creating your career plan:

1. Understand yourself
2. Research your career options
3. Make a decision and map out your goals

Step 1: Understand Yourself

Students entering college can usually be classified into two groups. The first are those who have a well defined self-image, meaning they know themselves, their likes, dislikes, interests, etc. The other group could be described as those who are still in the process of defining, or redefining, themselves. How do you begin the process of understanding yourself?

There are several dimensions of ourselves that we can evaluate and then use that information for possible career choices.

- **Interests:** interests, as it relates to career interests, can be described as something that concerns, involves, draws the attention of, or arouses the curiosity of a person. Your interests develop from your experiences and beliefs. Your interests can continue to develop and change throughout the course of your lifespan.
- **Skills and Aptitudes:** by definition, skills are talents or abilities that are acquired or developed through training or experience. Skills are most often measured by past performance and almost always improve with practice. Some examples of skills would be public speaking, teaching, writing, and so on. Aptitudes, on the other hand, are natural talents or strengths and are the foundation of your skills. Musical ability and memory for numbers, words, etc., are examples of aptitudes.
- **Work Values:** Work values can be defined as the worth of something in terms of its importance or usefulness. Here, the word "value" refers to how you feel about work itself and the contribution it makes to society. Most people who pursue work that closely matches their values tend to feel more satisfied and successful in their careers. There-

fore, work values are very personal to the individual and can change over time. Work values can be divided into two categories:

- ◇ **Intrinsic**—values that relate to a specific interest in the activities of the work itself, such as helping others, or for the benefits that the work contributes to society, such as controlling environmental waste.
- ◇ **Extrinsic**—an extrinsic value relates to the favorable conditions that accompany an occupational choice like salary, physical setting, or company paid benefits.

◆ **Life Goals:** Life goals are long-term goals or aspirations. These are things individuals hope to accomplish over the course of their lives. Work plays an integral part in the achievement of or has an influence on our life goals. Examples of life goals are achieving success in a profession, having a satisfying marriage, and obtaining lifetime financial security.

◆ **Personality Type:** Personality develops over time and is what makes you *you*. Understanding your personality cannot be ignored when making career decisions. For example, the quiet, orderly, detail-oriented person would not thrive in an environment that is predominantly fast-paced and constantly changing (like a hospital emergency room) where having the ability to make quick decisions and being flexible are essential skills.

One way to uncover such personal characteristics is to use self-assessment tools. Assessment tools are designed to help identify interests, skills, personality type, and values and how they can best be matched with school or career pursuits. Many self-assessments make a correlation between your personal attributes and related career fields; however, they do not provide a definitive answer to the question "What career should I choose?" Instead, they give you suggestions of a variety of careers that might be a good match for you. You will benefit the most from self-assessment if you see a career counselor to assist you with interpreting the results.

There are scores of formal and informal self-assessment instruments available in print, and on the web, that an individual can use for career planning. The hallmark of *formal* assessments is that they have been subjected to scientific rigor; meaning, the authors and publishers have performed research on the instrument in an effort to ensure a quality product. These assessment tools measure most of the dimensions listed above, either individually, or in clusters. Dalton State College uses the following instruments for career planning:

◆ *Discover® from ACT*—a powerful comprehensive career planning program. It is Internet based and assists students with identifying their interests, skills/abilities, and work values. It also allows you to research possible career occupations and educational paths.

◆ *Strong Interest Inventory (SII)*—measures interests in eight different areas: occupations, school subjects, activities, leisure activities, types of people preferred as coworkers, preference between two activities, personal characteristics, and preference in the world of work.

◆ *Myers-Briggs Type Indicator (MBTI)*—measures personality types that can be related to typical profiles of groups of people who work in specific occupations or that can be used to develop teams or understand the interactions among team members.

◆ *Self Directed Search (SDS)*—designed to measure personality type and interest in six different occupational groups. The assessment yields a three-letter code that is matched with occupations based on the interests, values, and skills of the respondent.

◆ *Georgia Career Information Systems (GCIS)*—GCIS provides Georgia's students and adult learners with vital career information. GCIS contains self-assessment, exploration, and search strategies as well as a vast amount of occupational and educational information.

- *What Can I Do With This Major?*—a Website that connects majors with careers. It includes an outline of common career areas, typical employers, and strategies designed to maximize career opportunities. Links are available to find a list of Websites that provide information about listed majors and related careers.

In addition to self-assessment tools, there are other ways you can evaluate yourself. You can learn a great deal about your interests, skills, and values through real life experiences such as internships. Also, in-depth discussion with a career counselor can be helpful in evaluating your personal characteristics as they relate to careers.

Step 2: Research Career Options

Basic research into the occupation(s) or academic options you are considering may seem daunting but, in truth, is very easy. One pitfall to be aware of, however, is that we often make assumptions about a career field or occupation based on testimonials from one or two people you have met in the field, what you see in the media, or what you hear from peers and family members. But by gathering concrete information from objective sources, you can make better decisions about your future occupation. Here are some topics you want to research about an occupation:

- typical job duties
- training and educational requirements
- skills and abilities needed for job duties
- job outlook
- salary ranges
- major employers in the occupation

Check out the Websites below to obtain information about occupations and employment trends across many fields and industries. You can also use these resources to learn which undergraduate and graduate level majors are recommended for each occupation.

- ***Georgia Career Information System (GCIS)*** (http://www.gcic.peachnet.edu/): Provides current and accurate occupational and educational information to schools and agencies throughout Georgia in order to help young people and adults make informed career choices. *User name and password required.* You can obtain the user name and password information from Academic Resources.
- ***O*Net Online*** (http://online.onetcenter.org/find/): Provides information about tasks, knowledge, skills, and abilities for a wide range of career fields. Search for occupations by keywords, skills used, or your Theme Code from your Strong Interest Inventory results.
- ***Occupational Outlook Handbook*** (http://www.bls.gov/oco/): Information about more than 200 career fields from the U.S. Bureau of Labor Statistics.
- ***Jobprofiles.org*** (http://www.jobprofiles.org/): Insider information from professionals on a variety of careers for those exploring their options.
- ***Georgia College 411*** (www.gacollege411.org): A comprehensive Website for planning, applying, and paying for college. It includes a section on career planning and provides useful tools for career research.

The goal in this step is to look at any and all occupations that interest you. Keep a list of every occupation you want to research further. When you are ready to do your research, review each occupation with a critical eye. Actively engage yourself in the process of understanding that occupation. Consider whether the occupations you are considering meet your personal values. While reviewing all occupations on your list, notate those occupations that seem to best match with your interests, values, and abilities. Try to narrow your selection to 3–5 top occupations. From those 3–5, you will want to conduct more in-depth research, including, but not limited to:

- Conduct informational interviews
- Try job shadowing, if possible
- Talk with professors

Consider issues such as:

- Does my occupation require further education?
- If so, what are the sources of that education?
- How long does it take?
- What does it cost?
- Does my choice require any other sort of credentials, such as certification or licensing?
- If so, where do I go to apply for it and what steps must I go through to receive it?
- Should I try to get work experience or an internship related to my career and occupational goals?
- Where do such opportunities exist and how do I take advantage of them?

Step 3: Make a Decision and Map out Your Goals

After you have conducted more in-depth research on your top 3–5 occupation choices, you should be ready to make a decision. If more than one occupation seems interesting to you and you find it difficult to make a decision, don't worry, the occupations probably have a common educational major. If so, choose your major and, as you continue in your studies, you will find that developing a career path will become easier.

While you are enrolled in college courses, be sure to take on internships, cooperative education opportunities, or part-time jobs. The more exposure to real-world experience you get as a student, the better prepared you will be when you start to look for your first job.

Where to Go for Assistance

If you find the task of career planning too confusing or believe you will benefit from professional assistance, visit the Counseling and Career Services Office in Academic Resources. The counseling staff can work with you one-on-one to guide you through all three stages of career planning.

••• Sources

Gardner, P. (2007). *Recruiting Trends 2007–2008.* East Lansing, MI: Collegiate Employment Research Institute, Michigan State University.

Harpaz, I. (1999). The transformation of work values. *Israel Monthly Review,* 122, 46–50.

Seidman, A. (2006). *College Student Retention: Formula for Student Success.* Westport, CT: Greenwood Publishing Group.

Super, D. E. (1976). *Career Education and the Meaning of Work.* Washington, DC: Office of Education.

Life-Management Skills

Managing Time and Money

Learning Goals

The primary goal of this chapter is to strengthen your skills with respect to managing time and money.

Outline

The Importance of Time and Money Management
Managing Time
    Strategies for Improving Time Management
Elements of a Comprehensive Time-Management Plan
    Converting Your Time-Management Plan into an Action Plan
    Dealing with Procrastination
Managing Money
    Strategies for Managing Money Effectively
    Strategic Selection and Use of Financial Tools for Tracking Cash Flow
    Developing Personal Money-Saving Strategies and Habits
    Long-Range Financial Planning: Financing Your College Education
Summary and Conclusion
Learning More through Independent Research
Exercise: Financial Self-Awareness: Monitoring Money and Tracking Cash Flow
Case Study: Procrastination: The Vicious Cycle

Activate Your Thinking

When you read each of the following words, what are the first words that come to your mind?

Time: _____

Money: _____

The Importance of Time and Money Management

For many students, beginning college means the beginning of more independent living and the development of life-management skills. Two of those skills involve managing time and money. Each of them can serve as valuable resources to support your progress and success; however, they can also be sources of stress or distress that can block your progress. If you look back at your responses to "time" and "money" on the previous page, chances are that the first thoughts that came to your mind about these words were either very positive or very negative. Thus, we need to be consciously aware of these two key areas of our life and manage them effectively so that they work for us, not against us, and enable us to progress toward our life goals.

Strengthening your skills in each of these areas of life management will enhance your academic performance in college, as well as enrich your personal life and career performance beyond college.

Managing Time

Time management is a skill that grows in importance when your time is less structured or controlled by others, and you have more decision-making power about how your time will be spent. New students encounter an academic calendar and schedule in college that differs greatly from high school. It presents them with more free time to manage because less time is controlled or managed by others; for example, there is less mandatory "seat time" in college and less supervision by school authorities or parents.

Managing personal time is also an important issue for college students because they are expected to do more academic work on their own outside of class. Approximately four out of every five full-time college students are trying to complete this academic work while working part-time (U.S. Department of Education, 2002). Some students have family responsibilities outside of college as well. Thus, it is no surprise that research shows that the ability to manage time effectively plays a crucial role in college success (Erickson, Peters, & Strommer, 2006).

Simply stated, college students who have more difficulty managing their time have more difficulty managing college. In one study, sophomores who had an outstanding first year in college (both academically and socially) were compared with another group of sophomores who struggled during their freshman year. Interviews conducted with these students revealed one key difference between the two groups: The sophomores who experienced a successful first year repeatedly brought up the topic of "time" during the interviews. The successful students said they had to think carefully about how they spent their time and that they needed to budget time because it was a scarce resource. In contrast, the sophomores who experienced difficulty in their first year of college hardly talked about the topic of time at all during their interviews, even when they were specifically asked about it (Light, 2001).

Studies of working adults also indicate that managing time plays a pivotal role in their professional and personal success. Setting priorities and balancing multiple responsibilities (work, family, school) that compete for our limited time and energy can be a juggling act and is often a major source of stress for people of all ages (Harriott & Ferrari, 1996).

> *Personal Story*
> I started the process of earning my doctorate a little later in life than some of my cohorts. I was a married father living with a preschool daughter. Since my wife left for work early in the morning, it was always my duty to get up and get my daughter's day going in the right direction. In addition, I had to do the same for me—which

---

STUDENT PERSPECTIVES

"The major difference [between high school and college] is time. You have so much free time on your hands that you don't know what to do for most of the time."
—First-year college student, Erickson & Strommer (1991)

"In high school we were given a homework assignment every day. Now we have a large task assigned to be done at a certain time. No one tells [us] when to start or what to do each day."
—First-year student, Rhoads (2005)

STUDENT PERSPECTIVE

"I cannot stress enough that you need to intelligently budget your time."
—Words written by a first-year student in a letter of advice to students who are about to begin college

in most cases was tougher than what I had to do for Sara, my daughter. Three days of my week was spent on campus in class or in the library. We did not have quick access to research on computers then as you do now. The other two days of the work week and the weekend was spent on household chores, family time, and studying. In my mind, for me to be successful and finish my Ph.D. in a reasonable amount of time and have a decent family life, I had to adopt a schedule to help me manage my time. Needless to say, I had a very strict schedule to follow each day of the week. I got up, drank coffee, read the paper, took a shower, got my daughter ready for school and fed her breakfast. I then took her to school. Once I returned home, I would put a load of laundry in the washer, study, write, research, and spend time concentrating on what I needed to do to be successful from 8:30–12:00 every day. For lunch I had a pastrami and cheese sandwich and a soft drink while rewarding myself by watching *Perry Mason* reruns until 1:00. I then continued to study until it was time to pick up my daughter from school. Sometimes, I would start dinner. Each night I spent time with my wife and daughter and prepared for the next day. As you can see, I lived a life that had a preset schedule. By following this schedule, I was able to successfully complete my doctorate in a reasonable amount of time while giving my family the time they needed. By the way, I still watch *Perry Mason* reruns.

—Aaron Thompson

For these reasons, time management should be viewed not only as a college-success strategy, but also as a life-management strategy and life-success skill. Studies show that people who manage their time well report they are more in control of their lives and feel happier (Myers, 1993). In short, when you gain greater control of your time, you experience greater satisfaction with your life.

Strategies for Improving Time Management

Developing Self-Awareness about How Your Time Is Spent

Have you ever asked yourself: "Where did all the time go?" or said to yourself: "I just can't seem to find the time!" One way to find out where your time went is by taking a time inventory (Webber, 1991) or doing a time analysis, which involves tracking your time by recording what you do and when you do it. By writing or mapping out how you spend time, you become more fully aware of how much time you actually have and where it actually goes, including patches of wasted time when you get little or nothing accomplished. You don't have to do this time analysis for more than a week or two; this should be long enough to give you a good sense of where your time is going and enough information to help you develop some strategies or habits for using time more effectively.

•—CLASSIC QUOTES—•

Doesn't thou love life? Then do not squander time, for that is the stuff life is made of.

—Benjamin Franklin, eighteenth-century inventor, politician, and co-signer of the *Declaration of Independence*

Time = Life. Therefore, waste your time and waste your life, or master your time and master your life.

—Alan Lakein, international expert on time management and author of the best-selling book, *How to Get Control of Your Time and Your Life*

Pause for Reflection
What is your greatest "time waster?"

Is there anything you can do right now to stop or eliminate it?

Itemize: Identify what specific tasks you need to accomplish and when you need to accomplish them.

Most of us have developed the habit of making lists for items we need to buy at the grocery store or lists of people we want to invite to a party. We make these lists to be certain that we don't forget anything or anybody. We can use exactly the same list-making strategy for tasks that we want to accomplish to ensure that we don't forget to do them, or forget to do them on time.

One practical strategy for itemizing your work tasks is by keeping an assignment booklet in which you list all your major assignments and exams for the term, along with their due dates. By pulling together all your work tasks from different courses in one place, you're less likely to overlook them or forget to do them.

Another itemizing option is to obtain a large calendar and record your commitments for the academic term and the dates they are due in the calendar's date boxes. Place the calendar in a location where it is in full view so you can't help but see it every day (e.g., on your bedroom or refrigerator door). If you regularly look at the things you should do, you're less likely to "overlook" and forget about them (or subconsciously push them out of your mind). Also, be sure that things you enjoy and look forward to are listed on the calendar and seen every day, because they can serve as strong incentives that motivate you to meet your work commitments.

Using an assignment book is an effective way to keep track of your assignments and exams.

Pause for Reflection

Do you have a calendar for the current academic term that you carry with you?

Do you carry a work list with you during the day?

If you carry either or both of the above items, why do you do so?

If you carry neither a calendar nor a work list, why do you think you don't?

Personal Story

As most of us who had moms in our household when we were kids, my mom was the person who ensured I got up for school on time. Once I got to school the bell would ring to let me know to move on to the next class. When I returned home I had to do my homework and chores. My daily and weekly schedule was dictated by someone else. When I came to college, I quickly realized that I needed to design a way to be organized, focused, and productive without the assistance of others. Where was mom when I really needed her? Since I came from a modest background, I had to work my way through college. Juggling schedules became an art for me. I knew the things that I could not miss (work and school) and the things I could miss (student organizations and girls). (Ok, not girls.) Thus, flexibility in my life existed only in terms of optional activities. After college, I spent 10 years in business, a world where I was measured on certain outcomes. It was during this time that I discovered a scheduling book. When I moved into academia as a professor I had other mechanisms to make sure I did what I needed to do when I needed to do it. This was largely based on when my classes were offered. Other time was dedicated to working out and spending time with my family. Now as an administrator, I have an assistant who keeps my schedule. She tells me where I am going, how long I should be there, and what I need to accomplish while I am there. Unless you take your parents with you or have an assistant, it is important to determine activities that are required and also allow time in your schedule for fun. Use a planner!

—*Aaron Thompson*

Prioritize: Rank your tasks in order of their importance.

Once your major commitments have been itemized by listing all the things that you need to do, they then need to be prioritized by deciding what order to do them in—i.e., what must be done first, what should be done next, and what could be done later. Prioritizing basically involves ranking your tasks in terms of their importance, with the highest ranked tasks appearing on the top of your list to ensure that they are tackled first.

How do you determine what tasks are most important and should be ranked highest? Two key criteria or standards of judgment can be used to help determine what tasks should be your highest priority:

1. **Urgency**—tasks that are closest to their deadline or due date should receive high priority (for example, finishing an assignment that's due tomorrow should receive higher priority than starting an assignment that's due next month);
2. **Gravity**—those that carry the heaviest "weight" should receive high priority (for example, if an assignment worth 100 points and another worth 10 points are due at the same time, working on the 100-point task should receive higher priority).

One strategy for making the task of prioritizing more manageable is to divide your tasks into "A," "B," and "C" lists (Lakein, 1973). The "A" list would include essential things—what you "must do," the "B" list would include important things—what you "should do," and the "C" list would include trivial things—what you "could do" or "might do" (e.g., if there's time left over after you've completed the tasks on lists "A" and "B").

Dividing our tasks in this fashion can help us decide how to divide our labor in a way that ensures we put "first things first." What we don't want to do is waste time doing less important things, and deceive ourselves into thinking that we're keeping busy and getting things done, when actually, we're doing things that just take our time (and mind) away from the more important things that should be done.

At first glance, itemizing and prioritizing may appear to be somewhat mechanical or clerical tasks. However, if we look at these mental tasks carefully, they require some key higher-level thinking skills such as:

a. analysis—breaking down commitments into specific tasks and breaking down time into its component elements or segments;
b. evaluation—critically evaluating our time-spending choices in terms of their importance or value; and
c. synthesis—organizing and integrating tasks into classes or categories based on priority.

Thus, developing self-awareness about how we spend time is a challenging exercise in self-reflection and higher-level thinking.

Develop a Time-Management Plan

Humans are creatures of habit. Regular routines help us organize and gain control of our life by doing things by design rather than leaving them to chance or accident, and planning our time increases the likelihood that we can make things happen for us rather than allowing them to happen to us—randomly or haphazardly. Thus, one valuable routine we can get into to help us organize our life and gain greater control of our life (and perhaps our destiny) is by planning how we're going to manage or spend our time.

Don't buy into the myth that you "don't have time to plan ahead" and that planning slows you down from getting started and getting things done. Time-management experts estimate that the amount of time you spend on planning your work time actually saves your total work time by a ratio of 3 to 1. In other words, for every one unit of time you spend planning, you save three units of time working; thus, 5 minutes of planning time will typically save you 15 minutes of total work time, and 10 minutes of planning time will save you 30 minutes of work time. This work-time savings probably results from the fact that planning ensures that before beginning our work, we know exactly what needs to be done and in what order to do it. This serves to reduce the number of mistakes we make due to "false starts"—starting our work but then having to re-start because we started off in the wrong direction, causing us to backtrack and reorganize our work after discovering its parts didn't fall naturally into an effective sequence or pattern. As the old proverb goes, "A stitch in time saves nine." Planning represents a "stitch" in time that saves "nine" stitches (units) of eventual work time.

> **STUDENT PERSPECTIVE**
>
> "The amount of free time you have in college is much more than in high school. Always have a weekly study schedule to go by. Otherwise, time slips away and you will not be able to account for it."
>
> –First-year student (Rhoads, 2005)

> **CLASSIC QUOTE**
>
> *Failing to plan is planning to fail.*
>
> –Alan Lakein, author, *How to Get Control of Your Time and Your Life*

Elements of a Comprehensive Time-Management Plan

Once we've accepted the notion that planning our time actually saves us time in the long run, the next thing to do is to design a time-management plan. Listed below are elements of an effective, total time-management plan.

A good plan should include:

a. a long-range plan for the entire academic term that identifies deadlines for reports and papers due toward the end of the term;
b. a mid-range plan for the upcoming month and week; and
c. a short-range plan for the following day.

The above timeframes may be integrated into a total time-management plan for the term by taking the following steps:

1. Identify the deadline dates of all assignments, i.e., the time when each of them must be completed (long-range plan),
2. Work backward from these final deadlines to identify dates when you plan to begin taking action on these assignments (short-range plan), and
3. Identify intermediate dates when you plan to finish particular parts or pieces of the total assignment (mid-range plan).

This three-stage plan should help you make steady progress throughout the term on assignments that are due later in the term, while reducing your tendency to procrastinate and your risk of running out of time at the end of the term.

A good time-management plan should include a balance of work and recreation.

A good plan should include reserve time to take care of the unexpected.

We should always hope for the best, but our plan should be built to anticipate and accommodate the worst. That is, our plan should include a buffer zone or safety net that builds in some extra time that can be used in case of any unforeseen or unexpected developments. Just as we should plan to save extra money in our bank in case emergency expenses crop up, we should also plan to save extra time in our schedule for the unexpected (e.g., unexpected tasks or tasks taking longer to complete than expected).

A good plan should include a balance of work and recreation.

Do not only plan work time; also plan time to relax, refuel, and recharge. Your overall plan shouldn't turn you into an obsessive-compulsive workaholic. Instead, your plan should contain a balanced blend of work and play, including activities that promote your mental and physical health—such as relaxation, recreation, and reflection.

Remember: A good time-management plan should help you stress less, learn more, and earn better grades, while leaving you more time for other important aspects of your life. Your plan should not only enable you to get your work done on time; it should also enable you to attain and maintain balance in your life.

• CLASSIC QUOTE • —

Murphy's Laws:
1. *Nothing is as simple as it looks.*
2. *Everything takes longer than it should.*
3. *If anything can go wrong, it will.*

—Named after Captain Edward Murphy, naval engineer, in 1949

STUDENT PERSPECTIVE

"It is just as important to allow time for things you enjoy doing because this is what will keep you stable."

—Words written by a first-year student in a letter of advice to new students

What activities do you engage in:

a. for fun?

b. to relieve stress?

Your plan should have some flexibility.

Your time-management plan should be flexible enough to allow you to occasionally bend it without breaking it. Some people are immediately turned off by the idea of developing a schedule and planning their time because they feel it over-structures their lives and limits their freedom. It's natural for us to prize our personal freedom and resist any attempts to restrict it in any way. However, when you create a personal time-management plan, remember: It is *your* plan—you own it and you run it; it shouldn't run or own you. A good plan actually preserves your freedom by helping you get done what must be done, reserving free time for you to do what you want and like to do.

A good time-management plan should not force you to become a slave to a rigid work schedule. Just as work commitments and family responsibilities can crop up unexpectedly, so too can fun opportunities and other pleasant experiences. Your plan should allow you the freedom to modify your schedule so that you can take advantage of these enjoyable opportunities and experiences. The only restriction is that you should plan to make up the work time you lost. In other words, you can borrow or trade work time for play time, but don't steal it—you should plan to pay back the work time you borrowed by planning to make up that work at another time in your schedule.

Converting Your Time-Management Plan into an Action Plan

Step one is planning the work; step two is working the plan. A good action plan is one that guides your work on a day-to-day basis, provides a preview of what you intend to accomplish, and allows you to review what you actually accomplished. You can implement such an action plan simply by drawing up a daily list, bringing that list with you as the day begins, and checking off items on the list after getting them done. At the end of the day, review your list, and identify what was completed and what still needs to be done. The uncompleted tasks should become high priorities for the next day.

If you find yourself left with many unchecked items on your daily to-do list at the end of the day, it's possible that you may be spreading yourself too thin by trying to do too many things in a single day. You may need to be more realistic about the number of things you can reasonably expect to accomplish on a daily basis by shortening your daily list. However, not getting many of your intended tasks done may also mean that you need to tweak your work schedule by adding work time or subtracting activities that are taking time and attention away from your work (e.g., taking cell-phone calls during your planned work times).

> **CLASSIC QUOTE**
>
> *Some people regard discipline as a chore. For me, it is a kind of order that sets me free to fly.*
>
> —Julie Andrews, Academy-award winning English actress who starred in the Broadway musicals, "Mary Poppins" and "The Sound of Music"

Pause for Reflection

1. Do you write down things you need to get done?

   ____ never

   ____ seldom

   ____ often

   ____ almost always

If you selected "never" or "seldom," why do think this is?

2. *By the end of a typical day, do you find that you accomplish most of the important tasks you hoped to accomplish?*

   ____ *never*

   ____ *seldom*

   ____ *often*

   ____ *almost always*

Why?

Dealing with Procrastination

Procrastination Defined

The word "procrastinate" derives from two roots: "pro" meaning "forward" and "crastinus" meaning "tomorrow." Thus, it could be said that procrastinators do not abide by the proverb, "Why put off to tomorrow what can be done today?" Instead, the procrastinator's philosophy is: "Why do today what can be put off to tomorrow?" This philosophy results in a perpetual pattern of postponing what needs to be done until the last possible moment, then rushing anxiously to get it done by sacrificing quality, getting it only partially done, or not getting it done at all.

Research shows that three out of four college students label themselves as "procrastinators" (Potts, 1987). Over 80 percent of them procrastinate at least occasionally (Ellis & Knaus, 1977), and almost half do so consistently (Onwuegbuzie, 2000). Furthermore, these percentages seem to be on the rise (Kachgal, Hansen, & Nutter, 2001). Procrastination is such a serious issue for college students that some colleges and universities have opened "procrastination centers," which provide help exclusively for students experiencing problems with procrastination (Burka & Yuen, 1983).

•—• **CLASSIC QUOTE** •—•

I wasted time, and now time doth waste me.

–The Tragedy of King Richard II, Act V, William Shakespeare (1595)

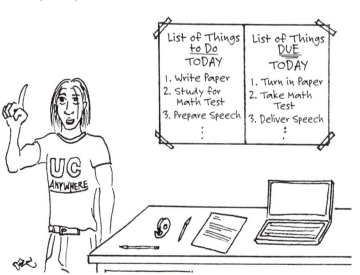

Next time, I'll start sooner!

A procrastinator's idea of planning ahead and working in advance often boils down to this scenario.

However, procrastination is by no means limited to college students. It is a widespread problem that afflicts people of all ages and occupations (Harriott & Ferrari, 1996), which is why you see lots of books on the subject of time management in the self-help section of any bookstore, and why you see lots of people at the post office mailing their tax returns at the last possible moment ("Haven't filed yet," 2003).

Myths That Promote Procrastination

Before there can be any hope of putting a stop to procrastination, people need to let go of two very popular myths or misconceptions about time and performance.

Myth 1: "I work better under pressure" (e.g., on the day or night before something is due).

It is true that people can work more rapidly and with more nervous energy when they're under pressure, but that does not mean they're working more *effectively* and are producing work of higher *quality*. Because they're playing "beat the clock," their focus is no longer on how *well* they can do the job, but how *fast* they can do it and whether they'll be able to get it done before running out of time. This is a classic case of "haste makes waste" and a formula that is destined to result in an inferior work product or work outcome.

Although you may work quicker under pressure, you are probably not working better.

Don't confuse rapidity with quality; it typically takes time to do a high-quality job, particularly if that job requires higher-level thinking skills such as critical thinking, creative thinking, or problem solving. Academic work in college often requires these forms of deeper learning and complex thinking, which cannot be rushed because they require time for reflection. Creative ideas take time to formulate, incubate, and eventually "hatch," which is not likely to happen under time pressure (Amabile, Hadley, & Kramer, 2002). Working under pressure on tasks that require higher-level thinking is like trying to complete a long, challenging test under a short time limit. What happens is we have less time to think, to attend to fine details, to double-check our work, and to fine-tune our final product.

Remember: Procrastinators often confuse desperation with motivation. Their belief that they "work better under pressure" is often just a rationalization to justify or deny the truth, which is that they will work *only* under pressure—i.e., they will work only when they are forced to work because they're under the gun to finally get the job done.

Myth 2: "Studying in advance is a waste of time because I'll forget it all by test time."

This misconception is commonly used to justify procrastinating with respect to preparing for upcoming exams. Distributed (spread-out) studying is more effective than massed (crammed) studying for producing deeper learning and stronger memory. Furthermore, last-minute studying the night before exams often results in lost sleep time due to the need to pull "late- or all-nighters." This practice reduces memory for information that has been studied and increases test anxiety because of lost dream (REM) sleep—which is needed for memory formation and stress management (Hobson, 1988; Voelker, 2004).

Lastly, working under time pressure adds to performance pressure and performance anxiety by leaving you no margin of error to correct mistakes, no opportunity to get help along the way, and no chance to work around random catastrophes that may arise at the last minute (e.g., a head cold or a family emergency).

Pause for Reflection

Do you tend to put off work for so long that getting it done turns into an emergency or panic situation?

If your answer is "yes," why do you think this happens? If your answer is "no," what is it that you do to prevent this from happening?

Psychological Causes of Procrastination

Sometimes, procrastination has deeper psychological roots. People may procrastinate for reasons not directly related to poor time-management skills, but because of emotional issues involving self-esteem or self-image. For instance, studies show that a psychological strategy that some procrastinators use to protect their self-esteem is *self-handicapping*. People use this strategy (consciously or unconsciously) to give themselves a handicap or disadvantage so that if their performance turns out to be less than spectacular, they can say it was caused by the fact that they were performing under a handicap (Smith, Snyder, & Handelsman, 1982). For example, if their academic performance does not turn out to be great, they can conclude that they could have attained a higher grade if they just had more time, and that they had the ability or potential to achieve an "A"; they just didn't put in enough time to demonstrate their true ability. Or better yet, if they happened to get a good grade despite procrastinating, they could conclude they got it without putting in much time, which really proves how brilliant they are! Either way, the procrastinator's self-image is totally protected from any possible damage because conditions are arranged to guarantee that any performance that's less than outstanding can be attributed to external factors (lack of time), and any outstanding performance can be attributed to something within the person (extraordinary ability).

In addition to self-handicapping, research also shows that there are other psychological factors that can contribute to procrastination, such as the following:

a. fear of failure—feeling that it's better to postpone the job or not do it at all, rather than fail at it (Burka & Yuen, 1983; Soloman & Rothblum, 1984);

b. perfectionism—having unrealistically high personal standards or expectations, which lead to the belief that it's better to postpone work or not do it at all than to risk doing it less than perfectly (Flett et al., 1992; Kachgal, Hansen, & Nutter, 2001);

c. fear of success—fear that doing well will show that the procrastinator has the ability to achieve success and will be expected to do "repeat performances" in the future (Ellis & Kraun, 1977; Beck, Koons, & Milgram, 2000); and

d. indecisiveness—difficulty making decisions, including decisions about what to do or how to begin doing it (Anderson, 2003; Steel, 2003).

CLASSIC QUOTE

We didn't lose the game; we just ran out of time.

—Vince Lombardi, legendary football coach

If these or any other issues are involved, it may mean that procrastination is merely a reflection of underlying psychological causes. These psychological causes must be dealt with first before procrastination can be overcome, and because they have deeper roots, it may take some time and professional assistance to uproot them. A good place to get such assistance is the Personal Counseling Office. The personal counselors on college campuses are professional psychologists who have been trained to deal with the psychological issues that can contribute to procrastination. Furthermore, these counseling psychologists are easily accessible to students because they provide their services on campus, and their services are free because their cost is covered by student tuition.

Self-Help Strategies for Combating the Procrastination Habit

Once inaccurate beliefs and emotional issues underlying procrastination have been dealt with, the next step is to overcome the actual habit of procrastinating. Listed below are our top strategies for minimizing or eliminating the procrastination habit.

Make the work meaningful.

> **CLASSIC QUOTE**
>
> *The future belongs to those who believe in the beauty of their dreams.*
>
> —Eleanor Roosevelt

Visualize your goals each time you feel procrastination rearing its ugly head. Take a moment to think about why the work is meaningful or important to achieve your goals and realize your dreams. Even if the nature of the work does not relate directly to your future aspirations, take a moment to think about how getting it done is a necessary stepping stone that will get you one step closer to your ultimate goal.

Make the start of work as inviting or appealing as possible.

Getting started can be a key stumbling block for many procrastinators. Procrastination often involves overcoming "start-up stress" that leads to work postponement and work avoidance (Burka & Yuen, 1983). If you have trouble starting your work, one strategy for jump-starting yourself is to arrange your tasks in a way that allows you to begin working on those tasks you find most interesting or are most likely to experience success. Once the work is begun, procrastinators may discover that the work wasn't as difficult, boring, or painful as they feared it would be; and as soon as they begin to make some progress, their apprehension starts to decline. As with any experience that's dreaded and avoided, the anticipation of the experience turns out to be worse than the actual experience itself. Once you are on a roll, you can ride the momentum you've created to attack your less appealing or more daunting tasks.

For many procrastinators, getting *started* is often their biggest obstacle.

Make the work manageable.

Work becomes less overwhelming and less stressful when it's handled in smaller chunks or pieces. You can conquer procrastination for large tasks by using a "divide and conquer" strategy: Divide the large task into smaller, more manageable units, then attack and defeat them one at a time.

Don't underestimate the power of short work sessions. They can be much more effective than longer sessions because it's easier to maintain maximum concentration and energy for shorter periods of time. If you're working on a large project or preparing for a major exam, dividing your work into short sessions gives you the opportunity to punch away at it in quick jabs and poke more and more holes in it. This will enable you to see the continual progress you're making and will gradually take away the pressure of having to go for the big "K.O." right before the bell.

Organization matters.

Research indicates that disorganization is a factor that contributes to procrastination (Steel, 2003). How well we manage and organize work materials can help us manage our time and reduce our tendency to procrastinate. Having the right materials in the right place at the right time can make our work easier to get to and easier for us to get going. When we've made a decision to get the job done, we don't want to waste time looking for the tools we need to begin doing it. For procrastinators, this time delay may give them just enough time to change their mind and not bother to start at all.

One simple but effective way to organize your college work materials is by developing your own file system. You can begin creating an effective file system by storing materials from different courses in different colored folders or notebooks. This will allow you to gather all materials relating to the same course in the same place, while keeping materials belonging to different classes in separate places. Such a system will help you get organized, help you beat procrastination by making it easier for you to start working, and help reduce stress caused by disorganization.

Location matters.

Where you work is as important as when and how you work. Distraction is a factor that has been found to contribute to procrastination (Steel, 2003). Thus, it may be possible for you to choose a work environment whose location and arrangement can combat procrastination by maximizing your concentration and minimizing distractions—which force you to stop and restart (or not restart at all).

Distractions tend to come in two major forms: social—e.g., people around who are not working, and media—e.g., cell phones, e-mailing, text messaging, CDs, and TV. Research indicates that the number of hours per week that college students spend watching television is *negatively* associated with academic success, including lower college GPA, less likelihood of graduating college with honors, and lower levels of personal development (Astin, 1993). So, pick a workplace and arrange your workspace to minimize media distractions.

> **STUDENT PERSPECTIVE**
>
> "Did you ever dread doing something, then it turned out to take only about 20 minutes to do?"
>
> —Conversation overheard in a coffee shop between two college students

Working in a location that limits your distractions will make it more difficult to procrastinate.

Remember: Remove anything and everything from your work place that is not relevant to your work.

Pause for Reflection

List your two most common sources of distraction while working, and next to each distracter, identify a strategy that you might use to reduce or eliminate it.

Source of Distraction   Strategy for Reducing This Source of Distraction

_____   _____

_____   _____

> **STUDENT PERSPECTIVE**
>
> "To reduce distractions, work at a computer on campus rather than using one in your room or home."
>
> —Suggestion for avoiding work distractions from a student in a first-year seminar class

Lastly, remember that you can arrange your work environment in a way that not only disables distractions but also enables concentration. You can "enable" your concentration by working in an environment that allows you easy access to work-support materials (e.g., class notes, textbooks, dictionary) and easy access to social support—such as working with a group of motivated students who help you stay focused and get your work done.

Adjust your sequence of work tasks to intercept procrastination at times when it's most likely to take place.

While procrastination frequently involves difficulty in starting work, it can also involve difficulty continuing and completing work (Lay & Silverman, 1996). As previously mentioned, if you have trouble starting work, it might be best to do your most stimulating tasks first. However, if you have difficulty maintaining or sustaining your work until it's finished, you might try scheduling work tasks that you find easier and more interesting *at the middle or end* of your planned work time. If tasks of greater interest and ease are scheduled at a time in the work sequence when you typically lose interest or energy, you may be able to maintain that interest and energy long enough to continue working until all your tasks are completed. Also, by doing your enjoyable tasks later, they can provide an incentive for completing your less enjoyable tasks first.

> **STUDENT PERSPECTIVE**
>
> "I'm very good at starting things but often have trouble keeping a sustained effort."
>
> —First-year student

Momentum matters.

It often takes less effort to finish a task that's close to completion than it is to restart a task, because you can ride the momentum that you've already created. Furthermore, finishing a task can give you a sense of closure—the feeling of personal accomplishment and self-satisfaction that comes from knowing you've "closed the deal." Seeing a checkmark next to a completed task and realizing that it's one less task to do can increase your energy and drive to accomplish all the other tasks on your list.

••• Managing Money

Just as time management is a key life-management skill, so is money management. In fact, managing time and managing money have a lot in common. You may be familiar with the expressions, "Time is money," "A day late and a dollar short," and "I lost track of my time (or money)." Also, when people commit a crime, they pay their "debt" to society by doing time (jail or doing community service) and/or paying a fine. Both time management and money management require self-awareness of how they're "spent"; both can be saved or wasted, and since both come in limited quantities, they need to be budgeted for and saved or else we'll "run out" of them. Lastly, and perhaps most importantly, how we spend our time and money can tell us a lot about what really matters to us or what we truly value.

For new college students, greater personal independence often brings with it greater demands for economic self-sufficiency, critical thinking about consumerism, and effective management of personal finances. The importance of money management for college students is growing for two major reasons. One is the rising cost of a college education, which is leading more students to work while in college and to work more hours per week (Levine & Cureton, 1998). The rising cost of a college education is also requiring students to make more complex decisions about what options (or combination of options) they will use to finance their college education. Unfortunately, research indicates that many students today are not choosing financial strategies that contribute most effectively to their educational success in college and their long-term financial success after college (King, 2005).

A second reason why money management is growing in importance for college students is the availability and convenience of credit cards. For students today, credit cards are easy to get, easy to use, and easy to abuse. College students can do everything right, such as getting solid grades, getting involved on campus, and getting work experience while in college, but a poor credit history due to irresponsible use of credit cards in college can reduce students' chances of obtaining credit after college and their chances of being hired immediately after graduation. Research also indicates that accumulating high levels of debt while in college is also associated with higher levels of stress (Kiecolt, et al., 1986), lower academic performance (Susswein, 1995), and greater risk of withdrawing from college (Ring, 1997).

On the positive side of the ledger, studies show that when students learn to use effective money-management strategies, they can decrease unnecessary spending, prevent accumulation of significant debt, and reduce personal stress (Health & Soll, 1996; Walker, 1996).

STUDENT PERSPECTIVE

"My money-management skills are poor. If I have money, I will spend it unless somebody takes it away from me. I am the kind of person who lives from paycheck to paycheck."

—First-year student

Strategies for Managing Money Effectively

Develop Financial Self-Awareness

Effectively managing any personal habit begins with the critical first step of self-awareness. Developing the habit of effective money management begins with awareness of *cash flow*—the amount of money we have flowing in and flowing out. As illustrated in Figure 1, cash flow can be tracked by:

◆ watching how much money you have coming in (income) versus going out (expenses or expenditures) and

◆ watching how much money you have accumulated but not spent (savings) versus how much money you've borrowed but not paid back (debt).

CLASSIC QUOTE

If we command our wealth, we shall be rich and free; if our wealth commands us, we are poor indeed.

—Edmund Burke, eighteenth-century author, political philosopher, and supporter of the American Revolution

Income for college students typically comes from one or more of the following sources:

a. scholarships or grants—which don't have to be paid back,
b. loans—which must be repaid,
c. salary earned from part-time or full-time work,

Figure 1 Two Key Avenues of Cash Flow

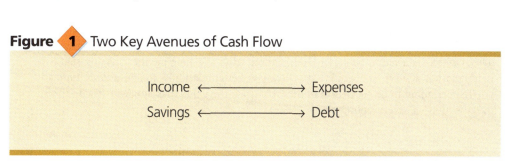

d. personal savings, and
e. gifts or other forms of monetary support from parents and other family members.

Sources of *expenses* (expenditures) may be classified into the following three categories:

1. Basic needs or essential necessities—expenses that tend to be fixed because you cannot do without them (e.g., expenses for food, housing, tuition, textbooks, phone, transportation to and from school, and health-related costs).
2. Incidentals or extras—expenses that tend to be flexible because spending money on them is optional or discretionary, i.e., you choose to spend at your own discretion or judgment. These expenses typically include:
    a. money spent on entertainment, enjoyment, or pleasure (e.g., CDs, movies, concerts, club hopping, spring-break vacations) and
    b. money spent primarily for reasons of promoting personal status or self-image (e.g., brand-name products, fashionable clothes, jewelry, or a "hot" new car).
3. *Emergency* expenses—unpredicted, unforeseen, or unexpected costs (e.g., money paid for doctor visits and medicine because of illnesses or accidents).

Pause for Reflection

What do you estimate to be your 2 to 3 most expensive incidentals (optional purchases)?

Do you think you should reduce those expenses or eliminate them altogether?

Personal Story   When I was four years old living in the mountains of Kentucky, it was safe for a young lad to walk the railroad tracks and roads alone. My mother knew this and would send me to the general store to buy a variety of small items we needed for our household. Since we had very little money, she was aware of the fact that we had to be cautious and only spend money on the staples we needed to survive. I could only purchase items from the general store that I could carry back home by myself and the ones my mother strictly ordered me to purchase. Most of these items cost less than a dollar and in many cases you could buy multiple items for that dollar in the early 1960s. At the store I would hand my mother's handwritten list to the owners. They would pick the items for me, and we would exchange the items for my money. On the checkout counter there were jars with different kinds of candy or gum. You could buy two pieces for $.01. As a hard-working good son who was fulfilling the wishes of my parents, I didn't think there would be any harm in rewarding myself with two pieces of candy after doing a good deed. After all, I could devour the evidence of my disobedience on my slow walk home. Upon my return, my mother being the protector of the vault and the sergeant-of-arms in our household, would count each item I brought home to make sure I had been charged correctly. She always found that I had either been overcharged by one cent or that I had spent one cent. In those days, parents believed in behavior modification. After she gave me the direction that I so richly did not deserve, she would say: "Boy, you better learn how to count your money if you're ever going to be successful in life." I learned the value of $1 and the discomfort of overspending at a very young age.

—*Aaron Thompson*

Develop a Money-Management Plan

Once you're aware of the amount of money you have coming in—and from what sources, as well as how much money you're spending—and for what reasons, the next step is to develop a plan for managing this cash flow. The bottom line is to ensure that money you have coming in is equal to or greater than the money going out. If the amount of money you're spending exceeds the amount you have coming in, you're "in the red" or have negative cash flow.

STUDENT PERSPECTIVE

"I keep track of my money on Excel."

—First-year student

Strategic Selection and Use of Financial Tools for Tracking Cash Flow

Several financial tools or instruments are available to us that can be used to track your cash flow and manage your money. These cash-flow instruments include:

- checking accounts,
- credit cards,
- charge cards, and
- debit cards.

Checking Account

Long before credit cards were created, a checking account was the instrument most people used to keep track of their money. Checking accounts are still used by many people in addition to (or instead of) credit cards.

A checking account may be obtained from a bank or credit union, and its typical costs include a deposit ($20–25) to open the account, a monthly service fee (e.g., $10), and small fees for checks. Some banks charge customers a service fee based on the number of checks written, which is a good option if you don't plan to write many checks each month. If you maintain a high enough balance of money deposited in your account, the bank may not charge any extra fees, and if you're able to maintain an even higher balance, the bank may also pay you interest—known as an "interest-bearing checking account."

Along with your checking account, banks usually provide you with an ATM (Automatic Teller Machine) card that you can use to get cash. Look for a checking account that does not charge you fees for ATM transactions, but provides this as a free service along with your account. Also, look for a checking account that doesn't charge you if your balance drops below a certain minimum figure.

Personal Story

> I clearly remember my younger sister (by three years) struggling with the concept of budgeting while she was in high school and working in her first job. She called me at college to share her frustration about not having any money in her account. She said to me, "How can I be overdrawn? I still have checks left!"
>
> —Viki Sox Fecas

Strategies for Using Checking Accounts Effectively

- Whenever you write a check or make an ATM withdrawal, immediately subtract its amount from your *balance*—i.e., amount of money remaining in your account to determine your new balance.
- Keep a running balance in your checkbook; it will ensure that you know exactly how much money you have in your account at all times. This will reduce the risk that you'll

write a check that "bounces," i.e., a check that you don't have enough money in the bank to cover. If you do bounce a check, you'll probably have to pay a charge to the bank and possibly to the business that attempted to cash your bounced check.

◆ Double check your checkbook balance with each monthly statement you receive from the bank. Be sure to include the service charges your bank makes to your account that appear on your monthly statement. This practice will make it easier to track errors—on either your part or the bank's part. (Banks can and do make mistakes occasionally.)

Advantages of a Checking Account

There are several advantages of a checking account:

◆ you can carry checks instead of cash;
◆ you have access to cash at almost any time through an ATM machine;
◆ it allows you to keep a very visible track record of income and expenses in your checkbook; and
◆ a properly managed checking account can serve as a good credit reference for future loans and purchases.

Credit Card (e.g., MasterCard, Visa, or Discover)

A credit card is basically money loaned to you by the credit-card company that issues you the card, which you pay back to the company on a monthly basis. You can pay the whole bill or a portion of the bill each month—as long as some minimum payment is made. However, for any remaining (unpaid) portion of your bill, you are charged a very high interest rate, which is usually about 18 percent.

Strategies for Selecting a Credit Card

If you decide to use a credit card, pay attention to its *annual percentage rate (APR)*. This is the interest rate you pay for previously unpaid monthly balances, and it can vary depending on the credit-card company. Credit-card companies also vary in terms of their annual service fee. You will likely find companies that charge higher interest rates tend to charge lower annual fees, and vice-versa. As a general rule, if you expect to pay the full balance every month, you're probably better off choosing a credit card that does not charge you an annual service fee. On the other hand, if you think you'll need more time to make the full monthly payments, you may be better off with a credit-card company that offers a low interest rate.

Another feature that differentiates one credit-card company from another is whether or not you're allowed a "grace period"—i.e., a certain period of time after you receive your monthly statement during which you can pay back the company without paying added interest fees. Some companies may allow you a grace period of a full month, while others may provide none and begin charging interest immediately after you fail to pay on the bill's due date.

Credit cards may also differ in terms of the credit limit (a.k.a., a "credit line" or "line of credit"), which refers to the maximum amount of money the company will make available to you. If you are a new customer, most credit-card companies will set a credit limit beyond which you will not be granted any additional credit.

Advantages of a Credit Card

If a credit card is used responsibly, it has some key advantages as a money-management tool. Its features can provide the following advantages:

- It helps you track your spending habits because the credit-company sends you a monthly statement that includes an itemized list of all your card-related purchases, which provides you with a "paper trail" of *what* you purchased that month and *when* you purchased it.
- It allows access to cash whenever and wherever you need it, because any bank or ATM machine that displays your credit card's symbol will give you cash up to a certain limit, usually for a small transaction fee. Keep in mind that some credit card companies charge a higher interest rate for cash advances than purchases.
- It enables you to establish a personal *credit history*. If you use a credit card responsibly, you can establish a good credit history that can be used later in life for big-ticket purchases such as a car or home. In effect, responsible use of a credit card shows others from whom you wish to seek credit (borrow money) that you're financially responsible.

Remember: Do not buy into the belief that the *only* way you can establish a good credit history is by using a credit card. It's not your only option; you can establish a good credit history through responsible use of a checking account and by paying your bills on time.

Strategies for Using Credit Cards Responsibly

While there may be advantages to using a credit card, you only reap those advantages if you use your card strategically. If not, the advantages of a credit card will be quickly and greatly outweighed by its disadvantages. Listed below are some key strategies for using a credit card in a way that maximizes its advantages and minimizes its disadvantages.

- **Use a credit card only as a convenience for making purchases and tracking the purchases you make; do not use it as a tool for obtaining a long-term loan.**

A credit card's main money-management advantage is that it allows you to make purchases with plastic instead of cash. The credit card allows you the convenience of not carrying around cash and enables you to receive a monthly statement of your purchases from the credit-card company, which makes it easier for you to track and analyze your spending habits.

The "credit" provided by a credit card should be seen simply as a short-term loan that must be paid back at the end of every month.

Remember: Do not use credit cards for long-term credit or long-term loans because their interest rates are outrageously high. Paying such a high rate of interest for a loan represents a very ineffective (and irresponsible) money-management strategy.

- **Limit yourself to one card.**

More credit cards mean more accounts to keep track of and more opportunities to accumulate debt. You don't need additional credit cards from department stores or gas stations, or any other profit-making business because they duplicate what your personal credit card already does (plus they charge extremely high interest rates for late payments).

- **Pay off your balance each month in full and on time.**

If you pay the full amount of your bill each month, this means that you're using your credit card effectively to obtain an interest-free, short-term (one-month) loan. You're just paying *principal*—the total amount of money borrowed and nothing more. However, if your payment is late and you need to pay interest, you pay more for the items you purchased than their actual ticket price. For instance, if you have an unpaid balance of $500 on your monthly credit bill for merchandise purchased the previous month, and you are charged the typical 18% credit-card interest rate for late payment, you end-up paying $590: $500 (merchandise) + $90 (18% interest to the credit-card company).

In fact, credit-card companies make their money or profit from the interest they collect from cardholders who do not pay back their credit on time. Just as procrastinating doing your work is a poor time-management habit, procrastinating paying your credit-card bills is a poor money-management habit that can cost you dearly in the long run because of the high interest rate you pay.

Avoid paying these huge interest rates and prevent credit-card companies from becoming rich at your expense by paying your total balance on time. If you cannot pay the total amount owed, pay off as much of it as you possibly can rather than making the minimum monthly payment. If you keep making only the minimum payment each month and continue using your credit card, you'll begin to pile up huge amounts of debt.

Remember: If you keep charging on your credit card while you have an unpaid balance or debt, you no longer have a grace period to pay off your charges; instead, interest is charged immediately on all your purchases.

> **CLASSIC QUOTE**
>
> *"You'll never get your credit card debt paid off if you keep charging on your card and make only the minimum monthly payment. Paying only the minimum is like using a Dixie cup to bail water from a sinking boat."*
>
> —Eric Tyson, financial counselor and national best-selling author of *Personal Finance for Dummies*

Pause for Reflection

1. Do you have a credit card?

2. If yes, do you pay off your entire balance each month?

3. a. If you don't pay off your entire balance each month, what would you say is your average unpaid balance per month?

   b. What changes would you have to make in your money-management habits to be able to pay off your entire balance each month?

Charge Card (e.g., American Express)

A charge card works very similar to a credit card in that you are given a short-term loan for one month; the only difference is that you must pay your bill in full at the end of each month, and you cannot carry over any debt from one month to the next. Its major disadvantage relative to a credit card is that it has less flexibility—no matter what your expenses may be for a particular month, you must still pay up or lose your ability to acquire credit for the next month. For people who habitually fail to pay their monthly credit-card bill on time, this makes a charge card a smarter money-management tool than a credit card because the cardholder cannot continue to accumulate debt.

Debit Card

A debit card looks almost identical to a credit card (e.g., it has a MasterCard or Visa logo), but it works differently. When you use a debit card, money is immediately taken out or subtracted from your checking account. Thus, you're only using money that's already in your account (rather than borrowing money), and you don't receive a bill at the end of the month. If you attempt to purchase something with a debit card that costs more than the amount of money you have in your account, your card will not allow you to do so. Just like a bounced check, a debit card will not permit you to pay out any money that is not in your account. Like a check or ATM withdrawal, a purchase made with a debit card should immediately be subtracted from your balance.

A major advantage of the debit card is that it provides you with the convenience of "plastic," just like a credit card, but it prevents you from spending beyond your means and accumulating debt. For this reason, financial advisors often recommend using a debit card instead of a credit card (Knox, 2004; Tyson, 2003).

> **CLASSIC QUOTE**
>
> *Never spend your money before you have it.*
>
> —Thomas Jefferson, third president of the United States, and founder of the University of Virginia

Financial Literacy: Understanding the Vocabulary of Money Management

As you read each of the financial terms in the following list, place a mark by any one whose meaning you did not previously know.

Account: a formal business arrangement in which a bank provides financial services to a customer (e.g., checking account or savings account).

Balance: amount of money in an account, or the amount of unpaid debt.

Budget: a plan for coordinating income and expenses such that sufficient money is available to cover or pay for expenses.

Credit: money obtained with the understanding that it will be paid back, either with or without interest.

Credit Line (a.k.a., *Credit Limit*): maximum amount of money (credit) made available to a borrower.

Debt: amount of money owed.

Default: failure to meet a financial obligation (e.g., a student who fails to repay a college loan "defaults" on that loan).

Deferred Student Payment Plans: a plan that allows student borrowers to temporarily defer or postpone loan payments for some acceptable reason (e.g., to pursue an internship or volunteer work after college).

Grant: money received that does not have to be repaid.

Insurance Premium: amount paid in regular installments to an insurance company in order to remain insured.

Interest: amount of money paid to a customer for deposited money (as in a bank account) or money paid by a customer for borrowed money (e.g., interest on a loan); interest is usually calculated as a percentage of the total amount of money deposited or borrowed.

Interest-Bearing Account: a bank account that earns interest if the customer keeps a sufficiently large sum of money in the bank.

Loan Consolidation: consolidating (combining) separate student loans into one new, larger loan in order to make the process of tracking, budgeting, and repayment easier. (Loan consolidation typically requires the borrower to pay slightly more interest.)

Loan Premium: amount of money loaned without interest.

Merit-Based Scholarship: money awarded on the basis of performance or achievement that does not have to be repaid.

Need-Based Scholarship: money awarded on the basis of financial need that does not have to be repaid.

Principal: the total amount of money borrowed or deposited, not counting interest.

Yield: revenue or profit produced by an investment above and beyond the original amount invested (e.g., higher lifetime income and other monetary benefits acquired from a college education that exceeds the amount of money invested in or spent on a college education).

Financial Tools for Saving Money

If you're taking in more money than you're spending, you are saving money, and you can invest the money you've saved in an account that will allow you to earn interest on your savings. This account can help you build up a *cash reserve* that can be used for future needs or used immediately for emergencies. Two major financial tools available to you for earning interest on savings are:

1. savings accounts and
2. money-market accounts.

Savings Account

A savings account can be opened at virtually any bank and will earn you interest on the money placed in your account. Usually, no minimum amount of money needs to be deposited to open a savings account, and you don't need to maintain a minimum amount of money in the account.

Money-Market Account

This account is just like a checking account; however, it allows you to write only a limited number of checks, and you're not charged for the checks you use.

If you plan on writing no more than three checks per month, and can continually maintain a minimum balance in your account, you're better off investing your savings in a money-market account than in a savings account because a money-market account will typically pay a higher rate of interest.

Developing Personal Money-Saving Strategies and Habits

The ultimate goal of money management is to save money and avoid debt. Here are some specific strategies for accomplishing this goal.

Prepare a personal budget.

A budget is simply a plan for coordinating income and expenses to ensure that your cash flow leaves us with sufficient money to cover your expenses. A budget helps you maintain awareness of your financial state or condition, and enables you to be your own accountant by keeping track of your money.

Just like managing and budgeting our time, the key first step in managing and budgeting our money involves prioritizing. In the case of money management, prioritizing first involves identifying our most important expenses—necessities that are indispensable and that we must have to survive—as opposed to incidentals that are dispensable because we can really live without them.

Some people can easily confuse essentials and incidentals. For instance, if a piece of merchandise happens to be on sale, what this means is that it may be a great bargain for consumers; however, it doesn't mean that we have to consume (purchase) it before somebody else does.

> **Remember:** Remaining consciously aware of the distinction between life's *essentials* that must be purchased, and *incidentals* that may or may not be purchased, is an important first step toward preparing an effective budget that enables you to save money and escape debt.

CLASSIC QUOTE

"A penny saved is a penny earned."

—Ben Franklin, eighteenth-century inventor, politician, and co-signer of the Declaration of Independence

STUDENT PERSPECTIVE

"I need to pay attention to my balance more closely and actually allot certain amounts for certain things."

—First-year student

STUDENT PERSPECTIVE

"I shouldn't buy random stuff (like hair dye) and other stuff when I don't need it."

—First-year student

We need to be aware of whether we're spending money on *impulse* or out of *habit* rather than out of actual need or after thoughtful reflection.

The fact is that humans spend money for a host of psychological reasons (conscious or subconscious) that are totally unrelated to actual need. For example, they spend to build up their self-esteem or self-image, to combat personal boredom, or to seek stimulation and an emotional "high" (Furnham & Argyle, 1998). Furthermore, people can become obsessed with spending money, shop compulsively, and become addicted to purchasing products. In fact, just as Alcoholics Anonymous (AA) exists as a support group for alcoholics, Debtors Anonymous (DA) exists as a support group for "shopaholics," and it includes a similar 12-step recovery program.

Make all your bills visible and pay them off as soon as possible.

When your bills are visible, they become memorable and you're less likely to forget to pay them, or forget to pay them on time. To increase the visibility of your bill payments, keep a financial calendar on which you record key fiscal deadlines for the academic year (e.g., due dates for tuition payments, residential bills, and financial-aid applications). Also, try to get in the habit of paying a bill as soon as you open it and have it in your hands, rather than setting it aside and running the risk of forgetting to pay it or losing it.

Live within your means.

This strategy is simple: Don't purchase what you can't afford. If you are spending more money than you're taking in, it means you're living *beyond* your means. To begin living *within* your means, you have two options:

1. Decrease your expenses (e.g., reduce your spending), or
2. Increase your income.

Since the vast majority of college students are already working while attending college (Orszag & Whitmore, 2001) and working so many hours that it's interfering with their academic performance or progress (King, 2005), the best option for most college students who find themselves in debt is to reduce their spending and begin living within their means.

Are you currently working for money while attending college?

If you're not working, are you sacrificing anything that you want or need because you lack money?

If you are working:

a. *How many hours per week do you currently work?*

b. *Do you think that working is interfering in any way with your academic performance or progress?*

c. *Would it be possible for you to reduce the number of weekly hours you now work and still be able to make ends meet?*

STUDENT PERSPECTIVE

"I need to save money and not shop so much and impulse buy."
—First-year student

It is preoccupation with possessions, more than anything else, that prevents us from living feely and nobly.
—Bertrand Russell, British philosopher and mathematician

STUDENT PERSPECTIVE

"What I don't do that I know I should do is pay my bills on time, i.e., cell phone and credit cards."
—First-year student

Economize

We can be frugal or thrifty without compromising the quality of our purchases by being intelligent consumers who use critical thinking skills when purchasing products. For example, we can pay less to see the exact same movie in the late afternoon than at night. Also, why pay more for brand-name products that are exactly the same as products with a different name? For instance, why pay 33 percent more for Advil or Tylenol when exactly the same amount of pain-relieving ingredient (ibuprofen or acetaminophen) is contained in generic brands? Often, when you pay extra for brand-name products, what you're paying for is the extra advertising that companies pay to the media and to celebrities to promote their products.

Remember: Advertising creates product familiarity, not product quality. The more money manufacturers pay for advertising and creating a "well-known" or "brand-name" product, the more money you pay for the product—not necessarily because you're acquiring a product of higher quality, but most often because you're covering its high cost of advertising.

Downsize

Cut down or cut out spending for products that you don't need. Don't engage in conspicuous consumption just to "keep up with the Joneses" (your neighbors or friends), and don't allow peer pressure to determine your spending habits. Let your spending habits reflect your ability to think critically rather than your tendency to conform socially.

Don't let peer pressure determine your spending habits.

Live with others rather than living alone.

Although you lose privacy when you live with others, you save money. There are also social benefits of living with others if you enjoy being with them.

Give gifts of time rather than money.

Spending money on gifts for family, friends, and romantic partners is not the only way to show that you care. The point of gift giving is not to show others you aren't cheap or to show off your lavish spending skills. Instead, show off your social sensitivity by doing something special or making something meaningful for them. Gifts of time and kindness can often be more personal and more special than store-bought gifts.

> **CLASSIC QUOTE**
>
> *"The richer your friends, the more they will cost you."*
>
> —Elisabeth Marbury, legal agent for theatrical and literary stars in the late nineteenth and early twentieth centuries

Personal Story

When my wife (Mary) and I were first dating, Mary was aware that I was trying to gain weight because I was on the thin side. (All right, I was skinny.) One day when I came home from school, I found this hand-delivered package in front of my apartment door. I opened it up and there was a homemade loaf of whole-wheat bread made from scratch by Mary. That gift didn't cost her much money, but the fact that she took the time to do it and remembered to do something that was important to me (gaining weight), it really touched me, and it's a gift that I've never forgotten. In fact, since I eventually married Mary and we're still happily married, I guess you could say that inexpensive loaf of bread was the "gift that kept on giving."

—Joe Cuseo

Develop your own set of money-saving strategies and habits.

You can save money by starting to do little things that can eventually become regular money-saving habits and add up to big savings over time. Consider the following list of habit-forming tips for saving money that were suggested by students in a first-year seminar class:

- Don't carry a lot of extra money in your wallet. (It's just like food; if it's easy to get to, you'll be more likely to eat it up.)
- Shop with a list—get in, get what you need, and get out.
- Put all your extra change in a jar.
- Put extra cash in a piggy bank that requires you to smash the piggy to get at it.
- Seal your savings in an envelope.
- Immediately get extra money into the bank (and out of your hands).
- Bring (don't buy) your lunch.
- Take full advantage of your meal plan—you've already paid for it, so don't pay twice for your meals by buying food elsewhere.
- Use e-mail instead of the telephone.
- Hide your credit card or put it in the freezer, so that you don't use it on impulse.
- Use cash (instead of credit cards) because you can give yourself a set amount of it and can clearly see how much of it you have at the start of a week and how much is left at any point during the week.

> **CLASSIC QUOTE**
>
> *The safest way to double your money is to fold it over and put it in your pocket.*
>
> —Kin Hubbard, American humorist, cartoonist, and journalist

Pause for Reflection

Do you use any of the strategies on the above list?

Have you developed any effective strategies that do not appear on the list?

When making purchases, always think in terms of their long-term total cost.

It's convenient and tempting for consumers to think in the short term ("I see it, I like it, and I want it now"). However, long-term thinking is one of the essential keys to successful money management and financial planning. Those small (monthly) installment plans that businesses offer to get us to buy expensive products may make the cost of products appear immediately attractive and affordable in the short run. However, if you factor in the interest rates you pay on monthly installment plans, plus the length of time (number of months) you're making installment payments, you get a much more accurate picture of the product's total cost over the long run. This longer-range perspective can quickly alert you to the reality that the product's total cost is actually quite expensive and perhaps "out of your league."

Also, a product's sticker price represents its immediate or short-term cost. However, its long-term price sometimes involves additional "hidden costs" that don't relate directly to the product's initial price, but which must be paid for the product's long-term use. For example, the sticker price we pay for clothes does not include the hidden, long-term costs that may be involved if those clothes require dry cleaning. By just taking a moment to check the inside label, we can save ourselves this hidden, long-term cost by purchasing clothes that are machine washable. Or, to use an example of a big ticket purchase, the extra money spent to buy a new car instead of a used car does includes not only paying a higher sticker price, but also paying the hidden costs of licensing and insuring the new car (as well as any interest fees, if the new car was purchased on an installment plan). When you include these hidden and long-term costs in a new car's total cost, buying a good used car instead of a new car is a very effective money-savings strategy.

> **Remember:** Avoid buying costly items impulsively. Instead, take time to reflect on the purchase you intend to make and do a cost analysis of its hidden or long-term costs, then integrate these invisible costs with the product's sticker price to generate an accurate synthesis and clearer picture of the product's total cost.

• CLASSIC QUOTE •

If you would be wealthy, think of saving as well as getting.

—Ben Franklin

Long-Range Financial Planning: Financing Your College Education

As we previously mentioned, an effective money-management plan should be time sensitive and include the following financial-planning timeframes:

- short-range financial plan—e.g., weekly income and expenses
- mid-range financial plan—e.g., monthly income and expenses
- long-range financial plan—e.g., projected or anticipated income and expenses for the entire college experience, and
- extended long-range financial plan that extends into the future—e.g., expected income and debt after graduation, including a plan for repayment of any college loans.

Thus far, our discussion has focused primarily on short- and mid-range financial planning strategies that will keep you out of debt on a monthly or yearly basis. We turn now to issues involving long-term financial planning for your entire college experience and for life after college. While there is no one "correct" strategy for financing a college education that works best for all students, there are some important research findings about the effectiveness of different financing strategies that college students have used, which you should be aware of when doing long-range financial planning for college and beyond.

One research finding shows that obtaining a student loan and working no more than 15 hours per week is an effective long-range strategy for students to finance their college education and meet their personal expenses. Students who use this strategy are more likely to graduate from college, graduate in a shorter period of time, and graduate with higher grades than students who work part-time for more than 15 hours per week while going to college full-time, or work full-time and go to college part-time (King, 2002; Pascarella & Terenzini, 2005).

Studies also show that borrowing money in the form of a student loan and working part-time for 15 or fewer hours per week is the most effective financial strategy for students at *all income levels*, and it is *especially effective for students with low incomes*. Unfortunately, less than 6 percent of all first-year students use this strategy. Instead, almost 50 percent of first-year students choose a strategy that research shows to be least associated with college success: borrowing nothing and trying to work more than 15 hours per week. Students who use this strategy increase their risk of lowering their grades significantly and withdrawing from college altogether (King, 2005), probably because they have difficulty finding enough time to handle the amount of academic work required by college on top of the work outside of college for more than 15 hours per week.

Other students decide to finance their college education by working full-time and going to college part-time. These students believe it will be less expensive in the long run to attend college on a part-time basis because it will allow them to avoid any debt from student loans. However, studies show that when students go to college part-time so that they can work full-time, it sharply reduces the likelihood that they will complete a college degree (Orszag, Orszag, & Whitmore, 2001).

Even students who manage to eventually graduate from college, but take longer to do so because they have worked more than 15 hours per week for extra income, will eventually lose money in the long run. The longer they take to graduate means the longer they must wait to "cash in" on their college degree and enter higher-paying, full-time positions that require a college diploma. The pay per hour for most part-time jobs that students hold while working in college is less than half what they will earn from working in a full-time position as a college graduate (King, 2005).

Furthermore, studies show that two out of three college students have at least one credit card, and nearly one-half of students with credit cards carry an average balance of more than $1,500 per month (Wahlstrom & Williams, 1997). Debt level this high is likely to push many students into working more than 15 hours a week to pay off their high level of debt. ("I owe, I owe, so off to work I go.") The result is that these students take longer to graduate and earn a college graduate's salary, because they tend to enroll in fewer courses per term to give themselves extra work time to earn enough money to pay off their credit-card debt.

Instead of paying almost 20 percent interest to credit-card companies for their monthly debt, these students would be much better off obtaining a student loan at a much lower interest rate, which they don't begin to pay back until six months after graduation—when they will be making more money in full-time positions as college graduates. Despite the clear advantages of student loans compared to credit card loans, only about 25 percent of college students who use credit cards take out a student loan.

"My school sends me portions of my diploma as I make partial payments on my student loans."

Compared to other loans, student loans have a much lower interest rate, and they don't need to be repaid until after students are awarded their college diploma—which is awarded in its entirety after graduation, not in parts until the entire loan is repaid!

> **CLASSIC QUOTE**
>
> "Unlike a car that depreciates in value each year that you drive it, an investment in education yields monetary, social, and intellectual profit. A car is more tangible in the short term, but an investment in education (even if it means borrowing money) gives you more bang for the buck in the long run."
>
> —Eric Tyson, financial counselor and national best-selling author of *Personal Finance for Dummies*

Remember: Student loans are provided by the American government with the intent of helping its citizens become better educated. In contrast, for-profit businesses such as credit-card companies, lend students money with no intent or interest in helping them become better educated, but with the intent of helping themselves make money—from the high rates of interest they collect from students who do not pay their debt in full at the end of each month.

Keep in mind that not all debt is bad. Debt can be good if it represents an investment in something that will *appreciate* with the passage of time, i.e., it will gain in value and eventually turn into profit for the investor. Purchasing a college education on credit is a good investment because it will appreciate over time—in the form of higher salaries for the remainder of the investor's life. In contrast, purchasing a car is a bad long-term investment because it immediately begins to depreciate or lose monetary value once it is purchased. The instant you drive that new car out of the dealer's lot, you immediately become the proud owner of a used car that's worth much less than what you just paid for it.

Pause for Reflection

In addition to college, what might be other good, long-term investments for you to make now or in the near future?

You may have heard the expression that "time is money." One way to interpret this expression is that when we spend more money, we must spend more time making money to pay for our spending habits. If you're going to college, spending more time to earn money to cover your spending habits often means spending less time studying, learning, completing classes, and earning good grades. You can avoid this vicious cycle by looking at your schoolwork as academic work that "pays" you back in terms of completed courses and higher grades. By putting in more academic time to complete more courses and earn better grades, you are "paid" back by increasing the likelihood you will graduate, graduate sooner, and start earning a full-time salary as a college graduate that will pay you about twice as much money per hour than you earn doing part-time work without a college degree (plus benefits such as medical insurance, dental insurance, and paid vacation time). Furthermore, the time you put into earning higher grades while in college should pay off immediately in your first full-time position after college because research shows that among students graduating in the same field, those with higher grades are more likely to earn higher starting salaries (Pascarella & Terenzini, 2005). Thus, our bottom-line recommendation is: **Work for better grades now; work for better pay later.**

> **CLASSIC QUOTE**
>
> "I invested in myself—in study, in mastering my tools, in preparation. Many a man who is putting a few dollars a week into the bank would do much better to put it into himself."
>
> —Henry Ford, founder of the Ford Motor Co., and one of the richest people of his generation

You may need to defer or delay satisfying all your immediate material desires and postpone consumer gratification by making high-priced purchases later. Ultimately, financing a college education may require that you give serious thought to your current lifestyle choices and make firm decisions about what you can live with and live without. For example, a new set of wheels or a more private and spacious apartment may have to wait until you graduate.

Finally, be sure you take full advantage of your Financial Aid Office during your time in college. This is the campus resource that has been designed specifically to help you finance your college education. If you are in any way concerned about whether you are currently using the most effective strategy for financing your education, make an appointment of see a professional in your financial aid office. Also, periodically check with this office to see if you qualify for additional sources of income through different avenues, such as:

◆ part-time employment on campus,
◆ low-interest loans,
◆ grants, or
◆ scholarships.

Lastly, keep a watchful eye out for notices posted near your Financial Aid Office about financial-aid reminders, application deadlines and updates, as well as information about campus workshops designed to help you finance your education and manage your money.

Postponing immediate or impulsive satisfaction of material desires is a key element of effective college financing and long-term financial success.

Do you need to work part time to meet your college expenses?

If yes, do you have to work more than 15 hours per week to make ends meet?

If yes, is there anything you can do to change that?

••• Summary and Conclusion

Mastering the skills of managing time and money are critical for success in college and in life beyond college. If we can gain better control over these practical aspects of our life, we can gain greater control over the quality of our life. On the other hand, if we ignore either one of them, we run the risk of increasing our stress level and decreasing our performance level. For instance, research indicates that procrastinators often feel miserable about their habit (Tice & Baumeister, 1997) and the work they produce is of poorer quality (Steel, Brothen, & Wambach, 2001; Wesley, 1994). Poor time management with respect to financial matters actually costs people money; for example, reports from H & R Block indicates that procrastinating on filing tax returns costs Americans an average of $400 a year, due to errors resulting from last-minute rushing to meet the deadline (Kasper, 2004).

There are two key features of both money and time management that cause both of these habits to be candidates for potential problems:

1. They are habits that people can fall into and practice so routinely that they do them without conscious self-awareness, and
2. The negative consequences of bad time- and money-management habits build up gradually and are not fully felt until a later point in time. Many years of research shows that the further away an event in time is, the less likely humans are to think about it and factor it into their day-to-day choices and decisions (Lewin, 1935; Ainslie, 1975; Elster & Lowenstein, 1992).

> **CLASSIC QUOTE**
>
> *Many people take no care of their money till they come nearly to the end of it, and others do just the same with their time.*
>
> —Johan Wolgang von Goethe, German poet, dramatist, and author of the epic, *Faust*

Just as problems of time and money management may have common causes, they may also have common solutions. The recurring themes of effective time and money management indicate that we should use the following higher-level thinking skills and related practices.

1. We should engage in reflective *analysis* of how we spend our time and money. This will allow us to become more consciously aware of our time-spending and money-spending habits, and enable us to know where all our time and money actually go.
2. We should engage in *synthesis* that integrates or "connects" our current decisions with their short-range, mid-range, and long-range consequences. This will allow us to see how our present actions affect the total, long-term picture (e.g., how current choices and decisions affect what happens at the end of the term, at the end of college, and life after college).
3. We should evaluate our priorities and create a plan that ensures we put our time and money into what we value the most (e.g., success in college and life).
4. We should apply our plan by putting into practice effective time- and money-management strategies on a day-to-day basis. Studies show that when people repeatedly practice effective life-management strategies, these strategies gradually become part of their regular routine and develop into natural habits. For example, when procrastinators repeatedly practice effective time-management strategies with respect to tasks that they procrastinate on, their procrastination habits begin to fade away and are replaced by more effective time-management habits (Ainslie, 1992; Baumeister, et al., 1994). The same results have been found for effective money-management habits (Health & Soll, 1996; Walker, 1996). Thus, when we become aware of what effective actions we should take and perform these actions consistently, they tend to turn into productive lifelong habits.

These four themes appear to be the keys to effectively managing time and money. They may also be the keys to effectively managing life.

Learning More through Independent Research

Web-Based Resources for Further Information on Managing Time and Money

For additional information relating to the ideas discussed in this chapter, we recommend the following Web sites:

Time Management
www.counseling.uchicago.edu/resources/virtualpamphlets/time_management.shtml
www.time-management-guide.com/procrastination.html

Money Management
www.youngmoney.com/money_management
www.students.gov

Name _____ Date _____

Financial Self-Awareness: Monitoring Money and Tracking Cash Flow

DIRECTIONS:

Step 1.
Use the worksheet that follows these directions to estimate what you expect your income and expenses are per month, and enter them in column 2.

Step 2.
Track your actual income and expenses for a month and enter them in column 3. (To help you do this accurately, keep a file of your cash receipts, bills paid, and checking or credit records for the month.)

Step 3.
After one month of tracking your cash flow, answer the following questions:

1. Did you enter any sources of income or expenses that were not listed on the worksheet? (If yes, what were they?)

2. Were your estimates generally accurate?

3. What specific items or areas had the largest discrepancies between what you estimated they would be and what they actually were?

4. Comparing your bottom-line total for income and expenses, are you satisfied with how your monthly cash flow seems to be going?

5. What changes could you make to create more positive cash flow—i.e., to increase your income or savings and reduce your expenses or debt?

6. How likely is it that you would actually make the changes you mentioned in your response to question #5?

333

FINANCIAL SELF-AWARENESS WORKSHEET

	Estimate	Actual
Income Source:		
Parents/Family		
Work/Job		
Grants/Scholarships		
Loans		
Savings		
Others:		
TOTAL INCOME		
Essentials (Fixed Expenses)		
Living Expenses: Food/Groceries		
Rent/Room & Board		
Utilities (gas/electric)		
Clothing		
Laundry/Dry Cleaning		
Phone		
Computer		
Household Items (dishes, etc.)		
Medical Insurance Expenses		
Debt Payments (loans/credit cards)		
Others:		
School Expenses: Tuition		
Books		
Supplies (print cartridges, etc.)		
Special Fees (lab fees, etc.)		
Others:		
Transportation: Public Transportation (bus fees, etc.)		
Car Insurance		
Car Maintenance		
Fuel (gas)		
Car Payments		
Others:		
Incidentals (*Variable* Expenses)		
Entertainment: Movies/Concerts		
DVDs/CDs		
Restaurants (eating out)		
Personal Appearance/Accessories: Haircuts/Hairstyling		
Cosmetics/Manicures		
Fashionable Clothes		
Jewelry		
Others:		
Hobbies		
Travel (trips home, vacations)		
Gifts		
Others:		
TOTAL EXPENSES		

CASE STUDY

Procrastination: The Vicious Cycle

Delilah has a major paper due at the end of the term. It's now past midterm and she still hasn't started to work on her paper. She tells herself, "I should have started sooner."

However, Delilah continues to postpone starting her work on the paper and is now beginning to feel anxious and guilty about it. To relieve her growing anxiety and guilt, she starts doing other tasks instead, such as cleaning her room and returning e-mails to people who have written her. This makes Delilah feel a little better because these tasks keep her busy, take her mind off the term paper, and give her the feeling that at least she's getting something accomplished. Time continues to pass, and the deadline for the paper is dangerously close. Delilah now finds herself in a position of having lots of work to do and very little time to do it.

Based on the procrastination research and counseling experiences of Jane Burka and Lenora Yuen, as reported in, *Procrastination: Why You Do It, What to Do About It.*

Reflection and Discussion Questions

1. What do you predict Delilah will do at this point?

2. Why did you make this prediction?

3. What grade do you think Delilah will receive on her paper?

4. What do you think Delilah will do on the next term paper she's assigned?

5. Other than starting sooner, what recommendations would you have for Delilah (and other procrastinators like her) to break this "cycle of procrastination" and prevent it from happening over and over again?

Financial Planning

Dianne Cox, *Director of Financial Aid*

Outline

Part I. The Cost of Attending College
Part II. Dalton State College Financial Aid
    Types of Financial Aid
    Who Can Receive Financial Aid?
    How to Apply for Financial Aid
    Calculating Financial Need
    Financial Aid Disbursements
    Financial Aid Refunds and Book Charges
    Georgia HOPE Program
Exercise: Calculating a HOPE GPA
    How Dropping and Withdrawing from Classes
        Affects Financial Aid
    Satisfactory Academic Progress (SAP) for Financial Aid
    Other Financing Options
Part III. Managing Your Money
    Basic Rules of Money Management
    Budgeting
Exercise—Creating a Budget
    College Expenses Budget
    Monthly Budget
    Money Saving Tips
    The Credit Card Trap
    Student Loans
    Identity theft
Exercise: What is Your Identity Theft Probability (ITP) Score?
    Maintaining Good Credit
Sources
    Additional References

Good financial planning is essential to completing a college education. There are costs associated with going to college, and decisions to make about how these expenses will be paid. If you're working to help meet expenses, it can be quite a balancing act. Money—or the lack of it—is often a deciding factor on whether students stay in college. Financial issues are cited as one of the top reasons that Dalton State freshmen do not return for their sophomore year in college.[1]

In this chapter, you will learn about the costs associated with attending college and financial aid resources available to help you attend. We'll also cover how to maintain eligibility to receive financial aid. Financial management skills will also be introduced, since spending habits and credit card debt, not lack of financial aid, is also a key reason that students drop out of college.[2]

••• Part I. The Cost of Attending College

Tuition, fees, books, and supplies are direct costs to attend Dalton State College. But, there are other costs associated with going to college—travel expenses, and normal living costs, such as rent, utilities, and food. Figure 1 below displays the estimated total cost for a full-time freshman to attend Dalton State for Fall 2009 and Spring 2010 semesters.

Figure 1 Estimated cost of attendance—full-time freshman at Dalton State College

	On-campus	w/ parent	Off-campus
Tuition & Fees	2970	2970	2970
Books & Supplies	950	950	950
Room & Board	6550	2250	6750
Transportation	770	1925	1925
Misc. Expenses	990	990	990
Total—Georgia resident	12230	9085	13585
Additional tuition & fees- non-res	5520	5520	5520
Total—non-resident students	17750	14605	19105

The good news is that financial aid is available to help students pay for tuition, fees, books and supplies, as well as reasonable living expenses. In the next section we'll examine the financial aid programs offered at Dalton State College, including information on how to apply, who qualifies, and how to maintain eligibility for financial aid.

Part II. Dalton State College Financial Aid

There are plenty of financial resources to help you attend Dalton State College, and around 90% of Dalton State students take advantage of some type of financial assistance.[3] It's important to be aware of the resources available—there's more than just HOPE—and also how to avoid the pitfall of losing financial aid eligibility.

Types of Financial Aid

There are two broad categories of financial aid—gift aid and self-help aid. We'll examine each type in more detail in a subsequent section.

Gift aid is financial aid that does not have to be repaid. Gift aid programs include scholarships and grants.

Scholarships are awarded due to ability—most are awarded for academic ability, but some are based on community service work, and some use your family's ability to pay for college as a factor.

Grants are generally awarded based on financial need—that is, based on family finances.

Self-help aid requires something from the recipient. Self-help aid includes:

Work Study, which offers students a chance to work on campus for wages. Dalton State offers both Federal Work Study, which requires financial need, and Campus Work Study.

Student Loans are low-interest loans, with repayment starting after graduation or after dropping below half-time enrollment.

Who Can Receive Financial Aid?

In addition to program-specific criteria, only United States citizens and eligible non-citizens who meet the following conditions may receive federal and Georgia aid:

- Making satisfactory academic progress for financial aid (see page 10 for detailed information);
- Have no defaulted student loans or refunds due to federal or state grant programs;
- Have registered for Selective Service by age 18 (males);
- Have not been convicted of drug offenses while enrolled in college and receiving federal financial aid;
- Students in mini-certificate programs of fewer than 16 credit hours do not qualify for federal aid.

How to Apply for Financial Aid

Scholarships:

Dalton State College Foundation Scholarship applications are available in December in the Office of Student Financial Aid and online at www.daltonstate.edu/scholarships.htm. The deadline for complete scholarship applications is February 1.

Private Scholarships—Many students also receive scholarships through private foundations, community organizations, and businesses. Pay attention to scholarship postings in local newspapers and postings on campus regarding scholarship opportunities. Scholarship notices received by the Office of Student Financial Aid are posted online at www.daltonstate.edu/finaid/outside_scholarships.htm.

Scholarship Searches—Free searches may be found at www.fastweb.com and www.finaid.org. We recommend that you *never* pay anyone to find scholarships for you. With a few hours of research, you can generally find as much, if not more, information on your own. Also, don't forget to research scholarships at Roberts Library.

Georgia HOPE—There are two ways to apply for HOPE:

- Go to www.daltonstate.edu/finaid, select HOPE Application Instructions and follow the instructions.
- Complete the Free Application for Federal Student Aid (FAFSA) at www.fafsa.ed.gov. The FAFSA application must be completed *each* academic year. See the next section for more details.

Federal Grants, HOPE, Work Study, and Student Loans:

Complete the Free Application for Federal Student Aid (FAFSA) after January 1 of each year. We recommend that you complete your federal tax return before starting on the FAFSA. The FAFSA may be completed online at www.fafsa.ed.gov to speed up processing, or call 1-800-4FED-AID to request a paper FAFSA. **This process must be completed annually.**

To make the FAFSA process paperless, both student and parent (dependent students only) should apply for a Department of Education Personal Identification Number (PIN) at www.pin.ed.gov. The PIN serves as your signature for the online FAFSA. If you have previously filed a FAFSA, you have already been assigned a PIN by the federal processor. If you cannot locate your PIN, go to www.pin.ed.gov and request that it be resent to you.

What You're Applying for with the FAFSA

Besides the following federal programs, your FAFSA serves as your *HOPE* application.

Federal Pell Grant/Federal SEOG, and LEAP Grants—These grants are awarded to students with exceptional financial need. The Pell Grant amount is determined by the cost of attendance, the Expected Family Contribution calculated by the FAFSA processor, and the student's enrollment status. Eligibility for Federal SEOG and LEAP Grants is based upon Pell Grant eligibility and exceptional financial need. A FAFSA filed by the priority deadline is recommended (June 1 for Fall, October 1 for Spring, and March 1 for Summer).

The Academic Competitiveness Grant is awarded to Pell-eligible students in their first or second year of college who have graduated from a rigorous high school program of study. First year recipients must have graduated from high school after January 1, 2006, and second year recipients after January 1, 2005. Second year students must have 30 earned hours with a 3.0 cumulative GPA to receive the Academic Competitiveness Grant at Dalton State College. Awards may not exceed unmet need.

SMART Grants are awarded to Pell-eligible students enrolled in their junior or senior year of study in Math, Biology, or Chemistry. To qualify, students must have a 3.0 cumulative GPA, including transfer hours, and be enrolled in classes necessary for their major; cumulative GPA is checked each semester before the SMART Grant is awarded. Students may receive up to $4,000 per academic year in SMART Grant funds, but awards may not exceed unmet need.

Work Study—A limited number of jobs are available on campus, with work schedules planned around student class schedules. Student workers receive a paycheck every other week for hours worked. Besides the FAFSA, a Campus Employment Application must be completed in the Office of Student Financial Aid. Students eligible for Federal Work Study (based on financial need) are invited to attend a Work Study Fair during the first week of class.

Stafford Loan—Students enrolled at least half-time (6 hours)* in programs eligible for federal aid may borrow low-interest Stafford Loans. There are two types of Federal Stafford Loans: 1) Subsidized—for students with financial need. The federal government pays the interest while the student is enrolled at least half-time and during the six-month grace period. For loans made after July 1, 2009, the interest rate on the Subsidized Stafford Loan is 5.6%; 2) Unsubsidized—the student pays the interest while in school and during the six-month grace period, or requests that the interest be added to the balance of the loan. The Unsubsidized Stafford Loan interest rate is 6.8%. For application instructions and detailed information on the Stafford Loan program, visit http://www.daltonstate.edu/finaid/loans.htm.

Financial Aid Deadlines

The deadline to submit Dalton State Scholarship applications is February 1. Priority deadlines for HOPE and federal aid applications (FAFSA) are listed below by semester. If an application is not filed by this date, aid may not be available when tuition and fees are due for the term. Students filing a FAFSA by the priority deadline date receive priority consideration for grants with limited funding.

Fall Semester	June 1
Spring Semester	October 1
Summer Semester	March 1

Dependency Status

Students applying for federal aid for the 2009–2010 year answer the questions in Figure 2 to determine dependency status for federal aid—you're considered "dependent" if you have to include your parents' financial information and "independent" if you don't.

Students who answer NO to all the questions listed above are considered dependent students, and must provide parent/stepparent income and investment information on their FAFSA application. Consult the FAFSA application for detailed information about which parent's (and stepparent, if married) information to report if your parents are divorced.

Federal regulations define a parent as a biological or adoptive parent. A legal guardian, foster parent, or grandparent is not considered a parent, and their information should not be used to complete the FAFSA. An appeal of dependency status may be made if a situation exists in your family that makes it unreasonable or impossible for you to obtain your parents' income and asset information. Examples include abandonment, parental drug/alcohol abuse, parental mental incapacity, physical or emotional abuse, parental incarceration, or severe estrangement. Dependency Status Appeal forms are available in the Office of Student Financial Aid.

What to Expect After You Complete a Financial Aid Application

The primary way the Office of Student Financial Aid contacts students regarding the status of aid applications is Dalton State College email, accessed through DSConnect. Review of your financial aid application normally takes place within two to four weeks after your financial aid

Figure 2 Dependency Status Questions

☐ Yes	☐ No	Were you born before January 1, 1986?
☐ Yes	☐ No	As of today, are you married?
☐ Yes	☐ No	Do you have children who receive more than half of their support from you?*
☐ Yes	☐ No	Do you have dependents (other than your children or your spouse) who live with you and receive more than half their support from you—now and through June 30, 2009?*
☐ Yes	☐ No	Are you currently serving on active duty in the U.S. Armed Forces for purposes other than training?
☐ Yes	☐ No	Are you a veteran of the U.S. Armed Forces?
☐ Yes	☐ No	When you were age 13 or older, were both of your parents deceased, were you in foster care or were you a ward/dependent of the court?
☐ Yes	☐ No	As of today, are you an emancipated minor as determined by a court in your state of legal residence?
☐ Yes	☐ No	As of today, are you in legal guardianship as determined by a court in your state of legal residence?
☐ Yes	☐ No	At any time on or after July 1, 2008, did your high school or school district homeless liaison determine that you were an unaccompanied youth who was homeless?
☐ Yes	☐ No	At any time on or after July 1, 2008, did the director of an emergency shelter program funded by the U.S. Department of Housing and Urban Development determine that you were an unaccompanied youth who was homeless?
☐ Yes	☐ No	At any time on or after July 1, 2008, did the director of a runaway or homeless youth basic center or transitional living program determine that you were an unaccompanied youth who was homeless or were self-supporting and at risk of being homeless?

*If you are independent ONLY because you have a child or a legal dependent, you must be able to provide documentation that you have income sufficient to provide *more than half* of their support. If not, you are required to provide parent information on your FAFSA application.

file is complete. Satisfactory Academic Progress for Financial Aid (see page 317) is reviewed for students, including transfer hours, when an aid application is received.

Students eligible for aid are emailed or mailed an award letter identifying the type and amount of financial aid being offered to them by Dalton State College. Students also receive notification if they do not qualify for HOPE and/or the Federal Pell Grant. Financial aid offers may be viewed through DSConnect; from the Banner menu select Student & Financial Aid Menu, then Financial Aid, then Financial Aid Award Letter.

FAFSA Filers Only: Students selected for *verification* must provide the Office of Student Financial Aid with a Verification Worksheet and submit signed copies of all required federal income tax returns and W2s. Additional documentation may be required after an initial review. If discrepancies occur between the information on the initial FAFSA and verification documentation, corrections are submitted electronically to the federal processor. The verification process must be complete in order to receive federal aid.

Calculating Financial Need

Financial need is required to qualify for need-based aid programs, such as federal grants. Financial need is calculated using the following formula:

Cost of Attendance − Expected Family Contribution (EFC) = Financial Need

Cost of Attendance: An estimate of the educational expenses a student will incur during an academic year. We presented an estimate of costs for entering Dalton State freshmen in Figure 1 on page 306. These expenses include direct costs (tuition and fees, books and supplies) and related educational expenses (living, transportation, and other miscellaneous expenses).

Expected Family Contribution (EFC): The US Department of Education calculates the Expected Family Contribution based on financial information provided on the Free Application for Federal Student Aid (FAFSA). The EFC calculation compares income and assets against standard living allowances based on the number of people in the household. FAFSA on the Web filers receive an estimate of their EFC when the application is completed online, and the federal processor also mails or e-mails a Student Aid Report to the applicant which includes the EFC.

Financial Need: The difference between the Cost of Attendance and the Expected Family Contribution (EFC).

The FAFSA is filed every year, since family income can vary from year to year. Income reported on the FAFSA is from the prior tax year. If the student's or parents' financial situation changes drastically due to circumstances such as illness, disability, unemployment, divorce or death of parent or spouse, request an Income Adjustment appeal from the Office of Student Financial Aid and Veteran Services.

Financial Aid Disbursements

Financial aid is first applied towards tuition, fees, and any book charges made through the Dalton State College Bookstore. If the financial aid award for a semester exceeds these charges, a financial aid refund is issued. At Dalton State, financial aid refunds are issued through HigherOne, Inc., a one-card banking and electronic funds disbursement system.

Students are mailed a HigherOne-issued debit card approximately two weeks after being admitted to the college. After receiving the HigherOne card, students choose a refund option at www.EasyRefundCard.com from the following choices:

- Refund balance placed into the HigherOne account. Funds may be withdrawn at an ATM machine on campus or at compatible off-campus ATMs ($500 per day limit), or the HigherOne card may be used as a debit card at merchants that accept MasterCard.
- Direct deposit into an existing checking or savings account.

Even students without financial aid should activate their HigherOne account, since this is the way that tuition refunds are distributed as well.

Financial Aid Refunds and Book Charges

HOPE Recipients: The HOPE book allowance is distributed through HigherOne, Inc., the week before classes begin for pre-registered students, with the exceptions listed below. Because HOPE does not cover all fees, students awarded *only* HOPE funds must either 1) sign an authorization form allowing Dalton State to take fees not covered by HOPE out of the HOPE book allowance, or 2) pay the additional fee amount not covered by HOPE to the

Figure 3 Financial Aid Eligibility Chart—*Not All Students Are Eligible for the Prorated Amount

Enrollment Status for Financial Aid

	Hope Scholarship/ Grant	Pell Grant	ACG/ SMART Grant	Stafford Loan	Campus Jobs
Full Time 12 Hours or more	Eligible	Eligible	Eligible	Eligible	Eligible
¾ Time 9 to 11 Hours	Eligible- Prorated Amount	Eligible- Prorated Amount	Eligible- Prorated Amount	Eligible	Eligible
½ Time 6 to 8 Hours	Eligible- Prorated Amount	Eligible- Prorated Amount	Eligible- Prorated Amount	Eligible	Eligible
Less than ½ time 5 or fewer Hours	Eligible- Prorated Amount	Eligible- Prorated Amount *	Not Eligible	Not Eligible	Not Eligible

Dalton State College Business Office prior to receiving the HOPE book allowance. Log into your DSConnect account and select Student Financial Aid Funds Authorization from the Banner menu to complete the authorization form.

Students who are not awarded HOPE until the week before classes begin may charge books in the Dalton State Bookstore through the fourth day of classes, as long as there is a credit balance available. Any credit remaining from the HOPE book allowance is distributed through HigherOne, Inc. at the end of the second week of classes, or within two weeks of the student receiving their award notification.

Federal Aid Recipients: Pre-registered students awarded federal aid prior to the beginning of the term may charge books in the Dalton State Bookstore through the fourth day of classes (if a credit balance remains after tuition, fees and housing charges are paid); remaining credit balances are distributed at the end of the second week of classes. Students awarded federal aid after classes begin may expect financial aid refunds within two weeks of receiving their award notification. **Exception:** Stafford Loans are not credited until funds are received from the lender. The first Stafford Loan disbursements for freshmen borrowers are not released until 30 days after school begins.

Enrollment status for financial aid purposes is determined at the end of the Drop/Add period each semester. The last day to drop in each term can be found in the college catalog; you may also access the academic calendar through www.daltonstate.edu—use DSC Quick Jump to go to Semester Schedule, then Academic Calendars.

Eligibility for financial aid is adjusted according to a student's enrollment status at the end of the Drop/Add period. HOPE and Pell Grant may be received for just one class; however eligibility for aid is prorated based on enrollment status, as direct college costs are less with fewer credit hours. Consult Figure 3 on page 312 for information on the aid available at different enrollment statuses.

Only classes taken for credit are eligible for financial aid. Audited and credit-by-exam (CLEP) classes are not eligible for aid.

C Session Classes: HOPE book allowances and federal grant aid for C session classes are applied to student accounts the week before C session begins. For students enrolled in both A or B and C session classes, this may delay any financial aid refund until the week before C session begins, and may even mean the student shows a balance due the college until that time.

Georgia HOPE Program

Almost 60% of Dalton State financial aid recipients receive HOPE Grant or Scholarship funds, so let's examine the HOPE program in more detail. To qualify for HOPE funding, students must be Georgia residents for at least one year. Eligible non-citizens must have eligible noncitizen status for at least one year prior to receiving HOPE funding.

As stated in the previous section, you do not have to be a full-time student to receive HOPE. For eligible students, HOPE pays 100% of tuition for *required classes* in the student's major program and partial fees. There is also a HOPE Book allowance of $150 per semester for 6 or more credit hours, or $75 per semester for five or fewer credit hours. HOPE may be received for a maximum of 127 combined-paid hours (HOPE Grant, Scholarship and ACCEL—for high school students taking college-level classes).

HOPE Grants are for students enrolled in Technical Division certificate or mini-certificate programs. The HOPE Grant may be received for a maximum of 63 paid hours.

HOPE Scholarships are for HOPE Scholars who enroll in associate and bachelor's degree programs. Students who were not HOPE Scholars following high school graduation may qualify for the HOPE Scholarship after attempting 30, 60, or 90 college credit hours with a 3.0 HOPE Grade Point Average (GPA).

HOPE Scholarship recipients must have a HOPE GPA of 3.0 at the end of each Spring Semester and after 30, 60, and 90 attempted hours. The HOPE GPA is calculated using all college credit hours—Dalton State and transfer hours. Students with attempted credit hours (Dalton State and transfer hours) of 127 hours or more do not qualify for the HOPE Scholarship.

Finding Your HOPE GPA on DSConnect

At the end of the 2004–2005 school year, 72% of first-year HOPE Scholars at Dalton State lost HOPE Scholarship eligibility. In order to make sure you don't become part of this statistic, it's important to know when and how you will be evaluated for on-going HOPE Scholarship eligibility.

Degree-seeking students may access their HOPE GPA on DSConnect. From the Banner menu select *Financial Aid*, then *HOPE Eligibility and HOPE GPA*. The HOPE GPA displayed is as of the last term grades were submitted. However, eligibility for HOPE is based on HOPE GPA after *certain* terms—after each Spring term (HOPE may be lost but not gained at a Spring checkpoint), and after 30, 60, and 90 attempted hours. For example, a student with a HOPE GPA of 2.9 after 30 attempted hours cannot regain the HOPE Scholarship with a 3.2 GPA after 42 attempted hours. This student must keep their HOPE GPA over 3.0 after attempting 60 hours, which is the next point they may gain HOPE Scholarship eligibility. Keep this in mind as you review your HOPE GPA on DSConnect.

Calculating a HOPE Grade Point Average (GPA)

The HOPE GPA is calculated for students in degree-seeking programs (associate and bachelor's) using all Dalton State college grades, plus all transfer hours. Here are how certain classes factor into your HOPE GPA:

Learning Support Classes—Learning Support classes count as attempted hours, but, since there are no letter grades, they will not count in your HOPE GPA. If you take *all* Learning Support classes in Fall and Spring Semester of your freshmen year, you will lose HOPE at the Spring checkpoint. If this happens, you may regain HOPE Scholarship eligibility after attempting 12 additional hours with a HOPE GPA of 3.0.

College Preparatory Curriculum (CPC)—Grades from these classes are included in your HOPE GPA, although they are not included in your Dalton State institutional GPA.

Name _____ Date _____

Exercise: Calculating a HOPE GPA

Let's calculate a HOPE GPA. Letter grades are given values used to calculate your GPA. The value assigned to a letter grade is multiplied by the number of credit hours for that course, to find the quality points (used in the GPA formula) earned for this course. Below are the values assigned to letter grades:

  A = 4
  B = 3
  C = 2
  D = 1
  F = 0

So, for example, if you receive a grade of A in a 3 credit hours class, you calculate the value of that class in the GPA formula by multiplying 3 (credit hours) by 4 (value of A grade) to get 12 quality points. You divide the total quality points by GPA credit hours to get your Grade Point Average. Learning Support classes do not factor into your Grade Point Average—you receive a grade of S (Satisfactory), IP (In Progress), or U (Unsatisfactory) for these courses.

Example—a student's Fall HOPE GPA is calculated below.

Fall Semester

Classes	Grade	Credit Hours	GPA Hours	Quality Points
First Year Experience	A	2	2	8
College Algebra	B	3	3	9
Learning Support English	U	4	0	0
Learning Support Reading	U	4	0	0
Fall Semester TOTAL		13	5	17

Fall Semester GPA is calculated by dividing total Quality Points by GPA hours:

  17 Quality Points ÷ 5 GPA hours = 3.4 GPA

This student has a 3.4 HOPE GPA after his/her first semester. Now calculate this student's *cumulative* (all terms enrolled) GPA after Spring Semester. Does this student keep the HOPE Scholarship at the Spring Checkpoint?

Spring Semester

Classes	Grade	Credit Hours	GPA Hours	Quality Hours
Fundamentals of Speech	C	3		
Weight Training	B	1		
Learning Support Reading	S	4		
Learning Support English	S	4		
Spring Semester TOTAL		12		

Now, calculate this student's cumulative HOPE GPA at the Spring Checkpoint. The cumulative GPA covers all terms enrolled.

Cumulative HOPE GPA = $\dfrac{\text{Fall Semester Quality Points} + \text{Spring Semester Quality Points}}{\text{Fall Semester GPA Hours} + \text{Spring Semester GPA Hours}}$

Cumulative HOPE GPA = $\dfrac{17 + \underline{}}{5 + \underline{}}$ = _____ = _____ HOPE GPA

How Dropping and Withdrawing from Classes Affects Financial Aid

Dropped classes or withdrawals may result in the suspension of financial aid—we'll cover this in the next section under Course Completion Rate and Maximum Timeframe, which are part of the Satisfactory Academic Progress calculation. Class attendance is monitored at the beginning of each term; students who never attend class(es) or stop attending are considered unofficially withdrawn. Aid recipients may be required to pay back all or a portion of aid if they withdraw, officially or unofficially.

If aid is received for classes later dropped or cancelled, money may be due back to financial aid programs. Check with the Office of Student Financial Aid before dropping classes to determine how the drop or withdrawal may affect your financial aid. The complete financial aid withdrawal policy is available in the Office of Student Financial Aid and in the Dalton State catalog.

Satisfactory Academic Progress (SAP) for Financial Aid

The calculation of Satisfactory Academic Progress is separate from the HOPE GPA calculation. The Grade Point Average (GPA) requirement is a lot lower than the HOPE GPA requirement, yet you can have a 4.0 GPA and still lose eligibility for financial aid, including the HOPE Scholarship. That's because Satisfactory Academic Progress standards include measures other than GPA, and the most common reason that students lose eligibility for aid is because they drop too many classes.

Federal regulations require institutions of higher education to establish minimum standards of Satisfactory Academic Progress (SAP) for students receiving federal aid. These standards apply to state aid and institutional work-study as well, and to all financial aid applicants, regardless of whether financial aid was received during the academic term(s) under review and regardless of when the classes were taken.

Satisfactory Academic Progress Standards

Students must meet requirements in all three areas listed below in order to make satisfactory academic progress: Grade Point Average, Course Completion Rate, and Maximum Time Frame.

Grade Point Average (GPA)

The minimum GPA for financial aid recipients is governed by Dalton State academic performance standards. In order to retain financial aid eligibility, the student must maintain the following cumulative GPAs based on Dalton State GPA.

1–14 GPA hours	1.0 cumulative GPA
15–29 GPA hours	1.6 cumulative GPA
30–44 GPA hours	1.8 cumulative GPA
45+ GPA hours	2.0 cumulative GPA

Financial aid is automatically suspended after a term where all grades are F, U, WF and/or WU, or a combination of these grades and Ws, or you are withdrawn from classes for nonattendance.

Course Completion Rate

Financial aid recipients must pass at least 67% of all hours attempted. Semester hours attempted include all hours on a transcript since high school graduation, except audit and credit-by-exam hours. Only grades of A, B, C, D, S and IP are considered satisfactory and passing for financial aid purposes.

Course Completion Rate is calculated by dividing cumulative earned hours by cumulative attempted hours. View your academic transcript on DSConnect to find these hours—from the Banner menu, select Student Menu, Student Records, Academic Transcript, then Submit. Scroll all the way down to the bottom to view your cumulative transcript totals.

Here is an example of what you'll see when you view your transcript on DSConnect:

TRANSCRIPT TOTALS (UNDERGRADUATE SEMESTER)

	Attempted Hours	Passed Hours	Earned Hours	GPA Hours	Quality Points	GPA
Total Institution	25.00	10.00	10.00	10.00	25.00	2.50
Total Transfer	0.00	0.00	0.00	0.00	0.00	0.00
Overall	25.00	10.00	10.00	10.00	25.00	2.50

This student's GPA is fine, but let's calculate Course Completion Rate. Divide Overall Earned Hours by Overall Attempted Hours to find this student's Course Completion Rate:

$$\frac{\text{Overall Earned Hours}}{\text{Overall Attempted Hours}} = \frac{10.00}{25.00} = .40 \text{ or a 40\% Course Completion Rate}$$

The following are considered when evaluating Course Completion Rate:

- Withdrawals (W, WF, WU), incompletes (I), failures (F), and unsatisfactory (U) grades are considered attempted, but not earned hours.
- Repeated courses and courses for which the student has been granted academic renewal are included in the calculation of both attempted and earned hours. Refer to the appropriate catalog for an explanation of how course repeats affect GPA.
- Audited courses are not considered in credits attempted or earned.
- Learning Support courses are included in the calculation of both attempted and earned hours. Financial aid will not pay for learning support classes in excess of 30 attempted hours.
- *Transfer credits*, including those earned during transient study, do not count in the calculation of your Dalton State GPA, but *are included in the calculation of both attempted and earned hours* to determine Course Completion Rate.

Maximum Time Frame

Eligible students may receive financial aid for up to 150% of the number of semester hours required to earn a degree or certificate. Attempted hours include both Dalton State and transfer hours, no matter when the classes were taken. Find the maximum attempted hours allowed by your program of study at www.daltonstate.edu/finaid/satisfactory_progress.htm.

Attempted hours for maximum timeframe are calculated in the following way:

Students with no prior certificates or degrees—all attempted hours (both Dalton State and transfer) count towards the maximum timeframe.

Students with Prior Certificates or Degrees—Students with prior certificates or degrees are given additional time to pursue additional educational goals; however, the following limits will be applied:

- A maximum of two degrees or certificates at the same level will be allowed.
- The overall maximum timeframe, based on the student's highest degree level is: Certificate—120 hours; Associate Degree—175 hours; Bachelor's degree—225 hours.

Students may be required to appeal to document certificates/degrees earned at other institutions.

When SAP Reviews Occur

Financial Aid Satisfactory Academic Progress is reviewed after Spring Semester (exceptions—students in the following scenarios are reviewed each term: 1) no passing grades for the term; 2) MINI certificate majors, due to program length; 3) students receiving aid under a SAP appeal waiver). Suspension notices are emailed within 48 business hours of the "grades due to Enrollment Services" date on the semester calendar. Financial aid applicants are also reviewed when application is made, if SAP status has not been evaluated since the last term enrolled at Dalton State, or if the student has transfer hours. Students not meeting the requirements listed above will be placed on probation or suspension. The Office of Student Financial Aid notifies students when they are on probation or suspended from receiving financial aid.

Probation—Students who do not meet the minimum GPA and/or course completion rate standards are placed on financial aid probation. During the semester of probation, the student is eligible to receive financial assistance.

- Probationary period—the probationary period ends at the end of the Spring Semester for students in Bachelor's, Associate and Certificate programs, and after the next term attended for MINI Certificate students, due to program length.
- GPA—a probationary period is allowed for students whose cumulative GPA falls below the minimum GPAs indicated on p. 317. *Exception: financial aid is automatically suspended after a term where all grades are F, WF and/or U in combination w/Ws.*
- Course Completion Rate—a probationary period is allowed for students whose cumulative course completion rate is below 67%.
- There is no probationary period for maximum timeframe.

At the end of the probationary period, the student will be removed from probationary status if all three financial aid satisfactory academic progress standards are met.

Suspension—If the above standards are not met, the student is placed on financial aid suspension. Eligibility may be regained by meeting all three financial aid satisfactory academic progress standards, or aid *may* be reinstated by appeal. Students who violate the Maximum Time Frame rule are automatically placed on financial aid suspension.

Appeal Procedure

Students on financial aid suspension may appeal in writing to the Director of Financial Aid, Pope Student Center, Room 15, 650 College Drive, Dalton, GA 30720, phone # (706) 272-4545, fax # (706) 272-2458. Appeals must be in writing, preferably using the Dalton State authorized appeal form. Documentation of mitigating circumstances, which may include medical problems, illness or death in the family, relocation, or employment changes is encouraged. Students who reference potential disabilities or mental health concerns in their appeal are referred to Disability Support Services and/or Counseling and Career Services for additional resources. Further documentation may be required. The director's decision may be appealed to the Satisfactory Academic Progress Appeals Committee. If an appeal is approved, the director or Committee may set specific terms for reinstatement of financial aid, which must be met in order for the student to receive aid. Appeal forms are available in the Forms section at www.daltonstate.edu/finaid, or in the Office of Student Financial Aid.

Appeal Deadlines

Appeals must be received in the Office of Student Financial Aid at least *one week* before the beginning of a term in order to have an appeal decision before the term begins. Appeals are reviewed on an on-going basis by the director. The SAP Appeals Committee will meet within the week before the beginning of each term. Appeal decisions are mailed or e-mailed within one week of review.

Other Financing Options

Besides the federal and Georgia aid programs reviewed at the beginning of this chapter, there are additional sources of aid available for eligible students. Some of these programs are summarized below.

Veteran Benefits and Veteran Dependent Benefits are available to qualified veterans and children of deceased or 100% disabled veterans. Active duty military personnel may have tuition benefits available through the military as well. A veteran certification official is available in the Office of Student Financial Aid and Veteran Services to provide more information and applications.

The ***HERO Scholarship*** provides educational grant assistance to members of the Georgia National Guard and U.S. Military Reservists who served in combat zones, or the children of such members of the Georgia National Guard and U.S. Military Reserves. See the Office of Student Financial Aid or www.gacollege411.org for more details.

Vocational Rehabilitation services may be available to students with physical or mental disabilities that impact ability to go to work. More information on Rehabilitation Services in Northwest Georgia is available at www.CareerDepot.org.

The ***Workforce Investment Act (WIA)*** provides college funding for students who meet specific criteria under the Workforce Investment Act, aimed at helping adult students retrain and update skills. Funding may also be available to assist with childcare and transportation. More information on Workforce Investment Training Programs is available at www.CareerDepot.org.

American Indian students may qualify for assistance through the ***Bureau of Indian Affairs' (BIA)*** Office of Indian Education. To qualify for funding, you must be at least one-quarter American Indian. Applications are available from the education office of the Tribe you are affiliated with.[4]

••• Part III. Managing Your Money

Good financial planning is an essential skill; however, money management can be especially difficult while you're attending college, since you may not be working, or you may be working fewer hours. Setting the goal of earning a college degree can be financially rewarding in the long run, and worth some financial sacrifices while you're attending college. People with bachelor's degrees, on average, earn a million dollars more in their lifetime than someone with a high school diploma.[5]

Basic Rules of Money Management

These ten basic rules of money management are provided in *The Road to Financial Health*, a publication produced by the Georgia Student Finance Commission and Consumer Credit Counseling Service:[6]

1. **Plan**—Plan for the future, major purchases, and periodic expenses.
2. **Set Financial Goals**—Determine short and long term financial goals.
3. **Know your financial situation**—Determine monthly living expenses, periodic expenses, and monthly debt payments. Compare expenses to monthly net income. Be aware of your total indebtedness.
4. **Develop a realistic spending plan**—Follow your budget as closely as possible. Evaluate your budget. Compare actual expenses with planned expenses.
5. **Don't allow expenses to exceed income**—Avoid paying only the minimum on your charge cards. Don't charge more every month than you are repaying to your creditors.
6. **Save**—Save for periodic expenses, such as car and home maintenance. Save 5 to 10% of your net income. Accumulate 3 to 6 months salary in an emergency fund.
7. **Pay your bills on time**—Maintain a good credit rating. If you are unable to pay your bills as agreed, contact your creditors and explain your situation. Contact Consumer Credit Counseling Service for professional advice.
8. **Determine the difference between wants and needs**—Take care of your needs first. Money should be spent for wants only after needs have been met.
9. **Use credit wisely**—Use credit for safety, convenience, and planned purchases. Determine the total you can comfortably afford to purchase on credit. Don't allow your credit payments to exceed 20% of your net income. Avoid borrowing from one creditor to pay another.
10. **Keep a record of daily expenditures**—Be aware of where your money is going. Use a spending diary to assist you in identifying areas where adjustments need to be made.

While some of these financial rules may be harder to follow while you're attending college, it's important to develop good habits during your college years. An especially important concept is living within your means, which means developing a realistic spending plan. Let's examine budgeting in more detail.

Budgeting

The concept of developing a budget is relatively simple in theory—figure your monthly income and your monthly expenses, then adjust monthly expenses as necessary to make sure they don't exceed monthly income. In reality, it can be pretty tough to make—and stick—to a budget. However, it is an important part of overall "financial health."

Name _____ Date _____

Exercise—Creating a Budget

It's a bit different to create a budget while you're attending college, since some of your expenses don't occur every month, but just two or three times per year. First, calculate your per semester college expenses. If you're a full-time student, you can use Figure 1 on page 306 to figure full-time tuition and an estimate of books and supplies; just divide by two to find the per semester amount.

College Expenses Budget

College Expenses—One Semester	Semester Amount
Tuition and Fees	$
Books	$
Supplies	$
Total Expenses	$
Resources to pay college expenses	$
Financial aid—scholarships	$
Financial aid— grants	$
Financial aid—student loan	$
Veteran benefits	$
Money from parents/relative/employer	$
Earnings from work	$
Other	$
Total Resources	$
Subtract Total Expenses from Total Resources	$

Subtract Total Expenses from Total Resources to find the bottom line figure. If this number is a negative number, you need to find additional resources to pay for college costs. Consult the information in Part II of this chapter, or visit the Office of Student Financial Aid to inquire about additional funding sources.

If the difference between Total Expenses and Total Resources is a positive number because of financial assistance, divide this number by 4—the number of months in a semester—to figure out the amount of assistance you should have available to pay for monthly living expenses.

Total College Expenses $ _____

Minus Total Resources $ _____ = $ _____

Positive Net Resources $ _____ ÷ 4 = $ _____ monthly resource

Now, estimate your monthly income and expenses. If you can't estimate your monthly expenses, start keeping track of daily expenditures to see where your money is going.

Monthly Budget

Income	Monthly Amount
Monthly net income from work (take home pay)	$
Spouse's net income from work	$
Monthly resource from financial assistance calculated above	$
Other monthly income source:	$
Other monthly income source:	$
Total Income	$
Expenses	**Monthly Amount**
Monthly Rent or Mortgage Payment	$
Home maintenance and repairs (home owners only)	$
Utilities—electric, gas, water	$
Phone bill(s)	$
Groceries/cleaning supplies/toiletries	$
Food away from home	$
Insurance—medical, car, life	$
Car payment	$
Gasoline	$
Car maintenance—oil changes and other maintenance	$
Child care expenses	
Monthly medical bills	$
Clothing—purchases, dry cleaning	$
Personal care—hair cut/color, nails	$
Charitable contributions—charities, church donations	$
Recreation—movie rental, concerts and sporting events, CDs/DVDs, travel, lottery tickets	$
Gifts/cards	$
Loan payments (credit cards, student loan)	$
Savings	$
Other Expense:	$
Other Expense:	$
Total Expenses	$

Subtract Total Expenses from Total Income to make sure you have enough money to cover monthly expenses.

Total Income $ _____

minus Total Expenses $ _____ = $ _____

If the difference is a positive number, you can actually put more money into savings. If the difference is negative you need to either increase your income or decrease your spending. The section on page 327 includes tips on decreasing spending.

Money Saving Tips

If your monthly expenses are greater than your monthly income, then you need to take a hard look at some of your expenses. Are some of your expenditures things you *want*, but don't *need?*

Here are some ideas for saving money:

- Get a roommate
- Buy used text books
- Use the labs on campus instead of buying a computer
- Brown bag lunches at least part of the time
- Use coupons for groceries and buy store brands
- Use e-mail instead of making long-distance calls
- Request basic phone service only
- Rent movies or go to matinees
- Eat at home instead of dining out
- Shop at consignment stores and discount stores
- Eliminate cable television
- Buy used furniture
- Pursue free or low-cost activities—such as biking, hiking, tennis, reading
- Purchase a low-cost vehicle—used instead of new
- Make an effort to save money on utilities, such as turning off lights in unoccupied rooms

The Credit Card Trap

It can be tempting to fill that gap between income and expenses with credit card purchases—but you'll pay in the long run . . . and pay! College students are targeted for credit card offers,[7] so beware of the temptation to use plastic to buy things you can't afford.

If you feel you need to have a credit card, limit yourself to one major credit card and use it for emergencies only. Before you purchase something with your credit card, give a good, hard look at whether you **really need** to purchase the item or service. Do you need to or just **want to?** Also, make sure you have enough income to pay the resulting monthly bill. Ideally, you should pay your credit card balance in full every month.

Selecting a credit card

If you decide to take out a credit card, here are some things you should compare:

- Annual Percentage Rate (APR)—look for the lowest annual interest rate.
- Annual fee—look for a card with no annual fee.
- Grace Period—this is the amount of time before interest charges begin after you make your purchase; some credit cards don't have a grace period. Since the goal is to pay your bill in full every month, you want a credit card with a grace period.
- Transaction fees—you'll pay more to use your credit card for cash advances, and a higher interest rate as well. Also, you may be slapped with a large late fee if you make a payment late.

Look for the best credit card terms online at www.bankrate.com.

The Lure of the Minimum Payment

It's tempting to use that credit card and only make the minimum monthly payment. But what does that cost you? The credit card calculator on www.bankrate.com was used to gather the information in Figure 4 - If you purchase an item on a credit card for $2,000, **purchase no further items**, and only pay the minimum balance, here's what you will pay, and for how long, at different interest rates:

Figure 4 Repayment of $2,000 Credit Card Balance Using Minimum Monthly Payments

Interest Rate	Time Needed to Repay	Total interest paid on $2000 purchase	Total purchase price
12%	158 months (13 years)	$1,180.05	$3,180.05
15%	184 months (15 years)	$1,758.16	$3,758.16
18%	222 months (18.5 years)	$2,615.43	$4,615.43
21%	284 months (almost 24 years)	$4,027.61	$6,027.61

Other Credit Card Tips

Here are some other tips regarding credit cards from the Consumer Response Center of the Federal Deposit Insurance Corporation (FDIC):[8]

- Avoid using multiple credit cards.
- Cancel unnecessary or unused credit cards.
- Make sure to keep your address updated with your credit card company.
- Keep copies of sales slips and compare with your bill when it arrives. If you find a billing error, put it in writing to the credit card company. Include your name, address, account number, and a description of the error.
- Do not let a friend use your credit card.
- Ignore offers to reduce or skip payments.

Student Loans

A better option for students than credit cards is a student loan. While this is the *last* type of financial aid you should consider, the terms of the student loan beat that of a credit card. Plus, if you qualify for a Subsidized Stafford Loan—you have to show financial need—you won't even be charged interest on the loan while you're in school at least half-time. However, regardless of family income, you can take out a Stafford Loan, as long as you don't have enough financial aid to pay your entire Cost of Attendance (see page 306 of this chapter). For application instructions and detailed information on the Stafford Loan program, visit http://www.daltonstate.edu/finaid/loans.htm. Let's look at some details on the Federal Stafford Loan Program.

Repayment begins six months after you graduate or drop below half-time enrollment. This six-month grace period is to allow you time to find a job before repayment begins on your Stafford Loan. You pick the private lender you want to use when you borrow a Stafford Loan at Dalton

State College. While the interest rate is the same because it's determined by the federal government, lenders offer different incentives for on-time and electronic payments, so you'll pay even less if you make on-time payments to take advantage of these incentives.

Subsidized Stafford Loan: You must have financial need (based on FAFSA results) to qualify for the Subsidized Stafford Loan. The interest rate for Subsidized Loans borrowed between July 1, 2009 and June 30, 2009 is 5.6%. You don't pay interest on a Subsidized Stafford Loan while in school or during grace or deferment periods—the government pays it for you.

Unsubsidized Stafford Loan: This version of the Federal Stafford Loan is not based on financial need. The borrower is responsible for all interest charges on an Unsubsidized Stafford Loan from the time the loan is received. The interest rate on Unsubsidized Stafford Loans is 6.8%. While you are not required to make payments while you're in school or during grace or deferment periods, we recommend that you pay interest quarterly. Any accrued interest that is not paid will be added (capitalized) to the loan balance when you enter repayment.

Annual Loan Limits: Federal Stafford Loan limits for a 12-month period (Fall-Spring-Summer) are:

- $3500 for freshmen
- $4500 for sophomores
- $5500 for students seeking a Bachelor's degree at the junior or senior level

Grade level is determined by hours earned and not hours attempted; students in one-year programs are considered freshmen regardless of attempted hours; students in two-year programs may not exceed sophomore level regardless of attempted hours. Independent students may be eligible to borrow additional Unsubsidized Stafford Loans of up to $6,000 per year at the freshmen or sophomore level and up to $7,000 per year at the junior or senior level. Dependent students may be eligible to borrow $2,000 per year in additional Unsubsidized Stafford Loan funds.

How Do I Repay My Federal Stafford Loan?

You are given a *six-month grace period* after you graduate or drop below half-time enrollment before repayment begins on your Stafford Loan. After the six-month grace period ends, you go into repayment on your loan. However, if you wish to start paying early, there are no penalties for early payment.

Interest accrues on an Unsubsidized Federal Stafford Loan from the time you receive the loan. Try to pay interest quarterly to keep the total cost of the loan down. Any unpaid interest will be added to your loan balance, called **capitalization**, when you enter repayment. Estimated quarterly interest on a $1,000 Stafford Loan at 6.8% interest is $17.00. Multiply $17.00 by the number of thousands you plan to borrow in Unsubsidized Stafford Loans, to estimate the quarterly interest charge (i.e., if you're borrowing a $4,000 Unsubsidized Loan, quarterly interest would be: 4 x $17 = $68.00).

Repayment Period: The standard repayment period for a Federal Stafford Loan is 10 years. The *minimum monthly payment is $50 per month*. Use the following chart to estimate how much your monthly repayment will be.

Figure 5 Federal Stafford Loan Repayment Chart[9]

Amount Borrowed	Number of payments	Minimum payment @6.8% maximum interest rate	Total Interest Charges	Total Payment with interest charges
$3,500	95 (8 years)	$50.00	$660.57	$4,160.57
$5,500	120 (10 years)	$67.46	$1,038.08	$6,538.03
$7,500	120	$91.99	$1,415.50	$8,915.50
$10,000	120	$122.65	$1,887.34	$11,887.34
$15,000	120	$183.98	$2,331.00	$17,831.00
$20,000	120	$245.31	$3,774.67	$23,774.67
$25,000	120	$306.63	$4,718.34	$29,718.34
$30,000	120	$367.96	$5,662.01	$35,662.01
$40,000	120	$490.61	$7,549.35	$47,549.35

Private Loans

You may receive offers to take out "quick" student loans that don't require you to file the Federal Aid Application. While you'll get the money quickly, the interest rates on these loans are generally much higher than the Stafford Loan interest rate. Students who are not making Financial Aid Satisfactory Academic Progress and are ineligible for Stafford Loans may want to compare private loan options at www.simpletuition.com/daltonstate to find the best deal.

Identity Theft

According to the FTC, identity theft cost the United States $52.6 billion in 2004. Every 79 seconds someone's identity is stolen – 50% of these identity thefts are committed by spouses, relatives, and close friends.[10] To see how much you know about preventing identity theft, take the following quiz, reprinted with permission from the authors, Mark Putman of the National Council of Higher Education Loan Programs and Lisa Curtis, Director of Consumer Services, Denver District Attorney's Office.[11]

Name _____ Date _____

Exercise: What is Your Identity Theft Probability (ITP) Score?

	Yes or No	If you answered yes, put this number in the Score column	Your Score
I pay bills with checks and place them in my mailbox or in a corner postal box.		5	
I do not use direct deposit or electronic transfer for paychecks, refund, or insurance claim checks.		10	
I have new boxes of checks mailed to my home.		10	
I have not "opted out" of my credit card marketing programs and receive "convenience" checks on my account in the mail.		10	
I carry a purse or wear my wallet in my back pocket.		10	
I use checks for shopping and carry my checkbook with me when in public.		5	
I have at least one item in my wallet that contains my Social Security number.		10	
I throw away my annual Social Security Earnings Statement without reviewing it.		10	
I have not copied the contents of my wallet (including the front and back of each credit card).		5	
I keep my auto registration, insurance card, checkbook, credit card receipts, or other identifying information in my car.		10	
I do not shred banking/credit information before trashing.		10	
I use a shredder, but it is not a cross-cut shredder.		5	
I have not called the credit reporting agencies "Opt-out Line" to be removed from credit card solicitations (888-567-8688).		5	
I have not ordered copies of my credit report in over a year.		10	
I have not notified the credit report agencies of the death of a relative or friend (letter and copy of death certificate).		10	
I have responded to e-mails or telephone calls from my Internet provider, financial institution, airlines, or companies like eBay or PayPal requesting verification of account numbers or passwords ('phishing').		10	
I use e-commerce, but do not use a secure browser, or I have a high-speed Internet service but no firewall protection.		10	
My ITP Score			

Scoring

80+ points—You are at high risk of being an identity theft victim. We recommend that you use the checklist below to reduce your vulnerability.

30–80 points—Your odds of being victimized are about average; higher if you have good credit. Use the checklist below to identify additional changes that will reduce your risk.

10–30 points—Congratulations. You have a high "IQ." Keep up the good work, but check the list below for anything you may have overlooked.

Minimize the Risk of Identity Theft

- Carry any document with sensitive information in a close-fitting pouch or in your front pocket, not in your purse or wallet. Sensitive documents include driver's license, credit and debit cards, checks, car registration, and anything with your Social Security Number.
- Don't carry your checkbook in public. Carry only the checks you need.
- If possible, remove anything from your wallet containing your SSN, including your Social Security card, Medicare/Medicaid card, or military ID card. If your SSN is on your driver's license—get a new license.
- Don't give any part of your Social Security, credit card or bank account numbers over the phone, email or Internet, unless you have initiated the contact to a verifiable company or financial institution.
- Request a free copy of your credit report once a year (see next section).
- Notify the credit reporting agencies of the death of a relative or friend to block the misuse of the deceased person's credit.
- Call the bank and credit card customer service and ask to "opt out" of marketing programs, including "convenience" checks mailings.
- Call the Credit Card Offer Opt-out Line to reduce the number of credit card solicitations you receive (888-567-8688 or www.optoutprescreen.com).
- Shred pre-approved credit card offers, convenience checks, and any document containing sensitive information with a crosscut (confetti) shredder.
- Mail bills to be paid at the Post Office, not in your mailbox or in street corner postal boxes. Consider using automated payment plans.
- Have new checks mailed to your bank or credit union and pick them up there instead of having them mailed to your home.

Maintaining Good Credit

To make sure you maintain a good credit history, and because of the possibility of identity theft, it is important to periodically check your credit report. There are three major credit reporting agencies in the United States–Equifax, Experian, and Transunion. According to the FDIC, "A credit report is similar to high school and college grade transcripts. Just like poor grades can negatively affect your career and academic options, a poor credit history can have far-reaching negative consequences."[12]

Because of the Fair and Accurate Credit Transactions (FACT) Act, a free credit report is available once a year. The **only** website where the free credit report is available is www.annualcreditreport.com. It is also available by calling (877) 322-8228. There are imposter websites which will charge you for the credit report, so make sure you go to the official website.

When you receive your credit report check that all of your personal and credit information is accurate. Report any errors in writing to the credit agency and follow up with them to make sure that corrections are made. If disputes remain unresolved, you may submit a written statement to the credit agency which will be included with the credit report given to potential creditors.

It is important to maintain a good credit history in order to get loans for major purchases such as a house or an automobile. Also, many employers check a prospective employee's credit history as a way of checking on the person's reliability and character. Here are tips from the FDIC on how to build a sound credit history:

- Keep your own checking account and savings account. Do not overdraw your account.
- Establish a credit card in your own name, and use it responsibly.
- Pay bills before the due date.
- Limit the number of credit cards you own. Too much open credit, even if the accounts have zero balances, will negatively affect your credit score.
- Close unused accounts—do not just cut the cards up—or the account will show as an open line of credit on your credit report. Ask the issuer to state on your credit report, "account closed by consumer."
- Limit the number of credit inquiries. Every time you apply for credit, it shows as an inquiry to your credit report. Too many inquiries are viewed negatively by lenders.
- A large number of recently established credit accounts may hurt your ability to be granted credit.
- Periodically obtain a copy of your credit report to verify that information reported is accurate and to look for ways that you can improve your credit.

••• Sources

1. Dalton State College, *Non-Returning Student Survey; First-Time, Full-Time, Degree-Seeking Students, Summary Report with Comments, Fall 2004–Fall 2005* (Dalton, GA: Office of Institutional Research and Planning, 2005) 1.
2. United States, General Accounting Office, *Consumer Finance: College Students and Credit Cards,* GAO-01-773 (Washington, DC, June 2001) 33–34.
3. Dalton State College, *2005 Facts and Figures,* (Dalton, GA: Office of Institutional Research and Planning, 2006) 129.
4. Office of Indian Education, "Higher Ed Grants." http://www.oiep.bia.edu/faqs_grantinfo.html
5. Jennifer Cheeseman Day and Eric Newburger, *The Big Payoff: Educational Attainment and Synthetic Estimates of Work Life Earnings,* P23–210 (Washington, DC: U.S. Census Bureau, 2002) 3.
6. *The Road to Financial Health* (Tucker, GA: Georgia Student Finance Commission and Consumer Credit Counseling, c. 2003), 2.
7. Dr. Robert Manning, Hearing on "The Importance of Financial Literacy Among College Students." (Washington, DC: U.S. Senate Committee on Banking, Housing, and Urban Affairs, Thursday, September 2, 2002), 2.
8. *Credit Card Savvy Students Handout,* (Washington, DC: Consumer Response Center, Federal Deposit Insurance Corporation, 2005), 2–3. [On-Line]. Available: http://www.fdic.gov/consumers/consumer/ccc/savvy.html
9. Repayment figures were calculated on the Loan Calculator at http://www.finaid.org/calculators/loanpayments.phtml.
10. Mark Putman, National Council on Higher Education Loan Programs (NCHELP), "Identity Theft," Georgia Association of Student Financial Aid Administrators Spring Conference, Savannah Riverfront Hotel, Savannah, GA, 15 May 2006.
11. Mark Putman, NCHELP and Lisa Curtis, Director of Consumer Services, Denver District Attorney's Office, "What is Your Identity Theft Probability (ITP) Score?," Georgia Association of Student Financial Aid Administrators Spring Conference, Savannah Riverfront Hotel, Savannah, GA, 15 May 2006.
12. Credit Card Savvy Students Handout; Consumer Response Center, Federal Deposit Insurance Corporation, www.fdic.gov/consumers/consumer/ccc/savvy.html

Additional References

2008–2009 Federal Student Aid Handbook, U.S. Department of Education, Division of Federal Student Aid. [On-line]. Available: http:www.ifap.ed.gov.

2008–2009 HOPE Program Regulations, Georgia Student Finance Commission. [On-line]. Available: http://www.gsfc.org/Main/publishing/pdf/2006/2006_hope_regs.pdf

Dalton State College 2008–2009 Catalog and Student Handbook. 36. Dalton, GA, 2007.

References

This section includes ALL references found within the full version of this text.

Abbey, A. (2002). Alcohol-related sexual assault: A common problem among college students. *Journal of Studies on Alcohol, 14,* 118–128.

AC Neilsen Research Services (2000). *Employer satisfaction with graduate skills.* Department of Education, Training and Youth Affairs. Canberra: AGPS. Retrieved October, 25, 2006, from http:www.dest.gov.au/ty/publications/employability_skills/final_report.pdf

Academic Integrity at Princeton (2003). *Examples of plagiarism.* Retrieved October 21, 2006, from http://www.princeton.du/pr/pub/integrity/pages/plagiarism.html

Ackerman, S. (1992). *Discovering the brain.* Washington, D.C.: National Academy Press.

Acredolo, C., & O'Connor, J. (1991). On the difficulty of detecting cognitive uncertainty. *Human Development, 34,* 204–223.

Adler, R. B., & Towne, M. (2001). *Looking out, looking in: Interpersonal communication* (10th ed.). Orlando, FL: Harcourt Brace.

Ahlum-Heather, M. E., & DiVesta, F. J. (1986). The effect of a conscious controlled verbalization of a cognitive strategy on transfer in problem solving. *Memory and Cognition, 14*(3), 281–285.

AhYun, K. (2002). Similarity and attraction. In M. Allen, R. W. Preiss, B. M. Gayle, & N. A. Burrell (Eds.), *Interpersonal communication research* (pp. 145–167). Mahwah, NJ: Erlbaum.

Ainslie, G. (1975). Specious reward: A behavioral theory of impulsiveness and impulse control. *Psychological Bulletin, 82,* 463–496.

Ainslie, G. (1992). *Picoeconomics: The strategic interaction of successive motivational states within the person.* New York: Cambridge University Press.

Alkon, D. L. (1992). *Memory's voice: Deciphering the brain-mind code.* New York: HarperCollins.

Allport. G. W. (1954). *The nature of prejudice.* Cambridge, MA: Addison-Wesley.

Amabile, T., Hadley, C. N., & Kramer, S. J. (2002). Creativity under the gun. *Harvard Business Review, 80*(8), 52–61.

Ambron, J. (1991). History of WAC and its role in community colleges. In L. C. Stanley & J. Ambron (Eds.), *Writing across the curriculum in community colleges* (pp. 3–8). New Direction for Community Colleges, no. 73. San Francisco: Jossey-Bass.

American College Testing (2003). *National college dropout and graduation rates, 2002.* Retrieved June 4, 2004, from http://www.act.org/news

American Heart Association (2006). *Fish, levels of mercury and omega-3 fatty acids.* Retrieved Jan. 13, 2007, from http://americanheart.org/presenter.jthml?identifier=3013797

American Obesity Association (2002). *Obesity in the U.S.* Retrieved April 26, 2006, from http://www.obesity.org/subs/fastfacts/obesity_US.shtml

American Psychiatric Association (1994). Diagnostic and Statistical Manual for Mental Disorders (4th ed.) (DSM-IV). Washington, DC: American Psychiatric Press.

American Psychiatric Association Work Group on Eating Disorders (2000). Practice guidelines for the treatment of patients with eating disorders. *American Journal of Psychiatry, 157,* 1–39.

Amir, Y. (1969). Contact hypothesis in ethnic relations. *Psychological Bulletin, 71,* 319–342.

Amir, Y. (1976). The role of intergroup contact in change of prejudice and ethnic relations. In P. A. Katz (Ed.), *Towards the elimination of racism* (pp. 245–308). New York: Pergamon Press.

Andersen, P. A. (1985). Nonverbal immediacy in interpersonal communication. In A. W. Siegmean & S. Feldstein (Eds.), *Multichannel integrations of nonverbal behavior* (pp. 1–36). Hillsdale, NJ: Lawrence Erlbaum.

Anderson, P. V. (1985). What survey research tells us about writing at work. In L. Odell & D. Goswami (Eds.), *Writing in nonacademic settings* (pp. 3–85). New York: Guilford Press.

Anderson, J. R. (2000). *Cognitive psychology and its implications.* Worth Publishers.

Anderson, C. J. (2003). The psychology of doing nothing: Forms of decision avoidance result from reason and emotion. *Psychological Bulletin, 129,* 139–167.

Anderson, J. R., & Bower, G. H. (1974). Interference in memory for multiple contexts. *Memory and Cognition, 2,* 509–514.

Anderson, M. & Fienberg, S. E. (2000). Race and ethnicity and the controversy over the U.S. census. *Current Sociology, 48*(3), 87–110.

Anderson, L. W., & Krathwohl, D. R. (Eds.)(2001). *A taxonomy for learning, teaching, and assessing: A revision of Bloom's taxonomy of educational objectives.* New York: Addison Wesley Longman.

Applebee, A. N. (1981). *Writing in the secondary school.* Urbana, Ill.: National Council of Teachers of English.

Applebee, A. N. (1984). Writing and reasoning. *Review of Educational Research, 54*(4), 577–596.

Applebee, A. N., Langer, J. A., Jenkins, L. B., Mullis, I. V. S., & Foertsch, M. A. (1990). *Learning to write in our nation's schools: instruction and achievement in 1988 at grades 4, 8, and 12.* Princeton, NJ: The National Assessment of Educational Progress.

Argyle, M., & Beit-Hallahmi, B. (1975). *The social psychology of religion.* London: Routledge.

Arnedt, J. T., Wilde, G. J. S., Munt, P. W., & MacLean, A. W. (2001). How do prolonged wakefulness and alcohol compare in the decrements they produce on a simulated driving task? *Accident Analysis and Prevention, 33,* 337–344.

Aronson, E., Wilson, T. D., & Akert, R. M. (2005). *Social psychology* (5th ed.). Upper Saddle River, NJ: Pearson/Prentice Hall.

Association of American Colleges & Universities (2002). *Greater expectations: A new vision for learning as a nation goes to college.* Washington, D.C.: Author.

Astin, A. W. (1993). *What matters in college?* San Francisco: Jossey-Bass.

Astin, A. W. (2004). Why spirituality deserves a central place in higher education. *Spirituality in Higher Education Newsletter, 1*(2), pp. 1–12.

Astin, A. W., Oseguera, L., Sax, L. J., & Korn, W. S. (2002). *The American freshman: Thirty-five year trends.* Los Angeles, CA: Higher Education Research Institute, Graduate School of Education & Information Studies, University of California, Los Angeles.

Astin, A. W., Parrot, S. A., Korn, W. S., & Sax, L. J. (1997). *The American freshman: Thirty year trends, 1966–1996.* Higher Education Research Institute, University of California, Los Angeles.

Astin, A. W., Vogelgesang, L. J., Ikeda, E. K., & Yee, J. A. (2000). *How service-learning affects students.* Higher Education Research Institute, University of California, Los Angeles.

Atkinson, R. C. (1975). Mnemotechnics in second-language learning. *American Psychologist, 30,* 821–828.

Audrain, J. E., Klesges, R. C., & Flesges, L. M. (1995). Relationship between obesity and the metabolic effects of smoking in women. *Health Psychology, 14,* 116–123.

Avolio, B. J. (2005). *Leadership development in balance: Made/born.* Mahwah, NJ: Lawrence Erlbaum Associates.

Ayers, L., Beaton, S., & Hunt, H. (1999). The significance of transpersonal experiences, emotional conflict, and cognitive abilities in creativity. *Empirical Studies of the Arts, 17*(1), 73–82.

Baer, J. M. (1993). *Creativity and divergent thinking.* Hillsdale, NJ: Erlbaum.

Bahrick, H. P., & Phelps, E. (1987). Retention of Spanish vocabulary over 8 years. *Journal of Experimental Psychology, Learning, Memory, & Cognition, 13,* 344–349.

Bailey, C. (1991). *The new fit or fat.* Boston: Houghton Mifflin.

Bandura, A. (1994). Self-efficacy. In V. S. Ramachaudran (Ed.), *Encyclopedia of human behavior, Volume 4* (pp. 71–81). New York: Academic Press.

Bandura, A. (1986). *Social foundations of thought and action: A social cognitive theory.* Englewood Cliffs, NJ: Prentice-Hall.

Bandura, A. (1997). *Self-efficacy: The exercise of control.* New York: Freeman & Co.

Barefoot, B. O. (Ed.) (1993). *Exploring the evidence: Reporting outcomes of freshman seminars.* Monograph Series No. 11. National Resource Center for The Freshman Year Experience. Columbia, SC: University of South Carolina.

Barefoot, B. O., Warnock, C. L., Dickinson, M. P., Richardson, S. E., & Roberts, M. R. (Eds.) (1998). *Exploring the evidence, Volume II: Reporting outcomes of first-year seminars.* (Monograph No. 29). Columbia, SC: National Resource Center for The First-Year Experience and Students in Transition, University of South Carolina.

Barker, L., Edwards, R., Gaines, C., Gladney, K., & Holley, F. (1980). An investigation of proportional time spent in various communication activities by college students. *Journal of Applied Communication Research, 8*, 101–110.

Barker, L., & Watson, K. W. (2000). *Listen up: How to improve relationships, reduce stress, and be more productive by using the power of listening.* New York: St. Martin's Press.

Baron, R. A., Byrne, D., & Brauscombe, N. R. (2006). *Social psychology* (11th ed.). Boston: Pearson.

Bartels, A., & Zeki, S. (2000). The neural basis of romantic love. *European Journal of Neuroscience, 12*, 172–193.

Basadur, M., Runco, M. A., & Vega, L. A. (2000). Understanding how creative thinking skills, attitudes, and behaviors work together. *Journal of Creative Behavior, 34*(2), 77–100.

Bassham, G., Irwin, W., Nardone, H., Wallace, J. M. (2005). *Critical thinking* (2nd ed.). New York: McGraw-Hill.

Bates, G. A. (1994). *The next step: College.* Bloomington, IN: Phi Delta Kappa.

Baumeister, R. F., Heatherton, T. F., & Tice, D. M. (1994). *Losing control: How and why people fail at self-regulation.* San Diego, CA: Academic Press.

Baxter Magolda, M. (1992). *Knowing and reasoning in college: Gender-related patterns in students' intellectual development.* San Francisco: Jossey-Bass.

Bean, J. C. (2003). *Engaging ideas.* San Francisco: Jossey-Bass.

Beck, A. T. (1976). *Cognitive therapy and the emotional disorders.* Boston: International Universities Press.

Beck, B. L., Koons, S. R., & Milgram, D. L. (2000). Correlates and consequences of behavioral procrastination: The effects of academic procrastination, self-consciousness, self-esteem and self-handicapping. *Journal of Social Behavior and Personality, 15*, 3–13.

Belenky, M. F., Clinchy, B., Goldberger, N. R., & Tarule, J. M. (1986). *Women's ways of knowing: The development of self, voice, and mind.* New York: Basic Books.

Bellah, R. N., Madsen, R., Sullivan, W. M., Swidler, A., & Tipton, S. M. (1985). *Habits of the heart: Individualism and commitment in American life.* Berkeley: University of California Press.

Benjamin, L. T., Jr., Cavell, T. A., & Shallenberger, W. R., III (1984). Staying with initial answers on objective tests: Is it a myth? *Teaching of Psychology, 11*, 133–141.

Benjamin, M., McKeachie, W. J., Lin, Y.-G., & Holinger, D. (1981). Test anxiety: Deficits in information processing. *Journal of Educational Psychology, 73*, 816–824.

Bennet, W., & Gurin, J. (1983). *The dieter's dilemma.* New York: Basic Books.

Bennis, W. (1989). *On becoming a leader.* Reading, MA: Addison-Wesley.

Benson, H., & Klipper, M. Z. (1990). *The relaxation response.* New York: Avon.

Biggs, J. B. (1987). *Student approaches to learning and studying.* Hawthorn, Victoria: Australian Council for Educational Research.

Biglan, A. (1973). The characteristics of subject matter in different academic areas. *Journal of Applied Psychology, 57*, 195–203.

Bishop, S. (1986). Education for political freedom. *Liberal Education, 72*(4), 322–325.

Bjork, R. (1994). Memory and metamemory considerations in the training of human beings. In J. Metcalfe & A. P. Shimamura (Eds.), *Metacognition: Knowing about knowing* (pp. 185–206). Cambridge, MA: MIT Press.

Blair, I. V. (2002). The malleability of automatic stereotypes and prejudice. *Personality & Social Psychology Review, 6*(3), 242–261.

Blakeslee, S. (1993, Aug. 3). Mystery of sleep yields as studies reveal immune tie. *The New York Times*, pp. C1, C6.

Bohme, K., & Budden, F. (2001). *The silent thief: Osteoporosis, exercises and strategies for prevention and treatment.* Buffalo, NY: Firefly.

Boice, R. (1994). *How writers journey to comfort and fluency: A psychological adventure.* Westport, CT: Praeger.

Bolles, R. N. (1998). *The new quick job-hunting map.* Toronto, Canada: Ten Speed Press.

Booth, F. W., & Vyas, D. R. (2001). Genes, environment, and exercise. *Advances in Experimental Medicine and Biology, 502*, 13–20.

Boudreau, C., & Kromrey, J. (1994). A longitudinal study of the retention and academic performance of participants in a freshman orientation course. *Journal of College Student Development, 35*, 444–449.

Bowen, H. R. (1977). *Investment in learning: The individual and social value of American higher education.* San Francisco: Jossey-Bass.

Bowen, H. R. (1997). *Investment in learning: The individual and social value of American higher education* (2nd ed.). Baltimore: The Johns Hopkins Press.

Bower, L. H. (1972). Mental imagery and associative learning. In L. W. Gregg (Ed.), *Cognition in learning and memory*. New York: Wiley.

Bower, G. H. (1973). "How to . . . uh . . . remember!" *Psychology Today* (October), 63–70.

Bower, G. H., Clark, M. C., Lesgold, A. M., & Winzenz, D. (1969). Hierarchical retrieval schemes in recall of categorized word lists. *Journal of Verbal Learning and Verbal Behavior, 8*, 323–343.

Bowlby, J. (1980). *Attachment and loss: Volume 3. Loss, sadness, and depression*. New York: Basic Books.

Boyer, E. L. (1987). *College: The undergraduate experience in America*. New York: Harper & Row.

Boyer, E. L. & Kaplan, M. (1977). *Educating for survival*. New Rochelle, NY: Change Magazine Press.

Bradshaw, D. (1995). Learning theory: Harnessing the strength of a neglected resource. In D.C.A. Bradshaw (Ed.), *Bringing learning to life: The learning revolution, the economy and the individual* (pp. 79–92). London, UK: The Falmer Press.

Bransford, J. D., Brown, A. L., & Cocking, R. R. (1999). *How people learn: Brain, mind, experience and school*. Washington, D.C.: National Academy Press.

Breivik, P. S. (1998). *Student learning in the information age*. American Council on Education, Oryx Press Series on Higher Education. Phoenix: The Oryx Press.

Bridgeman, B. (2003). *Psychology and evolution: The Origins of mind*. Thousand Oaks, CA: Sage.

Britton, J. and others (1975). *The development of writing abilities*. London: Macmillan.

Brody, J. E. (2003, August 18). Skipping a college course: Weight gain 101. *The New York Times*, p. D7.

Brown, R. D. (1988). Self-quiz on testing and grading issues. *Teaching at UNL, 10*(2), pp. 1–3. The Teaching and Learning Center, University of Nebraska-Lincoln.

Brown, D. (2003). *Career information, career counseling, and career development* (8th ed.). Boston: Allyn & Bacon.

Brown, T. D., Dane, F. C., & Durham, M. D. (1998). Perception of race and ethnicity. *Journal of Social Behavior & Personality, 13*(2), 295–306.

Brown, S. D., & Krane, N. E. R. (2000). Four (or five) sessions and a cloud of dust: Old assumptions and new observations about career counseling. In S. D. Brown & R. W. Lent (Eds.), *Handbook of counseling psychology* (3rd ed.)(pp. 740–766). New York: Wiley.

Brown, R. W., & McNeil, D. (1966). The "tip of the tongue" phenomenon. *Journal of Verbal Learning and Verbal Behavior, 5,* 325–327.

Brown, S. A., Tapert, S. F., Granholm, E., & Delis, D. C. (2000). Neurocognitive functioning of adolescents: Effects of protracted alcohol use. *Alcoholism: Clinical & Experimental Research, 24*(2), 164–171.

Bruffee, K. A. (1993). *Collaborative learning: Higher education, interdependence, and the authority of knowledge*. Baltimore: Johns Hopkins University Press.

Bryan, W. A., Mann, G. T., Nelson, R. B., & North, R. A. (1981). The co-curricular transcript—what do employers think? A national survey. *National Association of Student Personnel Administrators Journal, 9*(1), 20–34.

Buber, M. (1923). *I and thou* (Translation, 1970). New York: Touchstone.

Burka, J. B., & Yuen, L. M. (1983). *Procrastination: Why you do it, what to do about it*. Reading, MA: Addison-Wesley.

Bushman, B. J., & Cooper, H. M. (1990). Effects of alcohol on human aggression: An integrative research review. *Psychological Bulletin, 107*(3), 341–354.

Business Council of Australia and Australian Chamber of Commerce & Industry (2002). *Employability skills for the future*. Canberra, Australia: AGPS. Retrieved October, 25, 2006 from http:www.dest.gov.au/ty/publications/employability_skills/final_report.pdf

Business/Higher Education Round Table (1991). *Aiming higher: The concerns and attitudes of leading business executives and university heads to education priorities in Australia in the 1990s* (Commissioned Report no. 1). Melbourne, Australia.

Business/Higher Education Round Table (1992). *Educating for excellence part 2: Achieving excellence in university professional education* (Commissioned Report no. 2). Melbourne, Australia.

Buzan, T. (1991). *Use your perfect memory* (3rd ed.). New York: Penguin Books.

Caine, R. N., & Caine, G. (1991). *Teaching and the human brain*. Alexandria, VA: Association for Supervision and Curriculum Development.

Campbell, T. A., & Campbell, D. E. (1997, December). Faculty/student mentor program: Effects on academic performance and retention. *Research in Higher Education, 38*, 727–742.

Caplan, P. J., & Caplan, J. B. (1994). *Thinking critically about research on sex and gender*. New York: HarperCollins College Publishers.

Carducci, B. J. (1999). *Shyness: A bold new approach.* New York: HarperCollins.

Carney, R. N., & Levin, J. R. (2001). Remembering the names of unfamiliar animals: Keywords as keys to their Kingdom. *Applied Cognitive Psychology, 15*(2), 133–143.

Caroli, M., Argentieri, L., Cardone, M., & Masi, A. (2004). Role of television in childhood obesity prevention. *International Journal of Obesity Related Metabolic Disorders, 28* (Supplement 3), S104–108.

Carpenter, K. M., & Hasin, D. S. (1998). A prospective evaluation of the relationship between reasons for drinking and DSM-IV alcohol-use disorders. *Addictive Behaviors, 23*(1), 41–46.

Carroll, J. B. (1964). *Language and thought.* Englewood Cliffs, NJ: Prentice-Hall.

Carter, R. (1998). *Mapping the mind.* Berkeley and Los Angeles: University of California Press.

Cates, J. R., Herndon, N. L., Schulz, S. L., & Darroch, J. E. (2004). *Our voices, our lives, our futures: Youth and sexually transmitted diseases.* Chapel Hill, NC: University of North Carolina at Chapel Hill School of Journalism and Mass Communication.

Cheney, L. V. (1989). *50 hours: A core curriculum for college students.* Washington D.C.: National Endowment for the Humanities.

Chi, M., de Leeuw, N., Chiu, M. H., & LaVancher, C. (1994). Eliciting self-explanations improves understanding. *Cognitive Science*, 18, 439–477.

Chickering, A. W., & Schlossberg, N. K. (1998). Moving on: Seniors as people in transition. In J. N. Gardner, G. Van der Veer, & Associates, *The senior year experience* (pp. 37–50). San Francisco: Jossey-Bass.

Chronicle of Higher Education (2003, August 30). Almanac 2003–04. *The Chronicle of Higher Education, 49*(1). Washington, D.C.: Author.

Claxton, C. S., & Murrell, P. H. (1988). *Learning styles: Implications for improving practice.* ASHE-ERIC Educational Report No. 4. Washington D.C.: Association for the Study of Higher Education.

Coates, T. J. (1977). *How to sleep better: A drug-free program for overcoming insomnia.* Englewood Cliffs, NJ: Prentice-Hall.

Collins, A. M., & Loftus, E. F. (1975). A spreading activation theory of semantic processing. *Psychological Review, 82*, 407–428.

Colombo, G., Cullen, R., & Lisle, B. (1995). *Rereading America: Cultural contexts for critical thinking and writing.* Boston: Bedford Books of St. Martin's Press.

Conaway, M. A. (1982). Listening: Learning tool and retention agent. In A. S. Algier & K. W. Algier (Eds.), *Improving reading and study skills* (pp. 51–63). San Francisco: Jossey-Bass.

Connolly, P. (1989). Writing and the ecology of learning. In P. Connolly & T. Vilardi (Eds.), *Writing to learn mathematics and science* (pp. 1–14). New York: Teachers College Press, Columbia University.

Cook, S. W. (1984). Cooperative interaction in multiethnic contexts. In N. Miller & M. B. Brewer (Eds.), *Groups in contact: The psychology of desegregation.* New York: Academic Press.

Cook, L. (1991). Learning style awareness and academic achievement among community college students. *Community/Junior College Quarterly of Research and Practice, 15*, 419–425.

Cooper, K. (1982). *The aerobics program for total well-being.* New York: Bantam.

Corbin, C. B., Pangrazi, R. P., & Franks, B. D. (2000). Definitions: Health, fitness, and physical activity. *President's Council on Physical Fitness and Sports Research Digest, 3*(9), pp. 1–8.

Covey, S. R. (1990). *Seven habits of highly effective people* (2nd ed). New York: Fireside.

Covey, S. R., Merrill, A. R., & Merrill, R. R. (1996). *First things first: To live, to love, to learn, to leave a legacy.* New York: Fireside.

Cowan, N. (2001). The magical number 4 in short-term memory: A reconsideration of mental storage capacity. *Behavioral and Brain Sciences, 24*, 87–114.

Coward, A. (1990). *Pattern thinking.* New York: Praeger Publishers.

Craik, F. I. M., & Lockhart, R. S. (1972). Levels of processing: A framework for memory research. *Journal of Verbal Learning and Verbal Behavior, 11*, 671–684.

Craik, F. I. M., & Tulving, E. (1975). Depth of processing and the retention of words in episodic memory. *Journal of Experimental Psychology: General, 104*, 268–294.

Crawford, H. J., & Strapp, C. H. (1994). Effects of vocal and instrumental music on visuospatial and verbal performance as moderated by studying preference and personality. *Personality and Individual Differences, 16*(2), 237–245.

Cronon, W. (1998). "Only connect": The Goals of a Liberal Education. *The American Scholar* (Autumn), 73–80.

Crosby, O. (2002). Informational interviewing: Get the scoop on careers. *Occupational Outlook Quarterly* (Summer), 32–37.

Cross, K. P. (1982). Thirty years passed: Trends in general education. In B. L. Johnson (Ed.), *General education in two-year colleges* (pp. 11–20). San Francisco: Jossey-Bass.

Cross, K. P. (1993). Reaction to "Enhancing the productivity of learning" by D. B. Johnstone. *AAHE Bulletin, 46*(4), p. 7.

Csikszentmihalyi, M. (1996). *Creativity: Flow and the psychology of discovery and invention.* New York: HarperCollins.

Cummings, M. C. (2002). *Democracy under pressure* (9th ed.). Belmont, CA: Wadsworth.

Cuseo, J. B. (1991). *The freshman orientation seminar: A research-based rationale for its value, delivery, and content.* Columbia, SC: National Resource Center for The Freshman Year Experience, University of South Carolina.

Cuseo, J. B. (1996). *Cooperative learning: A pedagogy for addressing contemporary challenges and critical issues in higher education.* Stillwater, OK: New Forums Press.

Cuseo, J. B. (2002). *Igniting student involvement, peer interaction, and teamwork: A taxonomy of specific cooperative learning structures and collaborative learning strategies.* Stillwater, OK: New Forums Press.

Cuseo, J. B. (2003). Comprehensive academic support for students during the first year of college. In G. L. Kramer & Associates, *Student academic services: An integrated approach* (pp. 271–310). San Francisco: Jossey-Bass.

Cuseo, J. (2005). "Decided," "undecided," and "in transition": Implications for academic advisement, career counseling, and student retention. In R. S. Feldman (Ed.), *Improving the first year of college: Research and practice* (pp. 27–50). Mahwah, NJ: Lawrence Erlbaum Associates.

Cusinato, M., & L'Abate, L. (1994). A spiral model of intimacy. In S. M. Johnson & L. S. Greenberg (Eds.), *The heart of the matter: Emotion in marital therapy.* New York: Brunner/Mazel.

Czaja, R., Blair, J., Bickart, B., & Eastman, E. (1994). Respondent strategies for recall of crime victimization incidents. *Journal of Official Statistics, 10*(3), 257–276.

Dalton, J. C., Eberhardt, D., Bracken, J., & Echols, K. (2006). Inward journeys: Forms and patterns of college student spirituality. *Journal of College & Character, 7*(8), 1–21. Retrieved December 17, 2006, from http://www.collegevalues.org/pdfs/Dalton.pdf

Daly, W. T. (1992). The academy, the economy, and the liberal arts. *Academe* (July/August), 10–12.

Daniels, D., & Horowitz, L. J. (1997). *Being and caring: A psychology for living.* Prospect Heights, IL: Waveland Press.

Davidson, R. J., Kabat-Zinn, J., Schumacher, J., Rosenkranz, M. D., Santorelli, S. F., Urbanowski, F., Harrington, A., & Bonus, K. F. (2003). Alteration in brain and immune function produced by mindfulness meditation. *Psychosomatic Medicine, 65*(4), 564–570.

DeJong, W., & Linkenback, J. (1999). Telling it like it is: Using social norms marketing campaigns to reduce student drinking. *AAHE Bulletin, 52*(4), pp. 11–13, 16.

Dement, W. C. (1974). *Some must watch while some must sleep.* San Francisco: W. H. Freeman.

Dement, W. C., & Vaughan, C. (1999). *The promise of sleep.* New York: Delacorte Press.

Dement, W. C., & Vaughan, C. (2000). *The promise of sleep: A pioneer in sleep medicine explores the vital connection between health, happiness, and a good night's sleep.* New York: Dell.

DesMaisons, K. (1998). *Potatoes not Prozac.* London: Simon & Schuster.

Donald, J. G. (2002). *Learning to think: Disciplinary perspectives.* San Francisco: Jossey-Bass.

Dorfman, J., Shames, J., & Kihlstrom, J. F. (1996). Intuition, incubation, and insight. In G. Underwood (Ed.), *Implicit cognition.* New York: Oxford University Press.

Douglas, K. A., Collins, J. L., Warren, C., Kahn, L., Gold, R., Clayton, S., Ross, J. G., & Kolbe, L. J. (1997). Results from the 1995 national college health risk behavior survey. *Journal of American College Health, 46,* 55–66.

Drubach, D. (2000). *The brain explained.* Englewood Cliffs, NJ: Prentice-Hall.

Druckman, D., & Bjork, R. A. (Eds.)(1991). *In the mind's eye: Enhancing human performance.* Washington, D.C.: National Academy Press.

Dryden, G. & Vos, J. (1999). *The learning revolution: To change the way the world learns.* Torrance, CA & Auckland, New Zealand: The Learning Web.

Dudenhyer, J. P., Jr. (1976). An experiment in grading papers. *College Composition and Communication, 27(4),* 406–407.

Dunn, R., Dunn, K., & Price, G. (1990). *Learning style inventory.* Lawrence, KS: Price Systems.

Dunn, R., Griggs, S., Olson, J., Beasley, M., & Gorman, B. (1995). A meta-analytic validation of the Dunn and Dunn learning-styles model. *Journal of Educational Research, 88,* 353–362.

Dupuy, G. M., & Vance, R. M. (1996, Oct. 26). *Launching your career: A transition module for seniors.* Paper presented at the Second National Conference on Students in Transition, San Antonio, Texas.

Eaton, S. B., & Konner, M. (1985). Paleolithic nutrition: A consideration of its nature and current implications. *New England Journal of Medicine, 312,* 283.

Eble, K. E. (1966). *A perfect education.* New York: Macmillan.

Eckman, P., & Friesen, W. V. (1969). Nonverbal leakage and clues to deception. *Psychiatry, 32,* 88–106.

Education Commission of the States (1995). *Making quality count in undergraduate education.* Denver, CO: ECS Distribution Center.

Education Commission of the States (1996). *Bridging the gap between neuroscience and education.* Denver, CO: Author.

Einstein, G. O., Morris, J., & Smith, S. (1985). Note-taking, individual differences, and memory for lecture information. *Journal of Educational Psychology, 77*(5), 522–532.

Elbow, P. (1973). *Writing without teachers.* New York: Oxford University Press.

Elder, L., & Paul, R. (2002). *The miniature guide to taking charge of the human mind.* Dillon Beach, CA: The Foundation for Critical Thinking.

Ellin, A. (1993). "Post-parchment depression." *Boston Phoenix,* September.

Ellis, A. (1975). *A new guide to rational living.* Englewood Cliffs, NJ: Prentice Hall.

Ellis, A. (1995). Changing rational-emotive therapy (RET) to rational emotive behavior therapy (REBT). *Journal of Rational-Emotive & Cognitive Behavior Therapy, 13*(2), 85–89.

Ellis, A. (2000). *How to control your anxiety before it controls you.* New York: Citadel Press/Kensington Publishing.

Ellis, A. (2001). *Overcoming destructive beliefs, feelings, and behaviors: New directions for rational-emotive behavior therapy.* Amherst, NY: Prometheus Books.

Ellis, A., & Knaus, W. J. (1977). *Overcoming procrastination.* New York: Signet Books.

Engs, R. C. (1977). Drinking patterns and drinking problems of college students. *Journal of Studies on Alcohol, 38,* 2144–2156.

Engs, R., & Hanson, D. (1986). Age-specific alcohol prohibition and college students' drinking problems. *Psychological Reports, 59,* 979–984.

Entwistle, N. J., & Marton, F. (1984). Changing conceptions of learning and research. In F. Marton et al. (Eds.), *The experience of learning.* Edinburgh: Scottish Academic Press.

Entwistle N. J., & Ramsden, P. (1983). *Understanding student learning.* London: Croom Helm.

Erasmus, U. (1993). *Fats that heal, fats that kill.* Burnaby, British Columbia: Alive Books.

Erickson, B. L., Peters, C. B., & Strommer, D. W. (2006). *Teaching first-year college students.* San Francisco: Jossey-Bass.

Erickson, B. L., & Strommer, D. W. (1991). *Teaching college freshmen.* San Francisco: Jossey-Bass.

Ericsson, K. A., & Charness, N. (1994). Expert performance. *American Psychologist, 49*(8), 725–747.

Everly, G. S. (1989). *A clinical guide to the treatment of the human stress response.* New York: Plenum Press.

Ewell, P. T. (1997). Organizing for learning. *AAHE Bulletin, 50*(4), pp. 3–6.

Family Care Foundation (2005). *If the world were a village of 100 people.* Retrieved December 19, 2006, from http:www.familycare.org.news/if_the_world.htm

Feagin, J. R., & McKinney, K. D. (2003). *The many costs of racism.* Lanham, MD: Rowman & Littlefield.

Feldman, D. H. (1994). Creativity: dreams, insights, and transformation. In D. H. Feldman, M. Csikszentmihalyi, & H. Gardner (Eds.), *Changing creativity* (pp. 85–102). Westport, CT: Praeger.

Feldman, K. A., & Newcomb, T. M. (1997). *The impact of college on students.* New Brunswick, NJ: Transaction Publishers (originally published in 1969 by Jossey-Bass).

Feldman, K. A., & Paulsen, M. B. (Eds.) (1994). *Teaching and learning in the college classroom.* Needham Heights, MA: Ginn Press.

Felstead, A., Gallie, D., & Green, F. (2002). *Work skills in Britain 1986–2001.* Retrieved December 22, 2006, from http://www.kent.ac.uk/economics/staff/gfg/WorkSkills1986-2001.pdf

Ferris, K. R. (1982). Educational predictors of professional pay and performance. *Accounting, Organization, and Society, 7*(3), 225–230.

Feskens, E. J., & Kromhout, D. (1993). Epidemiologic studies on Eskimos and fish intake. *Annals of the New York Academy of Science, 683,* 9–15.

Festinger, L. (1954). A theory of social comparison processes. *Human Relations, 7,* 117–140.

Fidler, P., & Godwin, M. (1994). Retaining African-American students through the freshman seminar. *Journal of Developmental Education, 17,* 34–41.

Fiedler, F. E. (1993). The leadership situation and the black box in contingency theories. In M. M. Chemers & R. Ayman (Eds.), *Leadership theory and research* (pp. 2–28). New York: Academic Press.

Fingerhut, L. A., Kleinman, J. C., & Kendrick, J. S. (1990). Smoking before, during, and after pregnancy. *American Journal of Public Health, 80*(5), 541–544.

Fisher, J. L., Harris, J. L., & Harris, M. B. (1973). Effect of note-taking and review on recall. *Journal of Educational Psychology, 65*(3), 321–325.

Fixman, C. S. (1990). The foreign language needs of U.S.-based corporations. *Annals of the American Academy of Political and Social Science, 511*, 25–46.

Flavell, J. H. (1985). *Cognitive development* (2nd ed.). Englewood Cliffs, NJ: Prentice-Hall.

Fletcher, A., Lamond, N., van den Heuvel, C. J., & Dawson, D. (2003). Prediction of performance during sleep deprivation and alcohol intoxication using a quantitative model of work-related fatigue. *SleepResearch Online, 5*, 67–75.

Flett, G. L., Blankstein, K. R., Hewitt, P. L., & Koledin, S. (1992). Components of perfectionism and procrastination in college students. *Social Behavior & Personality, 20*, 85–94.

Ford, P. L. (Ed.) (1903). *The works of Thomas Jefferson*. New York: Knickerbocker Press.

Frankl, V. E. (1946). *Man's search for meaning*. London: Hodder & Stoughton.

Freund, K. M., Belanger, A. J., D'Agostino, R. B., & Kannel, W. B. (1993). The health risks of smoking. The Framingham study: 34 years of follow-up. *Annals of Epidemiology, 3*(4), 417–424.

Fromm, E. (1970). *The art of loving*. New York: Bantam.

Fromme, A. (1980). *The ability to love*. Chatsworth, CA: Wilshire Book Company.

Frost, S. H. (1991). *Academic advising for student success: A system of shared responsibility*. ASHE-ERIC Higher Education Report, No. 3. The George Washington School of Education and Human Development, Washington, D.C.

Furnham, A., & Argyle, M. (1998). *The psychology of money*. New York: Routledge.

Gamson, Z. F. (1984). *Liberating education*. San Francisco: Jossey-Bass.

Ganong, L. H., Coleman, M., Thompson, A., & Goodwin-Watkins, C. (1996). African American and European American college students' expectations for self and future partners. *Journal of Family Issues, 17*(6), 758–775.

Gardiner, L. F. (2005). Transforming the environment for learning: A crisis of quality. *To Improve the Academy, 23*, 3–23.

Gardner, H. (1983). *Frames of mind: The theory of multiple intelligences*. New York: Basic Books.

Gardner, P. D. (1991, March). *Learning the ropes: Socialization and assimilation into the workplace*. Paper presented at the Second National Conference on The Senior Year Experience, San Antonio, TX.

Gardner, H. (1993). *Multiple intelligences: The theory of multiple intelligences* (2nd ed.). New York: Basic Books.

Gardner, H. (1999). *Intelligence reframed: Multiple intelligences for the 21st century*. New York: Basic Books.

Gardner, J. N. (1987, January). *The freshman year experience movement: Present status and future directions*. Address delivered at The Freshman Year Experience Conference—West, Irvine, CA.

Garfield, C. A. (1984). *Peak performance: Mental training techniques of the world's greatest athletes*. Los Angeles: Tarcher.

Gemmil, G. (1989). The dynamics of scapegoating in small groups. *Small Group Behavior, 20*, 406–418.

Gere, A. R. (1987). *Writing groups: history, theory, and implications*. Carbondale, IL: Southern Illinois University Press.

Gershoff, S., & Whitney, C. (1996). *The Tufts University guide to total nutrition*. New York: HarperPerennial

Gibb, J. R. (1961). Defensive communication. *The Journal of Communication* (September) *11*, p. 3.

Gibb, H. R. (1991). *Trust: A new vision of human relationships for business, education, family, and personal living* (2nd ed.). North Hollywood, CA: Newcastle.

Giles, R. M., Johnson, M. R., Knight, K. E., Zammett, S., & Weinman, J. (1982). Recall of lecture information: A question of what, when, and where. *Medical Education, 16*(5), 264–268.

Giles, L. C., Glonek, F. V., Luszcz, M. A., & Andrews, G. R. (2005). Effect of social networks on 10-year survival in very old Australians: The Australia longitudinal study of aging. *Journal of Epidemiology and Community Health, 59*, 574–579.

Glass, J., & Garrett, M. (1995). Student participation in a college orientation course: retention, and grade point average. *Community College Journal of Research and Practice, 19,* 117–132.

Glassman, J. K. (2000, June 9). The technology revolution: Road to freedom or road to serfdom? *Heritage Lectures*, No. 668. Washington, DC: The Heritage Foundation.

Glenberg, A. M., Bradley, M. M., Kraus, T. A., & Renzaglia, G. J. (1983). Studies of the long-term recency effect: Support for a contextually guided retrieval hypothesis. *Journal of Experimental Psychology: Learning, Memory, and Cognition, 9*, 231–255.

Glenberg, A. M., Schroeder, J. L., & Robertson, D. A. (1998). Averting the gaze disengages the environment and facilitates remembering. *Memory & Cognition, 26*(4), 651–658.

Goffman, E. (1956). *The presentation of self in everyday life*. Edinburgh, UK: University of Edinburgh, Social Sciences Research Centre.

Goffman, E. (Ed.) (1967). *Interaction ritual: Essays in face-to-face behavior*. Chicago: Aldine.

Goleman, D. (1992, Oct. 27). Voters assailed by unfair persuasion. *The New York Times*, pp. C1–C3.

Goleman, D. (1995). *Emotional intelligence: Why it can matter more than IQ*. New York: Bantam Books.

Gordon, W. C. (1989). *Learning and memory*. Belmont: Wadsworth.

Gordon, V. N., & Steele, G. E. (2003). Undecided first-year students: A 25-year longitudinal study. *Journal of The First-Year Experience, 15*(1), 19–38.

Gottman, J. (1994). *Why marriages succeed and fail*. New York: Fireside.

Graf, P. (1982). The memorial consequence of generation and transformation. *Journal of Verbal Learning and Verbal Behavior, 21*, 539–548.

Green, M. G. (Ed.) (1989). *Minorities on campus: A handbook for enhancing diversity*. Washington, D.C.: American Council on Education.

Greenberg, R., Pillard, R., & Pearlman, C. (1972). The effect of dream (Stage REM) deprivation on adaptation to stress. *Psychosomatic Medicine, 34*, 257–262.

Griffin, C. W. (1982). *Teaching writing in all disciplines*. New York: Directions for Teaching and Learning, No. 12. San Francisco: Jossey-Bass.

Grunder, P., & Hellmich, D. (1996). Academic persistence and achievement of remedial students in a community college's success program. *Community College Review, 24,* 21–33.

Guilford, J. P. (1967). *The nature of human intelligence*. New York: McGraw-Hill.

Gullette, M. M. (1989). Leading discussion in a lecture course. *Change, 24*(2), pp. 32–39.

Haas, R. (1994). *Eat smart, think smart*. New York: HarperCollins.

Haberman, S., & Luffey, D. (1998). Weighing in college students' diet and exercise behaviors. *Journal of American College Health, 46*, 189–191.

Hall, E. T., & Hall, M. R. (1986). *Hidden differences: How to communicate with the Germans*. Hamburg, West Germany: Gruner & Jahr.

Hall, R. M., & Sandler, B. R. (1982). *The classroom climate: A chilly one for women*. Association of American Colleges' Project on the Status of Women. Washington, DC: Association of American Colleges.

Hall, R. M., & Sandler, B. R. (1984). *Out of the classroom: A chilly campus climate for women*. Association of American Colleges' Project on the Status of Women. Washington, DC: Association of American Colleges.

Halperin, A. C. (2002). *State of the union: Smoking on US college campuses*. Washington, DC: A report from the American Legacy Foundation. Retrieved August 13, 2006, from http:www.ttac.org/college/facts/references/html

Hamilton, D. L., & Sherman, S. J. (1989). Illusory correlations: Implications for streotype theory and research. In D. Bar-Tal, C. F. Graumann, A. W. Kruglanski, & W. Stroebe (Eds.), *Stereotyping and prejudice: Changing conceptions* (pp. 59–82). New York: Springer-Verlag.

Harriott, J., & Ferrari, J. R. (1996). Prevalence of procrastination among samples of adults. *Psychological Reports, 78*, 611–616.

Hart, L. A. (1983). *Human brain and human learning*. White Plains, NY: Longman.

Hartley, J. (1998). *Learning and studying: a research perspective*. London: Routledge.

Hartley, J., & Marshall, S. (1974). On notes and note taking. *Universities Quarterly, 28*, 225–235.

Harvey, L., Moon, S., Geall, V., & Bower, R. (1997). *Graduates' work: Organisational change and students' attributes*. Birmingham: Centre for Research into Quality, University of Central England.

Hashaw, R. M., Hammond, C. J., & Rogers, P. H. (1990). Academic locus of control and the collegiate experience. *Research & Teaching in Developmental Education, 7*(1), 45–54.

Hatfield, E., & Walster, G. W. (1985). *A new look at love*. Lanham, MD: University Press of America.

Hauri, P., & Linde, S. (1996). *No more sleepless nights*. New York: John Wiley & Sons.

"Haven't filed yet? Tackle those taxes." (2003, April 11). *USA Today*, p. 3b.

Health, C., & Soll, J. (1996). Mental budgeting and consumer decisions. *Journal of Consumer Research, 23*, 40–52.

Heath, H. (1977). *Maturity and competence: A transcultural view.* New York: Halsted Press.

Helkowski, C. & Shehan, M. (2004). Too sure, too soon: When choosing should wait. *About Campus*, (May/June), 19–24.

Herman, R. E. (2000). Liberal arts: The key to the future. *USA Today Magazine* (November), *129*, p. 34

Hersh, R. (1994). What our publics want, but think they don't get, from a liberal arts education: Ted Marchese interviews Richard Hersh. *AAHE Bulletin* (November), pp. 8–10.

Hersh, R. (1997). Intentions and perceptions: A national survey of public attitudes toward liberal arts education. *Change, 29*(2), pp. 16–23.

Higbee, K. L. (2001). *Your memory: How it works and how to improve it.* New York: Marlowe & Company.

Higher Education Council (1992). *The quality of higher education: Discussion papers.* (National Board of Employment, Education, & Training), Cantaberra, Australian Capital Territory: Australian Government Publishing Service.

Higher Education Institute (2004). *The spiritual life of college students: A national study of college students' search for meaning and purpose.* Los Angeles, CA: Higher Education Research Institute, Graduate School of Education & Information Studies. University of California, Los Angeles.

Hildenbrand, M., & Gore, P. A., Jr. (2005). Career development in the first-year seminar: Best practice versus actual practice. In P. A. Gore (Ed.), *Facilitating the career development of students in transition* (Monograph No. 43) (pp. 45–60). Columbia, SC: University of South Carolina, National Resource Center for The First-Year Experience and Students in Transition.

Hill, A. J. (2002). Developmental issues in attitudes toward food and diet. *Proceedings of the Nutrition Society, 61*(2), 259–268.

Hill, J. O., Wyat, H. R., Reed, G. W., & Peters, J. C. (2003). Obesity and environment: Where do we go from here? *Science, 299*, 853–855.

Hillocks, G. (1986). What works in teaching composition: A meta-analysis of experimental treatment studies. *American Journal of Education, 93*(1), 133–170.

Hobson, J. A. (1988). *The dreaming brain.* New York: Basic Books.

Hobson, E. H. (2004). *Getting students to read: Fourteen tips.* IDEA Paper #40. Manhattan, KS: The IDEA Center.

Hogan, R., Curphy, G. J., & Hogan, J. (1994). What we know about leadership: Effectiveness and personality. *American Psychologist, 49*, 493–504.

Holmes, K. K., Levine, R., & Weaver, M. (2004). Effectiveness of condoms in preventing sexually transmitted infections. *Bulletin of the World Health Organization, 82*, 254–464.

Horn, C. E. (1995). *Enhancing the connection between higher education and the workplace.* Denver, CO: The State Higher Education Executive Offices and The Education Commission of the States.

Horne, J. (1988). *Why we sleep: The functions of sleep in humans and other mammals.* New York: Oxford University Press.

Howard, A. (1986). College experiences and managerial performance. *Journal of Applied Psychology, 71*, 530–552.

Howard, P. J. (2000). *The owner's manual for the brain: Everyday applications of mind-brain research* (2nd ed.). Atlanta, GA: Bard Press.

Howe, M. J. (1970). Note-taking strategy, review, and long-term retention of verbal information. *Journal of Educational Psychology, 63*, 285.

Hugenberg, K., & Bodenhausen, G. V. (2003). Facing prejudice: Implicit prejudice and the perception of facial threat. *Psychological Science, 14*, 640–643.

Hunter, M. A., & Linder, C. W. (2005). First-year seminars. In M. L. Upcraft, J. N. Gardner, B. O. Barefoot, & Associates, *Challenging and supporting the first-year student: A handbook for improving the first year of college* (pp. 275–291). San Francisco: Jossey-Bass.

Indiana University (2004). *Selling your liberal arts degree to employers.* Bloomington, IN: Indiana University, Arts & Sciences Placement Office. Retrieved July 7, 2004, from http://www.indiana.edu/~career/fulltime/selling_liberal_arts.html

Insel, P. M., & Jacobson, L. (1975). *What do you expect? An inquiry into self-fulfilling prophecies.* Menlo Park: CA: Cummings Publishing.

Institute for Research on Higher Education (1995). Connecting schools and employers: Work-related education and training. *Change, 27*(3), pp. 39–46.

Institute of International Education (2001). *Open doors.* Retrieved July 7, 2005, from www.opendoorsweb.org/2001%20Files/layout_htm

Jablonski, N. G., & Chaplin, G. (2002). Skin deep. *Scientific American* (October), 75–81.

Jacobs, W. J., & Nadel, L. (1985). Stress-induced recovery of fears and phobias. *Psychological Review, 92*(4), 512–531.

Jakubowski, P., & Lange, A. J. (1978). *The assertive option: Your rights and responsibilities.* Champaign, IL: Research Press.

Janis, I. L. (1982). *Groupthink: Psychological studies of policy decisions and fiascoes.* (2nd ed.). Boston: Houghton Mifflin.

Jarvik, M. E. (1995). The scientific case that nicotine is addictive: Comment. *Psychopharmacology, 117*(1), 18–20.

Jemott, J. B., & Magloire, K. (1988). Academic stress, social support, and secretory immunoglobin. *Journal of Personality and Social Psychology, 55*, 803–810.

Jenkins, J. G., & Dallenbach, K. M. (1924). Oblivescence during sleep and waking. *American Journal of Psychology, 35*, 605–612.

Jensen, E. (1998). *Teaching with the brain in mind.* Alexandria, VA: Association for Supervision and Curriculum Development.

Johnsgard, K. W. (2004). *Conquering depression and anxiety through exercise.* New York: Prometheus.

Johnson, D. W., Johnson, R. T., & Smith, K. A. (1991). *Cooperative learning: Increasing college faculty instructional productivity.* ASHE-ERIC Higher Education Report No. 4. Washington, D.C.: Association for the Study of Higher Education.

Johnson, D., Johnson, R., & Smith, K. (1998). Cooperative learning returns to college: What evidence is there that it works? *Change, 30*, 26–35.

Joint Science Academies Statement (2005). *Global response to climate change.* Retrieved August 29, 2005, from http://nationalacademies.org/onpi/06072005.pdf

Jones, W. T. (1990). Perspectives on ethnicity. In L. V. Moore (Ed.), *Evolving theoretical perspectives on students* (pp. 59–72). San Francisco: Jossey-Bass.

Jones, W. H., Cheek, J. M., & Biggs, S. R. (1986). *Shyness: Perspectives on research and treatment.* New York: Plenum.

Jones, L., & Petruzzi, D. C. (1995). Test anxiety: A review of theory and current treatment. *Journal of College Student Psychotherapy, 10*(1), 3–15.

Joseph, R. (1988). The right cerebral hemisphere: emotion, music, visual-spatial skills, body-image, dreams, and awareness. *Journal of Clinical Psychology, 44*(5), 630–673.

Judd, C. M., Ryan, C. S., & Parke, B. (1991). Accuracy in the judgment of in-group and out-group variability. *Journal of Personality and Social Psychology, 61*, 366–379.

Julien, R. M. (2004). *A primer of drug action.* New York: Worth.

Kachgal, M. M., Hansen, L. S., & Nutter, K. J. (2001). Academic procrastination prevention/intervention: Strategies and recommendations. *Journal of Developmental Education, 25*, 14–24.

Kadison, R. D., & DiGeronimo, T. F. (2004). *College of the overwhelmed: The campus mental health crisis and what to do about it.* San Francisco: Jossey-Bass.

Kagan, S., & Kagan, M. (1998). *Multiple intelligences: The complete MI book.* San Clemente, CA: Kagan Cooperative Learning.

Karelis, C. H. (1986). A note on democracy and liberal education. *Liberal Education, 72*(4), 319–322.

Kasper, G. (2004, March). *Tax procrastination: Survey finds 29% have yet to begin taxes.* Retrieved June 6, 2006, from http://www.preweb.com/releases/2004/3/prweb114250.htm

Kassin, S. (2006). *Psychology in modules.* Upper Saddle Back River, NJ: Pearson.

Katz, J., & Henry, M. (1993). *Turning professors into teachers: A new approach to faculty development and student learning.* Phoenix: American Council on Education and Oryx Press.

Kaufman, J. C., & Baer, J. (2002). Could Steven Spielberg manage the Yankees?: Creative thinking in different domains. *Korean Journal of Thinking & Problem Solving, 12*(2), 5–14.

Kearns, D. (1989). Getting schools back on track. *Newsweek* (November), pp. 8–9.

Kember, D., Jamieson, Q. W., Pomfret, M., & Wong, E. T. T. (1995). Learning approaches, study time and academic performance. *Higher Education, 29*, 329–343.

Khoshaba, D. M., & Maddi, S. R. (1999–2004). *HardiTraining: Managing stressful change.* Newport Beach, CA: The Hardiness Institute.

Kielcolt-Glaser, J. K., & Glaser, R. (1986). Psychological influences on immunity. *Psychosomatics, 27*, 621–625.

Kiecolt, J. K., Glaser, R., Strain, E., Stout, J., Tarr, K., Holliday, J., & Speicher, C. (1986). Modulation of cellular immunity in medical students. *Journal of Behavioral Medicine, 9*, 5–21.

Kiewra, K. A. (1985). Students' note-taking behaviors and the efficacy of providing the instructor's notes for review. *Contemporary Educational Psychology, 10*, 378–386.

Kierwa, K. A. (2000). Fish giver or fishing teacher? The lure of strategy instruction. *Teaching at UNL, 22*(3), pp. 1–3. Lincoln, NE: University of Nebraska-Lincoln.

Kiewra, K. A., & Fletcher, H. J. (1984). The relationship between notetaking variables and achievement measures. *Human Learning, 3*, 273–280.

Kiewra, K. A., Hart, K., Scoular, J., Stephen, M., Sterup, G., & Tyler, B. (2000). Fish giver or fishing teacher? The lure of strategy instruction. *Teaching at UNL, 22*(3), Lincoln NE: Teaching & Learning Center, University of Nebraska.

Kincaid, J. P., & Wickens, D. D. (1970). Temporal gradient of release from proactive inhibition. *Journal of Experimental Psychology, 86*, 313–316.

King, A. (1990). Enhancing peer interaction and learning in the classroom through reciprocal questioning. *American Educational Research Journal, 27*(4), 664–687.

King, A. (1995). Guided peer questioning: A cooperative learning approach to critical thinking. *Cooperative Learning and College Teaching, 5*(2), pp. 15–19.

King, J. E. (2002). *Crucial choices: How students' financial decisions affect their academic success.* Washington, DC: American Council on Education.

King, J. E. (2005). Academic success and financial decisions: Helping students make crucial choices. In R. S. Feldman (Ed.), *Improving the first year of college: Research and practice* (pp. 3–26). Mahwah, NJ: Lawrence Erlbaum Associates.

King, P. M., & Kitchener, K. S. (1994). *Developing reflective judgment: Understanding and promoting intellectual growth and critical thinking in adolescents and adults.* San Francisco: Jossey–Bass.

Kintsch, W. (1968). Recognition and free recall of organized lists. *Journal of Experimental Psychology, 78*, 481–487.

Kintsch, W. (1970). *Learning, memory, and conceptual processes.* Hoboken, NJ: John Wiley & Sons.

Kintsch, W. (1982). *Memory and cognition.* Melbourne, FL: Krieger.

Kintsch, W. (1994). Text comprehension, memory, and learning. *American Psychologist, 49*, 294–303.

Kitchener, K., Wood, P., & Jensen, L. (2000, August). *Curricular, co-curricular, and institutional influence on real-world problem-solving.* Paper presented at the annual meeting of the American Psychological Association, Boston.

Klein, S. P., & Hart, F. M. (1968). Chance and systematic factors affecting essay grades. *Journal of Educational Measurement, 5*, 197–206.

Knapp, J. R., & Karabenick, S. A. (1988). Incidence of formal and informal academic help-seeking in higher education. *Journal of College Student Development, 29*(3), 223–227.

Knoll, A. H. (2003). *Life on a young planet: The first three billion years of evolution on earth.* Princeton, NJ: Princeton University Press.

Knouse, S., Tanner, J., & Harris, E. (1999). The relation of college internships, college performance, and subsequent job opportunity. *Journal of Employment Counseling, 36*, 35–43.

Knox, S. (2004). *Financial basics: A money management guide for students.* Columbus, OH: Ohio State University Press.

Kolb, D. A. (1976). Management and learning process. *California Management Review, 18*(3), 21–31.

Kolb, D. A. (1985). *Learning styles inventory.* Boston: McBer.

Kouzes, J. M., & Posner, B. Z. (1988). *The leadership challenge: How to get extraordinary things done in organizations.* San Francisco: Jossey-Bass.

Kowalewski, D., Holstein, E., & Schneider, V. (1989). The validity of selected correlates of unexcused absences in a four-year private college. *Educational and Psychological Measurement, 49*, 985–991.

Kruger, J., Wirtz, D., & Miller, D. (2005). Counterfactual thinking and the first instinct fallacy. *Journal of Personality and Social Psychology, 88*, 725–735.

Kuh, G. D. (1993). In their own words: What students learn outside the classroom. *American Educational Research Journal, 30*, 277–304.

Kuh, G. D. (1995). The other curriculum: Out-of-class experiences associated with student learning and personal development. *Journal of Higher Education, 66*(2), 123–153.

Kuh, G. D. (2002, February 17). *Student engagement in the first year of college.* Plenary address presented at the Annual Conference of The First-Year Experience, Kissimmee, Florida.

Kuh, G. D., Douglas, K. B., Lund, J. P., & Ramin-Gyurnek, J. (1994). *Student learning outside the classroom: Transcending artificial boundaries.* ASHE-ERIC Higher Education Report, No. 8. Washington, D.C.: George Washington University, School of Education and Human Development.

Kuhn, L. (1988). What should we tell students about answer changing? *Research Serving Teaching, 1*(8). Cape Girardeau, MO: Center for Teaching and Learning, Southeast Missouri State University.

Kulik, J. A., & Kulik, C.-L. C. (1979). College teaching. In P. L. Peterson & H. J. Walberg (Eds.), *Research on teaching: Concepts, findings, and implications*. Berkeley, CA: McCutcheon.

Kurfiss, J. G. (1988). *Critical thinking: theory, research, practice, and possibilities*. ASHE-ERIC, Report No. 2. Washington, DC: Association for the Study of Higher Education.

La Berge, D. (1995). *Attentional processing*. Cambridge, MA: Harvard University Press.

Ladas, H. S. (1980). Note-taking on lectures: An information-processing approach. *Educational Psychologist, 15*(1), 44–53.

Lakein, A. (1973). *How to get control of your time and your life*. New York: New American Library.

Lay, C. H., & Silverman, S. (1996). Trait procrastination, time management, and dilatory behavior. *Personality & Individual Differences, 21*, 61–67.

Langer, J. A., & Applebee, A. N. (1987). *How writing shapes thinking*. NCTE Research Report No. 22. Urbana, IL: National Council of Teachers of English.

Latané, B., Liu, J. H., Nowak, A., Bonevento, N., & Zheng, L. (1995). Distance matters: Physical space and social impact. *Personality and Social Psychology Bulletin, 21*, 795–805.

Laur-Ernst, U. (1990). German vocational education survey. In B. G. Scheckley, L. Lamdin, & M. T. Keeton (Eds.), *The skills employers seek and employees need: Employability in a high performance economy* (pp. 109–113). Chicago: Council for Adult and Experiential Education.

Leahy, R. (1990). What the College Writing Center is—and isn't. *College Teaching, 38*(2), 43–48.

LeDoux, J. E. (1996). *The emotional brain: The mysterious underpinnings of emotional life*. New York: Touchstone.

Lefcourt, H. M. (1982). *Locus of control: Current trends in theory and research*. Hillsdale, NJ: Erlbaum.

Lehrer, P. M., & Woolfolk, R. L. (1993). *Principles and practice of stress management*, Vol. 2. New York: Guilford Press.

Leibel, R. L., Rosenbaum, M., & Hirsch, J. (1995). Changes in energy expenditure resulting from altered body weight. *New England Journal of Medicine, 332*, 621–628.

Leuwerke, W. C., Robbins, S. B., Sawyer, R., & Hovland, M. (2004). Predicting engineering major status from mathematics achievement and interest congruence. *Journal of Career Assessment, 12*, 135–149.

Levin, D. T. (2000). Race as a visual feature: Using visual search and perceptual discrimination tasks to understand face categories and the cross-race recognition deficit. *Journal of Experimental Psychology: General, 129*(4), 559–574.

Levine, A. (1989). *Shaping higher education's future—demographic realities and opportunities, 1990–2000*. San Francisco: Jossey-Bass.

Levine, L. W. (1996). *The opening of the American mind: Canons, culture, and history*. Boston: Beacon Press.

Levine, A., & Cureton, J. S. (1998). *When hopes and fears collide*. San Francisco: Jossey-Bass.

Levitsky, D. A., Nussbaum, M., Halbmaier, C. A., Mrdjenovic, G. (2003, July). *The freshman 15: A model for the study of techniques to curb the 'epidemic' of obesity*. Annual meeting of the Society of the Study of Ingestive Behavior, University of Groningen, Haren, The Netherlands.

Levitz, R., & Noel, L. (1989). Connecting student to the institution: Keys to retention and success. In M. L. Upcraft, J. N. Gardner, & Associates, *The freshman year experience* (pp. 65–81). San Francisco: Jossey-Bass.

Lewin, K. (1935). *A dynamic theory of personality*. New York: McGraw Hill.

Liebertz, C. (2005a). Want clear thinking? Relax. *Scientific American Mind, 16*(3), pp. 88–89.

Liebertz, C. (2005b). A healthy laugh. *Scientific American Mind, 16*(3), pp. 90–91.

Light, R. L. (1990). *The Harvard assessment seminars*. Cambridge, MA: Harvard University Press.

Light, R. L. (1992). *The Harvard assessment seminars, second report*. Cambridge, MA: Harvard University Press.

Light, R. J. (2001). *Making the most of college: Students speak their minds*. Cambridge, MA: Harvard University Press.

Linn, R. L., & Gronlund, N. E. (1995). *Measurement and assessment in teaching* (7th ed.). Englewood Cliffs, NJ: Prentice-Hall.

Linville, P. W., Fischer, G. W., & Salovey, P. (1989). Perceived distributions of the characteristics of in-group and out-group members: Empirical evidence and a computer simulation. *Journal of Personality and Social Psychology, 57*, 165–188.

Lock, R. D. (2000). *Taking charge of your career direction* (4th ed.). Belmont, CA: Wadsworth/Thomson Learning.

Locke, E. (1977). An empirical study of lecture note-taking among college students. *Journal of Educational Research, 77*, 93–99.

Locke, E. A. (1991). *The essentials of leadership.* New York: Lexington Books.

Loftus, E. F. (1979). The malleability of human memory. *American Scientist, 67*(3), 312–320.

Loftus, E. F. (1980). *Memory: Surprising new insights into how we remember and how we forget.* Reading, MA: Addison-Wesley.

Lopez, G. E., Gurin, P., & Nagda, B. A. (1998). Education and understanding structural causes for group inequalities. *Journal of Political Psychology, 19*(2), 305–329.

Lorayne, H., & Lucas, J. (1974). *The memory book.* New York: Stein & Day.

Love, P., & Love, A. G. (1995). *Enhancing student learning: Intellectual, social, and emotional integration.* ASHE-ERIC Higher Education Report No. 4. Washington, D.C.: The George Washington University. Graduate School of Education and Human Development.

Elster, J., & Lowenstein, G. (Eds.) (1992). *Choice over time.* New York: Russell Sage Foundation.

Lubart, T. I. (1999). Creativity across cultures. In R. J. Sternberg (Ed.), *Handbook of creativity* (pp. 339–350). New York: Cambridge University Press.

Luotto, J. A., Stoll, E. L., & Hoglund-Ketttmann, N. (2001). *Communication skills for collaborative learning* (2nd ed.): Dubuque, IA: Kendall/Hunt.

Lutz, A., Greischar, N. B., Rawlings, M. R., & Davidson, R. J. (2004). Long-term meditators self-induce high-amplitude gamma synchrony during mental practice. *Proceedings of the National Academy of Science, 101*, 16369–16373.

MacGregor, J. (1991). What differences do learning communities make? *Washington Center News, 6*(1), pp. 4–9

Mackes (2003). Employers describe perfect job candidate. *NACEWeb Press Releases.* Retrieved July 13, 2004, from http://www.naceweb.org/press

MADD (2006). *Why 21?* Retrieved Dec. 16, 2006, from http://www/madd.org/stats/4846

Maddi, S. R. (2002). The story of hardiness: Twenty years of theorizing, research, and practice. *Consulting Psychology Journal: Practice and Research, 54*(3), 175–185.

Maes, J. D., Weldy, T. G., & Icenogle, M. L. (1997). A managerial perspective: Oral communication competency is most important for business students in the workplace. *The Journal of Business Communication, 34*(1), 67–80.

Magolda, M. B. B. (1992). *Knowing and reasoning in college.* San Francisco: Jossey-Bass.

Maier, N. R. F. (1970). *Problem solving and creativity in individuals and groups.* Belmont, CA: Brooks/Cole.

Mandler, G. (1967). Organization and memory. In K. W. Spence & J. T. Spence (Eds.), *The psychology of learning and motivation: Advances in research and theory* (Volume 1) (pp. 328–372). New York: Academic Press.

Marchese, T. J. (1990). A new conversation about undergraduate teaching: An interview with Professor Richard J. Light, convener of the Harvard Assessment Seminars. *AAHE Bulletin, 42*(9), 3–8.

Marshall, W. L., Boutilier, J., & Minnes, P. M. (1974). The modification of phobic behavior by covert reinforcement. *Behavior Therapy, 5*, 469–480.

Martin, P. Y., & Benton, D. (1999). The influence of a glucose drink on a demanding working memory task. *Physiology & Behavior, 67*(1), 69–74.

Marton, F., & Saljo, R. (1984). Approaches to learning. In F. Marton et al. (Eds.), *The experience of learning.* Edinburgh: Scottish Academic Press.

Marton, F., Housell, D. J., & Entwistle, N. J. (1997) (Eds.). *The experience of learning* (2nd ed.). Edinburg: Scottish Academic Press.

Marzano, R. J., Pickering, D. J., & Pollock, J. (2001). *Classroom instruction that works: Research-based strategies for increasing student achievement.* Alexandria, VA: Association for Supervision and Curriculum Development.

Massey, D. (2003). *The source of the river: The social origins of freshmen at America's selective colleges and universities.* Princeton, NJ: Princeton University Press.

May, M., Galper, L., & Carr, J. (2004). *Am I hungry? What to do when diets don't work.* Phoenix, AZ: Nourish Publishing.

McArthur, L. Z., & Friedman, S. A. (1980). Illusory correlation in impression formation: Variations in the shared distinctiveness effect as a function of the distinctive person's age, race, and sex. *Journal of Personality and Social Psychology, 39*, 615–624.

McGhee, P. (1999). *Health, healing and the American system.* Dubuque: Kendall/Hunt.

McGuiness, D., & Pribram, K. (1980). The neurophysiology of attention: Emotional and motivational controls. In M. D. Wittrock (Ed.), *The brain and psychology* (pp. 95–139). New York: Academic Press.

Mehrabian, A. (1972). *Nonverbal communication.* Chicago: Adline-Atherton.

Meilman, P. W., & Presley, C. A. (2005). The first-year experience and alcohol use. In M. L. Upcraft, J. N. Gardner, & B. O. Barefoot, & Associates, *Challenging and supporting the first-year student: A handbook for improving the first year of college* (pp. 445–468). San Francisco: Jossey-Bass.

Meyers, C. (1986). *Teaching students to think critically: A guide for faculty in all disciplines.* San Francisco: Jossey-Bass.

Middleton, F., & Strick, P. (1994). Anatomical evidence for cerebellar and basal ganglia involvement in higher brain function. *Science, 226,* 51584: 458–461.

Millard, B. (2004, November 7). *A purpose-based approach to navigating college transitions.* Preconference workshop presented at the Eleventh National Conference on Students in Transition, Nashville, Tennessee.

Miller, G. (1988). *The meaning of general education.* New York: Teachers College Press.

Miller, M. A. (2003). The meaning of the baccalaureate. *About Campus* (Sept./October), pp. 2–8.

Millman, J., Bishop, C., & Ebel, R. (1965). An analysis of test-wiseness. *Educational and Psychological Measurement, 25,* 707–727.

Milner, A. D., & Goodale, M. A. (1998). *The visual brain in action.* (Oxford Psychology Series, No. 27). Oxford: Oxford University Press.

Milton, O. (1982). *Will that be on the final?* Springfield, Ill.: Charles C. Thomas.

Minninger, J. (1984). *Total recall: How to boost your memory power.* Emmaus, PA: Rodale.

Mitler, M. M., Dinges, D. F., & Dement, W. C. (1994). Sleep medicine, public policy, and public health. In M. H. Kryger, T. Roth, & W. C. Dement (Eds.), *Principles and practice of sleep medicine* (2nd ed.). Philadelphia: Saunders.

Molnar, S. (1991). *Human variation: race, type, and ethnic groups* (3rd ed.). Englewood Cliffs, NJ: Prentice-Hall.

Monk, T. H. (2005). The post-lunch dip in performance. *Clinical Sports Medicine, 24*(2), 15–23.

Motley, M. T. (1997). *Overcoming your fear of public speaking: A proven method.* Boston, MA: Houghton Mifflin.

Multon, K. D., Brown, S. D., & Lent, R. W. (1991). Relation of self-efficacy beliefs to academic outcomes: A meta-analytic investigation. *Journal of Counseling Psychology, 38*(1), 30–38.

Murname, K., & Shiffrin, R. M. (1991). Interference and the representation of events in memory. *Journal of Experimental Psychology: Learning, Memory, & Cognition, 17,* 855–874.

Murray, D. M. (1984). *Write to learn* (2nd ed.). New York: Holt, Rinehart, & Winston.

Murray, D. M. (1993). *Write to learn* (4th ed.). Fort Worth: Harcourt Brace.

Myers, I. B. (1976). *Introduction to type.* Gainesville, FL: Center for the Application of Psychological Type.

Myers, D. G. (1993). *The pursuit of happiness: Who is happy—and why?* New York: Morrow.

Myers, D. G., & McCaulley, N. H. (1985). *Manual: A guide to the development and use of the Myers-Briggs Type Indicator.* Palo Alto, CA: Consulting Psychologists Press.

Nadel L., & Willner, J. (1980). Context and conditioning. A place for space. *Journal of Comparative and Physiological Psychology, 8,* 218–228.

Nagda, B. R., Gurin, P., & Lopez, G. E. (2003). Transformative pedagogy for democracy and social justice. *Race, Ethnicity, & Education, 6*(2), 165–191.

Nagda, B. R., Gurin, P., & Johnson, S. M. (2005). Living, doing and thinking diversity: How does pre-college diversity experience affect first-year students' engagement with college diversity? In R. S. Feldman (Ed.), *Improving the first year of college: Research and practice* (pp. 73–110). Mahwah, NJ: Lawrence Erlbaum Associates.

Naisbitt, J. (1982). *Megatrends: Ten new directions transforming our lives.* New York: Warner Books.

Narciso, J., & Burkett, D. (1975). *Disclose yourself: Discover the "me" in relationships.* Englewood Cliffs, NJ: Prentice-Hall.

Natale, V., & Ciogna, P. (1996). Circadian regulation of subjective alertness in morning and evening types. *EDRA: Environmental Design Research Association, 20*(4), 491–497.

National Association of Colleges and Employers (NACE) (2003). *Job Outlook 2003 survey.* Bethlehem, PA: Author.

National Forum on Information Literacy (2005). *Forum overview.* Retrieved Oct. 17, 2005, from http://www.infolit.org

National Institute of Mental Health (2001). *Eating disorders: Facts about eating disorders and the search for solutions.* Retrieved August 7, 2006, from http://www.nimh.nih.gov/publicat/eatingdisorders.cfm

National Institute of Mental Health (2006). *The numbers count: Mental disorders in America.* Retrieved December 16, 2006, from http:www.nimh.nih.gov.pulicat/numbers.cfm

National Research Council (1989). *Diet and health: Implications for reducing chronic disease risk.* Committee on Diet and Health, Washington, DC: National Academy Press.

National Resources Defense Council (2005). *Global warming: A summary of recent findings on the changing global climate.* Retrieved Nov. 11, 2005, from http://www.nrdc.org/global/Warming/fgwscience.asp

National Wellness Institute (2005). *The six dimensional wellness model.* Retrieved August 11, 2006, from http://www.nationalwellness.org/SitePrint.ph?id=391&tiername=Free%20Resource%20

Neer, M. R. (1987). The development of an instrument to measure classroom apprehension. *Communication Education, 36,* 154–166.

Newell, A., & Rosenbloom, P. S. (1981). Mechanisms of skill acquisition of the law of practice. In J. R. Anderson (Ed.), *Cognitive skills and their acquisition.* Hillsdale, NJ: Erlbaum.

Newton, T. (1990, September). *Improving students' listening skills.* IDEA Paper No. 23. Manhattan, KS: Center for Faculty Evaluation and Development.

Nicholas, R. W. (1991). Cultures in the curriculum. *Liberal Education, 77*(3), 16–21.

Nichols, M. P. (1995). *The lost art of listening.* New York: Guilford Press.

Nichols, R. G., & Stevens, L. A. (1957). *Are you listening?* New York: McGraw-Hill.

Niles, S. G., & Harris-Bowlsbey, J. (2002). *Career development interventions in the 21st century.* Upper Saddle River, NJ: Pearson Education.

Noel, L. (1985). Increasing student retention: New challenges and potential. In L. Noel & Associates (Eds.), *Increasing student retention* (pp. 1–27). San Francisco: Jossey-Bass.

Norman, D. A. (1982). *Learning and memory.* San Francisco: W. H. Freeman.

Nummela, R. M., & Rosengren, T. M. (1986). What's happening in students' brains may redefine teaching. *Educational Leadership, 43*(8), 49–53.

Nystrand, M. (1986). *The structure of written communication: Studies in reciprocity between writers and readers.* Orlando, FL: Academic Press.

Office of Research (1994). *What employers expect of college graduates: International knowledge and second language skills.* Washington, D.C.: Office of Educational Research and Improvement (OERI), U.S. Department of Education.

Ogawa, K., Nittono, H., & Hori, T. (2002). Brain potentials associated with the onset and offset of rapid eye movement (REM) during REM sleep. *Psychiatry & Clinical Neurosciences, 56,* 259–260.

O'Keefe, J., & Nadel, L. (1978). *The hippocampus as a cognitive map.* Oxford: Clarendon Press.

Oller, D. K. (1981). Infant vocalizations: Exploration and reflectivity. In R. E. Stark (Ed.), *Language behavior in infancy and early childhood* (pp. 85–104). New York: Elsevier/North-Holland.

Onwuegbuzie, A. J. (2000). Academic procrastinators and perfectionistic tendencies among graduate students. *Journal of Social Behavior and Personality, 15,* 103–109.

Orszag, J. M., Orszag, P. R., & Whitmore, D. M. (2001). *Learning and earning: Working in college.* Retrieved July 19, 2006 from http://www.brockport.edu/career01/upromise.htm

Ottinger, C. (1990). College graduates in the labor market: Today and the future. *Research Briefs, 1*(5), pp. 1–2. Washington, D.C.: American Council on Education, Division of Policy Analysis & Research,

Pace, C. R. (1990a). Measuring the quality of student effort. *Current Issues in Higher Education, 2*(1), (Monograph). Washington, D.C.: American Association for Higher Education.

Pace, C. R. (1990b). *The undergraduates.* Los Angeles: Center for the Study of Evaluation, University of California, Los Angeles.

Paivio, A. (1990). *Mental representations: A dual coding approach.* New York: Oxford University Press.

Palank, J. (2006, July 17, 2006). *Face it: 'Book' no secret to employers.* Retrieved August 21, 2006, from http:www.washtimes.com/business/20060717-12942-1800r.htm

Palmer, P. J. (1999). *The active life: A spirituality of work, creativity and caring.* San Francisco: Jossey-Bass.

Paolini, S., Hewstone, M., Cairns, E., & Voci, A. (2004). Effects of direct and indirect cross-group friendships on judgments of Catholics and Protestants in Northern Ireland: The mediating role of an anxiety-reduction mechanism. *Personality and Social Psychology Bulletin, 30,* 770–786.

Papalia, D. E., & Olds, S. W. (1990). *A child's world: Infancy through adolescence* (5th ed.). New York: McGraw-Hill.

Pascarella, E. T. (2001). Cognitive growth in college: Surprising and reassuring findings from The National Study of Student Learning. *Change* (November/December), pp. 21–27.

Pascarella, E., Flowers, L., & Whitt, E. (1999). *Cognitive effects of Greek affiliation in college: Additional evidence.* Unpublished manuscript, University of Iowa, Iowa City.

Pascarella, E., Palmer, B., Moye, M., & Pierson, C. (2001). Do diversity experiences influence the development of critical thinking? *Journal of College Student Development, 42*, 257–291.

Pascarella, E. & Terenzini, P. (1991). *How college affects students: Findings and insights from twenty years of research.* San Francisco: Jossey-Bass.

Pascarella, E. T., & Terenzini, P. T. (2005). *How college affects students: A third decade of research* (volume 2). San Francisco: Jossey-Bass.

Paul, R. (1995). *Critical thinking: How to prepare students for a rapidly changing world.* Dillon Beach, CA: The Foundation for Critical Thinking.

Paul, R. W., & Elder, L. (2002). *Critical thinking: Tools for taking charge of your professional and personal life.* Upper Saddle River, NJ: Pearson Education.

Paul, R., & Elder, L. (2004). *The nature and functions of critical and creative thinking.* Dillon Beach, CA: The Foundation for Critical Thinking.

Peele, S., & Brodsky, A. (1991). *Love and addiction.* New York: Signet Books.

Peigneux, P. P., Laureys, S., Delbeuck, X. & Maquet, P. (2001, Dec. 21). Sleeping brain, learning brain: The role of sleep for memory systems. *Neuroreport, 12*(18), pp. A111–124.

Perry, W. G. (1970, 1999). *Forms of intellectual and ethical development during the college years: A scheme.* New York: Holt, Rinehart & Winston.

Perry, R., Hechter, F., Menec, V., & Weinberg, L. (1993). Enhancing achievement motivation and performance in college students: An attributional retraining perspective. *Research in Higher Education, 34*, 687–723.

Peterson, C. (1990). Explanatory style in the classroom and in the playing field. In S. Graham & V. S. Folkes (Eds.), *Attribution theory: Applications to achievement, mental health, and interpersonal conflict.* Hillsdale, NJ: Erlbaum.

Peterson, C., & Barrett, L. (1987). Explanatory style and academic performance among university freshmen. *Journal of Personality and Social Psychology, 53*, 603–607.

Peterson, C., & Seligman, M. E. P. (2004). *Character strengths and virtues—a handbook and classification.* New York: Oxford University Press.

Peterson, C., Seligman, M. E. P., Yurko, K. H., Martin, L. R., & Friedman, H. S. (1998). Catastrophizing and untimely death. *Psychological Science, 9*, 49–52.

Piaget, J. (1978). *Success and understanding.* Cambridge, MA: Harvard University Press.

Piaget, J. (1985). *The equilibration of cognitive structures: The central problem of intellectual development.* Chicago, IL: University of Chicago Press.

Pinker, S. (1994). *The language instinct.* New York: HarperCollins.

Pintrich, P. R. (Ed.) (1995). *Understanding self-regulated learning.* New Directions for Teaching and Learning, no. 63. San Francisco: Jossey-Bass.

Plante, T. G., & Sherman, A. S. (Eds.) (2001). *Faith and health: Psychological perspectives.* New York: Guilford.

Policy Center on the First Year of College (2003). *Second national survey of first-year academic practices, 2002.* Retrieved August 10, 2005, from http://www.brevard.edu/fyc/survey2002/findings.htm

Pope, L. (1990). *Looking beyond the ivy league.* New York: Penguin Press.

Pope, R. L., Miklitsch, T. A., & Weigand, M. J. (2005). First-year students: Embracing their diversity, enhancing our practice. In R. S. Feldman (Ed.), *Improving the first year of college: Research and practice* (pp. 51–72). Mahwah, NJ: Lawrence Erlbaum Associates.

Postsecondary Education Opportunity (2000). Private economic benefit/cost ratios of a college investment for men and women, 1967–1999. *The Environmental Scanning Research Letter of Opportunity for Postsecondary Education*, Number 101 (November), pp. 1–6.

Postsecondary Education Opportunity (2001). *Enrollment rates for females 18 to 34 years, 1950–2000.* Number 113 (November). Washington, DC: Center for the Study of Opportunity in Higher Education.

Potts, J. T. (1987). Predicting procrastination on academic tasks with self-report personality measures. (Doctoral dissertation, Hofstra University). *Dissertation Abstracts International, 48*, 1543.

President's Council on Physical Fitness and Sports (2001). Toward a uniform definition of wellness: A commentary. *Research Digest*, Series 3, No. 15, pp. 1–8.

Pribram, K. H. (1991). *Brain and perception: Holonomy and structure in figural processing.* Hillsdale, NJ: Erlbaum.

Price, R. H., Choi, J. N., & Vinokur, A. D. (2002). Links in the chain of adversity following job loss: How financial strain and loss of personal control lead to depression, impaired functioning, and poor health. *Journal of Occupational Health Psychology, 7*(4), 302–312.

Purdue University Online Writing Lab (1995–2004). *Writing a research paper*. Retrieved August 18, 2005, from http://owl.english.purdue.edu/workshops/hypertext/ResearchW/notes.html

Purdy, M., & Borisoff, D. (Eds.) (1996). *Listening in everyday life: A personal and professional approach*. Lanham, MD: University Press of America.

Putman, R. D. (2000). *Bowling alone: The collapse and revival of American community*. New York: Simon & Schuster.

QHE (Quality in Higher Education) (1993). *Update (6)*. The newsletter of the quality in higher education project, University of Central England, Birmingham.

QHE (Quality in Higher Education) (1994). *Update (7)*. The newsletter of the quality in higher education project, University of Central England, Birmingham.

Rader, P. E., & Hicks, R. A. (1987, April). *Jet lag desynchronization and self-assessment of business-related performance*. Paper presented at the Western Psychological Association, Long Beach, CA.

Ramsden, P. (2003). *Learning to teach in higher education* (2nd ed.). London and New York: RoutledgeFalmer.

Ramsden, P., & Entwistle, N. J. (1981). Effects of academic departments on students' approaches to studying. *British Journal of Educational Psychology, 51*, 368–383.

Ratcliff, J. L. (1997). What is a curriculum and what should it be? In J. G. Gaff, J. L Ratcliff, and Associates, *Handbook of the undergraduate curriculum: A comprehensive guide to purposes, structures, practices, and change* (pp. 5–29). San Francisco: Jossey-Bass.

Redelmeier, D. A., & Tibshirani, R. J. (1997). Association between cellular-telephone calls and motor vehicle collisions. *New England Journal of Medicine, 336*(7), 453–458.

Reed, S. K. (1996). *Cognition: Theory and applications* (3rd ed.). Pacific Grove, CA: Brooks/Cole.

Reis, H. T., & Shaver, P. (1988). Intimacy as an interpersonal process. In S. W. Durck (Ed.), *Handbook of personal relationships* (pp. 367–389). New York: Wiley.

Rennels, M. R., & Chaudhari, R. B. (1988). *Eye-contact and grade distribution. Perceptual and Motor Skills, 67*(October), 627–632.

Rennie, D., & Brewer, L. (1987). A grounded theory of thesis blocking. *Teaching of Psychology, 14*(1), 10–16.

Resnick, L. B. (1986). *Education and learning to think*. Special Report. Pittsburgh: University of Pittsburgh, Commission on Behavioral and Social Sciences Education.

Rhoads, J. (2005). *The transition to college: Top ten issues identified by students*. Retrieved June 30, 2006, from http://advising.wichita.edu/lasac/pubs/aah/trans.htm

Richmond, V. P., & McCloskey, J. C. (1997). *Communication apprehension: Avoidance and effectiveness* (5th ed.). Boston, MA: Allyn & Bacon.

Riesman, D., Glazer, N., & Denney, R. (2001). *The lonely crowd: A study of the changing American character* (revised ed.). New Haven, CT: Yale University Press.

Ring, T. (1997, October). Issuers face a visit to the dean's office. *Credit Card Management, 10*, 34–39.

Riquelme, H. (2002). Can people creative in imagery interpret ambiguous figures faster than people less creative in imagery? *Journal of Creative Behavior, 36*(2), 105–116.

Roediger, H. L., III, & McDermott, K. B. (2000). Tricks of memory. *Current Directions in Psychological Science, 9*, 123–127.

Roffwarg, H. P., Muzio, J. N., & Dement, W. C. (1966). Ontogenetic development of the human sleep-dream cycle. *Science, 152*, 604–619.

Roos, L. L., Wise, S. L., Yoes, M. E., & Rocklin, T. R. (1996). Conducting self-adapted testing using MicroCAT. *Educational and Psychological Measurement, 56*, 821–827.

Rose, S. P. R. (1993). *The making of memory*. New York: Anchor Books.

Rosenfield, I. (1988). *The invention of memory: A new view of the brain*. New York: Basic Books.

Rosenthal, R., & Jacobson, L. (1968). *Pygmalion in the classroom*. New York: Holt, Rinehart & Winston.

Rosenthal, T. L., & Steffek, B. D. (1991). Modeling methods. In F. H. Kanfer & A. P. Goldstein (Eds.), *Helping people change*. Elmsford, NY: Pergamon.

Rothblum, E. D., Solomon, L. J., & Murakami, J. (1986). Affective, cognitive, and behavioral differences between high and low procrastinators. *Journal of Counseling Psychology, 33*(4), 387–394.

Rotter, J. (1966). Generalized expectancies for internal versus external controls of reinforcement. *Psychological Monographs: General and Applied, 80*(609), 1–28.

Ruggiero, V. R. (2004). *Beyond feelings: A guide to critical thinking.* New York: McGraw-Hill.

Rudman, L. A., & Fairchild, K. (2004). Reactions to counter-stereotypic behavior: The role of backlash in cultural stereotype maintenance. *Journal of Personality and Social Psychology, 87,* 157–176.

Rumberger, R. W., & Levin, H. M. (1987). *Computers in small business.* Washington D.C.: Institute for Enterprise Advancement.

Runco, M. A. (2004). Creativity. *Annual Review of Psychology, 55,* 657–687.

Saarni, C. (1999). *The development of emotional competence.* New York: Guilford.

Sadker, M., & Sadker, D. (1994). *Failing at fairness: How America's schools cheat girls.* New York: Charles Scribner's Sons.

Salovey, P., & Mayer, J. D. (1990). Emotional intelligence. *Imagination, Cognition, and Personality, 9,* 185–211.

Sapolsky, R. (2004). *Why zebras don't get ulcers.* New York: W. H. Freeman.

Savitz, F. (1985). Effects of easy examination questions placed at the beginning of science multiple-choice examinations. *Journal of Instructional Psychology, 12*(1), 6–10.

Sax, L. J. (2003). Our incoming students: What are they like? *About Campus* (July–August), pp. 15–20.

Sax, L. J., Astin, A. W., Korn, W. S., & Mahoney, K. M. (1999). *The American freshman: National norms for fall 1999.* Los Angeles, CA: Higher Education Research Institute, UCLA Graduate School of Education & Information, Studies.

Sax, L. J., Lindholm, J. A., Astin, A. W., Korn, W. S., & Mahoney, K. M. (2004). *The American freshman: National norms for fall, 2004.* Los Angeles: Higher Education Research Institute, UCLA.

Schab, F. R. (1990). Odors and the remembrance of things past. *Journal of Experimental Psychology: Learning, Memory, and Cognition, 16*(4), 648–655.

Schacter, D. L. (1992). Understanding implicit memory. *American Psychologist, 47*(4), 559–569.

Scheckley, B. G., & Keeton, M. T. (1997). *A review of the research on learning: Implications for the instruction of adult learners.* College Park, MD: Institute for Research on Adults in Higher Education, University of Maryland.

Schlosser, E. (2001). *Fast food nation: The dark side of the all-American meal.* Boston: Houghton Mifflin.

Schmeck, R. (1981). Improving learning by improving thinking. *Educational Leadership, 38,* 384–385.

Schneider, W., & Chein, J. M. (2003). Controlled and automatic processing: Behavior, theory, and biological mechanisms. *Cognitive Science, 27,* 525–559.

Schutte, N. S., Malouff, J. M., and others (1998). Development and validation of emotional intelligence. *Personality and Individual Differences, 26,* 167–177.

Schutte, N. S., & Malouff, J. M. (2002). Incorporating emotional skills content in a college transition course enhances student retention. *Journal of The First-Year Experience, 14*(1), pp. 7–21.

Secretary's Commission on Achieving Necessary Skills (SCANS) (1992). *Learning a living: A blueprint for high performance. SCANS Report for America 2000.* Washington, D.C.: U.S. Department of Labor.

Sedlacek, W. (1987). Black students on white campuses: 20 years of research. *Journal of College Student Personnel, 28,* 484–495.

Segall, M. H., Campbell, D. T., & Herskovits, M. J. (1966). *The influence of culture on visual perception.* Indianapolis: Bobbs-Merrill.

Seligman, M. E. P. (1991). *Learned optimism.* New York: Knopf.

Senge, P. (1990). *The fifth dimension.* New York: Currency/Doubleday.

Shanley, M., & Witten, C. (1990). University 101 freshman seminar course: A longitudinal study of persistence, retention, and graduation rates. *NASPA Journal, 27,* 344–352.

Shatz, M. A., & Best, J. B. (1987). Students' reasons for changing answers on objective tests. *Teaching of Psychology, 14*(4), 241–242.

Shelgon, R. (2003). *No direction home: The life and music of Bob Dylan.* New York: William Morrow.

Sherif, M., Harvey, D. J., White, B. J., Hood, W. R., & Sherif, C. W. (1961). *The Robbers' cave experiment.* Norman, OK: Institute of Group Relations.

Sidle, M., & McReynolds, J. (1999). The freshman year experience: Student retention and srudent success. *NASPA Journal, 36,* 288–300.

Simopoulos, A. P., & Pavlou, K. N. (Eds.) (1997). Genetic variation and dietary response. *World Review of Nutrition and Dietics.* Bosel, Switzerland: S Karger.

Simunek, M., Schutte, N. S., Hollander, S., & McKenley, J. (2000). *The relationship between ability to understand and regulate emotions, mood, and self-esteem.* Paper presented at the Conference of the American Psychological Society, Miami, FL.

Singh, N. A., Clements, K. M., & Fiatarone, M. A. (1997). A randomized controlled trial of the effect of exercise on sleep. *Sleep, 20*, 95–101.

Slavin, R. E. (1995). *Cooperative learning* (2nd ed.). Boston: Allyn & Bacon.

Smith, B. L. (1983–84). An interview with Elaine Maimon. *1983–84 Current Issues in Higher Education*. Washington, D.C.: American Association for Higher Education.

Smith, R. L. (1994). The world of business. In W. C. Hartel, S. W. Schwartz, S. D. Blume, & J. N. Gardner (Eds.), *Ready for the real world* (pp. 123–135). Belmont, CA: Wadsworth Publishing.

Smith, D. (1997). How diversity influences learning. *Liberal Education, 83*(2), 42–48.

Smith, D. D. (2005). Experiential learning, service learning, and career development. In P.A. Gore (Ed.), *Facilitating the career development of students in transition* (Monograph No. 43) (pp. 205–222). Columbia, SC: University of South Carolina, National Resource Center for The First-Year Experience and Students in Transition.

Smith, A. P., Clark, R., & Gallagher, J. (1999). Breakfast cereal and caffeinated coffee: Effects on working memory, attention, mood, and cardiovascular function. *Physiology & Behavior, 67*(1), 9–17.

Smith, S. M., Glenberg, A., & Bjork, R. A. (1978). Environmental context and human memory. *Memory & Cognition, 6*, 342–353.

Smith, T., Snyder, C. R., & Handelsman, M. M. (1982). On the self-serving function of an academic wooden leg: Test anxiety as a self-handicapping strategy. *Journal of Personality & Social Psychology, 42*, 314–321.

Smith, J. B., Walter, T. L., & Hoey, G. (1992). Support programs and student self-efficacy: Do first-year students know when they need help? *Journal of The Freshman Year Experience, 4*(2), 41–67.

Snyder, C. R., Harris, C., Anderson, J. R., Holleran, S. A., Irving, L. M., Sigmon, S. T., Yoshinobu, L., Gibb, J., Langelle, C., & Harney, P. (1991). The will and the ways: Development and validation of an individual-differences measure of hope. *Journal of Personality and Social Psychology, 60*, 570–585.

Soloman, L. J., & Rothblum, E. D. (1984). Academic procrastination: Frequency and cognitive-behavioral correlates. *Journal of Counseling Psychology, 31*, 503–509.

Spear, K. (1988). *Sharing writing: Peer response groups in English classes*. Portsmouth, NH: Boynton/Cook.

Spilka, B., Hood, R. W., Hunsberger, B., & Gorsuch, R. (2003). *The psychology of religion: An empirical approach* (3rd ed.). New York: Guilford Press.

Sprenger, M. (1999). *Learning and memory: The brain in action*. Alexandria, VA: Association for Supervision and Curriculum Development.

Squire, L. (1986). Mechanism of memory. *Science, 232*, 1612–1619.

Stangor, C., Sechrist, G. B., & Jost, T. J. (2001). Changing racial beliefs by providing consensus information. *Personality and Social Psychology Bulletin, 27*, 486–496.

Stark, J. S., Lowther, R. J., Bentley, M. P., Ryan, G. G., Martens, M. L., Genthon, P. A., & Shaw, K. M. (1990). *Planning introductory college courses: Influences on faculty*. Ann Arbor: University of Michigan: National Center for Research to Improve Postsecondary Teaching and Learning. (ERIC Document Reproduction Services No. 330 277 370)

Starke, M. C., Harth, M., & Sirianni, F. (2001). Retention, bonding, and academic achievement: Success of a first-year seminar. *Journal of The First-Year Experience & Students in Transition, 13*(2), 7–35.

Staudinger, U. M., & Baltes, P. B. (1994). Psychology of wisdom. In R. J. Sternberg (Ed.), *Encyclopedia of intelligence, Volume 1* (pp. 143–152). New York: Macmillan.

Steel, P. (2003). *The nature of procrastination: A meta-analytic and theoretical review of self-regulatory failure*. Retrieved June 28, 2006, from www.haskayne.ucalgary.ca/research/workingpapers

Steel, P., Brothen, T., & Wambach, C. (2001). Procrastination and personality, performance, and mood. *Personality & Individual Differences, 30*, 95–106.

Stein, B. S. (1978). Depth of processing reexamined: The effects of the precision of encoding and testing appropriateness. *Journal of Verbal Learning and Verbal Behavior, 17*, 165–174.

Sternberg, R. J. (2001). What is the common thread of creativity? *American Psychologist, 56*(4), 360–362.

Stolerman, I. P., & Jarvis, M. J. (1995). The scientific case that nicotine is addictive. *Psychopharmacology, 117*(1), 2–10.

Strage, A. A. (2000). Service-learning: Enhancing student learning outcomes in a college-level course. *Michigan Journal of Community Service Learning, 7*, 5–13.

Strommer, D. W. (1993). Not quite good enough: Drifting about in higher education. *AAHE Bulletin, 45*(10), pp. 14–15.

Suinn, R. M. (1985). Imagery rehearsal applications to performance enhancement. *Behavior Therapist, 8*, 155–159.

Sullivan, R. E. (1993, March 18). Greatly reduced expectations. *Rolling Stone*, pp. 2-4.

Sundquist, J., & Winkleby, M. (2000, June). Country of birth, acculturation status and abdominal obesity in a national sample of Mexican-American women and men. *International Journal of Epidemiology, 29*, 470-477.

Susswein, R. (1995). College students and credit cards: A privilege earned? *Credit World, 83*, 21-23.

Svinicki, M. D., & Dixon, N. M. (1987). The Kolb model modified for classroom activities. *College Teaching, 35*(4), 141-146.

Tafjel, H. (1982). *Social identity and intergroup behavior*. Cambridge, England: Cambridge University Press.

Taylor, S. E., Peplau, L. A., & Sears, D. O. (2006). *Social psychology* (12th ed.). Upper Saddle River, NJ: Pearson/Prentice-Hall.

Tchudi, S. N. (1986). *Teaching writing in the content areas: College level*. New York: National Educational Association.

Teigen, K. H. (1994). Yerkes-Dodson—A law for all seasons. *Theory & Psychology, 4*, 525-547.

Terenzini, P. T., & Pascarella, E. T. (2004, July). *How college affects students: A third decade of research*. Plenary address to the Academic Affairs Summer Conference of the American Association of State Colleges and Universities. Albuquerque, New Mexico.

Thayer, R. E. (1996). *The origin of everyday moods: Managing energy, tension, and stress*. New York: Oxford University Press.

The Board of Trustees of the University of Illinois (2005). *Career Preparation*. College of Liberal Arts & Sciences, University of Illinois at Urbana Champaign. Retrieved December 16, 2006, from http://www.las.uiuc.edu/students/career/businesscareers.html

The Conference Board of Canada (2000). *Employability skills 2000+*. Ottawa: The Conference Board of Canada.

The Echo Boomers (2004, Oct. 3). Retrieved Oct. 22, 2004, from http://www.cbsnews.com/stories/2004/10/01/60minutes/printable646890.shtml

The Pennsylvania State University (2005). *How to avoid plagiarism*. Retrieved Oct. 15, 2005, from http://tlt.its.psu/suggestions/cyberplag/cyberplagexamples.html

Thomson, R. (1998). University of Vermont. In B. O. Barefoot, C. L. Warnock, M. P. Dickinson, S. E. Richardson, & M. R. Roberts (Eds.) (1998). *Exploring the evidence, Volume II: Reporting outcomes of first-year seminars* (Monograph No. 29) (pp. 77-78). Columbia, SC: University of South Carolina, National Resource Center for The First-Year Experience and Students in Transition.

Thompson, R. F. (1981). Peer grading: some promising advantages for composition research and the classroom. *Research in the Teaching of English, 15*(2), 172-174.

Thornburg, D. D. (1994). *Education in the communication age*. San Carlos, CA: Starsong.

Tice, D. M., & Baumeister, R. F. (1997). Longitudinal study of procrastination, performance, stress, and health: The costs and benefits of dawdling. *Psychological Science, 8*, 454-458.

Tierney, W. G. (Ed.) (1998). *The responsive university: Restructuring for high performance*. Baltimore: Johns Hopkins Press.

Tillich, P. (1952). *The courage to be*. Newhaven: Yale University Press.

Tinto, V. (1993). *Leaving college: Rethinking the causes and cures of student attrition* (2nd ed.). Chicago: University of Chicago Press.

Tinto, V. (1997). Classrooms as communities: Exploring the educational character of student persistence. *The Journal of Higher Education, 68*, 599-623.

Tinto, V. (2000). Linking learning and leaving: Exploring the role of the college classroom in student departure. In J. M. Braxton (Ed.), *Reworking the student departure puzzle* (pp. 81-94). Nashville: Vanderbilt University Press.

Tisdell, E. J. (2003). *Exploring spirituality and culture in adult and higher education*. San Francisco: Jossey-Bass.

Tobias, S. (1985). Test anxiety: Interference, defective skills, and cognitive capacity. *Educational Psychologist, 20*(3), 135-142.

Tobolowsky, B. F. (2005). *The 2003 national survey on first-year seminars: Continuing innovations in the collegiate curriculum* (Monograph No. 41). Columbia, SC: University of South Carolina, National Resource Center for The First-Year Experience and Students in Transition.

Torrance, E. P. (1963). *Education and the creative potential*. Minneapolis: The University of Minnesota Press.

Torres, V. (2003). Student diversity and academic services: Balancing the needs of all students. In G. L. Kramer & Associates, *Student academic services: An integrated approach* (pp. 333–352). San Francisco: Jossey-Bass.

Tulving, E. (1983). *Elements of episodic memory.* Oxford: Clarendon Press/Oxford University Press.

Tulving, E. (1985). Memory and consciousness. *Canadian Psychology, 26,* 1–12.

Tyson, E. (2003). *Personal finance for dummies.* Indianapolis: IDG Books.

Ulus, I. H., & Wurtman, R. J. (1977). Trans-synaptic induction of adrenomedullary tyrosine hydroxylase activity by choline: Evidence that choline administration can increase cholinergic transmission. *Proceeding of the National Academy of Science, 74*(2), 798–800.

Underwood, B. J. (1983). *Attributes of memory.* Glenview, IL: Scott, Foresman, & Company.

United States Bureau of Labor Statistics (2005). *Number of jobs, labor market experience, and earnings growth: Results from a longitudinal survey.* Washington, D.C.: Author. Retrieved September 24, 2005, from http://www.bls.gov/news.release/nlsoy.toc.htm

U.S. Census Bureau (2000). *Racial and ethnic classifications in census 2000 and beyond.* Retrieved December 19, 2006, from http://census.gov/population/www/socdemo/race/racefactcb.html

U.S. Census Bureau (2003). *Current population survey, March 2002.* Washington, DC: Government Printing Office.

U.S. Census Bureau (2004). *The face of our population.* Retrieved December 12, 2006, from http://factfinder.census.gov/jsp/saff/SAFFInfojsp?_pageId=tp9_race_ethnicity

U.S. Department of Education, National Center for Education Statistics (2002). *Profile of undergraduate students in U. S. postsecondary institutions: 1999–2000.* Washington, DC: Government Printing Office.

U.S. Department of Health & Human Services (2000). *Healthy people 2010: Understanding and improving health.* Washington, DC: Government Printing Office.

U.S. National Center for Health Statistics (2003). *National vital statistics report,* Volume 51, No. 5.

Van Dongen, H. P. A., Maislin, G., Mullington, J. M., & Dinges, D. F. (2003). The cumulative cost of additional wakefulness: Dose-response effects on neurobehavioral functions and sleep physiology from chronic sleep restriction and total sleep deprivation. *Sleep, 26,* 117–126.

Van Overwalle, F. I., Mervielde, I., & De Schuyer, J. (1995). Structural modeling of the relationships between attributional dimensions, emotions, and performance of college freshmen. *Cognition and Emotion, 9*(1), 59–85.

Veechio, R. (1997). *Leadership.* Notre Dame, IN: University of Notre Dame Press.

Viorst, J. (1998). *Necessary losses.* New York: Fireside.

Voelker, R. (2004). Stress, sleep loss, and substance abuse create potent recipe for college depression. *Journal of the American Medical Association, 291,* 2177–2179.

Vogler, R. E. & Bartz, W. R. (1992). *Teenagers and alcohol: When saying no isn't enough.* Philadelphia: The Charles Press.

Vogt, P. (1994). Students, professors point out each other's irritating behaviors. *Recruitment and Retention in Higher Education, 8*(7), p. 1.

Vygotsky, L. S. (1978). Internalization of higher cognitive functions. In M. Cole, V. John-Steiner, S. Scribner, & E. Souberman (Eds. & Trans.), *Mind in society: The development of higher psychological processes* (pp. 52–57). Cambridge: Harvard University Press.

Wadden, T. A., Thomas, A., Foster, G. D., Letizia, K. A., & Mullen, J. L. (1990). Long-term effects of dieting on resting metabolic rate in obese outpatients. *Journal of the American Medical Association, 264,* 707–711.

Waddington, P. (1996). *Dying for information: An investigation into the effects of information overload in the USA and worldwide.* London: Reuters Limited.

Wade, C. & Tavris, C. (1990). Thinking critically and creatively. *Skeptical Inquirer, 14,* 372–377.

Wagner, U., Gais, S., Haider, H., Verleger, R., & Born, J. (2004). Sleep inspires insight. *Nature, 427,* 352–355.

Wagner, M. J., & Tilney, G. (1983). The effect of "superlearning" techniques on the vocabulary acquisition and alpha brainwave production of language learners. *TESOL Quarterly, 7*(1), 5–17.

Wahlstrom, C., & Williams, B. K. (1997, Spring). Dealing with students' naïveté about money. *The Keystone* (Newsletter of the Wadsworth College Success Series), pp. 4–5.

Walker, C. M. (1996). Financial management, coping, and debt in households under financial strain. *Journal of Economic Psychology, 17,* 789–807.

Walsh, K. (2005). *Suggestions from more experienced classmates.* Retrieved June 12, 2006, from http://www.uni.edu/walsh/introtips.html

Walter, T. W., Knudsbig, G. M., & Smith, D. E. P. (2003). *Critical thinking: Building the basics* (2nd ed.). Belmont, CA: Wadsworth.

Walter, T. L., & Smith, J. (April, 1990). *Self-assessment and academic support: Do students know they need help?* Paper presented at the annual Freshman Year Experience Conference, Austin, Texas.

Watkins, D. A. (1983). Depth of processing and the quality of learning outcomes. *Instructional Science, 12*, 49–58.

Webber, R. A. (1991). *Breaking your time barriers: Becoming a strategic time manager.* Englewood Cliffs, NJ: Prentic-Hall.

Weschsler, H., & Wuethrich, B. (2002). *Dying to drink: Confronting binge drinking on college campuses.* Emmaus, PA: Rodale.

Weinstein, C. E. (1982). A metacurriculum for remediating learning-strategies deficits in academically underprepared students. In L. Noel & R. Levitz (Eds.), *How to succeed with academically underprepared students.* Iowa City, Iowa: American College Testing Service, National Center for Advancing Educational Practice.

Weinstein, C. F. (1994). Students at risk for academic failure. In K. W. Prichard & R. M. Sawyer (Eds.), *Handbook of college teaching: Theory and applications* (pp. 375–385). Westport, CT: Greenwood Press.

Weinstein, C. F., & Meyer, D. K. (1991). Cognitive learning strategies. In R. J. Menges & M .D. Svinicki (Eds.), *College teaching: From theory to practice* (pp. 15–26). New Directions for Teaching and Learning, no. 45. San Francisco: Jossey-Bass.

Weinstein, C. E., & Underwood, V. L. (1985). Learning strategies: The how of learning. In J. W. Segal, S. F. Chapman, & R. Glaser (Eds.), *Thinking and learning skills* (pp. 241–258). Hillsdale, NJ: Erlbaum.

Wesley, J. C. (1994). Effects of ability, high school achievement, and procrastinatory behavior on college performance. *Educational & Psychological Measurement,* 54, 404–408.

Wheelright, J. (2005). Human, study thyself. *Discover* (March), pp. 39–45.

Whitman, N. A. (1988). *Peer teaching: To teach is to learn twice.* ASHE-ERIC Higher Education Report No. 4. Washington, D.C.: Association for the Study of Higher Education.

Wilder, D. A. (1984). Inter-group contact: The typical member and the exception to the rule. *Journal of Experimental Psychology, 20*, 177–194

Wilhite, S. (1990). Self-efficacy, locus of control, self-assessment of memory ability, and student activities as predictors of college course achievement. *Journal of Educational Psychology, 82*(4), 696–700.

Williams, J. M., Landers, & Boutcher, S. H. (1993). Arousal-performance relationships. *Sport Psychology: Personal Growth to Peak Performance, 3*, 170–184.

Willingham, W. W. (1985). *Success in college: The role of personal qualities and academic ability.* New York: College Entrance Examination Board.

Wilson, T. D., & Linville, P. W. (1982). Improving the academic performance of college freshmen: Attribution therapy revisited. *Journal of Personality and Social Psychology, 42*, 811–819.

Wilson, T. D., & Linville, P. W. (1985). Improving the academic performance of college freshmen using attributional techniques. *Journal of Personality and Social Psychology, 49*, 287–293.

Wilson, R., Mendes, C., Barnes, L., and others (2002). Participation in cognitively stimulating activities and risk of incident Alzheimer's disease. *Journal of the American Medical Association, 287*(6), 742–748.

Winsor, J. L., Curtis, D. B., & Stephens, R. D. (1997). National preferences in business and communication education: A survey update. *JACA, 3*(September), 170–179.

Wolvin, A. D., & Coakley, (1993). *Perspectives on listening.* Norwood, NJ: Ablex Publishing.

Wright, D. J. (Ed.) (1987). *Responding to the needs of today's minority students.* New Directions for Student Services, No. 38. San Francisco: Jossey-Bass.

Wyckoff, S. C. (1999). The academic advising process in higher education: History, research, and improvement. *Recruitment & Retention in Higher Education, 13*(1), pp. 1–3.

Yerkes, R. M., & Dodson, J. D. (1908). The relationship of strength and stimulus to rapidity of habit formation. *Journal of Neurological Psychology, 184*, 59–82.

Young, K. S. (1996, Aug. 10). *Pathological Internet use: The emergence of a new clinical disorder.* Paper presented at the annual meeting of the American Psychological Association, Toronto, Canada.

Zaccaro, S. J., Foti, R. J., & Kenny, D. A. (1991). Self-monitoring and trait-based variance in leadership: An investigation of leader flexibility across multiple group situations. *Journal of Applied Psychology, 76*, 308–315.

Zajonc, R. B. (2001). Mere exposure: A gateway to the subliminal. *Current Directions in Psychological Science, 10*, 224–228.

Zeidner, M. (1995). Adaptive coping with test situations: A review of the literature. *Educational Psychologist, 30*(3), 123–133.

Zimbardo, P. G. (1977, 1990). *Shyness: What it is, what to do about it.* Reading, MA: Addison-Wesley.

Zimbardo, P. G., Johnson, R. L., & Weber, A. L. (2006). *Psychology: Core concepts* (5th ed.). Boston: Allyn & Bacon.

Zimmerman, B. J. (1995). *Self-efficacy and educational development.* In A. Bandura (Ed.), Self-efficacy in changing societies. New York: Cambridge University Press.

Zinsser, W. (1988). *Writing to learn.* New York: HarperCollins.

Zohar, D., & Marshall, I. (2000). *SQ: Connecting with your spiritual intelligence.* New York: Bloomsbury.

Zull, J. E. (1998). The brain, the body, learning, and teaching. *The National Teaching & Learning Forum, 7*(3), pp. 1–5.

Glossary

This section includes ALL terms found within the full version of this text.

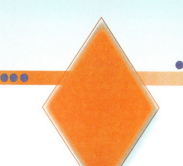

Ability (Aptitude): the capacity to do something well or to have the potential to do it well.

Academic Advisor: a professional who advises college students on course selection, helps students understand college procedures, and helps guide their academic progress toward completion of a college degree.

Academic Dismissal: denying a student to continue college enrollment because of a cumulative GPA that continues to remain below a minimum level (e.g., below 2.0).

Academic Probation: A DSC student whose grade point average falls below the required minimum level will be placed on academic probation and will be expected to see his/her academic advisor. Students on academic probation may be advised to reduce their class load and are not eligible to hold office on the Student Activities Council or to serve on any official college committee. Minimum grade point averages:

Credit Hours Attempted	Minimum GPA
15	1.60
30	1.80
45 or more	2.00

Academic Standing: The status of a student's academic career; usually determined by the *Grade Point Average* and other considerations.

Academic Support Center: place on campus where students can obtain individual assistance from professionals and trained peers to support and strengthen their academic performance.

Academic Suspension: Any DSC student on academic probation who fails to raise his/her GPA to the minimum level (*see academic probation*) after attempting 15 additional credit hours will be placed on academic suspension. Students on suspension are not eligible to register for any courses at DSC unless they appeal the suspension to a Readmissions Committee and are approved for readmission by the Vice President for Academic Affairs.

Academic Year: Usually this refers to the August–May school year. In some cases it refers to the entire year (including summer semester).

Administrators: college personnel whose primary responsibility is the governance of the college or a unit within the college, such as an academic department or student support service.

Admission: Approval for a student to attend an educational institution. The admission process usually involves an application form and may require transcripts or other supporting documents.

Advisor: A member of the college faculty or staff who assists students with planning semester schedules as well as their overall programs of study.

Application: The first step in requesting admission to an institution of higher education. Usually there is a form to fill out by a certain deadline; sometimes there is an application fee to pay.

Areas A–F: Areas A–F represent the *core curriculum* for a degree and Area F represents courses to be taken in the *major* field. Consult the latest DSC Catalog online to see the *core curriculum* and Area F requirements for a particular degree.

Associate's Degree: A diploma earned after successfully completing a required program of study in a community or technical college. It typically requires 62 or more credits and takes 2 years of full-time study. Some Associate degrees enable students to transfer to baccalaureate colleges and universities (Transfer Associate Degrees), others prepare students to go right into the workforce in a professional/technical field (Associate of Applied Science Degrees).

Attendance Policy: The policy set by the college or university, department or division, or individual instructor that states the maximum number of allowable absences from a *course*.

Baccalaureate or Bachelor's Degree: A college degree which can often be earned by following a 4-year instructional program. A baccalaureate institution, sometimes informally called a "4-year college," is a college or university which is entitled to grant a baccalaureate or Bachelor's degree. DSC currently offers Bachelor's degrees in Business, Early Childhood Education, and Social Work.

Board of Regents: An 18-member Board governing the University System of Georgia. The Board establishes minimum academic standards for the University System of colleges and universities. State funds for the University System are requested by, made to, and distributed by the Board of Regents.

CAAP (Collegiate Assessment of Academic Proficiency) Exam: The CAAP exam is required of all students graduating with an Associate's degree. The test assesses college students' academic achievement in core general educational skills and measures how well DSC curriculum has prepared its graduates. Exam sessions are offered twice each academic year, in December and April.

Career: the sum total of vocational experiences throughout an individual's work life.

Career Advancement: working up the career ladder to higher levels of decision-making responsibility and socioeconomic status.

Career Development Center: key campus resource for learning about the nature of different careers and for strategies on how to locate career-related work experiences.

Career Development Courses: college courses that typically include self-assessment of career interests, information about different careers, and strategies for career preparation.

Career Entry: gaining entry into a career and beginning a career path.

Catalog: A comprehensive resource listing college regulations, program and course descriptions, degree and graduation requirements, transfer requirements, and other essential information.

Certificate: A document granted by a college or university indicating that a student has successfully completed specified courses and requirements (compare with degree, which usually requires more time and coursework).

Citation: an acknowledgment of the source of any piece of information included in a written paper or oral report that doesn't represent one's own work or thoughts.

Class Schedule:
1. A publication listing detailed course and section information (days, times, room numbers, etc.) for a specific semester.
2. The specific courses that an individual student is taking or plans to take for a given semester.

CLEP (College Level Examination Program): Testing program of The College Board designed to measure prior learning. CLEP is a series of exams that test college level knowledge gained through coursework, independent study, travel, special interests, military service schools, and professional development. A student may earn college credits by achieving a specified level of performance on a CLEP exam. CLEP tests cost $75.00 and are given by appointment on Fridays in the CLEP Testing Lab in the Pope Student Center on the DSC campus.

Co-Curricular Experience: learning and development that occurs outside the classroom.

College Preparatory Classes (CPC): Students seeking a degree (A.S., A.A., or B.S.) who have graduated from high school in the past 5 years must have acquired 4 units of English, 3 units of science, 4 units of mathematics, 3 units of social science, and 2 units of foreign language (in a single language). If you are lacking one or more of these requirements, you have a CPC deficiency.

Commencement: The ceremony at the end of an academic year when students receive their degrees or diplomas (compare to graduation).

Communication Skills: skills necessary for accurate comprehension and articulate expression of ideas, which include reading, writing, speaking, listening, and multimedia skills.

Commuter Students: college students who do not live on campus.

COMPASS (Computer-Adaptive Placement Assessment and Support System) Exam: The COMPASS exam determines the current skill level in the area(s) tested so that students entering DSC can be placed appropriately. The COMPASS exam is taken to exit Learning Support/Developmental Studies courses in English, reading, or mathematics.

Concentration: a cluster of approximately three courses in the same subject area.

Concept: a larger system or network of related ideas.

Concept (Idea) Map: a visual diagram that represents or maps out main categories of ideas and their relationships in a visual-spatial format.

Cooperative Education (Co-op) Programs: programs in which students gain work experience relating to their college major, either by stopping their course work temporarily to work full-time at the co-op position, or by continuing to take classes while working part-time at the co-op position.

Cooperative Education/Internship: A program providing students with professional work experience related to an academic field of study. Co-ops generally last a full semester and can be used for course credit.

Core Courses: courses required of all students, regardless of their particular major.

Core Curriculum: An established set of courses that all students pursue during their early college career.

Co-Requisite: A course that must be taken at the same time as another course.

Course:
1. Often means the same as class.
2. A planned sequence of instruction in a particular topic; may include class meetings, lectures, readings, demonstrations, exercises, assignments, examinations, etc.; offered repeatedly to different groups of students.

Course Load: The total credit value of the courses a student is currently enrolled in.

Cover (Application) Letter: letter written by an applicant who is applying for an employment position or admission to a school.

Cramming: packing study time into one study session immediately before an exam.

Creative Thinking: a form of higher-level thinking skill that involves producing a new and different idea, method, strategy, or work product.

Credit: A unit of measure for college work. Generally speaking, one credit hour represents one hour of classroom attendance each week for one term, plus the study time, homework, etc., that go along with it.

Critical Thinking: a form of higher-level thinking that involves making well-informed evaluations or judgments.

CRN (Course Reference Number): A five digit number used to identify each course section offered in a semester. Fall semester CRNs begin with the number 6, spring semester CRNs begin with the number 2, and summer semester CRNs begin with the number 5.

Culture: a distinctive way or style of living that characterize a group of people who share the same social system, heritage, and traditions.

Cum Laude: graduating "with honors" (e.g., achieving a cumulative GPA of 3.3).

Cumulative GPA: a student's grade-point average for all academic terms combined.

Curriculum: (plural: curricula)
1. An established sequence of information to be learned, skills to be acquired, etc., in a specific *course* or in a complete instructional *program*.
2. Collectively, all the courses offered by a *department, division*, or college.

Dean's List: Includes the names of students who earn a grade point average of 3.5 or greater and receive no grade of WF or U during a term in which they are enrolled for 12 or more semester hours of academic credit. The Dean's List is published at the end of each semester.

Degree: A rank awarded by a college or university and earned by a student who has successfully completed specified courses and requirements (compare with certificate, which usually requires less time and coursework).

Department: An organizational unit within a college or university, offering courses about closely related topics (at a small school there may be one foreign languages department, at a large school there may be separate departments for Spanish, French, Japanese, etc.).

Diploma: An official document issued by a college or university indicating that a student has earned a certain degree or certificate.

Diversity: interacting with and learning from peers of varied backgrounds and lifestyles.

Diversity Appreciation: becoming interested in and valuing the experiences of different groups of people and willingness to learn more about them.

Diversity (Multicultural) Courses: courses designed to promote diversity awareness and appreciation of multiple cultures.

Documentation: information sources that serve as references to support or reinforce conclusions in a written paper or oral presentation.

Drop: To cancel *registration* in a *course* after enrolling into it. Students often add and drop courses before settling on a *class schedule* for a particular *semester*. This process involves completing a form and submitting it to Enrollment Services. See also *withdrawal*.

DSC: Dalton State College

DSConnect: This secure site provides DSC students, faculty, and administrative staff with Intranet and Internet services. All DSC students are assigned a DSConnect account where they are expected to check e-mail, class schedules, financial aid status, and grades.

Elective: A *course* that is not required for a particular instructional *program*. Many programs require a certain number of elective *credits*, and many recommend certain electives for students to choose from.

Enrollment Services: Enrollment Services is responsible for implementing DSC academic policies and procedures and maintaining complete and accurate academic records for all DSC students. The department evaluates the transcripts of students transferring to DSC. Students currently or previously enrolled at DSC can obtain official academic transcripts from this office. Students also contact Enrollment Services to change personal information (address, name changes) and to change academic majors.

Experiential Learning: out-of-class experiences that promote learning and development.

Faculty: The instructors or teaching staff at a school. College and university faculty rankings are: instructor, assistant professor, associate professor, and professor.

FAFSA (Free Application for Federal Student Aid): The application required for students to be considered for federal student *financial aid*. The FAFSA is processed free of charge and is used by most state agencies and colleges. There is a form for each academic year. FAFSA forms are available from high schools and online at http://www.fafsa.ed.gov.

Federal Work-Study: On-campus, student employment where the student's salary is paid through financial aid channels. See also *student assistant*.

FERPA: The Family Educational Rights and Privacy Act (FERPA) (a.k.a. the Buckley Amendment) is the legislation that ensures that students' educational and personal information is protected by educational institutions.

Final: An examination administered at the end of an academic *term*. Final exam can be cumulative (covering all material presented during the *term*) or partial (covering material only presented since the *midterm*).

Financial Aid: Money available from various sources to help students pay college expenses. These funds come as *loans, grants,* or *scholarships* (HOPE) from the state or federal government or other organizations. *Work-study* is also a form of financial aid.

Financial Aid Appeal: Students on financial aid suspension or probation may appeal to the Director of Financial Aid.

Free Electives: courses that students may elect to enroll in, which count toward your college degree but are not required for either general education or an academic major.

Freshman: A student in the first year of a typical 4-year *baccalaureate degree* program (or one who has earned fewer than 30 *semester* credits so far).

Full-Time Student: This is normally a student taking 12 or more credit hours in a semester.

FYES 1000 (First Year Experience): A 2-hour institutional credit course required for all new freshmen DSC students. FYES 1000 helps students develop strategies and attitudes to maximize academic success; to familiarize students with campus resources and how to use them; to assist students in developing positive relationships with faculty, student leaders, and peers; and to increase retention of first time students.

General Education: At DSC, a set of requirements designed to help every graduating student achieve competence in a variety of learning outcome areas.

Grade Points: the amount of points earned for a course, which is calculated by multiplying the course grade multiplied by the number of credits carried by the course.

Grade Point average (GPA): The GPA is computed by multiplying the number value of the *grade* earned in each *course* (generally, A = 4, B = 3, C = 2, D = 1, F = 0) times the number *credits* for each *course*, then dividing the result by the total number of credits taken.

Graduate Assistant (GA): a graduate student who receives financial assistance to pursue graduate studies by working in a university office or college professor.

Graduate School: university-related education pursued after completing a four-year, bachelor's degree.

Graduation: The formal completion of an instructional *program* or course of study. Students graduate after successfully meeting all *credit* and *course requirements* and other criteria set by the college or university (compare to *commencement*).

Grant: A type of *financial aid* that does not have to be paid back after the student leaves school. Grants are available through the federal government, state agencies, and educational institutions.

Higher-Level Thinking: thinking at a higher or more complex level than merely acquiring factual knowledge or memorizing information.

Higher One Easy Refund Card: All DSC student refunds, including financial aid refunds, are distributed to students through Higher One's Easy Refund Card. With an Easy Refund, the student's money is deposited into their Higher One Account as soon as Dalton State College releases it. This allows instant access to that money with the Higher One Easy Refund Card, which is a debit card accepted at stores worldwide.

History and Constitution Requirements: State of Georgia legislative requirements. Before being certified as having met all degree requirements, students must satisfy the Georgia legislative requisites of demonstrating proficiency in United States and Georgia history and the United States and Georgia constitutions. The requirements are *usually* satisfied by completing American History and Political Science courses at a University System of Georgia college or university. Students who have taken these courses at schools outside of the University System of Georgia should consult the latest DSC online to see the other ways the requirements may be satisfied.

Holistic (or Whole Person) Development: development of the total self, which includes intellectual, social, emotional, physical, spiritual, ethical, vocational, and personal development.

HOPE: The Georgia HOPE program (Helping Outstanding Pupils Educationally) is a scholarship funded by the Georgia Lottery.

Human Diversity: the variety of differences that exist among people who comprise humanity (the human species).

Humanities: The branches of knowledge, such as philosophy, literature, and art, which are concerned with human thought and culture.

Humanity: the common elements of the human experience that are shared by all human beings.

Hybrid Class: A course that is taught both online and on campus. Students enrolled in the class might attend one scheduled class per week and complete and submit other assigned course work online. Students are required to participate in both portions of the class.

Hypothesis: an informed guess that might be true, but still needs to be tested to confirm or verify its truth.

Illustrate: to provide concrete examples or specific instances.

Incomplete: A temporary *grade* given to a student who is doing satisfactory work but is forced by illness or other emergency to miss an exam or a major assignment. The instructor and student arrange how and when the student will complete the work and have the "I" changed to a final letter grade.

Independent Study: An arrangement that allows a student to earn college credit through individual study and research, usually planned with and supervised by a faculty member.

Information Literacy: the ability to find, evaluate, and use information.

Intellectual (Cognitive) Development: acquiring knowledge, learning how to learn, and how to think deeply.

Interdisciplinary: courses or programs that are designed to help students integrate knowledge from two or more academic disciplines (fields of study).

Interests: what someone likes or enjoys doing.

International Student: a student attending college in one nation who is a citizen of a different nation.

International Study (Study Abroad) Program: doing coursework at a college or university in another country that counts toward graduation, and which is typically done for one or two academic terms.

Internship: A supervised short-term apprenticeship or temporary job in a real-world setting closely related to a student's field of study. The student may or may not be paid but earns college *credit* for the work experience. See also *practicum*.

Interpret: to draw a conclusion about something, and support that conclusion with evidence.

Job Shadowing: a program that allows a student to follow (shadow) and observe a professional during a typical workday.

Junior: A student in the third year of a typical 4-year *baccalaureate* degree program (or one who has earned 60–90 *semester* credits so far).

Justify: to back-up one's arguments and viewpoints with evidence.

Leadership: ability to influence people in a positive way (e.g., motivating your peers to do their best), or the ability to produce positive change in an organization or institution, (e.g., improving the quality of a school, business, or a political organization).

Leadership Courses: courses in which students learn how to advance and eventually assume important leadership positions in a company or organization.

Learning Commons: A comfortable student study area in the DSC Derrell Roberts Library with a lounge area and a computer lab. The computer lab has a library staff person available for assistance and all printing is free.

Learning Community: a program offered by some colleges and universities in which the same group of students takes the same block of courses together during the same academic term.

Learning Style: the way in which individuals prefer to perceive information (receive or take it in), and process information (deal with it once it has been taken in).

Learning Support: Instruction that helps students improve their English, math, or reading abilities and prepare themselves for college-level study. At DSC, learning support courses are numbered 0098 or below.

Liberal Arts: the component of a college education that provides the essential foundation or backbone for the college curriculum, and which is designed to equip students with a versatile set of skills to promote their success in any academic major or career.

Lifelong Learning Skills: skills that include learning how to learn and how to continue learning that can be used throughout the remainder of one's personal and professional life.

Loans: A type of *financial aid* that must be repaid to the government agency or other lending organization when the student leaves school.

Magna Cum Laude: graduating with "high honors" (e.g., achieving a cumulative GPA of 3.5).

Major: Specialization in one academic *discipline* or field of study.

Mentor: someone who serves as a role model and personal guide to help students reach their educational or occupational goals.

Merit-Based Scholarship: money awarded on the basis of performance or achievement that does not have to be repaid.

Meta-Cognition: thinking about the process of thinking.

Midterm: 1. Middle of an academic term (semester or quarter).
2. An examination administered in the middle of an academic *term*.

Minor: a second field of study that is designed to complement and strengthen a major, which usually consists of about half the number of courses required for a college major (e.g., 6–7 courses for a minor).

Mnemonic Devices (Mnemonics): specific memory-improvement methods designed to prevent forgetting, which often involve such memory-improvement principles as: meaning, organization, visualization, or rhythm and rhyme.

Multicultural Competence: ability to understand cultural differences and to interact effectively with people from multiple cultural backgrounds.

Multidimensional Thinking: a form of higher-level thinking that involves taking multiple perspectives and considering multiple theories.

Multiple Intelligences: the notion that humans display intelligence or mental skills in many other forms besides their ability to perform on intellectual tests, such as the IQ or SAT.

Need: a key element of life planning that represents something stronger than an interest, and which makes a person's life more satisfying or fulfilling.

Need-Based Scholarship: money awarded to students on the basis of financial need that does not have to be repaid.

Netiquette: applying the principles of social etiquette and interpersonal sensitivity when communicating online.

Noncredit: Courses or instructional programs which do not require extensive homework or examinations and which do not offer college credit. Students frequently take noncredit courses for basic skills improvement, job training or career enhancement, or personal enrichment.

No-show: A student who *registers* into a *course* but never goes to *class*.

Online Resources: resources that can be used to search for and locate information including online card catalogues, Internet search engines, and electronic databases.

Oral Communication Skills: ability to speak in a concise, confident, and eloquent fashion.

Orientation: An event attended by new and transfer students prior to attending their first class at an institution.

Overload: At DSC, an overload is a course load of more than 18 credit hours in one semester. Students may receive permission from the Vice President for Academic Affairs to enroll for more than the normal load if they were placed on the Dean's List at the end of their last semester of enrollment, if they have a cumulative average above 3.0 on 18 or more hours completed at DSC, or if they are in their last semester of enrollment before graduation.

Oversubscribed (Impacted) Major: a major that has more students interested in it than there are openings for students to be accepted.

Paraphrase: restating or rephrasing information in one's own words.

Part-to-Whole Method: a study strategy that involves dividing study time into smaller parts or units, and then learning these parts in several short, separate study sessions in advance of exams.

Pass/Passing: At most schools, a student will earn *credit* and "pass" a *class* with a *grade* of "A" through "D." A student who earns an "F" grade fails the class and earns no credit. Different schools have different standards, so a student who passes a class with a "D" may or may not be able to use that class to meet *prerequisites* or fulfill *requirements*.

Plagiarism: deliberate or unintentional use of someone else's work without acknowledging it, giving the impression that it is one's own work.

Portfolio: a collection of work materials or products that illustrate an individual's skills and talents, or demonstrates that individual's educational and personal development.

Postsecondary: Refers to all educational *programs* for students past high school age; it includes community and technical colleges and job training programs as well as *baccalaureate* colleges and universities.

Practicum: A *course* that includes job-related activities and stresses the practical application of theory in a field of study. See also *internship*.

Prerequisite: A *course* that must be completed (often with a certain minimum *grade*) or a skill that must be demonstrated before a student can enroll in a more advanced course (for example, first-year French is a prerequisite for second-year French).

Primary Sources: information obtained from first-hand sources or original documents.

Process-of-Elimination Method: a multiple-choice test-taking strategy that involves "weeding out" or eliminating choices that are clearly wrong and continuing to do so until the choices are narrowed down to one answer that seems to be the best choice available.

Procrastination: the tendency to postpone making a decision or taking action until the very last moment.

Professional School: formal education pursued after a bachelor's degree in school that prepare students for an "applied" profession (e.g., Pharmacy, Medicine, or Law).

Professional/Technical: A *course* or instructional *program* that emphasizes job skills training for a particular field of work; often called "occupational" or "vocational" education and often contrasted with "academic" or "transfer" education.

Purge of Classes: Loss of classes for which student has registered due to failure to pay tuition (or lack of financial aid) by payment due date.

Recall Test Question: a type of test question that requires students to generate or produce the correct answer on their own, such as a short-answer question or an essay question.

Recitation (Reciting): a study strategy that involves verbally stating information to be remembered without looking at it.

Recognition Test Question: a type of test question that requires students to select or choose a correct answer from answers that are provided to them (e.g., multiple-choice, true-false, and matching questions).

Reconstruction: a process of rebuilding a memory part-by-part or piece-by-piece.

Records: Refers to all the information the college might keep regarding a student; it includes *registration* activity (*enrollment, withdrawal,* etc.), *grades*, payments, awards received, *financial aid* applications and award notices, and notes on *disciplinary* actions, as well as address, phone number, and student identification number.

Re-entry Student: a student who matriculated as a traditional (just out of high school) student, but who left college to meet other job or family demands and has returned to complete a degree or obtain job training.

Reference (Referral) Letter: a letter of reference typically written by a faculty member, adviser, or employer, for students who are applying for entry into positions or schools after college, or for students during the college experience when they apply for special academic programs, student leadership positions on campus, or part-time employment.

Reflection: a thoughtful, personal review of what one has already done, is in the process of doing, or is planning to do.

Refund: *Tuition and fees* that are paid back to a student who has *withdrawn* from a course. Usually, the amount to be refunded depends on how many *credits* the student is taking and exactly when the student dropped the course(s). At DSC, refunds are normally disbursed through the Higher One Debit Card Program.

Regents' Test: The Regents' Test is an examination to assess the competency level in reading and writing of all degree-seeking students enrolled in undergraduate programs in the University System of Georgia institutions.

Register/Registration: To sign up or *enroll* in a *course* or courses. "Registration activity" includes enrolling, dropping/withdrawing, making payments, etc.

Research Skills: ability to locate, access, retrieve, organize, and evaluate information from a variety of sources, including library and technology-based (computer) systems.

Resident: For purposes of calculating a student's *tuition and fees*, someone who has lived in the state for a specified length of time as shown by specified types of evidence.

Restricted Electives: courses that students must take, but have the option of choosing them from a restricted set or list of possible courses that have been specified by the college.

Resume: a written summary or outline that effectively organizes and highlights an individual's strongest qualities, personal accomplishments, and skills, as well as personal credentials and awards.

Rough Draft: an early stage in the writing process whereby a first (rough) draft is created that converts the writer's major ideas into sentences, without worrying about the mechanics of writing (e.g., punctuation, grammar, or spelling).

Scholarly: a criterion or standard for critically evaluating the quality of an information source; typically, a source is considered to be "scholarly" if it has been reviewed by a panel or board of impartial experts in the field before being published.

Scholarship:
1. A type of *financial aid grant*. Organizations may give scholarships according to academic achievement, financial need, or any other basis. Usually there is a competitive *application* process.
2. A person's ability and expertise in a particular *discipline* of study ("I've always admired Dr. Smith's scholarship in literature.").

School: An organizational unit within a college or university consisting of two or more related *departments*.

Secondary Sources: publications that rely on or respond to primary sources that have been previously published (e.g., a textbook that draws its information from published research studies or an article that critically reviews a published novel or movie).

Self-Assessment: process of evaluating one's own characteristics, traits, or habits, and their relative strengths and weaknesses.

Self-Monitoring: the process of maintaining awareness of one's own thoughts or actions, and how effective they are.

Semester: Some schools organize the *academic year* into two main periods—Fall and Spring Semesters—plus a shorter Summer Semester. Each DSC semester has an A Session (classes scheduled full semester); a B Session (classes scheduled first half of semester); and a C Session (classes scheduled second half of semester).

Semester (Term) GPA: GPA for one semester or academic term.

Senior: A student in the fourth year of a typical 4-year baccalaureate degree program (or one who has earned 90–120 *semester* credits so far).

Senior Seminar (Capstone) Course: course designed to put a "cap" or final touch on the college experience, helping seniors to tie ideas together in their major and/or make a smooth transition from college to life after college.

Service Learning: a form of experiential learning in which students serve or help others, while they simultaneously acquire skills through hands-on experience that can be used to strengthen their resume, and explore fields of work that may relate to their future career interests.

Shadow Majors: students who have been admitted to their college or university, but have not yet been admitted to their intended major.

Shallow (Surface-Oriented) Learning: an approach to learning in which students spend most of their study time repeating and memorizing information in the exact form that it was presented to them.

Social Sciences: The fields of sociology, anthropology, economics, psychology, political science, and history are grouped into the broader academic area referred to as social sciences.

Sophomore: A student in the second year of a typical 4-year *baccalaureate* degree program (or one who has earned 30–60 semester credits so far).

Student Development (Co-Curricular) Transcript: an official document issued by the college that validates a student's co-curricular achievements which the student can have sent to prospective employers or schools.

Student ID Card: A multi-purpose card with students' identification number. The card identifies Dalton State College students and is used as a library card and for other campus services.

Study Abroad Program: In this program, students take some of their credit work at a college or university in another country. The program is designed to offer students an opportunity to experience life in another culture, to see the world and human relationships from a broader, more informed perspective, and to add an international or cross-cultural dimension to their educational experience.

Summa Cum Laude: graduating with "highest honors" (e.g., achieving a cumulative GPA of 3.8).

Syllabus: (plural: syllabi) An outline plan for a particular *class*, including textbook requirements, class meeting dates, reading assignments, examination dates, and the instructor's grading standards, etc.

Synthesis: a form of higher-level thinking that involves building up ideas by integrating (connecting) separate pieces of information to form a larger whole or more comprehensive product.

Teaching Assistant (TA): a graduate student who receives financial assistance to pursue graduate studies by teaching undergraduate courses, leading course discussions, and/or helping professors grade papers or conduct labs.

Test-Wise: the ability to use the characteristics of the test question itself (such as its wording or format) to increase the probability of choosing the correct answer.

Theory: a body of conceptually related concepts and general principles that help to organize, understand, and apply knowledge that has been acquired in a particular field of study.

Thesis Statement: an important sentence in the introduction of a paper that serves as a one-sentence summary of the key point or main argument a writer intends to make, and support with evidence, in the body of the paper.

Transcript: An official *record* of the *courses* and *semester* or *quarter credits* a student has taken at a college or university, the *grades* and *degrees* or *certificates* earned, and any awards and honors received. The term "official transcript" indicates that the document was issued directly to someone other than the student. A transcript cannot be termed "official" if it has passed through the student's hands in any way.

Transfer: To move from one college or university to another and have the second institution recognize and accept some or all of the *courses* taken and *credits* earned at the first.

Transferable Skills: skills that can be transferred or applied across a wide range of subjects, careers, and life situations.

Transient Student: Temporary admission to another college or university with the intent to transfer completed course work back to your home school. DSC students must complete a transient permission form prior to attending another institution as a transient student.

Tuition and Fees: Tuition is a student's basic payment toward the cost of instruction at a college or university. Most institutions also charge fees for laboratory equipment and materials, computer use, parking, and other miscellaneous costs.

Undergraduate: A student who has not yet earned a Bachelor's degree; also refers to the *courses* and instructional *programs* such a student enrolls in.

University System of Georgia: Includes all state operated institutions of high education in Georgia—4 research universities, 2 regional universities, 13 state universities, 2 state colleges, and 13 associate degree colleges. These 34 public institutions are located throughout the state.

Visual Aids: charts, graphs, diagrams, or concept maps that improve learning and memory by enabling the learner to visualize information as a picture or image and connect separate pieces of information to form a meaningful whole.

Visual Memory: memory that relies on the sense of vision.

Visualization: a memory-improvement strategy that involves creating a mental image or picture of what is to be remembered, or by imagining it being placed at a familiar site or location.

Vocational (Occupational) Development: exploring career options, making career choices wisely, and developing skills needed for career success.

Waive: to give-up a right to access information (e.g., waiving the right to see a letter of recommendation).

WebCT—VISTA: Short for "Web Course Tools." A software program that manages a course allowing the teacher to provide the course over the Internet. It is interactive with the student and teacher and includes a multitude of features including e-mail, course calendar, online assessments, group discussions, and much more.

Withdrawal: The process of formally *dropping* a *class* or classes after the *term* has started. This process involves completing a form in Enrollment Services.

Work-Study: A type of *financial aid* which pays students to work part-time, often on campus, during the *academic year*.

Index

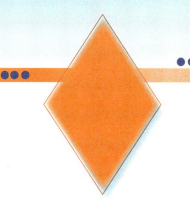

A

Ableism, 241
Academic advising, 145–152
   advisor responsibility, 146
   to advisees, 146
   college plan, 151
   first session/first advisement, registration, 151
   fourth, future session(s)/advisement, 152
   registration, 152
   second session/follow-up appointment, 151
   session expectations, 151–152
   student responsibilities, 146–150
   third session/second advisement, registration, 152
Academic Competitiveness Grant, 340
Achievement, 260
Acrostics, 160–161
Active class participation, 5–7
Active involvement, 2–8, 107
Active listening, 4–5
Active reading, 7–8
Ad hominem argument, 204
Advisor responsibility, 146
   to advisees, 146
Affiliation, 260
Ageism, 241
Analysis, 47, 190–191, 215
Analytical thinking, 190–191
Annual loan limits, 361
Anti-semitism, 241
Anxiety, 173
Apartheid, 240
Application letters, 280–282
Aptitudes, 295
Assignment-review teams, 23
Assistance, sources of, 298
Attendance rates, course grades, relationship, 4
Attention, nonverbal signals indicating, 86
Attention system, 79
Authority, appealing to, 204
Autonomy, 260

Awareness of career options, 270–271
Awareness of options, 131

B

Balanced thinking, 191, 197–199, 215
Begging question, 204
Behavioral sciences, 43
Benefits of higher-level thinking, 215–216
Biological rhythms, adjusting academic work to, 102
Biological wiring of brain, 74–75
Brain
   attention system, 81
   human attention system, 79
   outer surface, functions, 155
Brain-based learning principles, 74–78
Brainstorming, 206
Budget, 355–357
Budgeting, 353

C

Caffeine prior to test, avoiding, 169
Calculating HOPE GPA, 347–348
Campus resources, 8–15, 31–35, 108–109
   academic advisement, 10–11
   career development center, 11
   college library, 10
   counseling center, 12
   disability services, 10
   health center, 12
   learning center, 9
   writing center, 9
Capstone courses for seniors, 278
Career advancement, 271
Career choices, 260
Career development course, 264
Career entry, 271
Career mobility, 271
Career plan, importance of, 293–295
Career preparation, 257–289, 291–299
   assistance, sources of, 298
   career advancement, 271
   career development course, 264

career entry, 271
career exploration, 259–284
   awareness of options, 262–269
   reading about careers, 262–263
   step self-awareness, 259–262
career mobility, 271
career options, criteria, 271–273
career plan, importance of, 293–295
career plan initiation, 258
co-curricular programs, 263–264
cooperative education programs, 266–267
creation of, 295–298
degree attainment, 294
Dictionary of Occupational Titles, 263
Encyclopedia of Careers and Vocational Guidance, 263
financial benefits, 272
impact of career on personal life, 272–273
independent research, 286
information interviews, 264
internships, 265–266
less time to graduate, 294–295
major, career, correlation of, 292
majors, careers, distinguished, 293
mapping goals, 298
marketability, 293–294
observing people at work, 264–265
Occupational Outlook Handbook, 263
part-time work, 268–269
persistence, 294
research career options, 297–298
self-marketing, 275
   co-curricular experiences, 278–279
   college transcript, 276–278
   letters of application, 280–282
   letters of recommendation, 282
   networking skills, 282–284
   personal interviews, 284
   personal portfolio, 279–280
   personal resume, 280
self-monitoring, 273–276
step awareness of career options, 270–271

step entry into career of choice, 273
success, 233
time to graduation, 294–295
true, false quiz, 292
true or false quiz, 292
understanding of self, 295–297
volunteer service, 267–268
work conditions, 271
Career success, 49–51
Careers, web-based resources, 286
Cash flow, financial tools for tracking, 317–322
Categorizing people, 238
Changing things up, 99–100
Checking accounts, 317–318
Checking notes, 89
Checklist summary, college-success principles, 29–30
Chronological perspective, 58
   elements of, 59–60
   contemporary element, 59
   futuristic element, 59
   historical element, 59
Classism, 240
Co-curricular experiences, 278–279
Co-curricular programs on career planning, development, 263–264
Co-curriculum, 55–57
Cognitive dissonance, 212–213
Collaborative learning groups, 249
College community, connections with members of, 24
College library, 10
College major, decision regarding, 114–115
College major planning, 141–142
College plan, 151
College success diamond, 2
College success information, web-based resources, 30–36
College success principles, 1–36
   active class participation, 5–7
   active involvement, 2–8
   active listening, 4–5
   active reading, 7–8
   campus resources, 8–15, 31–35
      academic advisement, 10–11
      career development center, 11
      college library, 10
      counseling center, 12
      disability services, 10
      health center, 12
      learning center, 9
      writing center, 9
   checklist summary, college-success principles, 29–30
   experiential learning resources, 12–14
      co-curricular experiences on campus, 13–14
      service learning, 14
      volunteerism, 14

feedback, 27–28
future, reflection of, 28–29
independent research, 15, 30–36
interaction with mentor, 18–19
interaction with peers, 19–20
note-taking, 4–5
peers, collaboration with, 21–24
   assignment-review teams, 23
   learning communities, 23–24
   library research teams, 22
   note-taking teams, 21–22
   reading teams, 22
   team-instructor conferences, 22–23
   test results-review, 23
   writing teams, 22
research-based principles, 2
self-assessment, 25–26
self-monitoring, 26–27
self-reflection, 24–29
social interaction, 15–24
student-advisor interaction, 17–18
student-faculty interaction, 16–17
time spent in class, 3
time spent on coursework outside classroom, 3–4
Web-based resources, college success information, 30–36
College transcript, 276–278
Communication skills, 47, 49
Community, social consciousness, 60
Compare, contrast, 96–97
Comparing, 96–97
Compatible major, discovering, 131–137
Composition, 44
Comprehension self-monitoring strategies, 105–106
Computation skills, 47
Concept map, nervous system, 159
Contemporary element, 59
Convergent thinking, 215
Cooperative education programs, 266–267
Cost of attending college, 338
Course completion rate, 350
Course grades, attendance rates, relationship, 4
Cover letters, 280–282
Cox, Dianne, Financial Aid Director, 337–367
Creative thinking, 191, 205–207, 215
   strategies for, 213–215
Creativity, 47
Credit, maintaining, 365–366
Credit cards, 318–320, 359–360
   selecting, 359
Credit line, 321
Critical thinking, 47, 191, 200–205, 215
   to evaluate deductive reasoning, 201–202
Cross-cultural courses, 277–278
Culture, defined, 225
Curriculum, 41–44

D

Dalton State College Financial Aid, 339–346
Dalton State College Foundation Scholarship applications, 339
Deadlines, financial aid, 341
Debit cards, 320–321
Debt, 321
   default, 321
Decisions about college major, 115–116, 122–137
   learning styles, 125–131
   multiple intelligences, 124–125
   personal abilities, 123–124
   personal interests, 123
   personal values, 124
Declarative knowledge, 106
Deductive reasoning, 199–200, 215
Deferred student payment plans, 321
Defining, classifying forms, 190–207
Denial, 203
Dependency status, 341
Dependency status questions, 342
Developing, applying, 207–215
Dialectical thinking, 196–197, 215
Diamond of college success, 2
Dictionary of Occupational Titles, 263
Disability services, 10
Discrimination, 235–236
   causes of, 236–241
Distractions, 95–96
Divergent thinking, 215
Diversity, 223–255
   advantages of experiencing, 230–233
   career preparation, success, 233
   college experience and, 228–229
   culture, defined, 225
   discrimination, 235–236
      causes of, 236–241
   ethnic group, defined, 225–226
   familiarity, influence of, 237–238
   group membership, 239–241
   group perception, 239
   independent research, 251–252
   interpersonal interaction, 244–251
   majority group member attitudes, 239
   power of liberal arts education, 230–231
   prejudice, 234–235
      causes of, 236–241
   racial group, defined, 226–228
   self-awareness, 231, 241–243
   self-esteem, 239–241
   self-reflection, 241–243
   social development, 233
   stereotyping, 234
   stranger anxiety, influence of, 237–238
   tendency to categorize people, 238
   tolerance, 241–243
Dividing information, 97–98

Divisions of knowledge, subject areas, 42–44
   behavioral sciences, 43
   fine arts, 42
   humanities, 42
   mathematics, 42
   natural sciences, 42–43
   physical education, 43–44
   social sciences, 43
   wellness, 43–44
Dogmatism, 203
DOT. *See* Dictionary of Occupational Titles
Double standard, 203
Downsizing, 324
Dropping classes, effect on financial aid, 349
Dualistic thinking, 215
Durability, 46

E

Economizing, 324
Educational planning, 113–144
   awareness of options, 131
   college major, decision regarding, 114–115
   college major planning, 141–142
   compatible major, discovering, 131–137
   decision about college major, 115–116
   decisions about college major, 122–137
      learning styles, 125–131
      multiple intelligences, 124–125
      personal abilities, 123–124
      personal interests, 123
      personal values, 124
   graduation plan, 142–143
   independent research, 139
   long-range educational planning, 116–117
   myths about relationship between majors, careers, 117–122
   self-awareness, 122–131
   web-based resources, 139
   Web-based resources, educational planning, 139
Electives, 133
Emotion, appealing to, 205
Emotional development, 53, 56
Emotional learning, 103
Encyclopedia of Careers and Vocational Guidance, 263
English composition, 44
Entry into career of choice, 273
Episodic knowledge, 106–107
Ethical development, 53, 56
Ethnic group, defined, 225–226
Ethnocentrism, 240
Evaluation, 47
Experiential learning resources, 12–14
   co-curricular experiences on campus, 13–14
   service learning, 14
   volunteerism, 14

F

Factual information memorization, 77
FAFSA, 340–341
Fallacies, 203–205
Familiarity, influence of, 237–238
Federal grants, 340
Federal Pell Grant, 340
Federal SEOG, 340
Federal Stafford Loan, 341
   repayment, 361–362
Feedback, 27–28
Fight-or-flight reaction, 237
Financial aid, 339
   application, after completion of, 341–342
   application for, 339–343
   deadlines, 341
   disbursements, 343
   eligibility chart, 344
   refunds, book charges, 343–345
   types of, 339
Financial literacy, 321
Financial needs, calculating, 343
Financial planning, 337–367
   budget, 355–357
   calculating HOPE GPA, 347–348
   cost of attending college, 338
   Dalton State College Financial Aid, 339–346
   managing money, 353
   theft probability score, 363–364
Financial self-awareness, 315–316
Financial tools for saving money, 322
Fine arts, 42, 45
Focus attention, 84
Follow-up appointment, 151
Form study groups, 103–104
Free recall, 165
Fundamental skills acquisition, 46–48
Future, reflection of, 28–29
Futuristic element, 59

G

General education, college majors, careers, relationship, 118
Georgia Career Information System, 297
Georgia College 411, 297
Georgia HOPE program, 340, 345–346
Gift aid, 339
Gifts of time *vs.* money, 324
Glittering generality, 204
Global perspective, social consciousness, 61
GPA. *See* Grade point average
Grade point average, 346, 349
   computing, 181–182
Graduation plan, 142–143
Grants, 321, 339
Group membership, 239–241
Group perception, 239

H

Hasty generalization, 203
Health education, 45
Heterosexism, 241
Hierarchy of needs pyramid of Maslow, 20
Higher-level thinking, 187–222
   analysis, 190–191
   balanced thinking, 191, 197–199
   benefits of higher-level thinking, 215–216
   cognitive dissonance, 212–213
   creative thinking, 191, 205–207
      strategies for, 213–215
   critical thinking, 191, 200–205
      to evaluate deductive reasoning, 201–202
   defining, classifying forms, 190–207
   developing, applying, 207–215
   dialectical thinking, 196–197
   forms of, 209–210
   independent research, 217
   inductive reasoning, 202–205
   inferential reasoning, 191, 199–200
      deductive reasoning, 199–200
      inductive reasoning, 200
   listening strategies, 211
   multidimensional thinking, 190, 192–196
   multiple perspectives, 192–195
   multiple theories, 195–196
   reading strategies, 212
   self-questioning strategies, 207–211
   synthesis, 190–192
   web-based resources, 217
   Web-based resources, higher-level thinking, 217
Historical element, 59
History, 44
Holistic development, 51
   abilities associated with, 52–55
Homophobia, 241
Honors courses, 276–277
HOPE program, 340, 345–346
Human differences, 223–255
   advantages of experiencing, 230–233
   career preparation, success, 233
   college experience and, 228–229
   culture, defined, 225
   discrimination, 235–236
      causes of, 236–241
   diversity, 241–251
   ethnic group, defined, 225–226
   familiarity, influence of, 237–238
   group membership, 239–241
   group perception, 239
   independent research, 251–252
   interpersonal interaction, 244–251

majority group member attitudes, 239
power of liberal arts education, 230–231
prejudice, 234–235
    causes of, 236–241
racial group, defined, 226–228
self-awareness, 231, 241–243
self-esteem, 239–241
self-reflection, 241–243
social development, 233
stereotyping, 234
stranger anxiety, influence of, 237–238
tendency to categorize people, 238
tolerance, 241–243
Humanities, 42
Humanity, 228

I

Identity theft, 362
    risk of, 365
Individuality, 228
Inductive reasoning, 200, 202–205, 215
Inferential reasoning, 191, 199–200
    deductive reasoning, 199–200
    inductive reasoning, 200
Information interviews, 264
Insurance premium, 321
Integrating information, 97
Intellectual development, 52, 56
Intelligence, multiple forms of, 125
Interaction with mentor, 18–19
Interaction with peers, 19–20
Interdisciplinary courses, 277
Interest, 321
Interest-bearing account, 321
Interests, 295
International courses, 277–278
International world, social consciousness, 61
Internships, 265–266
Interpersonal interaction, 244–251
Interviews, 284

J

Jobprofiles.org, 297
Jumping to conclusions, 204

K

Knowledge, comprehension, higher-level thinking, relationship, 190
Knowledge awareness strategies, 106–107
    declarative knowledge, 106
    episodic knowledge, 106–107
    procedural knowledge, 106

L

Leadership courses, 277
LEAP Grant, 340
Learning, stages in, 82

Learning center, 9
Learning communities, 23–24
Learning research, 73–112
    active involvement, 107
    biological wiring of brain, 74–75
    brain-based learning principles, 74–78
    campus resources, 108–109
    changing things up, 99–100
    compare, contrast, 96–97
    comprehension self-monitoring strategies, 105–106
    distractions, 95–96
    dividing information, 97–98
    emotional learning, 103
    focus attention, 84
    form study groups, 103–104
    independent research, 109–112
    integrating information, 97
    knowledge awareness strategies, 106–107
        declarative knowledge, 106
        episodic knowledge, 106–107
        procedural knowledge, 106
    lecture listening, 83–90
    meaning in terms, 96
    memory, 103
    motor learning, 102
    new knowledge is built on knowledge already possessed, 76
    note-taking, 83–90
    notes
        checking, 89
        reflecting on, 89
        reviewing before class, 88
    part-to-whole method of studying, 98–99
    review, beginning with, 99
    seating posture, 86
    self-assessment, 111–112
    self-reflection, 104–108
    social interaction/collaboration, 108–109
    social seating position, behavior in classroom, 85
    stage retrieval, 81–82
    stages in learning, memory, 78–82
        stage perception, 78–80
        stage storage, 80–81
    study different subjects in different places, 100
    study strategies, 95–104
    textbook-reading comprehension
        after reading, 94
        before beginning to read, 90–91
        retention, improving, 90–94
        while reading, 91–92
    use all of senses, 100–102
    visual learning, 101
    Web-based resources, 109–112
Learning skills, 49
Learning styles, 125–131
Learning Styles Inventory, learning styles measured by, 128

Lecture listening, 83–90
Letters of application, 280–282
Letters of recommendation, 282–283
Letters of reference, 282
Liberal arts
    college majors, careers, relationship, 118
    web-based resources, 67
Liberal arts education, 37–72
    analysis, 47
    career success, 49–51
    chronological perspective, 58
        contemporary element, 59
        elements of, 59–60
        futuristic element, 59
        historical element, 59
    co-curriculum, 55–57
    communication skills, 49
    community, social consciousness, 60
    creativity, 47
    curriculum, 41–44
    divisions of knowledge, subject areas, 42–44
        behavioral sciences, 43
        fine arts, 42
        humanities, 42
        mathematics, 42
        natural sciences, 42–43
        physical education, 43–44
        social sciences, 43
        wellness, 43–44
    emotional development, 53
    ethical development, 53
    evaluation, 47
    fundamental skills acquisition, 46–48
    global perspective, social consciousness, 61
    holistic development, abilities associated with, 52–55
    independent research, 67
    intellectual development, 52
    international world, social consciousness, 61
    liberal arts education, planning, 69–71
    Liberal Arts Education-Planning Form, 70–71
    lifelong learning skills, 49
    meaning, purpose of, 38–40
    multi-dimensional perspective, 45–46
    multi-media communication skills, 47
    nation, social consciousness, 60
    personal development, 55
    physical development, 54
    planning, 69–71
    planning checklists, 71–72
    power of, 230–231
    skills, 49–51
    social development, 53
    social-spatial perspective, 57
    social spatial perspective, elements of, 60–62

society, social consciousness, 60
spiritual development, 54
synoptic perspective, 62–63
synthesis, 47
thinking skills, 49
universe, social consciousness, 61
value of, 44–48
vocational development, 54
Web-based resources, liberal arts, 67
whole person, development of, 51–55
world, broadening perspective of, 57–63
Liberal Arts Education-Planning Form, 70–71
Library research teams, 22
Life goals, 296
Lifelong learning skills, 49
Link system, 161–162
Listening skills, 47
Listening strategies, 211
Literature, 44
Living with others, 324
Loan consolidation, 321
Loan limits, 361
Loan premium, 321
Loci system, 162–163
Logical fallacies, 203–205
Long-range educational planning, 116–117
Long-range financial planning, 326–329
Long-term total costs, 325–326
LSI. *See Learning Styles Inventory*

M

Major, career, correlation of, 292
Majority, appealing to, 205
Majority group member attitudes, 239
Majors, careers, distinguished, 293
Mapping goals, 298
Marketability, 293–294
Maslow, Abraham, 20
Mathematics, 42, 44
Maximum time frame, 350–351
MBTI. *See Myers-Briggs type indicator*
Meaning, purpose of, 38–40
Meaning in terms, 96
Meaningful association, 155–156
Memorization, factual information, 77
Memory, 103, 153–186
   free recall, 165
   independent research, 183
   learning and, 154
   memory retrieval, 166–167
     on day of test, 169–171
     recitation, 166–167
     retrieval cues, 167–168
     during test, 171–178
   paired-associate recall, 165
   recall memory, testing of, 165–166
   recall test questions, 164
   recognition test questions, 164
   serial recall, 166
   stages in, 82
   strategies for memorization, 154–163
     acrostics, 160–161
     link system, 161–162
     loci system, 162–163
     meaningful association, 155–156
     mnemonic devices, 154–155
     organization, 157
     rhyme, 159–160
     rhythm, 159–160
     visualization, 157–159
   test-taking strategies, 163–182
     before test, 164–169
     troubleshooting test-taking errors, 178–182
   web-based resources, 183
Memory retrieval, 81–82, 166–167
   on day of test, 169–171
   during test, 171–178
Memory storage, 80–81
Merit-based scholarship, 321
Mnemonic devices, 154–155, 163
Money, tips for saving, 359
Money management, 314–329, 353
   cash flow, financial tools for tracking, 317–322
   checking account, 317–318
   credit cards, 318–320
   credit line, 321
   debit cards, 320–321
   debt, 321
     default, 321
   deferred student payment plans, 321
   financial self-awareness, 315–316
   financial tools for saving money, 322
   grant, 321
   insurance premium, 321
   interest, 321
   interest-bearing account, 321
   loan consolidation, 321
   loan premium, 321
   long-range financial planning, 326–329
   merit-based scholarship, 321
   money-management plan, 317
   money-market account, 322
   money-saving strategies, 322–326
     downsizing, 324
     economizing, 324
     gifts of time *vs.* money, 324
     living with others, 324
     long-term total costs, 325–326
     money-saving strategies, 325
     personal budget, 322–323
   need-based scholarship, 321
   savings account, 322
   strategies, 315–317
Money-management, plan, 317
Money-market account, 322
Money-saving strategies, 325
Motor learning, 102
Multi-dimensional perspective, 45–46
Multi-media communication skills, 47
Multicultural courses, 278
Multidimensional thinking, 190, 192–196, 215
Multiple forms of intelligence, 125
Multiple intelligences, 124–125
Multiple perspectives, 192–195
Multiple theories, 195–196
Muscle memory, 102
Myers-Briggs type indicator
   learning style, writing style, 127
   traits, learning styles measured, 126
Myths about relationship between majors, careers, 117–122

N

Nation, social consciousness, 60
Nationalism, 240
Natural sciences, 42–43, 45
Need-based scholarship, 321
Nervous system, concept map, 159
Networking, 282–284
Networking skills, 282–284
New knowledge is built on knowledge already possessed, 76
Nonverbal signals indicating attention, 86
Note-taking, 4–6, 83–90
Note-taking teams, 21–22, 108
Notes
   checking, 89
   reflecting on, 89
   reviewing before class, 88
Nutritional strategies, strengthening academic performance, 170

O

Observing people at work, 264–265
Occupational Information Network, 263, 297
Occupational Outlook Handbook, 263, 297
Optical illusion, 232
Oral communication skills, 47
Organization, 3, 157
Outer surface of brain, functions, 155
Outside classroom, working independently, 58

P

Paired-associate recall, 165
Part-time work, 268–269
Part-to-whole method of studying, 98–99
Peers, collaboration with, 21–24
   assignment-review teams, 23
   learning communities, 23–24
   library research teams, 22
   note-taking teams, 21–22

reading teams, 22
team-instructor conferences, 22–23
test results-review, 23
writing teams, 22
Peeves of professors, 87
Pell Grant, 340
Perception, 78–80
Persistence, 294
Personal abilities, 123–124
Personal budget, 322–323
Personal characteristics, career choice and, 261
Personal development, 55–56
Personal interests, 123
Personal interviews, 284
Personal life, impact of career on, 272–273
Personal portfolio, 279–280
Personal resume, 280
Personal values, 124
Personality types, 296
Physical development, 54, 56
Physical education, 43–45
Planning for college major, 141–142
Political science, 44
Popularity, appealing to, 205
Portfolio, 279–280
Power of liberal arts education, 230–231
Prejudice, 234–235, 240
causes of, 236–241
Prestige, appealing to, 204
Private loans, 362
Private scholarships, 340
Procedural knowledge, 106
Procrastination, 39–40, 309–314
myths promoting, 310–311
psychological causes of, 311–312
self-help strategies, 312–314
Promotion, 271
Psychology, 44

R

Racial group, defined, 226–228
Racism, 240
Reading about careers, 262–263
Reading skills, 47
Reading strategies, 212
Reading teams, 22, 108
Recall memory, testing of, 165–166
Recall test questions, 164
Recitation, 166–167
Recitation for memory retrieval, 166–167
Recognition test questions, 164
Recommendation letters, 282
Red herrings, 204
Reference letters, 282
Reflecting on notes, 89
Regionalism, 240
Registration, 151–152
Religious bigotry, 241

Research
brain-based learning principles, 74–78
independent research, 109–112
lecture listening, 83–90
self-assessment, 111–112
self-reflection, 104–107
stages in learning, memory, 78–82
stage perception, 78–80
stage storage, 80–81
study strategies, 95–104
textbook-reading comprehension
after reading, 94
before beginning to read, 90–91
retention, improving, 90–94
while reading, 91–92
Research-based principles, 2
Research career options, 297–298
Research skills, 47
Resume, 280
construction of, 281
Retention, improving, 90–94
Retrieval, 81–82
memory, 81–82, 167–168
Reviewing notes before class, 88
Reviews, beginning with, 99
Rhetorical deception, 204
Rhyme, 159–160
Rhythm, 159–160
Risk of identity theft, 365

S

SAP reviews, 351
Satisfactory academic progress
financial aid, 349–352
standards, 349
Savings account, 322
Schmidt, Amy, Academic Advising Director, 145–152
Scholarship searches, 340
Scholarships, 339–340
Seating posture, 86
Selective perception, 203
Self-assessment, 25–26, 111–112
Self-awareness, 122–131, 231, 241–243, 259–262
time expenditure, 303–305
Self-esteem, 239–241
Self-help aid, 339
Self-marketing, 275
co-curricular experiences, 278–279
college transcript, 276–278
letters of application, 280–282
letters of recommendation, 282
networking skills, 282–284
personal interviews, 284
personal portfolio, 279–280
personal resume, 280
Self-monitoring, 26–27, 104–107, 273–276
Self-questioning strategies, 207–211

Self-reflection, 24–29, 104–108, 241–243
Semantic knowledge, 106
Senior seminars, 278
Seniors, capstone courses, 278
Sensory stimulation, 260
SEOG, 340
Serial recall, 166
Session expectations, academic advising, 151–152
first session/first advisement, registration, 151
fourth, future session(s)/advisement, registration, 152
second session/follow-up appointment, 151
third session/second advisement, registration, 152
Sexism, 241
Skill knowledge, 106
SMART Grants, 340
Smoke screen, 204
Social development, 53, 56, 233
Social interaction, 15–24
Social interaction/collaboration, 108–109
Social sciences, 43
Social seating position, behavior in classroom, 85
Social-spatial perspective, 57
elements of, 60–62
Society, social consciousness, 60
Sociology, 44
Speaking, 3
Special needs, students with, 10
Speech, 44
Spiritual development, 54, 56
Stafford Loan, 341, 361
repayment, 361–362
Stages in learning, memory, 78–82
stage perception, 78–80
stage storage, 80–81
Stereotypes, 240
Stereotyping, 234
Storage, 80–81
Storage of memory, 80–81
Stranger anxiety, influence of, 237–238
Strategies for saving money, 322–326
downsizing, 324
economizing, 324
gifts of time vs. money, 324
living with others, 324
long-term total costs, 325–326
money-saving strategies, 325
personal budget, 322–323
Straw man argument, 204
Student-advisor interaction, 17–18
Student-faculty interaction, 16–17
Student loans, 339–340, 360–361
Student responsibilities, 146–150
Students with special needs, 10
Study strategies, 95–104

Study teams, 108
Studying different subjects in different places, 100
Subsidized Stafford Loan, 361
Synoptic perspective, 62–63
Synthesis, 47, 190–192, 215

T

Team-instructor conferences, 22–23
Teamwork, 249
Terrorism, 241
Test anxiety, 173
Test performance, 153–186
   free recall, 165
   independent research, 183
   learning and, 154
   memorization, 154–163
      acrostics, 160–161
      link system, 161–162
      loci system, 162–163
      meaningful association, 155–156
      mnemonic devices, 154–155
      organization, 157
      rhyme, 159–160
      rhythm, 159–160
      visualization, 157–159
   memory retrieval, 166–167
      on day of test, 169–171
      recitation, 166–167
      retrieval cues, 167–168
      during test, 171–178
   paired-associate recall, 165
   recall memory, testing of, 165–166
   recall test questions, 164
   recognition test questions, 164
   serial recall, 166
   strategies, 163–182
      before test, 164–169
      troubleshooting errors, 178–182
      web-based resources, 183
Test results review, 23, 108
Test-taking strategies, 163–182
   before test, 164–169
   troubleshooting test-taking errors, 178–182
Textbook-reading comprehension
   after reading, 94
   before beginning to read, 90–91
   retention, 7
   improving, 90–94
   while reading, 91–92
Theft probability score, 363–364
Thinking, defined, 188–189
Thinking skills, 49
Time management, 302–306
   importance of, 302
   improving, 303–305
   procrastination, 309–314
      myths promoting, 310–311
      psychological causes of, 311–312
      self-help strategies, 312–314
   self-awareness, time expenditure, 303–305
   time-management plan, 306–314
      converting into action plan, 308–309
Time-management plan, 306–314
   converting into action plan, 308–309
Time spent in class, 3
Time spent on coursework outside classroom, 3–4
Tolerance, 241–243
Tradition, appealing to, 205
Transcript, 276–278
Transferability, 46
Troubleshooting test-taking errors, 178–182

U

Understanding of self, 295–297
Universe, social consciousness, 61
Unsubsidized Stafford Loan, 361
Use all of senses, 100–102

V

Visual learning, 101
Visualization, 157–159
Vocational development, 54, 56
Volunteer service, 267–268

W

Wellness, 43–44
Whole person, development of, 51–55
Whole-person development, 51
Wishful thinking, 203
Withdrawing from classes, effect on financial aid, 349
Work conditions, 271
Work study, 339–341
Work values, 295–296
Working independently outside classroom, 58
World, broadening perspective of, 57–63
Writing, 3
Writing center, 9
Writing teams, 22
Written communication skills, 47

X

Xenophobia, 241